Staging the World

Spoils, Captives, and Representations in the Roman Triumphal Procession

IDA ÖSTENBERG

OXFORD

UNIVERSITY PRESS

OXFORD
UNIVERSITY PRESS

Great Clarendon Street, Oxford OX2 6DP

Oxford University Press is a department of the University of Oxford.
It furthers the University's objective of excellence in research, scholarship,
and education by publishing worldwide in

Oxford New York

Auckland Bangkok Buenos Aires Cape Town Chennai
Dar es Salaam Delhi Hong Kong Istanbul Karachi Kolkata
Kuala Lumpur Madrid Melbourne Mexico City Mumbai Nairobi
São Paulo Shanghai Taipei Tokyo Toronto

Oxford is a registered trade mark of Oxford University Press
in the UK and in certain other countries

Published in the United States
by Oxford University Press Inc., New York

A catalogue record for this title is available from the British Library

Library of Congress Control Number: 2008943417

Typeset by SPI Publisher Services Ltd, Pondicherry, India
Printed in Great Britain
on acid-free paper by
CPI Antony Rowe, Chippenham, Wiltshire

ISBN 978-0-19-921597-3

1 3 5 7 9 10 8 6 4 2

For Per, Sigrid, and Ivar

PREFACE

This book started out as a doctoral thesis that was defended at Lund University, Sweden, in December 2003. I would like to express my gratitude to my examiner, Kathleen Coleman, whose kind and important comments helped in rewriting the text. Profound thanks are due to my Ph.D. supervisor Anne-Marie Leander Touati, and to Marianne Wifstrand Schiebe, who both guided me through the original project with inestimable advice and stimulating discussions. I am also thankful to Magnus Wistrand and Örjan Wikander, who scrutinized the thesis and offered accurate comments and corrections.

In working with Oxford University Press, I have been blessed with having Dorothy McCarthy as editor. Her kind and quick responses to my many questions have helped me through countless difficulties. I am deeply grateful to the OSACR committee, in particular Simon Price, for obliging kindness and for straight suggestions for improvements, which helped me in refining my thinking on some crucial points. I owe a particular debt to Mary Beard for encouragement and important suggestions. Her own recent work on the triumph has been a true inspiration in the process of transforming the thesis into a book. Many thanks are also due to the participants of the stimulating meeting on the Roman triumph that Mary Beard arranged in Cambridge in March 2008.

Earlier versions of some of the material in this book, along with other papers on the Roman triumph, were presented at seminars in Cambridge, Lund, Gothenburg, Heidelberg, Helsinki, Rome, and Stockholm. Comments and questions from the participants at those occasions greatly helped in improving the text. For sharing ideas and suggestions, I am particularly indebted to Fanni Faegersten, Tanja Itgenshorst, Lena Landgren, Lennart Lind, Bengt Pettersson, Eva Rystedt, and Jenny Wallensten.

My work has been greatly facilitated by the generous grants and scholarships from the following foundations: Kungliga Vetenskaps- och Vitterhetssamhället i Göteborg (The Royal Society of Arts and Sciences in Gothenburg), Birgit och Gad Rausings stiftelse för humanistisk forskning, Stiftelsen Torsten och Ingrid Gihls fond, Gyllenstiernska Krapperupsstiftelsen, Crafoordska stiftelsen, Helge Ax:son Johnsons stiftelse, Stiftelsen Svenska Institutet i Rom, Ingenjör C. M. Lericis stipendium, Stiftelsen Harald och Tonny Hagendahls minnesfond, Stiftelsen Lars Hiertas Minne, and Inga och John Hains stiftelser för vetenskaplig medicinsk och humanistisk forskning. In arranging for permissions and illustrations from the Italian Museums, I have been much helped by Stefania Renzetti at the Swedish Institute in Rome.

My deepest gratitude goes to my family and to many friends, who have supported and encouraged me during all these years that I have spent in close company with the Roman triumphs. Above all, I thank my husband Per and children Sigrid and Ivar for offering limitless support, heartening hugs, and true joy. To them, I dedicate this book.

I.Ö.

Lund, 25 June 2008

CONTENTS

FIGURES

ABBREVIATIONS

ANRW	H. Temporini and W. Haase (eds.), *Aufstieg und Niedergang der römischen Welt* (Berlin and New York, 1972–)
BMCRE	H. Mattingly *et al.* (eds.), *Coins of the Roman Empire in the British Museum* (London, 1923–)
CAH	*The Cambridge Ancient History* (Cambridge, 1924–)
CIL	T. Mommsen *et al.* (eds.), *Corpus Inscriptionum Latinarum* (Berlin, 1862–)
DAI	Deutsches Archäologisches Institut, Rome
Degrassi, *Inscr. It.* 13:1, 2, 3	A. Degrassi, *Inscriptiones Italiae* 13:1, 2, 3: *Fasti et elogia* (Rome, 1947, 1963, 1937).
EAA	*Enciclopedia dell'arte antica, classica e orientale* (Rome, 1958–84)
EV	*Enciclopedia virgiliana* (Rome, 1984–91)
FGrHist	F. Jacoby *et al.* (eds.), *Die Fragmente der griechischen Historiker* (Berlin and Leiden, 1923–)
IGLS	L. Jalabert et al. (eds.), *Inscriptions grecques et latines de la Syrie* (Paris, 1929–)
ILS	H. Dessau (ed.), *Inscriptiones Latinae Selectae* (Berlin, 1892–1916)
Keil, *Gramm. Lat.*	H. Keil, *Grammatici Latini* (Leipzig, 1855–1923)
LIMC	*Lexicon Iconographicum Mythologiae Classicae* (Zurich and Munich/Düsseldorf, 1981–99)
LSJ	H. G. Liddell, R. Scott, and H. S. Jones (eds.), *A Greek–English Lexicon* (Oxford, 1940; with revised supplement by P. G. W. Glare, 1996)
LTUR	E. M. Steinby (ed.), *Lexicon Topographicum Urbis Romae* (Rome, 1993–2000)
NP	H. Cançik and H. Schneider (eds.), *Der Neue Pauly*: *Enzyklopädie der Antike* (Stuttgart, 1996–2003)
OLD	P. G. W. Glare (ed.), *Oxford Latin Dictionary* (Oxford, 1982)
RE	A. Pauly, G. Wissowa, and W. Kroll (eds.), *Real-Encyklopädie der klassischen Altertumswissenschaft* (Stuttgart, 1893–1978)
Roscher	W. H. Roscher (ed.), *Ausführliches Lexikon der griechischen und römischen Mythologie* (Leipzig, 1884–1937)
TLL	*Thesaurus Linguae Latinae* (Leipzig and Stuttgart, 1900–)
Trionfi romani	E. La Rocca and S. Tortorella (eds.), *Trionfi romani*. Catalogue of the exhibition held at Colosseum in Rome, 5 Mar.–14 Sept. 2008 (Rome, 2008)

ONE

Introduction

The Roman triumphal procession was a magnificent spectacle. Winding its way along the streets of the city, embracing the civic sphere by its very movement, the procession saw the victorious general and his army as they returned to the Capitol from the scene of war. Before his chariot, the triumphator paraded the fruits of victory: spoils, captives, and representations of peoples and places conquered. Josephus attests to the visual splendour of the triumph as it appeared in AD 71, when Vespasian and Titus put their Jewish victory on parade:

Silver and gold and ivory in masses, made in all kinds of forms, might be seen, not as if carried in procession, but flowing so to speak, like a river; fabrics were borne along, some made of the rarest purple, others embroidered by Babylonian technique with perfect representation; transparent gems, some set in golden crowns, some in other fashions, swept by in such profusion as to correct our erroneous supposition that any of them was rare.

(*BJ* 7.134–6)

The parade was an ostentatious performance, abundant not only in wealth, but also in colour, sound, imitation (*mimesis*), and emotion. The massed spectators were active partakers. Along with crowds of guests from outside, the people of Rome occupied every part of the urban space in order to catch the best view. As the pageant passed by in slow motion, the spectators awaited, watched, read, admired, applauded, ridiculed, lamented, explained, and discussed the wide variety of displays.

The triumphal procession manifested the victories of Rome as well as the defeat of her enemies. By rights of war, Rome took up the peoples and places that were led and carried before the triumphator as possessions of the *res publica* and offerings to its gods. Yet, spoils, captives, and representations also symbolized and presented the defeated to the gaze of the Roman people. At this crowded civic celebration, spectators met with coins from Spain and Asia, Jewish temple treasures, silver plate and furniture from royal opulent feasting, trees from eastern gardens, Punic elephants appearing as in battle, kings, long known by name only, and ferocious barbarians, tall in stature and wearing outlandish costumes. People read on placards names that sounded curiously exotic—*flumen Nathabur, mons nomine Niger, oppida Baracum, Buluba, Alasit, Galsa, Balla, Maxalla*. They witnessed images of foreign rivers and peoples brought into subjugation, represented in miserable vanquishment and grief. They watched many of these displays in unprecedented numbers, and often, they saw them for the first time. Indeed, the triumphal procession brought the world to Rome.

Rome was no static concept, however, nor was the world. During the period in focus here, from the early third century BC to the time of Trajan, Rome was exposed to constant change, as was, in close symbiotic interplay, the surrounding world. Questions of identity were crucial as the city and empire expanded, and ritual played a significant role in forming and affirming sense of community. The triumphal parade was particularly apt to perform and shape such concepts. Time and time again, it staged the prime Roman myth of conquest and supremacy, featuring the defeated 'other' as opposed to the victorious 'self' in a dramatic role-playing. This study takes as its theoretical premise that the ritually recurrent and visually emphatic triumphal processions both conveyed and constructed Roman views of self and other, and that they can be studied as formative expressions of such conceptions. Aiming at approaching issues of Roman identity constructs by unfolding meanings and functions of the triumphal performance, the study is basically an inquiry into how Rome presented and perceived the defeated on triumphal display. Spoils, captives, and representations are the objects, and the basic questions strive to establish both contents and context. What was displayed? How was it paraded? What was the response? The approach does not exclude discussions of the triumph as a religious rite and as a political act. But in the present study performance is the key word, and attention is in the first place paid to the visual expressions and schemes of the parade and to the interplay between these and the spectators.

PREVIOUS STUDIES

Modern scholarly enquiries into the triumph have, since Gibbon's study in 1764, focused strongly on its religious and political significations.[1] Indeed, the triumph was both a pregnant political manifestation and a significant sacred rite. Aiming at the religious centre of Rome, the procession formed part of a traditional religious feast that comprised also sacrifice, meal, and games. Hence, the parade included no small number of white oxen destined to be sacrificed on the Capitol, and attendants of many kinds led the animals along. Several scholars have read the

---

[1] E. Gibbon, 'Sur les triomphes des Romains', *Miscellaneous works*, ed. John, Lord Sheffield, III (Dublin, 1796), 123–63, esp. 159–60, noted by Bonfante Warren (1974). Important larger studies on the triumph are Goell (1854); Pais (1920); Ehlers (1939); Degrassi, *Inscr. It.* 13:1; Barini (1952); Payne (1962); Künzl (1988); Auliard (2001); and recently, with new questions asked, Itgenshorst (2005); Beard (2007).

triumph as a rite concluding the war, a *voti solutio* corresponding to the *nuncupatio voti* performed on the Capitol before going into battle.[2] Others stress the triumph as an entrance rite that crossed the *pomerium* from the sphere of war (*militiae*) to that of peace (*domi*), again corresponding to the processional departure from the city at the inaugural moment of the campaign.[3] Yet others emphasize the purifying aspects, stressing that the general and his army were cleansed from blood-guilt and slaughter as they passed through the *porta triumphalis*, and that, as a lustration rite, the triumph performed an *ambulatio* of the city around the Palatine.[4]

Discussions of the religious meaning of the triumph have focused predominantly on the Roman triumphator. Many studies have scrutinized his identity as king or god, analysing carefully dresses, insignia, and attributes, such as the red-painted face, the purple robe, sceptre, and chariot.[5] Either, it has been argued, the triumphator embodied Jupiter himself, carrying his costume and attributes, or, adorned in royal attire taken up from the Etruscans, he represented the *rex*.[6] Versnel, in his now classic *Triumphus: An Inquiry into the Origin, Development and Meaning of the Roman Triumph*, accounts for the two standpoints, and attempts to reconcile them. Accordingly, the triumphator was god, but king too, as the iconography of Jupiter gained force only with Etruscan kingship.[7] The question of the triumphator's identity forms part of a larger issue concerning the origin of the triumph, which constitutes a recurrent topic in modern studies: to what extent was the rite native Roman (or Latin) and in what ways did the Etruscans contribute?[8] Within this theme, the meaning of the term *triumphus* has also been addressed,[9] as has the relation between the triumph, the *pompa circensis*, and the funeral procession.[10] Questions of origins continue to attract,[11] and in 2006, a major debate evolved, as Jörg Rüpke proposed to redate the earliest

[2] Laqueur (1909: 220–30); Beseler (1909); Rüpke (1990: 225–6).

[3] Versnel (1970: esp. 388); Rüpke (1990: 226–30).

[4] Bonfante Warren (1970*a*: esp. 52–7).

[5] Warde Fowler (1916); Versnel (1970: 56–93); Bonfante Warren (1970*a*: 57–64); Weinstock (1971: 64–79); Künzl (1988: 85–108).

[6] For a review of scholarly discussions of the triumphator's divine aspects, see now Beard (2007: 219–56).

[7] Versnel (1970: 56–93). Bonfante Warren (1974) offers a detailed review of Versnel's study.

[8] Goell (1854: 1–7); Bonfante Warren (1970*a*); Lemosse (1972); Amiotti (2001). Wallisch (1955) sees the triumph as a Dionysiac θρίαμβος ceremony imitated by the Romans only in the 3nd cent. BC. Versnel (1970: esp. 201–303), interprets the ceremony as being in its essence an eastern New Year's festival, taken up in Rome by way of the Etruscans. For an up-to-date discussion of 'the myth of origins', see Beard (2007: 305–18).

[9] e.g. Versnel (1970: 11–55); Bonfante Warren (1970*b*); Amiotti (2001).

[10] *Pompa circensis*: Versnel (1970: 94–131); *pompa funebris*: Brelich (1938); Richard (1966); Versnel (1970: 94–131).

[11] Amiotti (2001), cf. Amiotti (2002). Auliard (2001) and Holliday (2002: 22–30) both offer very traditional descriptions of the triumph, its origins, development, and meaning.

triumphs to the late fourth century BC when the practice of erecting honorific statues commenced.[12] The theory was strongly contested by Versnel.[13]

The triumphator is also in focus when scholars approach is the triumph as a political manifestation. Quite naturally so, since the triumph brought the highest honour, prestige, and power upon the celebrating general and his family, contemporary and future.[14] The triumph was highly strived after, fiercely fought for, and once performed, it was used as a means of self-advertisement to win yet other glorious commissions and offices. In consequence, many historical studies have approached the triumph as an expression of personal authority and discussed it as a consequential pawn in the constant power game within the oligarchic circle of Republican Rome. Questions concerning the *ius triumphandi* abound; several scholars have explored the issue of who had the right to triumph and how this changed over time.[15] In fact, constitutional propriety has since Mommsen received much attention, along with the triumph's political values and consequences.

Due to the pronounced emphasis on the personal authority of the triumphator, any changes and developments in the triumphal celebration have been linked to prominent individuals. The famed Philhellenes M. Claudius Marcellus and Scipio Africanus, who celebrated major parades after the falls of Syracuse and Carthage in 211 and 201 BC respectively, are often pointed out as two main characters in the process of change. In bringing abundant and lavish booty to Rome, it is argued that Marcellus and Scipio triggered the transformation of the triumph from its original purification ritual, largely concerned with the gods, into opulent honorific celebration announcing individual glory and prestige.[16] The development continued rapidly with the enormous influx of luxury items brought in by the generals celebrating triumphs over Hellenistic kings in the first part of the second century BC. Certainly, many Roman victories over the Greek cities and kingdoms meant that Rome saw both masses of richness and novelties on display. But, as has been rightly pointed out lately, the idea of a triumph that developed from an honest religious ritual to individual, rich show-offs on parade is oversimplified and depends far too much on ancient authors' rhetorical emphasis on the moral decline in Rome.[17]

A true break in the triumphal history of Rome occurred with Augustus.[18] The triumph now became an honour restricted to members of the Imperial family and

[12] Rüpke (2006).
[13] Versnel (2006).
[14] Itgenshorst (2005) seeks to tone down Roman nobles' quest for triumphal honours.
[15] Goell (1854: 8–21); Mommsen (1887: 126–36); Laqueur (1909); Versnel (1970: 164–98); Richardson (1975); Develin (1978); Gruen (1990: 129–33); Richard (1992); Wardle (1994); Brennan (1994).
[16] Bruhl (1929); Bonfante Warren (1970a: 49, 64–5); Holliday (2002: 22–30).
[17] Itgenshorst (2005: 212–18); Itgenshorst (2006).
[18] Hickson (1991); Beard (2007: 295–305); Östenberg (2009); Itgenshorst (2008).

incorporated into the Imperial ceremonial.[19] Compared to that of the Republic, the Imperial procession seems, at least at first glance, more static and, disconnected from the political struggles of the nobility, has been rejected as 'mere spectacle'. However, in recent times, several scholars have started to take a fresh look at the Imperial triumphs as vivid and important expressions of their own time, not least as dynamic manifestations of dynastic proclamations.[20]

To sum up, there has been a strong tendency to discuss the triumph as political and religious constitution and institution rather than procession and performance. Certainly, the traditional issues are justified, offering countless valid and important insights. Still, it is surprising that work on the Roman triumph has been so little influenced by the stream of ritual and performance studies that have flourished in historical discussions during the last decades. By contrast, many inquiries into Greek processions have since the 1980s addressed performative aspects and civic implications.[21] Scholars have written substantially on both specific parades and on general issues with an anthropological approach.[22]

Still, Roman studies have not been untouched by tendencies to analyse spectacle, ritual, and performance, with their imprints particularly left in vital discussions on games, theatres, and the arena.[23] Processions have also attracted some attention,[24] and the triumph's dramatic force and emotional impact have been noticed. In a ground-breaking article of 1999, Richard Brilliant discussed the triumphal procession as public theatre, emphasizing the staging of visions, texts, and sounds that 'put ceremony before history'.[25] Brilliant moved the focus to the spectators and drew attention to their participation, stressing the emotional effect created in the common psychological space by the vivid imagery on display. In Brilliant's study, the triumphator still stands out as the main character, but here, he is contextualized, placed in a ritual act that addressed and reflected Roman society.

In 2003, Mary Beard openly and stimulatingly questioned Roman historians' traditional focus on the triumphator as an isolated figure of ritual and political solitude.[26] She proposed to integrate him in the procession as a whole, not however in 'the noisy, messy, probably rowdy, and almost entirely irrecoverable events of the ceremony "as it really happened"',[27] but above all in the written

---

[19] There is one exception. In AD 47, A. Plautius held an ovation over Britannia, accompanied, however, by the emperor Claudius on his way to the Capitol, Suet. *Claud.* 24.

[20] e.g. Balbuza (2002, 2004); Beard (2007), *passim*; Itgenshorst (2008).

[21] This is certainly due to what Feeney calls 'the structuralist revolution in Greek studies' (1998: 116). The anthropological approach has not to the same extent influenced Roman studies, which seem more closely tied to traditional historical methods.

[22] Rice (1983); Connor (1987); Rogers (1991: 80–126); Wikander (1992); Portefaix (1993); Chaniotis (1995); Graf (1996); Köhler (1996); Neils (1996); Walbank (1996); Maurizio (1998); Kavoulaki (1999, 2000); Thompson (2000).

[23] Bergmann (1999).   [24] Flaig (1995); Flower (1996: 91–127).

[25] Brilliant (1999).   [26] Beard (2003*b*).   [27] Beard (2003*b*: 28).

triumphs, the literary representations as preserved in the ancient accounts. Beard is sceptical about our capacity to unveil the historical triumphs behind all that representation and instead addresses the role of *mimesis* itself, in the parades as in the literary descriptions. In the theatrical context of representation, imitation, and performance, the triumphator played but one role in the game; he was no god, no king, but dressed up as god and king for the day, acting in the shadowland between reality and representation. The triumphator, as everything else, was imitation.

Two major monographs on the triumph have appeared in recent years: Tanja Itgenshorst's *Tota illa pompa: Der Triumph in der römischen Republik* (2005) and Mary Beard's *The Roman Triumph* (2007). The books are very different in character and style, but both share in having deconstructive aims. The authors provide useful reminders of the fragmentary nature of our sources and stress how much of our 'common knowledge' of the triumph is in fact based on writers living centuries after the events they describe. In particular, this goes for the early triumphs, supposedly held in Rome's mythical past. Itgenshorst's main purpose is to uncover characteristics of the Republican celebrations by isolating contemporary evidence only. Beard paints a broader canvas and addresses a number of triumphal aspects; a main point is that the triumph was not only glorification of military success but also provided an arena for ambivalence and critique.

LOOKING AT PROCESSION AS PERFORMANCE

This book proposes to discuss meanings and functions of the triumph in historical times. It does not strive to reconstruct and explain the distant beginnings of the ritual. In fact, like Beard and others, I remain sceptical about finding the meaning of the ritual in its origins.[28] As argued by Marshall, if all attention focuses on recovering the original meaning of the triumph, this implies that, in later periods, the procession having turned into a lavish manifestation of power, the celebration would in fact have lost its meaning.[29] Feeney puts it this way: 'The hunt for the origin removes the ritual from the cultural context which makes it possible for it to be significant.'[30]

Nor is this book specifically about the Roman triumphator. It will be argued that individual generals had both the will and power to affect the appearance of single parades. But the triumphator is not treated as a director, transmitting

---

[28] Versnel himself points out that '*origin* is not to be identified with *meaning*' (1993: 242).

[29] Marshall (1984: 123–7). Marshall stresses that the key to the meaning of the triumph lies in its contemporary performance, in the celebrating generals and crowds, who would have had only vague conceptions of the distant background of the parade; cf. Feeney (1998: 115–16).

[30] Feeney (1998: 118).

messages of propaganda to non-participant spectators.[31] Rather, my aim is to discuss the triumph as a ritualized play, in which the triumphator acted (prominently) together with other participants and spectators in a communal drama.

Looking at the triumph as performance, this study follows the path taken by Brilliant and Beard. Contrary to Beard, however, the principal object of analysis is not the construct of *mimesis* in the textual reconstructions of parade, but the procession itself, its staging and reception. I propose to discuss how Rome met with the surrounding world by analysing how spoils, captives, and representations were displayed and received. In its theoretical framing, the inquiry could be labelled performance analysis, with an aim to pay close attention to processional contents and sequence, acted roles, visual interplay, spectator participation, and emotional effect.[32]

Performance analysis has its basis in the cultural approach to ritual that developed in anthropology in the 1970s, promoted not least by the works of Victor Turner and Clifford Geertz.[33] Rituals are seen as reflections and expressions of community; they comment on society and its relations with the outer world.[34] Rather than being one-way communications of propaganda, rituals involve spectators as active participants. They establish and reinforce feelings of participation and community by addressing congregations of people in strong evocation of emotion.[35] In his classic essay on Balinese cockfighting, Geertz proposed the central device that interprets the ceremony as 'a story they tell themselves about themselves'.[36] Several historians working with different periods and settings have analysed procession from this approach, stressing that parades are forms of self-representation, directed at self-understanding, whether performed in classical Athens, Renaissance Venice, eighteenth-century Montpellier, or nineteenth- and twentieth-century America.[37] This does not mean that the processions were exact replicas of communal order. Rather, as events performed out of normal time, in a 'time out of time',[38] they staged the ideal pattern of social life.[39]

---

[31] By focusing on the triumphator, the triumph has been read as one of several media through which the general or emperor spread messages of propaganda. As there is at the moment again a tendency to discuss authority and power in the term of (more direct) propaganda, it is likely that studies will continue to focus on questions of the triumphator, certainly, though, with new questions posed.

[32] Cf. Kavoulaki (1999: 293).

[33] e.g. Turner's *From Ritual to Theatre: The Human Seriousness of Play* (New York, 1982), and *The Anthropology of Performance* (New York, 1988); for Geertz, see in particular Geertz (1973). See also Bell (1997: 61–8).

[34] Muir (1981: 5); Connor (1987: 41).

[35] Snickare (1999: 11); Brilliant (1999: 223); Chaniotis (2006).

[36] Geertz (1973: 448).

[37] Athens: Connor (1987); Neils (1992); Graf (1996); Venice: Muir (1981); Montpellier: Darnton (1985: 113–21); America: Davis (1986); Ryan (1989); Glassberg (1990); Schultz (1994).

[38] Falassi (1987: 4).

[39] J. Skorupski (1976) writes: 'Ceremony says, "look this is how things should be, this is the proper, ideal pattern of social life" ', quoted from Ryan (1989: 132); cf. Muir (1981: 5).

Critical voices have pointed out that in reading ritual as inclusive reflections of civic order and public consensus, scholars have tended to overlook tensions, diversities, and social strata within society. Although ritual and processions certainly do express community, they may also expose contrasts and competition. What might be read as expressions of civic unity may conceal exposure of internal power structure and social striving.[40] For example, Maurizio argues that the Panathenaic procession was both inclusive and exclusive, as it on one hand staged Athens as one community of religious identity and, on the other, exposed individual status.[41]

It is valid to read the triumph as visible hierarchy. Social orders were inevitably performed among participants as well as spectators. Furthermore, as Itgenshorst has rightly emphasized, there were heavy tensions inherent in a ritual that brought the successful general back from solitary leadership into the civic sphere.[42] Emotionally loaded mass congregations are potential arenas for all sorts of outbreaks, and there was always a risk that the celebration could go very wrong. As Mary Beard stresses throughout her book, there was a fine line between glory and scorn, and the triumphator always risked being brought down by hubris and discontented spectators.[43]

Still, the triumph had what many other civic parades lack—a pronounced other, the defeated, whose presence served as an antipode of normative community and reinforced a sense of oneness among all Roman participants. Leading and viewing subdued, formerly feared elephants or dreaded Germanic leaders in parade, grasping their crimes against civic order and participating in acts of humiliation, by necessity created strong feelings of belonging that confirmed and shaped Roman identity.[44] The emphatic exhibition of an emphasized other did perhaps make this ritual less potent in exposing differences within Roman society itself, as discontent, fear, and grief could always be directed at a present, outer enemy.

Culturalists have read procession as a communicative ritual by which community represents itself to itself.[45] With such a reading, in the triumph, 'Rome showed Rome to Rome'. Still, ritual cannot be restricted to mere communication, and the triumphal procession did more than reflect views of the world; it also formed an active role in shaping such values. In fact, many scholars working with concepts of performance stress that ritual had the capacity to not only

---

[40] Chaniotis (2006).

[41] Maurizio (1998: esp. 316–17).

[42] Itgenshorst (2005); cf. O'Neill (2004).

[43] Beard (2007).

[44] Cf. Hopkins (1991: 485); Coleman (1999: 241).

[45] Robert Darnton, in his famed study on Montpellier, writes in similar words of the city's main procession that it existed 'as sheer expression, a social order representing itself to itself' (1984: 121). Edmund Leach formulates similar arguments, stating that in ritual 'the performers and the listeners are the same people. We engage in rituals in order to transmit collective messages to ourselves', *Culture and Communication: The Logic by which Symbols are Connected* (Cambridge, 1976), 45.

express but also construct cultural patterns.[46] The point is not that the triumphal procession was no communication—quite clearly, Rome did show Rome to Rome—but rather that the procession was both expression and construction.

The triumph possessed characteristics that made it particularly suited to construct worldviews. The procession not only repeated certain forceful schemes, it also frequently introduced novelties to Rome. Following each foreign campaign close in time, the triumphal procession was in fact *the* public ritual that presented the outside world to Rome. In consequence, many peoples and places, items and individuals, people saw for the first time in the triumphal parade. Cicero attests to this function of the triumph, stating that the Gallic people was made known in Rome by way of triumphs and monuments, *triumphis ac monumentis notati*.[47] Among other examples, elephants made their first appearance in Rome in Dentatus' parade of 275 BC, and in 61 BC, Pompey introduced a number of spectacular objects and also put trees on parade for the first time. All these displays drew much attention and produced strong emotions. Without doubt, they played a decisive role in creating images of the world in Rome.

The introduction of novelties is not only an issue of reception but also concerns presentation. The explosive expansion of Rome brought about an influx of novel objects and the close meeting of unfamiliar lands and peoples, all of which 'Rome was now to show to Rome'. The triumph thus meant a true challenge as how to view and to stage the novel conquests, in itself dependent both on the traditional processional form and on pre-existing concepts. Indeed, the very existence of a triumphal procession forced Rome to consider how she (consciously or unconsciously) perceived the world and how she was to present it.

In examining spoils, captives, and representations, I propose to look both at the form, meaning, and function of the single displays and at the syntax of the parade, stressing such factors as categorization, sequence, interplay, and the composition of the totality.[48] In 1987, Marin suggested such an approach to procession along with issues of space and time.[49] As modern studies on the triumph have focused mainly on the Roman general, syntactic issues of the parade itself have been very sparsely addressed. Most studies that do comment on the order follow Ehlers, who states that there were three main groups in the procession: a first part, consisting of the booty, images of the subdued places, written placards, golden crowns, hostages, and prisoners; a second, centred on the triumphator; and a third, consisting of the

---

[46] Bell (1997: esp. 72–6, 82–3, 159–64); Schultz (1994: 19–20); Feeney (1998: 119); Kavoulaki (1999: 306); Bourque (2000: 21).

[47] Cic. *Font.* 12.

[48] A characteristic trait of performance theory is that it addresses questions both of semantics and syntax in the search for meaning, Bell (1997: 72–3).

[49] See Marin (1987: esp. 225). For such approaches, see M. Vovelle, *Les Métamorphoses de la fête en Provence de 1750 à 1820* (Aubier, 1976), 226–52; Muir (1981: 190–211).

army.[50] In its basic division, the tripartite categorization holds; in fact, it formed the principal grouping that signalled matters of identity. As we shall see, other placements and categorizations gave the parade further meaning and function.

Josephus, in his account of the triumph held by Titus and Vespasian in AD 71, partly quoted above, maintains that 'silver and gold and ivory in masses, made in all kinds of forms, might be seen, not as if carried in procession, but flowing so to speak, like a river . . . transparent gems . . . swept by in such profusion as to correct our erroneous supposition that any of them was rare . . . The spoils in general were borne in unordered heaps'.[51] His depiction conjures up images of a pageant in abundant disorder, as does Mantegna's vivid late fifteenth-century *Triumphs of Caesar*, where spoils, captives, images, soldiers, banners, arms, musicians, oxen, and elephants move along in dense disarray (Fig. 1).[52] In fact, the recent understanding of the triumph as a spectacle of noise, colour, and affect has nourished tendencies to paint the procession in carnival-like colours, as a called-for contrast to its previous characterization as lifeless institution detached from the very smelly, crowded streets it once paraded. Thus, in current scholarship, the triumph is 'noisy, messy, probably rowdy and almost irrecoverable', Mantegna paints a vivid echo of the 'herky-jerky movements of the parading troops', and the vivacity of the display has been illustrated by Bacchic sarcophagi with their 'hurly-burly of the Dionysiac cortège . . . and the disorderliness of the Bacchic ensemble'.[53]

The triumphal procession *was* a flourishing spectacle, a total experience for all senses, and a boiling-pot of full emotions. The effects of crowd, noise, visions, and colour *must* be stressed in order to interpret and understand the procession, its enormous visual impact and civic meaning. Still, the triumph was not a free-for-all-to-join carnivalish pageantry, but a highly ritualized procession, a well-planned political parade with deep roots in Roman tradition. As all rituals, the triumph was characterized by formality and repetition.[54] This goes not only for the celebrations of the distant past, when the 'original meaning' was still at work and the gods were revered in solemn simplicity, but also for the lavish processions of wealth and novelty in the second century BC as in the Imperial parades. These processions were ostentatious in performance, extravaganza, and abundance, but they were still ritual. Even behind the noise and colour, 'the rowdy, herky-jerky, and hurly-burly', there was formal sequence and choreography.

[50] Ehlers (1939: 501–11). See e.g. Favro (1994: 154); Holliday (1997: 133–4, based on Favro); Holliday (2002: 27).

[51] Joseph. *BJ* 7.134–6, 148.

[52] For Mantegna's painting, see Martindale (1979); Beard (2007: 153–9).

[53] Beard (2003b: 28); Brilliant (1999: 223–4), who takes Mantegna as 'an amalgamation of ancient testimonies perhaps closest to Josephus' report'. Note that I agree with Brilliant and Beard in their analyses of the triumph as powerful and vivid experiences. Both authors are well aware that the procession was also careful choreography and the quotes here are rather specimens of a general tendency, which forms my point of departure for a discussion of spectacle *vs.* structure.

[54] Bell (1997: 139–53); Rappaport (1999: 33–7); Snickare (1999: 11); Kavoulaki (2000: 145).

Mantegna's *Tri-
umphs of Caesar*.
Canvas 11: *The
Bearers of Stand-
ards and Siege
Equipment*. This
displays a pot-
pourri of people
and objects
thought to have
appeared in a
Roman triumph:
statues carried and
drawn on carts,
female personified
heads carrying
images of cities,
catapults, armour,
banners, and
written labels. The
text shows that the
painting intends
to represent Cae-
sar's triumph
over Gaul, held
in 46 BC.

Processional sequence was no 'mere form' arranging the contents. Rather, in ritual performance, contents and form are inseparable, and order a bearer of meaning. Syntax is semantics too, and indeed, the internal sequence of a parade determines the presentation and defines the participants.[55] As Muir states in his account of the Ducal parade in Renaissance Venice: 'In procession, position was everything.'[56] In analysing the triumphs as reflections and constructions of Roman worldviews, processional sequence and visual interplay are therefore central.[57] My approach here is to look at the composite whole by analysing in depth its parts, which, in their turn could be understood only by their place in the whole.[58] I propose to decode the parade by analysing its smallest units and place their

---

[55] Darnton (1985: 120); Marin (1987: 222); Maurizio (1998: 298–9).

[56] Muir (1981: 190).

[57] Kavoulaki (2000: 145): 'The composite character of such a ritual performance is based on the interaction and interconnectedness of its compound elements.'

[58] Cf. Kavoulaki (2000: 146).

contents in context, exploring their syntagmatic (sequential) and paradigmatic (interchangeable and contrasted) relations. At the same time, the study gives prime attention to the procession as spectacle and drama. Procession might be read as text, as the notion of semantics and syntax suggests,[59] but performance is the key word.[60] Thus, in this study, participants and spectators alike are partakers; there is constant interplay between actors, audience, and stage, and the formalization of ritual forces the participants into fixed roles.[61]

The study follows the procession as Rome expanded from being one of several notable states on the Italian peninsula to world power. One of the challenges in looking at ritual and performance in a longer historical perspective is the constant dialogue and tension between structure (characteristic of ritual) and change (characteristic of history). During the period in discussion here, Rome changed, as did the world, the city, the cultural context, and the value system. The procession too was exposed to changes, from internal as well as external pressures, challenged by constant novelties and invited to put the world, in all its variance and transformation, on stage. The procession was bound to change to be capable of interpreting and shaping values and perceptions, and to stay a vital force in each specific historical context.[62] At the same time, the power of the triumph was its ritual persuasiveness and its traditional reiteration. One of the discussions in the following will be the balance between frame and flexibility.

ROME: STAGE AND SPECTATORS

The triumphal procession was closely linked to the city of Rome. As the victorious general approached the city, Rome herself, her senators, magistrates, and people, went out to meet and welcome him. Later on, the very entrance into the city formed a key moment of the ritual. Ancient depictions often chose the passing through the *porta triumphalis* as a symbolic representation of the procession as a whole, and countless triumphal arches encapsulate this ritual crossing. Also, Livy, in his abundant triumphal accounts, frequently uses verb compounds with *trans-*, like *transferre, transvehere, traducere*, reflecting the transference of the spoils and booty across (*trans*) the *pomerium*.[63] As the general met with the senate outside the gates, his official request was to be allowed to enter the city in

---

[59] Ryan (1989: 133).

[60] Marin (1987: 227).

[61] Graf (1996: 57–8); Bell (1997: 140).

[62] Plattus (1983: 97); Bell (1997: 81–3). Today, there is an emphasis on rituals' flexibility to change, see e.g. Stavrianopoulou (2006: 10). Variance in ritual patterns is also discussed. For instance, Wiseman (2007) has suggested that the triumphal route was perhaps not all that fixed. At the same time, it is quite clear that rituals need repetition to be recognizable; both reiteration and change are crucial.

[63] Phillips (1974*a*).

triumph, *triumphans urbem inire* (*invehi*),[64] a phrase reflecting the importance of the passage from the military theatre of war and killing to the civic sphere of peace and order.

Once entered, the procession moved through and took up the civic space, defined the city and left imprints on its physical plan.[65] At the same time, the city led the procession along. It proceeded in slow pace on narrow streets—hence we should not picture full-blown military parades as in Mussolini's retrospective inauguration of the Via dell' Impero, parallel to the Via Sacra. On its way up to the Capitol, the triumph passed temples vowed by previous triumphators and it took in open spaces, theatres, and circuses that offered good views; very likely, the procession occasionally halted to perform specific rituals and dramas.[66] Route is central in understanding any processional performance. The triumphal route has received much scholarly interest, though still many uncertainties remain.[67] A number of basic elements are clear. In Republican times, the procession set off from the Circus Flaminius, entered the *porta triumphalis*, went up the Circus Maximus, moved along the Via Sacra, and came to an end at the Capitol. In the details of the passing through the Velabrum and the assumed encirclement of the Palatine, there are question marks that I hope to discuss in a subsequent article. In this study, I will not address the specifics of the spatial outline and there will be no attempt to locate the *porta triumphalis* or to rearrange the route. The discussion will, however, recurrently refer to the city as setting and interactive space. In the triumph, the city constituted the stage that set the event and defined the procession as a civic concern. After battle with close neighbours in the early third century BC as well as after having fought far abroad in the second century AD, Rome was the central point of victorious celebration. It took up Samnite weapons after the victory of Papirius Cursor and it embraced Jewish captives after the success of Vespasian and Titus. All through territorial expansion, the city embodied Rome and confirmed its conquest. Rome celebrated the triumph and the triumph celebrated Rome.

The spatial frame of the triumph was by nature both non-defined (the city as community) and strictly defined (a more or less fixed route). Similarly, the ritual

[64] Phillips (1974*a*; 1974*b*: 226–69).

[65] Laurence (1993) stresses that the Roman conception of the city was defined through ritual. Cf. Graf (1996: esp. 57–9), for Greek processions of the centripetal type, leading sacrificial animals from the outside to the city centre, sacred and political.

[66] Such stops were performed along the route of many Greek processions; see Kavoulaki (1999: 295, and n. 12, with further references). In the triumph, one stop is well known, the halt at the foot of the Capitoline hill in order to await the execution of the enemy leader (which seems not to have been compulsory), but as we shall see, there were probably others as well.

[67] Goell (1854: 44–57); Makin (1921); Coarelli (1968); Pfanner (1980); Plattus (1983: 99–103); Pietilä-Castrén (1987); Rüpke (1990: 228–9); Favro (1994); Brands and Maischberger (1995); Isager (1997); Coarelli (1997*a*: 118–35); Coarelli (1997*b*); Miller (2000); Wiseman (2007); Valli (2007); Beard (2007: 92–105).

was at once very specified in time (*triumphavit pridie kalendae Martiae*) and timeless. Founded, according to tradition, at the very point of birth of the city, each procession, reiterated and recognizable, also reflected and restaged previous celebrations.[68] As in all rituals, past and present merged.[69]

The city of Rome was also its spectators and, in Hopkins's words 'participation, as actor or observer, was a symbol of belonging to the community of Rome, which identified itself by its religious rites and traditions'.[70] Set in the city and fixed in tradition, the triumph defined the spectators, humans and gods, as Romans. This does not mean that all onlookers were Romans. People from all over the known world travelled to the city to view and be viewed on that day, and distinguished foreign guests were invited as a rule. Their presence lent occasion to the event and enhanced its recognition and status.[71] Also, they represented a viewer set between victors and the defeated, who on one hand renounced all affiliation with the conquered by joining in the celebration, but on the other hand was not fully incorporated as a member of Rome. The triumph staged symbolic statements also to these viewers,[72] as to those given notice of its splendour afterwards, though letters, oral narrative, literary accounts, and visual arts.

METHODS AND SOURCES

Discussions of Roman identity, perceptions of the world, and processional interplay require a thorough empirical analysis of triumphal contents. Since no such study as yet exists, in effect, a major part of this book is concerned with establishing the single displays and interpreting them in terms of contents, meaning, function, processional placing, categorization, and reception. Arms, ships and rams, coins and bullion, sculptures and paintings, art and valuables, golden crowns, prisoners, hostages, animals, and trees are all examined below in separate sections, as are the representations that were made specifically for the occasion: models and personifications of cities, peoples, rivers, and tableaux staging scenes from the war. The single displays are grouped in the modern categories spoils, captives (both obtained through war), and representations (produced for processional display); the study aims to reconstruct the ancient classification. The analysis also notes objects and people that were not shown, the negative displays.[73]

---

[68] Cf. Kavoulaki (2000: 145).

[69] Laurence (1993: 79–80, referring to Maurice Bloch); Stavrianopoulou (2006: 9).

[70] Hopkins (1991: 483).

[71] Baumann (1992: 110).

[72] Ibid., esp. 100–1.

[73] Darnton (1985: 119): 'One could not read a procession properly without noting the blank spots as well as the units that bulged with pomp and circumstance.'

As always when we approach antiquity, the sources are fragmentary and give far from a complete picture. To be able to discuss the Roman triumphal procession as expression and construction of worldviews, I have chosen to engage in an empirical inquiry of the complete corpus of ancient sources, literary and pictorial. It is my belief that the combined testimony from a wide variety of sources has the capacity to tell a very different story than would the fragments in isolation. To collect the relevant texts, I have used the list of triumphs and sources as presented by Degrassi in his edition of the *Fasti triumphales*, as well as the Latin and Greek databases.[74] In the following, I have used Loeb translations for longer quotes of Latin and Greek texts, but modified them as required. Translations of shorter passages are my own. Other translators are noted in footnotes. For entries in the *Fasti triumphales*, and for dates of specific triumphs, I have followed Degrassi's edition in the *Inscriptiones Italiae* (Rome, 1947).

The state of the sources sets the limits to the study. Several Greek accounts provide details of Roman triumphs held before the early third century BC. However, as Itgenshorst has recently emphasized,[75] the stories in Dionysius of Halicarnassus, Plutarch, and Zonaras of the processions held by heroes such as Romulus and Camillus are literary monuments rather than historical documents. Livy too notes as many as sixty-seven triumphs for the period 753–293 BC, but tells very little of the specifics of these parades. Things change in 293 BC, when Livy starts giving the contents of processions in some detail, and even more so around 200 BC, when lists of displays become rather comprehensive. Hence, from the third century BC, we are on firmer ground, and this is when this study sets off. Sources set limits also to chronological ends. After the triumphs held by Trajan, the *Historia Augusta* becomes close to being the sole source. This text is not only problematic in itself; it also gives very few details of processional contents and sequence. There are exceptions, and the *Historia Augusta* will occasionally figure in the analysis below, only, however, as testimony to generalized triumphal issues and not as a source for the specifics of the triumphs held after Trajan, which fall outside this study.

For much of the Republican triumphal history, Livy forms a main source. Hence, we are provided with quite detailed accounts of the triumphs held in the first part of the second century, but have difficulties in analysing processions between 167 BC, when Livy's text disappears, and the late Republic, which is rich in other sources. For example, although several authors suggest the magnificence of the three triumphs held in 146 and 145 BC (Metellus over Macedonia, Scipio Aemilianus over Carthage, and Mummius over Achaia and Corinth), we lack item-by-item accounts on the contents of these processions.

In books 21–45 (219–167 BC), Livy describes thirty-eight triumphs and ovations, some in a few words only, others in some detail. His accounts are

---

[74] Degrassi, *Inscr. It.* 13:1; databases: the PHI and TLG CD-Roms.
[75] Itgenshorst (2005: esp. 13–41).

mostly taken as trustworthy historical documentations.[76] This does not mean that his lists are complete or that they are unerring in detail. Quite clearly, his accounts did also fill literary purposes.[77] Still, Livy's standardized and strict lists of contents and number with little additional comment very likely provide a link to their post-processional documentation. Cicero gives testimony that detailed contents of triumphs were recorded by the *arearium* in the late Republic,[78] and imported wealth was probably listed from an earlier date. Livy's reiterated accounts echo such recordings, and even if not exactly replicas of any archives, they clearly give insights into the processional contents and appearance, and most importantly into Roman views of the displays.

This study strives to establish the contents of triumphs and frequently discusses specific displays, but the precise reconstruction of each parade in its detailed appearance is not the main aim; it is of little relevance whether or not, for example, Livy is accurate when he ascribes the display of the exact amount of 43,270 pounds of silver bullion to Flamininus in the parade of 194 BC. Flamininus might have displayed more or less; the point here is that silver bullion was counted as an important display at the time, that it was paraded in enormous quantities, and that the Roman archives found it relevant to record the amount in such detail. For the same reason, the testimonies of the Latin poets, Ovid being the prime example, are treated as equals to the historical accounts. Although the poets do not claim historical accuracy, as spectators, their descriptions transmit the Roman experience of the procession. They also reflect the appearance of the display and the emotions caused by the encounter with the subjugated on parade.

Greek and Latin texts both contribute to the analysis; as we shall see, they often expose differences. Although Greek and Latin writers of the period in general terms form part of a common culture, Greek authors clearly looked at the triumph from the outside. Compared to the Latin writers, they appear more independent in their approach to the traditions of triumph, and their descriptions, frequently presented in long, detailed narrative, are more often elaborate literary productions with their own internal ekphrastic considerations. In contrast, Latin writers, historians and poets alike, describe the procession from an inside perspective, and their accounts seem embedded in triumphal tradition. In generalizing terms, the Greek accounts describe, while the Latin descriptions reproduce the processions. Thus, while the detailed Greek depictions give inestimable information, detail, and colour, the Latin accounts are often closer

---

[76] Phillips (1974*b*: esp. 271–2); Oakley (1997: 56–7). For Livy's credibility concerning in particular the coins and bullion paraded: Frank (1933: 127); Jacobsthal (1943: 307); De Sanctis (1968: 607); Crawford (1974: 621 n. 2, 630 n. 6); Harris (1979: 59); Harl (1991: *passim*).

[77] I agree with Itgenshorst (2005) that Livy had rhetorical purposes with his triumphal accounts, but I believe her to be too sceptical in judging his descriptions as unreliable due to their repetitive style.

[78] Cic. *Verr.* II.1.21.57.

FIGURE 2 Eastern side of the arch of Titus in Rome with the preserved part of the long and narrow frieze that once encircled the entire monument. The triumphal procession shows, to the left, a personified river carried on a bier, and, further to the right, senators, and sacrificial oxen with their attendants.

keys to the processional meanings and to Roman views of the world. Both angles are crucial, however; they contrast and they interact. It is the variety of sources, Latin and Greek, prose and poetic, by contemporary eyewitnesses or based on archival record, that provides the possibility to analyse broad issues of procession and reception, identity, structure, and change.

Besides the written testimonies, there are some preserved reliefs with depictions of triumphal processions.[79] The representations are quite varied in style and intent. Some focus exclusively on the triumphator, who appears in splendid isolation standing in his triumphal car.[80] Such images are rather numerous, in sculpture and on coins, but for this study, they have but little relevance. Other depictions represent excerpts from the processional sequence, showing loads of booty or captives as they are carried through an arch (Figs. 4, 10). Our preserved examples are quite detailed and seem to aim at rendering the specifics of parade. For example, on the arch of Titus in Rome, it is quite clear that the large panels, although certainly not in all details historically correct, do represent the Jewish triumph of AD 71. There is also the newly discovered relief from Nicopolis by Actium,[81] which without any doubts refers specifically to Octavian's triumph in 29 BC.

[79] Künzl (1988: 160–3); *Trionfi romani*, 114–46.   [80] Beard (2007: 219–21).   [81] Zachos (2003).

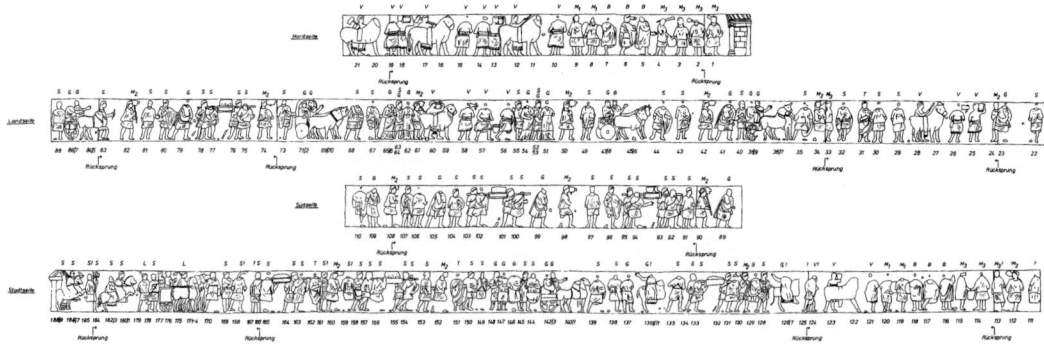

FIGURE 3 Like the arch of Titus in Rome, Trajan's arch at Benevento was decorated with a narrow frieze that depicted a triumphal procession at its length, encircling the arch on all sides. At Benevento, the whole sequence has been rather well preserved. At the top, sacrificial oxen with their attendants approach the temple of Jupiter Capitolinus, while the bottom left (north-western corner of the arch) shows the triumphator in his chariot at the rear of the parade. Behind the celebrating general, some officials are seen, but the larger mass of soldiers is not depicted. The frieze has booty, captives, and not least sacrificial animals represented all along the parade.

Still other representations are narrow, elongated friezes that once showed the procession at its length. Depictions of this kind encircled buildings like triumphal arches and temples. For example, the temple of Apollo Sosianus has left fragments of such a linear documentation (Fig. 16). In Benevento, a triumphal frieze still encircles the arch of Trajan, depicting a triumphal procession from beginning to end (Figs. 3, 11, 14, 15, 17), and the arch of Titus in Rome has preserved fragments of a similar depiction (Figs. 2, 24). In their details, the friezes reveal several matters of processional contents and appearance, but they are much more unspecific compared to the larger panels at the arch of Titus and the reliefs at Nicopolis. Besides their monumental placing, there is nothing in the narrow friezes to link the parades to any particular historical triumph.[82] They emphasize musicians, sacrificial oxen, and attendants of sacrifice. In this, they in fact expose the iconographical traits of 'procession', as traditionally represented in ancient art,[83] defining the ritual as a gift to the gods and encapsulating civic piety. The friezes are, in my view, representations of unspecific ritual iteration. They contrast with the larger panels and also with many written accounts, which frequently go into length and detail to describe the appearance of spoils, prisoners, and representations but tell only sparsely of the sacrificial aspects. Different media clearly had different aims, but in different ways, they all contribute to this study.

[82] With Andreae (1979); *contra* Adamo Muscettola (1992).   [83] Neils (1996: 178).

TWO

Spoils

ARMS, ARMY EQUIPMENT, ARTILLERY

Arms and armour stripped from defeated enemies on the battlefield (*spolia*, σκῦλα)[1] constituted the traditional spoils of ancient warfare. In Rome, the most prestigious spoils of arms were the *spolia opima*, weapons and armour captured from an enemy chief when killed by a Roman general in single combat.[2] According to the Roman tradition, *spolia opima* had been rightfully captured and dedicated only thrice: by Romulus, celebrating the defeat of King Acron of Caenina in 753 BC,[3] by A. Cornelius Cossus, after he had killed Lars Tolumnius, king of Veii, probably in 437 BC,[4] and finally by M. Claudius Marcellus in 222 BC, celebrating the besting of King Viridomarus, the Insubrian Gaul, at Clastidium.[5]

Ancient sources claim that Romulus, Cossus, and Marcellus carried the *spolia opima* themselves in parade and dedicated them to Jupiter Feretrius in his temple on the Capitoline hill.[6] As in Greece, it was common procedure in Rome to offer arms captured in war to the gods, and besides the rare pieces that ended up in the abode of Jupiter Feretrius, captured arms found their way to various other shrines in the city.[7] The spoils were either placed inside the temple or fixed to

---

[1] *RE* 2:e Reihe III (1927–9), s.v. 'spolia', 1843–5 (F. Lammert). Booty in the general sense is mostly labelled *praeda* and λάφυρα (Pritchett, 1991: 132–47).

[2] For the *spolia opima*, see e.g. *RE* 2:e Reihe III (1927–9), s.v. 'spolia opima', 1845–6 (F. Lammert); Latte (1960: 204–5); Versnel (1970: 304–13); Rich (1996); Schneider (1990: 187–205); Flower (2000); Gerding (2002: 116–25); Inglehart (2007)—all with further references.

[3] Liv. 1.10; Prop. 4.10; Dion. Hal. 2.33.2–34.4; Val. Max. 3.2.3; Plut. *Rom.* 16.5–8, *Marc.* 8.3; Fest. p. 202–4 L, s.v. 'opima spolia'; Ampel. 21.1; Serv. *ad Aen.* 6.859; Solin. 1.20; *vir. ill.* 2.3–5; Degrassi, *Inscr. It.* 13:3, 70, no. 86. Ogilvie (1965), 70–3.

[4] Liv. 4.19–20; Prop. 4.10; Dion. Hal. 12.5 (Ambr. Exc.); Val. Max. 3.2.4; Plut. *Rom.* 16.7–8, *Marc.* 8.3; Front. *Str.* 2.8.9; Flor. *Epit.* 1.6.9; Fest. p. 204 L, s.v. 'opima spolia'; Manil. *Astr.* 1.788; Ampel. 21.1; Serv. *ad Aen.* 6.841, 6.855, 6.859; *vir. ill.* 25.1–2. Ogilvie (1965), 557–8, 562–7.

[5] Cic. *Tusc.* 4.22.49–50; Liv. *Per.* 20; Verg. *Aen.* 6.855–9; Prop. 4.10; Val. Max. 3.2.5; Sil. *Pun.* 1.133, 3.587, 12.278–80; Plut. *Marc.* 8, *Rom.* 16.7–8, *Comp. Pel. Marc.* 1.2; Flor. *Epit.* 1.20.5; Fest. p. 204 L, s.v. 'opima spolia'; Front. *Str.* 4.5.4; Ampel. 21.1; Serv. *ad Aen.* 6.855, 6.859; Manil. *Astr.* 1.788; Oros. 4.13.15; Eutrop. 3.6; *vir. ill.* 45.1–4. Flower (2000).

[6] Romulus: Liv. 1.10.5; Plut. *Rom.* 16.6–8. Putnam (1985); Schneider (1990), *passim*, Abb. 21–2; Cossus: Liv. 4.20.2–3; Marcellus: Plut. *Marc.* 8.1–2.

[7] Spoils were often dedicated in temples vowed by the general in battle; for such manubial shrines, see Pietilä-Castrén (1987); Orlin (1997).

the doorposts or the outer walls. According to Plutarch, it was prohibited to take down or repair arms thus dedicated.[8] Spoils of arms were also used to decorate public places. According to the tradition, the Samnite shields captured by L. Papirius Cursor and displayed in his triumphal parade in 309 BC were used to embellish the Forum Romanum.[9] Much later, after his triumph in 101 BC, Q. Lutatius Catulus constructed a *porticus* on the Palatine to house the arms captured in the campaign against the Cimbri.[10] Not all of the arms won in battle and displayed in triumphs stayed in Rome, though. Many spoils were offered to allied cities, also to decorate temples and public places.[11]

The Roman custom of embellishing temples and public places with spoils of arms had Greek parallels, but unlike the Greeks, the Romans did not favour a placement of captured arms in their tombs.[12] Typically Roman rather than Greek was instead the practice of hanging up conquered weapons on the doors and walls of their houses.[13] Latin sources describe arms thus placed as being fixed, using mostly forms of *figere*, on the doorposts, *postes*, or at other locations at the entrance of the house (*circa limina*, *in vestibulo*, *in foribus*, etc.).[14] The same terms apply to arms attached to temples,[15] and there are other affinities between spoils placed on houses and those in shrines as well. In a well-known passage, Pliny the Elder argues that it was prohibited to take down the spoils fastened to the doors and outer walls of a Roman house even if the owner changed.[16] This is

---

[8] Plut. *Mor.* 273c–d.

[9] Liv. 9.40.15–17. When Livy later (10.46.2–6) describes the Samnite triumph held by the younger Papirius Cursor in 293 BC, he claims that the Roman people compared the spoils with those won by the triumphator's father and still decorating public places. The historical value of this episode has been doubted, though, see Rawson (1990: 164–6).

[10] Cic. *Dom.* 38.102, 43.114; Val. Max. 6.3.1c. *LTUR* iv (1999), s.v. 'porticus (monumentum) Catuli', 119 (E. Papi). Marius put up spoils from the same campaign around the Forum, Cic. *De orat.* 2.266; Quint. *Inst.* 6.3.38.

[11] e.g. Livy (24.21.9–11) states that the temple of the Olympian Jupiter in Syracuse was adorned with spoils captured from the Gauls and the Illyrians, which had been presented to Hiero by the Roman people. See also Cic. *Verr.* 11.1.21.55–6. Waurick (1977: 41).

[12] Flower (1998: 231). The custom was, however, widespread in many other Italian cultures, Polito (1998: 26–7). Gerding (2002: esp. 121–3) proposes that Crassus placed the controversial *spolia opima* taken in 27 BC in the tomb of his mother, Caecilia Metella.

[13] Polyb. 6.39.10; Cic. *Phil.* 2.28.68; Liv. 6.20.7, 10.7.9, 23.23.6; Verg. *Aen.* 5.393, 7.183–6; Prop. 3.9.26; Ov. *Trist.* 3.1.33–4; Tib. 1.1.53–4; Val. Max. 7.6.1b; Sil. *Pun.* 6.445–6; Plin. *Nat.* 35.2.6; Suet. *Nero* 38.2; Serv. *ad Aen.* 7.183, cf. Verg. *Aen.* 2.504; Ov. *Met.* 8.154. Rawson (1990); Wiseman (1987: esp. 393–9); Polito (1998: 26).

[14] Cato, *Orat. Fr.* 97 Malc.; Cic. *Phil.* 2.28.68; Liv. 10.7.9, 23.23.6, 38.43.10; Verg. *Aen.* 2.504, 7.183; Ov. *Met.* 8.154; Prop. 3.9.26; Plin. *Nat.* 35.2.7; Sil. *Pun.* 6.445–6.

[15] Verg. *Aen.* 3.286–8, 5.359–60, 8.721–2, 11.778–9; Hor. *Carm.* 4.15.6–8; Liv. 10.2.14, 10.7.9, 24.21.9–11; Sil. *Pun.* 14.649, 15.674–5; Pers. 6.45; Gallus, in Anderson *et al.* (1979: 138); Serv. *ad Aen.* 7.183. See also Wiseman (1987: esp. 393–9, with further references).

[16] Plin. *Nat.* 35.2.7.

just what Plutarch tells of the arms that hung in temples. Captured spoils of arms, those dedicated in temples and those fixed to houses, were all looked upon as inviolable.

Nonetheless, necessity at times forced the Romans to make use of all weapons available. In the crisis after the battle of Cannae in 216 BC, the senate ordered that the ancient spoils of arms should be taken down from temples and porticoes and be used in the defence of the city.[17] Later in the same year, Livy describes how six thousand men were armed with the weapons that C. Flaminius had carried in his triumph over the Gauls in 223 BC.[18] Spoils were used in internal conflicts as well. In 121 BC, M. Fulvius Flaccus and his sympathizers, supporting the case of C. Gracchus, armed themselves with the spoils that hung around Flaccus' house, weapons that had been captured from the Gauls and displayed in his triumph two years earlier.[19]

The houses most distinguished by captured spoils from defeated enemies were those owned by triumphant generals.[20] But sources show that the honour was, at least in the middle Republic, bestowed not on commanders only.[21] Polybius states that the men who had been awarded with diverse crowns for their courage in battle were noted in Rome by being the only ones to wear their decorations in religious processions and by having spoils hung up in their houses.[22] Livy too equates the men who had been rewarded with crowns with the ones who had spoils of war fastened to their houses. Describing the shortage of senators after the disaster at Cannae, Livy maintains that new members were elected primarily among those who had held offices, then from those who had arms of the enemy fixed to their doors or had received a civic crown.[23]

Arms and armour hung up at houses could have been won as *spolia provocatoria* in a formal single combat after challenge (*ex provocatione*),[24] or given the soldier as prizes of bravery after battle. Possibly, at an early date, soldiers carried their *spolia* themselves in the triumphal processions.[25] Later on, all booty was paraded before the general, and soldiers bore instead decorations of crowns and other *dona militaria*. The earliest trustworthy evidence of *dona* comes from Polybius, but

[17] Liv. 22.57.10–11; cf. Val. Max. 7.6.1b.
[18] Liv. 23.14.4, cf. Liv. 22.46.4, 24.21.9–11.
[19] Plut. *C. Gracch.* 15.1; triumph: Vell. Pat. 2.6.4; Plut. *C. Gracch.* 18.1.
[20] See e.g. Cic. *Phil.* 2.28.68; Liv. 38.43.10; Ov. *Trist.* 3.1.33–4.
[21] Rawson (1990: 161), assumes that the custom of having spoils fixed to houses commenced *c*.300 BC.
[22] Polyb. 6.39.10.
[23] Liv. 23.23.6–7.
[24] Val. Max. 3.2.24; Plin. *Nat.* 7.28.101–2; Gell. 2.11. Oakley (1985: esp. 397, 409 and n. 141); Rawson (1990: 160).
[25] Livy (3.29.4–8) claims that the soldiers in L. Quinctius Cincinnatus' triumph of 458 BC followed laden with booty, *secutus exercitus praeda onustus*.

the custom was in all probability older.[26] The institution developed rapidly during the late Republic, and Maxfield has convincingly proposed that the *dona* might have replaced the earlier practice of soldiers taking personal spoils.[27]

The tradition of decorating houses with spoils of war eventually disappeared, and Augustan poets provide our last evidence of a contemporary practice.[28] Later on, Pliny writes of the custom as having been one of the ancestors, *apud maiores*,[29] and Suetonius describes the houses still decorated with spoils that were destroyed in the fire of AD 64 as *domus priscorum ducum*.[30]

Arma telaque—*personal weaponry as piles and trophies*

Arms and armour seized from vanquished enemies were self-evident components of the Roman triumphs, where they customarily appeared in the initial part of the parades.[31] Textual evidence is abundant and depictions in art exist too. However, both literature and reliefs paint rather general pictures of martial spoils on triumphal parade. Thus, less than could be expected can be deduced on their specific appearance, origin, and numbers.

The Latin sources are particularly unspecific. Except for a few short mentions of shields, greaves, and bows,[32] arms on parade appear simply as *spolia*, *arma*, or *tela*.[33] The joint expression *arma telaque* suggests that both defensive and offensive weapons were put on show.[34] A few times, Livy notes the presence of *spolia Gallica*,[35] but apart from this, Latin accounts do not reveal the provenance of any captured arms. Nor do they suggest that the crowd ever revealed any emotional reactions when confronted with the captured weaponry. This limited interest in and very unspecific descriptions of arms on triumphal parades strongly contrast with the ever-present battle narratives in Latin texts, with

[26] Polyb. 6.39. Maxfield (1981: 45, 62).

[27] Maxfield (1981: 60–1). Duels also became rarer, which resulted in fewer opportunities to win the *spolia provocatoria*, Oakley (1985: 410).

[28] Ovid (*Trist.* 3.1.33–4) on the house of Augustus on the Palatine; Propertius (3.9.26) on Maecenas' house; Tibullus (1.1.53–4) on the house of Messalla.

[29] Plin. *Nat.* 35.2.6.   [30] Suet. *Nero* 38.2.

[31] Arms and armour are listed in the beginning of triumphal accounts at e.g. Liv. 26.21.7–10, 34.52.4–12, 36.40.11–14, 45.43.4–7; Diod. Sic. 31.8.10–12 (apud Sync.); Dion. Hal. 6.17.2; Ov. *Pont.* 3.4.103–12.

[32] Shields: Liv. 34.52.5–6; Ov. *Pont.* 3.4.103; greaves: Ov. *Pont.* 3.4.103; bows: Prop. 3.4.17. Livy and Ovid describe the shields and greaves in their capacity as objects of worth rather than arms.

[33] *Arma, tela*: Liv. 34.52.4, 39.5.15–16; Ov. *Pont.* 2.1.40. *Spolia* are mentioned in countless descriptions, see e.g. Liv. 10.46.4, 23.14.4, 33.23.4–5, 33.23.8–9, 33.37.11, 45.43.4–5. *Spolia* could be both captured weapons and other kinds of booty.

[34] For *arma et tela* as defensive and offensive weapons, *OLD* s.vv. 'arma' (2), 'telum' (1b); Briquel (1986: 66).

[35] Liv. 23.14.4, 33.23.4–5, 39.7.2.

in-depth commentaries on armoury details on both sides.[36] Roman art too provides abundant representations of weapons with thorough renderings of shapes and ornaments.[37]

A few Greek descriptions present the paraded arms in more detail. In his account of the Macedonian triumph held by Flamininus in 194 BC, Plutarch points out that the most beautiful sight in the procession was provided by the spoils of war, Greek helmets and Macedonian shields and pikes, Ἑλληνικὰ κράνη καὶ πέλται Μακεδονικαὶ καὶ σάρισαι.[38] The *sarissa* was a typical weapon of the Macedonians, the *pelta* of eastern peoples in general,[39] and both types likewise appear in Plutarch's vivid description of the arms shown by Aemilius Paullus in his Macedonian triumph of 167 BC (*Aem.* 32.5–8):

τῇ δ' ὑστεραίᾳ τὰ κάλλιστα καὶ πολυτελέστατα τῶν Μακεδονικῶν ὅπλων ἐπέμπετο πολλαῖς ἁμάξαις, αὐτά τε μαρμαίροντα χαλκῷ νεοσμήκτῳ καὶ σιδήρῳ, τήν τε θέσιν ἐκ τέχνης καὶ συναρμογῆς ὡς ἂν μάλιστα συμπεφορημένοις χύδην καὶ αὐτομάτως ἐοίκοι πεποιημένα κράνη πρὸς ἀσπίσι καὶ θώρακες ἐπὶ κνημῖσι, καὶ Κρητικαὶ πέλται καὶ Θρᾴκια γέρρα καὶ φαρέτραι μετὰ ἱππικῶν ἀναμεμιγμέναι χαλινῶν, καὶ ξίφη γυμνὰ διὰ τούτων παρανίσχοντα καὶ σάρισαι παραπεπηγυῖαι, σύμμετρον ἐχόντων χάλασμα τῶν ὅπλων, ὥστε τὴν πρὸς ἄλληλα κροῦσιν ἐν τῷ διαφέρεσθαι τραχὺ καὶ φοβερὸν ὑπηχεῖν, καὶ μηδὲ νενικημένων ἄφοβον εἶναι τὴν ὄψιν.

On the second [day], the most beautiful and costly Macedonian arms were paraded in many wagons. The arms themselves sparkled with freshly polished bronze and iron, and were carefully and artfully arranged to look exactly as though they had been piled together in heaps and at random, helmets lying upon shields and cuirasses upon greaves, while Cretan shields and Thracian wicker shields and quivers were mixed up with horses' bridles, and through them projected naked swords and pikes planted among them, all the arms being so loosely packed that they smote against each other as they were borne along and gave out a harsh and dreadful sound, and the sight of them, even though they were spoils of a conquered enemy, was not without its terrors.

Besides the Macedonian weaponry, Plutarch tells of Cretan πέλται and Thracian γέρρα, wicker shields and φαρέτραι, quivers. Cretan as well as Thracian auxiliaries fought in Perseus' army,[40] and their arms were quite likely present among other

[36] See e.g. Liv. 9.40.1–6 with Rouveret (1986), and Liv. 22.46.1–7, 37.30, 37.39–43, 38.29.3–8.

[37] Although many Roman artistic representations of arms are extremely thorough in detail, each shield, cuirass, or greave is often rendered 'incorrectly'. Weapon friezes many times display a mixture of Greek, barbarian, and at times possibly even Roman pieces, contemporary as well as historical. They reflect primarily an antiquarian interest in details. Also, Roman depictions of arms were highly influenced by the Hellenistic weapon friezes at Pergamon. Waurick (1983); Schneider (1990: 174–6); Polito (1998).

[38] Plut. *Flam.* 14.1.

[39] Sarissa: Markle (1977, 1982); Nylander (1983). Servius writes (*ad Aen.* 7.664): *pilum proprium est hasta Romana, ut gaesa Gallorum, sarissae Macedonum.* On πέλται in Roman weapon friezes, Polito (1998: 44–5). The *pelta*, a characteristic weapon of the Amazons, was originally used by the Thracians, but came later to be employed by other peoples of the East as well.

[40] Plut. *Aem.* 18.5, 23.6–11.

spoils paraded.[41] If so, they transmitted a message of Roman military supremacy that reached outside the specific area of Macedonian conquest.

Plutarch's description of the arms is exceptionally detailed when compared to Diodorus Siculus, the other Greek source of Aemilius Paullus' parade.[42] It is assumed that both Diodorus and Plutarch based their accounts on Polybius,[43] and in view of the difference between the two, much of the vivid and detailed ekphrasis of the weaponry was probably Plutarch's own. Most importantly, his account strongly contrasts with Livy's sober and standardized enumerations and thus also with the Roman annalistic documentation and tradition.[44] The Roman archives and literary sources contented themselves with referring to the exhibition of arms in very general terms.

Most descriptions of Republican triumphal processions stress that captured arms were transported on wagons.[45] The weapons were not grouped according to types, but instead, Greek and Latin texts emphasize that they were piled up in heaps seemingly at random. For example, Dionysius of Halicarnassus maintains that A. Postumius in the beginning of the fifth century BC showed heaps of weapons on many wagons,[46] and much later, Ovid depicts captured arms on triumphal display as *armaque cum telis in strue mixta sua*, 'defensive and offensive weapons in a mixed pile'.[47] In his account of Aemilius Paullus' Macedonian triumph, Plutarch (quoted above) tells of how the arms, glittering with freshly polished bronze and iron 'were carefully and artfully arranged to look exactly as though they had been piled together in heaps and at random'.[48]

---

[41] Cretan arms need not have been limited to auxiliaries from Crete. Appian (*Syr.* 32) tells us that there were in Antiochus III's army stone throwers, archers, javelin throwers, and peltasts from Phrygia, Lycia, Pamphylia, Pisidia, Crete, Tralles, and Cilicia, all armed in Cretan fashion.

[42] Diod. Sic. 31.8.10–11 (apud Sync.).

[43] Plutarch: Vianoli (1972: 81–2); Swain (1989: 317, 325–6). Diodorus: *RE* V (1905), s.v. 'Diodoros' (38), 689 (E. Schwartz); Cànola (1982: 763). Liedmeier (1935) argues that Diodorus' account is the one closest to Polybius, but that there might be traces of the Polybian description in Plutarch's version as well. Contrary to this view, Jacobsthal (1943: 310 and n. 24) holds that Plutarch's version reflects the Polybian original, while Diodorus' account is untrustworthy. Swain (1989: 325), notes the difficulty in reconstructing the Polybian original. Remarkably, the preserved text of Polybius contains no detailed triumphal descriptions; there are only a few rather general, shorter accounts. Possibly, the reason should be sought in the historical circumstances of Polybius' transferral to Rome. He was taken to Rome as one of a thousand Achaeans after Perseus' defeat and saw his friends and associates led in Aemilius Paullus' triumph. In fact, it cannot be excluded that Polybius himself was forced to walk in the procession.

[44] Unfortunately, the larger part of Livy's description of Paullus' triumph is lost, but the difference between him and Plutarch is evident in their accounts of Flamininus' celebration. Here, Livy produces a detailed list of the three days of display, Plutarch a short general overview only. Plutarch quotes Tuditanus for the amount of coins that Flamininus showed, but writes nothing of his other sources.

[45] On wagons: Liv. 33.23.4–5, 33.37.11, 36.40.11, 39.7.2; Dion. Hal. 6.17.2; Diod. Sic. 31.8.10 (apud Sync.); Plut. *Aem.* 32.5–8; App. *Mith.* 116. On biers: Plut. *Luc.* 37.3–4.

[46] Dion. Hal. 6.17.2: θριάμβῳ κοσμούμενος ὅπλων τε σωρὸν ἐφ' ἁμάξαις πολλαῖς κομίζων...

[47] Ov. *Pont.* 2.1.40.

[48] Josephus (*BJ* 7.148) writes, similarly, of the spoils shown in Vespasian and Titus' Jewish triumph that they were shown in unordered heaps, χύδην.

The triumphal exhibition of mixed piles of captured enemy arms cannot but bring to mind the heaps of weapons that the Romans regularly collected on the battlefield after a victorious battle or larger campaign. The arms were piled up, and the general had them burnt as an offering to Vulcan, Lua, Mars, or Minerva. For example, Livy tells us that at Amphipolis in 167 BC, Aemilius Paullus brought the captured Macedonian bronze shields into the ships, but put the rest of the arms of all kinds on a great heap, made his prayers and set fire to the pile.[49] Other texts provide similar accounts, the last example of which relates to the year 86 BC.[50]

Unlike the heaps constructed on the battlefield, the piles displayed in the triumphal processions were not set on fire, and the parallel between the two is not a strict one. Still, both types were consecrated to the gods: the arms brought together in the field by way of prayer and fire, the ones in Rome by way of the triumphal rite and by their subsequent fixing to the doorposts of temples and houses, both sacred and untouchable. By being piled up in seemingly disordered heaps, the arms in the triumphs connoted 'spoils' rather than 'arms'. This is no small matter, in view of the prohibition of bringing weapons inside of the *pomerium*. Weapons taken from the enemy were believed to still possess powers, which might cause danger if brought into the city.[51] Had the weapons been exhibited in proper order, sword by sword and lance by lance, they would have indicated arms of a still-threatening enemy force at combat. Thrown in disordered piles, 'helmets lying upon shields and cuirasses upon greaves', they instead provided visual allusion to the heaps collected in the field and affirmed Roman conquest of now-decommissioned weapons about to be dedicated to the gods.

During the first century BC, trophies replaced the earlier rite of burning enemy weapons on the battlefield.[52] After Ovid, there is also little evidence that heaps of mixed weapons were shown in triumphs. Instead, from the late Republic onwards, again parallel to the battlefield constructions, trophies appear on

[49] Liv. 45.33.1–3.

[50] App. *Mith.* 45. See also e.g. Liv. 8.30.8, 10.29.18–19, 30.6.9, 41.12.6; Sil. *Pun.* 10.547–57; Plut. *Mar.* 22.1–3; App. *Pun.* 48, 133, *Iber.* 57, *Syr.* 42; Serv. *ad Aen.* 8.562. For 'Waffenverbrennung', see Rüpke (1990: 198–202). The funeral pyres of Pompey, Caesar, and Augustus included piles of weapons, Polito (1998: 26–7). Tacitus (*Ann.* 2.22) states that Germanicus constructed a *congeries armorum*, which was left untouched on the battlefield after the second defeat of Arminius, and Florus maintains that Drusus built a monument of the captured weapons at the bank of the River Elbe, Flor. *Epit.* 2.30.23–4. Picard (1957: 20, 120, 301–4, 318–19); Polito (1998: 27). Leaving unburnt piles of captured weapons on the battlefield was a Celtic tradition, which is believed to have inspired the behaviour of Germanicus and Drusus (Rüpke, 1990: 202).

[51] Latte (1960: 129); Versnel (1970: 309); Rüpke (1990: 200, 211). Versnel claims that the *spolia opima* and the *spolia provocatoria* formed exceptions among the arms. They were harmless and could consequently be brought back to Rome and fastened to temples and houses without further precautions.

[52] Woelcke (1911); *RE* 2:e Reihe VII:1 (1939), s.v. 'τρόπαιον', 670–3 (E. Kirsten); Picard (1957: 103–63); Rüpke (1990: 201).

FIGURE 4
This second-century relief shows a triumphal procession passing under an arch. Laurel-wreathed soldiers carry a trophy flanked by prisoners on a decorated *ferculum*. The prisoners are very small in scale and have been read as dummies. But the trophy is disproportionately small too, and I suspect rather that the whole display on the bier has been cut down in size to give prominence to the Roman participants.

triumphal parade. Florus provides the earliest testimony. Describing Marius' triumph held in 101 BC over the Cimbri and the Teutones, he maintains that Teutobodus, king of the Teutones 'towered above his own trophies' (*super tropaea sua eminebat*).[53] This date fits rather well with the earliest reference, also in Florus, to a stone trophy erected at the battle scene in 121 BC.[54] After Marius, texts confirm the presence of *tropaea* in the triumph of Pompey in 61 BC and, besides, there are a few general remarks on their processional exhibition in the writings of Ovid and Seneca.[55] Anthropomorphic trophies with prisoners seated below also appear on a number of Imperial reliefs that depict excerpts from

[53] Flor. *Epit.* 1.38.10.
[54] Flor. *Epit.* 1.37.6. Trophies are depicted on Republican coins from 131 BC, Schneider (1990: 194–6, with further references).
[55] Pompey: Plut. *Pomp.* 45.4; Dio Cass. 37.21.2. Further references: Ov. *Pont.* 2.1.41; Sen. *Tro.* 150.

triumphal processions (Figs. 4, 16).[56] Here, the weaponry hanging on the trophies give a rather harmless impression. Far from the frights of the battlefield or the fearful noisy heaps in Plutarch's version of Paullus' triumph, the trophies with their seated captives appear rather as well-composed decorations than deadly arms.

The sources for the Imperial triumphs are far too meagre to allow us to reconstruct the development in detail. In all probability, however, the post-battle tradition on the field inspired the Romans to pile captured weapons in the Republican parades and display trophies in the Imperial.

There was in Rome a tradition that in older times, weapons on display in the triumphs and dedicated to the gods had been both broken and bloody.[57] Florus dates the change to a richer display to Dentatus' triumph over Pyrrhus in 275 BC, which showed art and riches from Tarentum in particular. Before this date, writes Florus, the only things seen were the cattle of the Volscians, the flocks of the Sabines, the *carpenta* of the Gauls, the broken arms (*fracta arma*) of the Samnites.[58] Plutarch prefers to see Marcellus' ovation over Syracuse in 211 BC, likewise famed for the display of Greek art and riches, as the turning point. Before this date, Rome was, in Plutarch's version, full of barbaric arms and bloody spoils (ὅπλων δὲ βαρβαρικῶν καὶ λαφύρων ἐναίμων ἀνάπλεως).[59]

There are of course standard explanations for Rome's later luxury habits and moral decline. Just how bloody and broken the arms once on display were is very hard to tell.[60] It is clear, though, that accounts of late Republican and Imperial triumphs lack descriptions of bloodstained, fragmented spoils. The burning of arms on the battlefield not only had a ritual function but a practical one too. Large amounts of weapons were normally captured from the enemy and far from all could be transported for display in Rome. Thus, the damaged and less valuable items were given up to the flames, while the untouched, worthy, and spectacular were shipped to the city. Hence, Livy tells that it was only after

---

[56] The relief from the temple of Apollo Sosianus (Fig. 16): Ryberg (1955: 144–6, pl. LI, figs. 78a–d); La Rocca (1985: 94–6, figs. 22, 24); Viscogliosi (1988: Kat. 41, 144–5); Zanker (1990: 70, fig. 55); *Trionfi romani* (2008), 120–1, no. 1.2.3. A relief from Museo Nazionale Romano (Fig. 4): Gabelmann (1981: no. 1, 437–8, Abb. 1); Palma and Lachenal (1983: no. 83, 195–8); Koeppel (1986: Kat. 44, 15–16, 85–6, Abb. 50); Künzl (1988: 76–7, Abb. 44); Beard (2007: 146, fig. 26); *Trionfi romani* (2008), 138–9, no. 1.2.16.

[57] See e.g. Sil. *Pun.* 1.620.

[58] Flor. *Epit.* 1.13.27. In Republican Rome, there was a marked interest in Samnite weaponry, see Briquel (1986).

[59] Plut. *Marc.* 21.2.

[60] A hydria from Capua, painted by the so-called Triumph-painter in the second half of the 4th cent. BC, shows two warriors in Oscan dress with a prisoner of war in front of them and carrying on poles bloodstained clothes from the enemy. Schneider (1990: 193–4, Abb. 24 and n. 128); Benassai (2001: 187–209).

Aemilius Paullus had taken the precious shields on board that the captured weapons were heaped up and burnt.[61] After the destruction of Carthage in 146 BC, Scipio Aemilianus had the arms, war engines, and ships unfit for use burnt to Mars and Minerva.[62] Somewhat later, Plutarch reports that Marius, after his victories against the Teutones, 'collected the weapons and spoils of the barbarians that were excellent, entire, and fitted to offer a magnificent sight in his triumphal procession; all the rest he heaped up on a huge pyre and offered a magnificent sacrifice'.[63]

On parade, the heaped weapons' visual appearance was thoroughly worked out. The arms were polished and carefully arranged. But the display did not stress the importance of any particular piece or type of weapon, nor did it emphasize the precise number of arms or groups of arms shown. Shields form the one exception to this rule. They were paraded as objects of physical value, and the ancient authors often point out that they were made of bronze, silver, or gold.[64] In Lucullus' triumph of 63 BC, there was even 'a wonderful shield adorned with precious stones'.[65] In contrast to other weaponry, shields were often displayed in separate groups, and their number was at times recorded. Diodorus Siculus states that, besides the wagons loaded with mixed weapons, Aemilius Paullus paraded 1,200 wagons filled with white shields and as many with bronze shields (clearly too high figures)[66] on the first day of his Macedonian triumph of 167 BC.[67] The second day's procession, which displayed statues, coins, and riches, also included golden shields.[68] Thus, these shields were exhibited not as arms, which in Diodorus' account dominated the opening day, but together with and as valuable objects and works of art. Livy's account of Flamininus' three-day-long triumph in 194 BC reflect a similar procedure. Here, the *arma* and *tela* opened day one, while the shields appear only in the following day's procession, which focused on the display of gold and silver.[69] Livy lists ten shields of silver among various other silver objects, and one shield, completely of gold, among the items of gold.

The special emphasis on shields as objects of worth could perhaps be explained by the fact that they were heavy objects, which often carried a substantial amount

---

[61] Liv. 45.33.1–3.

[62] App. *Pun.* 133, cf. *Pun.* 48.

[63] Plut. *Mar.* 22.1: Μετὰ δὲ τὴν μάχην ὁ Μάριος τῶν βαρβαρικῶν ὅπλων καὶ λαφύρων τὰ μὲν ἐκπρεπῆ καὶ ὁλόκληρα καὶ πομπικὴν ὄψιν τῷ θριάμβῳ δυνάμενα παρασχεῖν ἐπέλεξε, τῶν δὲ ἄλλων ἐπὶ πυρᾶς μεγάλης κατασωρεύσας τὸ πλῆθος ἔθυσε θυσίαν μεγαλοπρεπῆ.

[64] Liv. 9.40.15–16, 34.52.5–6; Diod. Sic. 31.8.10 (apud Sync); Plut. *Luc.* 37.3.

[65] Plut. *Luc.* 37.3: θυρεός τις διάλιθος.

[66] Liedmeier (1935: 254–5), suspects that Diodorus has mixed up Polybius' figures, which would have referred to the number of shields rather than wagons.

[67] Diod. Sic. 31.8.10 (apud Sync.). Plutarch states that at Pydna, the Thracians were distinguished by their gleaming white shields and greaves, *Aem.* 18.5.

[68] Diod. Sic. 31.8.11–12 (apud Sync.).   [69] Liv. 34.52.5–6.

of valuable metal.[70] Shields were also visually prominent status symbols, highly suitable for display. Vanquished enemies often had to turn over their complete arsenal of arms as well as their art treasures.[71] Many of the gold and silver shields exhibited in the triumphs of Flamininus and Aemilius Paullus, not to mention the one decorated with gems displayed by Lucullus, probably came from the royal treasuries of the East, not from the battlefields.

There are almost no Imperial references to the display of weapons in triumphs at all. As mentioned above, the practice of fixing arms to the houses also ceased around the time of Augustus. The two phenomena should probably be read as a result of the same development, in which captured weapons had lost much of their former strength as symbols of enemy defeat. Rome was now the world power, confident in its military superiority. Also, the Roman employment of foreign auxiliaries and the adoption of different types of weaponry that had earlier characterized their enemies may have played a part. By and by, many of the weapons that had symbolized the Gallic, Parthian, or Scythian forces, were used in the defence of Rome. As foreign weaponry became more and more familiar, it may well have lost some of its original power to induce fear and terror in the Romans, the soldiers in the field as well as the spectators in the city.

On Imperial reliefs depicting triumphal processions, arms do appear, but mostly as part of trophies and at a few times as ornaments of *fercula* and transport wagons. Even the military emperor Vespasian seems to have emphasized riches rather than arms in his triumph. In his long and detailed description of the Jewish triumph of AD 71, Josephus mentions abundant quantities of gold, silver, and ivory, but no arms. The spoils in focus were instead the sacred objects from the temple of Jerusalem.[72] Josephus cannot be trusted as unbiased; yet the arch of Titus also gives the temple treasures the place of honour among spoils. Our one Imperial source to emphasize the display of arms is Pliny the Younger, as he in his Panegyric (16–17) envisions Trajan's return from Dacia and the triumph to come:

Accipiet ergo aliquando Capitolium non mimicos currus nec falsae simulacra victoriae, sed imperatorem veram ac solidam gloriam reportantem, pacem tranquillitatem et tam confessa hostium obsequia, ut vincendus nemo fuerit ... Videor iam cernere non spoliis provinciarum et extorto sociis auro, sed hostilibus armis captorumque regum catenis triumphum gravem ... mox ipsum te sublimem instantemque curru domitarum gentium tergo, ante currum autem clipeos, quos ipse perfoderis.

---

[70] Perhaps the function of the shields as defensive rather than offensive, more dangerous weapons, also encouraged their display as art objects rather than arms.

[71] See e.g. Zonar. 8.18.1, discussed by Flower (1998: 230).

[72] Joseph. *BJ* 7.132–57.

And so the day will come when the Capitol shall receive no phoney chariots and false images of victory, but an emperor returning with true and genuine honour, bringing peace and the end of strife, and the submission of his enemies so evident that none shall be left to conquer...Already I seem to see before me a triumph filled not with spoils from our provinces and gold extorted from our allies, but with our enemies' arms and the chains of the captured kings...then, close behind the conquered peoples your own self standing high in your chariot, before which are the shields pierced by your own hand.

Pliny's vision of Trajan's future triumph emphasizes the exhibition of captured arms, including shields, which the emperor himself would have conquered and captured. The message is one of true military victories in contrast to the earlier mock triumphs, probably in particular those of Domitian. Similarly, the monuments of Trajan's Rome, not least the buildings at his Forum, were filled with representations of enemy weapons, which marked the emperor's defeat of the barbaric Dacians. Most interestingly, Polito has stressed the particularity and innovative force of the depictions of arms in Trajanic art.[73] While the majority of Imperial friezes depicting arms simply recalled images of weaponry introduced in the late Republican and early Imperial times and applied them as stock motives, the Trajanic friezes produced new iconographic sets of motives. It seems likely then, that while most Imperial triumphs included arms mainly as rich decorations, Trajan deliberately chose to manifest his success by stressing the subjected warlike powers of the Dacians. Consequently, he emphasized the captured arms in his triumphs as well as in the artistic commemoration of the victories, a display through which he could also allude to the military and moral strength of earlier days, Republican and Augustan.

Chariots: vehicles in mass and on singular display

Several types of chariots were displayed as spoils of war in the Roman triumphal procession. Among these, royal cars, which had been captured from or presented by eastern kings, will be discussed as part of the regal displays (pp. 95–7). Here, the discussion focuses on chariots with a primary battle function. Three kinds are attested in the sources: the scythed war chariots, the Gallic so-called *carpenta*, and the British war chariots labelled *esseda*.[74]

The scythe-bearing chariots, as they are named in modern literature, were labelled ἅρματα δρεπανηφόρα in Greek and *currus falcati* or *quadrigae falcatae* in

---

[73] Polito (1998: 191–8).

[74] Roman poets depict captured chariots fixed as dedications to the doors and doorposts of temples and houses, and wheels appear among other spoils on a number of Roman reliefs, *Aen.* 7.184; Sil. *Pun.* 1.618; Sen. *Thy.* 660. Reliefs: Polito (1998: 57–8).

Latin. The terms refer to the δρεπάναι and *falces*, that is sickles, scythes, or hooks that were fastened to the wheels or axes of the chariots.[75] The four-horsed scythed chariot was a Persian invention, known to have been employed by Darius III against Alexander at Gaugamela.[76] It was adopted by the Seleucids and used by Antiochus in the battle against Scipio Asiaticus at Magnesia in 190 BC.[77] Later, Archelaus employed scythed vehicles against Sulla at Chaeronea.[78] The accounts of Scipio and Sulla's triumphs describe no war chariots, but in Sulla's case, the sources are very fragmentary.[79] Livy's description of Scipio Asiaticus' triumph, on the other hand, is rather detailed,[80] but scythed chariots are lacking. This is especially noteworthy, as Livy puts quite an effort into describing their appearance and actions in the battle itself.[81] True, Livy most certainly used different sources when describing the battle (Polybius) and the triumph (archival material preserved in the annalists), and this circumstance might explain his shift of interest.[82] Still, Magnesia was the first occasion where Rome encountered these feared eastern war machines and, if displayed by Scipio, they would have made quite an impression in the parade. One would have expected to find some trace of this either in Livy or in some other source.

Later on, Plutarch tells that Lucullus showed ten scythed chariots in the triumph held over Mithridates and Tigranes.[83] We do not know how the chariots ended up in Lucullus' hands; but possibly, they formed part of Tigranes' army at the decisive battle at Tigranocerta.[84] Lucullus most likely took the trouble of transporting the chariots to Rome to call attention to the military success of his command, of which he had been deprived in favour of Pompey. There might also have been an allusion to Alexander's famed eastern victories, as the young king's handling of the scythed chariots in the battles against the Persian army was

---

[75] Rivet (1979: 130–2); Briscoe (1981: 352–3); Piggott (1983: 233–4).

[76] Diod. Sic. 17.53.1–2; Curt. 4.9.4–5; Arr. *Anab.* 3.8.6. Another kind of scythed chariot, called the *covinnus*, was associated with the Celts, especially the Britons, but chariots thus labelled never appear in the descriptions of any triumph celebrated over these peoples.

[77] Liv. 37.40.12, 37.41.5–12.

[78] Front. *Str.* 2.3.17.

[79] Cic. *Manil.* 3.8; Val. Max. 2.8.7; Plin. *Nat.* 33.5.16; Plut. *Sulla* 34.1; App. *BCiv.* 1.101; Eutrop. 5.9.1.

[80] Liv. 37.59.

[81] Liv. 37.41.5–12. Because of Livy's rather confusing description, it has been argued that he never himself set eyes on scythed vehicles, but rather misunderstood the description in Polybius: Rivet (1979: 130); Briscoe (1981: 352–3).

[82] Livy focuses more on the worth brought into Rome and less on 'curiosities' such as rare war machines. Still, he does report on the display of catapults and *ballistae* in a few triumphs of these years.

[83] Plut. *Luc.* 37.3: καὶ τῶν δρεπανηφόρων ἁρμάτων δέκα παρῆλθον, Much later, the biographer of the *Historia Augusta* has Alexander Severus making a speech, in which he claims to have captured 200 scythed chariots from the Parthian enemy, but has refrained from having them displayed in his triumph, performed in AD 233, S.H.A. *Alex. Sev.* 56.4–5.

[84] Plut. *Luc.* 27–8; App. *Mith.* 85–6. Keaveney (1992: 107–11).

famed. By displaying scythed cars, Lucullus exhibited the Roman defeat of these still rather unfamiliar war machines of the East, and could also allude to former celebrated victories of his famous model.

Vehicles labelled *carpenta* appear above all in Livy's descriptions of five Gallic triumphs held between 197 and 187 BC.[85] Besides, Florus attests to the general presence of Gallic *carpenta* in the triumphs of older days and to the specific appearance of a *carpentum* in the triumph held by Fabius Maximus over the Allobroges and Bituitus, king of the Arverni, in 120 BC.[86]

Clearly, the *carpenta* on triumphal display were intimately connected to parades celebrating victories over Gauls. With the exception of the triumph held by L. Furius Purpureo in 200 BC, in which no spoils at all were displayed,[87] all Livy's descriptions of triumphs held over the Gauls in the period 219–167 BC (books 21–45) include *carpenta*. No such vehicles are listed in any non-Gallic triumph. Both Livy and Florus describe the *carpenta* as *Gallica*,[88] and in Livy's accounts, the *carpenta* shown by Cethegus (197 BC) and Manlius Vulso (187 BC) were used to transport *spolia Gallica*.[89] In Manlius Vulso's parade held over the Galatians, the larger part of the procession consisted of coins, bullion, and luxurious objects captured during his long field tour in Asia.[90] Vulso also displayed Gallic arms and spoils, transported on *carpenta* to announce the defeat of the Galatians. Livy's account seems to reflect a divided display, in which the Gallic victory, marked by the *carpenta*, was exhibited apart from the riches manifesting the defeat of the kingdoms of the East.

In Latin literature, the term *carpentum* was applied to a variety of vehicles.[91] For example, Livy states that the Republican *matronae* rode the *carpentum* as a special honour bestowed on them by Camillus.[92] Later, riding a wagon labelled *carpentum* was the privilege of the women of the Imperial household,[93] and Messalina even participated in the British triumphal procession of her husband

---

[85] Liv. 33.23.4–9, 33.37.9–12, 36.40.11–14, 39.7.1–3.

[86] Flor. *Epit.* 1.13.27, 1.37.5–6.

[87] Liv. 31.49.1–3. Münzer has proposed that Livy's description of the battle at Cremona (31.21), which precedes Purpureo's triumph, is unauthentic, *RE* VII (1912), s.v. 'Furius' 86, 862–4. The account echoes the description of C. Cethegus' victory at the Mincio, Liv. 32.30.5–13. Livy maintains that Hamilcar was killed during Purpureo's campaign, but later on, Hamilcar appears as captive in Cethegus' triumph (33.23.5). See also Pais (1920: 128–31); Briscoe (1973: 110–15); Richardson (1975); Ziolkowski (1990: 26–7).

[88] Liv. 36.40.11; Flor. *Epit.* 1.13.27.

[89] Liv. 33.23.4, 39.7.2.

[90] Liv. 39.7.1–5.

[91] Abaecherli (1935/6: 5). The word *carpentum* is Celtic in origin and forms part of a rather substantial vocabulary for vehicles that the Latin language absorbed from the Gauls: Bulle (1943: 139–40); Piggott (1983: 230–4). Some scholars think that the car itself was imported from Gaul, others that it came from Etruria. Pagnotta (1977/8: 160–2) accounts for the various scholarly positions.

[92] Liv. 5.25.9.

[93] Abaecherli (1935/6: esp. 5–7); Bulle (1943: 140–1); Pagnotta (1977/8); Jucker (1980); Flory (1998: 492–3).

Claudius in a *carpentum*.[94] Such *carpenta* appear on several Imperial coins, depicted as two-wheeled covered vehicles, often drawn by mules or asses.[95] *Carpenta* were also included among the processional wagons of the *pompae circenses*.[96]

As for the *carpenta* present in the triumphal processions of the Republic, there are basically two possibilities: they could be supply wagons or war chariots. In favour of the first interpretation is the fact that *carpenta* appear in the parades not only as spoils but also as means of transport for captured arms and other spoils.[97] A few Imperial reliefs with battle scenes and triumphal processions also show rough two-wheeled carts carrying prisoners and occasionally spoils of war too. For example, male captives appear in such wagons on the smaller triumphal frieze on Trajan's arch at Benevento.[98] In modern literature, these wagons are often labelled *carpenta*,[99] implying that they were similar to the ones described by Livy as captured in battle and displayed in the Gallic triumphs of the years 197–187 BC.

However, several circumstances suggest that the *carpenta* on Gallic parade were war chariots rather than supply wagons. Florus, when accounting for Caesar's first encounter with the army of the Britons, describes the panic inflicted on the chariots (*carpenta*) of the enemy when they caught sight of the Romans.[100] More importantly, when Florus describes the triumph of Fabius Maximus over the Allobroges and Bituitus, the king of the Arverni, in 120 BC, he claims that the defeated king was displayed in his many-coloured arms standing in his silver *carpentum*, just as he had appeared in battle.[101]

As the principal source of the triumphal display of Gallic *carpenta*, Livy's use of the term is crucial. With few exceptions,[102] Livy applies the term to Gallic vehicles,[103] most of which were captured in battle or shown in triumphs, and

[94] Suet. *Claud*. 17.3. Flory (1998: 492–3). Eventually, *carpentum* became a general word for a two-wheeler, Piggott (1992: 34), cf. Piggott (1983: 231).

[95] Bulle (1943: 140–1, fig. 73); Lucchi (1968); Jucker (1980); cf. Piggott (1992: 34).

[96] Abaecherli (1935/6: 5).

[97] Liv. 33.23.4–5: *multa Gallica spolia captivis carpentis transvexit*, 33.37.11: *multa spolia hostium captivis carpentis travecta*, 36.40.11: *in eo triumpho Gallicis carpentis arma signaque et spolia omnis generis travexit*, 39.7.2: *et arma spoliaque multa Gallica carpentis travecta*.

[98] Andreae (1974: Abb. 425). Captives driven on two-wheeled wagons also appear on a few Campana plaques representing triumphal parades, see Gabelmann (1981: nos. 5–7, 453–6, Abb. 14–16); Tortorella (2008). Female prisoners and children are transported on rough carts on the column of Marcus Aurelius (see e.g. scene LXXXV, Köhler (1995: Taf. 97.2)) and on the Belvedere sarcophagus (Abaecherli (1935/6: 6–7, pl. V.4); Köhler (1995: Taf. 96.2)).

[99] Abaecherli (1935/6: 6–7); Köhler (1995: 377).

[100] Flor. *Epit*. 1.45.17. However, Piggott (1983: 231), reads Florus' *carpentum* as 'a personally favoured word with a generalized "chariot" connotation, rather than denoting a specific type of barbarian vehicle'.

[101] Flor. *Epit*. 1.37.5–6.

[102] Livy uses *carpentum* for the vehicles used by Tarquinius Priscus, Tanaquil, Tullia, and Camillus' *matronae*: 1.34.8, 1.48.5–7, 5.25.9, 34.1.3–4, cf. 34.3.9.

[103] In his description of the battle at Sentinum, Livy reports that the combined enemy forces of Gauls, Etruscans, Samnites, and Umbrians had at their disposal a thousand *carpenta*, here without doubt war chariots, 10.30.4–6. Livy himself doubts the high numbers of wagons. At 10.28.9, Livy calls the Gallic wagons employed at Sentinum *esseda carrique*.

also explicitly defined as *capta*.[104] In battle descriptions, Livy normally gives the number of captured *carpenta* together with the number of seized standards and enemy soldiers killed or captured.[105] These *carpenta* were clearly spoils of war. What is more, they appear as a characteristic category of Gallic booty in these years, a particularity that fits poorly with ordinary supply wagons.[106] Clearly then, the *carpenta* in these contexts should be interpreted as Gallic war chariots. In fact, chariotry was a traditional mark of Celtic warfare, and the war chariot was linked to the Celtic culture in the writings of many ancient authors.[107] As war chariots, each vehicle probably carried modest loads of spoils in the triumphal processions. But Diodorus Siculus states that the Gauls used two-wheeled chariots both for journeys and in battle, implying that the *carpenta* had double functions as war chariots and travelling carts.[108] Thus, they would also have been apt for the processional assignment of carrying spoils.

Livy's accounts of Gallic battles in these years provide the number of dead and captive enemies together with the number of standards and *carpenta* captured. In contrast, when describing the subsequent triumphs, Livy gives no exact numbers of *carpenta* paraded (nor of standards and once only of the captives). This difference in exactness might be explained by the sources used. The precise numbers given in the battle descriptions should probably be traced back to the general's own account of his achievements. After a victorious battle or campaign, the general sent laurelled letters to Rome announcing the success and accounting for his deeds, and once back in the city, he recounted his exploits in speeches held in front of the senate and the people.[109] Not least important was the hearing, usually held in the temple of Bellona, when the senate decided on the granting of a triumph.[110] Here, the commander reported (certainly, sometimes in exaggerated manners) the number of enemies he had killed and captured, the number of

---

[104] Capture: 31.21.17, 32.30.12–13, 33.36.13, 35.5.14, 36.38.6.

[105] Liv. 31.21.17, 32.30.11–13, 33.36.13–14, 35.5.13–14, 36.38.6. In one place Livy includes the number of torcs captured (33.36.13–14) and once the number of horses (36.38.6).

[106] In his depiction of Furius Purpureo's victory over the Gauls outside of Cremona in 200 BC (31.21.17), Livy states that the Romans captured more than 200 Gallic *carpenta* laden with much booty (*carpentis Gallicis multa praeda oneratis plus ducentis*), which could be read as if they were supply wagons. However, Livy's descriptions of the battle at Cremona and Purpureo's triumph are both highly problematic and indeed untrustworthy (cf. n. 87 above). Livy's *carpentis Gallicis multa praeda oneratis plus ducentis* is a standardized phrasing used for triumphal descriptions that fits poorly with a battle account. Also, his claim (31.49.1–3) that Purpureo's triumph showed no spoils and no prisoners fits poorly with his earlier account of booty taken.

[107] Piggott (1983: 195–238).

[108] Diod. Sic. 5.29.1. Piggott (1983: 230, 232).

[109] Letters: Cic. *Pis.* 17.39; Liv. 37.47.3, 41.12.4; Pers. 6.43. Rüpke (1990: 215–16). Speeches to the people (held before or after the triumph): Liv. 45.40.9–42.1; Vell. Pat. 1.10.4; Plut. *Sulla* 34.2. Cf. Phillips (1974*b*: 226–68).

[110] See e.g. Liv. 28.38.2–3, 31.47.7, 33.22, 36.39.5–6, 37.58.3 (temple of Apollo), 38.44.9–11, 39.29.4–5, 41.6.4, 42.21.6–7.

battles fought, cities taken, tribes subjected, and ships sunk. Livy's testimony suggests that the number of captured war chariots was included when battles had been fought against Gauls. Seized *carpenta* made up one of the precise numbers that was of importance for the general who, based on the greatness of his deeds, sought to obtain a triumph. The absence of similarly precise figures for the chariots once displayed in the triumphs probably reflects the primary interest of the *aerarium* in recording the amount of coins and other valuables, while items of less material worth, such as *carpenta*, were registered only in the second place.[111]

Still, it is likely that the *carpenta* were paraded in large numbers. In battle, Livy claims that they were captured in hundreds,[112] and in the triumphs he stresses that they were used to transport bulks of spoils.[113] When Minucius Rufus triumphed over the Gauls on the Alban Mount in 197 BC, Livy maintains that his procession almost equalled that of his colleague in Rome as regards the military standards, *carpenta*, and spoils displayed,[114] thereby attesting to the importance of exhibiting a large number of chariots. Thus, in the Gallic triumphs of 197–187 BC, the *carpenta* were most probably displayed as a rather anonymous mass of weaponry, a fact that also explains their fairly unglamorous task of acting as transport vehicles for other spoils.

In sharp contrast to this picture stands Florus' description of King Bituitus in 120 BC: *Nihil tam conspicuum in triumpho quam rex ipse Bituitus discoloribus in armis argenteoque carpento, qualis pugnaverat*, 'Nothing in the triumph was as conspicuous as king Bituitus himself, dressed in his many-coloured arms and standing in his silver chariot, just as he had appeared fighting'.[115] Here, Florus stresses the emphatic exhibition of one vehicle of rich material, reserved for carrying the enemy king. The *carpentum* distinguished royal status in the procession, as in battle. Thus, though still displayed in a Gallic triumph, Bituitus' chariot was more a social than an ethnic mark; it connoted first and foremost the defeat of a king, and only in the second place that of the Gauls. The importance of this display is probably reflected on some Roman silver coins, dated to 118 or 92 BC and referring to this Gallic campaign (Fig. 5).[116] A nude warrior, very possibly Bituitus, is depicted standing with his arms on a chariot

---

[111] Livy provides us with the precise sums of coins and bullion from 293 BC but starts (after the break in his text) giving the numbers for other items only from about 190 BC.

[112] According to Livy, Cethegus captured more than 200 chariots (32.30.13), M. Claudius Marcellus 732 (33.36.13), Scipio Nasica 247 (36.38.6). Some of the figures stem from Valerias Antias and were doubted by Livy himself.

[113] Liv. 33.23.4–5, 33.37.9–12, 39.7.2, cf. 36.40.11.

[114] Liv 33.23.8–9.

[115] Flor. *Epit.* 1.37.5–6.

[116] Carson (1978: no. 104, 36); Albrethsen (1987: 104, fig. 4 and n. 10).

FIGURE 5 Gallic warrior, probably Bituitus, pictured standing in his war chariot. The scene most likely refers to his appearance in the triumph held by Fabius Maximus in 120 BC.

drawn by two horses. A *carnyx* (i.e. a Celtic trumpet used in battle) identifies the scene as Gallic.

The difference in display between the early and late second century, as well as the later absence of any references to Gallic *carpenta* taken as spoils or shown in a triumph, should be seen as a reflection of the gradual disappearance of the war chariot from the Gallic battlefield. Chariots did continue to be used in Gaul in the later Republic, but their function had changed from vehicles widely used in battle to status symbols of the nobility.[117] As such, it proclaimed the nobility of King Bituitus in the triumph of Fabius Maximus.

War chariots were now instead used by the Britons. Accordingly, Caesar mentions no encounter with war chariots on Gallic ground and marvels when he later in Britain finds himself engaged in combats with enemy chariots, which he calls *esseda*.[118] British chariots were also captured as spoils of war, and coins minted by Caesar and his supporters around 50 BC depict trophies, weapons and two-wheeled war chariots as symbols of the British success.[119] In his vision of Caesar's Gallic triumphal procession, Lucan (3.76–8) depicts chariots appearing together with the Rhine, the Oceanus, the Britons, and a personification of Gaul:

---

[117] Frey (1976).

[118] Caes. *Gall.* 4.33; Cic. *Fam.* 7.7.1; Prop. 2.1.76. Frey (1976: 172); Piggott (1983: 232). The term *essedum* is quite commonly used for Celtic war chariots in Latin literature, but should not be confused with the British scythed chariot, the *covinnus*. Later on, *esseda* were prestigious travel wagons, just like *pilenta* and *petorrita*. According to Pomponius Porphyrio, in his commentary on Horatius' *Epistulae* (2.1.189–93), royal prisoners were driven in such vehicles in the triumph.

[119] Crawford (1974: no. 448, 463–4, pl. LIII.8, no. 482, 495, pl. LVII.22, 736 and n. 2).

ut vincula Rheno
Oceanoque daret, celsos ut Gallia currus
Nobilis et flavis sequeretur mixta Britannis.

...that he might have put chains on the Rhine and the Oceanus, and had noble Gaul follow lofty chariots together with fair-haired Britons.[120]

The term *currus* is often used to denote the triumphal car, and modern commentators have interpreted the word here as referring to the chariot of the victorious general.[121] However, in this passage, the consequence would be that the captives, *Gallia* and the Britons, would have followed the triumphator in the procession, a procedure unheard of throughout Roman history.[122] The *currus* here, indicated in the plural sense, are better interpreted as chariots, and specifically the war chariots, which Caesar encountered and captured on British grounds.[123] Thus, from having been an emblem of Gallic success, the war chariot now turned into a marker of victories performed on the other side of the Oceanus. As such it seems later to have been adopted by Caligula. Persius, describing the farcical triumph held by the emperor over the Germans and Britain in AD 40, states (6.43–7):

O bone, num ignoras? missa est a Caesare laurus
insignem ob cladem Germanae pubis et aris
frigidus excutitur cinis ac iam postibus arma,
iam chlamydas regum, iam lutea gausapa captis
essedaque ingentesque locat Caesonia Rhenos.

My dear man, didn't you hear? A laurel's come from Caesar
to announce his triumph over the German tribes. They're clearing
the altars of cold ashes. Caesonia's already
hiring the arms to hang on doorposts, royal cloaks,
war chariots, blond wigs for prisoners, giant Rhines.[124]

Having crossed the Rhine and encountered the Morini in a smaller fight, Caligula had his army entering ships to cross over to Britain, only to return immediately.

---

[120] Lucan complains that Caesar chose to celebrate triumphs not only for his victories in enemy Gaul but over his fellow Romans as well. The passage quoted above forms part of a vision of how his glorious manifestation of Gallic victory would have appeared had it been the only parade performed. Without doubt, Lucan modelled his image on the Gallic triumph, as it had already been celebrated. The passage is discussed by Daut (1984: 118–20).

[121] Hunink (1992: 69).

[122] Hunink (ibid.) admits that prisoners usually preceded the triumphator and tries to solve the problem by maintaining that *sequi* here could be read more vaguely as 'to accompany, to escort'.

[123] Daut (1984: 119) reads the *currus* as Celtic war chariots.

[124] Translation by Lee (1987).

In spite of the failure, Caligula forced his soldiers to gather shells as spoils and send them to Rome as markers of his victory over the Oceanus.[125] He also sent a letter (*missa est a Caesare laurus*) to the city to announce that the whole of Britain had been subdued.[126] *Esseda* commonly refers to war chariots employed by the British,[127] and clearly it was Caligula's intention to symbolize his British conquest by the display of these chariots.[128] Flory has demonstrated that Caligula collected pearls in *imitatio* of Caesar's defeat of the Oceanus.[129] Most probably, the *esseda* filled a similar function, bringing the former exhibition of the British chariots by Caesar to mind.

Military standards: signs of success

Ancient sources confirm the display of captured military standards (*signa*, *signa militaria*, σημαίαι) in several Republican triumphs. As often, Livy provides most of the evidence. He maintains that standards were carried ahead (*signa militaria praelata*) when Cincinnatus triumphed over the Aequi in 458 BC,[130] and later, from 197 to 167 BC, he attests to the display of standards in seven triumphal parades.[131] Besides, Polybius describes the presence of *signa* at the triumphal celebration held by Aemilius Papus over the Gauls in 225 BC.[132]

To the Romans, their own military ensigns were of utmost tactical, religious, and symbolic importance.[133] Placed in the frontline of the battle formation, the standards of the different divisions upheld the order of the army in action.[134] Their significance was particularly evident in the turmoil of close combat, where the *signa* acted as bearings for the individual soldiers and subdivisions and as means of assistance to the general, who used the standards to direct the

[125] Suet. *Cal*. 46; Dio Cass. 59.25.1–5 (apud Joann. Antioch.). Flory (1988).

[126] Suet. *Cal*. 44.2.

[127] Caes. *Gall*. 4.33; Cic. *Fam*. 7.7.1; Prop. 2.1.76; cf. Strab. 4.5.2. Piggot (1983: 231–5).

[128] Cf. Némethy (1903: 334–5).

[129] Flory (1988).

[130] Liv. 3.29.4.

[131] C. Cornelius Cethegus *de Gallis Insubribus Cenomanisque* in 197 BC (Liv. 33.23.4–8), Q. Minucius Rufus on the Alban Mount *de Gallis Liguribusque* in 197 BC (33.23.8–9), M. Claudius Marcellus *de Gallis Insubribus* in 196 BC (33.37.10–12), P. Cornelius Scipio Nasica *de Gallis Boiis* in 191 BC (36.40.11–14), M'. Acilius Glabrio over the Aetolians and Antiochus in 190 BC (37.46.1–6), L. Cornelius Scipio Asiaticus over Antiochus in 189 BC (37.59), L. Anicius Gallus over King Gentius and the Illyrians in 167 BC (45.43.1–8).

[132] According to Polybius (2.31.5–6), Aemilius sent the standards and the torcs captured from the Gauls to adorn the Capitol, while the rest of the spoils and the prisoners were led in his triumph.

[133] Domaszewski (1885); *RE* 2:e Reihe II (1921), s.v. 'Signa (*militaria*)', 2325–47 (W. Kubitschek); Kraeling (1942); Rostovtzeff (1942); Rüpke (1990: 184–8); Panciera (1994); Stoll (1995*a*: 38–68); Stoll (1995*b*).

[134] Domaszewski (1885: 1–12).

movements of the army according to his overall plan.[135] The standards also kept the divisions of the army in proper order during parades and processions.[136]

In early times, when combats were fought in the vicinity of Rome, the standards were, when not in use, placed in the *aerarium*,[137] a circumstance that clearly reveals the value, actual and symbolic, attached to them. Later on, they were placed in camp shrines, where the soldiers took turns to guard them.[138] The loss of *signa* meant not only the utmost disgrace, but also, since the standards were irreplaceable, the very disintegration of the division.[139]

In view of the Roman concern for their own standards, it needs not surprise us that foreign *signa* were looked upon as desirable spoils of the conquered enemy. Captured standards appear among other *spolia* on Roman reliefs,[140] and they were dedicated in temples and used to decorate public places.[141] The number of *signa* taken in battle formed a basic result of a successful Republican campaign. This is clear from Livy's many battle accounts, which normally list the number of seized ensigns together with the number of enemies killed and captured.[142] These numbers were effective measures of the magnitude of the victory, quantifying the losses of enemy divisions and men.

In the Gallic triumphs held between the late third century and the late second century BC, captured *signa* formed one of a number of recurrent items, together with *carpenta*, torcs, and the more undefined *Gallica spolia*. But while *carpenta* and torcs appear exclusively in Gallic parades, ensigns were present in triumphs over other enemies too, as diverse as the Aequi, the Illyrians, the Aetolians, and King Antiochus. Livy gives numbers of *signa* collected on the battlefield in campaigns against Macedonians, Carthaginians, Ligurians, and Celtiberians. He also tells that *signa militaria omnis generis* were fixed as spoils in the temple of Jupiter on

---

[135] Ibid. 2.

[136] Stoll (1995*a*: 39); Stoll (1995*b*: 108).

[137] Liv. 3.69.8, 4.22.1, 7.23.3.

[138] Kraeling (1942: esp. 275–6); Panciera (1994: 612); Stoll (1995*a*: 38–52; 1995*b*); *OCD* (1996), s.v. 'Standards, cult of', 1437–8 (C. R. Phillips).

[139] Rostovtzeff (1942: 98–9); Panciera (1994: 613); Stoll (1995*a*: 53, 65–6). For Augustus' return in 19 BC with the standards lost by Crassus at Carrhae, see now Östenberg (2009).

[140] Polito (1998: esp. 59–60).

[141] Liv. 40.51.3–4.

[142] See e.g. Liv. 26.47.7 (74 *signa*), 29.36.9 (11 *signa*), 30.6.9 (174 *signa*), 30.18.13–14 (22 *signa*), 30.36.8 (72 *signa*), 31.49.7 (78 *signa*), 32.6.7 (132 *signa*), 32.30.12–13 (130 *signa*), 33.10.9 (249 *signa*), 33.36.13 (87 *signa*), 35.1.10 (134 *signa*), 35.5.13–14 (212 *signa*), 36.19.12 (230 *signa*), 36.38.6 (124 *signa*), 40.33.7–8 (62 *signa*), 40.48.7 (37 *signa*), 40.50.5 (72 *signa*), 42.7.10 (82 *signa*). Many numbers stem from Valerias Antias, and Livy himself doubts their credibility, see e.g. 33.10.8–9, 36.19.12, 36.38.7. Oakley (1998: 358); Erdkamp (2006). It has long been recognized that Valerias Antias took a special interest in recording the number of captured standards, Walsh (1961: 127 n. 2); Ogilvie (1965: 411); Ziolkowski (1990: 17); Erdkamp (2006: esp. 169–71). See also Prachner (1994).

the Capitol.[143] Here, as in the triumphs, the standards' appearance probably signalled their origins, as *signa* depicting wild boars and wolfs were typical of the Gauls, and those reproducing dragons characteristic of the Scythians and the Dacians.[144]

As spoils of war, captured standards were customarily placed at the beginning of the triumphal processions. Livy describes the *signa* shown in Cincinnatus' parade as being *praelata*, and in most of his other triumphal accounts too, the standards appear first in line.[145] In the rear of the parade, Roman standards probably led the divisions of the army on parade behind the triumphator.[146] In this way, the standards of the defeated opened and those of the victors closed the parade.

Livy claims that M'. Acilius Glabrio showed 230 *signa militaria* in his triumph over the Aetolians and Antiochus in 190 BC and that Scipio Asiaticus exhibited 224 standards when celebrating his triumph over Antiochus the following year.[147] In most other triumphal accounts, Livy merely states that the ensigns displayed were many.[148] Thus, there is some discrepancy between the exact figures given for standards captured in battle and the vaguer depiction of ensigns shown in triumphs as being *multa*. As in the above discussion of *carpenta*, the explanation should probably be sought in the different primary sources used. The number of standards shown by Glabrio and Scipio was comparatively high, which might have encouraged a more precise recording. Many battle reports state figures for captured standards well below a hundred, so the good two hundred *signa* that started off the celebrations of these two generals announced victories of great dimensions.

Even when their exact number eludes us, Livy's descriptions show that the standards were paraded in great numbers. In fact, the major visual point of the display of the standards lay in their quantity, as the *signa* were measures of the number of enemy divisions routed and thus manifested the vastness of the Roman military success. Standards were also regarded as highly trustworthy proof of victory. This is clearly illustrated by the handling of the standards after the defeat

---

[143] Liv. 40.51.3–4. Cf. Sil. *Pun.* 1.627.

[144] Wild boar and wolf: Picard and Hatt, in Amy, Duval, and Formigé (1962: 86); Polito (1998: 59–60). Dragon: Coarelli (1967: 50); Polito (1998: 60). Several animal types were eventually taken up also as symbols on Roman standards, Domaszewski (1885: 54–6, 73–5); Coarelli (1967: 50); Rüpke (1990: 185–6, discussing Renel); Polito (1998: 59). Polito argues that the Romans included animals among many other emblems in their standards, while on barbarian standards the animal figures appear on their own.

[145] Cincinnatus: Liv. 3.29.4. Of Livy's remaining seven accounts that include standards, six list the contents in an order that probably reflects the sequence of the processions. Of these, standards appear first in four cases (33.23.4–8, 37.46.1–6, 37.59, 45.43.1–8), grouped among the first in one (36.40 11–14), and second in one (33.37.9–12).

[146] Plutarch (*Aem.* 34.7), states that the army followed the triumphator by companies and divisions. In the same procession, according to Livy (45.40.4), after the triumphator and his sons 'came the cavalry by troops, and the units of infantry, rank by rank', see also Dion. Hal. 2.34.2; cf. Joseph. *BJ* 7.123.

[147] Liv. 37.46.3, 37.59.3.

[148] Liv. 33.23.4, 33.23.8–9, 33.37.11, 45.43.4.

of the Cimbri by the combined forces of Marius and Lutatius Catulus in 102–101 BC. According to Plutarch, the private property of the enemy accrued to the soldiers of Marius, but the spoils of battle, consisting of standards and Gallic trumpets (*carnyces*), were brought to the camp of Catulus, who later used these items to prove that the victory had been his, not Marius.[149] Sources do not give the contents of Catulus' subsequent triumph; nevertheless the standards most certainly played a significant role together with the rest of the spoils of arms and probably the trumpets.[150] After his triumph, Catulus built a *porticus* where the arms from the Gallic campaign were placed.[151] Again, the major purpose was certainly to gain credit for the Cimbric success at Marius' expense, and again, Catulus probably gave the exhibition of the standards (and trumpets) a prominent place.

Artillery: the war engines of Syracuse and Ambracia

Larger war engines were put on show by Marcellus in 211 BC to manifest his conquest of Syracuse, and later in the triumph celebrated by Fulvius Nobilior in 187 BC over the Aetolians and Cephallania. According to Livy, Marcellus carried *catapultae ballistaeque et alia omnia instrumenta belli* in his procession and Fulvius Nobilior paraded large amounts of arms as well as catapults, *ballistae*, and all kinds of artillery (*ad hoc catapultae, ballistae, tormenta omnis generis*).[152] Plutarch also claims that Lucullus at the time of his triumph over Mithridates and Tigranes in 63 BC decorated the Circus Flaminius with a large number of captured arms and with the royal engines of war (μηχανήματα).[153]

Livy uses three different terms to describe the types of war engines paraded: *tormenta*, *catapultae*, and *ballistae*. Of these, *tormentum* was a general denomination for all types of artillery.[154] *Catapultae* were machines that worked similarly to crossbows, throwing various types of arrows, lances, bolts, and stone bullets, whereas *ballistae* (being closer to what we today think of as catapults) were more powerful machines in the form of mechanical slings that hurled above all larger

---

[149] Plut. *Mar.* 27.4.

[150] Brief mentions of Catulus' triumph: Diod. Sic. 38.4.2; Val. Max. 9.12.4; Plut. *Mar.* 27.6, 44.5; Eutrop. 5.2.2. *Carnyces* appear quite frequently on coins celebrating this victory, as on coins commemorating other larger successful campaigns against the Gauls and other northerners, see Albrethsen (1987); Vendries (1999); Hunter (2001).

[151] Cic. *Dom.* 38.102, 43.114; Val. Max. 6.3.1c.

[152] Liv. 26.21.7, 39.5.16.

[153] Plut. *Luc.* 37.2–3: ... ἀλλὰ τοῖς μὲν ὅπλοις τῶν πολεμίων οὖσι παμπόλλοις καὶ τοῖς βασιλικοῖς μηχανήμασι τὸν Φλαμίνειον ἱππόδρομον διεκόσμησε· καὶ θέα τις ἦν αὐτὴ καθ᾽ ἑαυτὴν οὐκ εὐκαταφρόνητος, 'but he decorated the Circus Flaminius with the arms of the enemy, which were plentiful, and with the royal war engines; and this was a great spectacle in itself, and far from contemptible'.

[154] Marsden (1969, 1971); Baatz (1994).

stones.[155] Artillery was primarily employed in sieges, both by the besiegers and the besieged. Assumed to have been developed in Syracuse under Dionysius I in the beginning of the fourth century BC,[156] larger artillery was widely employed in the Hellenistic kingdoms and well known to the Romans at least from the time of the First Punic War.[157]

Catapultae and *ballistae* were quite difficult and time-consuming to transport, and a Roman general on campaign seldom brought the machines long distances. Rather, it was customary either to construct the engines at the site of a siege or to require them from subjects and allies.[158] After the campaign, captured artillery was at times left with allies located close to the scene of the war.[159] At other times, the machines must have been incorporated into the Roman forces. For example, the large number of various types of artillery captured by Scipio Africanus at Carthago Nova in 209 BC and the catapults surrendered to Rome by Carthage during the Third Punic War were in all probability incorporated into the Roman arsenal.[160] In light of the logistic problems, it seems unlikely that victorious generals often took the trouble to transport the ungainly machines in large numbers back to the city only to display them in their triumphal processions. As always, it is extremely difficult to determine the frequency of a particular display from the fragmentary sources. Nevertheless, both Marcellus' Syracuse and Fulvius Nobilior's Ambracia clearly constituted quite special cases, where the sieges were much discussed already at the time, and where the exhibition of the captured war engines was of particular symbolic importance to the triumphant generals.

In fact, Marcellus' siege and final conquest of Syracuse constituted one of the most famed victories of Roman warfare. After the conquest, Greek works of art were brought in enormous quantities to Rome as war booty. But the struggle itself was just as renowned. Syracuse was defended by extraordinary war engines, constructed by the highly renowned Archimedes,[161] and his artillery managed to stop several Roman attacks from land as well as from sea. Not only did it fire the

---

[155] The engines could also throw pots with burning oil and even poisonous snakes. *Ballistae* appear as spoils on a few Pergamene and Roman weapon reliefs, Polito (1998: 57 and figs. 30, 146, 149). Sometime between AD 100 and 300, the vocabulary changed. *Catapultae* then came to mean one-armed stone hurlers and *ballistae* bolt-shooting devices only (Marsden, 1969: 1).

[156] Marsden (1969: 48–64).

[157] Ibid. 65–85.

[158] Ibid. 174–9.

[159] Livy (24.40.15–16) tells us that after Apollonia, with the help of Rome, had managed to defeat the Macedonian forces that had besieged the city, Rome took possession of most of the spoils, while Apollonia took the catapults and *ballistae*, for future use.

[160] Nova Carthago: Liv. 26.47.5–7; Carthage: App. *Pun.* 80.

[161] Liv. 24.33.9–34.16; Plut. *Marc.* 14–19. Eckstein (1987: 157–69).

usual missiles at long range, but the machinery also included smaller catapults built into the lower part of the walls for precision shots at close range.[162] Obviously a novelty, these machines surprised the Romans. Marcellus was left with no choice but to put his hope in a long siege, which after two years resulted in success. In 212 BC, Syracuse was captured and, much to the sorrow of Marcellus, Archimedes killed.

Despite his great success, the senate hesitated to grant Marcellus a triumph. His campaign had not concluded the war in Sicily and the army had not been brought back to Rome, and so he was permitted to celebrate a minor *ovatio* only. Marcellus protested by conducting a *triumphus* proper on the Alban Mount, and on the next day he entered Rome in ovation.[163] Livy's describes the display of arts, riches, and elephants, but starts off his account with a description of a representation of the captured Syracuse, catapults, *ballistae*, and other war equipment:

Pridie quam urbem iniret in monte Albano triumphavit; inde ovans multam prae se praedam in urbem intulit. Cum simulacro captarum Syracusarum catapultae ballistaeque et alia omnia instrumenta belli lata et pacis diuturnae regiaeque opulentiae ornamenta, argenti aerisque fabrefacti vis, alia supellex pretiosaque vestis et multa nobilia signa, quibus inter primas Graeciae urbes Syracusae ornatae fuerant. Punicae quoque victoriae signum octo ducti elephanti; et non minimum fuere spectaculum cum coronis aureis praecedentes Sosis Syracusanus et Moericus Hispanus, ...   (26.21.6–10)

On the day before he entered the city, he triumphed on the Alban Mount. Then in his ovation, he brought a great amount of booty before him into the city. Together with a representation of the captured Syracuse, catapults and ballistae and all the other war equipment were carried, and the adornments of a long peace and of royal wealth, a quantity of silverware and bronze ware, other furnishings and costly fabrics, and many notable statues, with which Syracuse had been adorned as highly as the foremost cities of Greece. As a sign that the Carthaginians had been defeated as well, eight elephants were led in the procession. And not the least spectacle, as they walked before the general, wearing golden wreaths, were Sosis of Syracuse and Moericus the Spaniard ...

Livy's enumeration of the display (arms, art, animals, and triumphator) follows the traditional processional sequence. It seems adequate to assume, therefore, that in Marcellus' parade the engines of war were paraded in the beginning of the

---

[162] Liv. 24.34.9–10; Plut. *Marc.* 16. Marsden (1969: 108–9, 122). Plutarch (*Marc.* 16.2) writes that Archimedes had built most of his engines under/at the foot of the wall, ὑπὸ τὸ τεῖχος, which, according to Marsden (1969: 109), 'probably means they were in front, and at the base, of the walls among the outworks'.

[163] Liv. 26.21.6; Plut. *Marc.* 22.1; *vir. ill.* 45.6–7.

procession together with the representation of Syracuse. The emphatic *cum* placed in the beginning of the list is unique in Livy's strictly standardized triumphal accounts and suggests that these items were attributed a certain prominence. In view of the background, this is only to be expected. Marcellus obviously felt a great disappointment over the fact that he had not been allowed to celebrate a proper triumph. His parade on the Alban Mount is an explicit demonstration of this dissatisfaction.[164] On entering Rome, he clearly wished to emphasize the greatness of his deeds in Sicily, and the larger part of the procession was dedicated to a display of his major success in capturing Syracuse. By opening his procession with a representation of Syracuse and the large war engines that had resisted the Roman forces for years, he trumpeted forth the message that his military achievements had been of such scale as to merit a proper triumph. Another function of the captured artillery would have been to demonstrate that the city had been properly taken by force, thereby justifying Marcellus' looting of temples. And the fame of their inventor may have meant that the exhibition of the artillery may have been a tribute to Archimedes as well.

After Marcellus' procession, war engines next appear in the triumph of M. Fulvius Nobilior in 187 BC held over the Aetolians and the island of Cephallania. Besides golden crowns, silver, gold, coins and bullion, bronze and marble statues, arms, prisoners, and a representation of the captured Ambracia, Livy also reports that catapults, *ballistae*, and all kinds of artillery were displayed.[165]

Sources mention two larger sieges by Nobilior that could have resulted in the capture and subsequent display of artillery in his triumph. One was held at the city of Same, located on Cephallania, which was captured after four months of siege.[166] The other, much more renowned, took place at the city of Ambracia, which was rich in art as former royal residence of Pyrrhus. After a long siege, the Aetolians were persuaded to have Ambracia open her gates in order to discuss peace.[167] Nobilior seized the opportunity to loot the city of its paintings and statues,[168] but since Ambracia had not been taken by force, which formed the customary condition for plundering, the conduct met with strong opposition both in Ambracia and Rome. The consul even carried a *senatus consultum* stating that it seemed that Ambracia had not been taken by force (*Ambraciam vi captam*

---

[164] Flower (2000: 40).

[165] Livy describes the contents of the triumph at 39.5.13–17. The representation of the captured Ambracia is not included in this list, but appears in the debate that preceded the triumph, Liv. 38.43.10. Here, it is noted that Nobilior intended to show an *Ambracia capta* in his procession.

[166] Liv. 38.28.5–38.29.11.

[167] Liv. 38.9.5–9.

[168] Liv. 38.9.13–14.

esse non videri).[169] Only after an intense debate, held in the absence of the consul, was Fulvius Nobilior able to secure his desired triumph.[170]

In view of the debate, Fulvius Nobilior must have considered the display of captured war engines an essential to legitimate his actions in war. Together with the representation of the captured Ambracia (*Ambracia capta*), the siege machines transmitted a clear message that the city had been taken properly by force. The combined display of war engines and a representation of the captured city brings Marcellus' ovation to mind, and it is in fact quite likely that Fulvius Nobilor himself aimed at alluding to this famous general and the renowned conquest of Syracuse.

After Fulvius Nobilior, we hear of no more catapults or *ballistae* in triumphal processions. The large engines probably constituted quite unusual exhibitions, but it is nevertheless probable that they were occasionally paraded. Thus, Caesar very plausibly had war engines on display in his Gallic triumph to announce his success in capturing Massilia. At the time of the conquest in 49 BC, this city was the site of a renowned artillery arsenal.[171] Caesar's victory was accomplished only after a long and famed siege, in which the large artillery had initially effectively pressed back the attacking Roman forces.[172] As might have been expected, Caesar's procession included a representation of the city of Massilia.[173] Artillery was most certainly displayed as well.

Plutarch provides the last evidence for a triumphal exhibition of catapults and *ballistae* in his description of Lucullus' triumph over Mithridates and Tigranes in 63 BC.[174] Unlike Marcellus and Nobilior, Lucullus chose not to drive the royal engines of war, μηχανήματα, through the city, but left them together with a large amount of arms to decorate the Circus Flaminius. Plutarch maintains that this was 'a great spectacle in itself and far from contemptible', but provides very little other information. He states only that they were royal, and they must therefore have formed part of either Mithridates' or Tigranes' forces, which Lucullus encountered during his campaign in the East.[175] Plutarch does not explain why Lucullus preferred to decorate the Circus Flaminius with the artillery rather than have it driven in his procession. We might note, however, that the Circus Flaminius formed an essential part of the processional space. It was the starting-point for the Republican parades as well as the location where triumphators-to-be placed their prisoners and booty while waiting to enter the city.[176] In the

---

[169] Liv. 38.44.6. Gellius (5.6.24–6) describes how Cato accused Nobilior of having distributed crowns to his soldiers also for the smallest of achievements.

[170] Liv. 39.5.6.   [171] Caes. *Civ.* 2.2.

[172] Caes. *Civ.* 2.6–16. Marsden (1969: 95, 112–13).

[173] Cic. *Off.* 2.8.28, *Phil.* 8.6.18.   [174] Plut. *Luc.* 37.2–3.

[175] For Lucullus' campaign against Mithridates, see Keaveney (1992: 75–98), and against Tigranes (ibid. 99–128).

[176] Liv. 39.5.17, 45.39.14.

particular case of Lucullus, the waiting had been long, to say the least. Lucullus had returned to Rome in 66 BC, and it was only in 63 that he was allowed to triumph.[177] If we assume that Lucullus used the Circus Flaminius for storage of his spoils, the arms and the war engines described by Plutarch had probably been there for quite some time. In fact, the exhibition of catapults and the other arms might well have seemed almost permanent. Lucullus' decision to leave certain spoils behind in the Circus Flaminius may have been a leftover of the preceding years and a marking of his dissatisfaction of having had to use the very starting-point of the procession as a years-long waiting room.

SHIPS AND RAMS

Literary sources write about the display of ships or rams (*rostra*, ἔμβολοι or ἔμβολα) in four triumphal processions: Lucullus in 63 BC, Pompey in 61 BC, Octavian in 29 BC, and Vespasian and Titus in AD 71.[178] Also, Horace includes *naves* in his depiction of a triumphal procession shown in the theatres.[179] Long before Lucullus' triumph, however, rams were brought to Rome as spoils of war. The best-known examples are the rams that were taken from the ships of Antium in 338 BC and fixed to the speakers' platform on the Roman Forum, accordingly labelled *rostra*.[180] The rams had not been taken as spoils in a proper sea battle, but belonged to ships that were confiscated after C. Maenius' victory over the Volscians, who at the time held Antium. It was only about eighty years later, in 260 BC, that C. Duilius defeated Hannibal and the Carthaginians at Mylae in the first major Roman victory at sea. Several honours, including a *columna rostrata* adorned with the captured beaks, were bestowed on the victor.[181] A memorial inscription from the column has been preserved. The text praises the great deeds of the first general who equipped Roman ships and trained crews, and who captured a large number of Carthaginian vessels and sank others.[182] Polybius

[177] Keaveney (1992: 129–36).

[178] Plut. *Luc.* 37.3; App. *Mith.* 116; Prop. 2.1.35; Joseph. *BJ* 7.147–8.

[179] Hor. *Epist.* 2.1.192: *esseda festinant, pilenta, petorrita, naves*, 'chariots, carriages, wagons, and ships make haste'. In his commentary to the passage, Pomponius Porphyrio suggests that captives taken in battle were transported on all these vehicles.

[180] Liv. 8.14.12; Plin. *Nat.* 16.3.7–8, 34.11.20; Varro *Ling.* 5.155; Flor. *Epit.* 1.5.10.

[181] Plin. *Nat.* 34.11.20; Sil. *Pun.* 6.663–6; Quint. *Inst.* 1.7.12. Several ancient texts state that Duilius was also given the honour of having a flautist and a torch bearer accompany him home from dinners at night, Degrassi, *Inscr. It.* 13:3, no. 13, 20–1; Cic. *Cato* 13.44; Liv. *Per.* 17; Flor. *Epit.* 1.18.10–11; Val. Max. 3.6.4; Sil. *Pun.* 6.667–70; Amm. 26.3.5; *vir. ill.* 38.

[182] Degrassi, *Inscr. It.* 13:3, no. 69, 44–9, esp. 46 (cf. *CIL* i. 195; *CIL* i². 2, 25): *Enque eodem mac[istratud bene | r]em navebos marid consol primos c[eset copiasque | c]lasesque navales primos ornavet pa[ravetque] | cumque eis navebos claseis Poenicas omn[is item ma- | x]umas copias Cartaciniensis praesente[d Hanibaled] | dictatored*

maintains that the Carthaginians lost fifty ships in the battle, of which the Romans captured at least thirty, and similar figures are provided by later literary sources.[183]

No texts specify whether or not the beaks captured from the Antiates and Carthaginians were displayed in the triumphs of Maenius in 338 BC and of Duilius in 260 BC respectively. Nevertheless, since both groups of beaks were transported to Rome, this is likely to have been the case, most probably so in the case of Duilius. His beaks were renowned spoils of the enemy, celebrated as tokens of the first major Roman victory at sea.[184]

Naval triumphs

In Rome, Duilius' sea victory was celebrated by the first *triumphus navalis*.[185] All in all, the *Fasti triumphales* record eleven such naval triumphs, the majority of which were held during the First Punic War, when seven out of the sixteen registered triumphs were *navales*.[186] After this war, only four more naval triumphs are recorded, the last of which was celebrated by Cn. Octavius in 167 BC after the defeat of Perseus.[187]

---

ol[or]om in altod marid pucn[ad vicet] | vique nave[is cepe]t cum socieis septer[esmom I, quin- | queresm]osque triresmosque naveis X[XX, merset XIII. |...| Triump]oque navaled praedad poplom [donavet multosque] Cartacinie[ns]is [ince]nuos d[uxit ante currum— — —]eis [— — —] capt[— — —]. 'And in the same command, he as consul was the first Roman to perform an exploit in ships at sea. He was the first to fit out and train ships and crews and, with these, he defeated in battle on the high seas all the Carthaginian ships and their mighty naval personnel, in the presence of Hannibal, their commander-in-chief. By force he captured one 'seven' and thirty quinqueremes and triremes along with their crews, and he sank thirteen... He brought the people booty from a sea battle and led freeborn Carthaginians before his car in triumph'. Translation based on Warmington (1940: 129–31) and Casson (1991: 148). To what degree the preserved inscription reflects the original Republican one is a matter of debate, see e.g. Frank (1919); Warmington (1940: 128 n. 1); Bona (1960: 139–40 and n. 82); LTUR i (1993), s.v. 'Columna rostrata C. Duilii (Forum)', 309 (L. Chioffi). The inscription was still present to be seen by Quintilian (Inst. 1.7.12).

[183] Polyb. 1.23. According to Eutropius (2.20), 31 ships were captured and 14 sunk, while Orosius (4.7.10) accounts for 31 captured and 13 sunk. Zonaras (8.11) states only that many ships were sunk and many captured.

[184] In his account of the battle, Polybius (1.23) describes how the Romans managed to capture Hannibal's ship, a seven-banked galley that had formerly belonged to King Pyrrhus. This is in all probability the *septer*... described as captured in the memorial inscription of Duilius. Whether this ship was displayed in the triumph, or otherwise exhibited, we do not know.

[185] Degrassi, *Inscr. It.* 13:3, no. 13, 20–1; Liv. *Per.* 17; Tac. *Ann.* 2.49; Plin. *Nat.* 34.11.20; Flor. *Epit.* 1.18.10; cf. Sen. *Dial.* 10.13.3; Eutrop. 2.20; Oros. 4.7.10; *vir. ill.* 38.

[186] C. Duilius in 260 BC, C. Atilius Regulus in 257 BC, L. Manlius Vulso Longus in 256 BC, Ser. Fulvius Paetinus Nobilior and M. Aemilius Paullus in 254 BC, C. Lutatius Catulus and Q. Valerius Falto in 241 BC.

[187] Cn. Fulvius Centumalus over the Illyrians in 228 BC, L. Aemilius Regillus in 189 BC and Q. Fabius Labeo in 188 BC, both over Antiochus, Cn. Octavius over Perseus and the Macedonians in 167 BC. In 102 BC, M. Antonius held a triumph over the pirates of Cilicia, after which he decorated the speakers' platform with *manubiae*, presumably *rostra*, Cic. *Orat.* 3.3.10. De Souza (1999: 102–8). Unfortunately, we do not know if Antonius' parade was registered as a *triumphus*, *ovatio*, or *navalis*.

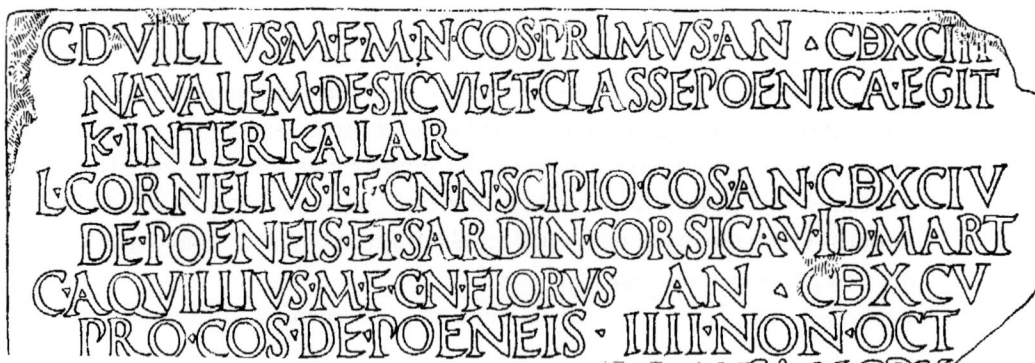

FIGURE 6 The entry for C. Duilius' triumph in 260 BC. The *Fasti triumphales* specifically labels it *triumphus navalis*, and also points out that Duilius was the first to perform this kind of celebration.

The *triumphus navalis* must have formed a particular type of triumphal celebration, just as the *ovatio* was seen as one specific kind and the ones held on the Alban Mount as another.[188] These triumphs are all specifically marked out in the *Fasti* as *ovationes* (e.g. *M. Fabius Ambustus ovans de Herniceis*), on the Alban Mount (*C. Cicereius ex Corsica in monte Albano*) or naval (*Q. Fabius Labeo ex Asia de rege Antiocho navalem egit*). The *Fasti* also record the first time that the *navalis* and the triumph on the Alban Mount were celebrated, thereby distinguishing them as particular varieties of the triumph (Fig. 6).[189] Furthermore, while the triumphs on the Alban Mount were held on the general's own initiative, the senate chose to grant a general the right to enter the city either *triumphans*, *ovans*, or to hold a *triumphus navalis*.[190]

The *ovatio* and the triumph on the Alban Mount were both ranked below the *triumphus* proper. The ovation was often given to a general who, though he had been successful in war, had failed to fulfil the traditional requirements for a *triumphus*.[191] According to our sources, while the general celebrating a *triumphus* rode through Rome in a chariot driven by four horses, dressed in a *toga picta*, and wearing a laurel wreath, the commander who was granted an *ovatio* wore the *toga praetexta* and a myrtle wreath, either walking or riding on horseback. Another difference was that flutes were employed instead of trumpets. Triumphs held on the Alban Mount are recorded only four times, and we know very little of the

[188] Ehlers (1939: 496–7); Versnel (1970: 165–8).
[189] 260 BC: *C. Duilius M. f. M. n. co(n)s(ul) primus an. CDXCIII | navalem de Sicul(eis) et classe Poenica egit | k. Interkalar.*; 231 BC: *C. Papirius C. f. L. n. Maso co(n)s(ul) ann. DXXII | de Corseis primus in monte Albano | III nonas Mart.*
[190] Liv. 36.40.9–10, 37.59.1–2 (*triumphus*), Liv. 26.21.4–5, 31.20 (*ovatio*), Liv. 37.58.3, 37.60.6–7 (*navalis*).
[191] *RE* XVIII:2 (1942), s.v. 'ovatio', 1890–1903 (G. Rohde); Ogilvie (1965: 276–7); Versnel (1970: 166–8); Richardson (1975: 54–63).

appearance and effect of the celebrations.[192] However, as these parades were held by generals whose requests for a triumph had been turned down by the senate, they were bound to be less prestigious than the triumphs held in the city.[193]

By contrast, the *triumphus navalis* seems to have constituted an exceptional honour at the time of its introduction. When Duilius defeated the Punic naval force in 260 BC, the event opened a new era of Roman mastery at sea as well as on land. The long-lasting consequences of Mylae were naturally clear to later times only, yet the many honours bestowed on Duilius leave no doubt that the victory was considered an extraordinary achievement at the time as well. The traditional *triumphus* celebrated for centuries to honour victories on land seems simply not to have sufficed to emphasize the novelty of the success. The less ostentatious *ovatio* would not have matched its importance. Hence, the *navalis* was introduced, as an equal in status and honour to the *triumphus* proper.

In spite of the prestige attached to Duilius' deeds and manifestations, the defining characteristics of the naval procession are unknown.[194] This might partly be explained by the state of the sources, as many of the naval triumphs were celebrated during the First Punic War, a period for which the account of Livy is missing. Later and once only, a source describes the spoils put on naval parade. Livy's account of L. Aemilius Regillus' *triumphus navalis* held in 189 BC after the defeat of Antiochus tells of the exhibition of 34,200 Attic tetradrachmae, 132,300 cistophori, and 49 golden crowns.[195] The display was less spectacular than contemporary processions, and Livy himself points out that the money paraded by Regillus in no way matched the splendour of the triumph. Apart from this circumstance, there is nothing unusual about the display. After his procession, a *tabula* praising Regillus' deeds was placed on the Capitol, a common honour also for generals who had celebrated the traditional *triumphus*.[196]

Thus, the *triumphus* and the *triumphus navalis* were similar in arrangement and they were initially placed on an equal footing. Still, they were classified as two different types of celebrations. An explanation for this may, in my opinion, be that the *navalis* was distinguished only by a singular display, which the *triumphus* lacked, namely captured rams. If rams formed the distinctive feature of the naval

---

[192] According to Pliny the Elder (*Nat.* 15.38.125), Papirius Maso, who in 231 BC was the first to hold a triumph on the Alban Mount, wore a wreath of myrtle at the public games, cf. Val. Max. 3.6.5; Fest. p. 131 L, s.v. 'Murtea corona'. Papirius probably wore the wreath as a reminder of his victory and triumph, and he is likely to have carried myrtle in the procession as well, see Brennan (1996: 323), and Baudou (1997: with further references). For the triumphs held on Alban Mount, see Brennan (1996).

[193] Liv. 33.23.8–9.

[194] Ehlers (1939: 496–7); Briscoe (1981: 392); Künzl (1988: 101–2).

[195] Liv. 37.58.3–5.

[196] Keil, *Gramm. Lat.* 6, p. 265. A *tabula* inscribed with an identical text hung above the doors of the temple of the Lares Permarini, vowed by L. Aemilius Regillus and dedicated in 179 BC by the censor M. Aemilius, Liv. 40.52.4–7.

triumph, this would explain why the sources never account for their presence in these processions. Being the very emblems of the *navalis*, such information would have been superfluous indeed.

Since frequent naval triumphs followed Duilius' celebration during the First Punic War, after which only a few *navales* are recorded, the *triumphus navalis* seems to have been intimately connected to the period when Roman power was first established at sea. Thereafter, the practice by and by fell out of fashion, and in the late Republic generals no longer performed naval triumphs to celebrate their victories at sea. Thus, when Octavian defeated Sextus Pompeius in a naval battle in 36 BC, although *columnae rostratae* were raised in honour of both him and Agrippa,[197] Octavian did not celebrate a naval triumph, but an ovation.[198] It seems that, with the ongoing success at sea after Duilius, the *navalis* soon turned from the particular to the ordinary, and thus lost its original value as a symbol of exceptional honour. Regillus' comparatively modest display in his *navalis* in 189 BC might reflect such a change. In the following year, Q. Fabius Labeo obtained a naval triumph over Antiochus even though he had fought no real war at all, having only secured the release of some Roman and Italian prisoners on the island of Crete.[199] The decline of the *triumphus navalis* is also manifested in the last one recorded, held by Cn. Octavius in 167 BC. Celebrating the defeat of Perseus, Octavius' *navalis* was a simple pendant to the glorious manifestation of Aemilius Paullus. While Paullus displayed captives and spoils in abundance,[200] Livy maintains that Octavius showed neither prisoners nor booty in his procession.[201] Still, some beaks were most certainly present to mark the parade as a naval triumph. Interestingly, then, when Aemilius Paullus arrived at Rome after Perseus' defeat, he came up the Tiber in a huge regal vessel adorned with Macedonian spoils and royal textiles.[202] There is no evidence whether or not Paullus showed this ship in his three-day-long procession,[203] but quite clearly, Octavius had to content himself with adornments from smaller vessels. By arriving in the foremost ship of the enemy, Paullus usurped any naval achievements as his own. Perhaps, it was this occasion that gave the *triumphus navalis*, already in decline, its final blow.

[197] App. *BCiv.* 5.130. Zanker (1990: 39–42); *LTUR* I (1993), s.v. 'Columnae rostratae Augusti', 308 (D. Palombi).

[198] Degrassi, *Inscr. It.* 13:1, 569; Aug. *Anc.* 4; Suet. *Aug.* 22; App. *BCiv.* 5.130; Dio Cass. 49.15.1; Oros. 6.18.34, 6.20.6. *Fasti Barberiniani* record a *triumphus*: Degrassi, *Inscr. It.* 13:1, 569.

[199] Liv. 37.60, 38.47.5–6.

[200] Liv. 45.40; Diod. Sic. 31.8.10–12 (apud Sync.); Plut. *Aem.* 32–4.

[201] Liv. 45.42.2–3. Even if Octavius showed no spoils, he nevertheless distributed money to his soldiers (Liv. 45.42.3). He also built the *Porticus Octavia*, Plin. *Nat.* 34.7.13; Pietilä-Castrén (1987: 120–3).

[202] Liv. 45.35.3; Cic. *Fin.* 5.24.70; Plut. *Aem.* 30.2–3; Eutrop. 4.8. For the historical and literary *exemplum* of solemn arrivals in Rome on the Tiber, see Görler (1993).

[203] Livy (45.42.12) states that after Paullus' triumph, royal Macedonian ships of sizes not previously seen were hauled up into the Campus Martius.

Terra marique

Our first literary descriptions of triumphs displaying ships and rams pertain to celebrations held only about a century after Octavius naval triumph (Lucullus in 63 BC, Pompey in 61 BC, Octavian in 29 BC, and Vespasian and Titus in AD 71).[204] As will be seen in the following, in contrast to generals who performed *triumphi navales*, these triumphators all displayed ships or rams in processions that were only partly dedicated to the celebration of victories at sea.[205] Their beaks and ships added symbols of success on sea to the ones showing victory on land in one and the same triumph.

Plutarch states that among a lavish display of valuable objects, Lucullus in 63 BC showed 110 bronze-beaked ships.[206] Certainly, the general's aim was to emphasize that although the war had mainly been fought on land, he had been successful at sea as well. The number of 110 vessels is quite astonishing considering that it has been calculated that Mithridates had about 120 ships at his disposal in his main fleet while fighting Lucullus,[207] many of which went down during the war.[208] If we are to put any trust in the number, Lucullus must have acquired some of the vessels elsewhere, as booty or as gifts. The ships paraded certainly implied Roman mastery at sea, although, in fact no Roman vessels had contributed to the success. The senate had offered to supply Lucullus with a fleet, but the general had declined, preferring to rely on the ships of the allies in the East.[209]

Led by his desire to outshine Lucullus, Pompey two years later paraded captured beaks together with placards announcing his conquest of 800 or more pirate ships with bronze beaks.[210] Pompey's triumph in 61 BC in many aspects aspired to claim his conquest of the world,[211] and the ships and *rostra* filled an important role in this display, boasting maritime success along with the terrestrial victories.

In his triple triumph of 29 BC, Octavian clearly challenged Pompey (and Caesar) as the true world conqueror, and in his three-day-long celebration, he paraded peoples from all three parts of the world.[212] The battle of Actium played a prominent part in Octavian's victory image,[213] and the *rostra Actia* depicted by Propertius were most probably given a conspicuous role in the procession.[214] These symbols of

---

[204] When describing the games held after Caesar's triumphs, Suetonius refers to staged naval battles that employed ships from the Tyrian and Egyptian fleets, Suet. *Iul.* 39.4; cf. Dio Cass. 43.23.4. Perhaps these ships had been displayed in the preceding processions as well.

[205] This is not to say that the *triumphi navales* always celebrated sea victories exclusively. For example, Duilius' triumph in 260 BC manifested his victories on land as well (Lazenby, 1996: 67–8). Without doubt, however, the *triumphi navales* focused primarily on the naval success of the general in question.

[206] Plut. *Luc.* 37.3. [207] Morrison (1996: 117). [208] App. *Mith.* 78.

[209] Plut. *Luc.* 13.4; App. *Mith.* 77. Keaveney (1992: 84–5).

[210] App. *Mith.* 116–17; Plut. *Pomp.* 45.2.

[211] Östenberg (1999). [212] See Östenberg (1999).

[213] Hölscher (1984, 1985); Zanker (1990: esp. 79–98). [214] Prop. 2.1.35.

naval domination were matched by a lavish display of terrestrial mastery, as the riches from Alexandria filled most of the three days of parades.[215] The dual message of victory on land and at sea was also announced at Nicopolis, where, on the victory monument displaying enemy rams from Actium, Octavian proudly inscribed that he had achieved peace on land and at sea, *pace parta terra marique*.[216]

In AD 71, Vespasian and Titus displayed ships in a triumph that celebrated a campaign fought almost completely on land. In this, they too put Roman universal supremacy on parade by exhibiting sea victories side by side with land conquests. The vessels on display may have been the ones Vespasian seized when he defeated the pirate force of Anicetus in AD 69.[217] The ships could also have been captured in the battle on Lake Gennesareth in AD 67,[218] although this has been doubted.[219] The boats of the Galilean force were very small and rough (σκάφη μικρά), and they fit poorly into Titus and Vespasian's spectacular triumphal display. Moreover, they do not match the ships (νῆες) that Josephus describes in the triumph.[220] However, Vespasian himself made quite a point out of the naval victory on Lake Gennesareth, which marked the end of the revolt in Tiberias and Tarichaeae. Coins with the legend VICTORIA NAVALIS were issued, and Jones points out that this was the only war event of the years 67/8 that attracted such attention.[221] Obviously, Vespasian took the opportunity to launch a smaller achievement at sea as a major naval success, and the ships displayed in the triumph played the same role. The exhibition might have included some of the vessels taken at Lake Gennesareth as those seized from Anicetus. To merit the Josephan label of νῆες, perhaps some larger ships confiscated by other means were paraded as well.

To sum up, ships and beaks displayed in the *triumphi navales* emphasized that the preceding victories had been earned at sea rather than on land and thus announced the beginning of the Roman maritime takeover. The ones shown from the late Republic and onwards instead formed part of triumphs that

---

[215] Dio Cass. 51.21.7–8.

[216] Murray and Petsas (1989: 62–77). The part *pace parta terra* has been preserved on different blocks, and *marique* is supplemented from *terra*. In Rome, an inscription on the *columna rostrata* erected in honour of Octavian and Agrippa after the battle against Sextus Pompeius stated: 'Peace, long disturbed, he re-established on land and sea', App. *BCiv*. 5.130. At this time, Agrippa was awarded a *corona navalis*, Verg. *Aen*. 8.682–4; Liv. *Per*. 129; Ov. *Ars* 3.392; Sen. *Benef*. 3.32.4; Plin. *Nat*. 16.3.7–8; Dio Cass. 49.14.3–4. Coins minted in Rome depict Agrippa wearing a mural and a naval crown, stressing his success both on land and at sea, *BMCRE* i (1923: 23, nos. 110–11, pl. 4.6); Carson (1980: 10, no. 335).

[217] Tac. *Hist*. 3.47. De Souza (1999: 208–9). After the fall of Jerusalem, there were also some piratical activities at Joppa, which were soon crushed by the Romans.

[218] Joseph. *BJ* 3.522–31.

[219] Michel and Brauernfeind (1969: 246).

[220] Ibid. The same may be said in arguing against the possible presence of Anicetus' pirate vessels.

[221] Mattingly and Sydenham (1926: 73, 75, 79, 85, 88, 95, 97, 102, 105, 108); Jones (1989: 131).

celebrated victories both on land and at sea. The Romans were now firmly established masters *terra marique*, and the role of the ships and the *rostra* was not to stress the specific importance of the naval victories, but rather to add symbols of the mastery of the sea to the spoils earned on land. Before the eyes of the spectators, the display embodied the world dominated by Rome.

Ships sailing by

The triumphal processions exhibited not only beaks but also entire ships. Plutarch explicitly states that Lucullus paraded 110 χαλκέμβολοι νῆες μακραί, bronze-beaked warships, in his triumph, and Josephus describes the display of many ships, πολλαὶ νῆες, in Vespasian and Titus' Jewish procession.[222] Horace's depiction of a triumphal procession shown on a theatre stage includes *naves*, not *rostra*, and Pomponius Porphyrio's comment that these had been captured in a naval battle in no way indicates that ships were an unusual form of display.[223] Propertius' description of how beaks from Actium ran along the Sacred Way, *Actiaque in Sacra currere rostra Via*, could be taken as evidence that Octavian showed rams rather than vessels. On the other hand, the poet's *rostra* might just as well be read as an allusion to the foremost and most conspicuous part of entire ships on display.

In the parades, the ships must have been transported on wheels. A painting from Ostia depicting a procession held in honour of Neptune provides a glimpse of such an operation.[224] Among other things it shows a ship with its topsail set being towed on a two-wheeled carriage by two men. Although the ships displayed in the triumphal processions were much larger in size and weight, the procedure must have been similar. Parts of the sails might even have been set, thus transmitting an image of vessels still sailing the seas. In fact, none of the descriptions of the ships shown in the triumphal processions describe them as being pulled or drawn with force. Propertius' *rostra* (which might well be ships) are described as actively *currere*, a verb commonly applied to vessels at sea, furrowing the waves of their own strength.[225] Plutarch states that the ships shown by Lucullus παρεκομίσθησαν, and although παρακομίζω in the passive sense often means 'to be carried, transported', it is also specifically employed for ships in the meaning 'sail beside, coast along'.[226] Similarly, according to Josephus, the ships shown by Vespasian and Titus in the Jewish triumph

[222] Plut. *Luc.* 37.3; Joseph. *BJ* 7.147–8.

[223] Hor. *Epist.* 2.1.192.

[224] *Archeo*, 11/6 (136) (1996) 66–7.

[225] See e.g. Prop. 1.14.3; Verg. *Aen.* 5.862, and for further references *TLL*, s.v. 'curro' (C3); *OLD*, s.v. 'curro' (3a).

[226] LSJ, s.v. 'παρακομίζω' (II.1), referring to this passage.

εἵποντο, 'followed' (from ἕπομαι), which also suggests that they were displayed seemingly moving by their own force.

After the triumph, the Romans may have incorporated some of the captured ships into their fleet.[227] Livy states that some of the ships from Antium were hauled up in the Roman docks in 338 BC, and Tacitus writes that Octavian stationed a captured squadron from Actium to serve the Roman cause at Forum Iulii.[228] Another possibility was to present the ships as gifts to allies. Thus, 220 smaller boats (*lembi*) taken from King Gentius of Illyria were given to the peoples of Corcyra, Apollonia, and Dyrrhacium after the triumph of Anicius Gallus in 167 BC.[229] Ships might also be exhibited as show pieces and trophies of war or dedicated to the gods.[230] At the sanctuary of Apollo at Cape Actium, Octavian dedicated ten entire vessels, of different sizes, representing the single ship classes that he had fought and vanquished.[231] These particular ships could not have been shown in the triumph in Rome first, but other dedications probably had. Captured ships were also at times burnt, some perhaps after the triumph, but most ships probably at the scene of battle. For example, the ships from Antium that were not reused by the Roman fleet were instead burnt, and Scipio Africanus had fire consume the larger part of the fleet of the Carthaginians at the end of the Second Punic War.[232]

Beaks in abundance

When captured warships were destroyed, their bronze beaks and other valuable equipment were usually saved for later use in ships or as ornaments or offerings to the gods. As was the case with other weapons, the Romans hung various parts of ships in temples as dedications, in public places as memorials or even on and in the houses of the victorious generals.[233] Anchors, figureheads, stern ornaments, tridents, steering oars might all be employed as trophies of war fought at sea.[234]

---

[227] This probably explains why Appian emphasizes that Pompey brought 700 undamaged ships to the harbours, *Mith.* 116.

[228] Antium: Liv. 8.14.12; Actium: Tac. *Ann.* 4.5.1. Similarly, Scipio transferred some of the ships captured in Spain to the Roman fleet, Liv. 28.38.1–2; App. *Iber.* 23, cf. 38.

[229] Liv. 45.43.10.

[230] See e.g. Liv. 45.42.12.

[231] Murray and Petsas (1989: esp. 6, 99, 115–16, 125, 142).

[232] Antium: Liv: 8.14.12; Carthage: Liv. 30.43.12; Zonar. 9.14.11.

[233] Temples: Liv. 10.2.14–15; Sil. *Pun.* 14.649. Public places: Silius Italicus (*Pun.* 1.621–3) includes naval spoils in his depiction of the *spolia* fixed to the door of the Curia (a public place and a *templum*). Houses: Pompey fixed beaks from the captured pirate ships in the *vestibulum* of his house, appropriately located on the Carinae ('the Keels'), Cic. *Phil.* 2.28.68 (Guilhembet, 1992). Vergil has the palace of Latinus decorated with several kinds of spoils, among them ships' beaks (*Aen.* 7.186).

[234] The reliefs on the arch at Arausio (modern Orange) show a variety of naval spoils, P. M. Duval, in Amy *et al.* (1962: 94–106, tav. 24–7, 50–2, 84–8). See also Polito (1988: 58, with further references).

Still, the favourite naval spoil among both Greeks and Romans was the ram, and the ram is the only part of the ship that we know was displayed in the triumphal processions. Besides Propertius' description of the beaks that sailed along the Sacred Way, our evidence for the triumphal exhibition of rams stems from Appian's account of Pompey's two-day-long procession commemorating his victories against the pirates and Mithridates. Appian states that Pompey led νεῶν ἔμβολα in the triumph, and the Greek historian's sober listing leaves no doubt that rams rather than vessels are intended. The beaks are listed among several items that Pompey led by (παρῆγε).[235] Unlike the ships, the rams did not move forward of their own, but had to be pulled.[236]

Appian provides no clue as to the number of beaks exhibited by Pompey. But both Plutarch and Appian maintain that placards shown in the triumph announced the conquest of 800 ships, while Pliny claims that the tablet put up by Pompey for Minerva stated that he had sunk or captured 846 ships.[237] These figures are astonishingly high. According to Appian, Pompey captured or received 377 pirate ships, and Plutarch states that the pirates in Cilicia had 90 beaked ships at their disposal.[238] However, Plutarch also maintains that all together, the pirates at the time had over 1,000 ships available,[239] and the 800 (or 846) ships must refer to Pompey's entire campaign against the pirates, from the initial operation in the West to the final blow in Cilicia. Even so, there might well be, as often in these contexts, an overstatement in Pompey's figures.[240]

Unlike Lucullus, Pompey preferred beaks to entire ships. In effect, an exhibition of hundreds of ships in Pompey's processions would have overemphasized the naval success in relation to the marvellous accomplishments in the lands of the East. Parading beaks from a large number of ships together with an announcement of the total number of vessels captured was much more effective. In this way, Pompey manifested that, while Lucullus had staged what must have seemed an endless row of ships in his one-day procession, the number of vessels captured by Pompey so far exceeded the achievements of his predecessor that not even during two days of triumph was there time and space enough to show them all in their entirety.

---

[235] App. *Mith.* 116.

[236] If, however, Propertius intends beaks only, not entire vessels, by the *rostra* that are described as *currere*, this distinction between ships that move forward by their own force and beaks that have to be pulled is less valid.

[237] Plut. *Pomp.* 45.2 (800 pirate ships); App. *Mith.* 117 (800 bronze-beaked ships); Plin. *Nat.* 7.26.97.

[238] App. *Mith.* 96; Plut. *Pomp.* 28.2. For Pompey's campaigns against the pirates, see e.g. Morrison (1996: 117–19); De Souza (1999: 161–78); Schulz (2000a: 437–8).

[239] Plut. *Pomp.* 24.4–5.

[240] Dreizehnter (1975: 225–33).

Financially and symbolically, beaks were by far the most valuable part of an ancient ship of war. The rams in the triumphs of Lucullus and Pompey were of bronze, and as such they represented a true monetary value.[241] Murray estimates that the bronze ram found outside of Athlit in Israel, stemming from a Hellenistic warship, was worth 1,116.2 drachmas of silver in the late fourth century.[242] This ram weighs 465 kg, is 226 cm in length and 76 cm in its maximum width, and has a maximum height of 95 cm, and Murray argues that it once belonged to a so-called 'four' or a 'five'.[243] Although by no means all captured rams were as heavy—the rams of the classical triremes are calculated to have had a weight of around 200 kg minimum[244]—they must have been desirable for their worth alone.

When the Athlit ram was found, its enormous weight attracted much attention. Since then, Murray and Petsas have carried out their investigation of Octavian's victory monument at Nicopolis and been able to conclude that the majority of the rams captured from the fleet of Cleopatra and Antony at Actium and fixed there were heavier than the Athlit ram, the largest ones having had a weight of around two tons.[245] Practical considerations must have played part in the decision to erect the monument on the spot rather than transporting these particular beaks to Rome. Still, Octavian sent other beaks and possibly entire ships as well back to the city. This is clear from Propertius' *rostra Actia* and from the fact that the senate decreed that rams from Actium should be fastened to the *aedes Divi Iulii*.[246] These beaks were clearly much smaller than those left at Nicopolis. Analysing depictions on reliefs and coins, Murray concludes that the rams from Actium and others that were suspended off the ground and fixed to the speakers' platforms and the honorary columns in Rome cannot have originated from ships larger than triremes.[247]

Similarly, the beaks paraded by Pompey must have been of sizes smaller than the Athlit ram and the ones on display at Nicopolis. Indeed, the trademark of the typical pirate ship was speed and lightness, and the rams shown in Pompey's triumph most likely did not stand out for their massiveness. Rather, their large number was what made an impression, reflecting the complete defeat of the pirates.

[241] Murray (1985) discusses the trade in damaged rams in 4th-cent. Athens.

[242] Ibid. Murray, in Murray and Petsas (1989: 127 n. 16). The Athlit ram in general: Murray and Petsas (1989: *passim*).

[243] Murray, in Murray and Petsas (1989: 103–5).

[244] Ibid. 105.

[245] Ibid. 85–6, 111–14. Ancient testimonies to the monument: Strab. 7.7.6, 17.1.10; Suet. *Aug.* 18.2, 96.2; Plut. *Ant.* 65.3; Philippus, in *Anth. Pal.* 6.236; Dio Cass. 51.1.3.

[246] Dio Cass. 51.19.2.

[247] Murray, in Murray and Petsas (1989: 95–114, esp. 110–13, and 143): 'The weapons at his camp literally dwarfed the examples he sent to Rome for mounting in the *Forum Romanum*.'

In fact, although ancient authors at times mention the size of a ship captured, their major concern was the number of vessels and beaks conquered and paraded.[248] Also, just like the general who had been successful on land told and retold how many cities he had seized, the Roman naval commander stressed the number of ships he had sunk or captured.[249] For example, the commemorative tablets put up to Regillus stress that he had captured over forty ships, and it was this number that granted him a naval triumph over Antiochus.[250] War vessels in fact were likened to enemy cities. They were equipped with towers and artillery.[251] Arrows, stones, and even fire were launched from catapults and *ballistae* in defence of the vessels, and, as the *corona muralis* on land, the soldier who first managed to board an enemy ship was given the *corona navalis*.[252] Ships were maritime fortresses, and the inscription that accompanied Duilius' *columna rostrata* stresses that the ships of the Carthaginians had been captured by force, *vique nave[is cepe]t*, which is also the standard formula used to announce the conquest of cities. As always, numbers may well be both exaggerated and corrupt, but it is nevertheless quite clear that Rome took great concern in measuring victories at sea by recording the number of ships sunk or captured. Like the ubiquitous notes of cities sized and of enemies killed or taken prisoner these numbers emphasized the magnitude of the deeds of a particular general and the extent of Roman military conquest.[253]

The Mediterranean became *mare nostrum*. The treaty after Zama allowed the Carthaginians to keep ten ships only,[254] a common clause forced on the vanquished. The fleet of Antiochus was destroyed after Apamea,[255] as was that of Perseus after Pydna, and the Macedonians were also prohibited from any future cutting of timber to build a new fleet.[256] Pompey deprived the pirates of all their ships in his campaign, thereby removing the very means of their former trade. Ships and beaks paraded in Rome, together with placards announcing the conquest, destruction, and confiscation of other vessels, symbolized the complete takeover of the enemy fleet, ensuring also future control of the sea.

---

[248] There are a few possible exceptions. If Duilius showed Hannibal's vessel (inherited from Pyrrhus) and Aemilius Paullus' royal Macedonian ships, these would have been spectacular showpieces indeed.

[249] e.g. Liv. 28.38.2; Plin. *Nat.* 7.26.97; Plut. *Pomp.* 45; App. *Mith.* 117.

[250] Liv. 37.58.3, 40.52.5–7.

[251] See e.g. App. *BCiv.* 5.118; Plut. *Ant.* 66.2, and the discussion in Marsden (1969: 169–73). For representations of ships with towers, see Morrison (1996: figs. 29, 31c, 36); Hölscher (1984: Abb. 11, 208).

[252] Maxfield (1981: esp. 74–6).

[253] On the tablet put up to Minerva, Pompey stressed three numbers: enemies killed or taken prisoners (12,183,000), ships sunk or captured (846), and cities and forts brought under Roman supremacy (1,538), Plin. *Nat.* 7.26.97.

[254] Polyb. 15.18.3–4; Liv. 30.37.3; App. *Pun.* 54; Dio Cass. 17.58.82; Zonar. 9.14.11.

[255] Liv. 38.39.2–3.   [256] Liv. 45.29.14.

COINS AND BULLION

Coins and bullion were regularly displayed in the Roman triumphal processions. Our first notice pertains to the year 293 BC, when L. Papirius Cursor and Sp. Carvilius Maximus both triumphed over the Samnites. Livy states that Papirius Cursor showed 2,533,000 pounds of *aes grave* and 1,830 pounds of silver in his procession, while Carvilius Maximus brought 380,000 pounds of *aes grave* into the treasury.[257] After this date, Livy's text is missing for larger parts of the third century BC, but other sources occasionally attest to coins captured or deposited in the public treasury at the time of a triumph.[258] For one, there is the inscription from the *columna rostrata* of C. Duilius.[259] The text was set up in commemoration of his naval victory over the Carthaginians in 260 BC and specified the quantity of gold, silver, and bronze pieces captured. The inscription as it stands today is of Augustan date, but it probably copies the Republican text rather accurately.

Throughout Roman Republican history, the amount and types of coins and bullion captured, displayed in the triumphs, and deposited in the *aerarium* were scrupulously registered. This is reflected particularly in Livy's books 28–45, which form the basis for our knowledge of the triumphs held between 207 and 167 BC.[260] During this period, Livy describes the contents of thirty-five triumphs in some detail, in thirty-one of which he records the amount of coins and bullion shown and deposited in the treasury.[261] In the remaining four cases, Livy specifically

[257] Liv. 10.46, esp. 5–7, 14–16. In Papirius' case, Livy explicitly states that the bronze and silver were carried in his procession, whereas for Carvilius, he writes only that the bronze was carried into the *aerarium*. Zonaras (8.1.9) states that in 294 BC, the year before the triumphs of Papirius Cursor and Carvilius Maximus, M. Atilius Regulus placed the money realized from the spoils of war in the treasury.

[258] Dion. Hal. 19.16.3–4 (fr.); Eutrop. 2.27.

[259] Degrassi, *Inscr. It.* 13:3, no. 69, 44–9: [*Aur*]*om captom numei* (*tria milia septingentei*), | [*arcen*]*tom captom praeda numei* (*centum milia*) [– – –; | *omne*] *captom aes* (*inter undetricies et tricies quater centena milia*). 'Gold taken: 3,700 pieces. Silver taken, together with that derived from the booty: 100,000 (. . . and more) pieces. Total amount, in bronze . . . (between 2,900,000–3,400,000 pieces)'. Signs representing the sums have been preserved but are incomplete. Crawford (1974: 626 n. 2) assesses the silver as 200,000–300,000 pieces and the bronze, like Degrassi, as 2,900,000–3,400,000 pounds. The gold was in all probability captured as booty from the enemy, together with at least some of the silver. Some silver might also have come from the selling of booty, as did the bronze, Mommsen, *CIL* i. 195; Degrassi, *Inscr. It.* 13:3, no. 69, 44–9; Warmington (1940: 130–1); Bona (1960: 139–41, with further references); Shatzman (1972: 186); Pietilä-Castrén (1987: 31).

[260] Between the reappearance of Livy's text at 219 BC and 207 BC, few triumphs were held. Livy's account of Marcellus' ovation in 211 BC, celebrating the victory at Syracuse (26.21.6–10), includes no specification of the coins and bullion on display. Livy does not describe the triumph held by Fabius Maximus over Tarentum in 209 BC, but Plutarch states that 3,000 talents were brought into the treasury at this occasion, Plut. *Fab.* 22.4–5.

[261] For some of these triumphs, Livy does not spell out explicitly that the items were displayed in the processions, only that an amount was brought into the treasury (e.g. 28.9.16–17, 30.45.3, 34.10.4–5). However, there can be little doubt that the money was shown in the processions as well.

stresses that no money was shown, a circumstance which was obviously note-worthy in itself.[262] Moreover, in as many as nineteen of the thirty-one triumphal accounts that include figures of worth, Livy records the sums of bronze, silver, and gold displayed but mentions no other spoils or captives.[263] Thus, of all the items displayed, only the coins and bullion were recorded.

The importance of the financial assets is also evident from the fact that the precise amount of coins and bullion paraded appear earlier than for other types of display. Livy provides us with precise sums of coins and bullion from 293 BC, and after the reappearance of his triumphal accounts in 211 BC, he starts giving specified numbers of other spoils, like military standards, statues, and captives only from 190 BC.[264] Before this date, Livy uses rather vague wordings to say that, for example, a great quantity of Gallic spoils (*multa Gallica spolia*) and many noble Gauls (*multi nobiles Galli*) were led in Cornelius Cethegus' triumph of 197 BC, and that, three years later, Flamininus showed many noble captives and hostages (*multi nobiles captivi obsidesque*).[265] At the same time, the money displayed by Cethegus is defined as 237,000 bronze asses and 79,000 silver bigati and that by Flamininus as 43,270 pounds of silver bullion, 84,000 Attic tetradrachmae, 3,714 pounds of gold, and 14,514 gold Philippics.[266] As always, we should be careful to trust any exact figures. Still, whatever their credibility per se, these numbers reflect the Roman will both to parade large

[262] P. Cornelius Cethegus and M. Baebius Tamphilus led only sacrificial animals in their triumphs *de Liguribus Apuanis* in 180 BC (40.38.8–9); Q. Fulvius Flaccus' triumph *de Liguribus* in 179 BC showed *nullam pecuniam admodum* (40.59.2–3). Cn. Octavius' naval triumph held over Perseus in 167 BC lacked both captives and spoils (45.42.2–3). L. Aemilius Paullus' triumph over the Ligurians in 181 BC showed 25 golden crowns, but no other gold or silver (Liv. 40. 34.7–8). This triumph is included among the thirty-one that list the gold and/or silver displayed.

[263] M. Livius Salinator and C. Claudius Nero in 207 BC (Liv. 28.9), L. Cornelius Lentulus *ovans* in 200 BC (31.20.6–7), L. Furius Purpureo in 200 BC (31.49.2–3), Cn. Cornelius Blasio and M. Helvius *ovantes* in 196 and 195 BC (33.27.1–3, 34.10.3–5), Q. Minucius Thermus in 195 BC (34.10.6–7), M. Porcius Cato in 194 BC (34.46.2–3), M. Fulvius Nobilior *ex Hispania ulteriore* in 191 BC (36.21.10–11), L. Aemilius Regillus' *navalis* in 189 BC (37.58.3–5), L. Manlius Acidinus Fulvianus in 185 BC (39.29.4–7), C. Calpurnius Piso and L. Quinctius Crispinus in 184 BC (39.42.1–4), A. Terentius Varro *ovans* in 182 BC (40.16.11), L. Aemilius Paullus in 181 BC (40.34.7–8), Q. Fulvius Flaccus in 180 BC (40.43.6–7), Ti. Sempronius Gracchus in 178 BC (41.7.1–3), L. Postumius Albinus in 178 BC (41.7.1–3), C. Claudius Pulcher in 177 BC (41.13.6–8). In some of these triumphal accounts, describing victories in Spain, Livy includes records of the number of golden crowns. In L. Furius Purpureo's triumph in 200 BC, Livy states that no spoils or captives were shown. Still, Purpureo brought bronze and silver coins to the treasury.

[264] The number of golden crowns appears from 194 BC and of torcs from 191 BC.

[265] Liv. 33.23.4–5, 34.52.4–10.

[266] Liv. 33.23.7, 34.52.5–7. In the triumph held by M. Claudius Marcellus over the Gallic Insubres in 196 BC, Livy (33.37.10–11) describes the spoils and the standards as having been *multa*, while the asses and silver coins are recorded to the exact amount of 320,000 and 234,000 respectively.

sums of money in the triumphs and also to specify their conquests in precise financial terms.[267]

The importance of the worth is also reflected in the behaviour of some generals who were unable to enter the city by way of a triumph. When Scipio Africanus returned to Rome in 206 BC after his success in Spain, he brought with him captured warships loaded with prisoners and booty.[268] He was, however, denied a triumph as he had fought in Spain as *privatus*,[269] and thus found himself standing outside the walls of Rome with captives, weapons, ships, money, and large numbers of other spoils. What became of the captives and the spoils is unclear, but we do know what happened to the coins and bullion. Livy describes Scipio's actions in 206 BC in the following way: *Senatu misso urbem est ingressus argentique prae se in aerarium tulit decem quattuor milia pondo trecenta quadraginta duo et signati argenti magnum numerum*, 'After the senate had been dismissed, he entered the city, and carried before him 14,342 pounds of silver and a great number of silver coins into the treasury'.[270] Although Scipio held no triumph, the coins and bullion were thus brought into the treasury, and Livy's formal wording *prae se in aerarium tulit* even implies an official entrance and delivery of the silver.[271]

The finances of the Roman state were extremely strained during the Second Punic War,[272] and the treasury must have been in a far too desperate need of the money obtained by Scipio not to have it brought into the city. There are, however, other examples of similar behaviour. When L. Stertinius returned from his victories in *Hispania ulterior* in 199 BC, which he had achieved as *privatus* with proconsular *imperium*, he did not even try to obtain a triumph. Still, he brought 50,000 pounds of silver into the treasury.[273] Similarly, in the late

---

[267] Cf. Harris (1979: 59): 'If the figures recorded by Livy for the *praeda* gained in many of the campaigns of the 290s are authentic, as most of them may well be, they show a degree of interest in measuring and recording that was not typical of that time.'

[268] App. *Iber.* 23, 38; Liv. 28.38.1–2.

[269] Liv. 28.38.2–5; Plut. *Pomp.* 14.1–2; Dio Cass. 17.56 (fr.). Appian (*Iber.* 38) states that Scipio did triumph, while Polybius (11.33.7) writes more vaguely that he brought home a brilliant triumph and victory to Rome (κάλλιστον θρίαμβον καὶ καλλίστην νίκην τῇ πατρίδι κατάγων). The Greek authors give no description of the appearance or contents of the triumph, and modern scholars tend rather to trust the testimony of Livy, see e.g. Richardson (1975: 52); Develin (1978: 432–3).

[270] Liv. 28.38.5–6.

[271] Indeed, Dio Cassius points out that, although Scipio was not given the honour to celebrate any triumph, he was allowed to sacrifice 100 white oxen on the Capitol and to celebrate a festival, 17.56 (fr.). His entrance thus included quite a few triumphal elements, a circumstance, which probably caused the confusion in the ancient sources concerning the nature of the celebration. Cf. Liv. 45.4.1.

[272] Buraselis (1996: 168–9).

[273] Liv. 33.27.3–5. Stertinius erected two arches, *fornices*, the first of their kind, *de manubiis*, see Pietilä-Castrén (1987: 71–4).

Republic, Lucullus not only displayed a large amount of coins and bullion in his triumph over Mithridates, he also advertised by placards the sums of money already paid to the treasury.[274] It seems that some money had been brought in while Lucullus waited outside the city walls to be allowed a triumph. Rome could await the weapons, the art objects, and the captives, but not the liquid assets.

From triumph to treasury

Livy at times describes the coins and bullion as being carried in the procession (*lata, tralata, travecta in triumpho*; *prae se tulit*, etc.), at others as being carried into the treasury (*in aerarium tulit*, etc.). The expressions *in triumpho tulit* and *in aerarium tulit* seem to be interchangeable variations in language rather than demarcations in meaning. This suggests that the money paraded in the triumphal processions was also deposited in the treasury.[275] Such a practice is further implied by the conduct of L. Manlius Acidinus Fulvianus in his ovation for victories in Spain in 185 BC. Fulvianus carried 52 golden crowns, 132 pounds of gold, and 16,300 pounds of silver in his procession.[276] On the same occasion, he declared that his quaestor Q. Fabius was bringing an additional 10,000 pounds of silver and 80 of gold to Rome, and that he was going to place this money too in the treasury (*id quoque se in aerarium delaturum*). The expression suggests that the gold and silver carried in Fulvianus' procession was brought to the *aerarium*.

On its way from the Forum up to the Capitol, the triumphal parade passed close by the *aerarium* of the *aedes Saturni*.[277] One might wonder, then, if the alternately used expressions *in aerarium tulit* and *in triumpho tulit* could perhaps reflect an actual ceremonial delivery, performed during or after the triumphal procession itself. Little is known of how the booty and captives were taken care of immediately after the procession, nor is it certain that the entire train was driven up to the Capitol.[278] Sources do relate that, at times, the procession halted at the foot of the Capitoline hill whilst the leader of the conquered enemy was led aside and executed. Perhaps then, the procession halted also to make room for the direct

---

[274] Plut. *Luc.* 37.4.

[275] As always, we should avoid taking Roman conducts and traditions as absolute rules. According to Orosius (5.18.26–7), when Pompeius Strabo triumphed in 89 BC, he left no money to the treasury; cf. Plut. *Pomp.* 4.1.

[276] Liv. 39.29.6–7.

[277] For the *aerarium* and its location in the temple of Saturn, Corbier (1974); Richardson (1980); De Libero (1998: 112–13); *LTUR* iv (1999), s.v. 'Saturnus, aedes', 234–6 (F. Coarelli).

[278] Horace (*Carm.* 4.2.33–6) suggests that prisoners were led all the way up on the Capitoline hill.

deposit of coins and bullion into the *aerarium* as part of the triumphal ritual. The deposit could of course have taken place after the conclusion of the procession.[279]

Manubial activities and distributions to soldiers

Of all the coins, bullion, and other valuable items brought as booty to Rome, the *aerarium* got a substantial part,[280] but shares were also bestowed on the soldiers.[281] Another portion was reserved for the erection of buildings and celebration of games *de manubiis*. What about these shares? Were they included in the display of coins and bullion in the triumphs and brought to the *aerarium*, controlled by the senate, before being distributed to the soldiers or used for manubial activities, or were they kept apart from the triumphal ceremony and the *aerarium* altogether? Peculiarly enough, this is an issue that has not been discussed in the rather vast modern scholarship on *praeda* and *manubiae*.[282]

Whether the money was later used for manubial activities, like the building of temples or the arrangements of games, the sources do not agree. At times, the evidence suggests that the sums brought into the *aerarium* and the ones used for the manubial building were kept separate from each other. Thus, when Sp. Carvilius Maximus triumphed in 293 BC, Livy states that 380,000 pounds of *aes grave* was brought to the treasury, and that the rest of the money was used to let out the contract for the temple of Fors Fortuna.[283] At other times, the manubial share was clearly included in the sum paraded in the triumph and deposited in the treasury, later to be redrawn. When Fulvius Nobilior was granted permission to hold a triumph in 187 BC, he informed the senate that he had vowed *ludi magni* to Jupiter at the time of his capture of Ambracia and that the cities had contributed 100 pounds of gold for this purpose. He now asked to

[279] Describing the triumph held by C. Fabricius Luscinus in 282 BC, Dionysius of Halicarnassus states that the triumphator brought 400 talents to the treasury after the triumph, μετὰ τὸν θρίαμβον, Dion. Hal. 19.16.3–4 (fr.). Similarly, Livy has Fulvius Nobilior declare that a certain sum of money was to be delivered to the treasury after it had been shown in the triumph, Liv. 39.5.8–9. These passages do not, however, exclude the possibility of a delivery as part of the procession. After all, the triumph was almost completed as the train reached the *clivus Capitolinus*.

[280] Note also that Livy (33.23.8–9) suggests that the *aerarium* paid for costs of the triumph, not however for parades on the Alban Mount. Cicero, on the other hand, implies that the general contributed to triumphs in Rome too, *Att.* 6.9.2, 7.1.9.

[281] The celebrating general may also bestow money on the people of Rome, App. *BCiv.* 2.102; Degrassi, *Inscr. It.* 13:3 (1937), no. 69, 46.

[282] In 1972, Shatzman in an influential article argued that the victorious general could do whatever he liked with the spoils of war. His standpoint was contested only in 1999, Churchill (1999). See also e.g. *RE* XXII:1 (1953), 1200–13, s.v. 'praeda' (K.-H. Vogel); Bona (1960); Gruen (1990: 133–45); Liou-Gille (1992); Orlin (1997: esp. 116–39).

[283] Liv. 10.46.14–16. Orlin (1997: 122–4 and n. 24).

earmark this sum out of the money he was planning to display in his triumph and deposit into the treasury, so that it could later be used for the games.[284] The request was granted on condition that the sum spent on the games did not exceed 80,000 sesterces.[285] In this case, the share to be later withdrawn for manubial activities was thus included among the coins and bullion shown in the procession and delivered into the treasury.

What then about the allotments bestowed on the soldiers? Did they form part of the sums paraded as booty in the triumphs and deposited in the treasury? Livy customarily concludes his triumphal reports by accounting for the soldiers' rations, a procedure which could be taken to indicate that this distribution was performed only after the procession had been completed. Indeed, Appian states that Caesar bestowed the money promised and more on his soldiers immediately after his triumph had been completed from the sums displayed in the procession.[286] However, it is not all that evident how to interpret this comment, since Appian describes all four triumphs celebrated by Caesar in 46 BC as one procession only. Also, by the time of the late Republic, the senate had lost much of its former control of the *aerarium*, and Caesar was renowned for treating the assets of Rome as his own.[287] Caesar's procedures are therefore not bound to agree with the practice of the earlier Republican age.

In fact, if we return to Livy, his testimony suggests that the soldiers' share was kept apart from the sums displayed as booty in the processions and brought into the treasury. Livy states that in 293 BC, Papirius Cursor delivered all the gold and silver obtained from the Samnites to the treasury and gave nothing to the soldiers, conduct that aroused much ill will in Rome.[288] The share of the *aerarium* and that of the soldiers are here clearly contrasted. Later, the soldiers who had taken part in Aemilius Paullus' campaign against Perseus tried to block his triumph as they thought they had been given less than could be expected from the royal booty, which Paullus had instead reserved for triumph and treasury. The quotation from Livy (45.37.10–11) clearly reflects the distinction between the sums bestowed on the soldiers on one hand and the ones displayed in the triumph and brought into the treasury on the other: *Cum te praeda partienda locupletem facere posset, pecuniam regiam translaturus in triumpho est et in aerarium*

---

[284] Liv. 39.5.8–9: *petere ut ex ea pecunia, quam in triumpho latam in aerario positurus esset, id aurum secerni iuberent.*

[285] Liv. 39.5.10–11. Scipio Africanus also arranged games from the money that he had brought into the treasury after his victories in Spain, but this money had not been delivered by way of a proper triumph, Liv. 28.38.14; cf. Dio Cass. 17.56 (fr.).

[286] App. *BCiv.* 2.102.

[287] Plin. *Nat.* 33.17.56; Plut. *Pomp.* 62.1–2. Frank (1933: 337); Crawford (1974: 639–40); Barlow (1977); De Libero (1998).

[288] Liv. 10.46.5–7. Orlin (1997: 122–4).

laturus, 'Although he could have made you rich by dividing the spoils, he will carry the royal money in his triumph and deposit it into the treasury'.[289]

Furthermore, the soldiers' share and the money paraded as booty are often registered in different kinds of denomination. Livy records the monetary distributions to the soldiers in bronze asses until Scipio Asiaticus introduced the denarius as payment in 189 BC. However, already some time before this date, asses ceased to be included in the records of the coins shown in the processions and carried into the treasury.[290] Thus, when M. Porcius Cato in 194 BC displayed 25,000 pounds of silver bullion, 123,000 silver denarii, 540,000 Oscan silver coins, and 1,400 pounds of gold in his triumph over Spain, he gave his soldiers 270 asses each.[291] When Scipio Asiaticus a few years later began to present payments to the soldiers by the denarius, Roman currencies were themselves absent from his procession. Instead, Scipio paraded silver bullion, Attic tetradrachmae, cistophori, and Philippic gold coins.[292] Nor are denarii mentioned in the accounts of the subsequent triumphs, while at the same time, this Roman silver denomination was used for the distribution of money to the soldiers.

In all probability, then, the distributions to the soldiers were not included among the sums of coins and bullion paraded as booty in the triumphal processions, at least not during most of the Republic. At the same time, the fact that Livy reports on the military provisions as part of his triumphal accounts indicates that these sums were often distributed at the triumph and therefore duly recorded together with the coins and bullion presented to the treasury.

For the Republican period, the practice of distributing payments to the soldiers at the triumphs is reflected in the actions of the consuls of 207 BC, M. Livius Salinator and C. Claudius Nero, as they celebrated their joint victory over the Carthaginians and Hasdrubal. Since the victorious battle had been fought under Livius' auspices and *imperium* and his army had been brought back and Claudius' had not, Livius was granted a *triumphus* proper and entered the city in a quadriga, while his colleague followed on horseback.[293] Livy follows his usual formula and states that 3,000,000 sesterces and 80,000 asses were brought into the treasury, and that Livius' soldiers were given 56 asses each. Then he makes the more

---

[289] Cf. Liv. 45.35.6–7: *de praeda parcius, quam speraverant ex tantis regiis opibus, dederat nihil relicturis, si aviditati indulgeretur, quod in aerarium deferret*, 'he had given them less of the booty than they had hoped from such lavish royal resources, though had he given rein to their greed, they would have left nothing to be deposited in the treasury'.

[290] Liv. 30.45.3–4. Appian, *Pun.* 66, writes in general terms of how gold, silver coins, and bullion appeared in the procession.

[291] Liv. 34.46.2–3. See similarly Liv. 30.45.3–4.

[292] Liv. 37.59.

[293] Liv. 28.9. For the arrangement of this celebration, see Richardson (1975: 55); Develin (1978: 433).

unusual remark that Claudius promised his absent soldiers the same sum, to be distributed on his return.[294] This implies that the bestowal of soldiers' money from the booty normally took place at the triumph. Since Claudius' army was not present at this occasion, the payment had to be postponed, and the triumphal allotment was replaced with an official announcement of the distribution to come.[295]

From Livy's accounts it is also evident that the specific sums given to the soldiers were well known both to the soldiers themselves and to the spectators of the processions. At Papirius Cursor's celebration in 293 BC, the onlookers lamented the fact that the triumphator so highly aspired to the glory that came from bringing large sums to the treasury that nothing was given to the soldiers, an act that caused a severe burden of large taxes on the citizens.[296] Later, in the triumph of C. Claudius Pulcher *de Histris et Liguribus* in 177 BC, the Roman soldiers were given more than double the pay of the allies, who reacted by walking silently in the procession to show their anger.[297]

The ceremonial allotment to the soldiers could have taken place on the day of the triumph, as the army lined up to enter the city. At this meeting, the general delivered a speech to his soldiers and distributed *dona militaria* to the ones who had distinguished themselves by exceptional courage.[298] What better occasion for the donatives to be delivered than this moment of gathering before the army was about to parade triumphantly through the streets of Rome, singing songs of joy and praise of the general, whose car they followed? In fact, Zonaras maintains that the soldiers were bestowed with *dona* as well as money just before the procession set off.[299] More important is the testimony of Livy, who, in describing the triumph held by Fulvius Nobilior in 187 BC, suggests such a procedure. After the account of the contents of the procession, Livy adds the usual specification of the money distributed to the soldiers, and also, for once, presents a possible setting for such a bestowal. Livy writes (39.5.17):

Multos eo die, priusquam in urbem inveheretur, in circo Flaminio tribunos praefectos equites centuriones, Romanos sociosque, donis militaribus donavit. Militibus ex praeda vicenos quinos denarios divisit, duplex centurioni, triplex equiti.

---

[294] Liv. 28.9.16–18.

[295] The practice might have been followed by other generals, who later triumphed without their armies being present.

[296] Liv. 10.46.5–7.

[297] Liv. 41.13.8: *Sociis dimidio minus quam civibus datum. Itaque taciti, ut iratos esse sentires, secuti sunt currum.*

[298] See e.g. Liv. 39.5.17; Ov. *Pont.* 2.1.29–30. *Dona* were also distributed on the battlefield, see e.g. Liv. 26.48.13–14, 38.23.11; Joseph. *BJ* 7.5–17; Plut. *Pomp.* 38.1–2. Maxfield (1981: 132–4).

[299] Zonar. 7.21.

On that day, before he rode into the city, in the Circus Flaminius, he presented many tribunes, prefects, cavalrymen, and centurions, Romans and allies, with military decorations. To the soldiers, out of the booty, he gave twenty-five denarii each, twice that amount to each centurion, and thrice to each cavalryman.

Although Livy does not explicitly say that the money was distributed together with the *dona* at the Circus Flaminius, it seems reasonable to read the two sentences as part of the same context. If this is correct, Livy here confirms the practice of money distributions as part of the inaugural ceremonials of the triumph.[300]

Triumphal displays and Roman finances

The wealth obtained by way of victorious military campaigns formed a primary source of income for the Roman state, and the sums paraded must at times have been very impressive.[301] For example, Aemilius Paullus is credited with having brought in between 120,000,000 and 300,000,000 sesterces in his Macedonian triumph of 167 BC,[302] and Caesar displayed more than 600,000,000 sesterces in his five triumphs of 46–45 BC.[303] When Octavian held his triple triumph in 29 BC after the subjection of Egypt, the riches were so abundant that property prices rose steeply and interest rates fell dramatically.[304]

Correspondingly, periods with few victories and triumphs meant a severe drain of wealth in the treasury.[305] Thus, although Rome did financially fairly well during the First Punic War,[306] Polybius reports that in 241 BC her resources

---

[300] If this interpretation is correct, the soldiers probably brought their monetary shares with them in the triumphal procession, just as they did the *dona militaria*.

[301] Howgego (1992: 4–8).

[302] Livy (45.40.1–2) cites Valerias Antias for an amount of 120,000,000 sesterces (more than 30,000,000 denarii) but adds that the total sum was probably higher. Polybius (18.35.4–5) states that a sum of 6,000 talents (roughly 36,000,000 denarii) was taken from the treasury of the palace of Perseus alone. Plutarch (*Aem.* 32–3) describes the display of 2,250 talents of silver and 231 talents of gold. Diodorus 31.8.11–12 (apud Sync.) has 1,000 talents of coined money, 2,200 talents of silver, and undefined talents of gold. Velleius Paterculus (1.9.6) gives a higher amount, 200,000,000 sesterces. Pliny (*Nat.* 33.17.56) records a sum of 300,000,000 sesterces, which Frank (1933: 137) assumes to have been caused by a misreading of the figure presented by Livy; cf. De Sanctis (1923: 351–2 n. 302).

[303] Velleius Paterculus (2.56.2) states that 600,000,000 sesterces were shown in the triumphs (about 150,000,00 denarii). Appian (*BCiv.* 2.102) records the display of 60,500 talents and 2,822 golden crowns, weighing 20,414 pounds (equivalent to around 390,000,000 denarii).

[304] Suet. *Aug.* 41.1; Dio Cass. 51.21.5. Reinhold (1988: 156); Howgego (1992: 5), who points out that under Augustus sudden dramatic increases in wealth by way of war booty came to an end. The major exception was the sack of Jerusalem in AD 70.

[305] The following brief survey of the Republican finances basically follows the picture painted by Crawford (1974: 634–40).

[306] Ibid. 634–5.

were exhausted.[307] No triumph had been held for nine years, and Rome must have welcomed the conclusive victory at the Aegates islands, celebrated in two naval triumphs in that year.[308] Large amounts of gold and silver were brought to Rome as war booty,[309] and an indemnity of 3,200 talents was imposed on Carthage, to be paid over ten years.[310]

If the situation was strained during the First Punic War, it was nearly catastrophic during the second. The war lasted for seventeen years, devastated large parts of the Italian peninsula and truly challenged the very existence of Rome. By 214 BC, the financial resources were exhausted and the treasury empty.[311] Various methods had to be applied in order to raise money, among which were special levies and voluntary temporary contributions from the citizens.[312] After the hardships of the Second Punic War, it is not difficult to imagine the relief and joy felt at the sight of Scipio Africanus' triumphal procession in 201 BC. Polybius describes how, when setting eyes on the prisoners and the rest of the display, the spectators were reminded of the dangers that had threatened their very being and thanked the triumphator and the gods for their rescue.[313] The relief felt must have been caused by the financial display as well. Livy states that Scipio brought in 123,000 pounds of silver, and Appian writes in more general terms of the gold and silver coins and bullion paraded.[314] Besides the value of the actual booty, a substantial indemnity was imposed on Carthage to be paid over the next fifty years.[315] We do not know whether or not the first payment of the indemnity was included among the booty staged in the procession, but, if not, there was probably at least some kind of advertisement of its extent.

Even if the booty and the indemnity from the Carthaginians helped to put Rome financially back on its feet, the state was far from rich.[316] In fact, Rome was unable to make the third and final repayment of the contributions from her citizens that was due in 200 BC. It was the following years of victories in Greece

[307] Polyb. 1.58.9–1.59.1.

[308] C. Lutatius Catulus and Q. Valerius Falto both held naval triumphs in 241 BC. For the battle and the treaty, see Lazenby (1996: 152–9).

[309] Eutrop. 2.27.2.

[310] Polyb. 1.62.9–1.63.3. Frank (1933: 67).

[311] From 211 BC the situation improved somewhat, due both to the inflow of booty from Syracuse, Capua, and Tarentum and to the opening of the Spanish mines in 209 BC, Crawford (1974: 33 and n. 2, 635).

[312] Buraselis (1996: 155–72). These years also saw the collapse of the old coinage system and the introduction of the denarius system, see Crawford (1964).

[313] Polyb. 16.23.5–6.

[314] Liv. 30.45.3; App. *Pun.* 66.

[315] Both Polybius (15.18.7–8) and Livy (30.37.5–6) state that the indemnity amounted to 10,000 silver talents. Pliny (*Nat.* 33.15.51) records 800,000 pounds of silver, agreeing roughly with Polybius' and Livy's figure.

[316] Crawford (1974: 635); Buraslis (1996: 171 n. 60).

and Asia that brought richness to Rome, manifested by actual imports of unprecedented sums of gold and silver into the city's treasury by way of the triumphal processions of Flamininus, Scipio Asiaticus, and others.[317] Finally, in 187 BC, the money displayed by Cn. Manlius Vulso in the triumph held to celebrate his campaign against the Galatians was used to refund the contributions by the Roman citizens.[318] The pleasure felt by the spectators when setting eyes on the very fortunes that were to end up in their own purses can easily be imagined, as can the sentiments twenty years later, when the immense royal riches displayed by Aemilius Paullus signified the abolition of taxes for Roman citizens.[319]

After 89 BC, the Roman economy was again in crisis. During the period 88–63 BC, the *aerarium* was, as Crawford puts it 'chronically short of money'.[320] The social and civil wars again saw battles fought on Italian soil, and both Sulla in his campaign against Mithridates and Sulla's opponents in Italy found themselves forced to confiscate temple treasuries in order to raise money.[321] Such was the situation when in 61 BC, Pompey celebrated his magnificent triumph over the pirates and the kingdoms of the East. The riches on display at this occasion were immense. Placards announced that besides the 20,000 talents, which he brought into the treasury and the ones already distributed to the soldiers, 85,000,000 drachmae were added from the territories newly subdued and made tributary.[322] Again, the money brought in by way of a triumphal procession celebrating victories in the East put Roman finances back on track.

Visualizing the wealth

To the spectators, the value of the coins and the bullion exhibited in the triumphal processions was far from clear from their display alone. Textual explications were needed and we know that both Lucullus and Pompey showed written

---

[317] I will not go into the much debated issue as to what extent prospects of booty and improved finances were primary motivations in the Roman declarations of war, see e.g. Harris (1979: esp. 54–104); Ziolkowski (1986); Buraselis (1996).

[318] Liv. 39.7.5: *...senatus consultum factum est ut ex pecunia, quae in triumpho translata esset, stipendium conlatum a populo in publicum, quod eius solutum antea non esset, solveretur.* Crawford (1974: 635) and Buraselis (1996: 165–6), are both convinced that Vulso's reimbursement covered several contributions from the time of the Second Punic War and onwards.

[319] Plin. *Nat.* 33.17.56. The *tributum* was only briefly reintroduced in the late Republic, Buraselis (1996: 165). Crawford (1977: 44) argues that the imposition of taxes on the Greek East from this date must have meant more to the Roman finances than this one-time import of booty by Paullus.

[320] Crawford (1974: 637).

[321] Val. Max 7.6.4; Plin. *Nat* 33.5.16. For Sulla's various methods of raising money, see Crawford (1974: 637–8, with references).

[322] Plut. *Pomp.* 45.3; see also Plin. *Nat.* 37.6.16; App. *Mith.* 116, with Heftner (1995: 311–12). Placards announced that, while the public incomes from the taxes had been 50,000,000 drachmae, Rome now received 85,000,000 from the areas that Pompey had subjected.

placards which proclaimed the sums on parade.[323] According to Pliny, Sulla's triumph in 81 BC included a *titulus* announcing that 14,000 pounds of gold and 6,000 pounds of silver were brought in from Praeneste.[324] The placard also explained that this was the money that the younger Marius had previously taken to Praeneste from the temple of Jupiter Capitolinus and other shrines. By way of the triumphal procession, in a symbolically pregnant manifestation, Sulla thus brought back the treasure to its rightful abode, the Capitoline hill. Figures were publicly advertised, and written placards were one of the means employed. The accounts of the triumphs of Lucullus and Pompey tell of such written announcements.

Placards announced the precise quantity of wealth brought in, but sums and weight were emphasized in other ways too. In the *triumphus per triduum* celebrated by Aemilius Paullus in 167 BC, Plutarch states that the second day's procession saw 3,000 men, who carried coined silver in 750 vessels, ἀγγεῖα.[325] Each vessel contained three talents and was borne by four men. The third day instead saw gold coins carried in 77 vessels, each vessel holding three talents.[326] Three talents in each vessel mean 78.6 kg, divided between four bearers.[327] According to the calculation of Jacobsthal, the largest *stamnoi* from the Delian treasury had a capacity of about one third of this, 1 talent,[328] so, if Plutarch is correct, the vessels used in the triumph of Aemilius Paullus must have been impressive in both size and weight. Four bearers were employed, carrying, according to Diodorus Siculus, the coins on φορήματα,[329] a term that reappears in Plutarch's account of Lucullus' triumph.[330] Φόρημα is the Greek equivalent

---

[323] Plutarch (*Luc.* 37.4) states that Lucullus showed placards (δέλτοι), with lists of the sums of money that he had already paid Pompey for the war against the pirates, to the quaestors who were in charge of the *aerarium* and to his soldiers. The same author states (*Pomp.* 45.3–4) that the placards displayed in Pompey's triumph recorded, among other things, the sums already paid to the soldiers. They had received at least 1,500 drachmae each.

[324] Plin. *Nat.* 33.5.16: . . . , *quod ex Capitolinae aedis incendio ceterisque omnibus delubris C. Marius filius Praeneste detulerat, XIIII pondo, quae sub eo titulo in triumpho transtulit Sulla et argenti VI.* Cf. Crawford (1974: 637), who identifies this money as the temple treasures melted down in Rome to finance the last struggle against Sulla, Val Max. 7.6.4. The gold and silver from Praeneste was paraded during day two of Sulla's celebration. Day one saw the money obtained from the rest of his victories, amounting to 15,000 pounds of gold and 115,000 pounds of silver, Plin. *Nat.* 33.5.16.

[325] Plut. *Aem.* 32.8: ἄνδρες ἐπεπορεύοντο τρισχίλιοι νόμισμα φέροντες ἀργυροῦν ἐν ἀγγείοις ἑπτακοσίοις πεντήκοντα τριταλάντοις.

[326] Plut. *Aem.* 33.3–4: εἶτα μετὰ τούτους οἱ τὸ χρυσοῦν νόμισμα φέροντες, εἰς ἀγγεῖα τριταλαντιαῖα μεμερισμένον ὁμοίως τῷ ἀργυρίῳ. τὸ δὲ πλῆθος ἦν τῶν ἀγγείων ὀγδοήκοντα τριῶν δέοντα.

[327] Jacobsthal (1943: 308–9).

[328] Ibid.

[329] Diod. Sic. 31.8.12 (apud Sync.): . . . , χρυσοῦ τάλαντα ἐν φορήμασι διακοσίοις εἴκοσι, . . . According to Diodorus Siculus, 1,000 talents of coined money and 2,200 talents of silver were displayed the second day and talents of gold borne on 220 carriers on the third.

[330] Plut. *Luc.* 37.3.

FIGURE 7 A Roman soldier carries a *ferculum* laden with spoils in a triumphal procession on this fragment of a relief from the later part of the first century AD. Note the cushion that eases the burden and emphasizes the heavy weight. The Roman bearer is wreathed, as opposed to non-Roman participants in the parade.

for *ferculum*,[331] the bier commonly employed in Roman processions.[332] As in Plutarch's description, preserved depictions of triumphs and other parades include *fercula* that are mostly carried by four bearers. To ease the burden the bearers use supporting stakes in their hands and cushions on their shoulders (Fig. 7). These items emphasize the heaviness of the booty, on the reliefs, as also in the processions.

In Lucullus' triumph, held about a century later, Plutarch writes that the procession showed twenty litters of silver vessels, while another thirty-two contained gold beakers, armour, and coined money. Men carried all this. Besides, eight mules bore golden couches, fifty-six bore silver ingots, and one hundred and seven carried silver coins, almost 2,700,000 pieces.[333] Hence, the wealth amounted to such a weight that men could carry only part of it. The 171 mules employed clearly manifested the multitude and heaviness of the riches brought into the city.

[331] LSJ, s.v. 'φόρημα'.

[332] On *fercula* and other biers employed in the Roman processions, see Abaecherli (1935/6), for the *ferculum*, esp. 1–5.

[333] Plut. *Luc.* 37.3–4: ... καὶ φορήματα εἴκοσι μὲν ἀργυρῶν σκευῶν, χρυσῶν δ' ἐκπωμάτων καὶ ὅπλων καὶ νομίσματος δύο καὶ τριάκοντα. ταῦτα μὲν οὖν ἄνδρες παρεκόμιζον· ἡμίονοι δ' ὀκτὼ κλίνας χρυσᾶς ἔφερον, ἓξ δὲ καὶ πεντήκοντα κεχωνευμένον ἀργύριον, ἄλλοι δ' ἑκατὸν ἑπτὰ νομίσματος ἀργυροῦ, μικρῷ τινι δεούσας ἑβδομήκοντα καὶ διακοσίας μυριάδας.

Most of Livy's triumphal accounts reveal nothing of where in the procession the coins and bullion were paraded. Occasionally, though, they appear as integrated parts of lists that seem to reproduce the sequence of the processions. As one would expect, Livy describes the coins and bullion among the booty in the initial part of the trains, mostly, but not always, after the military spoils of standards and arms.[334] In Flamininus' three-day-long celebration in 194 BC, the coins and bullion appeared together with the other items of bronze, silver, and gold on the second day.[335] Weapons and statues were shown on the first and prisoners on the last day. In Aemilius Paullus' triumph in 167 BC, Diodorus Siculus and Plutarch present slightly divergent versions, but both describe divisions of the train that were similar to that of Flamininus. According to the Greek authors, Aemilius Paullus paraded coins and bullion on days two and three, after the weaponry and before the prisoners, who concluded the display of the subjugated.[336]

Two much discussed currencies

Livy's descriptions show that the Republican triumphal processions regularly displayed coins and bullion of varied forms and currencies. Yet, no other source suggests such diversified displays. Latin authors (besides Livy) give the figures of coins and bullion on parade either in weight by the pound or in sum by the sesterce, and Greek writers mostly record the total amount in drachmae or in talents. This means that, when describing Republican triumphs, save Livy, ancient authors often recalculated the coins and bullion once displayed into drachmae, talents, pounds, or sesterces. A clear example of recalculation is when Pliny records the money brought into the treasury by Aemilius Paullus as 300,000,000 sesterces,[337] for Rome only commenced to reckon by the sesterce in 141 BC.[338] The information about talents, drachmae, pounds, and sesterces provides a sense of the dimensions of the booty involved but gives no clue to the types of currencies actually put on show in the Republican processions.

Fortunately, Livy's accounts give clear evidence that it was common procedure at least for the generals of the first half of the second century BC to exhibit gold and silver in a variety of shapes (wrought and unwrought) and coins in a number of currencies. Besides gold and silver bullion and the domestic denominations of

---

[334] After the weapons and standards: 26.21.7–10, 34.52.4–7, 37.46.2–6, 37.59.3–6. Before military spoils: 39.5.14–17, 39.7.1–2.

[335] Liv. 34.52.4–5: *secundo [die] aurum argentumque factum infectumque et signatum [transtulit]*. The golden crowns form an exception, as they opened the procession on day three only.

[336] Plut. *Aem.* 32–3; Diod. Sic. 31.8.10–12 (apud Sync.).

[337] Plin. *Nat.* 33.17.56.

[338] Crawford (1974: 621–5).

asses, bigati and denarii, Livy attests to the display of several non-Roman currencies. Spanish *argentum oscense* and Illyrian victoriati were paraded in triumphs
held over these specific areas, while Philippics, cistophori, and Attic tetradrachmae were regularly displayed in the processions held to celebrate victories in the
East. Many triumphs included a number of different currencies, all exhibited
together. For example, the triumph of Cn. Manlius Vulso over the Asian Gauls in
187 BC paraded, in Livy's testimony, 220,000 pounds of silver, 2,103 pounds of
gold, 127,000 pieces of Attic tetradrachmae, 250,000 cistophori, and 16,320
Philippics.[339]

Livy's descriptions of coins and bullion paraded are mostly taken as trustworthy, as are his triumphal accounts in general.[340] There are, however, a couple
of question marks concerning the identification of some of the specific currencies
that appear in his lists: the Attic tetradrachma, the *argentum oscense*, and the
cistophorus. The problem with the Attic tetradrachma centres on a remark on
the Macedonian triumph of Flamininus in 194 BC. Livy attests to the processional
display of 84,000 Attic tetradrachmae, and adds, as an explication, that they were
equivalent to three denarii.[341] However, the Attic drachma and the Roman
denarius basically correspond, so Livy's remark is curious indeed. There has
been no agreement on the coin type implied, but Harl has suggested that the
sum could represent an indemnity paid in some unknown local denomination.[342]

For the *argentum oscense* and the cistophori, the problem is a different one. In
both these cases, the issue is whether or not the coinages were actually in
circulation as early as the 190s BC, when Livy starts attesting to their presence
in triumphal processions. It cannot be excluded that Livy, or more probably his
sources, anachronistically relabelled some of the coins with names of currencies
that were in circulation in their own days but did not yet exist at the time of
the recorded triumphs. In fact, Livy at a few times clearly uses anachronistic
recalculations. When describing the triumphs of M. Livius Salinator (207 BC),
Aemilius Paullus, and Anicius Gallus (167 BC), he records the sum in sesterces,
although Rome started to count by this denomination in 141 BC only. Two of

[339] Liv. 39.7.1–2.
[340] Frank (1933: 127); Jacobsthal (1943: 307); De Sanctis (1968: 607); Crawford (1974: 621 n. 2, 630 n. 6);
Harris (1979: 59); Harl (1991: *passim*). The sums given by Livy (34.52.5–7) for the coins and bullion
displayed by Flamininus in 194 BC match the ones provided by Plutarch almost to the coin. Plutarch
(*Flam.* 14), who quotes Tuditanus as his source, accounts for the same amount of silver bullion (43,270
pounds) and Philippics (14,514) as Livy, but has 3,713 pounds of gold bullion instead of Livy's 3,714. Except
for the coins and bullion, the two accounts differ substantially from each other, and most probably, Livy
and Plutarch used different sources here. This circumstance adds to the credibility of the sums and weight
of coins and bullion recorded.
[341] Liv. 34.52.6. Livy uses the contracted form *tetrachma*, see Briscoe (1981: 129–30, 362–3).
[342] Harl (1991: 292).

these cases are particularly doubtful as Livy explicitly (and here only) cites Valerias Antias on the sums,[343] but it cannot be excluded that mechanisms of recalculation were in force in the cases of *argentum oscense* and cistophori as well. However, the issue is far from clear, and voices in defence of the historicity of the Livian accounts of the coinages on triumphal display have been raised. It has been noted that most of Livy's coinage anachronisms stem from his speeches, while outside of this sphere, the figures and currencies appear mostly to be historically correct.

Livy attests to the display of the silver coinage labelled *argentum oscense* in four triumphs and ovations held by M. Helvius, Q. Minucius Thermus, M. Porcius Cato, and Q. Fulvius Flaccus in 195–180 BC, all celebrating victories in Hispania.[344] The *argentum oscense* is commonly identified with the Spanish denarius that was struck predominantly in the town of Osca.[345] Its date of introduction has been intensely debated,[346] not least due to its close correspondence with the Roman denarius, which it imitated. The introduction of the Roman denarius was for a long time dated to 187 BC, which caused Livy's statement of the existence of the *argentum oscense* already in the 190s to be dismissed as anachronistic. The scene changed when the Roman denarius was redated to the now generally accepted 211 BC.[347] Both Crawford (in 1969) and Knapp (in 1977) argued that Livy's report of the *argentum oscense* in the triumphal processions of the early second century should be taken historically.[348] The problem is, however, that there exists no useful hoard evidence to support or to reject this early dating, which consequently has not generally been accepted. Not least important is Crawford's own redating (in 1985) of the *argentum oscense* to the middle of the second century, which has received considerable acceptance.[349]

[343] Liv. 45.40.1–2, 45.43.8.

[344] 119,439 coins by Helvius, 278,000 by Minucius Thermus, 540,000 by Cato and 173,200 by Fulvius Flaccus (Liv. 34.10.4–5, 34.10.7, 34.46.2–3, 40.43.6). Knapp (1977: 2 n. 3).

[345] Modern Huesca. The native legend on the coinage was BOLSCAN, latinized as OSCA. Since the Oscan denarii were among the earliest and most abundant, the name might later have been extended to denote the whole Iberian coinage, Crawford (1969: 83); Knapp (1977: 2–4).

[346] See Thomsen (1961: 185–91); Crawford (1969); Knapp (1977); Crawford (1985: 84–102); Knapp (1987: all with further references).

[347] Crawford (1964); Knapp (1977: 5–6); Crawford (1985: 52–62).

[348] Crawford (1969); Knapp (1977). Crawford followed Mommsen and saw the appearance of the Iberian denarius as related to the Roman organization of the two Spains in 197 BC. Knapp uses literary evidence to support his argument that the Iberian coinage was in circulation by 180/179 BC. In particular, he refers to Livy, 40.47.1–10, and the payment made by the town of Certima of 24,000 *nummi* (probably Spanish denarii) to Tiberius Gracchus in 180/179 BC.

[349] Crawford (1985: 95–6) relates the beginning of the Iberian denarius coinage to the switch in payment of Roman soldiers from bronze to silver. Richardson (1996: 74–5) agrees, although he did earlier (1976) propose a date of 180/179 BC. Knapp (1987: 22–3) sticks to his early dating but adds some reservations.

To solve this issue, it has been proposed that the coins displayed in the Spanish triumphs should be identified with some earlier kind of Spanish silver coinage known to have existed from the end of the third century BC. The Spanish numismatists Gómez-Moreno and Amorós, later followed by Thomsen, argued that the coins paraded are to be identified with the Iberian drachmae with Pegasus types and perhaps also some Hispano-Punic silver coins.[350] Their idea was that the triumphal archives recorded 'Spanish silver coins', which Livy's sources interpreted as *argentum oscense*.[351] Against this solution, Knapp pointed out that other Spanish coinages were more frequent than the *argentum oscense* in the 80s BC, when Livy's principal sources were active. Thus, it seems unlikely that they would have chosen this particular label for the Spanish denarii.[352] Another hypothesis, launched by Villaronga, proposes that the coinage shown in the Spanish triumphs was either silver coinage from Emporion or the so-called horsemen denarii from Kese.[353] Both types were in circulation at this early date but disappeared later, possibly due to the very circumstance that large amounts of booty were extracted by the Roman generals.[354] Villaronga's assumption is not that Livy's sources relabelled the coins into comprehensible currencies, but that the native script of the coins was mistaken as 'Oscan' already at the time of the triumphs and registration of the sums. These are all numismatic specifics, and no attempt at a solution will be proposed here. For our discussion, the important issue is that, in all the modern interpretations, Livy's *argentum oscense* represents some kind of Hispanic coinage. That is, whether or not the coinage should be identified with the *argentum oscense* existing later on, its appearance in Livy's triumphal accounts reveals that the victorious generals brought home some kind of non-Roman currency as booty from Spain and paraded it in their processions.

The problem with the cistophori is much the same as that of the *argentum oscense*. The cistophori were silver tetradrachmae, equivalent to the weight of three drachmae only. They were issued within the Pergamene domain, and due to their overvaluation they did not circulate widely outside of Asia Minor. Livy reports on their exhibition in four triumphal processions between 190 and 187 BC, all celebrating victories over Antiochus and the East. According to Livy, M'. Acilius Glabrio displayed 249,000 cistophori in his triumph of 190 BC, L. Aemilius

---

[350] Thomsen (1961: 189–91), with references to Gómez-Moreno and Amorós. Knapp (1977: 45–6) points out that, although Thomsen himself preferred a dating of the Roman denarius to 211 BC, on the issue of the *argentum oscense*, he followed the dating of Gómez-Moreno and Amorós that depended on the supposed introduction of the Roman denarius only in 187 BC.

[351] Thomsen (1961: 191).

[352] Knapp (1977: 4).

[353] Villaronga (1979: 114).

[354] Knapp (1987: 23) points out that many dies but few coins have been preserved of these silver coins, a fact that gives some support to Villaronga's suggestion.

Regillus 132,300 cistophori in his *navalis* held in 189 BC, Scipio Asiaticus 321,070 cistophori in 189 BC, and finally Cn. Manlius Vulso 250,000 cistophori in 187 BC.[355] The figures given by Livy are taken as plausible,[356] but as in the case of the Oscan silver coinage, the issue is whether or not the coinage itself was in circulation at the time of the triumphs. There is very little agreement among numismatists on the introduction of the cistophorus, and a wide range of dates from 215 to 133 BC has been suggested.[357] In effect, for anyone who advocates a date after 190 BC, Livy's descriptions of cistophori in the triumphs held over Antiochus become anachronistic. There is also the fact that the cistophori were the coinage not of Rome's enemies, but of her ally, the Pergamene Eumenes II. Their display as booty in the triumphal procession has therefore puzzled scholars.[358]

Livy or his sources are unlikely to have deliberately added the presence of cistophori in these accounts. Therefore, if the coinage was introduced only after the triumphs in question, the only reasonable explanation is again one of anachronistic translation into an understandable currency. Accordingly, it has been proposed that since cistophori were in wide circulation when Livy's sources were active, Valerias Antias and Claudius Quadrigarius relabelled the currency recorded in the triumphal records into a well-known denomination of their own time.[359] The problem with this interpretation is to determine the original coin term registered in the archives and later corrupted. Thomsen suggests tetradrachmae of some kind,[360] but this seems unlikely since all the lists from the triumphs in question also include Attic tetradrachmae, which formed the basis of Antiochus' silver coinage.

The most recent major contribution to the discussion is that of Harl, who in 1991 proposed a revaluation of the Livian accounts.[361] Harl conducted a thorough investigation of the numismatic evidence and concluded that it in no way impedes a date of 190 BC for the earliest striking of the cistophori. He also proposed two different possibilities for how the coinage of Pergamon might have ended up in Roman triumphs over Antiochus.[362] One was that the cistophori had been taken as booty by the Seleucids when they raided the Pergamene kingdom in 190 BC, the other that they should be recognized as indemnities

[355] Glabrio: Liv. 37.46.3, Regillus: 38.58.4–5, Scipio: 37.59.4, Vulso: 39.7.1.
[356] Harl (1991: 290).
[357] At the extreme opposites, Frank favoured an early date of 215–210 BC, Mommsen a late one of 133 BC. Crawford (1985: 158) prefers a date between 180 and 160 BC. Harl (1991) provides an account of the previous cistophoric scholarship.
[358] Thomsen (1961: 147); Harl (1991: 269, 291–4).
[359] Thomsen (1961: 148). Note, however, that when Livy explicitly cites Valerias Antias, he refers to the amount in sesterces (45.40.1–2, 45.43.8). In these cases (the triumphs of Aemilius Paullus and Anicius Gallus in 167 BC), Antias thus recalculated the currencies into a Roman denomination, which is something quite different from changing the name of the coin types as they appeared in the original archival records.
[360] Thomsen (1961: 148).   [361] Harl (1991).   [362] Ibid. 291–4.

paid by cities of Asia Minor to Rome rather than booty taken from Antiochus. Harl finds the second solution the more appealing and points out that large indemnities were customarily imposed by Rome and were most certainly included in the triumphal exhibitions. Although indemnities were regularly calculated in talents, payment in local currencies, like cistophori, were clearly accepted too. Harl specifically stresses how Manlius Vulso imposed several fines and sold immunities during his touring campaign of Asia on his way to fight the Galatians, money that was most probably put on show in his triumph in 187 BC.[363]

A manifold display

Harl's proposal underlines an important circumstance that is often forgotten in the discussions of what could reasonably have been paraded in the triumphs and what not, namely that besides the pure booty taken from defeated enemies, there were items on parade obtained in various other ways as well. In the case of coins and bullion, a few different sources and methods of extraction are observable.

Large amounts of wealth naturally consisted of what we normally call booty, money confiscated from the treasuries of captured cities, camps, and palaces. For example, Polybius describes how Aemilius Paullus found 6,000 talents in the palace of Perseus, money later paraded in the triumph of 167 BC.[364] Another important part consisted of incomes obtained from the selling of captives and spoils. A variety of currencies might then simply reflect the circumstance that traders from widespread regions had been involved. As Harl shows, still other money on triumphal display formed part of indemnities forced on the conquered party to compensate for Roman economic losses during the campaigns. For example, the Aetolians were imposed a fine of 500 talents in 189 BC, of which 200 was to be paid immediately,[365] money which was in all probability exhibited in the procession of Fulvius Nobilior two years later.[366] An indemnity of 2,500 talents of silver paid by Antiochus to Manlius Vulso as part of the treaty of Apamea was partly lost on the return journey, but a substantial portion of this money, labelled *pecunia publica*, must have been included among Vulso's triumphal display.[367]

---

[363] Harl (1991). For Vulso's campaign and triumph, see also Zecchini (1982); Grainger (1995).

[364] Polyb. 18.35.4–5.

[365] Polyb. 21.30.1–3; Liv. 38.9.9.

[366] Harl (1991), 291–2.

[367] Indemnity: Liv. 38.37.9; loss: Liv. 38.40.6–15; triumph: Liv. 39.7.1–5. Harl (1991: 291–4) maintains that indemnities almost certainly were included among the coins and bullion paraded in the processions of Flamininus (194 BC), Scipio Asiaticus (189 BC), and Manlius Vulso (187 BC). He also interprets the sums of *argentum oscense* shown in the Spanish triumphs as indemnities.

The triumphal trains also included sums of money paid to the general to buy immunity for a city or a group of people. All along his march towards the Galatians, Manlius Vulso sold immunities to the cities in Caria, Pisidia, and Pamphylia.[368] Livy gives the amounts by the talent, but the payment might well have been made in local currencies. Livy also states that the town of Cibyra paid in the form of a golden crown. Both golden crowns and large sums of money later appeared in Vulso's triumph and the cities' payments were most probably included. Another, much earlier example is the triumph held by Sp. Carvilius Maximus over the Samnites in 293 BC. During his earlier campaign in Etruria, Carvilius had agreed with 470 of the richest inhabitants in the city of Troilum that they should pay a large sum of money in order to go free. The rest of the population and the city were captured.[369] Further sums were obtained by granting a year's truce to the Faliscans, who paid 100,000 pounds of *aes grave* and a year's pay to the soldiers.[370] Back in Rome, Carvilius officially triumphed for his victories over the Samnites, but Livy's description suggests that the sums obtained in Etruria were included in the parade.[371] This case implies both that immunity payments formed part of the triumphal monetary exhibitions and that the displays included riches obtained from places outside of the specific area over which the triumph was held.

Of more voluntary character were the gifts from the cities that Fulvius Nobilior included among the monetary display in his triumph over the Aetolians in 187 BC. Fulvius claimed that he had been presented with a hundred pounds of gold from the cities as a contribution for the great games to Jupiter, vowed during the campaign. In the procession, the hundred pounds formed part of the total sum of 243 pounds of gold staged.[372] Thus, they constituted no small part of the financial display.

The diverse ways in which the coins and bullion had been obtained were reflected in the variety of bullion, currencies, and denomination displayed in the processions and entered in the records. This does not mean that large quantities of foreign currencies were actually placed in the *aerarium* or circulated on Italian soil. In fact, Pliny's description of the contents of the *aerarium* in 157, 91, and 49 BC includes no foreign money at all,[373] and very few hoards in

---

[368] See Harl (1991: 292–3) for a list of places and sums, cf. Grainger (1995).

[369] Liv. 10.46.10–11.

[370] Liv. 10.46.12–13.

[371] Liv. 10.46.13: *His rebus actis ad triumphum decessit, ut minus clarum de Samnitibus quam collegae triumphus fuerat ita cumulo Etrusci belli aequatum*, 'Having completed these deeds, he departed to celebrate his triumph, which, though less distinguished than his colleague's as regards the Samnite victory, nevertheless equalled it when the Etruscan war was counted in'.

[372] Livy (39.5.14–15) records 243 pounds of gold among the triumphal display. He has previously stated (39.5.8–9) that Fulvius intended to include the 100 pounds provided by the cities in the parade.

[373] Plin. *Nat.* 33.17.55–6.

Republican Italy contain foreign coins.[374] It seems that, as soon as the foreign coins had been exhibited in the triumphal parades and their amount been properly recorded, they were melted down and restruck. Thus, the choice to parade foreign currencies was a most deliberate one. There was a clear alternative of melting down the money before instead of after the triumph and giving the sums obtained in weight or in Roman denominations. Such a practice would in fact have facilitated the understanding of the amounts displayed for the spectators, who could relate to pounds and denarii, but only with difficulty to Philippics or Illyrian victoriati. Obviously, the primary aim of having the diverse currencies on parade was not that their precise financial implications should be comprehensible to most spectators. In fact, in the case of the cistophori, the main purpose would not even have been the financial value itself, as this currency had very little exchange value outside of the Pergamene kingdom. Still, their triumphal staging was important. First and foremost, the vast and heavy sums brought in by large numbers of men and mules together with the announcements of names of foreign currencies, cistophori, Philippics, tetradrachmae, victoriati, and *argentum oscense* implied the vastness of the Roman financial and political domination.

The transfer of large numbers of foreign currencies was also an act with financial consequences. In fact, the Roman acquisition of booty and gifts in many cases led to the extinction of the currencies in question. For example, the huge sums of gold displayed in Caesar's triumphs of 46 BC resulted in a situation where the gold coinage of Macedon, Carthage, Ptolemaic Egypt, and Gaul ceased to circulate, while Rome itself started to produce a gold coinage for the first time since the Second Punic War.[375] Foreign currencies flowed into Rome by way of the triumphal processions and were transformed to Roman wealth, symbolic and financial. In this very process, Rome absorbed the currencies of the other.[376] After Livy's testimonies to the first half of the second century BC, we have no more evidence for the display of such varieties of foreign currencies, and the financial

[374] Crawford (1977: 52), referring to M. Thompson, O. Mørkholm, and C. M. Kray (eds.), *An Inventory of Greek Coin Hoards* (New York, 1973), nos. 2053–7.

[375] Howgego (1992: 5). Booty and gifts of coins and bullion were regularly transformed into valid coinage in the ancient world, see the examples presented by Howgego (1990: 4–6). Howgego also emphasizes that large amounts of gold poured into the Roman treasury, while Rome itself did not strike a gold coinage between the Second Punic War and 46 BC. According to Pliny's description of the contents of the *aerarium*, there was a substantial amount of gold stored. Crawford maintains that the gold was exchanged for bronze and silver to be coined, but Howgego (1990: 12–15) proposes that some payments could also have been made in gold bullion.

[376] Howgego (1992: 5): 'The siphoning off of the gold and silver of the Mediterranean world into Roman hands had a numismatic corollary in the ending and withdrawal from circulation (whether gradual or not) of most of the existing non-Roman precious metal coinages.'

exhibitions of the Imperial processions are likely to have been much more stand-ardized. This was incorporation of the subjugated at its extreme.

STATUES AND PAINTINGS

Ancient sources attribute the first lavish triumphal display of captured statues to M. Claudius Marcellus. His *ovatio* in 211 BC paraded an unprecedented abundance of Greek art that had been taken at Marcellus' renowned capture of Syracuse.[377] Before this date, the display of statues and paintings are noted only twice. Livy claims that in 380 BC, T. Quinctius Cincinnatus carried a statue of Jupiter Imperator taken from the captured Praeneste in his triumphal procession and dedicated it on the Capitol.[378] About a hundred years later, after the defeat of Pyrrhus at Beneventum in 275 BC, M'. Curius Dentatus celebrated a triumph that according to Florus included both statues and paintings.[379]

After Marcellus, looted statues and paintings appear in several triumphal parades, often listed together as *signa et tabulae pictae*.[380] Besides, ancient authors quite often tell that triumphators dedicated specific statues or paintings, and although this is not explicitly spelt out, these pieces had probably first appeared in the triumphal parades.[381] Moreover, the frequent and general statement that

---

[377] Liv. 26.21.8–9: *et multa nobilia signa, quibus inter primas Graeciae urbes Syracusae ornatae fuerant*, 'and many notable statues, with which Syracuse had been adorned as highly as the foremost cities of Greece'. Gruen (1992: 84–130) seeks to tone down the importance of the capture of Syracuse and stresses that Romans were accustomed to seeing looted art pieces in their temples and public places long before 211 BC. Certainly, the defeat of Pyrrhus caused some import of Greek art into Rome. But several of the other examples quoted by Gruen were single statues, called to Rome by way of *evocatio*, solitary examples of cultic imports that cannot be seen in the same context as the enormous amount of art brought to the city by Marcellus and later triumphators. Cf. McDonnell (2006).

[378] Liv. 6.29.8–10. Cf. pp. 83–4.

[379] Flor. *Epit.* 1.13.27. Waurick (1977: 6–9).

[380] Flamininus in 194 BC: Liv. 34.52.4; Fulvius Nobilior in 187 BC: Liv. 39.5.15, cf. 38.9.13–14, 38.43.5–6, 9–10; Aemilius Paullus in 167 BC: Diod. Sic. 31.8.11–12 (apud Sync.); Plut. *Aem.* 32.4–5; Flor. *Epit.* 1.28.12–14; cf. Liv. 45.39.4–6; Scipio Aemilianus in 146 BC: App. *Pun.* 135; Mummius in 145 BC: Liv. *Per.* 52; Plin. *Nat.* 33.53.149–50; Eutrop. 4.14; cf. Polyb. 39.2 (apud Strab. 8.6.28); Liv. *Per.* 52; Plin. *Nat.* 34.17.36, 35.8.24, 37.6.12; Vell. Pat. 1.13.4–5; Zonar. 9.31.5–6; *vir. ill.* 60.3; Servilius Vatia in 74 BC: Cic. *Verr.* II.1.21.57; Pompey in 61 BC: Plin. *Nat.* 37.6.14. For Roman plundering of Greek art, see Pape (1975).

[381] Pliny (*Nat.* 34.16.34) states that the Romans were accused of having captured Volsinii in 264 BC for the sake of its 2,000 statues of bronze. Fragments of a statue base with a dedicatory inscription, which names the conqueror of Volsinii, M. Fulvius Flaccus, have been found in the area of S. Omobono, Torelli (1968); Cagiano de Azevedo (1972); Hölscher (1978: 320–1); Wiseman (1986: 95–9). In the absence of Livy, there is no evidence on whether Fulvius Flaccus showed any statues in his triumph over the Volsinienses. Similarly, we know that Fabius Maximus took a colossal Hercules from the captured Tarentum, but not if the statue was shown in his triumph of 209 BC. Pliny (*Nat.* 34.19.54) accounts for a statue representing Athena, which Aemilius Paullus placed in the temple of Fortuna Huiusce Diei. The statue was probably

spolia were shown in a triumph might refer to all kinds of booty, sculptures and paintings included.

Syracuse and Ambracia: the question of sacrilege

M. Claudius Marcellus' conquest of Syracuse and his display of large amounts of Greek works of art in 211 BC were much discussed in the ancient texts. Latin and Greek writers both blame Marcellus for having triggered the taste for Greek art in Rome. In the long run, several writers argue, the sack of Syracuse paved the way for a general preference for eastern luxury and the dissolution of Roman traditional values.[382] Marcellus was also accused of having looted not only profane but sacred contexts as well. Such a procedure was particularly delicate when it came to the capture of statues as these could be seen as the embodiments of the gods they represented.[383] Consequently, to take statues from temples could be regarded not merely as stealing from the gods, but as stealing the gods themselves away from their abodes.[384]

True, Cicero maintains that, although Marcellus did transfer much of the art of Syracuse to Rome, he left the gods undisturbed.[385] But Cicero's portrait of the moderate conduct of Marcellus on Sicily is clearly painted as a contrast to Verres' unscrupulous plundering of the island. Polybius judges Marcellus more severely,[386] as does Livy, who claims that the looting of the temples of Syracuse triggered sacrileges on an even larger scale.[387] Livy also tells how in 210 BC a group of delegates from Syracuse arrived in Rome to complain to the senate that their sanctuaries had been despoiled and the gods themselves (*di ipsi*) carried away.[388] They also accused Marcellus of having turned down peace offers to be able to take

shown in the triumph held in 167 BC. Another example is the statue of Hercules that stood by the *rostra* on the Forum, Plin. *Nat.* 34.19.93, see Pape (1975: 47–9). One of its inscriptions proclaimed *L. Luculli imperatoris de manubiis*, but no such statue appears in Plutarch's description of Lucullus' triumph of 63 BC, *Luc.* 37; cf. Plin. *Nat.* 34.17.36.

[382] See e.g. Lintott (1972); Gruen (1992: 84, 94–103).

[383] I will not discuss here to what degree the image of the god and the god itself were seen as identical, see e.g. Köves-Zulauf (1993: 161 and n. 17, with further references).

[384] In the discussion of statues taken as war booty from sacred contexts, the source material does not allow us to distinguish between cult statues and statues put up as dedicatory offerings.

[385] Cic. *Verr.* 11.4.54.121, cf. *Verr.* 11.4.58.130.

[386] Polybius (9.10) maintains that, by bringing the looted pieces of art to the city, Rome imitated the fashion of the conquered and exposed themselves to envy and hatred.

[387] Liv. 25.40.1–3. See also Liv. 34.4.4, for the classic quote from Cato the Elder: *Infesta mihi credite, signa ab Syracusis illata sunt huic urbi. Iam nimis multos audio Corinthi et Athenarum ornamenta laudantes mirantesque et antefixa fictilia deorum Romanorum ridentes*, 'They are threats, believe me, those statues that have been brought into the city from Syracuse. For now I hear far too many people praising and marvelling at the ornaments of Corinth and Athens and laughing at the terracotta antefixes of our Roman gods.'

[388] Liv. 26.30, esp. 9–10.

the city by force (*vi capere*), thereby justifying its plunder.[389] Only after an intense debate did the senate decide to ratify Marcellus' actions in war and as a victor.[390]

Plutarch also attributes the first import of large amounts of Greek art into Rome to Marcellus. He states that Marcellus brought with him the most beautiful of the dedicatory offerings (ἀναθήματα) in order that they might grace his triumph and adorn the city.[391] He also claims that Marcellus was blamed for leading not only men but gods as well in his victory procession.[392] Marcellus' behaviour is strongly contrasted to the conduct of Fabius Maximus, who celebrated a triumph for the capture of Tarentum in 209 BC. According to the famous story, Fabius preferred to leave the angered gods—their statues and paintings—to the people of Tarentum.[393]

After Marcellus, the issue of sacrilege again arose in the debate that preceded the triumph of M. Fulvius Nobilior over the Aetolians and the city of Ambracia in 187 BC.[394] Although Fulvius Nobilior had not managed to take Ambracia by force, which formed the customary condition for plundering, he emptied the city of its many treasures.[395] Ambracia had previously housed the palace of Pyrrhus, and it was therefore no small amount of statues and paintings that Fulvius Nobilior transported to Rome to be displayed in his triumph.[396] But he met with opposition in the senate. The consul M. Aemilius Lepidus, bitter enemy of Fulvius, even carried a *senatus consultum* stating that Ambracia seemed not to have been taken by force (*Ambraciam vi captam esse non videri*).[397] There was a severe debate on

---

[389] Liv. 26.30, esp. 5–7.

[390] Liv. 26.32.6. The delegates from Syracuse begged him to forgive them and to take the city of Syracuse under his protection and patronage, an offer that Marcellus accepted, Liv. 26.32.8. For the implications of this event, see Rives (1993).

[391] Plut. *Marc.* 21.1.

[392] Plut. *Marc.* 21.4: οὐ μόνον ἀνθρώπων, ἀλλὰ καὶ θεῶν οἷον αἰχμαλώτων ἀγομένων ἐν αὐτῇ καὶ πομπευομένων, . . .

[393] Plut. *Fab.* 22.5, *Mor.* 195f. See also Liv. 27.16.7–8 and Aug. *Civ.* 1.6. Both Plutarch and St Augustine suggest that Fabius' motives were not all virtuous. It was when he heard that many statues were of a huge size and armed that he decided to leave them in their anger for the people of Tarentum. Livy also stresses that the statues were colossal, and represented gods as warriors.

[394] The senate debated sacrilege at other times too. For example, in 173 BC, the censor Q. Fulvius Flaccus robbed the temple of Juno Lacinia at Croton of its marble roof to adorn the shrine of Fortuna, which he had dedicated in Rome (Liv. 42.3). The senate opposed this and voted that the roof should be brought back to Croton. The discussion in this chapter, however, focuses on generals who celebrated triumphs and showed statues and paintings in their processions.

[395] Polyb. 21.29–30; Liv. 38.9.13; Plin. *Nat.* 35.36.66. The people of Ambracia had voluntarily agreed to open their gates in order to discuss peace.

[396] Among the statues taken from Ambracia, Nobilior placed a group representing the Muses (Plin. *Nat.* 35.36.66) in the *Aedes Herculis Musarum* at the Circus Flaminius in Rome.

[397] Liv. 38.44.6. The senate also decided to hand over the issue to the pontiffs, Liv. 38.44.5–6. Cf. Liv. 26.34.12 on the proceedings after the fall of Capua in 210 BC, when the pontiffs were to decide which of the captured statues were *sacra* and which were *profana*.

whether or not to grant a triumph, and the Ambracians themselves appeared to state their complaint. In Livy's version, they lamented that Fulvius Nobilior had stripped their temples of their ornaments and that the representations of the gods, or rather the gods themselves (*di ipsi*), had been carried away. Left for the Ambracians to adorn were but empty walls and doorposts.[398]

Thus, the accounts in Livy and Plutarch of the conquests and triumphs of Marcellus, Fabius Maximus, and Fulvius Nobilior include several indications that in taking the paintings and above all the statues from the temples of the vanquished people, the very gods of these places were captured as well. Fabius is supposed to have left the gods in Tarentum when he refrained from taking the works of art with him, and the pillage of statues from Syracuse and Ambracia is equated with the capturing of the gods. Most important for the present discussion is Plutarch's remark that Marcellus was blamed for showing not only men, but gods too as captives in his procession. Plutarch thus implies both that statues of gods were put forth in the triumphal processions and that they were presented and perceived as captive deities not unlike the human enemy prisoners on display. This is a most noteworthy comment that demands to be looked thoroughly into. In view of the debate on the issue of sacrilege, once taken as booty, how were the statues and paintings presented in the Roman triumphal processions? As captive gods or as mere spoils of war?

Gods or goods?

When on triumphal display, paintings are simply referred to as *tabulae* or *tabulae pictae* by the Latin authors and γραφαί in our one Greek source.[399] *Tabula* is an art technical term, signifying 'painting' in the strictest sense.[400] Neither this term nor γραφή reveal anything about the type of subject depicted. The terms used for the statues on triumphal display are more revealing. The Greek sources use a varied vocabulary, which reveals that statues on parade represented both men and gods. Plutarch, Appian, and Diodorus Siculus use ἀνδριάντες (statues of men) as well as ἀγάλματα (statues of gods), and κολοσσοί (colossal statues).[401] For example, in his

---

[398] Liv. 38.43.5–6: *et, quod se ante omnia moveat, templa tota urbe spoliata ornamentis; simulacra deum, deos immo ipsos, convulsos ex sedibus suis ablatos esse; parietes postesque nudatos, quos adorent, ad quos precentur et supplicent Ambraciensibus superesse*, 'and, what disturbed them most of all, the temples throughout the city had been stripped of their ornaments; the images of the gods, or rather the gods themselves, had been torn from their seats and carried away; bare walls and doorposts, they said, had been left for the Ambracians to adore, to pray to, and to supplicate'.

[399] *Tabulae (pictae)*: Liv. *Per.* 52; Plin. *Nat.* 33.53.149; Flor. *Epit.* 1.13.27, 1.28.13; Eutrop. 4.14; γραφαί: Plut. *Aem.* 32.4.

[400] Daut (1975: 13 n. 8).

[401] ἀνδριάντες: Diod. Sic. 31.8.11 (apud Sync.); Plut. *Aem.* 32.4; ἀγάλματα: Diod. Sic. 31.8.11; App. *Pun.* 135; κολοσσοί: Plut. *Aem.* 32.4.

account of Aemilius Paullus' Macedonian triumph of 167 BC, Diodorus Siculus
states that there were ἀγάλματα as well as ἀνδριάντες on display.[402]

In contrast, among the variety of terms applied to statues in Latin literature in
general, *imago, statua, effigies, species, simulacrum,* and *signum,* only *signum* is ever
applied to the statues when exhibited as booty in a triumphal procession.[403] In
Latin literature in general, the term *signum* has multiple meanings, but it is most
commonly applied to statues representing gods. In fact, as has been shown in the
study by Daut, of the many Latin terms used for sculptures, only *simulacra* and
signa were applied to statues that represented deities.[404] These two terms bring
out different aspects of the statue: *simulacrum* predominantly applies to cult
statues and stresses the sacred function of the statue, whereas *signum* emphasizes
its material status.[405] The complete absence of any *simulacra* in the Latin descriptions implies that to the Romans, the statues on triumphal display were neither
sacred statues nor embodiments of the gods themselves. Rather, the exclusive use
of the term *signum* encourages us to interpret them as spoils of war, the prime
function of which was their material value.[406]

This assumption is strengthened by the fact that any additional information
about the *signa* concerns their material character. Latin texts frequently point out
that the statues shown in the triumphs were made of gold, bronze, marble, or
ivory: they were *signa aurea, aenea, marmorea, eburnea.*[407] The names of the gods
whose images were shown in the parades, on the other hand, appear only twice.
Pliny refers to the presence of golden statues of Minerva, Mars, and Apollo, *signa
aurea tria Minervae, Martis, Apollonis,* in the triumph held by Pompey in 61 BC.[408]
And, according to Livy, in the triumph over Praeneste in 380 BC, T. Quinctius
Cincinnatus led a *signum Iovis Imperatoris* that he dedicated on the Capitol.[409]
However, the historical value of this remark is doubtful. Festus maintains that
Cincinnatus dedicated a golden crown, and Cicero attributes the dedication of the
statue of Jupiter Imperator on the Capitol to another Titus Quinctius, the

---

[402] Diod. Sic. 31.8.11 (apud Sync.).

[403] *Signa*: Cic. *Verr.* II.1.21.57; Liv. 6.29.8–9, 26.21.8–9, 34.52.4, 39.5.15, *Per.* 52, cf. 45.39.5–6; Plin. *Nat.*
33.53.149; Flor. *Epit.* 1.13.27, 1.28.13; Eutrop. 4.14. The terms *simulacrum, imago,* and *effigies* do appear in
triumphal descriptions, but only to describe representations of cities, peoples, and rivers produced for
processional display.

[404] Daut (1975: 32–8, 141–5).

[405] Ibid. 32–8, esp. 36–7, 141–5.

[406] When the Ambracians made their complaints in Rome, they called their looted statues *di ipsi* and
simulacra deum, stressing their capacity as gods, Liv. 38.43.5–6. The same statues were then exhibited in the
triumph as *signa,* Liv. 38.43.10, 39.5.15.

[407] Liv. 34.52.4, 39.5.15, 45.39.5, *Per.* 52; Europ. 4.14; Plin. *Nat.* 37.6.14.

[408] Plin. *Nat.* 37.6.14. The statues are embedded in a list of other items of worth shown by Pompey;
gems, pearls, and gold.

[409] Liv. 6.29.8–10.

Flamininus who triumphed in 194 BC after his defeat of Philip of Macedon.[410] Livy's statement forms part of no regular triumphal list, which, based on annalist records, first appear in his descriptions of the early third century BC. Had this been the case, the name of the god would in all probability not have been spelt out.[411]

Even in the two special cases where gods are named, the statues are still described as mere works of art, not as embodiments of the gods. That is, Pompey did not show Minerva, Mars, and Apollo themselves, but only representations of them, *signa Minervae, Martis, Apollonis*, and Cincinnatus' statue was a *signum Iovis Imperatoris* rather than Jupiter in person. The omnipresent *signum* emphasizes that they were first and foremost statues. This is significant, not least since, as we shall see later, sculptured personifications shown in the parades lacked such a denomination.

Furthermore, sculptures taken as booty were without exception listed among other objects in the opening part of the parades, never among the prisoners further back.[412] Their categorization as spoils is particularly evident in the triumphs of Flamininus and Aemilius Paullus, which both lasted for three days and for which the contents of each individual day are listed in several sources. Livy, who attests to the division of Flamininus' *triumphus per triduum* in 194 BC, states that the bronze and marble statues were displayed on the opening day together with the arms and weapons. Day two staged more spoils of gold and silver and only day three saw the exhibition of captives, followed by the triumphator and his army.[413] Similarly, prisoners appeared only on day three of Aemilius Paullus' triumph in 167 BC, while the first two days saw arms and riches, among them the captured statues and paintings.[414]

The unexceptional use of *signa* as denomination for the looted statues, the rare revelations of their divine identities, the frequent references to their material

[410] Fest. p. 498 L, s.v. 'trientem tertium'; Cic. *Verr.* II.4.57.128–58.131. Modern scholars have treated the evidence variously. For example, De Sanctis (1960: 237 n. 31) and Cornell (1995: 461 n. 81) prefer the testimony of Livy, while Oakley (1997: 608–9, referring also to Heurgon and Beloch) trusts the evidence of Cicero. Combès (1966: 38–49) argues that there were several statues and that we should take both Livy and Cicero historically here. He also assumes that the cult of Jupiter Imperator was specifically connected to the Quinctii.

[411] Probably, Livy took it for granted that the statue with its inscription had been shown in a triumph, as had so many other Capitoline deposits.

[412] Being spoils of war, Latin authors describe the statues and paintings as being carried. They use forms of *ferre* or occasionally of *vehere* to refer to the processional transportation, which are by far the most common terms employed for the booty. Animate captives are instead mostly described either as being led, using forms of *ducere*, or actively walking, with forms of *ire*. In his account of Dentatus' triumph over Pyrrhus in 275 BC, Florus explicitly separates the *captivi* on one hand and the *pompa*, consisting of the booty of riches, statues and paintings included, on the other, Flor. *Epit.* 1.13.27.

[413] Liv. 34.52.4–12.

[414] Plutarch (*Aem.* 32–4) and Florus (*Epit.* 1.28.12–14) both have the statues displayed on the first day, while the arms and the riches were shown on day two. Diodorus Siculus (31.8.9–12) prefers the opposite order and places the statues on day two. Plutarch describes 250 wagons loaded with statues, Diodorus 500.

appearance and the location of them among the spoils leads us to conclude that the statues on parade were presented and perceived as spiritless goods rather than captive gods. As a matter of fact, Waurick has shown that, outside the processional space too, looted statues were treated no differently from other booty.[415] Inscriptions often gave the name of the victor, and the statues were placed in temples and public places, in Rome as in allied cities.[416]

In fact, Plutarch's remark on the indignation in Rome that even gods were led in the triumphal processions is unique.[417] No Latin author suggests that statues or paintings were presented or perceived as captured gods in the triumphal parades, not even Ovid, whose many triumphal depictions reveal a pronounced non-interest in the inanimate spoils and a corresponding fascination for the appearance and sentiments of prisoners and personifications alike. In his descriptions, Ovid is almost obsessed with the dresses, hairstyle, grief, and wrath of prisoners, peoples, and places, and it is nearly impossible to imagine that he would have missed the chance to dwell on the outlook of captive gods, had such been present.

All the evidence taken together, it seems most reasonable to take Plutarch's remark as a Greek reading of the phenomenon rather than a Roman practice. In contrast to the exclusive use of *signa* for all kinds of statues in the Latin accounts, the Greek variety of terms, ἀγάλματα, ἀνδριάντες, and κολοσσοί, suggests a more pronounced desire to distinguish between profane and sacred in this context. The Greek preference to see the statues as gods was certainly caused by the fact that the captured statues themselves were Greek. In Livy's accounts too, complaints of gods being stolen from temples come from the Greek inhabitants of Syracuse and Ambracia. Had it been the other way around and the Latin authors had discussed the foreign looting of statues from Roman temples, they are not likely to have debated them as works of art or booty only. Rather, they would most certainly have expressed indignation that their very gods had been violated.

As it was, the senate discussed the question of sacrilege only in the cases of Marcellus and Fulvius Nobilior. To our knowledge, no such debates occurred when other generals showed statues in their triumphs. Quite the contrary, as long

---

[415] Waurick (1977: esp. 40–6).

[416] Inscriptions: Cic. *Verr.* II.4.34.74, II.4.35.78–79, II.4.44.97, II.5.72.186. In 293 BC, L. Papirius Cursor bestowed the Latin *socii* with arms taken from the Samnites (Liv. 10.46.8–9). Similarly, Mummius distributed statues from Corinth to a multitude of places in Italy and Greece as well as to Pergamon. See further Waurick (1977: *passim*).

[417] Besides Plutarch's comment on Marcellus, Appian attests to the display in Pompey's triumph of 'representations of barbarian gods dressed according to the fashion of their countries', *Mith.* 117. These gods are interpreted below as sculptured personifications of subjected peoples (pp. 219–21). Josephus (*BJ* 7.136) also mentions gods in his detailed description of the contents of Vespasian and Titus' Jewish triumph: ἐφέρετο δὲ καὶ θεῶν ἀγάλματα τῶν παρ' αὐτοῖς..., where παρ' αὐτοῖς probably means that the statues represented Roman rather than captured gods.

as the aim was not private enrichment but public display, many of the Republican generals were even praised for having captured sacred statues. Scipio Aemilianus was complimented for not permitting his soldiers to plunder the temples of Carthage, but reserving the votive gifts for the triumph in Rome.[418] In his inscription set up for Minerva, Pompey even points out that the dedication to the goddess has become possible through the confiscation of sacred statues.[419]

Senatorial debates

Fulvius Nobilior and Marcellus form exceptions in that their victory celebrations were preceded or followed by debates on sacrilege. In the case of Nobilior, the opposition in the senate has been interpreted almost exclusively as a political attack from his personal enemies, who aimed at preventing him from achieving the honour of a triumph.[420] The animosity between Nobilior and Lepidus is well known. Still, it is my belief that the issue had deeper implications and that the discussions of sacrilege reflect a true anxiety over the fact that Ambracia had not been justly captured by force. Only by taking a city by force (*vi capere*) was the general entitled to exercise his rights of war and despoil a city of all its possessions, profane and sacred. After all, to plunder shrines and to abduct consecrated statues was a delicate affair, as was the practice of bringing the sacred objects to Rome, to lead them over the ritual border of the city and to rededicate them in new contexts. Such acts had to be performed in accordance with established rituals and principles of the *ius belli* in order to maintain good relations with worldly and divine powers.[421] This is why, again as a contrast to the behaviour of Verres, Cicero stresses that the statues that P. Servilius Vatia showed in his triumph in 74 BC had been taken 'in accordance with the rights of war and his powers as general' (*belli lege atque imperatorio iure*) and had been removed from the enemy city that had been 'captured by force and by his valour' (*vi et virtute capta*).[422]

In the case of Marcellus, the senate's reason for refusing him a *triumphus* proper was that he had not brought back his army.[423] Again, personal animosity

---

[418] App. *Pun.* 133, 135.

[419] Diod. fr. 40.4 (Const. Exc.): τούς τε ἀνδριάντας καὶ τὰ λοιπὰ ἀφιδρύματα τῶν θεῶν καὶ τὸν λοιπὸν κόσμον τῶν πολεμίων ἀφελόμενος ἀνέθηκε τῇ θεῷ χρυσοῦς μυρίους καὶ δισχιλίους ἑξήκοντα, ἀργυρίου τάλαντα τριακόσια ἑπτά, 'by confiscation of the statues and the other images set up to [or of] the gods as well as other ornaments taken from the enemy, he has dedicated to the goddess 12,060 pieces of gold and 307 talents of silver'. For the inscription, see Vogel-Weidemann (1985).

[420] Zecchini (1982: 170–6); Gruen (1984: 229; 1990: 70–1, 132; 1992: 107–10); Evans (1993: 183).

[421] Giovannini (1996: 24–8) discusses the looting of temples in general and the Jerusalem temple in particular.

[422] Cic. *Verr.* II.1.21.57. For the importance of the concept *vi capta*, Tarpin (1999: 288–91).

[423] Liv. 26.21.1–5; Plut. *Marc.* 22.1.

and *invidia* are pointed out as underlying political motives.[424] In addition, scholars emphasize that the complaint of Marcellus' looting came from much later writers, who blamed him for having brought Greek culture to Rome rather than for the very act of looting statues of gods as such.[425] These arguments are all valid, and it is also quite clear that the contrast between the conduct of Marcellus and that of Fabius Maximus is overemphasized in the sources. Despite the story of how Fabius left the gods in Tarentum, both Livy and Strabo maintain that the Roman general did in fact confiscate many of the objects dedicated on the acropolis of Tarentum.[426] Strabo, Pliny, and Plutarch also state that Fabius took a colossal statue of Hercules and placed it on the Capitol,[427] and Pliny maintains that the only reason why he did not bring with him another famous statue made by Lysippus was because it was too heavy to transport.[428]

Still, Livy's report of the senatorial debate that followed the complaints of the Syracusan delegation reveals that Marcellus' plundering of temples caused contemporary reactions as well. In contrast to Ambracia, Syracuse had been taken by force, but there was instead some doubt whether the conquest itself was justified. The people of Syracuse accused Marcellus of ignoring peace offers in order to be able to capture the city and loot its art treasures. The fall of Syracuse took place at a time that was turbulent in political as well as religious matters.[429] With Hannibal at the city gates, foreign religion had invaded Rome and traditional rites had suddenly been abandoned. In response, the senate intervened in 212 BC and confiscated all books on prophecy and ritual and forbade all foreign rites.[430] In all probability, it was the novelty of the large-scale plunder at this very critical point that caused the ambiguity and impelled the debate about sacrilege. In the end, however, the senate chose to ratify Marcellus' conduct and accomplishments.

To the treasury!

Not only were the statues and paintings paraded as spoils of war rather than sacred objects or embodiments of captured gods; their value as works of art was also passed over. Except for Livy's remark that the statues from Syracuse were *nobilia signa*, the ancient authors never comment on the aesthetic value of the

---

[424] Pape (1975: 81); Eckstein (1987: 169–77). Cf. Plut. *Marc.* 22.1.

[425] Pape (1975: 81–5); Gruen (1992: 94–102).

[426] Strab. 6.3.1; Liv. 27.16.7–8. According to Livy, the quantity of riches, statues, and paintings almost rivalled the booty from Syracuse.

[427] Strab. 6.3.1; Plin. *Nat.* 34.18.40–1; Plut. *Fab.* 22.5–6; *vir ill.* 43.6–7.

[428] Plin. *Nat.* 34.18.40–1.

[429] Springer (1952); Ridley (2000: 18).

[430] Liv. 25.1.6–12.

sculptures.[431] They give no names of artists, no dates, and no marvellous stories attached to the sculptures. Furthermore, in contrast to the many reactions of joy, fear, and relief from the spectators when confronting the captives and personifications, no sources reveal that the looted statues and paintings made any visual impression on the audience. Apparently, the statues and paintings were not staged as individual objects of art, but rather as an anonymous mass of booty. As such, quantity counted. Livy states that Marcellus displayed *multa signa* and he stresses that Flamininus had captured more (*plura*) statues from Philip than he had obtained from the Greek cities. Livy also specifies the statues shown in Fulvius Nobilior's triumphs as 785 made of bronze and 230 of marble, while in their accounts of the triumph held by Aemilius Paullus, Plutarch maintains that the statues filled 250 wagons and Diodorus Siculus 500 wagons.[432]

Besides their number, the only thing we learn about the statues is whether they were made of bronze, marble, gold, or ivory. In this too, the statues were just any rich spoils on parade, all of which were counted in number, weight, material, and money. Cicero's account of the triumph of Servilius Vatia reveals that the statues were carefully recorded by the *aerarium* after the triumph,[433] as does Livy's description of the debate that preceded the triumph of Aemilius Paullus. Here, one of the arguments in favour of a triumph concerns the fate of the captured statues and other valuables if not put on processional display: *Quo signa aurea, marmorea, eburnea, tabulae pictae, textilia, tantum argenti caelati, tantum auri, tanta pecunia regia? An noctu tamquam furtiva in aerarium deportabuntur?* 'What of the statues of gold, marble, ivory, the paintings, textiles, all the embossed silver, all the gold, all the royal money? Shall they be carried to the treasury by night as if stolen?'[434] The passage

---

[431] According to Pape (1975: 65), no artistic criteria were applied when choosing pieces of art as booty. Welch (2006) discusses what she calls the 'booty mentality', which also permeated Roman ways of selecting and setting up sculptures in private contexts. She argues that Roman and Greek ways of thinking about art differed, in that Greeks saw artists and subject matters, where Romans saw numbers, sizes, poses, and materials.

[432] Liv. 26.21.8–9, 34.52.4, 39.5.15; Plut. *Aem.* 32.4–5; Diod. Sic. 31.8.11–12 (apud Sync.). Klar (2006) argues very convincingly that large numbers of statues were used to decorate the *scaenae frons* of temporary theatres in Rome, thus contributing highly to the self-aggrandizement of victorious generals.

[433] Cic. *Verr.* II.1.21.57: *P. Servilius, quae signa atque ornamenta ex urbe hostium, vi et virtute capta, belli lege atque imperatorio iure sustulit, ea populo Romano apportavit, per triumphum vexit, in tabulas publicas ad aerarium perscribenda curavit. Cognoscite ex litteris publicis hominis amplissimi diligentiam. Recita. RATIONES RELATAE P. SERVILII. Non solum numerum signorum sed etiam unius cuiusque magnitudinem, figuram, statum litteris definiri vides,* 'The statues and objects of art, which, in accordance with the rights of war and his powers as general, P. Servilius removed from the enemy city, captured by force and by his valour, he brought home to the Roman people, carried them in his triumphal procession, and had them thoroughly entered in publicly exposed tablets by the treasury. Learn from the public records of the carefulness shown by this eminent man. Read them, please. STATEMENT OF THE ACCOUNTS SUBMITTED BY P. SERVILIUS. You see carefully stated in these records, not only the numbers of the statues, but the size, shape, and attitude of each one of them.'

[434] Liv. 45.39.5–6.

reveals that the statues and paintings were normally brought to the *aerarium* in full daylight as part of the triumph and that they were categorized and registered as items of worth together with the gold, silver, coins, and bullion.

In the triumphs, the statues were goods of value, which together with the other spoils made visible the augmented richness achieved through the military success of Rome.[435] Hence, on the tablet put up for Minerva, Pompey explicitly specifies that the confiscation of statues has enabled him to donate 12,060 pieces of gold and 307 talents of silver to the goddess. It is in light of this practice that we should read the humorous story of how Mummius told the contractors who were going to bring his booty of art from Corinth to Rome that if any of the statues or paintings were lost on the way, they had to replace them with new ones.[436] The story is told to ridicule Mummius, but, in fact, demonstrates that the spoils of war, statues and paintings included, were counted in money.[437] It comes as no surprise that Fulvius Nobilior left only statues made of terracotta behind in Ambracia, although their artist was the renowned Zeuxis.[438]

On parade

Once placed in temples and public places after the triumph, the statues and paintings were doubtless admired as works of art. But in the procession that introduced them to the Roman audience, they were not presented as admirable art objects. More importantly, they were actively categorized as goods rather than captive gods. Was this choice unproblematic? That is, were the statues and paintings perceived as plain booty when they were captured and transported to Rome and thus simply paraded in the triumphs as the spoils they actually were? Or was it only their categorization in the triumph that made them spoils rather than gods? Were perhaps the statues and paintings viewed as still possessing some divine powers that could be turned against Rome—powers which were neutralized by exhibiting them as plain objects of value?

Much could be said in favour of an interpretation that tones down the difficulties in presenting the statues and paintings as plain spoils. One could, for example, maintain that to capture images of the gods did not mean that the gods themselves were imprisoned, only their material reflections.[439] In fact,

---

[435] The looted works of art could of course also be sold at or close by the scene of war. In these cases, they were represented by their money's worth in the triumph.

[436] Vell. Pat. 1.13.4–5.

[437] Cf. *RE* XVI:1 (1933), s.v. 'Mummius', 1199–1200 (F. Münzer); Gruen (1992: 124 and n. 202).

[438] Plin. *Nat.* 35.36.66.

[439] Köves-Zulauf (1993: 160–2).

Köves-Zulauf has argued that the very idea of a *deus captivus* was unthinkable to the Roman mind.[440] Thus, even if the statues were carried off to Rome, the gods themselves stayed put. We have also seen how debates of sacrilege appear only in connection with the parades held by Marcellus and Fulvius Nobilior. These two cases form exceptions, which rather confirm that the rights of war, *ius belli*, entitled the Romans to confiscate all things, profane and sacred, providing that the city had been properly captured by force in a justly fought war.[441] Once these requests had been fulfilled and the works of art were not intended for private use, there was no issue of sacrilege or of robbing gods from their temples. The statues were plain spoils of war and paraded as such in the triumphs.

At the same time, the Roman discussions on sacrilege regarding some of the triumphs cannot but reflect a certain uncertainty about how to treat the booty taken from sacred contexts without offending the gods. Fabius Maximus' decision to leave some of the statues of the gods in Tarentum since they were angered could also be read as a reflection of this anxiety. In addition, a precautionary handling of statues of foreign deities is suggested by the Roman practice of calling out the gods from the enemy city and inviting them to a new abode in Rome before the attack, the so-called *evocatio*. From what little we know, no cult statue taken over by way of *evocatio* was brought to Rome in a triumphal procession.[442] The canonical example, Juno Regina from Veii, was not even allowed into the city of Rome, but stayed outside on the Aventine.[443] Of course, our sources are far from complete and the very custom of *evocatio* obscure. Still, it seems clear that gods who had been called out of their cities went to obtain a new temple and a fresh cult in Rome, and they went voluntarily. Thus, the statue of Juno Regina nodded in approval as the Roman proposal was put forth. To be displayed in a triumphal procession, on the other hand, was by definition a disgrace and a sign of subordination. No captive, whether human or divine, walked in a triumph of his or her own free will. Perhaps, then, behind the idea of presenting the statues as mere spoils, there was an inherent paradox: that gods could not be captured, but that at the same time you had to take care not to capture them.

---

[440] Ovid describes a Minerva Capta in the *Fasti* 3.835–48, see e.g. Girard (1989); Köves-Zulauf (1993); Gustafsson (2000: 56–9). Köves-Zulauf reads the epithet *capta* as an active form of *capere* and interprets the goddess as one who 'takes up' rather than one who has been captured (1983: 164–5).

[441] The official formula of surrender included the phrase *divina humanaque omnia dedere*, see Liv. 1.38.2. Pape argues that no *res sacra* existed outside the *ager Romanus* and that the Romans therefore had no problems in taking statues from foreign shrines as booty (1975: 36–7).

[442] For the custom of *evocatio*, see Gustafsson (2000), who treats all the traditional examples in detail.

[443] Liv. 5.22.6–7. The temple to Vertumnus from Volsinii was also located on the Aventine.

ART AND VALUABLES

Roman triumphs showed art and valuables in some abundance from at least the third century BC.[444] Some parades included a few types of objects only, while others were extremely rich in the amount as in the variety displayed. The literary sources are both Latin and Greek, and the evidence derives almost exclusively from the prose writers. Latin poets occasionally mention gold, silver, and purple on parade, but tell nothing in detail of the objects shown.[445] Among Latin prose writers, most references stem from Livy and Pliny, who argue that the rare and costly commodities brought to Rome through the triumphs over the East led to the dissolution of Roman traditional values.[446] Both authors date the beginning of the moral decline to Scipio Asiaticus and Manlius Vulso's triumphs over Asia and Antiochus III. Pliny writes of Scipio's performance in 189 BC: 'It was the conquest of Asia that first brought luxury to Italy, for in his triumph L. Scipio carried along 1,400 pounds of chased silver and 1,500 pounds of gold vessels.'[447]

Pliny and Livy link the introduction of *luxuria* not to the encounter with the East in general, but very specifically to the triumphal celebrations held over Asia.[448] Luxury, they claim, was imported into Rome by way of the actual silver and gold, furniture, and textiles that were carried in the parades of Scipio Asiaticus and Manlius Vulso. Similarly, Marcellus was blamed for having introduced large amounts of Greek works of art in his ovation over Syracuse in 211 BC, thereby initiating the process of moral decline in Rome.[449]

The role attached to the triumphs as importers of *luxuria* attests to the strong visual impression made by the parades and to their abundance and wealth. Also, many kinds of artistic objects were seen for the first time in Rome when carried in triumph. Thus, the parades signified the very introduction of the items into the city. Livy emphasizes that it was during the triumphal celebrations over Asia that Rome first saw certain furniture and textiles. Pliny provides the same information and adds two other examples of the introduction of novel riches by way of victory

[444] Florus claims that M'. Curius Dentatus showed *aurum, purpura, signa, tabulae Tarentinaeque deliciae* in the triumph held over Pyrrhus and the Samnites in 275 BC, *Epit.* 1.13.27. Waurick (1977: 6–9).

[445] Ovid himself admits that he is far more fascinated by the prisoners and representations on display, *Pont.* 3.4.23–7.

[446] For Pliny's chapters on art and the concept of *luxuria*, see Isager (1991); Carey (2003: esp. 75–101).

[447] Plin. *Nat.* 33.53.148: *Asia primum devicta luxuriam misit in Italiam, siquidem L. Scipio in triumpho transtulit argenti caelati pondo mille et CCCC et vasorum aureorum pondo MD ...*; cf. *Nat.* 37.6.12 and Livy, 37.59.4–5, who includes 1,423 pounds of chased silver vases and 1,023 pounds of gold vases in his description of Scipio's triumph. Livy (39.6.7) blames the introduction of *luxuria* equally on Scipio and Manlius Vulso (187 BC).

[448] The import of *luxuria* was not always linked to triumphal processions. A turning point often stressed was the testament of Attalus, which left Pergamon to Rome in 133 BC, Plin. *Nat.* 33.53.148–9.

[449] Polyb. 9.10; Liv. 25.40.1–3, 34.4.4; Plut. *Marc.* 21.

celebrations: 'It was this victory of Pompey [over Mithridates] that first made pearls and gemstones fashionable. The victories of L. Scipio and Cn. Manlius had done the same for chased silver, garments woven with gold, and dining couches inlaid with bronze; and that of L. Mummius for Corinthian bronzes and paintings.'[450] Pliny also states that it was during Pompey's celebration in 61 BC that Rome first saw the expensive myrrhine ware.[451] Myrrhine bowls and cups were displayed in the triumph and afterwards dedicated to Jupiter Capitolinus.

The majority of the valuable objects paraded in triumphs had been taken as booty from captured camps, cities, palaces, and sanctuaries; others had been received as gifts.[452] In fact, many objects on display, such as silver plate and precious stones, constituted traditional (often royal) gifts in the kingdoms of the East.[453] This goes for ivory tusks too. According to Livy, Scipio Asiaticus showed 1,231 tusks in his triumph over Antiochus, and Diodorus Siculus maintains that Aemilius Paullus displayed 2,000 tusks, each three cubits long, when celebrating his victory over King Perseus of Macedon.[454] We are not told how the ivory tusks had been obtained, but since tusks were traditionally presented as gifts or as tribute in the eastern kingdoms, the Roman generals had most probably either captured them from royal treasuries or received them as gifts of loyalty.[455]

Once displayed in the triumph, there was no distinction between the objects taken as booty and those received as gifts. Nor was the difference always clear when transferred to Roman ownership, as gifts were often presented by individuals or peoples subjected to Rome and were many times rather involuntary in character. For example, Plutarch holds that when Stratonice, one of Mithridates' concubines and in charge of his richest fortress, surrendered to Pompey, she bestowed on him many gifts.[456] Of these, he accepted only the ones that might adorn the temples of Rome and, not least important, add splendour to his triumph. Plutarch adds that Pompey proceeded similarly with the couch, table, and throne, all of gold, which were sent to him as gifts from the Iberian king.[457] These priceless items were

---

[450] Plin. *Nat.* 37.6.12: *Victoria tamen illa Pompei primum ad margaritas gemmasque mores inclinavit, sicut L. Scipionis et Cn. Manli ad caelatum argentum et vestes Attalicas et triclinia aerata, sicut L. Mummi ad Corinthia et tabulas pictas*. For Vulso, see also Plin. *Nat.* 34.8.14.

[451] Plin. *Nat.* 37.7.18: *Eadem victoria primum in urbem myrrhina invexit, primusque Pompeius capides et pocula ex eo triumpho Capitolino Iovi dicavit.* Myrrhine is today commonly interpreted as flourspar, see Loewental and Harden (1949); Bromehead (1952); Harden (1954); Isager (1991), index, s.v. 'Fluorspar'. Seneca included *murrea pocula* among the *spolia luxuriae*, which also comprised tortoise shells, tables of (citrus) wood, crystal, pearls, and silk, *Benef.* 7.9.2–5; cf. Prop. 4.5.21–6.

[452] *Contra* Merten (1968: 108–11).

[453] See e.g. Plut. *Pomp.* 36.4–5; Flor. *Epit.* 1.40.28, 2.34.62–3. Klauser (1944: 130–3).

[454] Liv. 37.59.3; Diod. Sic. 31.8.12 (apud Sync.).

[455] Grainger (1995: 27) proposes that the tusks had been presented as gifts. In the grand procession of Ptolemy in Alexandria, Ethiopian tribute bearers carried 600 elephant tusks, Ath. 5.201a.

[456] Plut. *Pomp.* 36.6.   [457] Ibid. 36.7.

delivered to the quaestors; certainly, they too were staged in the triumph and dedicated in the temples.

As gifts were present among the valuables shown in the Roman triumphs, not all of the items displayed originated in the restricted areas of conquest. Often, they had wider geographic derivations and thus implied an extensive hegemony. The same mechanisms were involved in the pure war booty as well. After all, many objects confiscated by (as well as given to) the Romans had not been produced in the vanquished areas themselves, but had in their turn been collected either as spoils or as gifts from other places, far and near. This circumstance is clearly expressed by Appian, as he records the triumph held by Scipio Aemilianus after the destruction of Carthage in 146 BC (*Pun.* 135):

ὡς δὲ αὐτῷ πάντα ἐξετετέλεστο, διαπλεύσας ἐπιφανέστατα δὴ πάντων διεθριάμβευε πολύχρυσον θρίαμβον, ἀγαλμάτων τε γέμοντα καὶ ἀναθημάτων, ὅσα Καρχηδόνιοι χρόνῳ πολλῷ καὶ συνεχέσι νίκαις ἐκ πάσης γῆς συνενηνόχεσαν ἐς Λιβύην.

When all was finished, he sailed for home and celebrated the most glorious triumph ever, splendid with gold and filled with all the statues and votive offerings that the Carthaginians had brought together in Africa from all parts of the world during their long period of continuous victories.

Despite the worldwide origins of items on parade, we are seldom informed of their specific ethnic or geographic origins. In general terms, passages describing the most abundant riches refer to triumphs held over the Hellenistic kings. The East did provide Roman triumphs with a large proportion of their riches, not to mention many novelties during the Republican age, yet the fragmentary state of the sources is a difficulty. Several triumphs were labelled 'the most glorious ever', and for the period between 167 BC, when Livy's text disappears, and the late Republic, we are left with very general remarks on the spoils shown. When Caesar celebrated his five triumphs in 46 and 45 BC over Gaul, Egypt, Pontus, Africa, and Spain, the first, celebrating the victories in Gaul, was in fact regarded as the most splendid.[458] True, in comparison with the other areas, Caesar had been able to collect spoils in Gaul for a longer time; nevertheless, he explicitly wished for this particular province, since it was 'most likely to enrich him and furnish suitable material for triumphs'.[459]

---

[458] Suet. *Iul.* 37.1, cf. 54.2–3.

[459] Ibid. 22.1. Note also Velleius Paterculus' account (2.56.2) of the diverse materials employed in Caesar's triumphs of the years 46–45 BC. In the Gallic triumph, citrus wood was used for the *apparatus*. Citrus wood is very costly, and Deutsch interprets Caesar's choice as a manifestation of his desire to render the Gallic triumph the most magnificent, Deutsch (1924*b*: esp. 258–60).

Royal provenance and emblems

Ancient sources comment extensively on any kingly connections of paraded objects,[460] and clearly, numerous luxurious products had a royal provenance. Many objects had been taken from conquered camps of enemy kings;[461] others had been collected from royal palaces and treasuries. For example, much of the gold and silver that Aemilius Paullus shipped to Rome had been confiscated from the Macedonian royal treasuries.[462] Also, a great number of spoils were shipped to Pompey's triumph in Rome from the city of Talauri, which had been used by Mithridates for storage. This repository carried a wide range of royal connections, as many items had been inherited from the Persian King Darius I, yet others stemmed from the Ptolemaic Queen Cleopatra.[463] Appian lists: '2000 drinking-cups made of onyx inlaid with gold, and many cups and wine-coolers, drinking-horns, and ornamented couches and thrones, bridles for horses, and trappings for their breasts and shoulders, all ornamented in like manner with precious stones and inlaid with gold. The amount of spoils was so great that it took 30 days to transfer them.'[464]

Some of the paraded objects were royal emblems that symbolized the king. Thrones, sceptres, chariots, and diadems are all attested. As for thrones, our single explicit piece of evidence is Appian's statement that Pompey carried Mithridates' throne in 61 BC,[465] but Pompey must have shown other thrones as well. The king of the Iberians had sent him a golden throne that was delivered to the quaestors,[466] and thrones were among the items brought to Rome from the storage at Talauri.[467] On parade, Mithridates' throne might have held the king's sceptre, as Appian lists 'the throne of Eupator' and 'his sceptre' in close order.[468] The empty throne represented divine and royal sovereignty, and the symbolism was often strengthened by the display of regalia. Hence, in Babylon, just after Alexander's death, a royal throne decorated with the diadem, robe, arms, and ring of the king was put up in public.[469] In his grand procession held in Alexandria

---

[460] Liv. 26.21.7–8, 37.46.4; Suet. Aug. 41.1; Plin. Nat. 37.5.11; Plut. Aem. 33.4–5; App. Mith. 116.

[461] See e.g. Liv. 37.57.12–15.

[462] Polyb. 18.35.4–5; Plut. Aem. 28.10; Liv. 45.33.5–7.

[463] Alexander's cloak, which Pompey allegedly wore in the triumph, seems to have come from this repository, App. Mith. 117, cf. 115.

[464] App. Mith. 115.

[465] Ibid. 116.

[466] Plut. Pomp. 36.7.

[467] App. Mith. 115.

[468] Ibid. 116: καὶ τὴν Δαρείου τοῦ Ὑστάσπου κλίνην, καὶ τὸν τοῦ εὐπάτορος αὐτοῦ θρόνον. καὶ σκῆπτρον αὐτοῦ, καὶ εἰκόνα... 'and the couch of Darius, the son of Hystaspes, the throne and sceptre of [Mithridates] Eupator himself, and his image'.

[469] Curt. 10.6.4. In a dream of Eumenes of Cardia, the deceased Alexander orders that an empty throne carrying his diadem, sceptre, crown, and other royal insignia should be put up before an altar in his tent, Diod. Sic. 18.60.4–6; Polyaen. 4.8.1–2.

sometime in the first half of the third century BC,[470] Ptolemy Philadelphus displayed chryselephantine thrones that carried golden diadems, crowns, and horns, all divine and regal symbols.[471] In her commentary on the text of Callixenus of Rhodes describing Ptolemy's procession, Rice stresses the function of the throne as a 'symbol of authority of the absent deity or king whose imminent arrival was expected even as his invisible presence could be felt'.[472] When displayed as booty in the Roman triumphal procession, the message was reversed. The throne of the Iberians represented a king, who had surrendered his powers to Rome, and Mithridates' throne symbolized a king (the symbolism perhaps strengthened by way of the sceptre) who was dead, whose kingdom had been conquered, whose powers were gone. The irony of the display is evident, the empty throne denoting not the potent and omnipresent king, but the vanquished sovereign, who was not to return. Hence, the emptiness of the throne did not signify presence but absence.

The empty golden litter covered with purple cloth, which was paraded by Aemilius Paullus in 167 BC and which must have belonged to Perseus, transmitted a similar message, as did Perseus' ivory car, embellished with gold and precious stones.[473] This royal chariot, splendid but empty, also formed a clear visual contrast to the chariot of the victor, carrying the triumphator further back in the procession. A century after Aemilius Paullus' Macedonian celebration, Pompey showed chariots of gold and silver, probably of royal origins,[474] and later again, Aurelian is recorded to have exhibited three *currus regii* in the triumph held in AD 274. The contents and meaning of the later Roman triumphs lie outside the scope of this inquiry, but since the testimony given by the biographer in the *Historia Augusta* reveals several circumstances of general interest for the parades, it will be quoted here:

Currus regii tres fuerunt, in his unus Odaenathi, argento, auro, gemmis operosus atque distinctus, alter, quem rex Persarum Aureliano dono dedit, ipse quoque pari opere fabricatus, tertius, quem sibi Zenobia composuerat, sperans se urbem Romam cum eo visuram. Quod illam non fefellit; nam cum eo urbem ingressa est victa et triumphata.[475]

There were three royal chariots, of which the first, produced with much labour and adorned with silver and gold and jewels, had belonged to Odaenathus, the second, also

---

[470] The date of the procession has been much debated. Foertmeyer (1988) suggests the winter of 275/274 BC, which has won some acceptance.

[471] Ath. 5.202a–b. Rice (1983: 116–18); cf. Calmeyer (1974: 71–4).

[472] Rice (1983: 116). Thomson (2000: 278–9) maintains that the thrones bore a strong reference to Alexander.

[473] Diod. Sic. 31.8.12 (apud Sync.); Plut. *Aem.* 33.5–6. For the empty throne and the empty chariot as parallel motifs in the eastern Mediterranean art tradition, see Calmeyer (1974: esp. 71).

[474] Plin. *Nat.* 33.54.151–2.

[475] S.H.A. *Aurel.* 33.2–3. Merten (1968: 105–8).

made with similar care, had been presented as a gift to Aurelian by the king of the Persians, and the third Zenobia had made for herself, hoping in it to meet with the city of Rome. And this hope was not unfulfilled; for she did indeed enter the city together with it, but vanquished and led in triumph.

Just like the royal chariots displayed by Aemilius Paullus and Pompey, the *currus regii* here are described as being made of precious materials: gold, silver, and jewels. Two points should be made. First, the chariots taken as booty from Odaenathus and Zenobia were shown and listed together with the one presented as a gift by the Persian king. Spoils and gifts were obviously displayed without distinction, and this seems to have been a general procedure in Roman triumphal history. Second, there is a visual irony directed towards the vanquished regent. Zenobia's chariot was allegedly the one in which she had intended to see (that is, conquer) Rome. Now, she does indeed get to enter the city with this very vehicle; not, however, as *victrix* but as *victa*. What was once the emblem of a powerful ruler has been inverted into a symbol of her defeat, staging her crime in a twist of irony. Just like the empty throne, the triumphal exhibition of Zenobia's chariot made visible the broken pride and arrogance of an enemy of the Roman rule.

In Aemilius Paullus' Macedonian triumph, the regal connotations were strongly emphasized. Plutarch describes the display of 'Perseus' chariot, his arms, and his diadem, lying on the arms', which probably means that the arms and the diadem were both transported on the royal car.[476] The diadem was one of the more manifest royal emblems.[477] Accordingly, when Perseus fled from the battlefield at Pydna, he hid his purple coat and took off his diadem and carried it in his hand, in order to avoid recognition.[478] When he was later taken captive at Samothrace, he laid himself upon the ground and placed the diadem at the feet of the Roman leader, thus surrendering his powers and kingship.[479] The importance of the diadem and of its arrangement together with the royal chariot and arms is underlined by the fact that, in Plutarch's account, it was listed last in the line of the spoils, immediately preceding the royal captives.[480] The equipment and insignia of Perseus thus formed a processional transition between spoils and captives, leading the spectators (and the reader) from the display of lifeless items in the former part of the parade to the animate individuals further

---

[476] Plut. *Aem.* 33.5–6: τούτοις ἐπέβαλλε τὸ ἅρμα τοῦ Περσέως καὶ τὰ ὅπλα καὶ τὸ διάδημα τοῖς ὅπλοις ἐπικείμενον.

[477] Ritter (1965); Smith (1988*b*: 34–8).

[478] Plut. *Aem.* 23.1–2.

[479] Liv. 45.19.16, cf. 45.6.10. Tigranes placed his tiara (κίταρις) at Pompey's feet, Plut. *Pomp.* 33.3.

[480] Plut. *Aem.* 33, esp. 5–6. Diodorus Siculus, 31.8.12 (apud Sync.), tells a similar, if not identical, story. He has Perseus preceded by several items of royal origins, including the ivory chariot, a horse in battle array, a golden couch, and a golden litter covered with purple cloth.

back. Perseus himself walked behind his former emblems, deprived of all regal marks, but wearing the dark robe and the high boots of his country. Before him, the display of his diadem, chariot, and arms announced the complete defeat of the king's former powers, military, legal, and religious.

A royal diadem also appears among the spoils shown by Lucullus in the triumph of 63 BC, which celebrated his victories over Mithridates and Tigranes. The diadem had belonged to Tigranes, and Plutarch maintains that it was the sight of the paraded diadem that encouraged Crassus to attack Asia, as 'he thought that the barbarians were spoils and booty, and nothing else'.[481] The diadem must have been conspicuously displayed, in order to attract such attention from Crassus. In fact, in contrast to most spoils of value, described and displayed *en masse*, the royal emblems were accounted for as single pieces, reflecting a more pronounced processional exhibition. Crassus, renowned for his avarice, reacted not only to the splendour of the diadem itself, but to an even higher degree to the promise of further conquests that it transmitted. The captured diadem thus connoted the vanquishment of a king as well as royal riches for the taking.

Precious goods for show and banquets

In several accounts of triumphs held over the eastern kingdoms, Livy attests to the presence of *sup(p)ellex*,[482] a term which could signify either 'furnishings' in a general sense or furniture specifically.[483] Livy writes in quite unspecific terms that the *supellex* shown by Anicius Gallus was *regia* and the one by Acilius Glabrio *regia argentea*, royal and made of silver.[484] When describing the triumphs of Scipio Asiaticus and Manlius Vulso, Livy is more specific, defining *supellex* as one-legged tables and sideboards, here clearly furniture.[485] Looking closer at his other accounts, it becomes clear that *supellex* here too should be read primarily as 'furniture'. In Glabrio's triumph, Livy first states that a large number of silver vessels of great weight was displayed, after which he adds: *tulit et suppellectilem regiam argenteam ac vestem magnificam*. Here, *supellex* most probably refers to royal furniture made of silver or perhaps rather with silver inlays. If so, Glabrio's display would have included silver plate (*argentum*), furniture (*supellex*), and

---

[481] Plut. *Luc.* 36.7: ὡς λάφυρα καὶ λείαν τοὺς βαρβάρους, ἄλλο δ' οὐδὲν ὄντας. For the terms λάφυρα and λεία, see Pritchett (1991: 77–86, 132–47).

[482] Liv. 26.21.8, 37.46.4, 39.6.7, 45.43.5.

[483] *RE* 2:e Reihe IV (1932), s.v. 'supellex', 923–4 (A. Hug).

[484] Liv. 37.46.4, 45.43.5.

[485] Liv. 39.6.7: *quae tum magnificae supellectilis habebantur, monopodia et abacos Romam advexerunt.* The introduction of the one-legged tables and sideboards seems to have been specifically attributed to Manlius Vulso, cf. Plin. *Nat.* 34.8.14.

cloth (*vestis*), that is, all three major categories of Roman household goods.[486] Similarly, Pliny maintains that Scipio and Vulso's processions introduced couches of bronze (*triclinia aerata*), garments of gold (*vestes Attalicae*), and chased silver (*caelatum argentum*) into the city.[487] Again, these are the same categories of rich household equipment. In fact, the three groups—luxurious furniture, rare textiles, and costly plate—appear rather frequently in other sources too, not least in their descriptions of the parades held to celebrate victories over the Hellenistic kingdoms.[488]

What kinds of furniture were put on parade in the triumphs? Pliny maintains that Scipio Asiaticus and Manlius Vulso exhibited bronze couches (*triclinia aerata*),[489] and that Vulso was the first to show dining couches made of bronze, sideboards, and one-legged tables, *triclinia aerata abacique et monopodia*.[490] Livy too describes the display of dining couches of bronze (*lecti aerati*), tables with one leg, and sideboards (*monopodia et abaci*) in the parades of Scipio Asiaticus and Manlius Vulso.[491] Several other passages attest to the triumphal display of dining couches (*lecti*, *lecti tricliniares*, *triclinia*, κλίναι), which are by far the type of furniture most frequently attested. Some of the couches were made of bronze (Vulso and Scipio), others of gold, as stated for the parades of Aemilius Paullus, Lucullus, and Pompey.[492] Couches formed an essential part of the dining apparatus, as did sideboards and one-legged tables. All attested furniture thus originates from the context of the meal and the symposium.

On parade in the trains of Scipio and Vulso, there were also *vestes Attalicae*, textiles woven with gold, believed to have been invented by the Attalid kings.[493] Other processions included purple cloth.[494] The textiles were closely linked to

[486] *RE* 2:e Reihe IV (1932), s.v. 'supellex', 923–4 (A. Hug). This categorization of Roman household goods is reflected in Cic. *Phil.* 2.27.66: *Maximus vini numerus fuit, permagnum optimi pondus argenti, pretiosa vestis, multa et lauta supellex et magnifica multis locis non illa quidem luxuriosi hominis, sed tamen abundantis*, 'There was an immense amount of wine, a very great weight of the finest silver, costly fabrics, much elegant and magnificent furniture in many places, the belongings of a man not indeed lavish but fully supplied.'

[487] Plin. *Nat.* 37.6.12.

[488] Dentatus over Pyrrhus and the Samnites in 275 BC (Flor. *Epit.* 1.13.25–8); Marcellus over Syracuse in 211 BC (Liv. 26.21.8); Aemilius Paullus over Macedonia and Perseus in 167 BC (Diod. Sic. 31.8.10–12; Liv. 45.39.4–6; cf. Plut. *Aem.* 32–3); Anicius Gallus over the Illyrians and King Gentius in the same year (Liv. 45.43.4–6); Lucullus over Mithridates and Tigranes in 63 BC (Plut. *Luc.* 37.3–4); Pompey over Mithridates, Tigranes, and the eastern kingdoms in 61 BC (Plin. *Nat.* 37.6.12–14, 37.7.18; cf. App. *Mith.* 115); Vespasian and Titus in their Jewish triumph in AD 71 (Joseph. *BJ* 7.132–57).

[489] Plin. *Nat.* 37.6.12.   [490] Ibid. 34.8.14.   [491] Liv. 39.6.7.

[492] Aemilius Paullus: Diod. Sic. 31.8.12 (apud Sync.); Lucullus: Plut. *Luc.* 37.4; Pompey: App. *Mith.* 115; cf. Plin. *Nat.* 37.6.14. King Oroeses of Albania sent Pompey a golden couch (Flor. *Epit.* 1.40.28) that was most probably displayed in the triumph.

[493] Plin. *Nat.* 8.74.196, 33.19.63; Prop. 2.13.22, 3.18.19, 4.5.24; Val. Max. 9.1.5; Sil. *Pun.* 14.659.

[494] Flor. *Epit.* 1.13.27; Diod. Sic. 31.8.12. Josephus (*BJ* 7.134–5) writes that in Vespasian and Titus' triumph 'fabrics were borne along, some made of the rarest purple, others embroidered by Babylonian technique with perfect representation', καὶ τὰ μὲν ἐκ πορφύρας ὑφάσματα τῆς σπανιωτάτης φερόμενα, τὰ δ' εἰς

the furniture on parade. Livy twice connects the display of *supellex* with that of *vestis*. He maintains that Marcellus showed *alia supellex pretiosaque vestis* and that Acilius Glabrio *tulit et suppellectilem regiam argenteam ac vestem magnificam*.[495] Livy's now well-known account of the novelties brought in by Scipio Asiaticus and Manlius Vulso also focuses on these two categories (39.6.7):

Ii primum lectos aeratos, vestem stragulam pretiosam, plagulas et alia textilia et, quae tum magnificae supellectilis habebantur, monopodia et abacos Romam advexerunt.

They for the first time imported into Rome couches of bronze, valuable robes for coverlets, tapestries, and other products of the loom, and what at that time was considered luxurious furniture—tables with one leg and sideboards.

The term *vestis* has a wide range of meanings (clothing, garment, blanket, coverlet, tapestry, hangings) but in this passage *stragula* defines it as coverlets.[496] *Plagulae* were likewise coverlets, and specifically those used to cover the *lecti*, dining couches.[497] Livy's coupling of fabrics and furniture in the parades of Marcellus, Asiaticus, Vulso suggests that the coverlets were exhibited on the couches in the triumphs as well. In fact, Diodorus Siculus attests to such a combined display when he describes the presence in Aemilius Paullus triumph of 'a golden couch strewn with flowered coverlets'.[498] Like the furniture on parade, textiles too connoted rich banquets and feasts.

   The third group of household goods, the plate, is the one most frequently documented. At times, sources state in general wording that wrought gold, silver, or bronze were paraded. At others, the type of tableware shown is defined, in the clear majority of cases as plate connected to drinking. Vessels (*vasa*, σκεύη), mixing-bowls (κρατῆρες), wine coolers (ψυκτῆρες), bowls (φιάλαι), cups (κύλικες), beakers (ἐκπώματα), and drinking horns (κέρατα, ῥυτά) all appear in the triumphal accounts.[499] From all terms applied, it is clear that, while the Latin authors contented themselves with referring to the display of *vasa*, or even more generally of *aurum*, *argentum*, and *aes factum*, the terminology used by the

ἀκριβῆ ζωγραφίαν πεποικιλμένα τῇ Βαβυλωνίων τέχνῃ. In Rome, there was a distinction between Phrygian and Babylonian embroidery, the former being made in cross stitch, the latter in satin stitch. The Babylonian technique often applied golden threads and its designs were frequently many-coloured, *RE* 2:e Reihe III (1929), s.v. 'Stickerei', 2490–5 (A. Hug).

   [495] Liv. 26.21.8, 37.46.4, cf. Liv. 45.35.3, 45.39.5.

   [496] *RE* 2:e Reihe IV (1932), s.v. 'stragulum', 169–70 (A. Hug).

   [497] *Plagulae*: *RE* XX:2 (1950), s.v. 'plagula', 2006–7 (K. Schneider). Coverings for *lecti*: Apul. *Met.* 2.19, 2.21; Cic. *Mur.* 75; Sen. *Epist.* 95.72. D'Arms (1999), 302.

   [498] Diod. Sic. 31.8.12 (apud Sync.): κλίνη χρυσῆ στρωμναῖς πολυανθέσι κατεστρωμένη, . . .

   [499] The ψυκτῆρες and the ῥυτά are documented only in Appian's description of Mithridates' storehouse that was shipped to Rome for the triumph, *Mith.* 115. All the other terms stem from listings of processional contents. For precious drinking vessels as spoils in the Greek world, see Pritchett (1991: 174–9).

Greek authors was much more varied.[500] For example, according to Plutarch, day two of Aemilius Paullus' Macedonian triumph saw 'other men [carrying] mixing-bowls of silver, drinking horns, bowls, and cups, all and each arranged for visual display and extraordinary in size and in the height of their reliefs'.[501]

This was not all. On the last day of the celebration, Perseus' gold plate was exhibited together with bowls known as Antigonids, Seleucids, and Thera-cleian.[502] The Theracleian bowls originally owed their name to a famous Corinthian potter,[503] but Θηρίκλειος as a term was soon applied also to silver- and goldware. Verres tried eagerly to get his hand on some Θηρίκλειοι made of silver, and golden Θηρίκλειοι appear among the precious goods displayed in Ptolemy's grand Alexandrian procession.[504] The other two types were both named after kings, Antigonus and Seleucus respectively.[505] Listed with the royal golden tableware as one of final displays in Aemilius Paullus' splendid triumph, they too must have been made of a precious material.

An abundance of precious plate added to the richness of the parades, and the amount of tableware was ostentatiously stressed by way of the number of biers, people, animals, or carts needed to transport the precious objects through the city. Thus, Pliny writes that the gold vessels inlaid with gems shown by Pompey in 61 BC filled nine sideboards.[506] Plutarch maintains that Lucullus had men carrying twenty litters (φορήματα) of silver vessels and thirty-two of gold beakers, armour and coined money.[507] There were also eight mules that bore golden couches.

Wealth was also measured by weight. And clearly, the weight was of utmost importance, since it defined very precisely the value of the plate in question. In fact, as is attested by several archaeological finds, the weight of the individual pieces was often inscribed on ancient silver and gold,[508] and it was carefully recorded not least when tableware was presented as gifts or as donations in the temples.[509] Still, triumphal accounts never give the weight of single pieces on parade, but either provide the weight for all the plate together or include it in the

---

[500] Pliny (*Nat.* 37.7.18) does specify the myrrhine ware dedicated by Pompey to Jupiter from his triumph (*ex eo triumpho*) as being *pocula* and *capides*, but this passage does not come from an account of the triumph itself but is a specification of the objects dedicated to Jupiter afterwards.

[501] Plut. *Aem.* 32.9: ἄλλοι δὲ κρατῆρας ἀργυροῦς καὶ κέρατα καὶ φιάλας καὶ κύλικας, εὖ διακεκοσμημένα πρὸς θέαν ἕκαστα καὶ περιττὰ τῷ μεγέθει καὶ τῇ παχύτητι τῆς τορείας.

[502] Plut. *Aem.* 33.4–5: οἵ τε τὰς Ἀντιγονίδας καὶ Σελευκίδας καὶ Θηρικλείους καὶ ὅσα περὶ δεῖπνον χρυσώματα τοῦ Περσέως ἐπιδεικνύμενοι.

[503] Ath. 11.470e–f.

[504] Verres: Cic. *Verr.* II.4.18.38–9; Ptolemy: Ath. 5.199b, with Rice (1983: 73–4).

[505] Ath. 11.488e–f, 497 f.

[506] Plin. *Nat.* 37.6.14.

[507] Plut. *Luc.* 37.3–4.

[508] Strong (1966: 22–3); Oliver and Shelton (1979).

[509] Gasparri (1970). Trimalchio had his plate marked with its weight, Petron. 31.

total weight of all the wrought bronze, silver, or gold (*aes/argentum/aurum factum*).[510] Plutarch in our most detailed passage states that Aemilius Paullus showed silver plate, 'each and all arranged for visual display and extraordinary in size and in the height of their reliefs',[511] thus emphasizing the visual effects of the single huge vessels, but he does not specify how much each of them weighed or contained. In contrast, the descriptions of Callixenus and Polybius of the Hellenistic royal processions at Alexandria and Daphne provide the reader with much information about the capacity or weight of the particular vessels (as of the measures of the single pieces of furniture).[512] Some of the pieces were of very large dimensions. For example, Callixenus describes a golden wine cooler that held 30 μετρηταί (about 1,175 litres), and, more startling, a silver κρατήρ that held 600 μετρηταί (about 23,500 litres) and was drawn in a cart by 600 men![513] The latter figure is extraordinary (and unrealistically) high, and the enormous κρατήρ must have been a showpiece, perhaps even produced for the occasion. We might get a better idea of the sizes and weights involved in the Roman displays from the inscription that accounts for a royal donation of several precious vessels in the temple of Apollo at Didyma in 288–287 BC, among which there was a large silver ψυκτήρ, 38.79 kg in weight.[514] Such pieces might well have been paraded in the processions arranged by Aemilius Paullus and by others. Also, there is the well-preserved bronze krater with Mithridates' name inscribed that was found at Nero's villa at Antium in the mid-eighteenth century (Fig. 8).[515] The piece might have come to Italy by way of a triumph, and Pompey's celebration of 61 BC has been suggested. At least, it gives us a glimpse of what one of many rich objects on parade might have looked like.

At times, inscriptions on ancient plate also give the name of its owner.[516] Occasionally, the name of the craftsman appears too, provided that a famous artist was involved and the piece was of outstanding quality.[517] However, ancient

---

[510] The earliest testimonies to metal tableware give general statements of the kind 'embossed silver vessels in large numbers and of great weight', *vasa argentea caelata multa magnique ponderis*, referring to Glabrio's triumph in 190 BC (37.46.3–4). However, starting from the triumph of Scipio Asiaticus in 189 BC, the weight of the plate or of all the worked gold and silver has been preserved in the sources.

[511] Plut. *Aem.* 32.9.

[512] Alexandria: Ath. 5.197d–203a. Procession held by Antiochus IV at Daphne: Polyb. 30.25.16–19 (apud Ath. 5.195b–c). Each piece of silver plate weighed no less than a thousand drachmae.

[513] Ath. 5.199b–c, f.

[514] Gasparri (1970: 51).

[515] Musei Capitolini, Inv. MC 1068. Beard (2007: 10–11, fig. 2); *Trionfi romani*, 209, II.4.6. The krater is from the late 2nd or early 1st cent. BC, but its handles and foot are restored. It has a chased pattern of lotus leaves around the neck, inlaid with silver. The Greek inscription says: 'King Mithridates Eupator [gave this] to the Eupatoristae of the gymnasium.'

[516] Trimalchio had his name inscribed on his plate, Petron. 31.

[517] Strong (1966: 19–22).

FIGURE 8
A 70 cm high
bronze vessel
inscribed as being a
gift from
Mithridates VI
Eupator of Pontus.
Possibly, it travelled
from the East to
Italy by way of
Pompey's triumph.

accounts of triumphs never give the names of the artists behind the plate on parade. This is typical for all types of art objects on triumphal display. We are told of the items, their material, amount and/or weight, and at times something of the appearance, but never of the artists or former history of the items.

Moreover, the ancient authors only seldom comment on the aesthetics of the plate on parade.[518] Regarding the silver vessels, one circumstance though was of particular importance, namely if the vessels shown were *vasa caelata* (chased, embossed, engraved), thereby affirming their quality. The term *caelatus* probably refers to vessels with embossed figures, a common technique for gold- and silverware in the Hellenistic age.[519] For example, according to Livy, among the worked silver displayed by Flamininus, there were many vases of all kinds, and most of them were embossed (*caelata pleraque*), and the same applies to all of the 1,423 pounds of silver vases put on parade by Scipio Asiaticus (*omnia caelata erant*).[520] Plutarch, again a Greek source, is more detailed and states that the pieces of silver plate exhibited by Aemilius Paullus were 'extraordinary in size and in the height of their reliefs (τῇ παχύτητι τῆς τορείας)'.[521] Here again, embossed meant quality

[518] Livy, in accounting for the silver paraded by Flamininus in 194 BC, comments that some of the vases were of excellent workmanship (*quaedam eximiae artis*), 34.52.5. In his description of Scipio Nasica's triumph held over the Boii in 191 BC, Livy characterizes the vessels displayed as *Gallica vasa, non infabre suo more facta*, 'Gallic vases, not unskilfully wrought in their manner', 36.40.12.

[519] Milne (1941); Strong (1966: 7); Barr-Sharrar (1982: 132 and n. 41); Rice (1983: 74–7 and n. 115).

[520] Liv. 34.52.5, 37.59.4–5. Pliny (*Nat.* 37.6.12) claims that Scipio Asiaticus and Manlius Vulso made chased silver popular by way of their triumphs.

[521] Plut. *Aem.* 32.9. In this passage it is quite clear that figures in high relief are intended (Milne, 1941: 396). However, both τόρευσις and *caelatura*, and forms of these words, were employed to denote metal working in general (Strong, 1966: 7). See also Rice's commentary to Callixenus' text (1983: 74–7 and n. 115).

(τορεία is the equivalent for *caelatus*, embossed, engraved)[522] and the workman-ship was measured by the degree to which the technique has been taken.

But even if the ancient sources repeatedly state that the vessels on triumphal display were embossed, they at no time give the appearance or motives of single vases. This appears again in sharp contrast to Callixenus' description of the plate put on show in Ptolemy's procession in Alexandria, which includes several such depictions.[523] Thus, for the Roman triumphs, the ornaments tell the same story as the weight. Although the plate was 'each and all arranged for visual display', the appearance and characteristics of the individual pieces seem to have attracted very little attention in the archives and in the later writings.

Instead, plate was first and foremost exhibited and recorded as belonging to the categories of bronze, silver, and gold. In fact, in the parades themselves, the plate was at times presented according to its material, as when Lucullus had the silver vessels placed on *fercula* separately from the biers that carried the gold beakers.[524] In contrast, the types of plate did not make up processional categories. While some of the Greek sources specify the objects on display as cups, drinking-horns, and bowls, in the Latin descriptions of this Roman parade, the plate was simply *vasa*, or even just *aes*, *argentum*, or *aurum*. This fact could not be explained away by a richer terminology on part of the Greeks, since it has been established that Latin had twenty-five names for drinking-cups alone.[525] Even if the single masterpieces, excel-ling in size and decoration, must have made a strong impression on the spectators, this has left no trace in the sources. Rather, it was the mass of the display, the quantity of the glittering silver and gold, the number of biers, the heaviness of the total display that attracted attention. In short, the importance of the plate lay first and foremost in the amount of wealth brought into the treasury by way of its display.[526]

The recurrent and abundant displays of rich furniture, textiles, and above all plate, documented particularly in the triumphs held over the kingdoms of the East, echo the ostentatious exhibitions of gold and silver ware in the royal Hellenistic proces-sions.[527] Here too, vessels, mixing-bowls, cups, and wine coolers appear, and they appear in large quantities. As in Rome, the plate was counted in numbers and measured by its weight. Silver and gold were often shown in separate groups,[528] and

---

[522] Milne (1941); Strong (1966: 7).   [523] Ath. 5.197d–203a.

[524] Plut. *Luc.* 37.3–4. Plutarch's version of Aemilius Paullus' three-day-long parade also transmits an image of a categorization according to material, *Aem.* 32.8–33.6.

[525] Hilgers (1969: 15); cf. D'Arms (1999: 311).

[526] Several Greek sources also emphasize the mass of the display, see Plut. *Pomp.* 45.3 and Joseph. *BJ* 7.134–6.

[527] Polyb. 30.25 (apud Ath. 5.194c–195c); Ath. 5.197d–203a. Rice (1983: esp. 71–8); Wikander (1992: 147–8); Köhler (1996: esp. 80–4).

[528] Rice (1983: 73); Köhler (1996: 80–1).

the amount and weight of the plate was emphasized by the large number of men needed to transport the goods. But there were dissimilarities too. As has already been noted, Callixenus' account of Ptolemy's procession in Alexandria in particular reveals details which the descriptions of the Roman triumphs lack: the precise dimensions of the furniture and ornaments, and the capacity of the vessels. Another difference lies in the obvious emphasis on Dionysiaca in the Alexandrian procession, celebrating all stages of wine preparation.

Furthermore, while there were in Alexandria objects with pronounced cultic functions, such as altars, censers, and tripods, the valuables paraded as booty in the Roman triumphs reveal only limited cultic associations.[529] As a general rule, the tableware, textiles, and furniture shown in Rome were profane riches, connoting—besides wealth—banquets, symposia, and household exhibitions for show.[530] This is particularly clear in Pompey's triumph of 61 BC, where some of the gold vessels were displayed on *abaci*, sideboards,[531] imitating the common arrangement of the triclinium, where the richest plate was exhibited to be admired by the guests at the feast.[532] The furniture itself, the sideboards, the one-legged tables, and not least the dining couches and their costly coverlets transmitted the same image of banqueting and sumptuous display.

A large part of the furniture, plate, and textiles displayed in the triumphs stemmed from the camps, palaces, and treasuries of the Hellenistic kings, reflecting the major concern with feasting, especially drinking, at the Hellenistic royal banquets. Some of the objects which ended up in Rome might have functioned as mere showpieces, while others must have served more practical functions at the banquets held by the kings. The royal feast constituted an essential element of the Hellenistic kingdoms. Forming part of the central concept of *tryphê*, it was incumbent upon the king to organize feasts at which abundant offerings of food and drink went hand in hand with an ostentatious display of precious plate, furniture, and textiles.[533] The most famous of the

---

[529] This observation is strictly with regard to the objects displayed as booty. In the triumphs, there were, of course, victims and items connected to the sacrifice on the Capitoline hill.

[530] Aemilius Paullus showed a consecrated bowl on the last day of his Macedonian triumph, but this was an object which the triumphator himself had produced from ten talents of gold and precious stones, rather than an item taken directly as booty or bestowed as a gift, Diod. Sic. 31.8.12 (apud Sync.); Plut. *Aem.* 33.4. After his triumph, Camillus made three golden bowls out of the surplus, had his name inscribed, and placed them on the Capitol, Liv. 6.4.1–3, with Oakley (1997: 422–3); Diod. Sic. 14.93.3.

[531] Plin. *Nat.* 37.6.14.

[532] Strong (1966: 130); D'Arms (1999: esp. 311–13 and figs. 9–10).

[533] Murray (1996); Zimmer (1996); Nielsen (1998). Callixenus' description of the pavilion in Alexandria at the time of the grand procession is also revealing (Ath. 5.196a–197c). Here, set in an elaborately ornamented environment, there were 100 couches of gold, spread with purple cloth, and 200 gold tables with one leg. The plate put up for show on the tables weighed 10,000 silver talents (300 tons).

silversmiths of the time were tied to the royal palaces, and the production was large,[534] as was the amount of objects carried away to Rome. Staged in the triumphs, the household goods transmitted an image first and foremost of the newly conquered richness of Rome (gold, silver, purple), but they also connoted sumptuous feasting and royal submission. The king had been subdued, his riches confiscated, and despite, or rather due to, his luxurious living, he had not been able to defend his country and people against the Roman force. What is more—the objects of his feasts were displayed in a parade, which was itself immediately followed by a banquet, lavishly equipped. Organized by the Roman state and the victorious general and paid for out of the booty, a feast was given for the senate and the general at the Capitol, while the people celebrated in the precinct of Hercules Victor at Forum Boarium.[535] Thus, Rome went immediately from viewing the conquest of the other's banquet to celebrating one of its own.

Opulence in the extreme: pearls and gems

In book 37 of the *Naturalis Historia*, focusing on gems, Pliny describes some of the objects shown in Pompey's triumph in 61 BC. Pliny claims that the information stems from the records of Pompey's triumphs (*ex actis Pompei triumphorum*):

... transtulit alveum cum tesseris lusorium e gemmis duabus latum pedes tres, longum pedes quattuor—ne quis effetas res dubitet nulla gemmarum magnitudine hodie prope ad hanc amplitudinem accedente, in eo fuit luna aurea pondo XXX—, lectos tricliniares tres, vasa ex auro et gemmis abacorum novem, signa aurea tria Minervae, Martis, Apollinis, coronas ex margaritis XXXIII, montem aureum quadratum cum cervis et leonibus et pomis omnis generis circumdata vite aurea, musaeum ex margaritis, in cuius fastigio horologium. Erat et imago Cn. Pompei e margaritis, illa relicino honore grata, illius probi oris venerandique per cunctas gentes, illa, inquam, ex margaritis, illa, severitate victa et veriore luxuriae triumpho!

He carried in the procession a gaming-board with a set of pieces, the board being made of two precious gemstones and measuring three feet broad and four feet long. And lest anyone doubt that our natural resources have been exhausted, with none of today's gems even coming near such a size, there rested on the board a golden moon of 30 pounds. He also paraded three dining-couches; nine sideboards filled with gold

[534] Liv. 45.33.5–7. Strong (1966: 15); Zimmer (1996).

[535] Capitol: Liv. 45.39.13; Forum Boarium: Ath. 4.153c, 5.221f–222a; cf. Varro *Rust.* 3.2.16; Liv. *Per.* 115; Vell. Pat. 2.56.1–2; Plut. *Luc.* 37.4, *Caes.* 55.2. After the triumph held by Vespasian and Titus in AD 71, the triumphators dined with certain selected guests in the Imperial palace, while others were feasted in their homes, Joseph. *BJ* 7.156–7.

vessels inlaid with gems; three gold statues of Minerva, Mars, and Apollo; thirty-three pearl crowns; a square mountain of gold with deer, lions, and every variety of fruit trees on it, and a golden vine entwined around it; and a pearl shrine to the Muses bedecked with a sun-dial. There was also a portrait of Pompey made of pearls, that portrait so pleasing with the handsome growth of hair swept back from the forehead, the portrait of that noble head revered throughout the world—that portrait, I say, that portrait was rendered in pearls. Here it was austerity that was defeated and extravagance that more truly celebrated its triumph.[536]

The number, weight, and sizes of the gems and pearls put on parade by Pompey were extraordinary indeed. In fact, Pliny maintains that it was Pompey's victory that made pearls popular in Rome,[537] and the Roman general clearly made a spectacular show of these spoils. In another passage, Pliny states that Pompey dedicated Mithridates' gem collection (*dactyliotheca*) on the Capitol.[538] This assemblage had most probably been exhibited together with the other gems, pearls, and precious goods in the triumph as well.

After Pompey, we only once hear of pearls and gems displayed in a triumph. In the procession held by Vespasian and Titus to celebrate the victory over the Jews, Josephus attests to the presence of large numbers of transparent gems, of which some were set in golden crowns.[539] Pearls and gems, were, however, without doubt exhibited in other processions as well. We know that Caesar dedicated a cuirass made of British pearls in the temple of Venus Genetrix after his triumphs in 46 BC.[540] Flory has argued very convincingly that the pearl cuirass symbolized the defeated Ocean, from where the pearls stemmed.[541] Oceanus himself, the vanquished enemy, was present in the Gallic triumph, represented by a gold statue,[542] and the pearls of which he had been despoiled must have had their obvious place in the procession as well.

Octavian probably paraded pearls in his triple triumph of 29 BC. A few years later, in 25 BC, he bestowed on the statue of Venus in the Pantheon a pair of pearl earrings, produced by the cutting in two of one large pearl, which had been captured from Cleopatra.[543] This pearl had originally formed one of a pair, the

[536] Plin. *Nat.* 37.6.13–14, cf. 1.37. The fact that the passage is based on Pompey's *acta triumphorum* might explain why Pliny, although focusing on the display of gems and pearls, has included objects of pure gold as well.
[537] Plin. *Nat.* 37.6.12.
[538] Ibid. 37.5.11. Westall (1996: 90–2).
[539] Joseph. *BJ* 7.135.
[540] Plin. *Nat.* 9.57.116; cf. Suet. *Iul.* 47. The act was certainly in rivalry with Pompey, Flory (1988); Westall (1996: 87, 90–2).
[541] Flory (1988).
[542] Flor. *Epit.* 2.13.88–9.
[543] The story of Cleopatra's pearls stems from Pliny, *Nat.* 9.58.119–21 (cf. Macr. *Sat.* 3.17.14–18), and is discussed by Flory (1988: 502–4). See also Ullman (1957).

second of which Cleopatra herself had consumed at a renowned banquet in Alexandria. Having taken a bet with Antony that she could spend ten million sesterces on a single feast, she placed the pearl in a cup filled with vinegar and drank it down.[544] The surviving pearl was a famed object indeed. It was known as the largest ever seen and it had strong regal connotations, both in that it had been Cleopatra's, and in that she in her turn had inherited it from generations of eastern regents. In addition, it bore the memory of its former match and of this one's well-known disappearance. It is difficult to imagine that Octavian would have missed the chance to exhibit it in his triumph, where it would have filled many functions: displaying an object of extreme richness, challenging the demonstrations of pearls by Pompey and Caesar, exhibiting the vanquishment of an infamous female ruler, connoting royal subordinance and the failure of eastern opulence. However, unlike the massive display of pearls by Pompey, this one pearl, even being the largest ever, would not easily have been detachable if put on single display. The only possible means to do the pearl justice would have been to display it with the statue of Cleopatra, which was paraded on a bier in the parade.[545] If so, I would surmise that the cutting took place later, and that the statue carried but one earring. In that way, the present and the absent pearl would have complemented each other in telling the full story of the vanquished queen, her *luxuria* and arrogance.[546]

The triumphal display of gems and pearls reflects the difficulty in exhibiting these rather small items to the fullest visual effects in a moving parade. Rich as they may be, their opulence would not easily have been comprehensible if displayed on their own. Thus, gems were often exhibited as inlays in golden crowns and furniture, and Pompey showed them in the form of a gaming-board and as a *musaeum* as part of a larger scenery. Caesar probably showed the British pearls in the shape of the cuirass later dedicated to Venus, and Pompey even had pearls displayed in the form of his own portrait. Pliny reacted with disapproval against the effeminate exhibition of the general's face made of pearls, and probably also to the very fact that Pompey had his own image displayed in the triumph at all, a conduct otherwise unheard of.

Pearls and gems represented opulence in the extreme. They often originated in royal contexts and they were exceptionally costly. Furthermore, as is often stressed by the ancient authors, they represented the true wealth of Nature.

---

[544] Flory (1988: 502 n. 19) points out that the swallowing of pearls dissolved in vinegar was a topos in descriptions of the excessive living of the rich, see Hor. *Sat.* 2.3.239–42; Val. Max. 9.1.2; Suet. *Cal.* 37.1.

[545] Dio Cass. 51.21.8.

[546] Flory (1988: 502–4) stresses that, by dedicating a royal object to the gods instead of taking possession of it himself, Octavian demonstrated his disapproval of private luxury while at the same time disclaiming any royal associations.

Pliny calls Cleopatra's remaining pearl 'a truly unique work of Nature'.[547] He describes pearls in general as the most expensive products of the sea,[548] and he labels gems 'the supreme and perfect aesthetic experience of the wonders of Nature'.[549] Thus, when displayed in the triumphs, the gems and pearls were not only spoils of extreme wealth and royal origin. They also connoted Roman mastery over Nature itself.

Spolia Gallica: *some notes on the exhibition of torcs*

Ancient authors only seldom testify to the specific origin of objects displayed in the Roman triumphs. When such information does appear, it frequently concerns objects that are labelled Gallic. Livy occasionally refers to the display of *spolia Gallica*, without, however, defining its content.[550] More specifically, Scipio Nasica in his triumph of the Boii in 191 BC paraded *vasa Gallica*.[551] Another art object, the torc,[552] is never explicitly labelled Gallic, but nevertheless seems to have been linked specifically to victories and triumphs over the tribes of Gaul.

Our only explicit piece of evidence refers again to Scipio Nasica's triumph, in which Livy attests to the presence of 1,471 golden torcs.[553] Clearly, however, torcs were shown in other parades as well. Torcs appear as spoils captured on the battlefield, and they were dedicated as votive gifts after triumphs. According to Polybius, L. Aemilius Papus had captured standards and torcs decorating the Capitol at his Gallic triumph in 225 BC.[554] Two years later, according to Florus, C. Flaminius erected a *tropaeum* also on the Capitol out of the torcs captured in war.[555] In 196 BC, Livy claims that the younger Marcellus took many golden necklaces, *aurei torques multi*, in the battle against the Insubri.[556] One of the torcs was later dedicated as a gift to Jupiter, again on the Capitoline hill.[557] Finally, Eutropius states that Cn. Domitius Ahenobarbus brought a substantial amount

---

[547] Plin. *Nat.* 9.58.121: *gerebat auribus cum maxime singulare illud et vere unicum naturae opus.*

[548] Ibid. 37.78.204.

[549] Ibid. 37.1.1: *ad summam absolutamque naturae rerum contemplationem . . .*

[550] Liv. 33.23.4, 39.7.2.

[551] Liv. 36.40.11.

[552] On the torc in general, see *RE* 2:e Reihe VI:2 (1937), s.v. 'torques und torquis', 1800–5 (E. Schuppe); Agostinetti (1997).

[553] Liv. 36.40.12.

[554] Polyb. 2.31.5–6. The rest of the spoils and the prisoners were led in the parade.

[555] Florus (*Epit.* 1.20.4–5), maintaining that the Gauls had earlier vowed a necklace made of Roman spoils to their god of war.

[556] Liv. 33.36.13. Livy states that his information stems from Valerias Antias.

[557] Liv. 33.36.13–14, based on Claudius Quadrigarius. Livy accounts for Marcellus' triumph at 33.37.10–12, stating in very general terms that *multa spolia hostium* were displayed.

of booty 'from the Gallic torcs' to Rome after his victory over the Arverni in 120 BC.[558]

In all these examples, the torcs paraded, captured, and dedicated had been captured from Gauls. Not that Gauls and Celts were the only ones who used massive golden necklaces; several peoples, such as the Germans, Persians, and Scythians, carried the torc.[559] They were even worn by Hellenistic dynasts and royal princes of the East. Still, in ancient literature as well as in art, the torc was predominantly used as a symbol of the Gauls and the Celts.[560] Gauls wore torcs already in Pergamene art,[561] and in Roman art and literature golden necklaces were linked particularly to Gallia and the Gauls.[562] Eventually, the torc also became a Roman military symbol: at least from 89 BC, but possibly earlier, it was included among the *dona militaria* presented to soldiers who had distinguished themselves in battle.[563]

Torcs were taken as spoils on the battlefield. Many ancient authors confirm that the Gauls carried their necklaces in combat.[564] Livy tells the story of how T. Manlius defeated a giant Gaul in single battle and seized his torc, thereby acquiring the family name Torquatus.[565] Maxfield suggests that the taking of golden necklaces as booty might have predated the formalization of the torc as a *donum militarium*,[566] thereby indicating that the Romanization of the symbol would have lessened its value as spoils of war. This is a compelling thought, since no account of a Gallic victory celebration after 120 BC includes the presence of captured torcs. The distinguished soldiers carried their *dona* in the triumphal processions, and the presence of torcs that symbolized Roman victorious deeds may have lessened the desire to present them as spoils of a vanquished enemy.[567]

On one of the cups from Boscoreale, a *torquatus* walks behind Tiberius' triumphal car (Fig. 9).[568] However, it has been argued that soldiers did not

---

[558] Eutrop. 4.22: *Praeda ex torquibus Gallorum ingens Romam perlata est.*

[559] *RE* 2:e Reihe VI:2 (1937), s.v. 'torques und torquis', 1800–5 (E. Schuppe); Maxfield (1981: 86–7); Agostinetti (1997).

[560] Agostinetti (1997: esp. 497–8).

[561] The Dying Gaul in the Capitoline Museums, a marble copy of a bronze original made in the reign of Attalus I, wears a torc, Pollitt (1986: 85–90, figs. 85, 87c); Marszal (2000: fig. 70).

[562] *LIMC* viii Suppl. (1997), s.v. 'Gallia, Galliae', 594–6 (M. Henig); Houghtalin (1993: esp. 260–88).

[563] Maxfield (1981: esp. 86–8); Linderski (2001).

[564] Polyb. 2.29.8–9; Strab. 4.4.5; Prop. 4.10.43–4; Plin. *Nat.* 33.5.15.

[565] Liv. 7.9.6–7.10.14, with Oakley (1998: 113–48). See also Oakley (1985: 393–4 and n. 11, with further references).

[566] Maxfield (1981: 60–1, 87).

[567] However, it must be noted that accounts of the Gallic triumphal manifestations of the late Republic and early Empire are all very fragmentary.

[568] Kuttner (1995: pl. 24, 145–7); *Trionfi romani*, 124–5, I.2.6.

FIGURE 9 A silver cup from Boscoreale in Campania shows Tiberius riding in a triumphal chariot with a slave, smaller in size, standing behind him. Tiberius has a laurel sprig in one hand and a sceptre in the other. One of his followers carries a torc around his neck. Today the cup, one of a pair, is much damaged.

wear the torcs bestowed as *dona* around the neck,[569] and the *torquatus* has been interpreted as a Gallic or German commander, serving in Tiberius' auxiliary troops during his campaign in the North.[570] The torc here would then be one that marked his ethnic origin. However, Silius Italicus (*Pun.* 15.256) does describe how a torc, presented as a *donum*, hung around the neck of the rewarded soldier, and Pfanner maintains that torcs were applied around the neck also on the Roman soldiers, who had received them as *dona*.[571] The *torquatus* on the Boscoreale cup might then well be a Roman soldier distinguished by a *donum*. With this interpretation, the *torquatus* connotes 'Roman supremacy' rather than 'Gallic cooperation'.

Torcs were also used as votives and political gifts. Gauls presented Augustus with a golden torc weighing 100 pounds,[572] and similar gifts were sent in the opposite direction as well. In 170 BC, the Roman senate decided to send gifts to two royal Gallic brothers, consisting of silver vessels, horses, and two torcs made of five pounds of gold.[573] Torcs were not only ethnic markers, but social emblems as well. The Persians and the Scythians presented torcs as gifts to high-ranking foreign individuals,[574] and in Polybius' description of the battle at Talamone in 225 BC, only the young and distinguished among the Gauls, placed nude in the front line, carry the torc.[575] From what little we know, torcs were not, however, displayed with the prominent captives in the triumphs, but were presented as and among the other gold and valuable objects at the head of the procession. In Scipio Nasica's triumph of 191 BC, Livy groups the display of 1,471 golden torcs, 247 pounds of gold bullion, 2,340 pounds of silver, and 234,000 bigati coins.[576] Thus,

[569] Maxfield (1981: 88); Linderski (2001: 3).   [570] Kuttner (1995: 146–7).
[571] 1993: 75 and n. 253.   [572] Quint. *Inst.* 6.3.79–80.
[573] Liv. 43.5.8–9.   [574] Xenoph. *Anab.* 1.2.27.
[575] Polyb. 2.29.7–9.   [576] Liv. 36.40.12–13.

the torcs were presented as a rather typical rich object in the triumphal processions, emphasizing, above all, the quantity of wealth that was brought into Rome
by its display.

The Jewish temple treasures

In the passageway of the arch of Titus, two famed large panels show the Jewish
triumph held by Vespasian and Titus in AD 71. On our left, as we proceed towards
the Capitol, we face the well-known treasures from the temple in Jerusalem, being
carried on *fercula* by soldiers who are just about to enter a triumphal arch.[577] The
holy objects from Jerusalem also appear in Josephus' detailed account of the
triumph in his *Bellum Judaicum*.[578] The passage starts out with a general depiction
of the booty of riches (*BJ* 7.132–6), the animals (136–7), and the prisoners on
display (138–9). Josephus proceeds to more in-depth accounts of two specific
displays, the staged war scenes (139–47)[579] and the temple treasures, then concludes by noting the appearance of the triumphators themselves (148–52):

Λάφυρα δὲ τὰ μὲν ἄλλα χύδην ἐφέρετο, διέπρεπε δὲ πάντων τὰ ἐγκαταληφθέντα τῷ ἐν
Ἱεροσολύμοις ἱερῷ, χρυσῆ τε τράπεζα τὴν ὁλκὴν πολυτάλαντος καὶ λυχνία χρυσῆ μὲν ὁμοίως
πεποιημένη, τὸ δ' ἔργον ἐξήλλακτο τῆς κατὰ τὴν ἡμετέραν χρῆσιν συνηθείας. ὁ μὲν γὰρ μέσος ἦν
κίων ἐκ τῆς βάσεως πεπηγώς, λεπτοὶ δ' ἀπ' αὐτοῦ μεμήκυντο καυλίσκοι τριαίνης σχήματι
παραπλησίαν τὴν θέσιν ἔχοντες, λύχνον ἕκαστος αὐτῶν ἐπ' ἄκρον κεχαλκευμένος· ἑπτὰ δ' ἦσαν
οὗτοι τῆς παρὰ τοῖς Ἰουδαίοις ἑβδομάδος τὴν τιμὴν ἐμφανίζοντες. ὅ τε νόμος ὁ τῶν Ἰουδαίων
ἐπὶ τούτοις ἐφέρετο τῶν λαφύρων τελευταῖος. ἐπὶ τούτοις παρῆσαν πολλοὶ Νίκης ἀγάλματα
κομίζοντες· ἐξ ἐλέφαντος δ' ἦν πάντων καὶ χρυσοῦ ἡ κατασκευή. μεθ' ἃ Οὐεσπασιανὸς ἤλαυνε
πρῶτος καὶ Τίτος εἵπετο, . . .

The spoils in general were borne in unordered heaps; but conspicuous above all stood out
those captured in the temple at Jerusalem: a golden table, many talents in weight, and a
lamp stand, likewise made of gold, but constructed on a different pattern from those,
which we use in daily life. Affixed to a pedestal was a central shaft, from which there
extended slender branches, arranged trident-fashion, a wrought lamp being attached to
the extremity of each branch; of these there were seven, indicating the honour paid to that
number among the Jews. After these, and last in the row of spoils, the Jewish Law was
carried. After these went many men carrying images of Victoria, all made of ivory and
gold. Behind them drove Vespasian, followed by Titus . . .

At first sight, Josephus' description seems to indicate that the temple treasures were
carried just in front of the triumphators in the rear of the procession. Such a position

---

[577] The relief is thoroughly analysed by Pfanner (1983: 50–65, 71–6, Taf. 54–67). See also Ryberg (1955:
146, pl. LII, fig. 79b).

[578] For a discussion of the passage in Josephus, see Beard (2003a: esp. 548–52); Eberhardt (2005).

[579] The description of the war scenes concludes with a short note on the display of ships, 147–8.

would be remarkable indeed, as it is otherwise unheard of in the triumphal history of Rome.[580] For all that we know from the rather abundant sources, the spoils were placed at the beginning of the parade, the prisoners in the rear. And in fact, when we look closer at Josephus' text, it becomes clear that his narrative sequence is more complex than might first be assumed. As stated above, the initial part of the description (132–9) is rather general in style and reflects the traditional triumphal order: spoils, animals, prisoners. Thereafter, Josephus goes into far more detail when recounting the stages with scenes from the war (139–47) and the temple treasures (148–52). These two descriptions could be read as simply forming a more thorough continuation of the preceding sequence of spoils, animals, and prisoners. But they might also be taken as elaborated excursuses of the basic description of the parade already concluded, focusing on two exhibitions that stood out from the rest of the procession in appearance and importance.

Speaking in favour of a sequential description is the fact that Josephus seems recurrently to stress the order of the display: 'After these, and last of all the spoils, the Jewish Law was carried', 'After these went many men carrying images of Victoria, all made of ivory and gold', 'Behind them drove Vespasian, followed by Titus'. Still, there are several circumstances suggesting that we should interpret his description of the temple treasures as non-sequential excursuses.[581] Most importantly, Josephus starts out his account of the temple treasures with a reference to the display of the spoils in general, which were borne χύδην, 'in unordered heaps, as if poured out in floods'. In this, he undoubtedly reconnects to the introductory description of the procession (7.132–6), in which the abundance of riches are described and characterized as having been seen 'not as if carried in procession, but flowing so to speak, like a river' (7.134).[582] Among these spoils, and most conspicuous of them all, were the temple treasures from Jerusalem, λάφυρα ... διέπρεπε δὲ πάντων ... This suggests that the temple treasures belonged to the general group of spoils (λάφυρα), described in the beginning of Josephus' triumphal account and in all probability displayed in the initial part of the parade. In fact, Josephus explicitly states that the Law was shown not only after the other temple treasures, but more importantly τελευταῖος τῶν λαφύρων, 'last in the row of spoils'. This phrasing is crucial, as it tells us clearly that the Law

[580] Michel and Bauernfeind (1969: 246 n. 78): 'Es ist auffallend, daß der an sich rechtliche Begriff der "Beute" erst so spät in der Schilderung des Triumphzuges genannt wird.'

[581] Josephus marks his turn from the general introductory overview to the thorough descriptions of war scenes and temples treasure with emphatic phrases: 'But nothing in the procession excited so much astonishment as' (war stages), 'But conspicuous above all' (treasures).

[582] ... οὐχ ὥσπερ ἐν πομπῇ κομιζόμενον πλῆθος, ἀλλ' ὡς ἄν εἴποι τις ῥέοντα ποταμόν. Contra Michel and Bauernfeind (1969: 246 n. 78), who propose that Josephus in his introductory passage might be referring to the display of spoils from all over the world, while the latter description deals exclusively with the spoils from Palestine.

was shown last in the display of the very spoils which he has already accounted for in the initial part of the description.[583]

With this interpretation, Josephus has allowed himself a more detailed ekphrasis of what were in his eyes the two most prominent displays. The holy treasures formed, as we shall see, the very essence of Jewish culture, and the war scenes filled a crucial role in Josephus' literary monument, as they, as the historian himself maintains, explained the sufferings to which the Jews were destined when they revolted.[584] Both issues were crucial to a historian who not only possessed a profound knowledge of the Jewish religion and culture, but who also, as one of his principal messages, tried to show that the Jews themselves were to blame for their vanquishment and subsequent fate.[585]

Regardless of any difficulties involved, Josephus' text implies that the temple treasures from Jerusalem were placed last of all the spoils. Thus located, they were emphasized as a most important display. Their significance is further stressed by Josephus' description of how they, in contrast to all the other booty, shown in abundant and unsystematic heaps, distinguished themselves by a separate and conspicuous display. The very fact that Josephus provides a rather detailed description of these spoils suggests a pre-eminence out of the ordinary. As we have seen, the ancient authors seldom give thorough portrayals of the individual objects of booty on display.

Had Josephus' description constituted our only source for the display of the temple treasures in the Jewish triumph, his emphasis might well have been interpreted as a manifestation of his Jewish origin, involving both a certain familiarity and a particular interest in the sacred objects from Jerusalem. But, since several of the spoils from the temple also appear on one of the larger reliefs in the passageway of the arch of Titus, there can be no doubt that these objects were regarded as significant from a Roman point of view as well. On this Roman monument, the temple treasures were chosen from the display as *the* characteristics of the Jewish victory and triumph (Fig. 10). This is noteworthy, since very few such depictions of particular pieces of booty exist on our, albeit rather fragmentary, preserved reliefs with triumphal motifs. Being not just any precious goods, but the sacred objects of the Jews, the emphatic depiction of the temple treasures is indeed highly remarkable.

On the famous relief of the arch of Titus, two of the three temple treasures mentioned by Josephus are represented, the golden table and the lamp stand.

---

[583] This interpretation of Josephus' text complicates his description of the temple treasures being followed by images of Victoria, which in their turn precede the triumphators. It seems likely that Vespasian followed the images of Victoria, and that Josephus' μεθ' ἃ refers to the ἀγάλματα Νίκης. However, his description of how these images were seen ἐπὶ τούτοις, 'after these (things)' is very general and could be taken to refer to all of the preceding items and not just to the temple treasures.

[584] Joseph. *BJ* 7.145–6.   [585] Giovannini (1996).

FIGURE 10 Relief panel in the passageway of the arch of Titus in Rome. Three written labels, *tituli*, announce the booty following on biers, including the table of shewbread with vessels and trumpets, the holy Jewish lamp stand, and, probably intended after the third placard, the Jewish law.

Young men carrying placards on high poles walk just in front of each of the two displays. The placards are the written *tituli*, mentioned by literary sources.[586] Carried just in front of spoils, captives, and representations, they announced the identities of the objects and people who followed. Besides the two placards shown just in front of the table and the lamp stand, a third *titulus*, also carried by a young man, is depicted in the rear of the parade at the left end of the relief. No booty follows this third placard, but we should imagine the procession continuing to the left and the placard bearer preceding yet another object, in all probability the third renowned spoil from the Jerusalem temple mentioned by Josephus, the Jewish Law. Josephus describes this as ὁ νόμος, which is usually interpreted as a book scroll containing the Pentateuch.[587] The relief also shows two vessels and two trumpets, placed on and attached to the table respectively. Josephus in fact also mentions vessels of gold from the temple at the end of his

[586] The form and function of the triumphal *tituli* are analysed by Östenberg (forthcoming).
[587] Michel and Bauernfeind (1969: 248 n. 81, with further references).

long triumphal description, telling not of their processional display but stating that they were later dedicated in Vespasian's Templum Pacis.[588]

The objects depicted on the relief of the arch of Titus are customarily identified with the well-known sacred objects of the Jerusalem temple: the seven-branched *menorah*, the table of the shewbread, the vessels carrying frankincense that accompanied the twelve loaves on the table in the temple, and the silver trumpets (*hazozerot*). However, for each of these objects, there is an ongoing debate as to whether they are *the* true, most sacred items of the central Holy Place of the temple, or if they were rather some other lamp stand, table, vessels, and trumpets, also taken from the temple, but of less sacred value to the Jews.[589] The uncertainty of the precise origins of the objects is partly caused by another passage in Josephus, accounting for the sacred treasures that were brought to Titus after the destruction of the temple (*BJ* 6.388–9): 'two lamp stands similar to those deposited in the sanctuary, along with tables, bowls, and platters, all of solid gold and very massive; he further delivered the veils, the high-priests' vestment, including the precious stones, and many other articles used in public worship'. This passage shows that Titus confiscated more than just one lamp stand, one table and a few vessels. However, in the present work, focusing on the Roman context, it is sufficient to observe that, regardless of the precise sacred origin of the particular items, the objects represented on the arch of Titus and shown in the triumph undoubtedly came from, and were displayed as stemming from, the temple of Jerusalem.

Spoils of richness

Even if the Jewish temple treasures were objects of a sacred nature, in the triumph in Rome, they were presented in the traditional manner of precious goods. Hence, they were shown among the rest of the spoils, and their rich material and heaviness were particularly emphasized. Josephus stresses that the table and the lamp stand were made of gold, and he emphasizes that the table weighed many talents. On the arch of Titus, the table and the lamp stand are both transported on *fercula*, each *ferculum* being carried by as many as eight men (normally a bier required four men), stressing the heavy weight of the booty. The heaviness is further underlined by the cushions that each bearer carries on his weighed-down shoulder to ease the burden of the *ferculum* and also by the support-crutch that he holds in his free hand.[590] A larger number of bearers, cushions, and crutches are the customary iconographical traits present in most of

---

[588] Joseph. *BJ* 7.161–2.

[589] For a thorough discussion of the forms and origins of the objects depicted on the arch and for references to earlier works, Yarden (1991), see also Michel and Bauernfeind (1969: 247–8 n. 80).

[590] Pfanner (1983: 51–3, 72, Taf. 54–5, 57, 60–1).

the reliefs that show how pieces of heavy booty were transported in the triumphal parades.[591] Heaviness was of utmost importance when it came to exhibiting riches in the triumphs, and in this respect the temple treasures were no different from profane objects.

In view of the emphasis on the weight and the richness of the spoils of war, it is hardly a coincidence that the one item left out of the depiction on the arch of Titus is the Jewish Law. This was perhaps the most sacred of all the objects from the temple. Josephus states that when a synagogue in Caesarea was attacked, people hurried to protect not the place, but the Torah.[592] As an item of material worth and weight, its value was, however, subordinate to that of the table and the lamp stand, and if depicted, the representation would not have been one that underlined heaviness. Instead, ingeniously, the depiction ends with a *titulus*, marking the display to come without actually having to depict it.

As for the trumpets and the vessels, the vessels had their normal ritual placement together with the shewbread on the table, so their depiction here possibly reflects their processional appearance; the trumpets, on the other hand, were probably placed together with the table on the relief in order to add further objects of ritual importance and, not least, of great value and weight to the representation. The vessels were of gold and the trumpets of silver. Hence, again to emphasize weight and richness, it was not the more sacred *shofar* made of simpler horn, but the long and massive silver instruments that were chosen to represent the triumphal display.

Symbols of defeat

Although the temple treasures were represented as traditional spoils of value, it is still noteworthy that the sacred objects of the Jews were chosen from the abundant spoils to symbolize the triumph. The temple treasures were not just any spoils, but objects that strongly denoted a particular ethnic group. Their display transmitted a clear message of the defeat of the Jews in all aspects— military, political, cultural, and religious.

After the revolt in Judaea had been suppressed, the Roman superiors treated the Jews extremely harshly: thousands of captives were killed or enslaved, the temple was destroyed not to be rebuilt, and the Jewish temple tax was transformed to a Roman *fiscus Iudaicus*.[593] Both political and religious considerations were involved in the Roman conduct towards the Jews. Many Romans were highly sceptical of the religious particularity of the Jews, and criticized and wrote

---

[591] Koeppel (1983: Kat. 11, 71, 97, Abb. 12); Koeppel (1984: Kat. 4, 13, 24–5, Abb. 7, Kat. 20, 13, 49–50, Abb. 28–9); Künzl (1988: fig. 45).

[592] Joseph. *BJ* 2.285–91.

[593] Goodman (1987: 231–51).

ironically of their peculiar practices.[594] Not least, it was the monotheistic firm-
ness, the absence of any cult statue and the imperturbable celebration of the
Sabbath that aroused suspicion and scorn. The revolt in Judaea caused anti-
Jewish tendencies to grow stronger.[595] This is most clearly expressed by Tacitus'
harsh characterization of the Jews in his account of the conflict.[596] In the opinion
of the Roman historian, the customs (*instituta*) of the Jews were *sinistra foeda*,
evil and disgusting, their traditions (*mos*) *absurdus sordidusque*, preposterous and
mean.[597] Religion and politics went hand in hand, and in the Jewish religious
particularity there was an inherent and constant political threat to the Roman
order. This peril was reflected in the rumours that prevailed around this time,
prophecies foretelling that men coming from Judaea would rule the world,[598] and
it was confirmed by the Jewish revolt.[599]

The political threat and the religious otherness were linked also in that, when
the Jews rebelled against Rome, the Jewish state, which was proclaimed, was
centred on the temple in Jerusalem. This extremely rich place,[600] prospering not
least from the taxes paid from all around the Diaspora, now became the core of the
Jewish resistance, and as the rest of Judaea fell by and by, Jerusalem and above all
the temple turned into its last defence. Several walls, around the city, the palace,
and the sanctuary itself, protected the temple.[601] Tacitus attests to its fort-like
appearance: 'The temple was built like a citadel, with walls of its own, which were
constructed with more care and effort than any of the rest; the very colonnades
about the temple made a splendid defence.'[602] Protected by huge fortifications, the
temple and the city of Jerusalem as a whole were considered more or less impregnable. Several Roman generals had tried to conquer the city, but only Pompey had
previously succeeded. Titus certainly regarded it as a great achievement to have
been able to occupy and destroy the city. On the preserved inscription from
another arch built in his honour, placed at the Circus Maximus, we read:

Senatus populusque Romanus Imp. Tito Caesari divi Vespasiani f. Vespasiano Augusto
pontif. max. trib. pot. X. imp. XVII cos. VIII p.p. principi suo quod praeceptis patr.

---

[594] See e.g. Cic. *Flacc.* 28.66–9. Giovannini (1996: 17); Goodman (1997: 302–4); Beard *et al.* (1998*a*:
221–2); Hidal (2001). Beard *et al.* stress the *superstitio* of the Jewish people as opposed to the normative
religio of the Romans, cf. Tac. *Hist.* 5.13.1. They also point out that not all Roman writers were anti-Jewish,
but that the attitudes varied (1998*b*: 273–5); cf. Goodman (1987: 236–7).

[595] Goodman (1987: 237–9); Beard *et al.* (1998*b*: 273).

[596] Tac. *Hist.* 5.1–13. For Tacitus' view of the Jews, see Rosen (1996).

[597] Tac. *Hist.* 5.5.1, 5.5.5.

[598] Ibid. 5.13; Suet. *Vesp.* 4.1; Joseph. *BJ* 6.312–13.

[599] Tac. *Hist.* 5.10.2.

[600] Ibid. 5.8.1.

[601] Ibid. 5.8, 5.11–12. Giovannini (1996: 28).

[602] Tac. *Hist.* 5.12.1: *Templum in modum arcis propriique muri, labore et opere ante alios; ipsae porticus, quis
templum ambibatur, egregium propugnaculum.*

consiliisque et auspiciis gentem Iudaeorum domuit et urbem Hierusolymam omnibus ante se ducibus regibus gentibus aut frustra petitam aut omnino intemtatam delevit.

The senate and the Roman people [dedicated this] to the emperor Titus Caesar Vespasian Augustus, son of the deified Vespasian, pontifex maximus, holder of the tribunician power for the tenth time, imperator for the seventeenth time, consul for the eighth time, father of the fatherland, its princeps because by the example and advice of his father, and under his auspices, he subdued the Jewish people and destroyed the city of Jerusalem, which all generals, kings, and peoples before him had either attacked without success or left entirely unmolested.[603]

The inscription, although technically belonging to another monument, could be read as a caption to the relief on the arch of Titus.[604] Here, as in the procession, the sacred objects appeared as symbols of Jerusalem, a city thought to be almost impregnable. Titus had managed not only to take the city, but had also besieged and destroyed its innermost citadel, the strongly fortified temple, which had formed the centre of the Jewish rebellion. The holy objects thus connoted Roman military supremacy in that they symbolized a fallen walled citadel, not unlike the models of cities on display. Within this fort, the treasures also worked as symbols of the Holy Place, the heart of the temple and fort, from which they stemmed. Formerly accessible to the Jewish priests only, this place had only once before been entered by a Roman—Pompey, who did so by right of conquest (*iure victoriae*).[605] Also by right of conquest, Titus entered, emptied, and razed the temple with its Holy Place. The sacred objects on display showed that this kernel of Jewish resistance, formerly left outside of Roman control, had now been vanquished by the all-embracing hegemony of Rome.

Being symbols of the temple, the treasures on triumphal display also denoted the defeat of the Jewish religion and culture. The temple had been the uniting force and symbolic centre, not only of the Jews in Judaea, but of the entire Diaspora.[606] This was the only temple where, as a Jew, you sacrificed to God, either in person or by way of the taxes you sent there. By destroying the temple, by refusing to re-erect it, and by transforming the Jewish temple tax into the Roman *fiscus Iudaicus*, Vespasian and Titus struck at the very heart of Jewish identity. Tacitus states that, when some of his men urged that the temple should be spared, Titus and others opposed, 'holding the destruction of this temple to be a prime necessity in order to wipe out more completely the religion of

---

[603] *CIL* vi. 944; *ILS* 264; translation based on Goodman and Holloway (1987: 191).

[604] Holloway (1987: 190–1).

[605] Tac. *Hist.* 5.9.1: *Romanorum primus Cn. Pompeius Iudaeos domuit templumque iure victoriae ingressus est.* Del Medico (1964).

[606] Goodman (1997: 311–12).

the Jews'.[607] Once back in Rome, the suppression of Jewish beliefs and practices was manifested by the treasures, which Vespasian and Titus put on triumphal parade.

In the display of the temple treasures from Jerusalem, there also flows an undercurrent of irony and scorn, directed at the religious superstition and the political impertinence of the Jews. In terms of religion, the ritual objects symbolized the particular behaviour of the Jews, which at times resulted in unstrategic decisions, such as the reluctance to fight on the Sabbath or the preference to protect the Torah rather than a site.[608] The objects could thus be seen as representatives of a religiosity that had in fact brought about the fall of its own adherents. Politically, the captured objects might be read as ironical symbols of the Jewish rebellion. The prophecy, which had foretold that the future world rulers would stem from Judaea had turned out to be referring to Vespasian and Titus,[609] now riding in triumph over the very Jewish people who in their self-confident disobedience had assumed it to predict their own mastery.

GOLDEN CROWNS

The Roman triumphal procession also included golden crowns (*coronae aureae*) that had been presented to the triumphator mostly by allied and subdued cities, peoples, and states.[610] The *coronae* were paraded and described as gifts, but the degree of voluntariness in the giving varied highly, as Rome both expected and at times also demanded crowns from loyal and defeated states and leaders. Hence, on parade, the crowns transmitted double meanings, having been offered (more or less willingly) as gifts but received not very differently from other spoils.

Between 201 BC and AD 118, literary sources record golden crowns in more than twenty Roman triumphs and ovations.[611] The tradition continued too, as Servius

---

[607] Tac. *Hist. Frg.* 2: *At contra alii et Titus ipse evertendum in primis templum censebant quo plenius Iudaeorum et Christianorum religio tolleretur*, 'Yet others, and Titus himself, opposed, holding the destruction of this temple to be a prime necessity in order to wipe out more completely the religion of the Jews and the Christians'. The point was thus to wipe out both the Jewish and the Christian religion.

[608] Plut. *Mor.* 169c; Joseph. *BJ* 2.285–91.

[609] Tac. *Hist.* 5.13.

[610] *RE* II (1896), s.v. 'Aurum coronarium', 2552–3 (W. Kubitschek); *RE* IV (1901), s.v. 'corona', 1638–9 (H. O. Fiebiger); Klauser (1944); Millar (1977: 140–2); *NP* ii (1997), s.v. 'Aurum coronarium', 327 (E. Pack); Oakley (1998: 359–60).

[611] Scipio Africanus in 201 BC (App. *Pun.* 66); Flamininus in 194 BC (Liv. 34.52.8–9); M'. Acilius Glabrio in 190 BC (Liv. 37.46.4); L. Aemilius Regillus in 189 BC (Liv. 37.58.4); Scipio Asiaticus in 189 BC (Liv. 37.59.3–4); Fulvius Nobilior in 187 BC (Liv. 39.5.14); Cn. Manlius Vulso in 187 BC (Liv. 39.7.1); L. Manlius Acidinus Fulvianus in 185 BC (Liv. 39.29.6); C. Calpurnius Piso in 184 BC (Liv. 39.42.3); L. Quinctius Crispinus in 184 BC (Liv. 39.42.3–4); A. Terentius Varro in 182 BC (Liv. 40.16.11); L. Aemilius Paullus in 181 BC (Liv. 40.34.8);

FIGURE 11 Four men carry a huge golden crown on a richly adorned *ferculum*. This is one of two golden crowns still seen on the smaller frieze encircling the arch of Trajan at Benevento.

in his late fourth-century commentary on Vergil's *Aeneid* claims that crown gold was sent to triumphators by conquered peoples still in his day.[612] As often, Livy forms our most informative source. He lists golden crowns in twelve processions performed between 194 and 180 BC.

The crowns also appear on two reliefs representing triumphal processions. On the smaller frieze that encircles the arch of Trajan at Benevento, two large crowns can be seen (Fig. 11). The crowns appear quite apart from each other on separate

Q. Fulvius Flaccus in 180 BC (Liv. 40.43.6); L. Aemilius Paullus in 167 BC (Plut. *Aem.* 34.5; Diod. Sic. 31.8.12 (apud Sync.)); Pompey in 61 BC (crowns of pearls, Plin. *Nat.* 37.6.14); Caesar in 46 BC (App. *BCiv.* 2.102; cf. Dio 42.49.3, 42.50.2); L. Antonius in 41 BC (Dio Cass. 48.4.6); Cn. Domitius Calvinus in 36 BC (Dio Cass. 48.42.4–5); Octavian in 29 BC (*IGLS* iii. 718; *JRS* 63 (1973), 58; Millar (1977: 410–11); Verg. *Aen.* 8.721; cf. Aug. *Anc.* 21; Dio Cass. 51.21.4); Claudius in AD 44 (Plin. *Nat.* 33.16.54); Vespasian and Titus in AD 71 (Joseph. *BJ* 7.135); Hadrian, celebrating the posthumous triumph of Trajan in AD 118 (S.H.A. *Hadr.* 6.3–4). When L. Antonius triumphed in 41 BC, he boasted that he had been presented with far more crowns than Marius (Dio Cass. 48.4.6), thereby indicating that Marius too had displayed golden crowns in his triumphs. In 78 BC, according to Appian, over 2,000 golden crowns presented by cities, legions, and friends were carried in Sulla's funeral parade, App. *BCiv.* 1.106.

[612] Serv. *ad Aen.* 8. 721: *aurum coronarium dicit, quod triumphantibus hodieque a victis gentibus datur.* According to the *Historia Augusta*, Aurelian in AD 274 displayed golden crowns that had been presented by all the cities, S.H.A. *Aurel.* 34.3–4, with Merten (1968: 108–11).

FIGURE 12 This imperial relief shows a triumphal procession that includes a golden crown being carried on a *ferculum* by four bearers. They are followed by a group of prisoners, representing a family with mother, father, and child. A wide range of dates has been proposed, from the Augustan to the Severan age.

fercula, each *ferculum* being carried by four bearers.[613] Both crowns are fairly well preserved, and they display a similar design, with several protruding rather large flower heads. A relief in Naples, the date of which is debated, also depicts a triumphal parade that includes a golden crown carried on a *ferculum* by four bearers (Fig. 12).[614] This crown is shaped as a huge laurel wreath.[615]

From the time of the late Republic, Roman triumphators were also offered so-called *aurum coronarium*, crown gold,[616] and the emperors later collected crown gold as a more or less regular tax. Clearly, however, this new custom did not replace the old one altogether, and there was probably a mixed practice, in which sometimes crowns were sent, at others crown gold.[617] Perhaps, the gold was

[613] Andreae (1974: Abb. 425–6). Vessberg (1952: 130), believes that the depiction shows several crowns, each piled up on the other.

[614] Inv. no. 6722 (7516), from the Farnese collection in Rome. Abaecherli (1935/6: pl. II.2); Ryberg (1955: 149–50, pl. LIII, fig. 81c); Koeppel (1983: Kat. 11, 71, 97, Abb. 12); *Trionfi romani*, 123, I.2.5.

[615] Both Festus (p. 504 L s.v. 'triumphales') and Gellius (5.6.5–7) claim that the crowns had originally been made of laurel leaves.

[616] *RE* II (1896), s.v. 'Aurum coronarium', 2552–3 (W. Kubitschek); Klauser (1944); *NP* ii (1997), s.v. 'Aurum coronarium', 327 (E. Pack). The term *aurum coronarium* appears first in Cicero (*Pis.* 37.90), who tells of a law passed by Caesar in 59 BC, which prescribed that *aurum coronarium* was to be collected only when a triumph had been decreed.

[617] In 31 BC, the Syrian city of Rhosus sent Octavian a golden crown (*IGLS* iii. 718; *JRS* 63 (1973), 58; Millar (1977: 410–11)). For the triumph two years later, the cities of Italy offered Octavian crown gold, Aug. *Anc.* 21; Dio Cass. 51.21.4.

occasionally reshaped into crowns specifically for the triumphal display. Mostly, however, the *aurum coronarium* was probably taken up as gold bullion. Dio Cassius states that when Domitius Calvinus triumphed in 36 BC, he used some of the crown gold obtained from the Spanish cities to finance the triumphal celebration itself, while most of it was spent on the Regia.[618]

Golden crowns first appear in Appian's description of Scipio Africanus' triumph over the Carthaginians,[619] but this account is far too general to be read as proof of the historical parade of 201 BC.[620] Most objects, like the golden crowns, are listed without any specific number or weight. Appian also fails to mention the presence of the Numidian King Syphax and the Roman liberated senator Terentius Culleo, both recurrently noted in other sources as the two most conspicuous characters on parade.[621] Some parts of the account (such as the elephants) are most probably correct, but basically, the description should be read as a very general overview of the Roman triumph. Appian himself states as an introduction that: καὶ ὁ τρόπος, ᾧ καὶ νῦν ἔτι χρώμενοι διατελοῦσιν, ἐστὶ τοιόσδε, 'The form [of the triumph], which they still continue to use, is such as this'. Very likely, he included several objects, such as the golden crowns, to transform his own meagre information of Scipio's parade into a full description of a Roman triumph, as it was still performed in his own days.

Next, golden crowns appear in Livy's account of Flamininus' Macedonian triumph in 194 BC.[622] Livy does not explicitly state that this was the first time that golden crowns were seen in a Roman triumph, but two circumstances could nevertheless be taken as such an indication.[623] First, after his text picks up again with book 21, Livy describes in some detail thirteen triumphs and ovations taking place before Flamininus' procession without mentioning any golden crowns.[624] Second, Livy characterizes the 114 golden crowns paraded by Flamininus as gifts from *civitates*. When crowns next appear, in Acilius Glabrio's triumph over Antiochus and the Aetolians in 190 BC, Livy tells that they were 45 in number

---

[618] Dio Cass. 48.42.4–5.

[619] App. *Pun.* 66.

[620] Itgenshorst (2005: 15–17), reaches the same conclusion.

[621] Syphax: Polyb. 16.23.6; Val. Max. 6.2.3; Tac. *Ann.* 12.38; Sil. *Pun.* 17.172–5, 17.629–30; Ampel. 37.1. At 30.45.4–5, Livy maintains that Syphax died before the triumph, but in describing the triumph of Aemilius Paullus (45.39.6–8), he refers to the glorious display of Syphax in Scipio's parade. Culleo: Liv. 30.45.5–6, *Per.* 30, 38.55.1–3; Oros. 4.19.6; Plut. *Mor.* 196e; [Quint.], *Decl. Mai.* 9.20.

[622] Liv. 34.52.8–9: *dona civitatium*.

[623] Livy claims that foreign states had presented golden crowns to Rome at an earlier date. In 342 BC, Carthage sent a crown of 25 pounds to the temple of Jupiter on the Capitol, as Rome celebrated victories over the Samnites, Liv. 7.38.2, with Oakley (1998: 360).

[624] Liv. 26.21.6–10, 28.9.11–18, 30.45.1–6, 31.20, 31.49.2–3, 33.23.4–9, 33.27.1–3, 33.37.10–12, 34.10.3–7, 34.46.2–3.

and defines them as gifts from allied *civitates*.[625] Hereafter, Livy includes crowns in ten further triumphal accounts, without once noting the identity of the donors.[626] This suggests that Livy, or his sources, felt the need to specify the character of the golden crowns as being gifts from city states only when they first appeared in the triumphs. Later on, the crowns having turned into familiar objects, such general information on their obvious nature became superfluous.

Who sent the crowns?

The practice of presenting golden crowns to kings and victors had existed in Greece since at least the fifth century BC, and it was widely in use in the Hellenistic East.[627] When golden crowns first appear as part of the Roman triumphs, they also seem linked to victories in the East. Besides Flamininus and Acilius Glabrio, Livy also tells that L. Aemilius Regillus paraded 29 golden crowns, and Scipio Asiaticus 234 golden crowns, when they triumphed over King Antiochus in 189 BC.[628] Two years later, M. Fulvius Nobilior showed 112 pounds of golden crowns (or probably rather 112 crowns),[629] when performing his triumph over the Aetolians, and Cn. Manlius Vulso put forth 212 crowns after his victory over the Asian Gauls and the peace with Antiochus.[630] Crowns displayed in these eastern triumphs came from cities in or close to the area of the campaign. We know that one of the crowns in Fulvius Nobilior's parade had been given by the defeated city of Ambracia itself,[631] and in Manlius Vulso's triumph, the crowns on display had been presented by all the cities and tribes west of the Taurus Mountains.[632]

In the same period, there are no crowns in Livy's accounts of triumphs held for other victories, in Spain and Gaul.[633] Western triumphs start including crowns only with L. Manlius Acidinus Fulvianus' *ovatio* for his victories in *Hispania citerior* in 185 BC.[634] Crowns then appear in a number of parades held over Spain

[625] Liv. 37.46.4: *dona sociarum civitatium*.

[626] Liv. 37.58.4, 37.59.3–4, 39.5.14, 39.7.1, 39.29.6, 39.42.3–4, 40.16.11, 40.34.8, 40.43.6.

[627] Klauser (1944: 134–7); Millar (1977: 140). Callixenus claims that as many as 3,200 golden crowns were paraded by Ptolemy II Philadelphus in Alexandria, Ath. 5.202d.

[628] Liv. 37.58.4, 37.59.3–4.

[629] Livy (39.5.14) states that golden crowns with a total weight of 112 pounds were displayed in the triumph, but the one given by Ambracia alone weighed 150 pounds (Polyb. 21.30.10–11; Liv. 38.9.13), and Nobilior must have shown other crowns as well. Since all other Livy's reports on golden crowns shown in triumphs record their number, the 112 here probably refers to number rather than weight.

[630] Liv. 39.7.1.   [631] Polyb. 21.30.10–11; Liv. 38.9.13.

[632] Polyb. 21.34.4–5; Liv. 38.37.4–5, 39.6.1. When Acilius Glabrio had defeated Antiochus in 191 BC, Philip of Macedon sent a golden crown to the temple of Jupiter Capitolinus in Rome, Liv. 36.35.12–13. We do not know if Glabrio showed the crown in his triumph.

[633] Between 200 and 189 BC, twelve triumphs and ovations are recorded for victories in Spain and Gaul.

[634] Liv. 39.26.6: 52 crowns.

and Liguria down to 180 BC.[635] We do not know who sent these gifts. Possibly, the peoples of Spain and Liguria offered some of them. Others could have been sent from the cities in the East, who may well have continued the tradition of presenting gifts to Roman triumphators when they were successful in the West. We know that in the late Republic golden crowns came from areas far away from the scenes of battle. When Cn. Domitius Calvinus triumphed for his victories in Spain 36 BC, Dio Cassius states that he only accepted the crown gold from the Spanish cities,[636] thus implying that many other areas had offered gold as well. Later, among the crowns carried in Claudius' triumph over Britannia in AD 44, placards announced one as presented by *Hispania citerior* weighing 7,000 pounds and one from *Gallia comata* weighing 9,000 pounds.[637]

All through Roman history, crowns for triumphs were mainly given by allied and defeated cities, states, and monarchs who wanted to express their loyalty or manifest their submission. Tertullian calls golden crowns *coronae provinciales*,[638] and Servius claims that defeated peoples were the ones who gave crown gold.[639] Italy itself seldom appears among the donors, but in 47 BC, Caesar did collect crown money from the Italian cities.[640] The generals of the late Republic were often in desperate need of money to pay their soldiers, and it could be that this period saw extractions of gold from Italy that were not normally practised.[641]

In 41 BC, L. Antonius, the brother of the triumvir, went even further. When performing a triumph over some peoples in the Alps, he boasted that he had been given many golden crowns, particularly from the city, tribe by tribe.[642] This is an exceptional remark on what must have been a very special procedure. At no other time does Rome appear among the givers of golden crowns for a triumph,[643] and

---

[635] Liv. 39.42.3–4, 40.16.11, 40.34.8, 40.43.6: C. Calpurnius Piso and L. Quinctius Crispinus over the Lusitanians and the Celtiberians in 184 BC (83 crowns each), A. Terentius Varro over *Hispania citerior* in 182 BC (*ovatio*; 67 crowns), L. Aemilius Paullus over the Ligurians in 181 BC (25 golden crowns), Q. Fulvius Flaccus over the Celtiberians in 180 BC (124 crowns).

[636] Dio Cass. 48.42.4–5.

[637] Plin. *Nat.* 33.16.54: *Claudius successor eius, cum de Brittannia triumpharet, inter coronas aureas VII pondo habere quam contulisset Hispania citerior, VIIII quam Gallia comata, titulis indicavit.* Claudius also received crown gold for his British victory from a *synodos* of athletes at Hermopolis, Mitteis and Wilchen (1912: 184–7, no. 156); Millar (1977: 141).

[638] Tert. *Coron.*13.1. Klauser (1944: 139–40).

[639] Serv. *ad Aen.* 8.721.

[640] Caesar also collected crown money from foreign kings, Dio 42.49.3, 42.50.2.

[641] Dio states that those who managed to obtain a triumph through their friendships with Antony or Octavian in the mid-30s used this occasion as a pretext to demand large amounts of crown gold from the cities, Dio Cass. 49.42.3.

[642] Dio Cass. 48.4.6: καὶ παρὰ τοῦ δήμου κατὰ φυλήν, . . . Earlier on, Antonius had led a commission that distributed public lands to veterans and poor, for which he was appointed patron of the thirty-five tribes.

[643] According to the *Historia Augusta* (*Alex. Sev.* 32.5), Alexander Severus sent back *aurum coronarium* to Rome. We do not know why this gold was given.

according to Dio Cassius, Antonius boasted that he was the first victor to have been given crowns by the people. Dio explains this unusual procedure by referring to the influence of Fulvia, Antonius' famous sister-in-law, and to the bribes secretly distributed. In 29 BC, the *municipia* and *coloniae* of Italy also offered Octavian crown gold for his triumph, but both Dio Cassius and Augustus himself maintain that he chose not to accept it.[644] Octavian's choice was, I believe, very likely an explicit response to the highly untraditional act of his former enemy L. Antonius, the brother of his most bitter rival, Antony. As in so many other cases, Octavian's conduct seems to have set the standard. Later, Hadrian, when staging Trajan's posthumous triumph, also sent back the crown gold offered from Italy.[645]

Gifts or spoils?

The case of L. Antonius, although an exception, sheds light on the contradictory nature of the golden crowns. After all, in their capacity as personal gifts, crowns did not exclude domestic donors. Describing Scipio's triumph, Appian also states that the golden crowns had been presented as a reward for the triumphator's bravery by cities, allies, and even by the army itself.[646] Especially in the eastern tradition, crowns were tokens of personal glory, and cities and monarchs often presented them specifically to the Roman victorious commander. The custom is reflected in Diodorus Siculus and Plutarch's account of the triumph held by Aemilius Paullus, where 400 golden crowns appear immediately before the triumphator himself.[647] Thus located, they celebrated first the bravery and victory of Aemilius Paullus himself and were displayed only secondly as booty of Rome.

However, no Latin account suggests that golden crowns were specifically bestowed on or attached to the victorious general. According to Livy, in Flamininus' triumph held over the Macedonian King Philip in 194 BC, also lasting for three days, the crowns inaugurated the third day's celebration.[648] In other processions, Livy implies that the crowns were carried among other spoils in the opening part of the parade.[649] For example, he lists the contents of Scipio Asiaticus' triumph in 189 BC as: 224 military standards, 134 representations of cities, 1,231

---

[644] Aug. *Anc.* 21; Dio Cass. 51.21.4.

[645] Hadrian also reduced the sums sent from the provinces, S.H.A. *Hadr.* 6.5, cf. *Ant. P.* 4.10, *Alex. Sev.* 32.5.

[646] App. *Pun.* 66. As discussed, this passage is an account of the triumph in general rather than the specific parade held by Scipio Africanus in 201 BC.

[647] Diod. Sic. 31.8.12 (apud Sync.); Plut. *Aem.* 34.5.

[648] Liv. 34.52.8–9.

[649] Liv. 37.46.4, 37.58.4, 37.59.3–5, 39.5.14, 39.7.1, 39.29.6, 39.42.3–4, 40.16.11, 40.34.8, 40.43.6.

ivory tusks, 234 golden crowns, 137,420 pounds of silver, 224,000 Attic tetra-drachmae, 321,070 cistophori, 140,000 Philippic gold coins, 1,423 pounds of silver vases, and 1,023 pounds of gold vases.[650] The captives followed. When C. Calpur-nius Piso and L. Quinctius Crispinus triumphed in 184 BC, Piso first displayed 83 golden crowns and 12,000 pounds of silver.[651] According to Livy, Crispinus a few days later showed the same amount of gold and silver (*tantundem auri atque argenti*), thereby telling us indirectly that the crowns were counted as pure gold bullion and recorded as such in the treasury after the parade. Being rich spoils, their number and/or weight were clearly specified, on preceding *tituli* and in the official archives. Livy always provides the number of crowns on processional display, and Appian, for example, states that Caesar showed 2,822 golden crowns weighing 20,414 pounds.

The friezes on the arch of Benevento and in the National Museum in Naples tell the same story (Figs. 11, 12). These representations are very far from being photographical documentations of any exact triumphal order. Still, it is of importance that the crowns are depicted detached from the triumphator. On the relief from the Naples Museum, the crown precedes a group of prisoners, and no celebrating general is seen. On the arch at Benevento, the crowns appear far from the triumphator, in exactly the same way as the other spoils: preceded by *tituli* and carried on *fercula*. Their heavy weight is emphasized; four men are employed to carry the biers, and all are depicted with cushions on their shoulder and support-crutches in their hands.

Most of our evidence thus suggests that golden crowns were normally taken up as spoils of Rome. Rather than the private possessions of the triumphant general, in the Roman tradition, they were thought of (though perhaps not always treated) as public property.[652] Thus, the *lex Servilia*, proposed in 63 BC and opposed by Cicero, decreed that all gold and silver from spoils that had not been placed in the treasury or used for public building should be turned over to the decemvirs. There is no difference between the gold and silver taken as booty and the gold given as crowns; the spoils of worth are listed as: *aurum, argentum ex praeda, ex manubiis, ex coronario*.[653] We might also note that foreign peoples and rulers often sent crowns of gold as gifts to Rome, and asked to have them deposited in the temple of Jupiter on the Capitoline hill.[654] In this, there was a

---

[650] Liv. 37.59.3–5.

[651] Liv. 39.42.2–4.

[652] I will not here go into the controversial debate of *manubiae* and to what extent the general had rights to the war booty. The important point in this context is that whether the general took much or none of the booty for private use, the items chosen for public triumphal display were exhibited primarily as belonging to Rome.

[653] Cic. *Leg. Agr.* 2.22.59.

[654] See e.g. Liv. 7.38.2, 28.39.19, 36.35.12–13, 43.6.6, 44.14.3.

parallel tradition of bestowing on Rome, not the triumphators in private, golden crowns as signs of victory and loyalty.

To sum up, Appian, Plutarch, and Diodorus Siculus all suggest that golden crowns were to some degree presented as personal gifts of the triumphator. Their texts could be taken as historical comments on exceptional Roman behaviour, or as Greek literary reflections of traditional eastern expectations. In either case, their accounts imply that the crowns kept some of their character as private prizes for a brave and successful victor even when taken up and displayed as Roman spoils. In the late Republic, there are also some indications that crowns were collected as private property from domestic donors. Still, these instances appear as exceptions to the Roman tradition. On our preserved friezes, there is no doubt that the crowns are represented as spoils, and the literary sources paint a similar picture.

On parade in the triumphal processions, the crowns had on one hand a symbolic value, demonstrating that the Roman dominance ranged far outside the particular area of the victory celebrated; and on the other hand an actual value, specified by the amount of gold they contained. Their design as wreaths embodied triumph itself, and was paralleled by other crowns of victory and bravery carried in the parade, by the triumphator, cheering soldiers and Roman partakers alike. The donors of the crowns, as specified on written *tituli*, advertised far-flung subjugation and participation, and their multitude and weight gave form to tremendous monetary value.

THREE

Captives

PRISONERS

Human prisoners formed a key element in the Roman triumphal procession. Literary sources frequently mention captives on display, and they even suggest that when actual prisoners were lacking, others had to play their part in order to make the procession complete.[1] Prisoners on triumphal parade also appear on a number of preserved reliefs. In fact, human captives constitute a stock motive in Roman art in general,[2] depictions that both manifest foreign submission and evoke the common display of prisoners in the parades themselves.

Masses and leaders

A few literary passages claim that thousands of prisoners were led in some of the triumphs held in the fifth and fourth centuries BC.[3] The figures seem very high, but it is clear that captives were at times exhibited in considerable numbers. Livy, describing the debate that preceded the Macedonian triumph of Aemilius Paullus in 167 BC, refers to the *turba captivorum* that awaited the procession at the Circus Flaminius.[4] Many captives were, however, sold as slaves on or close by the battlefield, and the evidence mostly suggests a selective process, in which the captives fit to make a show in Rome were picked out for the triumph, while the rest were auctioned off immediately.[5] For example, after taking Numantia, Scipio Aemilianus selected fifty prisoners to be displayed in his triumph and sold the rest.[6]

For triumphs held after the mid-fourth century BC, no source specifies the total number of captives led on parade. This silence is highly revealing, suggesting

---

[1] Caligula and Domitian were both accused of having bought or dressed up captives in their triumphs, Pers. 6.43–7; Suet. *Cal.* 47; Tac. *Agr.* 39.

[2] See e.g. Levi (1952); Schneider (1986).

[3] Dion. Hal. 6.17.2; Eutrop. 2.5.2; Liv. 7.27.8–9.

[4] Liv. 45.39.14.

[5] e.g. Cic. *Att.* 5.20.5; Paus. 7.16.7–8; App. *Iber.* 98. As wars were fought further away from Rome, practical reasons alone often brought about an immediate selling of the captives. Hence, on tour in Galatia, Cn. Manlius Vulso sold his captives, as he had no possibility of arranging for their transportation, App. *Syr.* 42.

[6] App. *Iber.* 98.

that, unlike the valuables, which were precisely quantified, the precise total number of prisoners was not of primary importance to the records.[7] Numbers do occur, but only in respect of the prominent prisoners. Eminence was central, and out of the entire company of prisoners, attention was directed almost exclusively to the smaller group of distinguished captives on parade. Most figures stem from Livy, who maintains, for instance, that M'. Acilius Glabrio displayed thirty-six noble captives in 190 BC and that Scipio Asiaticus led thirty-two royal commanders, prefects, and nobles the year after.[8] Other authors provide similar figures. For example, Diodorus Siculus states that Aemilius Paullus led 250 officers in his parade and Plutarch that Lucullus showed 60 of Mithridates' friends and generals in 63 BC.[9]

Beside the principal opponent, there were two basic categories of distinguished prisoners on display. One was the family and the relatives of the king or chief, people related by blood and marriage to the principal adversary. The other category consisted of commanders and friends of the king or chief, captives whose bond to the enemy superior was political and who had been military opponents of Rome. Of the two groups, the family and relatives of the king or chief definitely attracted more attention than the political associates. For example, while the ancient accounts often give the identities of leading family members on parade, they seldom provide such information about the prominent political captives. As an example, we might look at Appian's description of Pompey's triumph in 61 BC (*Mith.* 116–17):

(116) ..., καὶ πλῆθος αἰχμαλώτων τε καὶ λῃστῶν, οὐδένα δεδεμένον ἀλλ' ἐς τὰ πάτρια ἐσταλμένους. (117) Αὐτοῦ δὲ τοῦ Πομπηίου προῆγον ὅσοι τῶν πεπολεμημένων βασιλέων ἡγεμόνες ἢ παῖδες ἢ στρατηγοὶ ἦσαν, οἱ μὲν αἰχμάλωτοι ὄντες οἱ δὲ ἐς ὁμηρείαν δεδομένοι, τριακόσιοι μάλιστα καὶ εἴκοσι καὶ τέσσαρες. ἔνθα δὴ καὶ ὁ Τιγράνους ἦν παῖς Τιγράνης, καὶ πέντε Μιθριδάτου, Ἀρταφέρνης τε καὶ Κῦρος καὶ Ὀξάθρης καὶ Δαρεῖος καὶ Ξέρξης, καὶ θυγατέρες Ὀρσάβαρίς τε καὶ Εὐπάτρα. παρήγετο δὲ καὶ ὁ Κόλχων σκηπτοῦχος Ὀλθάκης, καὶ Ἰουδαίων βασιλεὺς Ἀριστόβουλος, καὶ οἱ Κιλίκων τύραννοι, καὶ Σκυθῶν βασίλειοι γυναῖκες, καὶ ἡγεμόνες τρεῖς Ἰβήρων καὶ Ἀλβανῶν δύο, καὶ Μένανδρος ὁ Λαοδικεύς, ἵππαρχος τοῦ Μιθριδάτου γενόμενος.

(116) ... and a multitude of captives and pirates, none of them bound, but all arrayed in their native costumes. (117) Before Pompey himself went the chiefs, sons, and generals of

---

[7] In contrast, when giving battle results, Livy and others often provide the total number of captives taken (Ziolkowski, 1990).

[8] Glabrio: Liv. 37.46.4–5; Livy has previously stated (37.3.8) that Glabrio brought 43 *principes Aetolorum* to Rome as captives. If the figures are correct, some of the prisoners died or even escaped before the triumph (Briscoe, 1981: 363). In fact, Livy maintains that Damocritus, the leader of the Aetolians, killed himself a few days before the procession, as he was followed after having escaped from prison, 37.46.5. Scipio: 37.59.5–6. For more numbers, see Liv. *Per.* 19, 39.5.16–17, 39.7.2. At times, Livy labels the prisoners *multi*: 33.23.5, 34.52.9, 40.34.9.

[9] Diod. Sic. 31.8.12 (apud Sync.); Plut. *Luc.* 37.3. See also App. *Mith.* 117 for Pompey's triumph.

the kings against whom he had fought, who were present (some having been captured and others given as hostages) to the number of 324. Among them were Tigranes, the son of Tigranes, and five sons of Mithridates, namely Artaphernes, Cyrus, Oxathres, Darius, and Xerxes, also his daughters, Orsabaris and Eupatra. Olthaces, chief of the Colchians, was also led in the procession, and Aristobulus, king of the Jews, the tyrants of the Cilicians, and the female rulers of the Scythians, three chiefs of the Iberians, two of the Albanians, and Menander the Laodicean, who had been chief of cavalry to Mithridates.[10]

Appian describes two different groups of prisoners. First comes a multitude of prisoners and pirates, who are not identified by name, but form an anonymous mass, grouped according to their origins. Thereafter, Appian gives a rather detailed description of the eminent prisoners led before Pompey in the parade, specifying their number as 324. Emphasis is put on the defeated rulers and their families: Appian identifies only one of Mithridates' generals, but gives the names of all his seven children. To parade the royal family was obviously a greater achievement than to lead military commanders in the train.

To give another example, after the battle of Pydna, a thousand leading Achaeans, Polybius included, were taken to Rome accused of having collaborated with King Perseus.[11] Other Greek and Macedonian political leaders associated with King Perseus were publicly summoned to Rome,[12] and yet others were searched out at diverse locations by letters.[13] The testimonies give a rather detailed picture of the prominent prisoners who were transported to Rome, certainly to be displayed in the triumph.[14] Still, Plutarch and Diodorus Siculus summarize the presence of all Macedonian and Greek leaders in Paullus' parade in just a few words.[15] Instead, both go into exhaustive depictions of the weaponry and valuables on display, and Plutarch provides a lengthy account of Perseus, his children, and their attendants. Augustus' words in his *Res Gestae* reflect the same concern for displaying enemy kings and their families: *In triumphis meis ducti sunt ante currum meum reges aut regum liberi novem,* 'In my triumphs, nine kings or children of kings were led before the car'.[16] There is

[10] Cf. Plut. *Pomp.* 45.

[11] Polyb. 32.5.7; Liv. 45.34.9, 45.35.2. Tagliafico (1995).

[12] Liv. 45.32.3–7. All who had held some office under the king and also his friends were ordered to leave Macedonia and travel to Italy together with their sons over 15 years of age. Many Greek leaders were also searched out, Liv. 45.35.1–3, see also Polyb. 30.13.6–11; Liv. 45.31.9–11, 45.34.9.

[13] Polybius tells of how King Ptolemy by way of such a letter was ordered to send Polyaratus the Rhodian to Rome, Polyb. 30.9.

[14] Livy, 45.35.1–3, states that all the prisoners and hostages arrived in Rome before Aemilius Paullus: Perseus and Gentius with their families, the horde of other prisoners, the Macedonians, who had been ordered to come to Rome, and the leaders of Greece, who had been summoned there.

[15] Plut. *Aem.* 34.2; Diod. Sic. 31.8.12 (apud Sync.).

[16] Aug. *Anc.* 4.

no word of enemy commanders and no total numbers of prisoners displayed. Only the number of kings and their children was important enough to merit a place in Augustus' own summary of his deeds.

Kings and chiefs

Of all the *captivi nobiles* led in a Roman triumph, none attracted more attention than the principal adversary, the king or chief of the enemy. The inhabitants of Rome must often have had a rather vague conception of the precise nature of enemies and lands fought afar. The obvious exception was the enemy ruler, on whose actions, character, and physical appearance rumours and debate often focused. Once defeated and led through the city, the display of a Perseus or Jugurtha, famed kings and feared adversaries, made the strongest visual impressions on the spectators and afterwards reappeared as memorable moments of glory in the writings. Not for nothing had Caesar saved Vercingetorix for six years, only to have him displayed and executed in his Gallic triumph in 46 BC.[17]

The *dux* or *rex* was often conspicuously staged. When Fabius Maximus triumphed over the Gauls in 120 BC, he had Bituitus, king of the Arverni, displayed as in battle, dressed in his many-coloured arms and mounted on a silver chariot (Fig. 5).[18] Some twenty years later, in the triumph held by Marius over the Cimbri and Teutones, Teutobodus, the king of the Teutones made a similar spectacular sight (*insigne spectaculum*). According to Florus, the king, being of extraordinary stature, towered above the trophies of his defeat.[19] Placed aloft, the principal enemy commander was evidently staged as the visual antipode of the triumphator.[20] This is most clearly seen in the case of Bituitus, who, just like the triumphant general, rode in a chariot. But while the vehicle of the Roman general was that of victory and triumph, the one that carried the besieged enemy *rex* connoted his defeat and vain attempt to oppose Roman supremacy.

The visual interplay between the triumphator and the vanquished chief was strengthened by their close processional location. The superior enemy commander came last in line of spoils and captives, followed only by his friends and associates. Hence, his place was close in front of the triumphator. In this way, the

---

[17] Vercingetorix: Dio Cass. 40.41.3, 43.19.4; cf. Plut. *Caes.* 27.5. As an example of the sentiments felt in Rome at the sight of a previously feared enemy commander now led in chains, we might also quote Plutarch on Marius' exhibition of Jugurtha in 104 BC (*Mar.* 12.2): 'This was a sight which they had despaired of beholding, nor could anyone have expected, while Jugurtha was alive, to conquer the enemy; so versatile was he in adapting himself to the turns of fortune and so great craft did he combine with his courage.'

[18] Flor. *Epit.* 1.37.5–6.   [19] Flor. *Epit.* 1.38.10.

[20] Beard (2007) emphasizes that the triumphator always risked being visually outshone by the leading captive.

parade intensified as the objects passed by, culminating in the major exponents, the defeated king or chief, and the king of the day, the Roman triumphator. On the last day of Aemilius Paullus' Macedonian triumph, Plutarch tells how King Perseus with his retinue was seen just before the triumphator (Plut. *Aem.* 34):

Αὐτὸς δὲ τῶν τέκνων ὁ Περσεὺς καὶ τῆς περὶ αὐτὰ θεραπείας κατόπιν ἐπορεύετο, φαιὸν μὲν ἱμάτιον ἀμπεχόμενος καὶ κρηπῖδας ἔχων ἐπιχωρίους, ὑπὸ δὲ μεγέθους τῶν κακῶν πάντα θαμβοῦντι καὶ παραπεπληγμένῳ μάλιστα τὸν λογισμὸν ἐοικώς. καὶ τούτῳ δ᾽ εἵπετο χορὸς φίλων καὶ συνήθων, βεβαρημένων τὰ πρόσωπα πένθει, καὶ τῷ πρὸς Περσέα βλέπειν ἀεὶ καὶ δακρύειν ἔννοιαν παριστάντων τοῖς θεωμένοις ὅτι τὴν ἐκείνου τύχην ὀλοφύρονται τῶν καθ᾽ ἑαυτοὺς ἐλάχιστα φροντίζοντες. καίτοι προσέπεμψε τῷ Αἰμιλίῳ δεόμενος μὴ πομπευθῆναι καὶ παραιτούμενος τὸν θρίαμβον. ὁ δὲ τῆς ἀνανδρίας αὐτοῦ καὶ φιλοψυχίας, ὡς ἔοικε, καταγελῶν, " Ἀλλὰ τοῦτο γ᾽," εἶπε, "καὶ πρότερον ἦν ἐπ᾽ αὐτῷ καὶ νῦν ἐστιν, ἂν βούληται·" δηλῶν τὸν πρὸ αἰσχύνης θάνατον, ὃν οὐχ ὑπομείνας ὁ δείλαιος, ἀλλ᾽ ὑπ᾽ ἐλπίδων τινῶν ἀπομαλακισθεὶς ἐγεγόνει μέρος τῶν αὑτοῦ λαφύρων.

Ἐφεξῆς δὲ τούτοις ἐκομίζοντο χρυσοῖ στέφανοι τετρακόσιοι τὸ πλῆθος, οὓς αἱ πόλεις ἀριστεῖα τῆς νίκης τῷ Αἰμιλίῳ μετὰ πρεσβειῶν ἔπεμψαν. εἶτ᾽ αὐτὸς ἐπέβαλλεν ἅρματι κεκοσμημένῳ διαπρεπῶς ἐπιβεβηκώς, ἀνὴρ καὶ δίχα τοσαύτης ἐξουσίας ἀξιοθέατος, ἀλουργίδα χρυσόπαστον ἀμπεχόμενος καὶ δάφνης κλῶνα τῇ δεξιᾷ προτείνων. ἐδαφνηφόρει δὲ καὶ σύμπας ὁ στρατός, τῷ μὲν ἅρματι τοῦ στρατηγοῦ κατὰ λόχους καὶ τάξεις ἑπόμενος, ᾄδων δὲ τὰ μὲν ᾠδάς τινας πατρίους ἀναμεμιγμένας γέλωτι, τὰ δὲ παιᾶνας ἐπινικίους καὶ τῶν διαπεπραγμένων ἐπαίνους εἰς τὸν Αἰμίλιον περίβλεπτον ὄντα καὶ ζηλωτὸν ὑπὸ πάντων, οὐδενὶ δὲ τῶν ἀγαθῶν ἐπίφθονον.

Behind the children and their train of attendants walked Perseus himself, clad in a dark robe and wearing the high boots of his country, but the magnitude of his evils made him resemble one who is utterly dumbfounded and bewildered. He, too, was followed by a company of friends and intimates, whose faces were heavy with grief, and whose tearful gaze continually fixed upon Perseus gave the spectators to understand that it was his misfortune which they bewailed, and that their own fate least of all concerned them. And yet Perseus had sent to Aemilius begging not to be led in the procession and asking to be left out of the triumph. But Aemilius, in mockery, as it would seem, of the king's cowardice and love of life, had said: 'But this at least was in his power before, and is so now, if he should wish it,' signifying death in preference to disgrace; for this, however, the coward had not the heart, but was made weak by no one knows what hopes, and became a part of his own spoils.

Next in order to these were carried wreaths of gold, four hundred in number, which the cities had sent with their embassies to Aemilius as prizes for his victory. Next, mounted on a chariot of magnificent adornment, came Aemilius himself, a man worthy to be looked upon even without such marks of power, wearing a purple robe interwoven with gold, and holding forth in his right hand a spray of laurel. The whole army also carried sprays of laurel, following the chariot of their general by companies and divisions, and singing, some of them diverse songs intermingled with jesting, as the ancient custom was, and others paeans of victory and hymns in praise of the achievements of Aemilius, who was gazed upon and admired by all, and envied by no one that was good.

Aemilius Paullus and Perseus played the two central parts in the triumphal performance. They appeared not far from each other during the last day's parade, forming the visual climax of the manifestation. The account in Plutarch compares and contrasts the two principal characters. His antithetical ekphrasis certainly reveals a strong literary dramaturgy, but might not be that far away from how the main characters of a triumphal play were staged and perceived also on the streets of Rome.

Both Perseus and Aemilius Paullus were preceded and announced by golden objects intimately linked to their own persons: Perseus by his golden and rich belongings, Paullus by the golden crowns. Perseus' items were luxury personal possessions and royal insignia, of which he had now been deprived, symbolizing the very loss of his royal powers. Paullus' golden crowns also had royal connotations, but they were tokens of courage and victory, bestowed on the triumphator by the cities, and contrasting with the cowardliness and defeat of the Macedonian king. Furthermore, although symbolically linked to the triumphator, the golden crowns in reality belonged to Rome. Thus, in contrast to the display of Perseus' private luxuries, Paullus' crowns emphasized the moral superiority of the Roman triumphator. They also marked the loyalty towards Paullus and Rome of Perseus' former Macedonian subjects.

King and triumphator were also contrasted by way of the retinues that followed them. After Perseus came his friends and intimates, all focusing on the fate of their leader. Similarly, the retinue that followed Aemilius, the soldiers in the army, had their attention directed towards their general. The sentiments and behaviour of the two congregations are strongly opposed, Perseus' company lamenting the fate of their leader, Paullus' singing songs in praise of theirs. The ritual jests made at the expense of Paullus enhanced his status as victor, and as a contrast, Perseus was mocked for his cowardice.[21] In their outfit too, the two leaders were opposed. Aemilius wore the traditional festal royal dress of the triumphator, appearing as king. Perseus, the former king, instead was clothed in black, the customary colour of mourning.[22] And while Paullus is thought worthy of gaze even without his royal attire, Perseus appears at a loss when deprived of his.[23] To further enhance the contrasting effects, Plutarch states that while all eyes were directed at Aemilius, Perseus passed by almost unnoticed,

---

[21] Cf. Cic. *Tusc.* 5.40.118; Plut. *Mor.* 198b. Plutarch (*Aem.* 19), referring to Polybius, describes Perseus' cowardice on the battlefield, but also maintains that Posidonius defended the actions and character of the king.

[22] Zonaras 9.24.3–4, states that the royal prisoners were dressed in the fashion of captives, ἐν τῷ τῶν αἰχμαλώτων σχήματι.

[23] Cf. Flor. *Epit.* 1.28.13–14.

since much focus and compassion was instead conducted towards his children, who walked just in front of him. Some of Paullus' children were also present, accompanying his father behind his triumphal car.[24]

In Roman memory, Aemilius Paullus' triumph held a special place, a moment of glory that was largely due to the presence of the vanquished King Perseus. Of all the leaders fought, conquered, and paraded, the royal ones counted the most. In Pompey's triumph, placards trumpeted the names of kings conquered: Tigranes the Armenian, Artoces the Iberian, Oroezes the Albanian, Darius the Mede, Aretas the Nabatean, Antiochus of Commagene.[25] And while the entries in the *Fasti triumphales* give the specific people brought down (*de Liguribus, de Aetoleis*) or the place of campaign (*ex Asia, ex Hispania ulteriore*), the name of the principal adversary appears only when he was a king.[26] In these specific cases, the *Fasti* further stress the royal defeat by adding that the triumph was held *de rege*. For example, Dentatus celebrated his triumph in 275 BC *de Samnitibus et rege Pyrrho*, in 194 BC, Flamininus triumphed *ex Macedonia et rege Philippo*, and in 188 BC, Q. Fabius Labeo performed his naval triumph *ex Asia de rege Antiocho*.[27]

Triumphs held over kings were the ones most highly praised in the literary tradition, and the deeds of Dentatus and Flamininus garnered attention for generations even though they had not been able to lead Pyrrhus and Philip in person in their parades.[28] Nevertheless, the processions in which a defeated king

[24] The fate of the children adds to the contrasting effects between the two men, as two of Paullus' sons died within a few days of each other, at the very time of the triumphal celebration. Plutarch and other authors marvel at the freak of Fortuna, who has the children of the vanquished king led as captives but unharmed in the triumph, while Aemilius, saviour of Rome, suffers the personal misfortune of losing his, Liv. 45.40.6–46.12, *Per.* 45; Vell. Pat. 1.10.3–5; Val. Max. 5.10.2; Sen. *Dial.* 6.13.3–4; Plut. *Aem.* 35–6, *Mor.* 198c–d; App. *Mac.* 19; Ampel. 18.13.

[25] Some of the kings appeared in person, App. *Mith.* 117; Plut. *Pomp.* 45.4. Some were also named on the tablet that Pompey put up for Minerva, Diod. Sic. 40.4 (Const. Exc.), see also Oros. 6.5.6.

[26] Marcellus' triumph of 222 BC does name Viridomarus, but only in the lines added to call attention to the prime spoils of honour: *isque spolia opima rettu[lit] | duce hostium Virdumaro ad Clastid[ium | interfecto]*.

[27] Degrassi, *Inscr. It.* 13:1. The entry for Flamininus has been only partly preserved: *[ex Macedonia et rege] Philippo . . .*, cf. the *Fasti triumphales Urbisalvienses*, Degrassi, *Inscr. It.* 13:1, 338. The king's name has also been preserved, or can be reconstructed, in the entries for the following triumphs: M'. Valerius Maximus *de Poenis et rege Siculorum Hierone* in 263 BC, L. Aemilius Regillus and Scipio Asiaticus, who performed triumphs *ex Asia de rege Antiocho* in 189 and 188 BC, Aemilius Paullus and Cn. Octavius in 167 BC *ex Macedonia et rege Perse*, and L. Anicius Gallus triumphing *de rege Genfio* in the same year (the *Fasti triumphales Urbisalvienses* have *de rege Gentio*), Q. Fabius Maximus *de Allobrogibus et rege Arvernorum Betuito* in 120 BC, Q. Caecilius Metellus holding a triumph *de Numideis et rege Iugurtha* in 106 BC. The entry for Marius in 104 BC is heavily damaged, but without doubt, *de Numideis et rege Iugurtha* should be reconstructed here too, as proposed by Degrassi. Several other damaged entries once must have named the vanquished king, such as Scipio Africanus' triumph in 201 BC, which certainly recorded *de rege Syphace*.

[28] Dentatus: Cic. *Pis.* 24.58, *Mur.* 14.31, *Cato* 16.55; Liv. 45.38.11; Plut. *Cato* 2.1–2; Apul. *Apol.* 17; Flamininus: Cic. *Pis.* 25.61, *Mur.* 14.31; Liv. 45.39.1; Eutrop. 4.2.3.

was physically present made the most indelible impression on the spectators. These events formed high points in the collective memory and were time and again revisited in the ancient writings as Rome's most splendid moments. When Lucius Verus brought actors from Syria after the Parthian war, the biographer in the *Historia Augusta* writes ironically of how this was done 'as proudly as if he were leading kings to a triumph'.[29] Livy's words express the same attitude: *Illud spectaculum maximum, nobilissimus opulentissimusque rex captus*, 'that greatest of shows, a captive king of highest birth and greatest riches'.[30]

The case of Syphax, king of the Numidian tribe the Masaesyli, illustrates the importance of the king's physical presence. Syphax fought against Rome during the Second Punic War; after the defeat of Carthage, he was sent to Rome and led in Scipio Africanus' triumph in 201 BC.[31] Syphax had played only a secondary role in the war, and the victory was first and foremost one over Hannibal and Carthage.[32] Nevertheless, it was the exhibition of Syphax, a royal captive and a true king, that proved the grand display. In the debate that preceded the triumph of Aemilius Paullus, Livy draws attention to the former most glorious triumphal display, that of Syphax, and points out how in 167 BC people still remembered the crowds that had gathered to catch sight of the king.[33] Tacitus describes how the Emperor Claudius' capture of Caratacus was compared to former moments of glory, of which the exhibition of Syphax was put on footing with that of Perseus: *neque minus id clarum, quam quod Syphacem P. Scipio, Persen L. Paulus, et si qui alii vinctos reges populo Romano ostendere*, 'an incident as glorious as the exhibition to the Roman people of Syphax by Publius Scipio and Perseus by Lucius Paullus, and of other chained kings by other generals'.[34]

Family matters

Next only to the glory of exposing a captive king in a triumphal procession was that of displaying his royal family. Appian's description of Pompey's parades (quoted above) emphasizes the presence of the five sons and two daughters of Mithridates, who are all identified by name. We have also seen that Augustus claims as a major achievement to have led not only kings but their children too in his triumphs.[35] The same emphasis on royal children is seen in Livy's version of

---

[29] S.H.A. *Verus* 8.7: *quasi reges aliquos ad triumphum adduceret, sic histriones eduxit e Syria*, cf. Fronto, p. 209 N.

[30] Liv. 45.39.6.

[31] Polyb. 16.23.6; Val. Max. 6.2.3; Tac. *Ann.* 12.38; Sil. *Pun.* 17.172–5, 17.629–30; Ampel. 37.1.

[32] Livy (45.39.7) describes Syphax as an appendage to the war, *accessio Punici belli*.

[33] Liv. 45.39.6–8. At 30.45.4–5, Livy maintains that Syphax had died before the triumph.

[34] Tac. *Ann.* 12.38.1–2; cf. Val. Max. 6.2.3.

[35] Aug. *Anc.* 4.

FIGURE 13 On this denarius of a younger relative, L. Aemilius Paullus (in large perspective) stands by a trophy with his principal captives, King Perseus, hands bound back, and two royal children. The image reflects the importance of the royal prisoners in the memory of Paullus' family and of Rome. The inscription emphasizes that the victory was Paullus' third, TER PAULLUS.

the voices raised in favour of voting a triumph for Aemilius Paullus: 'Shall the captive king Perseus, shall the king's sons Philip and Alexander, such great names—shall they be removed from the sight of the citizens?'[36]

King Perseus' infant sons and daughters were led as captives in the triumph of Aemilius Paullus. In fact, they must have been central to the parade, as a denarius issued by a relative of Paullus about a century later shows the king with two children at the base of a trophy (Fig. 13).[37] In contrast to the captive grown-ups, the infant children could not be held guilty of the rebellion against Rome. Consequently, while most adult prisoners were mocked and scorned, the spectators of the triumph beheld the infants with pity and compassion (Plut. *Aem.* 33.6–8):

εἶτα μικροῦ διαλείμματος ὄντος ἤδη τὰ τέκνα τοῦ βασιλέως ἤγετο δοῦλα, καὶ σὺν αὐτοῖς τροφέων καὶ διδασκάλων καὶ παιδαγωγῶν δεδακρυμένων ὄχλος, αὐτῶν τε τὰς χεῖρας ὀρεγόντων εἰς τοὺς θεατὰς καὶ τὰ παιδία δεῖσθαι καὶ λιτανεύειν διδασκόντων. ἦν δ' ἄρρενα μὲν δύο, θῆλυ δὲ ἕν, οὐ πάνυ συμφρονοῦντα τῶν κακῶν τὸ μέγεθος διὰ τὴν ἡλικίαν· ᾗ καὶ μᾶλλον ἐλεεινὰ πρὸς τὴν μεταβολὴν τῆς ἀναισθησίας ἦν, ὥστε μικροῦ τὸν Περσέα βαδίζειν παρορώμενον· οὕτως ὑπ' οἴκτου τοῖς νηπίοις προσεῖχον τὰς ὄψεις οἱ Ῥωμαῖοι, καὶ δάκρυα πολλοῖς ἐκβάλλειν συνέβη, πᾶσι δὲ μεμιγμένην ἀλγηδόνι καὶ χάριτι τὴν θέαν εἶναι μέχρι οὗ τὰ παιδία παρῆλθεν.

Then, at a little interval, came the children of the king, led along as slaves, and with them a multitude of foster-parents, teachers, and tutors, all in tears, stretching out their own hands to the spectators and teaching the children to beg and supplicate. There were two boys, and one girl, and they were not very conscious of the magnitude of their evils

[36] Liv. 45.39.7–8: *Perseus rex captus, Philippus et Alexander, filii regis, tanta nomina, subtrahentur civitatis oculis?*
[37] Musei Capitolini, Rome, inv. 945. *Trionfi romani*, 192, II.3.1.

because of their tender age; wherefore they evoked even more pity in view of the time when their unconsciousness would cease, so that Perseus walked along almost unnoticed, while the Romans, moved by compassion, kept their eyes upon the children, and many of them shed tears, and for all of them the pleasure of the spectacle was mingled with pain, until the children had passed by.

As in the cases of both Paullus and Perseus, a large retinue of attendants accompanied the captive children. The people in this group cried for mercy and of grief, and their tears were paralleled by those of the spectators, whose attention was likewise focused on the children. Of these, the smallest ones evoked the strongest feelings of pity, caused by their fate and above all by their lack of understanding. The children were not at fault, but simply by being the sons and daughters of Perseus, they shared in their father's crime. It was their innocent unawareness that more than anything aroused sympathy, the very thought that the children one day would grasp the immense wrongdoings made by their own house against Rome.

Since small children led on triumphal parade by definition were innocent, they might be saved by being transformed into Romans. In fact, Perseus' son Alexander ended up an expert metalworker, adopted the Latin tongue, and became secretary to Roman magistrates.[38] Later on, another child, Ventidius Bassus, was led together with his mother and other captives from Asculum Picenum in the triumph celebrated in 89 BC by Pompey's father, Pompeius Strabo.[39] Some fifty years later, in 38 BC, Ventidius turns up in the triumphal lists again, this time as triumphator, celebrating a victory over the Parthians.[40] This is a most striking example of incorporation of a young captive into the Roman realm and of the ever-changing fancy of Fortune.[41] The particularity of the event was further enhanced by the circumstance that Ventidius' parade was the only Republican triumph held over the Parthians. Not surprisingly, ancient authors commented frequently upon the story.[42] Another fate that attracted attention was that of the historian Juba, son of the king of Numidia, who as a child of about five years in age was led among the captives in Caesar's African triumph in 46 BC. Plutarch characterizes Juba as 'the most fortunate captive ever taken, since from being a barbarian and a Numidian, he came to be enrolled among the most learned Greek historians'.[43] Plutarch's point of view is Greek, and consequently he

[38] Plut. *Aem.* 37.4.
[39] Vell. Pat. 2.65.3; Val Max. 6.9.9; Plin. *Nat.* 7.43.135; Gell. 15.4.2–3; Dio Cass. 43.51.4–5, 49.21.3.
[40] Vell. Pat. 2.65.3; Val Max. 6.9.9; Plin. *Nat.* 7.43.135; Plut. *Ant.* 34.4–5; Gell. 15.4.4; Dio Cass. 43.51.5–6, 49.21.2–3; Eutrop. 7.5.
[41] Plin. *Nat.* 7.43.135; Dio Cass. 49.21.2–3.
[42] Pliny (*Nat.* 7.43.135) refers to Masurius, Cicero, and 'many other authors', all of whom had written about Ventidius and his fate.
[43] Plut. *Caes.* 55.2: μακαριωτάτην ἁλοὺς ἅλωσιν, ἐκ βαρβάρου καὶ Νομάδος Ἑλλήνων τοῖς πολυμαθεστάτοις ἐναρίθμιος γενέσθαι συγγραφεῦσι; cf. App. *BCiv.* 2.101.

emphasizes Juba's transference from barbarian captive to Greek historian rather than to Roman citizen.[44] Nevertheless, the basic implication is not much different from that of a Roman perspective, emphasizing the role of Fortune and the incorporation of the still innocent child within the realm of civilization.

Not only the royal children attracted attention, but also the wives, brothers, sisters, and other kin of defeated kings and leaders. In the Illyrian triumph celebrated by Anicius Gallus in 167 BC, Livy points out that King Gentius was accompanied by his wife, his children, and his brother Caravantius.[45] Plutarch states that among the many captives paraded in Pompey's triumph of 61 BC were the son of Tigranes, the Armenian king, with his wife and daughter, and Zosime, a wife of King Tigranes.[46] An illustrative passage can also be found in Strabo, who, in describing the land of Germania, is led to give an account of the captives present in Germanicus' triumph over the Cherusci, Chatti, and Angrivarii in AD 17 (7.1.4):

ἔτισαν δὲ δίκας ἅπαντες καὶ παρέσχον τῷ νεωτέρῳ Γερμανικῷ λαμπρότατον θρίαμβον, ἐν ᾧ ἐθριαμβεύθη τῶν ἐπιφανεστάτων ἀνδρῶν σώματα καὶ γυναικῶν, Σεγιμούντός τε Σεγέστου υἱός, Χηρούσκων ἡγεμών, καὶ ἀδελφὴ αὐτοῦ, γυνὴ δ' Ἀρμενίου τοῦ πολεμαρχήσαντος ἐν τοῖς Χηρούσκοις ἐν τῇ πρὸς Οὔαρον Κουιντίλλιον παρασπονδήσει καὶ νῦν ἔτι συνέχοντος τὸν πόλεμον, ὄνομα Θουσνέλδα, καὶ υἱὸς τριετὴς Θουμέλικος· ἔτι δὲ Σεσίθακος, Σεγιμήρου υἱὸς τῶν Χηρούσκων ἡγεμόνος, καὶ γυνὴ τούτου Ῥαμίς, Οὐκρομίρου θυγάτηρ, ἡγεμόνος Χάττων, καὶ Δευδόριξ, Βαιτόριγος τοῦ Μέλωνος ἀδελφοῦ υἱός, Σούγαμβρος.

But they all paid the penalty, and afforded the younger Germanicus a most brilliant triumph—that triumph in which their most famous men and women were led captive, I mean Segimundus, son of Segestes and chieftain of the Cherusci, and his sister Thusnelda, the wife of Arminius, the man who at the time of the violation of the treaty against Quintilius Varus was commander-in-chief of the Cheruscan army and even to this day is keeping up the war, and Thusnelda's three-year-old son Thumelicus; and also Sesithacus, the son of Segimerus and chieftain of the Cherusci, and Rhamis, his wife, and a daughter of Ucromirus, chieftain of the Chatti, and Deudorix, a Sugambrian, the son of Baetorix, the brother of Melo.

Strabo, possibly an eyewitness,[47] announces that Germanicus' triumph had the most famous men and women, thereby admitting the importance of the female display. Still, both male and female captives were identified by way of their relations to the chief enemies, and for the women, having mostly played subordinate political roles, royal kinship counted as the prime merit. True, Thusnelda

---

[44] The contrast is strongly marked by the close placing of the words βαρβάρου καὶ Νομάδος Ἑλλήνων.

[45] Other noble captives were present as well, Liv. 45.43.6–7: *Ante currum ducti Gentius rex cum coniuge et liberis et Caravantius, frater regis, et aliquot nobiles Illyrii.*

[46] Plut. *Pomp.* 45.4. See also the triumphal ceremony that Claudius held over Caratacus, which included Caratacus' brothers, wife, daughter, and vassals, Tac. *Ann.* 12.36.

[47] Benario (2005: 176).

was probably well known in Rome for her own actions and character.[48] However, her fame and the conspicuousness of her display nevertheless stemmed from her being the sister of Segimundus, daughter of the pro-Roman Segestes (who actually watched the triumph) and, above all, wife of Arminius, the vanquisher of Varus. In the absence of Arminius, the display of Thusnelda, his high-born consort, was of the utmost importance.[49] The son too played a significant role here, marking that the offspring of Arminius had been captured and that the future of the Cherusci lay in the hands of Rome.[50] The tender age of the boy is again pointed out,[51] stressing his innocence and the possibility of his being saved.[52] The other captives, men as well as women, were responsible for their own fates and for this they paid the penalty, as Strabo writes. Both Arminius and Thusnelda held high places in nineteenth-century German nationalism, and Piloty's famed painting of Germanicus' triumph sets Thusnelda in the centre of all attention, proud and morally unbreakable (cover image).[53]

Of all the women known to have been displayed in Roman triumphs, the clear majority are described as wives or sisters of conquered leaders and mothers of royal children. In art too, this is how women on triumphal parade appear, together with men and children or children only. Such groups of captives, featuring a child, a woman, and a man, are seen both on a relief in the National Museum of Naples (Fig. 12) and on another in the Castelli-Baldassini collection in Pesaro.[54] In both cases the three form a very tight unit, with mother and father on the Naples relief protectively flanking their child. Both reliefs seem to have formed part of longer friezes showing a triumphal procession at length, where the groups, inserted between various other displays, probably conveyed a representative image of the captive family. On the frieze running around the arch of Trajan in Benevento, the captive men are instead represented either as single prisoners or depicted in sets of two seated in wagons (Fig. 14).[55] The women appear separately

[48] Tac. *Ann.* 1.57–8. *RE* 2:e Reihe VI:1 (1936), s.v. 'Thusnelda', 655–6 (A. Stein).

[49] Benario (2005: 177) claims that Thusnelda was the first woman shown as a prime captive in a Roman triumph. But Caesar had already in 46 BC displayed Arsinoë in this capacity, as Octavian later Cleopatra, by way of her image.

[50] The captive child must have appeared in strong contrast to the five children of Germanicus, who accompanied their father in his chariot, Tac. *Ann.* 2.41.3.

[51] Tacitus (*Ann.* 1.57–8) states that Thusnelda was expecting in AD 15, so possibly the boy was younger than the 3 years given by Strabo.

[52] Tacitus, *Ann.* 1.58, says that the boy met a humiliating destiny, but the book in which he describes the details is lost. We know only that Thumelicus was sent to Ravenna for upbringing. At *Ann.* 11.16, Tacitus implies that the boy has now died.

[53] Beard (2007: 107–11).

[54] Naples: Inv. no. 6722 (7516). Ryberg (1955: 149–50, pl. LIII, fig. 81c); Koeppel (1983: Kat. 11, 71, 97, Abb. 12); *Trionfi romani*, 123, I.2.5; Pesaro: Bacchielli (1988).

[55] Vessberg (1952: 134, bild 4); Pfanner (1983: 87 and Beil. 3). The arch of Trajan at Benevento includes prisoners of many types, Vessberg (1952); Ryberg (1955: 150–4, pl. LIV, figs. 82 a–e); Andreae (1979); Pfanner (1983: 86–7, Beil. 3); Adamo Muscettola (1992); *Trionfi romani*, 132–5, I.2.13–14.

FIGURE 14 On the narrow, long frieze of the arch of Trajan at Benevento, two prisoners are drawn on a cart by oxen. Both captives are male, dressed in barbarian style. One is bound, the other holds out his hands in grief, lament, and supplication. The frieze includes several similar groups of prisoners along the sides of the arch, most probably to give vivid glimpses of the parade from all views rather than to document the event in proper photographic order.

FIGURE 15 Soldiers lead a group of women and children in the triumphal procession represented on the arch of Trajan at Benevento. Before them, a young man carries a *titulus* that once named and explained the presence of the captives.

in two groups, together with children and infants (Fig. 15).[56] Thus, while the Naples and Pesaro reliefs focus on the family as a unit, the frieze in Benevento separates the captive men into one group and their families into a second. In both cases, as in literature, family members and units appear as important exhibits. While captured enemy soldiers and military leaders on parade gave form to martial superiority, family members testified to the complete takeover of the enemy elite and announced Roman control also of the domestic sphere.

Arsinoë and Cleopatra: female centrepieces

All general rules have exceptions, and ancient literature provides a few revealing examples of women who were displayed as individuals rather than as part of a collective group. In focus here stand Arsinoë, Cleopatra's younger sister, and Cleopatra herself, represented by her image.[57] Caesar exposed Arsinoë to the Roman gaze as part of his Egyptian parade conducted in 46 BC. Florus maintains that she was carried on a bier, and suggests that the three major displays of the Egyptian procession were the Nile, Arsinoë, and the Pharus.[58] Dio's description is more detailed and dwells in particular on the presence of Arsinoë (43.19.2–4):

καὶ τὰ μὲν ἄλλα ηὔφρανέ που τοὺς ὁρῶντας, ἡ δ' Ἀρσινόη ἡ Αἰγυπτία (καὶ γὰρ ἐκείνην ἐν τοῖς αἰχμαλώτοις παρήγαγε) τό τε πλῆθος τῶν ῥαβδούχων καὶ τὰ ἀπὸ τῶν πολιτῶν τῶν ἐν τῇ Ἀφρικῇ ἀπολωλότων πομπεῖα δεινῶς αὐτοὺς ἐλύπησεν [...] καὶ ἡ Ἀρσινόη γυνή τε οὖσα καὶ βασιλίς ποτε νομισθεῖσα ἔν τε δεσμοῖς, ὃ μηπώποτε ἔν γε τῇ Ῥώμῃ ἐγεγόνει, ὀφθεῖσα πάμπολυν οἶκτον ἐνέβαλε, κἀκ τούτου ἐπὶ τῇ προφάσει ταύτῃ καὶ τὰ οἰκεῖα πάθη παρωδύραντο.

Most of it, of course, delighted the spectators, but the sight of Arsinoë of Egypt (whom he also led among the captives), and the multitude of lictors and the symbols of triumph taken from the citizens who had fallen in Africa displeased them terribly . . . And the sight of Arsinoë, a woman and once called a queen, in chains—a spectacle which had never yet been seen, at least in Rome,—aroused very much pity, and with this as an excuse, they lamented their own misfortunes.

Female captives had long appeared in the triumphal processions of Rome, and Dio's main point of complaint is not that a woman was led in triumph, but rather that a woman was assigned the role of the principal royal prisoner on display. Arsinoë was not exhibited among other family members, nor was her prime function that of being a king's wife, sister, or daughter. Instead, carried aloft on a *ferculum*, she was exhibited as the principal enemy of the Egyptian campaign. In

[56] Pfanner (1983: 87 and Beil. 3). Currie (1996: 172–3).

[57] Zenobia, queen of Palmyra, forms another famed example of female presence, but her display falls outside the chronological scope of this study.

[58] Flor. *Epit.* 2.13.88–9: *Altera laurus Aegyptia: tunc in ferculis Nilus, Arsinoe et ad simulacrum ignium ardens Pharos.*

this, she did serve a deliberate purpose. It is quite obvious that Caesar, well aware of the fact that Rome did not appreciate a victory celebration over its own citizens, tried to present his triumphs as being held over foreign enemies. In this, the exhibition of principal non-Roman adversaries, leaders and kings, was essential. Vercingetorix, in his capacity as a true foreign leader captured on the battlefield, played a main part in the Gallic parade. Equally important was the younger Juba, whose presence Caesar used to transform the vanquishment of Metellus Scipio and Cato in Africa into a triumph over the Numidian king Juba, father of the young captive.[59] It is in this context that the prominent display of Arsinoë should be read. By playing the traditional role of the leading opponent she marked the Egyptian procession as a triumph over foreign enemies.

By tradition, however, the role of Rome's leading enemy character was played by a male military opponent. On parade, his status and deeds shed light on the triumphator and on the Roman accomplishment. In consequence, the character and acts of the main opponent had to be of such dignity and magnitude as to match his leading role. At the time of Caesar's triumphs, Arsinoë was a girl of about thirteen years of age. She lacked both the sex and status to fill the emphatic position bestowed on her. To present her as principal enemy was not thought worthy of a Roman triumphator, and in consequence, the display did not fall on good ground. Instead of affronting the prime captive with their customary mockery, the spectators pitied Arsinoë. Just as the fate of the small children of Perseus drove the spectators to tears, so too Arsinoë aroused sympathy rather than scorn. She too was innocent, not of the crime of opposing Rome in a general sense, but of the position of a leading captive in which she was placed.

Seventeen years later, Arsinoë's elder sister Cleopatra was presented, by way of an image, in a prominent position in the triple triumph of Octavian.[60] In contrast to Arsinoë, Cleopatra had been promoted as the major opponent all along in the civil war between Octavian and Antony, and she was pointed out as the true adversary of Rome, political and military. It was against Cleopatra that Octavian declared war,[61] and it was for his victory over the queen that Octavian was granted an arch and a triumph.[62] Of course, Octavian's stress on Cleopatra as the major enemy was again a way to cover the fact that, in reality, Romans had fought and defeated other Romans. Still, Cleopatra was perceived as a true threat, and her defeat at Actium was greeted with relief.[63] Describing Octavian's parades, Dio Cassius

---

[59] Plut. *Caes.* 55.1–2.

[60] Prop. 3.11.53–4; Plut. *Ant.* 86.3; Dio Cass. 51.21.8–9.

[61] Plut. *Ant.* 60.1; Dio Cass. 50.4.4–5.

[62] Liv. *Per.* 133; Dio Cass. 51.19.1, 4–5. Not dissimilarly, when the Emperor Aurelian was much later accused of showing Zenobia, a woman, in his triumph, he emphasized her former function as a traditional enemy opponent, a political and military leader, S.H.A. *Tyr. Trig.* 30.4–12, cf. 30.13–27.

[63] See e.g. Hor. *Carm.* 1.37. For the Augustan poets' treatment of Actium and Cleopatra's defeat, see Gurval (1995).

states that no mention was made of Antony or of any other Roman, but that the triumphs were held over the Egyptians as over Cleopatra.[64] Livy is even more explicit, stating the Octavian's third triumph was performed *de Cleopatra*.[65]

Unlike Arsinoë and despite being a woman, Cleopatra filled the traditional requirements of a principal military and royal adversary. Still, she too was a woman, and had she been displayed alive, there might have been similar voices raised against her exhibition in a leading triumphal position. In fact, Propertius wonders how much of a triumph it would have been, had Cleopatra, a woman, been led in the very streets that had seen the glorious exhibition of Jugurtha: 'Thank heaven! A fine triumph one woman would have made on streets where once Jugurtha was paraded!'[66] Many ancient authors testify to Octavian's ambition to lead the queen alive and his disappointment at her death.[67] But Propertius' verses could cause second thoughts concerning the death of Cleopatra, and some modern scholars have also expressed doubts on the suicide.[68] Did she, as reported, commit her famed suicide or should one suspect that she was somehow helped to her death? Octavian must have been well aware of the negative response that Caesar's exhibition of Arsinoë had caused. Would he in fact have preferred an image of the queen, as a deliberate attempt not to repeat the mistake of his adoptive father? Would he have feared that Cleopatra had sympathizers in Rome, both from her preceding visit and from her position as the mother of Caesar's child? The sources do not encourage us to interpret Cleopatra's death as a murder, but it is not unreasonable that Octavian agreed to let her take her own life, just as other defeated enemy leaders were offered that opportunity.[69] What is clear is that the queen's death offered Octavian the best political solution. By displaying her only in an image, he was able to perform the defeat of a proud, worthy adversary. At the same time, he avoided the emotional reaction that the queen would most certainly have evoked, had she walked alive dragged in chains.

Cleopatra's representation appeared on the third and final day's parade, which presented the Egyptian victory. Dio Cassius writes (51.21.8–9):

τά τε γὰρ ἄλλα καὶ ἡ Κλεοπάτρα ἐπὶ κλίνης ἐν τῷ τοῦ θανάτου μιμήματι παρεκομίσθη, ὥστε τρόπον τινὰ καὶ ἐκείνην μετά τε τῶν ἄλλων αἰχμαλώτων καὶ μετὰ τοῦ Ἀλεξάνδρου τοῦ καὶ Ἡλίου, τῆς τε Κλεοπάτρας τῆς καὶ Σελήνης, τῶν τέκνων, ὡς πομπεῖον ὀφθῆναι. μετὰ δὲ δὴ τοῦτο ὁ Καῖσαρ...

---

[64] Dio Cass. 51.19.1, 4–5.

[65] Liv. *Per.* 133.

[66] Prop. 4.6.65–6: *di melius! quantus mulier foret una triumphus, / ductus erat per quas ante Iugurtha vias!* (tr. G. Lee). Gurval (1995: 270–1).

[67] Plut. *Ant.* 86.4; Suet. *Aug.* 17.4; Dio Cass. 51.14.

[68] Groag (1915: 64–7); W. W. Tarn in *CAH* x (1934), 109–10, rep. in Tarn and Charlesworth (1965: 138–9). Whitehorne (1994: 194–6) accounts for, but dismisses, the doubts presented by others. Gurval (1995: 30) raises doubts on the suicide, but acknowledges the great difference in the display of Arsinoë and Cleopatra.

[69] Plut. *Aem.* 34.

Among other features, an image of Cleopatra, lying upon a couch in her death, was carried by, so that in a manner, she too appeared as a processional display together with the other captives and with her children, Alexander, also called Helios, and Cleopatra, called also Selene. Hereafter came Caesar, . . .

Similarly to primary enemy captives shown alive, the image of Cleopatra was exhibited together with her children immediately in front of the Roman triumphator.[70] Octavian entered the city only at the end of day three,[71] and his entrance formed the supreme moment of his *triplex triumphus*. The display of Cleopatra and her children at this very visual peak attests to the importance of their exhibition, and also shows that representations of principal adversaries worked as valid stand-ins for absent vanquished enemy leaders. Not that many Roman generals could boast captive regents, and to cover up for their absence, images took their place. The effigy of Cleopatra was displayed at the very location where the queen, if alive, would have walked. By way of her representation, as Dio writes, 'she too appeared as a processional display together with the other captives and with her children'.

Dio's account reveals very little of the specific appearance of Cleopatra's image, but we are told that she was carried on a bier and that the queen was shown by way of an image of death, ἐν τῷ τοῦ θανάτου μιμήματι. Plutarch too describes the image as one representing death: 'For in his triumph an image of Cleopatra herself with the asp clinging to her was carried'.[72] His description attests to the presence of a snake, by whose poison the queen is supposed to have taken her life.[73] As will be discussed further on, other known representations of principal enemies focused on their final fate and death, and by ἐν τῷ τοῦ θανάτου μιμήματι Dio probably refers to an image that represented the death of the queen rather than the queen already dead. This interpretation is supported by another description of this famous display, made by Propertius as he watched the parade pass by: *bracchia spectavi sacris admorsa colubris | et trahere occultum membra soporis iter*, 'I beheld the arms bitten by the sacred asps, and her limbs absorb the numbing poison as it spread unseen'.[74] In life, Cleopatra had managed to escape the triumph, but she could not prevent her death from being replayed for the spectators of Rome.

---

[70] It has been suggested that the two small children depicted in Octavian's triumphal car on the recently discovered relief at Nicopolis are Cleopatra's children (Zachos, 2003: 91–2). However, captives, adults as well as children, always are described as shown in front of the car, while those standing in the chariot were relatives of the triumpator. Therefore, I agree with Mary Beard that the children at Nicopolis belonged to Octavian's family and were in all probability Julia and Drusus (Beard, 2007: 224–5).

[71] Serv. *ad Aen*. 8.714: *tertio [die] ipse cum Alexandrino est ingressus triumpho*. Östenberg (1999).

[72] Plut. *Ant*. 86.3: ἐν γὰρ τῷ θριάμβῳ τῆς Κλεοπάτρας αὐτῆς εἴδωλον ἐκομίζετο καὶ τῆς ἀσπίδος ἐμπεφυκυίας. Cf. Verg. *Aen*. 8.696–7; Hor. *Carm*. 1.37.31–2.

[73] I will not here address the much-debated issue of whether Cleopatra was killed by one or two snakes, for references to the debate, see Gurval (1995: 29 n. 17). For the death of Cleopatra, see also Whitehorne (1994: 186–96).

[74] Prop. 3.11.53–4. For the translation, I have followed Camps (1966: 109, 54 (b)).

Parading varied origins

Roman citizens were not displayed as defeated in the triumphal procession. This is most clearly reflected in the total absence of any Roman deserters and defectors from the triumph. When captured, these men were severely punished, and at least at times, the punishment formed part of public spectacles.[75] Still, deserters and their public punishment were consistently kept away from the triumphal ritual, in which Rome and Romans by definition formed the victorious side.

The same concern is seen in Lucullus' conduct during his eastern campaign. Having captured three main Mithridatic commanders, the Roman Varius, Alexander the Paphlagonian, and Dionysius the eunuch, of whom the last immediately committed suicide, Lucullus proceeded diversely with the first two, not according to their deeds, but their origins.[76] Since it seemed improper to lead a Roman senator in the triumph, Varius was put to death immediately. Alexander, being a Paphlagonian, suited the role of a defeated foreign leader to the point and was saved to be exhibited in the triumph. Seventeen years after Lucullus' triumph, Caesar similarly refrained from displaying any citizens' names in his triumphs. Still, he could not resist showing his principal adversaries, many of them Romans, by way of images.[77] Only Pompey was absent, being still greatly missed. The exhibition of Romans in the traditional roles of defeated foreign enemies was clearly out of line.[78] Caesar's display was not well taken, and people groaned at the sight of Scipio, Cato, and Petreius in the process of committing suicide. Octavian obviously learnt from Caesar's mistake. No Roman citizens appear in the descriptions of his triumph, which instead focus on the defeat of Cleopatra. Antony was nowhere present, neither by name nor by images.

Besides Cleopatra and her children, Octavian paraded many other less-famed captives of diverse origins in his triumph. In his depiction of the shield of Aeneas, Vergil lists Nomades, Afri, Leleges, Carians, Gelonians, Morini, and Dahae,[79] and I have argued elsewhere that the depiction in all probability reflects the historical exhibition of 29 BC rather well.[80] The Morini also appear in Dio Cassius' description of the triumph, together with another northern people, the Suebi.[81] These two peoples, the Morini and the Suebi, had been brought down by Octavian's subordinate commander Gaius Carrinas, a campaign for which he triumphed in 28 BC. Still, Octavian incorporated their display in his Dalmatian

---

[75] Aemilius Paullus had allied deserters trampled to death by elephants, possibly as part of his games at Amphipolis in 167 BC, Liv. *Per.* 51; Val. Max 2.7.14. Ville (1981: 55); Ferrary (1988: 563 n. 61); Edmondson (1999: 79). Scullard believes that the executions took place at games in Rome (1974: 184–5). Scipio Aemilianus also threw deserters and fugiative slaves to the beasts at shows for the people (*in edendis populo spectaculis*), probably referring to *ludi* performed after the triumph, Val. Max 2.7.13–14; Liv. *Per.* 51: *Scipio exemplo patris sui Aemili Pauli, qui Macedoniam vicerat, ludos fecit transfugasque ac fugitivos bestiis obiecit.*

[76] App. *Mith.* 76–7.   [77] App. *BCiv.* 2.101.

[78] Cf. Gurval (1995: 23–5).   [79] Verg. *Aen.* 8.724–8.

[80] Östenberg (1999).   [81] Dio Cass. 51.21.5–6.

FIGURE 16 Soldiers raise a *ferculum* carrying two captives flanking a trophy. Frieze from the temple of Apollo Sosianus in Rome.

procession, the first of the three parades that formed the celebration of 29 BC. Perhaps, this is the event celebrated in stone on a relief that once adorned the temple of Apollo Sosianus (Fig. 16), representing Gallic prisoners carried on a *ferculum*.[82] As Sosius' triumph was held over the Jews, it has been argued that the frieze was a tribute to Octavian, exhibiting Gallic captives in remembrance of his *triplex triumphus*. This could well be so, especially if it turns out that the other cella walls showed days two and three of the triumph, thus reblazoning Octavian's worldwide triumphal acclaim.[83] If, on the other hand, only the Gallic parade was depicted, we should keep in mind that the frieze exhibits rather non-specific excerpts of triumph, and that Gallic prisoners could be a very symbolic manifestation. The northerners could represent Roman triumph in general, reflecting martial success in the widest sense at the very spot where Republican parades had long passed as they entered the city.

Octavian's purpose in parading Morini and Suebi was like the pronounced presentation of Cleopatra. By showing prisoners from near and far Octavian could tone down the domestic character of his war and victory.[84] But there was

[82] The idea of Octavian's triumph was launched by La Rocca, and has been widely accepted: La Rocca (1985: 94–6, figs. 22, 24); Viscogliosi (1988: 136–40, cat. 41); Zanker (1990: 70, fig. 55); Viscogliosi (1996: 75–81, figs. 87, 90); *Trionfi romani*, 120–1, I.2.3.

[83] Viscogliosi (1996: 81).

[84] Östenberg (1999); cf. Gurval (1995: esp. 19–36), for similar arguments.

more to the manifold exhibition of captives. The diverse displays in the *triplex triumphus* demonstrated that the entire world had been subdued, an exhibition by which Octavian challenged previous similar worldwide announcements, above all in the triumphs of Pompey and Caesar.[85] In fact, to parade as many ethnic groups as possible appears to have been a characteristic trait of the Roman triumphal procession in general. This goes not only for the manifestations of the great generals of the late Republic, who deliberately boasted the conquest of the world by way of a numerous and varied display, but for other celebrations too, announcing the complete subjection of smaller areas. Pompey himself, in the last and greatest of his triumphal shows, held in 61 BC, manifested the total subjection of the specific area of Asia by displaying captives and hostages from a large number of kingdoms. Pontus, Armenia, Cappadocia, Paphlagonia, Media, Colchis, Iberia, Albania, Syria, Cilicia, Mesopotamia, Phoenicia, Palestine, Judaea, Arabia, and the pirates were all represented in the processions of the two-day-long celebration and duly recorded afterwards.[86] Others proceeded similarly, also in smaller areas of conquest. For example, the records for Germanicus' triumph over the Cherusci, the Chatti, and the Angrivarii in AD 17 list captives not only from these tribes, but also from the Sugambri, Chaulci, Campsani, Bructeri, Usipi, Chattuarii, Landi, and Tubattii.[87]

The display of a large number of diverse peoples might thus denote the complete takeover of a certain area. At other times, the captives came from widespread areas and connoted further extended victories. Captives presented in the triumphs not infrequently originated in areas outside the specific sphere for which the triumph was held. For example, in 275 BC, Dentatus led Molossians, Thessalians, Macedonians, Bruttii, Apuli, and Lucanians in a triumph that according to the *Fasti* celebrated the defeat of the Samnites and King Pyrrhus.[88] By way of these captives, Dentatus and Rome laid claim to more widespread conquests. Parts of Greece were on display by way of their captives, as was southern Italy. The same idea is evident in the case of Octavian, who displayed the Morini and the Suebi, in a triumph that officially celebrated the victories in Dalmatia. Vergil labels the Morini *extremi hominum* and Pliny calls them *ultimi hominum*.[89] Their display

---

[85] Östenberg (1999).

[86] Plut. *Pomp.* 45.2. Pliny lists Asia, Pontus, Armenia, Paphlagonia, Cappadocia, Cilicia, Syria, the Scythians, Jews and Albanians, Iberia, Crete, the Basternae, Mithridates and Tigranes, *Nat.* 7.26.98. Appian (*Mith.* 116–17) maintains that many peoples were present in the procession, from Pontus, Armenia, Cappadocia, Cilicia, Syria, Albania, and Iberia. There were also Jews, Colchians, Heniochi and Scythians, Achaeans of Scythia, and a Laodicean, cf. Diod. Sic. 40.4 (Const. Exc.). The entry in the *Fasti* is rather poorly preserved, and, of the subdued peoples, it is possible to read clearly only [*Paphla*]*gonia, Cappadoc(ia)* . . . [*Alb*]*ania, pirateis.*

[87] Strab. 7.1.4; cf. Tac. *Ann.* 2.41.

[88] Flor. *Epit.* 1.13.27.

[89] Verg. *Aen.* 8.727; Plin. *Nat.* 19.2.8; see also Mela 3.2.

in the *triplex triumphus* showed that not only Dalmatia but also the very northern extremities of the world formed part of Octavian's conquests.[90]

Amazons and pirates: outsiders on display

According to the *Historia Augusta*, ten women, who had been captured in male dress among the Goths, were led as captives in Aurelian's parade, and a placard announced them as Amazons.[91] Pompey too led Amazons in parade. Plutarch claims that the Romans found Amazonian shields ($\pi\acute{\epsilon}\lambda\tau\alpha\iota$) and high boots on the field after the battle against the Albanians, but no women's bodies were discovered.[92] Appian similarly states that the Roman discovered only after the battle against the Albanians and Iberians that Amazons had fought among their enemies.[93] In his version, women were found among the captives and hostages. Since they had similar wounds to the men, they were supposed to be Amazons.

Neither Plutarch nor Appian explicitly mention the exhibition of Amazons or their military attire among Pompey's triumphal displays. Both do, however, report that among the captives Scythian women (Plutarch) or the female rulers of the Scythians (Appian) appeared,[94] and these are in all probability to be interpreted as the 'Amazons' defeated in the Caucasus. In both versions, the display was one of prominence. Plutarch includes the Scythian women in a very selective list of the most distinguished prisoners and hostages on parade.[95] In Appian too, the women appear among the most eminent captives, and their importance is further stressed by his identification of them as $\Sigma\kappa\upsilon\theta\hat{\omega}\nu\ \beta\alpha\sigma\acute{\iota}\lambda\epsilon\iota o\iota$ $\gamma\upsilon\nu\alpha\hat{\iota}\kappa\epsilon\varsigma$, the female rulers of the Scythians.[96] The prominence of these women was thus linked to their royal status, but also, in all probability, to their identification as the mythical Amazons. Written placards most certainly announced their identity as Amazons, and their weapons, the $\pi\acute{\epsilon}\lambda\tau\alpha\iota$, and their high boots may have been displayed too. Picard has attributed the increase in popularity of the $\pi\acute{\epsilon}\lambda\tau\alpha\iota$ among the weaponry depicted in Roman art to the victories of Pompey.[97] If this is correct, their exhibition in the triumph probably constituted a major impetus.

[90] Cf. the discussion in Östenberg (1999).
[91] S.H.A. *Aur.* 34.1. Zecchini (1996).
[92] Plut. *Pomp.* 35.3–4.
[93] App. *Mith.* 103, cf. *Mith.* 69. According to Appian, there were some uncertainties as to whether the Amazons formed a nation of their own, or if all warlike women were named Amazons.
[94] Plut. *Pomp.* 45.4; App. *Mith.* 117. Pliny (*Nat.* 7.26.98) includes Scythians among the peoples over whom Pompey triumphed. Dowden (1997: 115–16) attributes the story in Plutarch to Theophanes of Mytilene, who accompanied Pompey on his campaign, *FGrHist.* 188 F 4.
[95] Plut. *Pomp.* 45.4.
[96] App. *Mith.* 117.
[97] Picard (1957: 188–9). Polito (1998: 44–5), is sceptic. For the Amazonian *peltai*, see also Shapiro (1983: *passim*).

By having these mythical women warriors and possibly their weapons exhibited in his triumph, Pompey succeeded in transmitting several important messages. One was the allusion to previous famed mythical subjugators of Amazons, such as Hercules and Theseus, another the link to Alexander the Great, who according to the Alexander-historians met with the Amazon queen herself.[98] There may also have been another, more recent predecessor involved, namely Lucullus, who during his command in the Mithridatic war had sacked the city of Themiskyra, alleged residence of the Amazons.[99] The sources are silent on the matter, but Lucullus may well have boasted an Amazonian defeat in his triumphal manifestation, which would make the Pompeian display an obvious response. Another primary message concerned the nature of the Amazons. Being women, who dwelled in a mythic world on the very outskirts of the community, geographically as well as socially, their conquest showed the Roman subjection of the other in its most pronounced sense.[100] Amazons on triumphal display denoted a Roman conquest that not only embraced the known world, but the world beyond as well.

In comparison to the Amazons, pirates were probably paraded more often. Our sources explicitly attest to the presence of pirates as captives at two occasions: the triumph held in 74 BC by P. Servilius Vatia Isauricus after his victory over the pirates in Cilicia and Pompey's great procession of 61 BC, held to celebrate the defeat of the pirates and the kingdoms of the East.[101] Pirates were also probably displayed when M. Antonius triumphed in 102 BC after his victories in Cilicia, although no preserved source tells of the contents of the parade.[102] Q. Caecilius Metellus may have paraded some pirates in his triumph of 62 BC after the campaign in Crete.[103] Possibly, Octavian led pirates in his ovation after the defeat of Sextus Pompeius at Sicily in 36 BC,[104] and some captives may have been exhibited as pirates in Vespasian and Titus' Jewish triumph in AD 71.[105]

Our main source for the triumph of Servilius Vatia is Cicero, who depicts him as the positive antithesis of Verres.[106] Vatia is praised for having captured more

[98] Plut. *Alex.* 46 = *FGrHist.* Kleitarchos 137 F 15, Polykleitos 128 F 8, Onesikritos 134 F 1, Antigenes 141 F 1. See also Strab. 11.5.4; Diod. Sic. 17.77.2; Arr. *Anab.* 7.13. Dowden (1997: 114–16, with further references).

[99] App. *Mith.* 78. Dowden (1997: 100).

[100] Hardwick (1990); Dowden (1997).

[101] Vatia: Cic. *Verr.* II.5.26.66–7; Pompey: Plut. *Pomp.* 45; App. *Mith.* 116; cf. Diod. Sic. 40.4 (Const. Exc.); Val. Max. 8.15.8; Plin. *Nat.* 7.26.98; Petron. 240; Ampel. 47.

[102] Plut. *Pomp.* 24.6; cf. Liv. *Per.* 68; Obseq. 44. De Souza (1999: 102–8).

[103] Vell. Pat. 2.34.1–3, 2.40.4–5; App. *Sic.* 6; Flor. *Epit.* 2.13.9; Dio Cass. 36.19.3. Pompey deprived Creticus of some of his leading captives (Vell. Pat. 2.40.4–5; Dio Cass. 36.19.3), but others were probably present. For Creticus' campaign, see De Souza (1999: 157–61, 171–2).

[104] Augustus stressed that the war in Sicily had been one against pirates, *Anc.* 25.1: *Mare pacavi a praedonibus.* For the campaign against Sextus Pompeius, see De Souza (1999: 185–95).

[105] For Vespasian's campaign against the pirate force of Anicetus, Tac. *Hist.* 3.47. De Souza (1999: 208–9).

[106] Cic. *Verr.* II.5.26.66–7. For Vatia's campaign, see Ormerod (1922); Maróti (1989); De Souza (1999: 128–31).

pirate chiefs alive than all his predecessors together and above all, in contrast to Verres, for displaying these captives to the public in a parade. In Pompey's triumphal celebration, Plutarch attests to the display of pirate chiefs, ἀρχιπειράται, while Appian maintains that there was a large number of captives and pirates present.[107] The defeat of the pirates was also announced by way of placards and by the exhibition of a large number of rams from captured pirate ships.[108]

Pirates led on triumphal parade manifested that Rome had brought law and order to the sea. Thus, when Octavian had defeated Sextus Pompeius, he claimed to have pacified the sea from plunderers and re-established peace on land and at sea.[109] But pirates were not just about the sea. Appian states that Pompey showed 'a multitude of captives and pirates' (καὶ πλῆθος αἰχμαλώτων τε καὶ λῃστῶν).[110] Thus, he does not include the pirates in the larger group of captives, the αἰχμάλωτοι, but lists them as a separate category. This statement, which at first seems rather awkward, reflects the circumstance that the pirates lived outside the normative society. They were members of no *civitates* or *nationes*, but classed as bandits. Consequently, Valerius Maximus states that Pompey triumphed over kings (*reges*), states (*civitates*), peoples (*gentes*), and plunderers (*praedones*), thereby meaning the pirates.[111] In the procession itself, as seen in Appian's description, there were on one hand the normative captives, representing the social communities of *gentes* and *civitates*, on the other there were the pirates, non-citizens and outlaws.[112] Cicero expresses the same thought in the *De Officiis*, declaring that the usual codes were not applicable in the relations with pirates, since 'a pirate is not included in the category of lawful enemies, but is the common enemy of everybody'.[113]

In his speech against Verres, Cicero several times returns to the status of the pirates. Verres himself is compared to a pirate and is also accused of having accepted bribes to save a captured pirate chief rather than having him displayed to

---

[107] Plut. *Pomp.* 45.4; App. *Mith.* 116. For Pompey's campaigns against the pirates, see e.g. Morrison (1996: 117–19); De Souza (1999: 161–78); Schulz (2000a: 437–8).

[108] Plut. *Pomp.* 45.1–2; App. *Mith.* 116–17; cf. Plin. *Nat.* 7.25.93, 7.26.97.

[109] Aug. *Anc.* 25.1; App. *BCiv.* 5.130. See also Fugmann (1991) for the passage in the *Res Gestae* and for the *aemulatio* involved.

[110] App. *Mith.* 116.

[111] Val. Max. 8.15.8: *de Mithridate et Tigrane, de multis praeterea regibus plurimisque civitatibus et gentibus et praedonibus unum duxit triumphum*, 'He performed one single triumph over Mithridates and Tigranes, over many other kings and a large number of states, peoples, and bandits'; cf. Aug. *Anc.* 25.1. In this context, we might note that during the Republican era a few generals paraded their suppression of slave uprisings, most notably M. Licinius Crassus in 71 BC after the defeat of Spartacus, Cic. *Pis.* 24.58; Plut. *Crass.* 11.8; Plin. *Nat.* 15.38.125–6; Gell. 5.6.23. In contrast to the case of the pirates, only *ovationes* were granted for successes in servile wars, the enemy being thought not worthy enough to render true *triumphi* (Marshall, 1972).

[112] Plutarch too (*Pomp.* 45.4) separates the chief pirates from the rest of the captives in Pompey's triumph.

[113] Cic. *Off.* 3.29.107: *nam pirata non est ex perduellium numero definitus, sed communis hostis omnium*.

the people.[114] Verres' conduct is contrasted to the acts of Servilius Vatia, the triumphator of 74 BC (*Verr.* II.5.26.66–7):[115]

Unus plures praedonum duces vivos cepit P. Servilius quam omnes antea. Ecquando igitur isto fructu quisquam caruit, ut videre piratam captum non liceret? At contra, quacumque iter fecit, hoc iucundissimum spectaculum omnibus vinctorum captorumque hostium praebebat, itaque ei concursus fiebant undique ut non modo ex iis oppidis qua ducebantur sed etiam ex finitimis visendi causa convenirent. Ipse autem triumphus quam ob rem omnium triumphorum gratissimus populo Romano fuit et iucundissmus? Quia nihil est victoria dulcius, nullum est autem testimonium victoriae certius quam, quos saepe metueris, eos te vinctos ad supplicium duci videre.

One man, Publius Servilius, captured more pirate chiefs alive than all his predecessors put together. And when did he ever deny to anyone the satisfaction of seeing a captured pirate? On the contrary, wherever he journeyed, he offered everybody this most enjoyable spectacle of captured enemies in chains; and so, crowds gathered from all around to set eyes on the show not just from the towns through which the prisoners were led, but from the neighbouring towns as well. And why was the actual triumph the most welcome and pleasing of all triumphs to the Roman people? Because nothing is more delightful than victory, and there is no surer evidence of victory than for you to see those whom you often feared led in chains to their execution.

As bandits and outlaws, the pirates lacked all legal rights. Consequently, Cicero points out that the numerous pirate chiefs whom Vatia displayed were led in the triumph *ad supplicium*, to their execution.[116] Far from all enemy leaders were killed as part of the triumphal ritual, and Cicero's statement that the pirate chiefs suffered this destiny could possibly be taken to suggest that they were more harshly punished than enemy leaders in general.[117]

By capturing and killing the pirate leaders, Servilius Vatia removed 'the most cruel and deadly enemy of the Roman people', as Cicero puts it in another passage.[118] Accordingly, his triumph was greeted as *gratissimus et iucundissimus omnium triumphorum populo Romano*. Unlike many other enemies, the pirates constituted a constant threat not only to Rome but to other communities too. Being 'the common enemy of all the nations and peoples',[119] Vatia's exhibition of the captive pirates was clearly one that engaged people outside the city as well. All along the route, people gathered to catch sight of the spectacle, forming a universal triumphal parade that preceded and announced the great one of the *Urbs*.

---

[114] De Souza (1999: esp. 152–7, with references).

[115] Cf. the passage at *Verr.* II.5.30.76–7.

[116] *Supplicium* might mean simply 'punishment', but here it is likely that 'execution' is intended, cf. Cic. *Verr.* II.5.30.77.

[117] Cf. Coleman (1999: esp. 234–5), on the particularly severe punishment of *latrones*.

[118] Cic. *Verr.* II.5.30.76: *Hostem acerrimum atque infestissimum populi Romani,* . . .

[119] Ibid. II.5.30.76, cf. *Off.* 3.19.107.

Pompey proceeded rather differently with the pirates who were led in his triumph. Quite surprisingly, Appian claims that neither the pirates nor the other captives were chained and that the majority were sent home after the parade at public expense.[120] Still, Pompey's display of the pirates transmitted a message not much dissimilar to that of Vatia. The pirates were not killed, but neutralized by other means: by the conquest of their fleet and, above all, by their transformation into city-dwellers and farmers.[121] Pompey simply offered them a second chance and some land, softening their wild habits by 'a change of place, occupation and manner of life'.[122]

By displaying the captured pirates in public, the triumphator and Rome demonstrated that they had taken on the responsibility of upholding the law and order of the sea and of the entire world. The pirates formed one of the most severe threats to the public order of the *orbis terrarum*, and thus to Rome's role and reputation as the world's leading power as well. In fact, Polybius suggests that it was Rome's task to protect the Greeks from the (Illyrian) pirates, again described as a common enemy, and Plutarch states that the pirates' plundering was 'a disgrace to Roman supremacy'.[123] The overarching responsibility of Rome to deal with the pirates was formulated in a *lex de provinciis praetoriis* in around 100 BC, found on inscriptions at Delphi and Knidos.[124] It declares that the pirates were enemies of the Roman peoples, their friends, and allies, and it classes all attempts to assist them as acts of hostility towards Rome. Rome was the ruler of the world, and Rome was to keep the world's order. The manifestation of the captured pirates led in the triumphal parades of Servilius Vatia and Pompey thus confirmed and reinforced Rome's position as the dominant power of the *orbis terrarum*.

Captives as spectacle

The triumphal procession was a great spectacle, and not everyone was regarded as fit for display. Hence, the prisoners who were visually most apt for exhibition were chosen for the parade. Josephus preserves a very flagrant example in his description of the harsh treatment of the prisoners taken at the conquest of Jerusalem.[125] The old and weak were executed, as were many brigands, while the young and strong were sent to work in Egypt or presented as gifts to friends and allies, who were to use

[120] App. *Mith*. 117. De Souza (1999: esp. 169–72) discusses Pompey's *clementia* as opposed to Metellus Creticus' harsh handling of the pirates.
[121] Plut. *Pomp*. 28. Schulz (2000a: 437–8).
[122] Plut. *Pomp*. 28.3. Translation De Souza (1999: 175).
[123] Polyb. 2.12.4–6; Plut. *Pomp*. 24.4.
[124] De Souza (2000: 108–15, with further references).
[125] Joseph. *BJ* 6.416–19.

them for games in the amphitheatres. Children under 17 years of age were sold, and it was only the tallest and most handsome of the young men who were picked out for the triumph, where they were led adorned in beautiful dress.[126]

Once on parade, the visual effect of the captives was highly stressed. Preferably, the main opponent would be a king, rich, of high birth, conspicuous in stature and powerful in war. If not, he should at least be presented as such. Hence, Caligula arranged for *chlamydes regum*, kings', cloaks, for the captives to be carried in his ovation.[127] And Ovid, praising the deeds of Tiberius, writes of how a leading German prisoner is to be presented raised up, shining in Sidonian purple.[128] Made of Sidonian purple, the attire was in all probability a royal robe used by the Romans to costume leading captives as kings. The practice reappears in another triumphal description by Ovid, who tells of how captive kings demand garbs too rich to become their fate (*textaque fortuna divitiora sua*).[129] Besides robes, royal captives were decked out with chains of gold.[130] In the triumph of 104 BC, and in contrast to Marius' plain iron ring, Jugurtha had a golden earring.[131] The gold stressed his royal status, but also denoted the military and moral inferiority of the king as opposed to the Roman general.

Eminence was the most emphasized aspect of captives on parade. Another point was their ethnic origins. Hence, when Appian states that Pompey showed his prisoners arrayed in their native costumes (ἐς τὰ πάτρια ἐσταλμένους), the passive form ἐσταλμένους (from στέλλω, 'arrange, array, equip') shows that the prisoners did not wear their normal attire, but had been put into national dress for the processional occasion. The clothes helped in identifying and characterizing the diverse groups, as did the written placards that preceded each of the *nationes* or *gentes* on parade.[132]

From the practice of arraying captives in national dress, it was but a short step to dressing up non-captives to play the roles of prisoners. From the *Historia Augusta*, we hear that the Emperor Gallienus in his decennial procession included a group of Persians, who played the part of captives.[133] Also present were 'men dressed up as foreign peoples, as Goths, Sarmatians, Franks, and Persians, and no fewer than two hundred paraded in a single group'.[134] The practice was certainly

---

[126] Ibid. 7.138.

[127] Pers. 6.46.

[128] Ov. *Trist.* 4.2.27–8: *hic, qui Sidonio fulget sublimis in ostro,* | *dux fuerat belli . . .*

[129] Ov. *Pont.* 3.4.109–10.

[130] Prop. 2.1.33; Sil. *Pun.* 17.630; cf. S.H.A. *Aurel.* 34.3, *Tyr. Trig.* 30.24–7. See also Vell. Pat 2.82.3; Sen. *Tro.* 153–4.

[131] Golden earring: Plut. *Mar.* 12.3; iron ring: Plin. *Nat.* 33.4.11–12.

[132] Placards: S.H.A. *Aurel.* 34.1–2; cf. Plin. *Nat.* 5.5.36. Östenberg (forthcoming).

[133] S.H.A. *Gall.* 9.5: *nam cum <g>rex Persarum quasi captivorum per pompam (rem ridiculam) duceretur, . . .*

[134] S.H.A. *Gall.* 8.7–9.1: *ibant praeterea gentes simulatae, ut Gothi, Sarmatae, Franci, Persae, ita ut non minus quam duceni globis singulis ducerentur.* Merten (1968: 94–100).

not restricted to the later Empire. Tacitus blames Domitian for having bought men who possessed suitable physical appearance and hair to play the role of captives in his triumph over the Chatti.[135] Similar rumours concerned the *ovatio* that Caligula held in AD 40. Persius writes ironically of how weapons were acquired to appear as booty and how royal mantles and yellow wigs were prepared for the captives:

> O bone, num ignoras? missa est a Caesare laurus
> insignem ob cladem Germanae pubis et aris
> frigidus excutitur cinis ac iam postibus arma,
> iam chlamydas regum, iam lutea gausapa captis
> essedaque ingentesque locat Caesonia Rhenos.

My dear man, didn't you know? A laurel's come from Caesar to announce his triumph over the German tribes. They're clearing the altars of cold ashes. Caesonia's already hiring the arms to hang on doorposts, royal cloaks, war chariots, blond wigs for prisoners, giant Rhines.[136]

Suetonius provides a similar picture (*Cal.* 47):

Conversus hinc ad curam triumphi praeter captivos ac transfugas barbaros Galliarum quoque procerissimum quemque et, ut ipse dicebat, ἀξιοθριάμβευτον, ac nonnullos ex principibus legit ac seposuit ad pompam coegitque non tantum rutilare et summittere comam, sed et sermonem Germanicum addiscere et nomina barbarica ferre.

Then turning his attention to his triumph, besides the barbarian captives and deserters, he also chose all the tallest of the Gauls, and, as he himself expressed it, those who were 'worthy of a triumph', as well as some of the chiefs. These he reserved for his parade, compelling them not only to dye their hair red and to let it grow long, but also to learn the German language and to assume barbarian names.

The details of the story provided by the two authors are perhaps exaggerated, but the basic message of the costuming is most certainly historically correct. The triumph was a spectacular role-playing, in which the adding and improving of some displays cannot have been that uncommon. In fact, the younger Pliny speaks with disfavour of the *mimici currus* and *simulacra falsae victoriae* that appeared in earlier triumphs, all in contrast to the authentic procession that is to celebrate the true victories of Trajan.[137]

In staging his triumphal play, Caligula paid particular attention not only to the status of his 'captives', but to their ethnic appearance as well. German captives had to

---

[135] Tac. *Agr.* 39: *inerat conscientia derisui fuisse nuper falsum e Germania triumphum, emptis per commercia, quorum habitus et crines in captivorum speciem formarentur.*

[136] Pers. 6.43–7 (tr. G. Lee). I have followed the translation and commentary by Lee and Barr (1987: 163), and taken *gausapa* as wigs.

[137] Plin. *Pan.* 16.3, probably referring to the triumphs of Domitian in particular.

look German and, being Gauls, the men chosen simply did not appear barbarian enough. According to Strabo, compared to the Gauls, the Germans were wilder, taller, and had yellower (redder) hair.[138] Hence, Caligula's Gauls had to be transformed into true northern barbarians to suit their roles.

First and foremost, true Germans captives had to be men of stature. Consequently, the Gauls chosen by Caligula were the tallest, the *procerrissimi*. Many ancient authors stress the long and forceful bodies of the German people,[139] and in Marcellus' triumph over Germans and Gauls of 222 BC, Plutarch maintains that the captives were of gigantic size.[140] Florus also stresses the conspicuous stature of Teutobodus, the king of the Teutones, when displayed by Marius in 101 BC.[141] Tall, even gigantic bodies connoted a bellicose nature and applied to all northern barbarian peoples, especially the Germans and the Britons.[142] Oakley stresses that stories of defeated gigantic enemies are multipresent in Latin literature, since 'the Romans had a complex about their short stature when compared to the Celts or the Germans'.[143] Tall captives suggested martial skills and, not least, they suited the visual occasion of the triumphal procession. For prominent barbarians on display, tallness was almost a prerequisite.

Caligula's 'captives' were asked to colour their hair red and have it grow long.[144] Persius instead proposes golden wigs. Several ancient authors stress the (golden) red hair of the Germans.[145] The long loosely hanging hair also appears as a typical trait of barbarians in art, stressing their wild, uncivilized nature,[146] as opposed to the irreproachable coiffures of the Romans and Greeks.

The 'captives' were not only supposed to look German. Suetonius stresses that they were asked to assume barbarian names and learn the German language. The

---

[138] Strab. 7.1.2.

[139] Caes. *Gall.* 1.39, 4.1, *Afr.* 40.6; Colum. 3.8.2–3; Strab. 7.1.2; Tac. *Germ.* 4.2–3, *Agr.* 11.2, *Ann.* 1.64.2; Flor. *Epit.* 1.45.12–13; Mela 3.26; Iuv. 8.251–3; Manil. 4.715. Balsdon (1979: 214–15). The defeat of gigantic enemies, in particular Gauls and Germans, was also a literary topos, see Liv. 7.9.6–10.4, 7.26.1–10; Plut. *Marc.* 7.1; cf. Vell. Pat. 1.12.4. Oakley (1985: 407–8).

[140] Plut. *Marc.* 8.1. The *Fasti* label the triumph as one held over Gauls and Germans. Some have tried to explain this early mention of Germans by the fact that they were confused with the Gallic Gaesati, fought by Marcellus. Others think that the *Germani* were originally a Gallic tribe, who took part in the war. Pais (1920: 116–18, 401–16); Hafner (1968).

[141] Flor. *Epit.* 1.38.10.

[142] Britons: Strab. 4.5.2. Balsdon (1979: 215). Compared to Romans, Gauls were tall too: Caes. *Gall.* 2.30; Liv. 7.9.8, 38.17.2–4; Sil. *Pun.* 5.112–13.

[143] Oakley (1995: 407).

[144] The note on the growing of the hair suggests that the proposal was advanced quite sometime before the ovation. Alternatively, as Persius possibly suggests, the 'captives' would have worn wigs.

[145] Tac. *Germ.* 4.2; Liv. 38.17.2–4; Strab. 7.1.2. Germans reddened their hair: Amm. Marc. 27.2.2. Gauls were characterized as redheaded: Diod. Sic. 5.28.1.

[146] Liv. 38.17.2–4; Tac. *Germ.* 31.1. Balsdon (1979: 215–16).

names must have been advertised on placards in the parade, but what about the language?[147] When were the 'captives' supposed to speak? Possibly, they were requested to talk at some point before or after the procession. But Suetonius' passage focuses on Caligula's concern for the realization of the procession itself (*ad curam triumphi*, *ad pompam*). Probably, then, the men acting as Germans were obliged to utter some words in the parade itself. We have already seen how the teachers who accompanied the royal children in Paullus' triumph taught them how to beg and supplicate.[148] Such acts of supplication must have occurred in many triumphs, and it is unlikely that they were performed in silence. Vergil provides an indication of talking captives when depicting the shield of Aeneas. Here, the conquered peoples walked in a long row, as varied in languages and appearance as in their style of dresses and arms (*incedunt victae longo ordine gentes,* | *quam variae linguis, habitu tam vestis et armis*).[149] Again, the captives' language appears in a clear triumphal context. These passages suggest that the spectators actually heard the prisoners speak, and also that the many languages constituted one of the characteristics of each group of *nationes* and *gentes* on display, marking their origins. A large variety of languages heard, as in Vergil's version of Octavian's parade, denoted a conquest far spread. Also, foreign barbaric talk contrasted to the Latin of the victors, manifested not least in the written placards borne along.

Humiliation, mocking, and the role of fate

Pompey had his prisoners led on parade unbound, a performance that must have formed an exception. Normally, prisoners were shown chained or bound (Figs. 17, 18).[150] They were scorned and humiliated, and at times they were whipped and executed. Their very defeat justified the cruel treatment, as did their former misdeeds against Rome.

Humiliation constituted a main component in the display of the captives.[151] It was the fear of public disgrace, the thought of being dragged before the eyes of all people in chains deprived of former power and glory, that led Mithridates and Cleopatra to take their own lives to avoid being led in triumph. As a further means of disgrace, close relatives who had been fighting on Rome's side might be invited to watch the display, as might friendly kings.[152] When not dragged on

---

[147] Again, if the 'captives' were supposed to learn the German language, this must have been prepared some time in advance.

[148] Plut. *Aem.* 33.6–8.

[149] Verg. *Aen.* 8.722–3.

[150] For the Campana reliefs, see Abaecherli (1935/6: pl. VIII.1–3, 5); Borbein (1968: 40, Taf. 7); Gabelmann (1981: 453–5, Abb. 14–15); Ferris (2000: pl. 72); Tortorella (2008); *Trionfi romani*, 128–9, I.2.9–10.

[151] Coleman (1990: 46–7; 1999: esp. 239–40).

[152] Strab. 7.1.4; Eutrop. 4.8.4.

FIGURE 17 Prisoners
paraded in the tri-
umphs were usually
chained, whether
walking or, as here,
drawn on carts. The
photo shows a detail
from the frieze of the
arch of Trajan at
Benevento.

FIGURE 17 Prisoners paraded in the triumphs were usually chained, whether walking or, as here, drawn on carts. The photo shows a detail from the frieze of the arch of Trajan at Benevento.

foot in chains, the captives might be placed on biers, carried through the streets, their helplessness exposed.[153] They could also be used as decorative elements to form part of trophies together with the weaponry they once carried (Figs. 4, 16).[154] They might even be forced to play their own vanquished roles from the war. Josephus maintains that in Titus and Vespasian's Jewish triumph each defeated general was exhibited in the very pose in which he had been captured.[155] Humiliation cannot be carried much further.

Another means of exposing the captives to humiliation, much exploited in the triumphs, was that of ironical mocking.[156] Jests, aiming at the failed presumptuous intentions of the conquered party, were regularly made. In Marius' parade of 104 BC, Jugurtha was mocked for his former arrogant statement that Rome could be bought and would one day perish if it could only find a purchaser.[157] The prophecy had come to nothing, but instead the former king was led though the

[153] Sen. *Herc. O.* 109–10; *Dial.* 7.25.4.

[154] Sen. *Tro.* 149–50. Pomponius Porphyrio suggests that prisoners taken at sea were driven in the captive vessels, *ad Hor. Epist.* 2.1.192.

[155] Joseph. *BJ* 7.147.

[156] Cf. Coleman (1990: 47), discussing the Roman penal character in general. Among other examples, she cites the soldiers' mocking of Jesus, dressing him up as a king because of his alleged claims to be king of the Jews. Elsewhere, analysing the punishment of 'informers', Coleman (1999: 241–2) writes: 'This ironical inversion . . . is characteristic of Roman penal thinking.'

[157] Flor. *Epit.* 1.36.17–18.

FIGURE 18 Two bearded male prisoners represented in grief and lament on a triumphal scene in terracotta. The captives sit on an open cart, chained to their necks and ankles. Two attendants hold or even pull them by the chains, while a third leads the horses, which pull the pair forwards. This Campana plaque is dated to somewhere between the middle of the first to the early second century AD, but the earliest preserved similar depictions, though with female captives, stem from the Augustan age.

city of which he had dared to talk so provocatively in chains to his execution. The king had committed hubris and for this he was punished. The ironical mockery might also form part of the performance itself. Several authors tell the story of how the captive Gauls shown by Aemilius Papus in 225 BC were led wearing their breastplates, which were publicly removed as the parade reached the Capitol.[158] Again, the act was a response to an earlier arrogant statement on part of the vanquished, as the Gauls had promised not to take off their breastplates until they had mounted the Capitol. The triumph replayed their vow, but the scene was reversed from the prophesised victorious act to an ironical, humiliating scene of disgrace and defeat.[159]

The display of former kings and military leaders in the utmost pose of humiliation, deprived of all belongings and power and forced to pass the mocking spectators of Rome formed the utmost visual illustration of the changing turns of Fortuna. In consequence, literary triumphal descriptions frequently emphasize the role of fate.[160] Horace points out the part played by Fortuna as captive kings

[158] Flor. *Epit* 1.20; Dio Cass. 12.50.4 (Zonar. 8.20).

[159] Armed Gauls on the Capitol was a delicate affair, to say the least, and perhaps one might read the event as an apotropaic precaution against further Gallic attempts to invade Rome.

[160] See the illustrative passage in Sen. *Dial.* 7.25.4, and (in Swedish), Östenberg (2008).

are led in triumph, their hands bound back.[161] There was also the case of Andriscus, known as Pseudophilippus, an usurper to the Macedonian throne, who was defeated by Q. Caecilius Metellus Macedonicus and led in triumph in 146 BC.[162] Despite his fall, Florus stresses that 'Fortune thus far smiled upon him in his misfortune that the Roman people triumphed over him as if over a real king'.[163] The role of the principal enemy was by tradition one of status and dignity. Being only a pretender to the throne, Andriscus' processional display actually bestowed him with the royal status he had desired, if just for a day.

The fate of the captives paraded moved the spectators to a variety of emotions. Fates undeserved caused pity and lamentation, as when smaller children were exposed. Mostly, however, the principal captives were staged and perceived as true enemies of the Roman order, who deserved nothing but scorn. Thus, the spectators of Caesar's triumph applauded the images that showed the deaths of Achillas and Pothinus, and they laughed as they saw a representation of King Pharnaces in flight.[164]

The fascination for mankind's ever-changing fate concerned not only Fortuna and her favours as such, but to an even higher degree the human reactions to their destinies. Therefore, the captives' behaviour and facial expressions as they were led in the parade were closely studied. Ovid, exiled in Tomis, complains not that he has missed all the gold and purple of the triumphs in Rome, but rather *regum vultus, certissima pignora mentis*, 'the countenances of the kings, the most revealing indications of their minds'.[165] Ancient authors particularly stress how many leading prisoners walked with their gaze fixed towards the ground. Silius Italicus pictures King Syphax 'with the downcast eyes of a captive'.[166] Ovid maintains that while some prisoners appear as forgetful of their destinies, others turn their countenances to earth, as becomes the occasion.[167] A major point is that the captives, who formerly fought with open, rebellious gaze, have been pacified.[168] Their eyes directed towards the ground, the captives show that they have submitted to Fortune and accepted their subjection by Rome.

---

[161] Hor. *Epist.* 2.1.191; cf. Ov. *Pont.* 3.4.109–10; Dio Cass. 40.41.2.

[162] For Andriscus and his revolt, see Helliesen (1986).

[163] Flor. *Epit.* 1.30.5: *hoc quoque illi in malis suis indulgente fortuna, ut de eo populus Romanus quasi de rege vero triumpharet.*

[164] App. *BCiv.* 2.101.

[165] Ov. *Pont.* 3.4.27.

[166] Sil. *Pun.* 17.629–30.

[167] Ov. *Trist.* 4.2.23–4: *et cernet vultus aliis pro tempore versos, | terribiles aliis inmemoresque sui.*

[168] Ibid. 4.2.29–30: *hic, qui nunc in humo lumen miserabile fixit, | non isto vultu, cum tulit arma, fuit,* 'This one, who now has fixed his sad gaze on the ground, had not such countenance when he bore arms'; [Ov.] *Cons. ad Liv.* 275–6: *et tandem trepidos vultus inque illa ferocum | invitis lacrimas decidere ora genis,* 'and faces anxious at last, and the tears falling down unwilling, haughty cheeks'.

Death or remission?

Appian claims that after the triumph had been concluded, Pompey sent all prisoners, kings only excluded, home at the expense of the state.[169] This stands out as an exception in the triumphal history of Rome. In all probability, Pompey made a point out of leading the captives unbound, saving the grand part and sending many of them back, thus advertising the greatness of a leader and state in unthreatened power.[170] Most commonly, the mass of less-renowned prisoners would have been sold as slaves, put to labour, or employed in games. The more eminent captives were treated more individually, and met with destinies that varied highly depending on their status and former misdeeds. Some were executed as part of the triumphal ritual, while others were pardoned and at times even admitted into Roman citizenship. There were also those who ended up in prison and others who were spared but kept in custody, often in some minor city close to Rome.

Appian's comment on Pompey's acts highlights the enormous importance attached to the processional occasion itself. Pompey's captives were taken to Rome with the explicit purpose of being put on parade, after which the state itself covered the expense of their return. We do not know when the decision to send the captives back was taken, but at other occasions, the senate determined the prisoners' post-processional fates only after the triumph had been concluded. For example, it was only after Aemilius Paullus and Gnaeus Octavius had performed their Macedonian triumphs in 167 BC that the senate met to discuss the subsequent destinies of the prisoners displayed by Paullus.[171] At this occasion, they decided that Perseus and his family were to be placed in Alba Fucens, while Bithys, the son of the Thracian King Cotys, was to be sent to Carseoli together with the hostages for safe-keeping.[172] The rest of the prisoners were put in prison. The practice of postponing the decisions concerning the handling of captives until after the triumph shows that a prime reason for shipping them to Rome at all was their very processional display.

One matter had to be decided before the parade set off, though, and that was whether or not the principal enemy was to be executed as part of the ritual. If such an execution was to take place, the procession halted at the base of the Capitoline hill, while the principal enemy was led aside to the Carcer and killed by way of decapitation or strangulation. The literary sources tell of such triumphal

---

[169] App. *Mith.* 117.

[170] Appian's comment is probably somewhat exaggerated. Other sources state that many Jews settled in Rome after Pompey's victories. Perhaps the statement refers to the more distinguished prisoners only (except for the kings), while the large majority had to stay put.

[171] Liv. 45.42.4–5; cf. Diod. Sic. 31.9; Zonar. 9.24.

[172] Bithys and the hostages were soon afterwards sent back home, Liv. 45.42.6–12; Zonar. 9.24.

executions on several occasions, and in modern literature, they are described as being more or less compulsory.[173] However, most triumphal descriptions are silent on the matter, and although no conclusions can be drawn *e silentio*, it is nevertheless clear that there were processions which did not include an execution of the principal enemy. We have already seen how Perseus and Bithys were placed in custody rather than being put to death by Aemilius Paullus. The royal Illyrian prisoners led in parade by Anicius Gallus the same year were likewise conferred to safe-keeping,[174] and King Bituitus, the king of the Arverni, was sent to Alba Fucens after his display in the triumph of Fabius Maximus in 120 BC.[175] Appian states that only Aristobulus, king of the Jews, was killed during Pompey's triumph of 61 BC (and he is wrong; Aristobulus died in 49 BC),[176] Arsinoë was released after her appearance in Caesar's parade,[177] and Tiberius spared the life of Bato, chief of the Pannonians, in his triumph in AD 12.[178]

While it is thus clear that not all of the leading captives were executed as part of the ceremony, it is just as evident that many were. The sources explicitly name the following leading prisoners as having been put to death during the processions: the Samnite leader Gaius Pontius (291 BC), Aristonicus, who claimed to be a son of Eumenes II (126 BC), Jugurtha (104 BC), pirate chiefs (74 BC), Vercingetorix (46 BC), the Galatian King Adiatorix and Alexander of Emesa (29 BC), and Simon Bar Gorias (AD 71).[179] Besides, Appian describes how Britomaris, king of the Gallic Senones, was tortured and led in triumph in 283 BC.[180] Both Cicero and Appian describe the killing of the leading captive as a customary feature of the triumph.[181]

Why then were certain leading prisoners put to death while others were spared? Modern scholars have proposed different interpretations for the killing of the principal *captivi* as part of the triumphs. The executions have been read as part of a rite concluding the war, as a punishment effected by the killing of the enemy leader or as a ritual sacrifice for the dead.[182] This is not the place to enter into a profound discussion of the various possible interpretations. Still, it is

[173] Versnel (1970: 95); Lemosse (1972: 447); Künzl (1988: 90).
[174] Liv. 45.43.9–10.
[175] Liv. *Per.* 61; Val. Max. 9.6.3.
[176] App. *Mith.* 117. For Aristobulus, see Joseph. *AJ* 14.92–6; Dio Cass. 39.56.6. *RE* II (1895), s.v. 'Aristobulos' (6) (U. Wilchen), 909. Heftner (1995: 313). For Tigranes, cf. *Mith.* 105.
[177] Dio Cass. 43.19.4.
[178] Suet. *Tib.* 20; Ov. *Pont.* 2.1.45–6.
[179] Pontius: Liv. *Per.* 11; Aristonicus: Sall. *Epist. Mithr.* 8–9; Vell. Pat. 2.4.1; Eutrop. 4.20; cf. Liv. *Per.* 59; Flor. *Epit.* 1.35.6–7; Jugurtha: Liv. *Per.* 67; Plut. *Mar.* 12; Eutrop. 4.27.6; Oros. 5.15.19; pirate chiefs: Cic. *Verr.* II.5.26.66–7; Vercingetorix: Dio Cass. 40.41.3, 43.19.4; cf. Plut. *Caes.* 27.5; Adiatorix and Alexander: Strab. 12.3.6; Dio Cass. 51.2.2–3; Simon Bar Gorias: Joseph. *BJ* 7.153–5.
[180] App. *Samn.* 6.1, *Gall.* 4.11. Brennan (1994: 426–7).
[181] Cic. *Verr.* II.5.30.77; App. *Mith.* 117; cf. Liv. 26.13.15; Zonar. 7.21.11.
[182] Rüpke (1990: 210–11).

important to stress the circumstance, pointed out above, that the leading captive was at times saved and pardoned. The fact that not all processions included such a kill conflicts with the interpretation of the executions as a ritual sacrifice or as a rite concluding the war. Rites and rituals demand some repetitive actions, and would probably have required compulsory executions.

Instead, sources suggest that the executions were punishments for crimes committed towards Rome by the enemy leader.[183] By their conquest, the defeated peoples and their leader were *iure belli* at the mercy of the Romans.[184] Depending on their earlier acts, the leading captives could be pardoned, sentenced to custody, or to death. If capital punishment was chosen, the enemy would mostly be saved for triumphal exhibition, where the execution was also carried out. For example, Caesar condemned Vercingetorix to death at his defeat,[185] but waited until the Gallic triumph six years later to carry out the execution. The Roman people were to set eyes on their former enemy and partake in his punishment as well.

Lives were spared when enemy leaders had behaved well in the eyes of Rome. Hence, in AD 12, when the Pannonian leader Bato was led in triumph, he was not killed but sent to Ravenna afterwards furnished with gifts. The reason, Suetonius explains, was that in the preceding war, Bato had allowed Tiberius and the Roman army to escape when they had been caught in an ambush. Tiberius' treatment of Bato was thus a gesture of gratitude.[186] The reward came only after the triumph, though. Bato was by definition an enemy leader who had been defeated, and his processional display was required.

Vice versa, leaders who were executed as part of the triumph are pointed out in the sources as criminals. The chief of the Gallic Senones, Britomaris, had killed Roman *legati*, and as a punishment he was tortured, led, and in all probability killed in the triumph held in 283 BC.[187] Aristonicus, who was strangled as part of M'. Aquillius' triumph of 126 BC, had killed the Roman proconsul in Asia at the beginning of the war and for this he was sentenced to death.[188] Vercingetorix was denied mercy on grounds that he had betrayed the friendship with Caesar and Rome,[189] and Octavian had Adiatorix killed as part of his triumph since the Galatian had earlier attacked and killed Roman citizens.[190] In the *triplex triumphus* of 29 BC,

---

[183] *Contra* Lemosse (1972: 447). Rüpke (1990: 211) maintains that a punitive aspect, killing the responsible leader, is possible, but not verifiable. Bonfante Warren (1974: 580) discussing the work of Versnel, labels the executions 'human sacrifice'.

[184] When Zenobia was captured, she entered *in iura Romana*, S.H.A. *Tyr. Trig.* 30.3. See also e.g. Liv. 30.14.10–11, 30.15.5–6.

[185] Dio Cass. 40.41.2–3.

[186] Suet. *Tib.* 20; cf. Ov. *Pont.* 2.1.45–6.

[187] App. *Samn.* 6.1, *Gall.* 4.11. All the adult male Senones were killed, the women and children led into slavery.

[188] Vell. Pat. 2.4.1; Oros. 5.10; cf. Liv. *Per.* 59; Sall. *Epist. Mithr.* 8–9; Flor. *Epit.* 1.35.4–7.

[189] Dio Cass. 40.41.2.　　　[190] Strab. 12.3.6.

Alexander of Emesa in Arabia was also executed, on the grounds that he had achieved his kingdom as a reward for accusing Octavian.[191] In the Pseudo-Ovidian *Consolatio ad Liviam*, similarly, the author imagines a triumph in which the chief German captive is led to his death in the Carcer, thus paying the penalty for the death of Drusus.[192] There are more examples. Strabo stresses that the leading German prisoners paraded by Germanicus in AD 17 were led in the triumph as a penalty for their opposition in war.[193] And when Jugurtha died in the Carcer, Plutarch points out that he 'paid the penalty, which his crime deserved'.[194]

Crime and penalty were closely linked and both were on display. The public announcement of the crimes that justified the punishment formed an important part of the processional exhibition and added to the humiliation of the captives. The crimes were announced by way of written placards or they were shown by imagery, closely attached to the prisoners.[195] Outside the triumphal context too, placards stating their crimes preceded criminals led to their execution.[196] This practice forms a clear parallel to the emphatic announcement of the captives' misdeeds in the triumph that further strengthens the interpretation of the leading and killing of captives as a public punishment. The spectators of the procession, the Roman people and foreign guests, were not only to watch the enemies of Rome being dragged, whipped, humiliated, and even killed. They were also to participate in the punishment and fully to grasp the just causes.

HOSTAGES

Ancient writers tell of the presence of hostages in two triumphal parades only: Flamininus' victory procession held in 194 BC to celebrate the defeat of King Philip of Macedon and Pompey's great eastern celebration performed in 61 BC. According to Livy, Flamininus led many noble prisoners and hostages before his car on the third day of his triumph. Among these were Demetrius, the son of King Philip, and Armenas, the son of the Spartan King Nabis.[197] We know that Demetrius and Armenas were hostages rather than prisoners, as both Livy and Appian state that, according to the treaty, Philip had surrendered his son

---

[191] Dio Cass. 51.2.2–3.   [192] [Ov.] *Cons. ad Liv.* 277–8.

[193] Strab. 7.1.4.   [194] Plut. *Mar.* 12.4.

[195] Placards: Veyne (1983: esp. 285); Coleman (1999: 237–8); Östenberg (forthcoming).

[196] Suet. *Cal.* 32.2, *Dom.* 10.1; Dio Cass. 54.3.6–7. Note also the placard (τίτλος in John 19: 19) placed above the head of Christ on the cross, announcing his crime (αἰτία) of having aspired to be the king of the Jews, Mark 15: 26; Matth. 27: 37; cf. Luke 23: 38.

[197] Liv. 34.52.9–10: *et ante currum multi nobiles captivi obsidesque, inter quos Demetrius, regis Philippi filius, fuit et Armenes, Nabidis tyranni filius, Lacedaemonius*, cf. Eutrop. 4.2.3. Modern works and translations mostly refer to Nabis' son as Armenas, using the Spartan form of the name.

Demetrius and certain noble friends as hostages.[198] Nabis too had been forced to present Flamininus with hostages after his defeat. The terms of peace stated that they were to be five in number, that they had to be approved by the Roman commander, and that they should include Nabis' son.[199] Thus, according to our sources, apart from Demetrius and Armenas, the noble hostages led in Flamininus' triumph included prominent Macedonian royal friends and also at least four more hostages given by Nabis. After the triumph, Demetrius remained in Rome until 191/190 BC, when he was released as a reward for Philip's loyalty in the war against Antiochus.[200] The Spartan hostages were released too, except for Armenas, who had to stay in Rome and died there shortly afterwards.[201]

Flamininus' triumph officially celebrated the victory over Macedonia only. Still, his parade saw hostages given not only by Philip, but also by the Spartan Nabis. By leading Lacedaemonian hostages in his parade, Flamininus was able to include the suppression of the tyrant Nabis in the manifestation of his Greek success. Also, the display of Spartan hostages effectively concealed the fact that Nabis had contributed with troops in the campaign against Philip, whose defeat was now officially on parade.

Some 130 years later, in 61 BC, Pompey had hostages walk in his two-day-long parade. Appian states in rather general terms that 324 chiefs, sons, and generals of the kings whom Pompey had fought went ahead of the triumphator in the procession, and that some of these had been taken prisoners, others given as hostages.[202] Plutarch is more specific. According to his description, the hostages led by Pompey had been presented by the Caucasian peoples of Iberia and Albania and by the king of Commagene.[203] While we know nothing of the hostages from Commagene, Appian states that after their defeat, the Albanians and Iberians offered Pompey presents and hostages.[204] More specifically, Florus and Dio Cassius both maintain that Artoces, the king of the Iberians, was compelled to hand over his own children to Pompey as hostages.[205] Without doubt, these royal children were led in Pompey's triumphal train among the sons of defeated kings.

[198] Liv. 33.13.14, 33.30.10; App. *Mac.* 9.2; see also Plut. *Flam.* 9.5.

[199] Liv. 34.35.11, cf. 34.40.4.

[200] Polyb. 21.3; Liv. 36.35.13–14; App. *Mac.* 9.5; Zonar. 9.19.14. For Demetrius in the triumph and afterwards, Allen (2006: 1–10).

[201] Polyb. 21.3.

[202] App. *Mith.* 117: Αὐτοῦ δὲ τοῦ Πομπηίου προῆγον ὅσοι τῶν πεπολεμημένων βασιλέων ἡγεμόνες ἢ παῖδες ἢ στρατηγοὶ ἦσαν, οἱ μὲν αἰχμάλωτοι ὄντες οἱ δὲ ἐς ὁμηρείαν δεδομένοι, τριακόσιοι μάλιστα καὶ εἴκοσι καὶ τέσσαρες.

[203] Plut. *Pomp.* 45.4: ᾿Αλβανῶν δὲ καὶ ᾿Ιβήρων ὅμηροι καὶ τοῦ Κομμαγηνῶν βασιλέως,...

[204] App. *Mith.* 103. For the conflict with the Iberians and the Albanians, see Dreher (1996).

[205] Flor. *Epit.* 1.40.28; Dio Cass. 37.2.5–7.

In his article on hostages in Rome, Stephan Elbern distinguishes between hostages given at different kinds of peace treaties: the *deditiones*, the *foedera aequa*, and the *foedera iniqua*.²⁰⁶ The *deditio*, capitulation, was the most common form of treaty imposed by Rome on her 'barbarian' enemies. Normally, a large number of hostages were involved. They were treated not much differently from prisoners-of-war and accordingly had few rights.²⁰⁷ Elbern categorizes the hostages presented to Pompey by the Albanians and the Iberians as forming part of *deditiones*.

In contrast, the hostages given as part of a *foedus* were sacrosanct. The *foedus aequum*, applied when Rome chose not to restrict the sovereignty of the defeated state, constituted the customary agreement with the kingdoms of the Hellenistic East. Normally, only a few hostages were given and royal children included. The children were usually quite young, to allow them to be formed by Roman culture and education during their stay in Italy.²⁰⁸ According to Elbern, the hostages presented to Flamininus by Philip and Nabis belong to this category.²⁰⁹

In a *foedus iniquum*, finally, the function of the hostages was to force the inferior party to obedience towards Rome. Elbern classifies the hostages presented to Pompey by the king of Commagene as belonging to this category. This might well be correct, although little is known about the nature of the relations between Rome and Commagene during the Third Mithridatic War. Appian states only that Antiochus, the king of Commagene, at first resisted Pompey, but that he soon entered into friendly relations with the Roman general.²¹⁰ After the war, Pompey expanded the realm of Commagene to include Seleucia on the Euphrates as well as parts of the Roman conquests in Mesopotamia.²¹¹ According to Appian, Antiochus' name was included on the written placard that announced the defeated kings to the spectators of Pompey's parade.²¹² However, Commagene appears in no official list of the eastern nations over which Pompey held his triumph.²¹³

From Elbern's analysis, it is clear that the function and status of the hostages presented to Flamininus and Pompey varied. Still, when led in the triumphal

²⁰⁶ Elbern (1990: 98–100, 137–40). Elbern also discusses hostages given at armistices and short-term treaties as well as those handed over as securities of a continued dominance, ibid. 100–3, 140. Allen (2006: 13–22) stresses that the categories are overlapping.

²⁰⁷ Elbern (1990: 109).

²⁰⁸ Ibid. 107–8.

²⁰⁹ When first presented by Philip in 197 BC, the hostages were according to Elbern handed over as part of an armistice. Later, in 196 BC, the hostages were used to confirm the treaty as part of a *foedus aequum*. Ibid. 139–40.

²¹⁰ App. *Mith.* 106.

²¹¹ Strab. 16.2.3; App. *Mith.* 114. *RE* I (1894), s.v. 'Antiochos' (37), 2487–9 (U. Wilcken).

²¹² App. *Mith.* 117.

²¹³ Plut. *Pomp.* 45.2; Plin. *Nat.* 7.26.98; Diod. Sic. 40.4.

processions, the hostages all looked alike. In Flamininus' three-day-long triumph, the hostages were led together with the prisoners in the final day's parade. Livy stresses that they were *nobiles*, and they were followed by the triumphator and the army only.[214] Appian too, in describing Pompey's parade, writes that the leading prisoners and hostages walked just in front of the Roman general.[215] Plutarch includes the hostages given by the Iberians, Albanians, and the king of Commagene in his rather restricted list of prominent royal prisoners displayed. Clearly, the importance of the hostages was their status as royal relatives and friends. In comparison, any differences in origin and function mattered but little.

Hostages were led among and as prominent prisoners. In Flamininus' triumph, prisoners and hostages (*multi nobiles captivi obsidesque*) formed a joint display of important nobles shown in substantial numbers.[216] Livy emphasizes that the group included two royal sons, Demetrius and Armenas. Their capacity as hostages rather than prisoners is not pointed out, and their kingly status was clearly much more significant than their precise roles. In Pompey's triumph, Plutarch adds the hostages to his list of the most eminent prisoners on display.[217] Appian too emphasizes that chiefs, sons, and generals of the kings were led in the procession, after which he almost incidentally adds that some were prisoners, other hostages.[218] Identifying some of them, he makes no distinction as to which of the two categories they belonged to.

The fact that hostages were grouped among the prisoners is probably why they so seldom appear explicitly in the descriptions of Roman triumphal processions. The parade of prisoners is often likely to conceal joint exhibitions of prisoners and hostages. After all, the giving and accepting of hostages formed a customary part of treaties concluding wars, and the presence of hostages in the triumphs of Flamininus and Pompey in no way stands out as exceptional.

Among many examples, hostages were most likely led in the triumph held by Aemilius Paullus in 167 BC after the defeat of King Perseus and the Macedonians at Pydna. Livy maintains that after the triumph had been performed, the senate decided that Perseus should be taken to Alba Fucens and that Bithys, son of the Thracian King Cotys, should be sent to Carseoli together with the hostages.[219] No hostages appear in the literary descriptions of the triumph itself, which do, however, note the presence of both Perseus and Bithys.[220] Since the senate

---

[214] Liv. 34.52.9–10, quoted above.

[215] App. *Mith.* 117, quoted above.

[216] Liv. 34.52.9–10.

[217] Plut. *Pomp.* 45.4.

[218] App. *Mith.* 117.

[219] Liv. 45.42.4–5. Bithys had been presented as hostage to Perseus together with other Thracians. After Pydna, they passed into Roman hands, Polyb. 30.17.

[220] Perseus: Diod. Sic. 31.8.12 (apud Sync.); Liv. 45.40.6, 45.41.10–11; Plut. *Aem.* 34.1–4; Zonar. 9.24.3–4; Bithys: Zonar. 9.24.3–4.

discussed the fate of the hostages together with that of the prominent prisoners just after the triumph, they too must have been led in the parade. Some of the hostages presented by Antiochus III were very possibly exhibited together with the prisoners in the triumphs held by Scipio Asiaticus in 189 BC and Manlius Vulso in 187 BC.[221] In 187 BC, the hostages handed over by the Aetolians and Cephallenians might well have been led among the prisoners in Fulvius Nobilior's triumph.[222]

Thus, in the triumphal processions, the hostages were not presented as a distinct category. Instead, they were exhibited among and as prisoners. This is noteworthy, since the function and status of prisoners and hostages often differed substantially. Being led as a prominent prisoner in a Roman triumph was considered the utmost humiliation, and you might even be executed at the end of the procession. An eminent hostage, on the other hand, was sacrosanct.[223] After the parade, both prisoners and hostages were commonly kept under guard, but their conditions of life varied considerably. Prominent prisoners were mostly strictly controlled; they were often held in uncomfortable conditions and were sometimes even put to death.[224] In contrast, hostages of rank enjoyed a substantial amount of freedom. Younger eminent children in fact lived lives that did not differ much from those of royal sons sent to Rome for education by kings with friendly relations to Rome.[225] What is more, while both prisoners and hostages on parade manifested the achievements and outcome of the victorious war, the hostages also presented future obligations of the subjugated and loyal peoples towards Rome and their support for it.

In all probability, many triumphs once included larger groups of less prominent hostages, delivered as part of the conclusion of *deditiones* and led among the mass of anonymous prisoners. No such groups of hostages have been recorded in the sources, probably due to their lack of status, as well as their display among captives. As seen, sources do tell, however, that when distinguished hostages were put on triumphal parade, they were led among the most prominent prisoners, with whom they formed a category of exclusive noble and royal subjects.

---

[221] Polyb. 21.42.21–3; Liv. 38.38.15–16; Diod. Sic. 29.10 (Const. Exc.); App. *Syr.* 38–9. Livy states that 32 royal leaders, prefects, and nobles were led in Scipio Asiaticus' triumph (37.59.5–6), while Cn. Manlius Vulso paraded 52 enemy leaders (39.7.2).

[222] Liv. 38.11.6–7, 38.28.6. According to Livy (39.5.16–17), 27 leaders walked in Nobilior's triumph. They were Aetolians, Cephallanians, and commanders of Antiochus.

[223] Dion. Hal. 5.34.1. Elbern (1990: 109, 116–18).

[224] See e.g. Diod. Sic. 31.9 (Photius; Const. Exc.).

[225] Braund (1984: 14–15); Elbern (1990: 112–14). For example, Demetrius, the son of Seleucus IV, lived the life of a prince when held as hostage in Italy, see e.g. Diod. Sic. 31.18.1 (Const. Exc.). He was so loosely guarded that he was able to escape without anyone noticing it, Polyb. 31.11–15. Braund (1984: 13–14); Elbern (1990: 112–13); Allen (2006: 15, 89, 210–12).

ANIMALS

According to the *Historia Augusta*, some of the major processions arranged by Roman emperors in the third century AD included large numbers of exotic animals. Gordian III is said to have prepared a Persian triumph with, among others, 32 elephants, 10 elks, 10 tigers, 60 tame lions, 30 tame leopards, 10 hyenas, 6 hippopotami, 1 rhinoceros, 10 wild lions, 10 giraffes, 20 wild asses, and 40 wild horses.[226] Gordian died before he had the chance to carry out his triumphal plans, and the animals were inherited by Philip the Arab, who exhibited them in the secular games of AD 248 to celebrate Rome's millenary. When the Emperor Aurelian triumphed over Zenobia some twenty-five years later, he too is credited with displaying a variety of animals. According to the biographer of the *Historia Augusta*, the parade saw tigers, giraffes, and elks, together with 20 elephants and 200 tamed beasts of all kinds from Libya and Palestine.[227]

Foreign beasts in rows

In contrast to the descriptions in the *Historia Augusta* of parades rich in foreign species, there is only one earlier account to suggest the triumphal display of rows of exotic animals. Josephus writes of the Jewish triumph held in AD 71: 'Beasts of many species were led along, all decked out with appropriate adornments. The numerous attendants, who led each group, were dressed in garments of purple and gold . . .'.[228] Josephus is more concerned with the rich ornaments worn by the animals and their assistants than with the precise types of beasts displayed. Nevertheless, his account tells that the animals paraded were of many kinds, and that they were grouped, probably according to species. This is also how the *Historia Augusta* describes the beasts in the third century AD processions. Here, the precise figures indicate that elks, tigers, lions, and others were displayed not in an unordered zoological mass, but rather each kind separately. In fact, accounting for Aurelian's triumph, the biographer specifically states that the animals were shown *per ordinem*.[229] Paraded in ordered rows, the variety of exotic beasts marked the Roman control of the vast world of foreign fauna.

Nothing in Josephus' description suggests that the Jewish triumph would have been the only or the first to exhibit groups of animals of diverse species. In fact, this is very unlikely to have been the case. For one, processions in the eastern

[226] S.H.A. *Gord.* 33.1–2.
[227] S.H.A. *Aurel.* 33.4.
[228] Joseph. *BJ* 7.136–7: . . . ζῴων τε πολλαὶ φύσεις παρήγοντο κόσμον οἰκεῖον ἁπάντων περικειμένων. ἦν δὲ καὶ τὸ κομίζον ἕκαστα τούτων πλῆθος ἀνθρώπων ἁλουργαῖς ἐσθῆσι καὶ διαχρύσοις κεκοσμημένον, . . .
[229] S.H.A. *Aurel.* 33.4. In Ptolemy Philadelphus' grand procession, the animals clearly walked in groups according to their species, Ath. 5.197c–203b, esp. 5.200c–202a.

Mediterranean with exotic animals had long formed part of public demonstrations, and all sorts of beasts appeared in the lavish parades organized by the Hellenistic kings.[230] Clearly, the Roman processions were not unaffected by these spectacles. Also, from the earliest period, Romans had captured domestic cattle and led them in triumphs. For example, Florus maintains that before Dentatus' triumph over Pyrrhus in 275 BC, the victory processions in Rome had commonly contained *pecora Vulscorum* and *greges Sabinorum*.[231] Thus, way before the introduction of foreign beasts, Rome was used to witnessing animals being led along their streets in triumph.[232]

When then did Rome start to lead exotic animals in her parades? We know that M. Fulvius Nobilior arranged the first recorded *venatio*, with lions and *pantherae*,[233] in 186 BC as part of his *ludi votivi*,[234] and in 169 BC, the curule aediles presented games in the Circus Maximus that included sixty-three *Africanae*,[235] forty bears, and a number of elephants.[236] Shows then became more and more common, and in the last century BC the aediles put in large efforts and expenses in order to outdo each other in shows of magnitude and exoticism.[237] For our discussion of possible inclusion of animals in the triumphal processions, the most interesting games are the *ludi* held by victorious generals as votive games after the triumphs or given at the inauguration of temples vowed in battle.[238] The two spectacles, triumph and *ludi*, were often intimately connected, and in Fulvius Nobilior's case we know that the booty displayed in the triumph was later used to pay for the shows.[239] It cannot be ruled out that some beasts that fought during Nobilior's *ludi* were first presented to the Roman audience at his preceding triumph. The problem here is that we know only vaguely how much time passed between triumph and *ludi*; Livy tells that Nobilior triumphed in December 187 and that his games were held sometime during the next year.[240] For the same

---

[230] Philadelphus: Ath. 5.197c–203b, esp. 5.200c–202a. Rice (1983: 83–99); Köhler (1996: 106–7); Coleman (1996: 58–68).

[231] Flor. *Epit*. 1.13.27.

[232] Livy (9.31.16, cf. 9.31.7–8) also states that the Romans collected *praeda pecorum* after the victory of C. Iunius Bubulcus Brutus over the Samnites, celebrated by a triumph in 311 BC. Later, the triumph of L. Licinius Lucullus *de Vaccais et Cantabris* in 151 BC was preceded by a victory that rendered no gold and silver, only 10,000 cloaks, some cattle, and 50 hostages, given by the tribe of the Intercatii as part of the peace treaty (App. *Iber*. 54).

[233] Jennison (1937: 47, 183–7) interprets the *pantherae* as 'leopards'.

[234] Liv. 39.22.1–3.

[235] By *Africanae* or *Africanae bestiae*, the Latin authors mostly intend 'leopards' or 'lions, leopards, and other larger cats', Jennison (1937: 45–8).

[236] Liv. 44.18.8.

[237] Jennison (1937: 47–51); Kyle (1995: *passim*); Coleman (1996: 60–1).

[238] For the *ludi* held by victorious generals, see Bernstein (1998: 271–82).

[239] Liv. 39.5.7–11.

[240] Triumph: Liv. 39.5.13: *Triumphavit ante diem decimum Kal. Ianuarias*; games: Liv. 39.22.1–3. Fulvius Nobilior had planned to hold his triumph in Jan. 186 BC, but, as his bitter rival M. Aemilius Lepidus was on his way to Rome, clearly intending to prevent the triumph, Nobilior hurried to perform it in Dec. 187 BC.

animals to be in the parade, triumph and games would have needed to be very close in time, as the costs for feeding animals while awaiting the *ludi* quickly reached very high sums. Rome always kept the time span between the arrival of beasts on Italian soil and their appearance and disappearance in the Forum, circuses, and arenas to a minimum.[241] This is why it is very unlikely that the various exotic animals (elephants, lions, leopards, a Gallic lynx, a rhinoceros, Ethiopian monkeys) put on show by Pompey at the opening of his theatre complex and the shrine of Venus Victrix in 55 BC were shown in his great triumph six years earlier.[242]

In contrast, the large triumphal manifestations of Caesar and Octavian in 46 and 29 BC respectively included games with animal shows that closely followed triumphal processions.[243] Coupled with his four triumphs of 46 BC, Caesar organized spectacular games as a joint celebration of his victories and the inauguration of his Forum and the temple of Venus, both monuments closely tied to his wars and triumphs.[244] Octavian held his games, opening the *aedes divi Iulii*, on 18 August 29 BC, only a few days after his threefold triumph celebrated on 13–15 August.[245] Both Caesar and Octavian used captives from their triumphs in the subsequent games, and it is very likely that the beasts performed a similar dual role, going straight from the victory processions to the arena.[246] After all, both celebrations showed large eastern displays, not least from the conquest of Alexandria, which was famous for its zoological collections and rich in trade in

On this basis, one could argue that the games, which in addition to the animals also displayed actors from Greece and athletes, would have required some extra planning and that they could not have been held until later in 186 BC, months after the triumph. On the other hand, there are all through Roman history examples of generals who held lavish spectacles only days after their return.

[241] Kyle (1995: 184; 1998: 187). Immediately after his triumph in AD 274, Aurelian presented the elephants and the tamed beasts to private citizens in order that the costs of their feeding should not become a burden on the state, S.H.A. *Aurel.* 33.4. Also, the *vivaria*, the enclosures where the beasts were kept while awaiting the games, were intended for temporary holding only, Kyle (1998: 187 and n. 22).

[242] Games: Cic. *Fam.* 7.1.3; Plin. *Nat.* 8.7.20–2, 8.28.70–8.29.71; Sen. *Dial.* 10.13.6–7; Plut. *Pomp.* 52.4; Dio Cass. 39.38. Jennison (1937: 51–5); Bernstein (1998: 329–35).

[243] Cf. Coleman (1996: 61): 'But it is not until the fifties BC that exotic species are introduced at Rome and put on display for their curiosity value, . . .'

[244] The temple of Venus Genetrix was dedicated on 26 Sept. 46 BC, but we have no exact dates for Caesar's triumphs. Caesar returned to Rome in late July and the four triumphs were held *eodem mense, sed interiectis diebus*, Suet. *Iul.* 37.1. Thus, the triumphs were performed sometime in Aug. or Sept. Caesar's games also included *ludi funebres* in honour of his deceased daughter Julia. Games: Vell. Pat. 2.56.1–2; Plin. *Nat.* 8.7.22, 8.70.182; Plut. *Caes.* 55.2; App. *BCiv* 2.102; Suet. *Iul.* 39; Dio Cass. 43.22.2–23.6. For modern discussions of the games, see Jennison (1937: 55–9); Weinstock (1971: 80–90); cf. Bernstein (1998: 327–50). Monuments: Westall (1996).

[245] Dio Cass. 51.22.4–9.

[246] Horace's description of a triumphal procession staged at the theatres includes a giraffe and a white elephant. He might be painting a picture of *ludi* held after the procession, or perhaps he imagines animals led in the parade itself, Hor. *Epist.* 2.1.191–8.

exotic animals. It was probably from Alexandria that Caesar had obtained the giraffe which Pliny and Dio Cassius claim was seen for the first time in Rome at the games.[247] Octavian included the hippopotamus and the rhinoceros, also possibly taken from Alexandria, in his games. Again, Dio maintains that the event introduced these animals to a Roman audience.[248] He is mistaken, as Scaurus had displayed the hippopotamus in 58 BC and Pompey the rhinoceros in 55 BC.[249] Nevertheless, the animals must still have formed a spectacular sight for most people in Rome,[250] and they would have added eminence and novelty to the processions. Most likely, then, the triumphal parades of Caesar and Octavian included exotic beasts that were immediately taken into use in the arenas.

The beasts on triumphal display in Rome had neither participated in the preceding wars nor been taken as captives in battle. It is also unlikely that all the animals stemmed from the conquered lands only. At least in part, they had probably been presented as gifts from lands and kings who wished to compliment the commanders on the victories and express their own loyalty. Exotic animals constituted a traditional gift and tribute of the eastern Mediterranean.[251] Alexander was presented with various species on his way to India,[252] and several of the beasts on display in the Alexandrine procession of Ptolemy Philadelphus had been gifts from foreign kings.[253] The practice continued in Roman times, and Augustus is known to have received tigers, elephants, and snakes as gifts from Indian embassies.[254]

Horses and elephants displayed separately

Roman triumphal processions at times displayed groups of animals that were all of the same species. The literary sources provide information on two types of animals exhibited in this way: horses, mentioned only a few times, and elephants, rather substantially commented upon. In contrast to the rows of miscellaneous foreign animals, which had been taken as booty or offered as gifts from various areas only after the victory had been secured, most horses and elephants had

---

[247] Dio Cass. 43.23.1–2; Plin. *Nat.* 8.27.69. Besides the giraffe (called 'camelopard'), Caesar's games included elephants, lions, and bulls, fought by mounted Thessalians.

[248] Dio Cass. 51.22.4–9. As well as the hippopotamus and the rhinoceros, other wild beasts and tame animals were slain in great numbers.

[249] Scaurus: Plin. *Nat.* 8.40.96; Amm. 22.15.24; Pompey: Pliny (*Nat.* 8.29.71) states that the rhinoceros was by now already well known, but there might be some confusion as to the precise species involved, Toynbee (1973: 125–7).

[250] See e.g. Hor. *Epist.* 2.1.195.

[251] Bodson (1998: 71–5).

[252] Ibid. 72–4, with references.

[253] Ibid. 74–5; Rice (1983: 86–8, with references).

[254] Strab. 15.1.73; Flor. *Epit.* 2.34.62–3; Dio Cass. 54.9.8; cf. Hor. *Epist.* 2.1.196.

appeared as Roman opponents on the very battlefield where they had also been captured.[255]

Noble horses

According to Livy, P. Cornelius Scipio Nasica exhibited a herd of captured horses in his triumph over the Gallic Boii of 191 BC.[256] Livy tells nothing of the number of animals paraded. He does state in the earlier battle description that 1,230 horses were captured, but doubts this high figure himself as it stems from Valerias Antias.[257] In the triumph, Livy specifies that the horses were shown together with the high-ranking captives (*et cum captivis nobilibus equorum quoque captorum gregem traduxit*). The description seems to reflect certain esteem from the Roman point of view, suggesting that the horses had played an important part in the battle and that they were considered captives of significance. Livy's *nobiles*, although strictly referring to the captive humans, could allude to the horses as well. The Gauls were famed for their horsemanship,[258] and it is in fact noteworthy that this is our only comment on the capture and triumphal display of Gallic horses.[259]

Besides Livy's report on Nasica's triumph, there is but a single additional reference to the presence of captured horses in a triumphal procession. This time, the exhibition was one of a single animal rather than a group. According to Diodorus Siculus, Aemilius Paullus included in the third day's parade of his Macedonian triumph 'a horse dressed for battle with cheek-pieces set with jewels and the rest of its gear adorned with gold'.[260] Even if Diodorus emphasizes that the horse was shown in battle attire, his primary focus lies on the horse's costly appearance rather than its martial accomplishments. This is evident also from the fact that the horse is listed among a number of luxurious items which, in Diodorus' account, dominated the display that preceded the captured king on the third day of the triumph: talents of gold, a golden bowl with inlays of jewellery, gold works of all kind, elephant tusks, an ivory chariot adorned with gold and precious stones (here the horse is mentioned), a golden couch, and a

[255] This is a general, not an absolute, rule. Some of the displays of elephants included beasts that had been collected as part of peace treaties concluded after battle. Horses and elephants also appeared in parades made up of miscellaneous animals, where they represented first and foremost a variety of animal.

[256] Liv. 36.40.11–12.

[257] Liv. 36.38.6. Ziolkowski (1990: esp. 15).

[258] Plut. *Marc.* 6.4. Gallic cavalry was used in the Republican forces and it was prominent among the imperial Roman auxiliary *alae*, Hyland (1990: 20–2).

[259] On a few occasions, Livy includes the number of captured horses in his accounts of battle results, see 29.36.9, 30.6.9, 30.36.8, 32.6.7, 35.1.10, 35.5.13, 36.38.6, 40.33.7–8, 40.48.7, 40.50.5. However, except for the passage referring to Nasica (36.38.6), none of these passages describe victories over the Gauls.

[260] Diod. Sic. 31.8.12 (apud Sync.): ...ἵππος φαλάροις διαλίθοις καὶ τῇ λοιπῇ κατασκευῇ διαχρύσῳ πολεμικῶς κεκοσμημένος, ...

golden litter. The horse's lavish trappings and its appearance in the midst of various royal displays signalled none other than the king.[261]

Elephants exhibited

In comparison to the rather scant evidence of horses, sources give more evidence of elephants on parade. Ancient authors describe the presence of captured elephants in the triumphs and ovations of M'. Curius Dentatus in 275 BC, L. Caecilius Metellus in 250 BC, M. Claudius Marcellus in 211 BC, and Scipio Africanus in 201 BC. In particular, several writers comment rather extensively upon the earliest display of elephants by Dentatus and Metellus. Besides these exhibitions, elephants also appear in the late Republican triumphal celebrations of Pompey (around 80 BC) and Caesar (46 BC). However, these beasts were not presented as captives, but had other functions.

Lucanian oxen: the first encounter

When King Pyrrhus, responding to an appeal from Tarentum, landed on Italian soil in 280 BC, he brought with him a force of 25,000 men and 20 elephants.[262] Italy had never before seen such beasts, and the elephants aroused much attention; they were called Lucanian oxen, from the area in which they were first spotted.[263] The city of Tarentum celebrated their arrival by minting coins with images of Indian elephants.[264] Cruder depictions of elephants, in all probability referring to Pyrrhus' beasts, also appear on issues of *aes signatum* from central Italy during the first half of the third century BC (Fig. 19).[265] Pyrrhus' elephants caused the Roman army a great deal of trouble, and it was only at the battle of Beneventum in 275 BC that the consul M'. Curius Dentatus managed to drive the elephants back onto Pyrrhus' own lines, thereby forcing the Epirote king to retreat to Tarentum and later to Greece.[266] After the victory at Beneventum, Dentatus returned to Rome and celebrated a triumph over the Samnites and King Pyrrhus. Florus tells of the richness of the parade, but adds: 'nothing that

[261] Bridles and trappings for horses, made of gold and precious stones, formed part of Mithridates' royal repository in Talauri, which Pompey confiscated and, in all probability, showed in his triumph, App. *Mith*. 115. Horses with rich trappings were used as royal gifts, see Liv. 43.5.8; Plut. *Pomp*. 36.4.

[262] Plut. *Pyrrh*. 15.1; Zonar. 8.2.7.

[263] Plin. *Nat*. 8.6.16; cf. Lucr. 5.1302. The nickname remained in use even as late as the 3rd cent. AD, as can be seen on an inscription from Leptis Magna, Toynbee (1973: 51); Scullard (1974: 253–4).

[264] Scullard (1974: 103 and pl. XIVa).

[265] Toynbee (1973: 34 and pl. 6); Scullard (1974: 115–16 and pl. XIVb); Crawford (1974: no. 9.1, 132, 716–18); Callu (1976); Carson (1978: no. 3, 11). A 3rd-cent. BC painted dish from Capena depicting a turreted Indian cow elephant with her calf might also refer to Pyrrhus' herd, Scullard (1974: 113 and pl. VIIa); Toynbee (1973: 34 and pl. 2).

[266] Scullard (1974: 101–16) accounts for the roles played by the elephants in the battles between Pyrrhus and the Roman forces, 280 to 275 BC.

FIGURE 19 The elephant depicted on this *aes signatum* from the first half of the third century BC probably refers to Pyrrhus' beats. Contemporary representations such as this suggest that the elephants made a very deep first impression, on the battlefield as in the triumph.

the Roman people saw pleased them more than those beasts whom they had feared, carrying their towers and following the victorious horses with heads bowed low not wholly unconscious that they were prisoners' (*Sed nihil libentius populus Romanus aspexit quam illas, quas timuerat, cum turribus suis beluas, quae non sine sensu captivitatis summissis cervicibus victores equos sequebantur*).[267] According to Eutropius, Dentatus displayed four elephants, while Dionysius of Halicarnassus and Zonaras hold that the Romans captured eight beasts at Beneventum.[268]

Seneca, Pliny the Elder, and Eutropius all stress that Dentatus' triumph was the first time that the city of Rome saw elephants.[269] In the eighth book of his *Naturalis Historia*, Pliny expressly states that 'Italy saw elephants for the first time in the war against King Pyrrhus and called them Lucanian oxen because they were seen in Lucania in 280 BC; but Rome first saw them in a triumph five years later'.[270] In the seventh book, Pliny contradicts himself, writing that L. Caecilius Metellus, who triumphed over the Carthaginians in 250 BC, was the one *qui primus elephantos ex primo Punico bello duxit in triumpho*.[271] No other source claims that Metellus introduced Rome to elephants, and in view of the substantial evidence of Dentatus' capture and triumphal display of the beasts, this statement by Pliny must be erroneous. The error could possibly be explained away by maintaining that, by *primus*, Pliny intends to say not that Metellus was the first ever to show elephants in a triumph, but that he was the first to do so during the First Punic War.[272] But it might also be a simple factual mistake on Pliny's

---

[267] Flor. *Epit.* 1.13.26–28.

[268] Eutrop. 2.14.3; Dion. Hal. 20.12.3; Zonar. 8.6.6.

[269] Sen. *Dial.* 10.13.3; Plin. *Nat.* 8.6.16: Eutrop 2.14.3.

[270] Plin. *Nat.* 8.6.16: *Elephantos Italia primum vidit Pyrri regis bello et boves Lucas appellavit in Lucanis visos anno urbis CCCCLXXIV, Roma autem in triumpho V annis ad superiorem numerum additis*. The manuscript has *CCCCLXXII*, 282 BC instead of the correct 280 BC. Consequently, it places Dentatus' triumph seven years (*VII annis additis*) after this occasion instead of five; see the note by H. Rackham in the Loeb edn, 1947, which I have followed here.

[271] Plin. *Nat.* 7.43.139.

[272] Scullard (1974: 111). There have also been attempts to substitute the word *primus* for *plurimos* here, since Pliny elsewhere (*Nat.* 8.6.16) writes that the elephants Metellus captured and showed were *plurimos*.

part,[273] possibly influenced by the circumstance that, in the later Roman tradition, both Dentatus and Metellus were famed for having brought elephants to the city at this early time. Dentatus was praised for having been the first to show the beasts to Rome, Metellus for having displayed so many.[274] According to the somewhat divergent sources, Metellus transported between 120 and 140 animals from the battlefield in Sicily to Rome and displayed them in his triumph.[275] Seneca tells us that Metellus was the only one of all Romans (*unus omnium Romanorum*) to show (as many as) 120 captured elephants in his triumph.[276] Whatever the exact number of animals involved, the beasts quite clearly made a spectacular impression. In fact, Pliny even writes that Varro is said to have described an historical event by placing it, not in a year calculated according to his own Varronian chronology, but 'in the year that Metellus showed a great number of elephants in his triumph'.[277] The tradition of Metellus' deed was also much promoted by the Metelli themselves, who from the middle of the second century BC and all through the Republic issued coins that carried the image of an elephant in commemoration of the great achievement of their ancestor.[278]

Metellus' bringing of the elephants to Rome was an enterprise much eulogized by the ancient authors. Not least, the shipping of the herd on huge rafts filled with earth and bushes across the strait of Messina aroused praise, and Zonaras points out that the operation was so smooth that the elephants never sensed that they were travelling at sea.[279] We can easily imagine the excitement that Metellus and his extraordinary retinue caused all along the road to Rome, forming a triumph-like procession in itself. The triumphal exhibition, to and in the city, was also the sole reason for transporting the beasts at all. In fact, once the

---

Another point is that, since Pyrrhus' elephants had been Indian, Metellus was the first to show African beasts in his triumph. However, the ancient authors do not make this distinction in their descriptions of the triumphs. The African elephants used by the Carthaginians were not the huge bush elephants but the much smaller forest elephants, today extinct, Scullard (1974: 23–4, 60–3).

[273] Schilling (1977: 204).

[274] Both these triumphs, especially that of Dentatus, were held in high esteem in Rome for other reasons as well. Dentatus was famed for having expelled a great foreign king and for having afterwards returned to a life of simplicity, Cic. *Pis.* 24.58, *Mur.* 14.31, *Cato* 16.55; Liv. *Per.* 14, 45.38.11; Plut. *Cat. Mai.* 2.1–2; Flor. *Epit.* 1.18.26–8; Apul. *Apol.* 17. Metellus' victory and triumph was of great importance, since it constituted a turning point in favour of the Romans during the First Punic War, Liv. *Per.* 19; cf. Plin. *Nat.* 7.43.140–1. The capture of the Punic elephants was considered to have played a crucial part in the success, Polyb. 1.40.15–41.2.

[275] Liv. *Per* 19: 120 animals; Dion. Hal. 2.66.4: 138 animals; Plin. *Nat.* 8.6.16–17: 142 or 140 animals; Sen. *Dial.* 10.13.8: 120 animals; Front. *Str.* 2.5.4: 130 animals; Zonar. 8.14: 120 animals; Eutrop. 2.24: 130 animals; Oros. 4.9.14–15: 104 animals, 26 killed.

[276] Sen. *Dial.* 10.13.8.

[277] Plin. *Nat.* 18.4.17.

[278] Scullard (1974: 152, pl. XXIV, a–c, n. 90); Toynbee (1976: 274–5); Grassi (1999: 484–5).

[279] Zonar. 8.14; see also Plin. *Nat.* 8.6.16–17; Front. *Str.* 1.7.1.

triumph was over, Rome had no idea what to do with the elephants. It was decided that the beasts should not be kept nor be presented as gifts to foreign kings, and as a result, they ended up in the circus.[280] According to Pliny, there were two different later traditions, according to which the elephants were either killed by javelins or simply driven around the circus in order to increase contempt for them. Pliny adds that the advocates of the second theory are unable to explain where the elephants finally ended up.

The abundant descriptions in the ancient literature of the triumphs of Dentatus and Metellus, and the contemporary as well as later choice to picture the elephants on coins, testify to the indelible first impression that these animals made on the Roman audience. The strong sentiments were apparently caused by the awe that the first military confrontations had induced on the Roman side. Florus stresses that the elephants shown by Dentatus had been much feared even by the inhabitants of Rome,[281] who up to that date had never even set eyes on the animals, but merely heard frightening stories about them. Polybius describes the joy and relief that Metellus' capturing of the Punic beasts caused in Rome, now confident that the conclusive victory was near.[282]

To the Roman soldiers in the field, the beasts were unfamiliar and dreadful war engines, against which a special form of artillery had to be constructed.[283] The elephants were no less than attacking fortresses, carrying towers and warriors on their back and tusks that were at times armed with sharp iron or even with spears.[284] Florus maintains that Dentatus paraded the elephants *cum turribus suis*. Thus they appeared in Rome as in battle.

But the elephants were much more than inanimate war machines. To the Romans, still not used to their looks and behaviour, they appeared as wild and forceful monsters (*ferae, beluae, monstra*).[285] Florus describes how the Roman horses were terrified by their massive ugliness, smell, and trumpeting.[286] In fact, to inject fear into the enemy soldiers and horses was one of the principal functions of the elephants in the field; they often bore war paint, and they were occasionally even intoxicated with rations of wine before battle to augment their fury.[287]

The capture of the animals neutralized their formerly uncontrolled force, and their appearance as captives in the triumph made visible the taming of their

---

[280] Plin. *Nat.* 8.6.17.

[281] Flor. *Epit.* 1.13.28, quoted above.

[282] Polyb. 1.40.15–1.41.2, cf. 1.39.12–13 for the Roman fear of the elephants.

[283] Scullard (1974: 107–9).

[284] Lucr. 2.536–40, 5.1302–4; Sil. *Pun.* 9.570–98; Iuv. 12.108–10; App. *Syr.* 32; Zonar. 8.3.11.

[285] See e.g. Sil. *Pun.* 9.570–619; Front. *Str.* 2.5.4; Flor. *Epit.* 1.13.6, 1.13.8.

[286] Flor. *Epit.* 1.13.8.

[287] Seibert (1973: 349–50); Scullard (1974: 238).

ferocity.[288] Florus describes the elephants in Dentatus' triumph as walking with their heads bowed down, an attitude which not only signalled lost powers and captivity to the spectators of the parade, but also showed that the beasts themselves were conscious of and accepted their submission to Rome. In fact, the lowered head constituted a fitting attitude also for the human prisoners, who were forced to walk in the Roman triumphs; thus they bowed physically as well as symbolically to the power of Rome. The attitude of the elephants and the emphasis on their feelings suggest that, in the Roman triumphal processions, these animals were presented not unlike the human captives.[289] This circumstance is also reflected in their location in the train. Livy and Appian's descriptions of the parades performed by Marcellus and Scipio Africanus both place the elephants after the diverse spoils, before either the triumphator or the human prisoners.[290] Thus, similarly to the herd of horses led by Scipio Nasica, discussed above, the elephants were shown together with or close by the human prisoners.

Signum victoriae Punicae

After the spectacular displays of Dentatus and Metellus, elephants next appear in the *ovatio* held by Marcellus in 211 BC after the conquest of Syracuse. Livy describes the military spoils, art, and precious goods from the conquered Greek city, and adds: *Punicae quoque victoriae signum octo ducti elephanti*, 'as a mark that the Carthaginians had been defeated as well, eight elephants were led in the procession'.[291] Marcellus had captured the elephants when he overcame a Punic force near Agrigentum after the fall of Syracuse.[292]

Ten years later, Scipio Africanus triumphed after the conclusive battle at Zama. Appian records the presence of elephants in the procession,[293] and although his account must be treated with caution, such animals were most certainly present in the parade. Hannibal had had eighty elephants on his side at Zama, eleven were killed in battle, many others captured.[294] As part of the peace treaty, the Carthaginians were forced to surrender their remaining elephants to Rome, and to promise not to train any more animals in the future.[295] The victors bestowed some of the Punic elephants on Masinissa, the Numidian king who had fought on Scipio's side. The rest were shipped to Italy,[296] where they must have constituted a welcome contribution to the triumph, announcing the end of the Hannibalic war.

[288] See also Shelton (2004).
[289] Cicero (*Fam.* 7.1.3–4) describes the opening of Pompey's theatre in 55 BC, and people's sentiments at seeing the elephants forced to perform.
[290] Liv. 26.21.7–10; App. *Pun.* 66.
[291] Liv. 26.21.7–10.
[292] Liv. 25.41.7.
[293] App. *Pun.* 66.
[294] Polyb. 15.12.1–5; Liv. 30.33.1–7, 12–16, 30.35.3. Scullard (1974: 168–9).
[295] Polyb. 15.18.4; Liv. 30.37.3; App. *Pun.* 54; Dio Cass. 17.57.82.
[296] Zonar. 9.14.11.

After Scipio's triumph, we hear of no more elephants led in any triumph until the third century AD, when they appear as one of many kinds of exotic animals. Elephants ceased to be used on the battlefield at around the time of Caesar, and the beasts exhibited in the late Roman processions had not been captured in war, but had probably been collected after battle or presented as gifts. Rather than denoting a particularly fierce enemy defeated in combat, the elephants here, together with the other species, transmitted an image of the worldwide fauna, now embraced by the Roman hegemony.

However, up to the time of Caesar, elephants continued to be captured from enemy forces on the battlefield. Still, after Scipio Africanus, no sources describe elephants taken captive and led as such in a triumph. On some occasions, their display might simply not have left any traces in our sources, but at others it seems clear that Rome chose not to parade her captured beasts. For example, elephants formed an important part of Antiochus' army used against the Roman forces both in Aetolia and above all at Magnesia in 190 BC. At Magnesia, the Roman general Scipio Asiaticus managed to capture fifteen beasts,[297] and in the treaty of Apamea that followed, Antiochus was forced to hand over his remaining elephants and to promise not to possess any in the future.[298] Still, no sources suggest that elephants appeared in Scipio's triumph after Magnesia, or in Manlius Vulso's procession, which followed the treaty of Apamea.[299] Scipio preferred to display 1,231 ivory tusks, items he had probably taken from the royal treasury or been presented with as gifts from loyal states of the East. Vulso, as soon as he had received the elephants of Antiochus that formed part of the treaty, chose to present them as a gift to King Eumenes of Pergamon.[300]

There were probably a number of motives involved in the choice made by these generals not to follow the precedents set by Dentatus, Metellus, Marcellus, and Scipio Africanus of displaying captured elephants as part of their triumphal spectacles in Rome. For one, shipping the beasts to Rome was a considerable logistic undertaking.[301] Such practical matters would not have hindered a general determined to display elephants in his parade. But in these cases, the charm of the novelty had already passed; it probably did not seem worth the effort to transport the beasts all the way to Rome just to show them to an audience who now demanded more to be impressed. Their thirst for novelties probably motivated Scipio's ivory tusks, items, which, according to our knowledge, had never before been displayed in a triumph. By parading a large number of tusks, Scipio exhibited new and extraordinary riches and alluded to his defeat of Antiochus' elephants, without having to go through the trouble of shipping the beasts back home.

---

[297] Liv. 37.44.1; App. *Syr.* 36. For the role of the elephants, see the account in Scullard (1974: 178–82, esp. 181).

[298] Polyb. 21.42.12–13; Liv. 38.38.8.

[299] Scipio: Liv. 37.59.3–6; Vulso: Liv. 39.7.1–5.

[300] Liv. 38.39.5.

[301] Seibert (1973: 350–1) discusses the difficulties involved in transporting elephants.

From Titus Flamininus' war against Philip of Macedon at the beginning of the second century BC and all through the Republic, the Romans themselves occasionally employed elephants in war. The animals used were partly the ones taken by Scipio Africanus after Zama, partly those bestowed on Masinissa at the same occasion.[302] Later on, beasts were supplied by Masinissa's successors and most probably, other loyal allies contributed as well. Hence, by offering the elephants to Eumenes, Manlius Vulso would not only have endowed an ally with an appropriate gift. He would also have made sure that in the future, if necessary, Rome could rely on an additional supply of war elephants in the East.[303] The very circumstance that the Romans now employed elephants in their own lines might also have lessened the desire to present them as captive foreign beasts in the triumphal processions.

Scipio Asiaticus and Manlius Vulso were both victorious in the East, and it might well be that elephants at this time had become symbolically linked to Rome's glorious defeat of the Carthaginians. Livy states that Marcellus showed elephants as a *signum victoriae Punicae*.[304] In fact, during the First and Second Punic Wars, Roman warfare and sentiments had been much focused on how to fight these still unfamiliar beasts. The battle at Zama signified the breaking of their spell; Scipio had showed how to control their behaviour in battle, the power of the much-feared Hannibal, intimately connected to the elephants, had been broken, and the beasts delivered to Rome. After Zama, there is comparatively little concern and fear at the prospect of encountering elephants on the battlefield. The animals are no longer *ferae*; their powers are mastered and ready to be used by the Roman forces as well. The Roman spectators, who had earlier waited with eagerness to see the powerless elephants walk as captives in the triumphs, now had other expectations, other fears. It might be then that the triumph of Scipio Africanus in 201 BC, making visible the final mastery of the elephants, put an end to the desire to view and exhibit the elephants as captives in the Roman triumphal procession.[305]

'The wild beast knows the delight of peace'
In two late Republican triumphal manifestations, elephants again appear: Pompey's first triumph, held over Africa sometime between 81 and 79 BC,[306]

[302] For elephants provided by Masinissa and his successors: Liv. 31.36.4–5, 32.27.2, 36.4.8–9, 42.62.2–3; App. *Iber.* 46, 67, 89. Scullard (1974: 178–85, 190–8). Masinissa continued to send elephants to the Roman forces, even when they campaigned in the East.

[303] A note in Polyaenus (4.21) that the forces sent to fight Perseus were provided with Indian elephants from Antiochus might refer to the elephants earlier given up by the Syrian king at Apamea, Scullard (1974: 182).

[304] Liv. 26.21.9.

[305] Unfortunately, after Scipio's celebration in 201 BC, little is known of the contents of African processions, and we cannot tell if captured elephants continued to mark the triumphal celebrations over this continent.

[306] The date has been debated, see e.g. Badian (1955, 1961); Twyman (1979).

and Caesar's fourfold celebration in 46 BC demonstrating his success in Gaul, Egypt, Pontus, and Africa. Now, however, the role of the elephants had changed, and they were no longer led captives.

The story of the elephants' role in Pompey's triumph over Africa is both well known and amusing. Not yet a senator and performing his first triumph, Pompey tried to enter Rome in a quadriga drawn by four elephants.[307] However, the *porta triumphalis* was too narrow, and although Pompey tried twice, he finally had to give up his project and change to the traditional horses. Some thirty-five years later, in 46 BC, elephants appeared in Caesar's processions. There are two different versions of the role they played in these spectacles. Suetonius has it that forty elephants carrying torches flanked Caesar as he ascended the Capitol in his Gallic triumph.[308] Dio Cassius' account also includes elephants carrying torches, but in this version, they conducted Caesar home together with all the people after the dinner held on the last day's triumph.[309] Dio Cassius' description is usually taken to be the most probable one.[310] Triumphs conducted after nightfall are unheard of in Roman history,[311] while illuminated escorts home at night was an honour bestowed on prominent generals already at the time of the First Punic War.[312]

It was in his triumph over Africa that Pompey tried to employ elephants as beasts of burden.[313] If we are trust Dio Cassius, Caesar's elephants made their appearance on the last day of the four triumphs held in 46 BC when, similarly, the victory in Africa was celebrated.[314] Consequently, scholars have stressed the symbolic meaning of the elephants put on show by the two great generals as denoting the submission of Africa.[315] We also saw above that, with the exception

[307] Plin. *Nat.* 8.2.4 (referring to Procilius); Plut. *Pomp.* 14.4–5; Gran. Lic. 36, p. 31 F (34 C). For the event, see Mader (2006).

[308] Suet. *Iul.* 37.2.

[309] Dio Cass. 43.22.1–2. Earlier (43.21.2), Dio has stated that during the first day's triumph, i.e. the Gallic one, Caesar climbed the stairs of the Capitol on his knees.

[310] Weinstock (1971: 77–8); Scullard (1974: 197–8, 279 n. 140); Voisin (1983: 32–3).

[311] Torches do not necessarily indicate a procession held at night. For example, as Pompey returned to Rome in 50 BC, all through Italy he was greeted by people who carried garlands as well as lighted torches, Plut. *Pomp.* 57.2–3.

[312] Cic. *Cato* 13.44; Liv. *Per.* 17; Val. Max. 3.6.4; Sil. *Pun.* 6.667–70; Flor. *Epit.* 1.18.10–11; Amm. 26.3.5; *vir. ill.* 38; Degrassi, *Inscr. It.* 13:3, no. 13, 20–1, all referring to C. Duilius.

[313] Plutarch (*Pomp.* 14.4) says that Pompey shipped many elephants that he had captured from the kings to Rome. The plural 'kings' indicates that the elephants did not come only from King Iarbas, who helped Pompey and Sulla's adversaries in the war, but (as gifts) from others as well, Scullard (1974: 193).

[314] Caesar's elephants might have been the ones taken from Juba in Africa, but it is more probable that they were animals already present in Italy, see further below.

[315] Matz (1952: 30); Voisin (1983: 32–3, referring to W. Drumann and P. Groebe in *Geschichte Roms*, iii (Leipzig, 1906), 554 n. 2). Voisin also points out that the elephant was an emblem of the Metelli and that coins depicting these animals were issued by Caesar's adversary Metellus Scipio in Africa at the time of the conflict, see Carson (1978: no. 223, 61). By displaying elephants in his triumphs, Caesar would thus have been able to allude to the defeat of Metellus Scipio as well.

of Dentatus' parade, captured elephants were initially led in triumphs held over Carthage. In the late Republic, and especially during the Empire, the elephant was commonly used as an emblem of Africa.[316]

However, in the case of Caesar, Suetonius, in contrast to Dio, claims that the elephants appeared in the Gallic parade. And, even if Dio is correct, it is far from certain that the elephants were meant to evoke the African celebration in particular. In many ways, Caesar combined his four triumphs of 46 BC into one spectacle rather than four separate celebrations,[317] and the feast in question could well have concluded the entire fourfold performance rather than the specific African parade. Most importantly, in contrast to the beasts displayed by Dentatus, Metellus, Marcellus, and Scipio Africanus, the elephants described as taking part in the triumphs of Pompey and Caesar were not captives, but employed to transport and escort the triumphator himself. They were not staged as submissive prisoners of Rome, but now they rendered service to the victorious Roman leader.

In fact, Roman generals had employed elephants as victory symbols at least from the late 120s BC. After the campaign against the Allobroges and the Arverni, the victorious general Cn. Domitius Ahenobarbus celebrated his victory by riding through the province on an elephant's back escorted by his soldiers in a kind of a victory procession.[318] Rome's adversaries had used no elephants in the war, and Africa was not involved. The animal in question must have fought on the Roman side, after which it was picked up as a victory symbol for Rome and for Ahenobarbus. Even more interesting for the late Republican triumphs in question is the coin that Caesar issued in 54 BC (or later), inscribed with his own name and a depiction of an elephant trampling an object interpreted as a Gallic *carnyx* (Fig. 20).[319] Again, the elephant had nothing to do with Africa, and it had not been captured from a vanquished foe, but it was a representative of the supreme Romans and their triumphant leader.

Thus, although there might well have been a certain symbolic link between the elephants and the African triumphs of Pompey and Caesar, it seems more reasonable to stress the connection between these animals and the triumphing generals. This standpoint is further strengthened by the obvious references both to Alexander and to Dionysus and his triumphant return from India on an elephant's back. Describing Pompey's African triumph, Pliny himself makes

---

[316] Toynbee (1973: 50–3); *LIMC* i (1981), s.v. 'Africa', 250–5 (M. Le Glay); Salcedo Garcés (1991); Stribrny (1991); Salcedo Garcés (1996: esp. 123–30); Grassi (1999).

[317] Östenberg (1999: esp. 158).

[318] Suet. *Nero* 2.1–2. Flor. *Epit.* 1.37.5; Oros. 5.13.

[319] Albrethsen (1987: 105–6, fig. 8); Künzl (1988: 126, Abb. 85b). Albrethsen stresses that the *carnyx* frequently appear as a symbol of Gauls and other northern barbarians on Roman coins. There have been other interpretations of the object represented beneath the elephant as well, see Dayet (1960).

FIGURE 20
Elephant trampling
on an object that has
been interpreted as
a Gallic *carnyx*.
Obverse of denarius
struck for Caesar.

this connection when he states: *Romae iuncti primum subiere currum Pompei Magni Africano triumpho, quod prius India victa triumphante Libero patre memoratur*, 'At Rome they [the elephants] were first used in harness to draw the chariot of Pompey the Great in his African triumph, as they are recorded to have been used before when Father Liber went in triumph after his conquest of India'.[320] The idea of the triumphant Dionysus developed in the Hellenistic age, and was inspired by Alexander's campaign in India.[321] Alexander collected a substantial herd of elephants, which accompanied him on his way back from the East in celebration of his Indian tour.[322] From now on, the elephant *exuviae* appear on depictions of the head of Alexander, and both Alexander and Dionysus are shown either riding on or drawn by elephants. Ptolemy I minted a gold stater depicting Alexander in the guise of Zeus Ammon standing in a chariot drawn by four elephants,[323] and in the grand procession of Ptolemy Philadelphus, Dionysus and Alexander were represented riding on and drawn by elephants respectively.[324]

The idea of the elephants as escorts and symbols of victorious gods and semi-divine rulers was adopted in Rome, and it is in this context that the animals at Pompey and Caesar's triumphs should be seen. Already in 125 BC, a coin of one Caecilius Metellus showed Jupiter in an elephant biga,[325] and Augustus was

---

[320] Plin. *Nat.* 8.2.4. Much later, when the Emperor Caracalla ventured to drive an elephant chariot, Dio Cassius records that this was done 'in imitation of Alexander, or rather of Dionysus', Dio Cass. 78.7.4.

[321] Rice (1983: 83–6).

[322] Scullard (1974: 74, with further references).

[323] Matz (1952: 29); Toynbee (1973: 39); Scullard (1974: 254 and pl. XVc).

[324] Ath. 5.200d, 5.202a–b. Rice (1983: 83–6). Twenty-four quadrigae drawn by other elephants were also present, Ath. 5.200e–f. Rice (1983: 90–2).

[325] Crawford (1974: no. 269.1, 292–3).

FIGURE 21 Aureus from 17 BC representing an arch placed on a viaduct and celebrating Augustus' repairs of roads, specifically the Via Flaminia. The arch is crowned by a statue of the emperor, who stands in an elephant-drawn chariot accompanied by a winged Victoria.

depicted in triumphal dress on coins issued in 17 BC standing in a chariot drawn by two elephants (Fig. 21).[326] In commemoration of his successful achievements during the civil wars, L. Cornificius, a friend of Octavian, even used to ride about on an elephant whenever he dined out.[327] From early Imperial times, elephants were customarily employed to draw the images of deceased emperors and their family members in the *pompae circenses*.[328] This use of elephants reveals that they were connected not only with earthly victories, but also with life, light, and the victory over death as well.[329] The theme of Dionysus' triumphant return from India on an elephant's back was a frequent motif on Roman sarcophagi, and elephants were often used for candelabra in Roman art.[330] Caesar's use of the elephants as torch-bearers in his triumph might be seen in this context, and he was clearly also inspired by eastern precedents. Antiochus VI is known to have employed torch-bearing elephants, emphasizing his divine nature as victorious ruler.[331]

The elephants used by Pompey and especially by Caesar were very far from being the *monstra*, *ferae*, and *beluae* of the triumphs of Dentatus and Metellus. To be able to carry torches in a procession they had to be well trained, and Caesar's animals may have been raised and drilled in Italy rather than captured in Africa. In

[326] Matz (1952: 31); Toynbee (1973: 39–40); Scullard (1974: 255); Beard (2007: fig. 18). Several triumphal arches were crowned by statues of the emperors set in triumphal chariots drawn by elephants; for Domitian, see Mart. 8.65.9–10.

[327] Dio Cass. 49.7.6.

[328] Scullard (1974: 255–7); cf. Himmelmann (1973: 37–42, Taf. 56b, 57a).

[329] Matz (1952: *passim*).

[330] Sarcophagi: Matz (1952: 33–4; 1968–75: see index, s.v. 'Indischer Triumph'). Candelabra: Matz (1952: 36); Toynbee (1973: 47); Scullard (1974: 258).

[331] Gardner (1878: 66–7, nos. 42–8, pl. 19, no. 12); Matz (1952: 34); Toynbee (1973: 47).

fact, during his stay in Africa, Caesar actually sent for elephants from Italy.[332] These beasts might have originated in one of the state-owned herds that are known to have been present at least from early Imperial times, but which possibly existed earlier.[333] Elephants were now trained for ceremonies rather than for war and, as stated above, the beasts more or less disappear from the lines of battle during the last years of the Republic.[334] Their change of scene from the battles of war to the spectacles of the city is reflected in an epigram by Philip of Thessaloniki (*Ant. Pal.* 9.285):

No longer does the mighty-tusked elephant, with tower on back and ready to fight phalanxes, charge unchecked into battle; but in fear he has yielded his thick neck to the yoke, and draws the chariot of divine Caesar. The wild beast knows the delight of peace; throwing off the gear of war, he conducts instead the father of good order.[335]

Philip wrote these verses to commemorate the introduction of an elephant biga that carried the image of Divus Augustus at a circus procession organized by Tiberius or Caligula.[336] They fit perfectly also to describe the changing role of the beasts in the triumphal procession, from captured wild monsters of enemy armies to tamed escorts of the Roman victor.

TREES

Two passages in book 12 of Pliny's *Naturalis Historia* tell of trees shown in Roman triumphal processions:

1. *Romae eam Magnus Pompeius triumpho Mithridatico ostendit*, 'It [the ebony tree] was exhibited in Rome by Pompey the Great in his triumph over Mithridates'.[337] Solinus' version of this passage runs: *Hebenum ex India Mithridatico*

---

[332] Dio Cass. 43.4.1. Toynbee (1973: 47). These tame elephants were not brought into battle, but were employed to accustom the horse to the beasts.

[333] Toynbee (1973: 37, 47). Later, Juvenal speaks of a *Caesaris armentum* at Laurentum, Iuv. 12.102–7, esp. 106. There also existed a *procurator ad elephantos*, *ILS* 1578. Most of the elephants here stemmed from Africa and India, but some were probably born and raised in Italy, Ael. *NA* 2.11.

[334] Elephants were occasionally used on the battlefield, as during Claudius' invasion of Britain, Dio Cass. 60.21.2. Later, the elephants reappear in the Sassanid army, and the *Historia Augusta* even reports that Severus Alexander showed some captured elephants in his triumph over the Parthian Sassanids held in AD 233 (S.H.A. *Alex. Sev.* 56.3–4). It is far from clear, however, if this passage should be trusted, Scullard (1974: 200–1).

[335] Οὐκέτι πυργωθεὶς ὁ φαλαγγομάχας ἐπὶ δῆριν | ἄσχετος ὁρμαίνει μυριόδους ἐλέφας, | ἀλλὰ φόβῳ στείλας βαθὺν αὐχένα πρὸς ζυγοδέσμους, | ἄντυγα διφρουλκεῖ Καίσαρος οὐρανίου. | ἔγνω δ᾽ εἰρήνης καὶ θὴρ χάριν· ὄργανα ῥίψας |Ἄρεος, εὐνομίης ἀντανάγει πατέρα (translation based on Scullard, 1974: 257).

[336] Scullard (1974: 257).

[337] Plin. *Nat.* 12.9.20.

triumpho Romae primum Magnus Pompeius exhibuit, 'The ebony tree from India was displayed for the first time in Rome by Pompey the Great in his triumph over Mithridates'.[338]

2. *Ostendere arborum hanc urbi imperatores Vespasiani, clarumque dictu, a Pompeio Magno in triumpho arbores quoque duximus. Servit nunc haec ac tributa pendit cum sua gente*, . . . 'This kind of tree [the balsam tree] was exhibited to the city by the emperors Vespasian and Titus, and it is a remarkable fact that ever since Pompey the Great we have led even trees in our triumphal processions. The balsam tree is now a subject of Rome and pays tax together with the race to which it belongs . . .'[339]

Thus, according to Pliny, Pompey was the first to display trees in the triumphal processions at Rome (*a Pompeio Magno*).[340] Pliny maintains that Pompey exhibited the ebony tree as part of his great Asiatic triumph of 61 BC. Solinus states that the ebony stemmed from India and that Pompey's triumph was the first occasion (*primum*) that the tree was seen in Rome. Although not explicitly spelt out, Pliny's emphasized *ostendere* could suggest that the balsam tree too, in AD 71, was introduced to the city by way of a triumphal parade. Furthermore, the phrase *a Pompeio Magno* reveals that the processions of 61 BC and AD 71 were not alone in putting trees on parade. Rather, Pompey introduced a new element into the processional performance that was taken up by subsequent triumphators as well.

Pliny clearly refers to the ebony tree and not to ebony wood. This is evident both from his use of the feminine *eam* (for *ebenus, i, f.* rather than *ebenum, i, n.*) and from his specific statement that trees (*arbores*) had been led in triumphal trains since Pompey. The difference should be noted, since we know that the valuable ebony logs were used as tribute in the eastern Mediterranean.[341] In fact, Ptolemy Philadelphus is said to have displayed 2,000 ebony logs together with 600 ivory tusks in his grand procession in Alexandria.[342] But while ancient authors affirm the presence of ivory tusks in a few Roman triumphal processions held over the East,[343] they at no time tell of ebony logs being paraded.

The ebony tree displayed by Pompey could be interpreted either as the ancient Egyptian ebony tree (*Dalbergia melanoxylon*, originally from Senegal/Sudan) or

---

[338] Solin. 52.52 (55). Gaius Iulius Solinus based his work *Collectanea rerum memorabilium* (*c*.AD 200) almost entirely on Pliny and Mela.

[339] Plin. *Nat.* 12.54.111–12. I have followed Mayhoff's proposition of *arborum* in the Teubner edn, 1909.

[340] In the passage *a Pompeio Magno in triumpho arbores quoque duximus*, the *arbores* are sometimes misread as balsam trees rather than trees in general. Consequently, some scholars maintain that Pompey displayed not only the ebony tree but also the balsam tree in his triumph, *RE* II (1896), s.v. 'Balsambaum', 2837 (P. Wagler); Greenhalgh (1981: 174); Kuttner (1999: 345).

[341] Hdt. 3.97; Plin. *Nat.* 12.8.17–18.

[342] Ath. 5.201a.

[343] Liv. 37.59.3; Diod. Sic. 31.8.12 (apud Sync.).

the Indian ebony tree (from the *Diospyros* family, probably the *Diospyros ebenum*, which is the true ebony).[344] Solinus is clear in his opinion; he describes Pompey's ebony trees as coming *ex India*. Pliny, on whom the passage is based, does not give this information, but as his remark stems from the chapters dealing with the trees of India, we should take India as the provenance of Pompey's display.[345]

In fact, trees from India fitted perfectly into the message and meaning of Pompey's triumphal performance. To the Romans of this date, India was still an unknown wonderland on the eastern edges of the world, hitherto reached only by Hercules and Alexander. By parading ebony trees announced as coming from India, Pompey was able to make yet another strong reference to his great predecessor and model, Alexander. He also implied that his command had extended the Roman hegemony to the very borders of the inhabited world.

Unlike Alexander, Pompey never reached India on his eastern campaign. Therefore, *ex India* does not imply spoils from a land conquered by the Roman army. The trees may have been sent as gifts from India, but it is more plausible that they were taken as booty or bestowed as gifts from some royal garden in the lands subjected by Pompey. In fact, the royal garden formed a common feature of the Hellenistic palaces.[346] Its idea was based on an Assyrian-Babylonian tradition of the *paradeisos* filled with trees, bushes, and flowers from far and near, collected on journeys or taken as war booty.[347] The ebony tree fitted well into the royal *paradeisos*. For example, we know that Assurnassirpal collected ebony trees on a journey and planted it in his ninth-century palace garden at Nimrud.[348] Very probably, the Indian ebony grew in some of the Hellenistic royal gardens at the time of Pompey's campaign.

Later on, in AD 71, Vespasian and Titus displayed the balsam tree in their Jewish triumphal procession. The ancient authors describe the balsam tree as a shrub, and Pliny maintains that it did not exceed two cubits in height.[349] According to the tradition, the queen of Sheba presented the balsam tree as a gift to King Solomon,[350] after which the tree grew predominantly in Judaea. Pliny claims that it was restricted to two palace gardens, probably situated at Jericho and Ein

[344] Strab. 15.1.37, 17.2.2. *RE* V (1905), s.v. 'Ebenholzbaum', 1893 (M. C. P. Schmidt); Stol (1979: 36–8); *NP* iii (1997), s.v. 'Ebenholz', 860 (C. Hünemörder).

[345] While Pliny describes both the Indian and the Egyptian ebony tree, Vergil maintains that India was the only place where ebony grew, *Georg.* 2.116–17, *sola India nigrum | fert hebenum*; cf. Plin. *Nat.* 12.8.17. Bruère (1956: 234–5).

[346] Nielsen (1994); Sonne (1996); Nielsen (2001).

[347] Wiseman (1984); Sonne (1996: esp. 137–8); Nielsen (2001: esp. 171–2).

[348] Wiseman (1984: 38, 42).

[349] Plin. *Nat.* 12.54.113; Strab. 16.2.41; Tac. *Hist.* 5.6.1. For the tree, see also *RE* II (1896), s.v. 'Balsambaum', 2836–9 (P. Wagler); André (1985: 33); *NP* ii (1997), s.v. 'Balsam', 428 (C. Hünemörder); Cotton and Eck (1997). The balsam tree is today labelled *commiphora gileadensis*.

[350] Joseph. *AJ* 8.174.

Gedi.[351] The ownership of the gardens both before and after the Jewish war is uncertain and much debated. Pliny calls the gardens royal, and they had probably been in the possession of different dynasts since the Seleucids.[352] Later on, Antony presented the balsam plantations as a gift to Cleopatra, from whom Herod leased them.[353] After Actium, it is likely that the gardens were given back to Herod, and in AD 6, when Judaea became part of the Roman province of Syria, they were probably transferred into Roman ownership, though the Jews might still have leased them.[354]

Discussions of the fate of the balsam plantations after the triumph of Vespasian and Titus focus on a statement in Pliny that, from this date, the tree was cultivated by the *fiscus* (*seritque nunc eum fiscus*).[355] The *fiscus* here has earlier been understood as the private possession of the Roman emperor,[356] but Alpers has proposed that it should be read as the *fiscus Iudaicus*, a state-owned provincial chest, which formed part of the *aerarium populi Romani*.[357] Since the provincial *tributum* was paid to the Roman state rather than to the emperor, this reading allows for Pliny's declaration, quoted above, that the balsam tree now paid tax together with the race to which it belonged (*servit nunc haec ac tributa pendit cum sua gente*).

Ebony and balsam were both exotic trees, renowned for the high-priced luxury goods produced from them. Ebony was used mainly in costly furniture, while the balsam tree delivered the expensive oil *opobalsamum*, used as medicine and perfume.[358] In fact, so valuable was the balsam that during the Jewish war, actual battles were fought at the plantations, when the Roman army protected the trees from being destroyed in anger by the Jews.[359]

In view of the high value of their products, the trees on triumphal display suggested great future incomes secured for Rome. Still, on parade, emphasis was clearly given to ebony and balsam as trees rather than material for luxury products. In Pliny's description, quoted above, the trees appear as living beings rather than inanimate goods. Pliny not only equates the population of trees with that of human beings (*servit nunc haec ac tributa pendit cum sua gente*); he also employs

[351] Plin. *Nat.* 12.54.111; cf. Theophr. *Hist. Pl.* 9.6.1; Strab. 16.2.41; Joseph. *AJ* 9.7, 15.96, *BJ* 4.469. Cotton and Eck (1997: 153–4). Later on, balsam grew elsewhere in the area too, Cotton and Eck (1997: 161).

[352] Plin. *Nat.* 12.54.111. Cotton and Eck (1997: 155).

[353] Joseph. *BJ* 1.361–2, *AJ* 15.96; Plut. *Ant.* 36.2. Smallwood (1981: 62).

[354] Scholars argue that, after AD 6, the plantations were either owned by the Roman emperor, or they were public property; emperor: Millar (1963: 30); Cotton and Eck (1997: 155, 160–1); public property: Brunt (1966: 79); Baldacci (1969: 357–64); Alpers (1995: 296–8). Jewish leasing: Alpers (1995: 299 and n. 1052).

[355] Plin. *Nat.* 12.54.113.

[356] Millar (1963: 30); Cotton and Eck (1997: 155).

[357] Alpers (1995: 291–304, esp. 300). Cf. Brunt (1966); Smallwood (1981: 340).

[358] Meiggs (1982: 282–6) discusses the various uses of ebony. Balsam: Plin. *Nat.* 12.54.111, 23.7.92, 37.78.204.

[359] Plin. *Nat.* 12.54.113.

the particular phrase *arbores ducere* to describe their processional display. The verb *ducere* is never used to account for objects of booty on parade, but is by far the most common way to express how prisoners and animals (i.e. living creatures) were led. In fact, in ancient literature in general, trees were quite often described as breathing beings, much similar to humans.[360]

Since balsam and ebony were paraded as prisoners rather than spoils, they were probably carried upright as living trees rather than as felled trunks. In this way, the trees would have made a proud and conspicuous first entry into the city. Trees were displayed erect in other processions. For example, a painting from the Temple of Venus in Pompeii shows a sacred tree carried upright on a *ferculum* as part of an Isis procession.[361] Another possibility is that the trees were placed upright in carrying devices, which were suspended on poles carried by men. This is how Egyptian paintings depict myrrh and possibly balsam trees being brought from southern lands.[362] The specific species of the ebony tree shown by Pompey is unknown, whereas we know that the balsam trees were shrubs. They would easily have been carried upright through the city.

Living trees were most probably replanted after the procession. At least, this is how practice worked in the Near East, where trees and plants from distant lands were taken as war booty or collected on journeys and replanted in the royal palace gardens on home ground. Through the gathering of foreign trees and plants, the kings in the Near East created gardens that formed miniature cosmological entities. Visitors could gaze upon the flora of the surrounding world in one and the same place. Hellenistic rulers in the East adopted the tradition of the royal garden; in fact, the balsam tree and probably also the ebony tree shown in the Roman triumphs were taken from such contexts. Very likely, the idea was taken up in Rome too. Trees were most certainly replanted as evergreen memories of triumphal success, royal defeat, and Rome's embracing of the world.

We know of other successful transplantations of trees from the East to Italian soil in the late Republic.[363] It is probably no coincidence that it was Pompey's predecessor as commander in the Mithridatic War, Lucullus, who brought the cherry tree to Italy from Pontus.[364] Very likely, this tree transfer inspired Lucullus' rival Pompey to bring ebony to Rome and to make a spectacular display of these trees, even more highly valued than the costly cherry trees. In this way, as in so many others, Pompey trumped his predecessor in staging royal eastern booty in the city of Rome.

---

[360] Colum. 3.10.11; Ovid. *Met.* 1.549–62; Plin. *Nat.* 16.72.181. Gowers (2005).
[361] Abaecherli (1935/6: 3, tav. I.1); Ryberg (1955: 169–70, pl. LXI, fig. 99).
[362] Täckholm (1976: 182–5); Darby *et al.* (1977: 319, fig. 6.44). In Ptolemy Philadelphus' Alexandrian procession, men carried trees in which animals and birds hung, but we know nothing of how these trees were transported, Ath. 5.201b.
[363] White (1970: 258–9, 262).
[364] Plin. *Nat.* 15.30.102. White (1970: 258–9 n. 82).

FOUR
_____

Representations

REPRESENTATIONS AND 'TRIUMPHAL PAINTINGS'

Besides the various kinds of spoils and captives obtained in war, the Roman triumphs also paraded representations produced specifically for the processions. The representations were executed in many forms and showed a variety of topics. The primary types were conquered cities, subjected peoples and rivers, and war scenes. Thus, for example, the spectators who had gathered to witness the four triumphs held by Caesar during one and the same month in 46 BC saw representations of Gallia, the city of Massilia, and the Rivers Nile, Oceanus, Rhine, and Rhône, as well as scenes showing the flights and deaths of the triumphator's principal adversaries.[1]

As will be shown below, war scenes were staged as dramatic tableaux, which brought into play multiple artistic media. Around ten passages in the ancient literature testify to such tableaux, and the Greek historians Appian and Josephus provide the most detailed descriptions. Being the most complex category of representations, the tableaux will be discussed last in this chapter. Triumphal representations of conquered cities, subjected peoples (*nationes* and *gentes*), and rivers were three-dimensional single-subject representations shaped as models or personifications. In ancient literature, roughly thirty-five passages, almost all Latin, mention such representations. The texts most frequently tell of cities (in around twenty-five literary references), followed by rivers (thirteen) and peoples (eight). In addition, quite a few passages refer to mountains (seven), and there are single references to buildings and the *oikumene*.[2] There are also in art one or two preserved depictions of rivers on parade and one that depicts a building. These numbers probably reflect quite well the relative frequency of representations paraded.[3] As a comparison, we might use Pliny's account of L. Cornelius

---

[1] Cic. *Phil.* 8.6.18, *Off.* 2.8.28; Lucan. 3.76–8; App. *BCiv.* 2.101; Flor. *Epit.* 2.13.88–9.

[2] Ancient reality is not always easily transformed into exact categories, and the numbers given are all approximate. Some passages could describe single specific representations or refer to more general overviews of larger displays. Images of mountains, buildings, and the *oikumene* will be analysed among the other representations below.

[3] Also, Ovid and Zonaras refer vaguely to the display of lakes and seas (Ov. *Trist.* 4.2.37–8; Zonar. 7.21.10), but from these passages alone it is difficult to affirm what the representations looked like.

Balbus' triumph held in 19 BC for his African victories. According to Pliny, Balbus displayed eighteen or nineteen towns, four or five peoples, two rivers, and two mountains in his procession.[4]

Before we proceed to discuss the multifaceted display of cities, peoples, rivers, and war scenes, we need to dwell on a concept that has permeated modern debate on the representations on parade—the so-called 'triumphal paintings'. In the pursuit of the lost pictorial origins of Roman historical relief, scholars have for quite some time turned to descriptions in the ancient literature of representations shown in triumphs and of paintings with battle scenes displayed in public. These kinds of representations—labelled 'triumphal paintings'—are believed to bear testimony to a larger Republican tradition of narrative painting, which constituted the forerunner of Imperial historical painting and relief.[5]

In modern literature, a 'triumphal painting' implies a painting which, commissioned by a Roman general, depicted his achievements in a successful war campaign. Scholars assume that the painting glorified and commemorated the general's martial deeds by way of a twofold display: first in his triumphal procession, later in a temple or a public place. The 'triumphal paintings' are described as narrative in character, showing successive episodes, sometimes in one and the same painting, sometimes through a series of paintings, as depicted in Mantegna's fifteen-century painting *The Triumphs of Caesar* (Fig. 22).[6] Of documentary rather than aesthetic nature, they, according to general opinion, frequently made use of the so-called bird's eye perspective. That is, in order to indicate geographic and topographic locations as well as martial actions, the paintings represented people and structures, each in the most informative way, against a setting of landscapes and plans of cities. In surviving art, the most notable examples of this kind of narrative technique can be seen in the well-known painting from Pompeii depicting a riot at the amphitheatre and in the reliefs on Trajan's column, both of which are assumed to trace their origins back to Republican 'triumphal paintings'.[7] It is also frequently maintained that the development of 'triumphal paintings' gained from the arrival in the second

---

[4] Plin. *Nat.* 5.5.36–7.

[5] In 1959/60, Gerhard Zinserling published what is still the principal analysis on triumphal paintings, 'Studien zu den Historiendarstellungen der römischen Republik'. After Zinserling, the two main works on 'triumphal paintings' are the articles by Mansuelli (1979) and Holliday (1997). Among many other discussions, see e.g. Dawson (1944: 50–4); Blanckenhagen (1962: esp. 54–7); Felletti Maj (1977: 59–65); Hölscher (1978: 344–6); Bonfante (1978: 149–51); Holliday (1980: 5–7); Hölscher (1980: 352–5); Brilliant (1984: 26, 108–9); Koeppel (1985: 90–2); Blanckenhagen, in Blanckenhagen and Alexander (1990: 43–5); Kleiner (1992: 47–8); Amiotti (2002: 204); Holliday (2002: esp. 80–3, 104–14, 211–19); cf. Koortbojian (2002: esp. 37–40); Lusnia (2006: 285–96).

[6] Beard (2007: 153–9).

[7] Pompeii painting: Moffitt (1997: 240, fig. 5); Holliday (2002: 109–10, fig. 55); Trajan's column: Settis (1988: esp. 93–8, 232–41); Kleiner (1992: 214–20).

FIGURE 22 On
Mantegna's *Tri-
umphs of Caesar*,
bearers carry
painted war scenes
that are depicted in
rows on banners. It
is thought the
Mantegna was
inspired in particu-
lar by Josephus'
description of the
Jewish triumph
with war scenes
represented
on *pegmata*
(*BJ* 7.139–47).

century BC of topographers from Hellenistic Alexandria, who worked in a tradition of pictorial map-making of the type seen in the Nile Mosaic in Praeneste.[8] No actual 'triumphal painting' has survived, but it is assumed that an early reflection of the type can be seen in the early third-century BC painting from a tomb on the Esquiline hill. The paintings depict episodes from the Second Samnite War in honour of the commander and triumphator Q. Fabius Maximus Rullianus.[9]

It goes without saying that analyses of historical paintings provide many valuable discussions on the form and function of Roman art. Unfortunately, however, the term 'triumphal paintings' has brought about major misconceptions when it comes to the imagery put on display in the triumphal procession.

[8] Meyboom (1995); Moffitt (1997); Holliday (1997: 138–9).

[9] Bonfante (1978: 149–51, with further references); Hölscher (1978: 346–8); Mansuelli (1979: 45); Holliday (1980: 3–4); Kleiner (1992: 48); Holliday (1997: 136); Hölkeskamp (2000: 240–8); Holliday (2002: 83–91); *Trionfi romani*, 168–9, II.1.2.

First, modern works frequently group all the representations shown in the processions as 'triumphal paintings'.[10] However, though paintings were certainly present,[11] ancient sources show that triumphal representations were mainly produced in other artistic media, such as models, sculptures, and dramatic tableaux. Secondly, the conventional use of the term 'triumphal painting' to describe paintings with battle scenes put up in public locations and temples has brought about a well-established assumption that these paintings were first shown in the processions. As we shall see, the assumption lacks any support from the sources. In the following, I aim to show that the art works conventionally grouped as 'triumphal paintings' were of two quite different kinds. On one hand, there were the representations made for the triumphs. These took on varied artistic expressions but were not 'paintings' in the sense commonly assumed. On the other hand, there were commemorative paintings produced for stationary display in a public place or a temple. I will first focus on the second type, the commemorative paintings, arguing that this kind of 'triumphal paintings' was not intended for processional display. After that it will be possible to move on to an inquiry into the diverse representations actually put on parade.

Commemorative paintings

No actual 'triumphal painting' has been preserved, and the sources are all literary. Most modern discussions follow Pliny and take as their point of departure the painting that the triumphator M'. Valerius Messala displayed on the wall of the Curia Hostilia in 263 BC.[12] It represented his victory over the Carthaginians:

Plin. *Nat.* 35.7.22: Dignatio autem praecipua Romae increvit, ut existimo, a M'. Valerio Maximo Messala, qui princeps tabulam [picturam] proelii, quo Carthaginienses et Hieronem in Sicilia vicerat, proposuit in latere curiae Hostiliae anno ab urbe condita CCCCXC.

The dignified reputation of painting in Rome was, in my judgement, increased particularly by M'. Valerius Maximus Messala, who was the first to display a painting of a battle—the one in which he had defeated the Carthaginians and Hiero in Sicily—on a side wall of the Curia Hostilia in the 490th year from the foundation of the city.[13]

Pliny continues his account by describing two other 'triumphal paintings', which likewise appear in all modern discussions on the subject: one displayed on the

---

[10] This is all the more strange, since the misunderstanding was pointed out already by Zinserling (1959/60: 421, cf. 403).

[11] See the discussion below, pp. 247–8, 251–5.

[12] Vessberg (1941: no. 84, 26); Zinserling (1959/60: no. 4, 405, 436); Hölscher (1978: 344); Mansuelli (1979: *passim*); Holliday (1997: 135).

[13] Translation based on Pollitt (1998: 51).

Capitol by the triumphator of 189 BC, L. Scipio Asiaticus, representing his Asiatic victory,[14] and another commissioned by L. Hostilius Mancinus, who was the first man to break into Carthage during the Third Punic War.[15] Hostilius Mancinus' painting showed a plan of Carthage and the battles fought there. It was displayed in the Forum, where Mancinus himself explained the various scenes to the people looking at it. Pliny (*Nat.* 35.7.22–3) writes:

Fecit hoc idem et L. Scipio tabulamque victoriae suae Asiaticae in Capitolio posuit, idque aegre tulisse fratrem Africanum tradunt, haut inmerito, quando filius eius illo proelio captus fuerat. Non dissimilem offensionem et Aemiliani subiit L. Hostilius Mancinus, qui primus Carthaginem inruperat, situm eius oppugnationesque depictas proponendo in foro et ipse adsistens populo spectanti singula enarrando, qua comitate proximis comitiis consulatum adeptus est.

L. Scipio did the same thing; he placed a painting of his Asiatic victory on the Capitol. This is said to have annoyed his brother Africanus, and not without reason, as his son had been taken prisoner in that battle. Also L. Hostilius Mancinus, who had first broken into Carthage, committed a very similar offence with Aemilianus by displaying in the Forum a painting of the site of the city and of the attacks upon it and by himself standing by it and describing the events one by one to the people watching. This was a piece of affable behaviour, which won him the consulship in the next election.[16]

Besides the three paintings described by Pliny, modern analyses of 'triumphal paintings' also discuss the painting that the triumphator Ti. Sempronius Gracchus exhibited in the temple of Mater Matuta in 174 BC.[17] The painting had the shape of the island of Sardinia (where Gracchus had fought his war) and had battles depicted on it. Livy (41.28.8–10) maintains that it was accompanied by an inscribed text:

Eodem anno tabula in aede Matris Matutae cum indice hoc posita est: 'Ti. Semproni Gracchi consulis imperio auspicioque legio exercitusque populi Romani Sardiniam sub-egit. In ea provincia hostium caesa aut capta supra octoginta milia. Re publica felicissime gesta atque liberatis sociis, vectigalibus restitutis exercitum salvum atque incolumem plenissimum praeda domum reportavit; iterum triumphans in urbem Romam rediit. Cuius rei ergo hanc tabulam donum Iovi dedit.' Sardiniae insulae forma erat, atque in ea simulacra pugnarum picta.

In the same year a tablet was set up in the temple of Mater Matuta with this inscription: 'Under the command and auspices of the consul Ti. Sempronius Gracchus, the legion and the army of the Roman people conquered Sardinia. In this province more than eighty thousand enemies were killed or captured. The assignment having been most successfully carried out and the allies set free, the revenues restored, he brought back home the army

---

[14] Vessberg (1941: no. 145, 37); Zinserling (1959/60: no. 9a, 407); Mansuelli (1979: *passim*).

[15] Vessberg (1941: no. 150, 39); Zinserling (1959/60: no. 13, 409–10, 414–15); Hölscher (1978: 345); Mansuelli (1979: esp. 47–8); Holliday (1997: 134, 145).

[16] Tr. based on Pollitt (1998: 51).

[17] Vessberg (1941: no. 147, 38); Zinserling (1959/60: no. 11, 408–9, 416); Holliday (1997: 136–8).

safe and secure and enriched with booty; for the second time he returned to the city of Rome in triumph. In commemoration of this event he set up this tablet as a gift to Jupiter.' It had the form of the island of Sardinia, and on it representations of battles were painted.

Scholars have assumed that the types of painting exhibited in public by Messala, Scipio Asiaticus, and Tiberius Gracchus were primarily produced for display in these generals' triumphal processions and only put up publicly afterwards.[18] Even the painting commissioned by Hostilius Mancinus has been described as carried in his parade—though Mancinus actually never celebrated any triumph.[19] This kind of erroneous statement in a specialist article on the subject can only be explained by the use of the misleading term 'triumphal paintings' for these works of art, implying their processional use.

Hostilius Mancinus' 'triumphal painting' was not made for display in a triumphal procession. It was created with the specific purpose of being displayed and scrutinized in a public place. Likewise—it is argued in the following—the main intent of similar kinds of paintings depicting scenes from the victorious wars was not processional display, but commemorative exhibition in a public place or a temple.

No descriptions of the triumphs held by Messala, Scipio Asiaticus, and Tiberius Gracchus include any paintings with battle scenes.[20] More significantly, in the accounts of the paintings themselves, neither Pliny nor Livy mention any processional use, although these two authors otherwise provide abundant information of content in triumphal parades. Quite the contrary, both authors stress the public placing of the paintings by using forms of the verbs *ponere* or *proponere* and by emphasizing the settings employed: *in latere curiae Hostiliae, in Capitolio, in foro, in aede Matris Matutae*.[21]

Livy and Pliny describe the paintings as *tabulae*, adding, in some cases, forms of the verb *pingere* to define them as painted. Quite clearly, *tabulae* and *tabulae pictae* formed part of triumphal displays, but ancient authors employ these terms exclusively for paintings taken as booty and paraded as such, often together with looted statues (*signa tabulaeque*). In fact, no Latin author ever uses *tabula* to describe a representation specifically produced for exhibition in a triumphal

---

[18] Vessberg (1952: 131); Zinserling (1959/60: *passim*); Blanckenhagen (1962: 55); Bonfante (1978: 150); Hölscher (1978: 344; 1980: 352); Holliday (1980: 5); Brilliant (1984: 108); Koeppel (1985: 90–2); Bellen (1988: 874); Kleiner (1992: 48); Favro (1994: 154); Holliday (1997: *passim*; 2002: 30, 63, 80–3, 104–14, 211–19); Amiotti (2002: 204); Hölscher (2006: 40).

[19] Holliday (1997: 134, 136, 145), cf. Holliday (2002: 82, 214).

[20] Eutropius (2.19) briefly mentions Messala's triumph, and Livy's triumphal account of Tiberius Gracchus' triumph (in book 41) is missing. Livy's description of Scipio Asiaticus' parade is more substantial, Liv. 37.59.

[21] Cf. Mansuelli (1979: 45, 47).

parade.[22] Forms of *pingere* are also excluded. Instead, if given a specific term at all, these works are mostly called *simulacra*, or at times *imagines* and *effigies*, terms that could signify artistic representations of any kind or simply 'likeness' in a very general sense.[23] Thus, through their choice of terms, the Latin authors reveal that the paintings taken as booty and the representations produced for processional use were of two different kinds, as were these representations and the paintings of battles exhibited in public places.

The term *tabula* combined with a form of *pingere* appears in some further literary references to paintings depicting the military deeds of Roman generals. The *De viris illustribus* mentions the triumph held by L. Aemilius Paullus over the Ligurians in 181 BC in the following way: *de Liguribus triumphavit. Rerum gestarum ordinem in tabula pictum publice posuit*, 'He triumphed over the Ligurians. He put up a painting in public where the sequence of his achievements was depicted.'[24] Much later, the Emperor Maximinus (AD 235–8) had paintings depicting his war in Germania exhibited before the senate house. The text in the *Historia Augusta* runs: *Iussit praeterea tabulas pingi ita ut erat bellum ipsum gestum et ante Curiam proponi, ut facta eius pictura loqueretur. Quas quidem tabulas post mortem eius senatus et deponi iussit et exuri*, 'He also ordered that paintings, illustrating how the war itself had been conducted, should be produced and be put up before the senate house, in order that his achievements would be told by way of the art of painting. After his death, the senate ordered the paintings to be taken down and burned.'[25] Similarly, the Greek text of Herodian tells us that Septimius Severus, having fought successful battles in Parthia, wrote to the senate and the people, ordering that his achievements should be painted and publicly displayed: τάς μάχας τε καὶ τὰς νίκας δημοσίαις ἀνέθηκε γραφαῖς, 'the battles and the victories publicly displayed in paintings'.[26]

As in the passages of Livy and Pliny, the descriptions of the paintings commissioned by Aemilius Paullus, Maximinus, and Septimius Severus in no way suggest that the painted *tabulae* (γραφαί) had previously been shown in triumphal processions. Instead, the passages again emphasize the public placing of the paintings, underlined by the expressions *publice posuit* (Aemilius Paullus), *ante Curiam proponi* (Maximinus), and δημοσίαις ἀνέθηκε γραφαῖς (Septimius Severus). The author of the *De viris illustribus* claims first that Aemilius Paullus

---

[22] This circumstance has not been noticed in discussions on triumphal paintings. Hence, for instance, Holliday writes: 'They [the triumphal paintings] were sometimes executed on large panels, called *tabulae*, which could be easily carried in the procession,' Holliday (1997: 134; cf. 1980: 5).

[23] Daut (1975: 34); Flower (1996: 33, 35). Greek terms are εἰκών and μίμημα.

[24] *Vir. ill.* 56.

[25] S.H.A. *Max.* 12.10–11.

[26] Hdn. 3.9.12. Lusnia (2006) argues that the paintings were reproduced in stone on Severus' arch at the Forum.

triumphed and only afterwards did he display a painting in public. The painting depicted his deeds, very probably including the triumph itself. A similar procedure is suggested by a passage on Caracalla in the *Historia Augusta*, telling of a portico in Rome that showed Septimius Severus' paintings: *Reliquit et porticum patris nomine, quae gesta illius contineret et triumphos et bella*, 'In the name of his father, he [Caracalla] also left a portico, intended to contain his [father's] deeds, triumphs as well as wars.'[27] Here, the *res gestae* displayed explicitly included both wars and triumphs, suggesting that the paintings were executed only after Septimius Severus' procession had taken place. Herodian's description also excludes a processional exhibition, as he maintains that Septimius Severus sent orders that paintings showing his achievements should be exhibited in public while he was still in Parthia.

Returning to the *tabula* of Tiberius Gracchus, Livy's account (quoted above) in fact makes it clear that this painting was produced and put up in the temple of Mater Matuta only after Gracchus' triumph. According to Livy, the inscription, which accompanied Tiberius Gracchus' painting, first related his martial achievements on Sardinia and the successful outcome of the war. Thereafter it stated: *iterum triumphans in urbem Romam rediit. Cuius rei ergo hanc tabulam donum Iovi dedit*, 'for the second time he returned to the city of Rome in triumph. In commemoration of this event he set up this tablet as a gift to Jupiter.' Tiberius Gracchus' *tabula* thus memorialized both his achievements on Sardinia and his triumphal celebration, and must have been produced only after the procession had been concluded.[28]

In attempting to establish the nature of the publicly exhibited paintings representing Roman generals' successful achievements in war, the term *tabula* used by the Latin authors is revealing. In Latin literature, *tabulae* (literally signifying boards or planks) imply not only paintings, but also written dedicatory tablets hung up in temples and written official documents publicly displayed, such as laws, decrees of the senate, proscription lists, as well as *acta* and *commentarii* relating the achievements of a magistrate or a triumphator.[29] For example, after his triumph held in 74 BC, P. Servilius Vatia Isauricus displayed *tabulae publicae* by the *aerarium* with close descriptions of the booty that he had won in the war and displayed in his triumph.[30] Through a meticulous recording of each

---

[27] S.H.A. *Carac.* 9.6–7, cf. *Sev.* 21.12: *Exstat sane Romae Severi porticus gesta eius exprimens a filio, quantum plurimi docent, structa*, 'There is a portico of Severus in Rome which contains his exploits. Most men say that it was built by his son.'

[28] According to Festus, L. Papirius Cursor (triumph 272 BC) and M. Fulvius Flaccus (triumph 264 BC) displayed paintings in the temples of Consus and Vortumnus, depicting them as *triumphantes*, Fest. p. 228 L, s.v. 'picta'. Zinserling (1959/60: nos. 1 and 3, 404–5).

[29] *OLD* s.v. 'tabula'.   [30] Cic. *Verr*. II.1.21.57.

of the captured statues, of their number, sizes, shapes, and attitudes, these *tabulae* announced and commemorated in detail the achievements of the general.

The triumphator (or some other person in his honour) also often placed *tabulae* as written dedicatory tablets in the temple of Jupiter on the Capitoline hill and in a shrine vowed during the war and built from its spoils. Hence, above the doors of the temple of the Lares Permarini hung a written *tabula*, which commemorated the successful deeds of L. Aemilius Regillus, triumphator in 189 BC. Regillus had vowed the temple during his naval campaign against Antiochus, and his relative M. Aemilius Lepidus dedicated it as censor ten years later.[31] Livy accounts for the text inscribed on the *tabula* and also maintains that another *tabula* with the same text was put up above the doors of the Capitoline temple of Jupiter.[32] In fact, an excerpt from Regillus' Capitoline tablet, identical in wording to the *tabula* at the Lares Permarini, is quoted in the *De metris*, a grammatical treatise traditionally attributed to the first-century AD writer Caesius Bassus. The *De metris* also cites a passage from another Capitoline *tabula* of the same kind, relating the deeds of M'. Acilius Glabrio, who triumphed over the Aetolians and Antiochus in 190 BC.[33] Atilius Fortunatianus supplies further information on this practice. In the *De Saturnio*, he states that it was a common procedure for triumphators to dedicate *tabulae* celebrating their martial achievements on the Capitoline hill.[34]

---

[31] Pietilä-Castrén (1987: 92–3).

[32] Liv. 40.52.5–7: *Supra valvas templi tabula cum titulo hoc fixa est: 'Duello magno dirimendo, regibus subigendis, patrandae pacis causa haec pugna exeunti L. Aemilio M. Aemilii filio † Auspicio imperio felicitate ductuque eius inter Ephesum Samum Chiumque, inspectante eopse Antiocho, exercitu omni, equitatu elephantisque, classis regis Antiochi antehac invicta fusa contusa fugataque est, ibique eo die naves longae cum omnibus sociis captae quadraginta duae. Ea pugna pugnata rex Antiochus regnumque † Eius rei ergo aedem Laribus permarinis vovit.' Eodem exemplo tabula in aede Iovis in Capitolio supra valvas fixa est,* 'Above the doors of the temple, a tablet was fixed carrying the inscription: "For finishing a great war, for subduing kings, this battle, fought for the purpose of winning peace, [gave victory] to Lucius Aemilius, the son of Marcus Aemilius, as he left the field. Under his auspices and command, with his good fortune and generalship, in the area bounded by Ephesus, Samos, and Chios, under the eyes of Antiochus himself, of all his army, his cavalry and his elephants, the fleet of Antiochus, hitherto undefeated, was routed, shattered and put to flight, and there on that day forty-two ships were taken with all their crews. As a result of the finishing of this battle King Antiochus was defeated and his naval empire [overthrown . . .] By this reason, he vowed a temple of the Lares of the Sea." A tablet with the same text was set up in the temple of Jupiter on the Capitoline above the doors.' (Tr. based on E. T. Sage, Loeb classical library.) The passage is corrupt and the reading uncertain at various points. For the reading of *eodem exemplo* as 'with the same text', see *TLL*, s.v. 'exemplum', 1350 (IV.B2).

[33] Caesius Bassus, in Keil, *Gramm. Lat.* 6. p. 265: *Apud nostros autem in tabulis antiquis, quas triumphaturi duces in Capitolio figebant victoriaeque suae titulum Saturniis versibus prosequebantur, talia repperi exempla: ex Regilli tabula: 'duello magno dirimendo regibus subigendis', qui est subsimilis ei quem paulo ante posui, consulto producit eum quo sit impudentior; in Acilii Glabrionis tabula: 'fundit fugat prosternit maximas legiones'.*

[34] Atilius Fortunatianus, in Keil, *Gramm. Lat.* 6. p. 293–4: *maxime tamen triumphaturi in Capitolio tabulas huius modi versibus incidebant, [id est sic] 'summas opes qui regum regias refregit'.* The form

It is in the context of these written commemorative *tabulae* hung up by the triumphators that the publicly exhibited 'triumphal paintings' should be seen. Like their written counterparts, the painted *tabulae* memorialized the triumphator's achievements in war and often his triumphal celebration as well. Neither the written nor the painted *tabulae* were produced for parade. They were non-mobile records set up for display in a public place or temple compound.[35]

Some 'triumphal paintings' were publicly exhibited documentary *tabulae*, which, like Servilius Vatia's written ones, put forth in detail and celebrated the performed duties of a Roman official. Others were dedicatory tablets exposed in temples. Like the written *tabulae* hanging above the doors of the temple of the Lares Permarini and on the Capitol, they confirmed the deeds of the triumphator and offered thanks for the outcome of the war and for the triumph. This is particularly obvious in the case of the *tabula* set up by Tiberius Gracchus in the temple of Mater Matuta. Here, the pictorial documentation of the battles on Sardinia was accompanied by an inscription, which included an explicit dedication, not to the goddess of the temple, but to Jupiter. This circumstance can only be explained in light of Livy's statement that a written *tabula* similar to the one concerning Regillus in the temple of the Lares Permarini hung in the temple of the Capitoline Jupiter. In fact, it is most probable that a second example of Tiberius Gracchus' *tabula*, also dedicated to Jupiter, was placed on the Capitol. As the account in the *De Saturnio* reveals, it was common procedure for all triumphators to place tablets on the Capitoline hill. This circumstance also explains what Scipio Asiaticus' painted *tabula*, depicting his Asian victory, was doing *in Capitolio*, a location that has puzzled scholars.[36] By placing it there, Scipio simply followed the tradition of triumphators having *tabulae*, painted or written, documenting their martial deeds hung up as dedications on the Capitol, the destination of the triumphal procession.[37] These *tabulae* were potent reminders of Rome's former triumphs, adding a sense of timelessness to each

---

triumphaturi indicates that the tablets were put up by the triumphators before the triumph. Other sources suggest that this was done only after the parade. The important thing is that the *tabulae* were not produced for processional display, but had other functions.

[35] Pictorial documentations of the martial *res gestae* were also exhibited in houses and tombs. For example, the paintings from the Esquiline hill mentioned above were found in the tomb of the Fabii. For commemorative paintings placed in the atrium of the house of the triumphator, see Wiseman (1986: esp. 87–8).

[36] See e.g. Zinserling (1959/60: 417): 'Wenn Scipio Asiaticus ein Bild das seinen Sieg über Antiochos III verherrlichte, "in Capitolio posuit" so ist das ein besonders bemerkenswerter Umstand.'

[37] If this kind of commemorative *tabulae* were primarily dedicated to Jupiter Capitolinus, the practice was most probably an honour reserved exclusively for triumphators. Hence, our one example of a *tabula* put up by a person who did not celebrate a triumph, Hostilius Mancinus, was displayed 'in Foro'.

specific event. They expressed that Rome had been, was, and was to be eternally victorious and triumphant.

After his triumph held over Praeneste in 380 BC, Titus Quinctius Cincinnatus, according to Livy, dedicated a statue of Jupiter Imperator on the Capitol together with an inscribed *tabula* that commemorated his accomplishments and the help provided by the Roman gods.[38] Livy characterizes the written *tabula* as a *monumentum rerum gestarum*, thus providing us with a valid definition of the function of the written and painted *tabulae* discussed above: they were *monumenta* celebrating Roman generals' martial *res gestae*. The words of T. P. Wiseman in an article on historiography in the Roman Republic might conclude our discussion: 'First comes the *res gesta*, the exploit worthy of record; then the rewards for achievement, *honores* and the triumph; then the *monumentum* to preserve the memory of the deed; then the celebration of it by story-tellers and learned historians, for the unlettered multitude and the literate élite respectively.'[39]

CITIES AND TOWNS

Already in 1959/60, Zinserling argued that tower models were employed to represent both larger cities and smaller towns on triumphal parade. Still, modern literature most often assumes that 'triumphal paintings' were used,[40] either to display views of battles fought in the capturing of cities, or as allegoric representations, showing captured female personifications in painting (or as statues). Nothing in the ancient sources supports this assumption. There are no γραφαί, *tabulae* (*pictae*), and no forms of the verb *pingere*. Instead, the ancient authors often state only that *oppida victa*, the *captiva Corinthus* or Massilia were carried past. At other times, Latin writers group their display as *simulacra oppidorum*. Like the Greek words in use, εἰκών and μίμημα, *simulacrum* is rather non-specific in character, often denoting 'likeness' or 'representation' in general, and in itself reveals very little of the form employed.

Fortunately, there is also ancient testimony to confirm the specific artistic means employed. One passage suggests that personifications could be used. Silius Italicus, in his poetic depiction of the triumph celebrated by Scipio Africanus in 201 BC, includes the presence of the city of Carthage: *Mox victas*

[38] Liv. 6.29.9–10.

[39] Wiseman (1986: 87–8). Wiseman takes as his point of departure the story in Apuleius' *Metamorphoses* (book 6) of the girl who attempts to escape on an ass and imagines her future awards. First she will have a kind of triumph and only thereafter will her escape be recorded and painted for display in her atrium.

[40] See e.g. Daut (1975: 34–5 and n. 12); Felletti Maj (1977: 60); Mansuelli (1979: 46); Holliday (1980: 6); Köhler (1996: 110); Holliday (1997: 130, 136), Holliday (2002: 104–5); Amiotti (2002: 204, 112).

tendens Carthago ad sidera palmas | ibat, 'Next, Carthage went by, stretching her conquered hands to heaven'.[41] Silius' account echoes Vergil's triumphal description on the shield of Aeneas and cannot be taken as a historical commentary on Scipio's triumph.[42] It does, however, presuppose that Silius' own readers were familiar with the kinds of display depicted, and thus implies that, in the first century AD, cities might appear in personified forms in the triumphal pageants. Silius' description does not reveal whether Carthage was represented by an actor, a sculpture or a painting. Still, as it is quite clear that sculptured personifications were used for peoples and rivers (discussed below), such representations are likely to have been employed for cities as well.

Silius Italicus' Carthage forms our one unambiguous evidence of city personifications on triumphal display, and ancient sources far more frequently suggest the use of three-dimensional models. Zinserling, in his pioneering study, called them 'Der πύργος-Typ'.[43] The name is drawn from a passage in Appian, also describing the triumphal procession performed by Scipio Africanus in 201 BC: πύργοι τε παραφέρονται μιμήματα τῶν εἰλημμένων πόλεων, 'Towers were borne along as representations of the captured cities'.[44] Appian's statement is supported by a passage in Strabo, which, oddly enough, does not appear in discussions on triumphal representations. In his account of Celtiberia, Strabo writes:

Πολυβίου δ' εἰπόντος τριακοσίας αὐτῶν καταλῦσαι πόλεις Τιβέριον Γράκχον, κωμῳδῶν φησι τοῦτο τῷ Γράκχῳ χαρίσασθαι τὸν ἄνδρα, τοὺς πύργους καλοῦντα πόλεις, ὥσπερ ἐν ταῖς θριαμβικαῖς πομπαῖς.

But because Polybius went on to say that Ti. Gracchus destroyed three hundred of their cities, [Posidonius] makes fun of him, saying that the man did this merely to gratify Gracchus, for he called the towers cities just as they do in the triumphal processions.[45]

In these passages, Appian and Strabo confirm the use of towers to represent captured cities in the Roman triumphal processions. However, they do not reveal how the towers were rendered. To form a clearer conception of their appearance, we need to consult a couple of other references in the ancient literature.

After his victories in Spain in 45 BC, Caesar both celebrated a triumph of his own and allowed two of his subordinate commanders, Q. Fabius Maximus and Q. Pedius, to perform one triumph each for the same victory. The arrangement

---

[41] Sil. *Pun.* 17.635–6.   [42] e.g. Rawson (1990: 162–3).

[43] Zinserling (1959/60: 422–4).

[44] App. *Pun.* 66. Even these tower cities are at times discussed as 'triumphal paintings', Felletti Maj (1977: 60); Mansuelli (1979: 46); Holliday (1997: 136).

[45] Strab. 3.4.13. Ti. Sempronius Gracchus' campaign in Celtiberia rendered him a triumph in 178 BC.

was laughed at in Rome and jests circulated. One example has been preserved in Quintilian:

ut Chrysippus, cum in triumpho Caesaris eborea oppida essent translata, et post dies paucos Fabii Maximi lignea, thecas esse oppidorum Caesaris dixit.

When ivory towns were carried in Caesar's triumphal procession, and a few days later wooden ones were shown in the triumph of Fabius Maximus, Chrysippus remarked that the latter were cases for Caesar's ivory towns.[46]

Dio Cassius comments on the same event:

καὶ ἦν μέν που γέλως ἐπί τε τούτῳ, καὶ ὅτι καὶ ξυλίναις ἀλλ᾽ οὐκ ἐλεφαντίναις ἔργων τέ τινων εἰκόσιν ἄλλοις τε τοιούτοις πομπείοις ἐχρήσαντο, . . .

Naturally this occasioned ridicule, as did also the fact that they [Q. Fabius Maximus and Q. Pedius] used wooden instead of ivory representations of certain achievements together with other similar triumphal apparatus.[47]

Quintilian and Dio Cassius thus give clear evidence that the Spanish towns shown in 45 BC were executed in ivory and in wood, depending on the status of the triumphator. The witticism related by Quintilian that the wooden towns were *thecae*, cases, for the ivory ones, implies that these wooden and ivory towns were some kind of three-dimensional models.

Ovid too refers to the presence of ivory representations of towns. His poetic image of Tiberius' future triumph over Germania includes ivory towns encircled by turreted walls in such a way that the imitations seem real: *oppida turritis cingantur eburnea muris,* | *fictaque res vero more putetur agi.*[48] In one of his other triumphal depictions, Ovid paints a picture of barbarian towns made of silver in imitation of their razed walls: *protinus argento versos imitantia muros,* | *barbara cum victis oppida lata viris,* . . . [49]

The sources thus clearly show that conquered cities and towns were staged in the triumphal processions as three-dimensional models executed in diverse materials, such as ivory, wood, and silver.[50] Unfortunately, no such model has been preserved from antiquity. But Ovid's emphasis on the *muri* of the city walls taken together with the evidence in Strabo and Appian that the cities were shown by

---

[46] Quint. *Inst.* 6.3.61.　　[47] Dio Cass. 43.42.2.　　[48] Ov. *Pont.* 3.4.105–6.

[49] Ibid. 2.1.37–8: 'Right away, barbarian towns of silver were brought forth, imitating demolished walls with defeated men.' Some editors prefer *pictis* instead of *victis*, based on the foremost manuscripts. Cf. Beard (2004: 116). If this is correct, Ovid probably describes enemy men, who were 'painted, tattooed' as marks of their northern origins rather than men painted on the silver models of cities. However, to me, *victis viris* makes much more sense in this context of barbarian towns with razed walls.

[50] Other materials were most certainly used as well. Velleius (2.56.2) writes that citrus wood was used throughout Caesar's Gallic triumph, acanthus wood in the Pontic parade, tortoise shell in the Egyptian, ivory in the African, and finally, silver in the Spanish procession, *quinque egit triumphos; Gallici apparatus ex citro, Pontici ex acantho, Alexandrini testudine, Africi ebore, Hispaniensis argento rasili constitit.* The crucial

FIGURE 23 Model of a
bridge carried in tri-
umph. According to the
inscribed *titulus*, the
bridge represents *pons
Mulvius*. From this,
many but far from all
scholars, have inter-
preted the image as re-
ferring to Constantine's
victory over Maxentius
at the Milvian Bridge in
AD 312.

way of towers, πύργοι, suggest that the city walls formed the most significant part of
the representations.[51] Perhaps only the walls were shown or perhaps the models
showed important buildings of the cities enclosed by a wall, not unlike models held
in the hands of city patrons in medieval and later painting.[52] The plain notion of
πύργοι in Appian and Strabo points to the former, Ovid's (poetic) description of
towns encircled by turreted walls could be read as an indication of the latter.

   None of the preserved ancient reliefs with triumphal scenes include any representation of a conquered city or town. However, a relief from Cherchel in Algeria
shows a group of men carrying a model of a bridge on a *ferculum* (Fig. 23).[53] The
relief is of a late date but may well indicate how models were traditionally

term here is *apparatus*, which might embrace the representations, although Velleius' statement that silver
was used in the Spanish triumph does not fit the accounts of ivory models in Quintilian and Dio Cassius.
Cf. Suetonius, who writes that Caesar's triumphs were *diverso quemque apparatu et instrumento*, Suet.
Iul. 37.1–2. Deutsch (1924*b*). Much later, Claudian writes of the exhibition of *oppida facta metallo*, Claud.
24.22–3.

   [51] Latin authors use the general wording *simulacra oppidorum* for the representations. It might be
significant that *oppidum* often denotes a fortress or a town fortified and protected by a wall, *RE* XVIII:I
(1939), 708–25, s.v. 'Oppidum' (E. Kornemann); *TLL*, s.v. 'oppidum'. See also Boos (1989); Tarpin (1999).
   [52] See e.g. Cairola and Carli (1963: pl. 45).
   [53] The *ferculum* is preceded by a *tabula ansata* inscribed: PONS MVLVI | EXPEDITIO |
IMPERATORIS | coNstantini, *CIL* viii. 9356; *ILS* 686. Torelli (1982: 124–5, pl. V.6); Künzl (1988: 78–9,

presented in the triumphs. Florus also confirms that models of buildings were carried on *fercula* in the triumphs. He states that Caesar displayed Pharus, the lighthouse of Alexandria, on a bier in the Egyptian triumph performed in 46 BC.[54] Certainly, models of cities and towns were also carried on *fercula*. The models must have been rather large in structure, in order to be seen and recognized by the mass of spectators from long distances. As with the bridge on the relief from Cherchel, they would have required a substantial number of bearers.

The Roman model

Appian and Strabo's descriptions of the πύργοι, both quoted above, are crucial. Appian's line (*Pun.* 66) stems from his account of Scipio Africanus' triumph, which should clearly be read as a description of the Roman triumphal procession in general.[55] To introduce the passage, Appian himself states: καὶ ὁ τρόπος, ᾧ καὶ νῦν ἔτι χρώμενοι διατελοῦσιν, ἐστὶ τοιόσδε, 'The form [of the triumph], which they still continue to use, is such as this: . . .' The fact that Appian includes towers imitating cities in this passage suggests that, at the time of his writing, such models both constituted familiar components of the Roman triumph and were believed to have done so far back in time. Strabo's reference to how the Romans called towers cities in the triumphal processions transmits the same impression. By quoting Posidonius, his statement shows that city towers were customary not only in his own days but in the first half of the first century BC as well.

All three Greek authors, Posidonius, Strabo, and Appian, thus suggest that the use of towers to symbolize cities and towns was characteristic of the Roman triumph, in Republican as well as in Imperial times. Moreover, Strabo's description is permeated by a revealing tone of irony. Posidonius, writes Strabo, makes fun of Polybius for exaggerating the achievements of Tiberius Gracchus. What was in reality the subjugation of smaller forts only became the conquest of cities in Polybius' writings. But there is more to the irony. Through the statement 'he called the towers cities just as they do in the triumphal processions', Posidonius (and Strabo) make fun of the very display of cities in the Roman triumphal procession. They ridicule the Roman commanders' habit of exaggerating their

Abb. 47); *Trionfi romani*, 140, I.2.17. Torelli (1982: 124), interprets the relief as pertaining to Caracalla's Germanic campaign in AD 213 and reads: *Pons Mulvi | Expeditio | imperatoris | in Germa- | niam*. For quite some time, the relief was assumed to be a falsification, especially as regards the inscription. Today, there seems to be a general consensus regarding its authenticity.

[54] Flor. *Epit.* 2.13.88–9. At Caesar's funeral, a model of the temple of Venus Genetrix (*ad simulacrum templi Veneris Genetricis*) was placed on the Campus Martius, Suet. *Iul.* 84.1. A painting from Pompeii, depicting a procession, shows a model of a temple on a *ferculum*, Abaecherli (1935/36: 3, pl. I.1). Ryberg (1955: 169, pl. LXI, fig. 99).

[55] Cf. Itgenshorst (2005: 14–24).

own achievements, and also, I would argue, the very custom of representing cities by way of towers at all. What Strabo and Posidonius really say is that, unlike the Romans, the Greeks would never represent cities by way of simple depictions of their actual visual appearance. Thus, through the irony of the Greek authors, the Roman and the Greek ways of symbolizing cities are opposed. If we add the statement by Appian of how towers formed part of the typical Roman triumph, the impression given by the three Greek authors from Republican, Augustan, and Imperial times is that the habit of representing cities by way of models was not only characteristic of the Roman triumph, but also typically Roman as opposed to the Greek practice.

Indeed, the customary Greek way of symbolizing cities as well as other geographic, topographic, and ethnic entities was not by way of realistic depictions of their actual appearance, but in personified forms.[56] Influenced by this Greek practice, Roman official art from the late Republic and onwards produced a large number of allegoric representations of peoples and places, not least female personifications of *nationes* and *gentes*. Personifications of cities also appear, but are much rarer. Instead, the majority of city representations in Roman official art focus on the city walls,[57] a phenomenon that must be seen as a parallel to the preference for models in the triumphs.

The Roman inclination to emphasize the walls of cities and towns is mirrored by the *coronae murales*, the mural crowns, one type of *dona militaria* presented to the soldiers as rewards for their deeds in war and worn by them at the triumphal parades.[58] The *corona muralis* was given to the soldier who first mounted a city wall or broke into an enemy town.[59] Aulus Gellius maintains that the crown was ornamented with representations of the battlement of a wall.[60] His account matches the preserved depictions of mural crowns in Roman relief, which show three-dimensional circular models of city walls with detailed indications of stone works, battlements, gates, and windows.[61]

The earliest evidence of *coronae murales* comes from Polybius, but nothing in his description suggests that the practice was a new one.[62] Livy's account of the soldiers who participated in Papirius Cursor's triumph in 293 BC adorned with

---

[56] Personifications of cities appear in Greek art and literature from the early 5th cent. BC but become numerous only in Hellenistic times. For depictions of cities in ancient art, see Gardner (1888); Aubauer (1970); Ostrowski (1996); Parisi Presicce (1999).

[57] Aubauer (1970: 1–6).

[58] e.g. Liv. 10.46.3–4, 45.38.12; cf. Val Max 3.2.24. For *dona militaria*, see Maxfield (1981). In Republican times, *dona* were presented as awards for individual achievements to soldiers of any rank. In the Empire, they came to be given as standard distinctions to soldiers of higher ranks only.

[59] Maxfield (1981: esp. 76–9).

[60] Gell. 5.6.16–7.

[61] Maxfield (1981: 76–9, pl. 5bcd).

[62] Polyb. 6.39.5. Maxfield (1981: 43–5, with references); Oakley (1985: 393 n. 2).

diverse crowns, *civicae*, *vallares*, and *murales*, might be historically correct.[63] The custom continued throughout Republican and into Imperial times. On the triumphal frieze on Trajan's arch in Benevento, soldiers following the triumphator on horseback at the rear of the procession carry mural crowns aloft on high poles.[64]

Roman warfare focused on the sieges of cities, and there are strong affinities in form and function between the Roman *coronae murales* and the *simulacra oppidorum*. Both represented city walls by way of three-dimensional models. Both were displayed in triumphal processions from Republican times and onwards to symbolize the conquest of cities, by the triumphator (*simulacra oppidorum*) and the soldiers (*coronae murales*) respectively.[65] Both traditions reflect a traditional Roman way of representing the conquest of cities.

By displaying the cities and towns as models, which emphasized their walls, the Roman triumphs stressed the military success in the siege and conquest of these places. Caesar's model of Pharus transmitted similar messages.[66] Certainly, the lighthouse represented the city of Alexandria and the land of Egypt. A guide to ships at sea during day as well as night, Pharus was an emblem of the sea-borne trade of the Mediterranean, and its display connoted future Roman commercial control and incomes. Obviously, Pharus, in its capacity as one of the wonders of the world, was also of great symbolic value to Caesar. However, the model of the lighthouse, just like the tower cities on triumphal display, also manifested a successful military conquest. The island of Pharus was a fort, its lighthouse too, and, as in the conquest of cities, Caesar had promised rewards to the soldier who first managed to force an entry on the island. Pharus was a fortification that had been captured by the effective and brave Roman war machine.

City personifications in art

The display of towers in the triumphal processions should thus be seen in light of a general Roman preference for representing cities and towns by way of their walls. However, we might also turn the facts around and, along with the

---

[63] Liv. 10.46.3–4. Already way before this date, in the middle of the 5th cent. BC, a certain L. Siccius Dentatus allegedly owned a substantial collection of *dona*, among which were three *coronae murales*, Dion. Hal. 10.36.3–37.5; Val. Max. 3.2.24; Plin. *Nat.* 7.28.101–3; Gell. 2.11. Dentatus is most certainly a legendary figure.

[64] Andreae (1979: 326); Pfanner (1983: 87, Beil. 3).

[65] Just as each successful Roman general kept count of and in various way announced the number of triumphs celebrated, victories won, cities taken, enemies killed, etc., each soldier counted the number of battles he had fought, spoils he had taken, scars he had received, *dona* he had achieved, triumphs he had participated in, see Val. Max. 3.2.24; Gell. 2.11; Plin. *Nat.* 7.28.101–4. Oakley (1985: 409 and n. 141).

[66] Flor. *Epit.* 2.13.88–9.

preference for wall models, emphasize the hesitation to show city personifications in the triumphs, a reluctance that has parallels in art.

From the time of the late Republic, Roman official art produced female personifications of cities as well as so-called 'province personifications' or rather personifications of peoples and their lands (*nationes*, *gentes*). As will be further discussed in
the following chapter, personifications of peoples could basically be represented in
two ways in Roman art: either as adopted members of the Roman community or as
newly conquered or reconquered enemies.[67] The personifications of the first type—
labelled *provincia pia fidelis*—are mostly represented standing, in a friendly attitude.
They are predominantly Greek ideal in style, wearing Greek dress, hairstyle, and
often a mural crown. In the second type, commonly called *provincia capta*, the
personifications are more realistic in style. They wear national clothes and they are
often depicted in grief, wearing their long hair unbridled. They are shown in
submissive postures, denoting their defeat.

The female personifications of cities at first glance seem confusingly similar to
the personifications of peoples. In modern scholarship, they are frequently
discussed together as one coherent group.[68] There is, however, a fundamental
difference in their representations; in contrast to the twofold mode of representing personifications of *gentes* and *nationes*, personifications of cities seem to have
been depicted as adopted members of the Roman community only. There are a
couple of coins that possibly show personifications of cities kneeling to a Roman
general, but the cities are represented in a Greek ideal style and they are celebratory rather than submissive.[69] Personified cities were not, it seems, represented as
barbarian-styled subdued enemies of Rome. That is, it looks as if personified
cities could be shown as subjects of Rome, but not as subjugated by Rome.

In Greek art, where personifications of cities are much more numerous, we
note the same unwillingness to represent them as militarily subdued.[70] None of
the cities present in the grand procession held by Ptolemy Philadelphus in

[67] The categorization was first proposed in 1900 by Piotr Bienkowski, who named the two types
provincia pia fidelis and *provincia capta* respectively. Others have subsequently suggested different subdivisions and names. For instance, Kuttner calls them 'the celebratory or friendly and the domineering or
hostile' (1995: 74).

[68] e.g. Gardner (1888); Ostrowski (1996); Parisi Presicce (1999).

[69] Coins issued by Pompey's proquaestor M. Minatius Sabinus show a Pompeian soldier greeted by
female personifications, standing and kneeling, Crawford (1974: no. 470.1b, 480, pl. LV, 19). The kneeling
personification might represent Tarraco or some other Spanish city, but this is not clear. Hispania has also
been suggested, as has the land of Baetica, Houghtalin (1993: 319–20 and n. 23).

[70] It is significant that Ostrowski (1996) in his article 'Personifications of Countries and Cities as a
Symbol of Victory in Greek and Roman Art' can present only examples of countries. He includes no
example, Greek or Roman, of a city personification represented as military conquered; cf. Smith (1988*a*:
70–1).

Alexandria were displayed captured. The cities had been liberated by Alexander from the Persian rule, and were represented by women, γυναῖκες, either actors or statues, who wore costly dresses and golden crowns. Also crowned with a golden diadem, the city of Corinth, probably a statue, stood beside a statue of Ptolemy on the cart that preceded the liberated cities.[71]

City personifications also often appear on coins issued and monuments erected by the cities themselves, a practice that continued in Roman times. For example, the Puteoli base, a replica of a Tiberian monument in Rome, showed an assembly of fourteen Greek cities from Asia Minor represented in female form.[72] All are seen standing; they wear Greek dress and mural crowns. The Roman monument was erected by the cities in gratitude to Tiberius for his help with restorations after a major earthquake. Similarly, the very few personifications of cities on Roman-made official monuments are almost always representations of non-foreign, Italian cities. On a Claudian relief in the Louvre, three female city personifications with mural crowns are represented taking part in a religious procession, possibly a supplication in honour of the emperor.[73] One of the reliefs on Trajan's arch in Benevento depicts four female personifications.[74] They wear turreted crowns and are usually interpreted as cities of Italy. All these personifications are Greek in style; they wear Greek dress, Greek hairstyle, and mural crowns. They stand upright and are presented as equals to the Roman participants with whom they are depicted. Nowhere do we find examples of city personifications with barbarian appearance wearing native dress and loose hair. They are not depicted as prisoners or in conquered poses subdued by the Roman military supremacy. All in all, they lack all the characteristics of the *provincia capta*-type of female personifications, but fit well into the group of adopted members of the Roman community.

The evident unwillingness in art to represent city personifications as militarily subdued helps to explain their rare presence in the triumphal processions. When led in these parades, the cities were by definition captives. This is clear from our one unambiguously attested example, the personification of Carthage, which, as we saw, Silius Italicus places in the triumph of Scipio Africanus.[75] We know

[71] Ath. 5.201d. Rice (1983: 102–10). The other figures on the cart, Ptolemy, Alexander, and Arete are specified as ἀγάλματα, and it is therefore likely that Corinth, simply described as ἡ πόλις Κόρινθος, was shown by way of a statue as well.

[72] Vermeule (1981). A statue base from Cerveteri shows personifications of the cities of Vetulonia, Tarquinia, and Vulci. The relief probably once included representations of all the principal twelve Etruscan cities, see e.g. Hölscher (1988: 528–30, Abb. 4); Liveriani (1995: 224–7).

[73] Hölscher (1988: 530–1, Abb. 5).

[74] Kleiner (1992: 224–9, fig. 190). A relief in the Villa Medici dated to the middle of the 2nd cent. AD depicts two female turreted personifications kneeling on each side of a Victoria as she inscribes a shield. Veyne (1961) has interpreted the personifications as representations of Europe and Asia, cf. Cozza (1958).

[75] Sil. *Pun.* 17.635–6.

nothing of the dress or hairstyle of the personification, but she is clearly described as captured, both by way of the explicit *captae palmae* and her gesture—she raises her hands to heaven in supplication and despair. Silius testifies to an Imperial practice, and from the preceding discussion it seems reasonable to conclude that tower models formed the primary mode of representing cities and towns in the triumphal procession. By preferring to display the cities and towns as tower models, the Roman triumphs emphasized their conquest. By refraining, initially, from showing them as personifications, they avoided leading the cities 'in person' as captives in the parade. We saw above that Rome took care not to display the statues of gods taken as booty as animate captives in their triumphal processions. Similar considerations seem to have been involved also in the exhibition of conquered cities.

Syracuse and Ambracia: conquest confirmed

If it was a long-established Roman tradition to represent conquered cities and towns by way of models in the triumphal processions, it follows that it is close to impossible to determine when the usage began. Not only would the practice itself have been too familiar to draw attention. The models might also for quite some time have been rather simple towers, not conspicuous or extraordinary enough to be recorded in documents and by later historians.

In the fifth book of his histories, Livy alludes to the display of Veii in Camillus' triumph of 396 BC. Camillus pictures himself in Veii, the very city that was carried in his parade (*et ante oculos habere urbem latam in triumpho suo*).[76] Modern historians usually explain the passage in terms of anachronism.[77] Indeed, in contrast to his detailed lists of the contents of later triumphal processions, Livy's remark on the representation of Veii is vague, incidental, and isolated. Although it is not impossible that some form of tower models were in use already at this date, the testimony from Livy cannot be taken to prove such an early practice.

After Camillus, Livy again refers to a city on triumphal display when describing the ovation held in 211 BC by M. Claudius Marcellus after his victories on Sicily. Marcellus was one of the great Republican generals, and his conquest of the Greek metropolis of Syracuse after years of siege during the Second Punic War was both discussed and celebrated already in his own time. Marcellus

---

[76] Liv. 5.30.2.

[77] Zinserling (1959/60: no. 21a, 413); Hölscher (1978: 344–5 n. 148). The victories and triumphs of Camillus were legendary in Rome, and there might have been dramatic plays which showed his famed triumphal processions and inspired Roman historians. For the legend of Camillus and Roman historiography, see Bruun (2000: esp. 66–7), for the possible influence of drama.

brought enormous amounts of spoils to Rome, but in spite of his famed victory, he was refused a *triumphus* proper.[78] His campaign had not brought the war to an end and his army was still in Sicily, so the senate decided to grant Marcellus the simpler *ovatio* only. Marcellus reacted by performing a triumph on the Alban Mount, and on the following day, he entered Rome in ovation. Livy's description (26.21.6–10) of the parade again calls our attention:

Pridie quam urbem iniret in monte Albano triumphavit; inde ovans multam prae se praedam in urbem intulit. Cum simulacro captarum Syracusarum catapultae ballistaeque et alia omnia instrumenta belli lata et pacis diuturnae regiaeque opulentiae ornamenta, argenti aerisque fabrefacti vis, alia supellex pretiosaque vestis et multa nobilia signa, quibus inter primas Graeciae urbes Syracusae ornatae fuerant. Punicae quoque victoriae signum octo ducti elephanti; et non minimum fuere spectaculum cum coronis aureis praecedentes Sosis Syracusanus et Moericus Hispanus, . . .

On the day before he entered the city, he triumphed on the Alban Mount. Then in his ovation, he brought a great amount of booty before him into the city. Together with a representation of the captured Syracuse, catapults and *ballistae* and all the other war equipment were carried, and the adornments of a long peace and of royal wealth, a quantity of silverware and bronze ware, other furnishings and costly fabrics, and many notable statues, with which Syracuse had been adorned as highly as the foremost cities of Greece. As a sign that the Carthaginians had been defeated as well, eight elephants were led in the procession. And not the least spectacle, as they walked before the general, wearing golden wreaths, were Sosis of Syracuse and Moericus the Spaniard . . .

Marcellus' procession, loaded with spoils from Syracuse and preceded by much debate and rumour, must have made a profound impression on the spectators, still rather unaccustomed to such lavish displays. Interestingly, then, among all the contents of the procession, Livy emphasizes the representation of Syracuse by starting his description with a statement of its display: *Cum simulacro captarum Syracusarum* . . . The emphatic introductory *cum simulacro* is unique in Livy's standardized triumphal lists and suggests a certain prominence on part of the city. Most probably, the display was a novelty and a representation out of the ordinary. It must have acted as an inspiration for triumphators to come.

Scholars often argue that the *simulacrum* showed the capture of Syracuse from a map-like bird's eye perspective.[79] Even Zinserling, who drew attention to the use of tower models, maintains that Syracuse was shown by way of such a painting.[80] *Simulacrum captarum Syracusarum* is then read as 'a representation of the capture of Syracuse'. I have argued above that such paintings were put up

---

[78] Liv. 26.21.1–5; Plut. *Marc.* 22.1.

[79] Zinserling (1959/60: 428); Mansuelli (1979: 46). Comparions are made with the painting placed in the Forum by Hostilius Mancinus, Plin. *Nat.* 35.7.23.

[80] Zinserling (1959/60: 405, 428).

only after the triumph. Others interpret Livy's description of the *simulacrum captarum Syracusarum* as 'a representation of Syracuse made prisoner'. According to this reading, Syracuse was shown as a captured female personification, represented in painting or as a sculpture.[81] Scholars who prefer this interpretation stress that Marcellus, a famed hellenophile, introduced personifications in the triumphs inspired from the Greek practice of representing cities in female form.[82]

Looking closer at Livy's account of Marcellus' parade, it becomes clear that, in rough, his list follows the typical sequence of the triumphal train: weapons, valuables and art, captives (here animals), and the triumphator. In the opening part of his description, the word *lata* separates the introductory display of war engines and the subsequent appearance of valuables and art objects. If we take the account as reflecting the order of the display, the representation of Syracuse was carried ahead together with the artillery and other weaponry. The valuables of all kinds and the statues then followed.

The representation of Syracuse and the arms used in its defence thus formed a joint display in Marcellus' procession. While a personification would have been totally out of place in the company of huge catapults, *ballistae*, and other weaponry, a large city model with the walls emphasized fitted perfectly. The combined display of city model and war engines was also more than appropriate for the specific occasion of Marcellus' ovation. His famed conquest of Syracuse had been preceded by a siege lasting for years. A large number of catapults and other awesome war machinery had effectively prevented all Roman attempts to break through the walls of the city. The construction of the defence system and war engines was ascribed to the famous Archimedes, who, according to Plutarch, had placed most of the engines closely behind the wall.[83] As a result, the Romans felt that they were fighting against the gods, in that the evil came from an invisible source. It seemed almost as if the walls themselves were alive to fire at them. Having finally succeeded in taking the city, it comes as no surprise that Marcellus chose to open up his procession in Rome with the joint display of his two principal adversaries in Sicily, the weaponry of Archimedes and the fortifications of Syracuse. Catapults, weapons, and fortifications had together resisted the power of Rome, together they had had to surrender and together they were now displayed.

If the proposed interpretation is correct, *simulacrum captarum Syracusarum* could simply be read as 'a representation of Syracuse', where Livy adds *captarum* as a general statement that the city had been taken in the war rather than as a description of its visual appearance in the triumphal procession. Appian

---

[81] Holliday (1997: 130, 136; 2002: 112–13); McDonnell (2006: 83).
[82] Holliday (1980: 6); Köhler (1996: 110); Holliday (1997: 136).
[83] Plut. *Marc.* 16.2.

describes the towers imitating captured cities in similar terms, μιμήματα τῶν εἰλημμένων πόλεων.[84] On the other hand, it cannot be excluded that the conquest of the city was staged together with its representation. The war engines and weaponry displayed with the city model might have taken an active part in forming a kind of tableau, and the city walls might have been shown not intact but partly razed. In fact, Ovid suggests the display of such conquest scenes; writing of silver models of barbarian towns shown with its men and imitating razed walls (*muri versi*).[85]

Livy's stress on the display of Syracuse suggests the visual prominence given the city model. In view of the historical circumstances, this is only to be expected. As stated above, despite a major military success, Marcellus, formerly winner of the prestigious *spolia opima*, was refused a proper triumph. Clearly as an act of protest, he performed the untraditional parade on the Alban Mount.[86] Back in Rome, Marcellus chose to open the procession with an ostentatious announcement of his glorious military achievements: the inexpugnable city of Syracuse, now conquered, and Archimedes' marvellous war engines, now captured. Marcellus' message was clear: his achievements merited a *triumphus* proper.

Very possibly there was also a statement of justification involved. We saw in a preceding chapter that Marcellus' looting of the temples of Syracuse was debated at the time, and that there was even some discussion on the just procedure in the capture of the city.[87] A city taken by force formed the prerequisite of its looting. Hence, to Marcellus, the *simulacrum captarum Syracusarum*, represented with its walls, possibly to some degree shown razed, and displayed together with war engines, probably filled the function also of confirming that Syracuse had been *vi captae*, taken by force. Such a display would have justified his plundering of the temples.

About twenty-five years later, in 187 BC, M. Fulvius Nobilior performed a triumph over the Aetolians and Cephallania. The triumph was preceded by much debate, this time centred on the issue of Ambracia, principal city of the Aetolians. The senate opposed the fact that, although Nobilior had not managed to take Ambracia by force, he had emptied the city of its many treasures, thus violating the rights of war.[88] Fulvius' bitter enemy, the consul M. Aemilius Lepidus, even

---

[84] App. *Pun.* 66. The word μίμημα signifies both 'artistic representation', and, more generally, 'anything imitated'. Within the field of art and drama it was used to denote an imitation with as much likeness to reality as possible; hence the signification of the modern terms 'mime' and 'mimic'. Its closest equivalents in Latin would be *imitatio* and *simulacrum*, both words that not only denote an artistic representation but also imply a close imitation of reality. Therefore, Appian's μιμήματα τῶν πόλεων could basically be read as a translation of the Latin *simulacra oppidorum*, as was pointed out by Zinserling (1959/60: 422–3).

[85] Ov. *Pont.* 2.1.37–9.

[86] For triumphs held at the Alban Mount, see Brennan (1996).

[87] Pp. 80–2, 86–7.

[88] Polyb. 21.29–30; Liv. 38.9.13; Plin. *Nat.* 35.36.66. The people of Ambracia had voluntarily agreed to open the gates in order to discuss peace.

passed a *senatus consultum* to the effect that it seemed that Ambracia had not been taken by force (*Ambraciam vi captam esse non videri*).[89] In Livy's account of the discussions held in the senate, a representation of Ambracia (*Ambracia capta*) is singled out as one of the essential features of a future triumph.[90] When Fulvius Nobilior was later allowed to hold his triumph, Livy's description includes no representation of Ambracia.[91] Nevertheless, *Ambracia capta* was most probably displayed and, like Marcellus' Syracuse, given a prominent position. Like Marcellus, Fulvius paraded catapults, *ballistae*, and all kinds of artillery in his procession. In fact, ancient authors attest to the display of war engines only in the parades of Marcellus and Fulvius Nobilior, suggesting that they played a particularly important role here. In Marcellus' ovation, the war engines and the model of Syracuse formed a joint display, which manifested the great success of a famous Roman general and the just conquest of a celebrated city. Similarly, I would surmise that Nobilior, in reference to Marcellus, paraded the *Ambracia capta*, very probably a model too, and the siege machines together. Representations of the seizure might well have been staged as well, announcing Nobilior's main message that the city of Ambracia had been taken by force (*vi capta*) and thereby that it had been justly looted. Again, a city displayed together with its artillery manifested and confirmed its conquest.

Cities on parade: some concluding observations

The cities put on triumphal parade could arouse strong sentiments among the spectators. Hence, Cicero writes of how people in Rome reacted with anger when Caesar paraded the city of Massilia in 46 BC.[92] Massilia was Rome's former ally, and the display of that city in a place normally reserved for foreign enemy cities caused dismay and, according to Cicero, confirmed Caesar's ignorance of the people's will.

The absence of cities also caused emotional reactions. Florus writes ironically of how Caesar refrained from including Pharsalus, Thapsus, and Munda among the representations in his triumphs. After all, argues Florus, the victories won at these places were far greater than the ones for which he officially triumphed.[93] Sulla's triumph held in 81 BC also reveals that cities on display could be a delicate matter. The triumph lasted for two days and celebrated the victory over Mithridates as well as the subjugation of some hostile Italian towns conquered on Sulla's return from Asia.[94] Of the Italian adversaries, Praeneste had held a particularly important position. Once captured, Sulla spared the lives of the

[89] Liv. 38.44.6.   [90] Liv. 38.43.10, cf. Liv. 38.43.9.   [91] Liv. 39.5.13–17.
[92] Cic. *Phil.* 8.6.18, *Off.* 2.8.28.   [93] Flor. *Epit.* 2.13.88–9.   [94] Plin. *Nat.* 33.5.16.

Roman citizens but killed the Samnites and the Praenestines.[95] In the triumph, Sulla included the treasure previously transferred to Praeneste from Rome by the younger Marius.[96] According to Valerius Maximus, Sulla also showed many Asian and Greek cities, but no town inhabited by Romans citizens.[97] Thus, although Praeneste had been taken by force, many of its inhabitants slain, and its art objects paraded as booty, no representation of the city appeared in the procession. Cities on triumphal parade transmitted messages of the conquest and defeat. As the cities present (Massilia) and absent (Pharsalus, Thapsus, and Munda) in Caesar's triumphs also show, Roman cities and cities linked to a Roman cause were not suitable for triumphal exhibition.

In contrast to the visual emphasis attached to certain cities, Livy (37.59.3–6) lists the 134 *simulacra oppidorum* displayed by Scipio Asiaticus in 189 BC as one of many kinds of spoils:

Tulit in triumpho signa militaria ducenta viginti quattuor, oppidorum simulacra centum triginta quattuor, eburneos dentes mille ducentos triginta unum, aureas coronas ducentas triginta quattuor, argenti pondo centum triginta septem milia quadringenta viginti, tetrachmum Atticorum ducenta viginti quattuor milia, cistophori trecenta viginti unum milia septuaginta, nummos aureos Philippeos centum quadraginta milia, vasorum argenteorum—omnia caelata erant—mille pondo et quadringenta viginti tria, aureorum mille pondo viginti tria. Et duces regii, praefecti, purpurati duo et triginta ante currum ducti.

He carried in his triumph 224 military standards, 134 representations of towns, 1,231 ivory tusks, 234 golden crowns, 137,420 pounds of silver, 224,000 Attic tetradrachmae, 321,070 cistophori, 140,000 gold Philippics, 1,423 pounds of silver vases—all were embossed—and 1,023 pounds of vases of gold. Also, 32 royal commanders, prefects, and nobles were led before the car.

The 134 *simulacra oppidorum* appear second in the list, embedded in an enumeration of the booty. The *oppida* are not emphasized and, among those displayed, no particular city or town appears as significant. The importance of the display was rather one of quantity; Scipio boasted that he had conquered as many as 134 *oppida*. Many other parades showed large numbers of cities and towns. We saw that Sulla displayed many (*multa*) Greek and Asian cities.[98] Pliny's detailed account of L. Cornelius Balbus' African triumph in 19 BC lists eighteen or nineteen cities and towns, which far outnumbers the other kinds of representations on display.[99] Pliny states that the names of the places were announced on placards, and the Augustan poets also attest to the presence of *tituli* identifying the cities and towns on parade.[100] Confronted with rows of tens and even

[95] App. *BCiv.* 1.94; cf. Plut. *Sulla* 32. [96] Plin. *Nat.* 33.5.16.
[97] Val. Max. 2.8.7. [98] Val. Max. 2.8.7. [99] Plin. *Nat.* 5.5.36–7.
[100] Ov. *Pont.* 2.1.50, *Trist.* 4.2.20; Prop. 3.4.15–16. See Östenberg (forthcoming).

hundreds of representations, the *tituli* must have been indispensable in confirm-ing the presence of the individual cities and towns.

Marcellus' staging of the single city of Syracuse and Scipio Asiaticus' exhibition of as many as 134 *simulacra oppidorum* thus present dissimilarities in display and intent. But Livy's descriptions of the two also reveal certain affinities. According to Livy, Scipio's parade presented military equipment, *simulacra oppidorum*, spoils of valuables and art, and prisoners, in that order. The list reflects the processional sequence, which means that the *simulacra oppidorum* were presented at the beginning of the procession, between the military spoils of standards and the booty of art and valuables. Thus, they had a processional location very similar to the representation of Syracuse in Marcellus' parade.

Appian's description of Scipio Africanus' triumph reflects a similar processional placing.[101] In his account, Appian lists: spoils, tower models of cities, war scenes, valuables, animals, prisoners, triumphator, and army. Again, the list reflects the processional sequence, and again, the representations of cities appear at the begin-ning of the procession. Appian's account is of particular interest, as it claims to describe the typical Roman triumph, as it had been and was still performed in his own days. In all probability then, the customary Roman triumph paraded tower models of conquered cities in the introductory part of the procession.

In contrast, Silius Italicus depicts the personification of Carthage only behind the prisoners in his version of Scipio Africanus' triumph.[102] Carthage precedes other representations, which are immediately followed by the triumphator. Carthage, described as a living captive who walked (*ibat*) with hand raised to the sky in supplication, was thus allotted the traditional place of the prisoners further back in the parade.

To sum up, representations of cities and towns formed a regular part of the triumphal processions at least from around 200 BC. Hence, they are attested con-siderably earlier than the representations of peoples and rivers. Their processional exhibition at times stressed the conquest of a particular city, on other occasions the extent of the success. Models formed the primary Roman mode of representing captured cities. Our only clear evidence of the use of city personifications comes from Silius Italicus, writing in the last quarter of the first century AD. Several other authors confirm the Republican habit of displaying models, and there are the affinities with the Republican *coronae murales*. Most importantly, the Greek authors Posidonius, Strabo, and Appian attest to the practice of representing cities in the form of towers as something typical of the triumph and of the Romans in general.

As we have seen, the Romans refrained from representing defeated cities as personifications in art. The preference for tower models in the triumphs testifies to the same reluctance to show the cities as personified captives. Still, Silius

---

[101] App. *Pun.* 66.   [102] Sil. *Pun.* 17.635–7.

Italicus' description of Carthage bears witness to an Imperial practice, in which personifications of cities and towns were paraded as well. We do not know when the attitude changed, but, in all probability, the introduction of city personification in the triumphal scheme was influenced by the establishment of personified peoples and rivers among the display from around the middle of the first century BC. Pliny's detailed list of the representations of peoples, towns, rivers, and mountains led in Balbus' African triumph of 19 BC could possibly be taken as a reflection of such a development.[103] Pliny lists a large number of towns that mixed together with tribes, rivers, mountains, walked (*iere*) in the parade, a term more apt for personifications, present in person, than models. Also, he uses a form of *ducere* to describe Balbus' display of them, *ducere* being by far the most common term applied to prisoners, but never used for the inanimate booty. Pliny lists the representations in the order in which they paraded, thus revealing that the towns made a mixed appearance with peoples and rivers (and mountains), which were clearly shown by way of personifications.[104] Since we have seen that models and personifications were two very different types of display, normally exhibited in separate parts of the procession, one does not expect them to have been shown intermingled. It is then, perhaps, more reasonable to assume that in Balbus' triumph, the listed representations were all shown by way of personifications. Such compound displays, showing a mixture of representations of all kinds, all exhibited together, might well have contributed to introducing city personifications into the processional staging.

At the same time, it is quite clear that the practice of representing conquered cities and towns as models continued. Caesar showed models, and Ovid describes the towns to be displayed by Tiberius as models. Most importantly, Strabo and Appian suggest that the display of tower models was characteristic of the Roman triumph. These passages, and the parallel reluctance in Imperial art to show the conquered cities in personified form, imply that models continued to form the principal mode of triumphal representation also after the introduction of the personifications. By preferring to display the vanquished cities and towns by way of models representing their walls, the Romans emphasized the military conquest of these places.

PEOPLES AND RIVERS

Peoples and rivers paraded in the triumphs were shown as personifications. The literary sources are clear on this point, and there is also the triumphal frieze

---

[103] Plin. *Nat.* 5.5.36–37, quoted below.

[104] If towns as well as tribes were represented by female personifications in Balbus' triumph, this would explain Pliny's doubt as to whether Bubeium was an *oppidum* or a *natio*.

FIGURE 24 The
small frieze on the
arch of Titus in
Rome has
preserved a repre-
sentation of a
river, carried on a
ferculum in tri-
umph. As the
larger panels of
the arch show the
Jewish procession
of AD 71, the river
is most commonly
read as the Jordan.

preserved on the arch of Titus in Rome (Fig. 24).[105] Last in a sequence of
parading people and animals comes a group centred on a male figure, carried
by four soldiers on a *ferculum*. The male figure is rather poorly preserved, but his
general appearance is quite discernible. He has long hair and a full beard. A piece
of cloth covers his hips and legs but leaves the upper part of his body naked. He is
shown lying on his left side, resting his bent left arm on an overthrown urn, from
which water pours. His right arm rests along the upper part of his body, and in
his right hand, which falls on the abdomen, he holds a bundle of reeds. Thus, in
all aspects, the figure displays the typical iconography of a river personification.[106]

The male figure on the frieze of the arch of Titus confirms that rivers were
shown in personified three-dimensional form in the triumphal processions.[107] It
does not reveal, however, whether the figure was a sculptured personification or

---

[105] Pfanner (1983: 83–4 (Figur 35), 90, Abb. 47, Taf. 79.1–2, 80.2, 85.4, 86.4, 6–7, 87.1–2); Klementa
(1993: 108–9).

[106] Images of rivers are at times identified as river personifications, at others as river gods.

[107] Very possibly, the small frieze that encircles Trajan's arch at Benevento includes a similar representation of a river personification carried in triumph. Early works on the frieze describe the presence of such a
river image, Vessberg (1952: 132); Andreae (1979: 326). In later studies, however, there is no mention of the
representation, Pfanner (1983). The frieze has now been cleaned, rendering it far more legible, Adamo
Muscettola (1992: esp. 2). Up-to-date photographs reveal partly preserved remains of what might well
once have shown a river personification carried on a *ferculum*.

an actor playing the part of a river. Zinserling, arguing that statues would have been too heavy to carry, suggested that actors were employed as 'mimische Personifikationen'.[108] Still, the sources point rather to a use of sculptures. To our knowledge, the peoples and rivers never acted any scenes in the processions. Ancient authors describe one pose only, and for this no actors were needed.[109] More importantly, there is literary evidence to confirm the use of plastic art. Florus writes of Caesar's triumph over Gallia in 46 BC: *primum de Gallia triumphum trahens; hic erat Rhenus et Rhodanus et ex auro captivus Oceanus*, 'His first triumph was held over Gaul: here were the Rhine and the Rhône, and the captive Oceanus, made of gold'.[110] Being *ex auro*, of gold, must mean that the Oceanus was shown as a sculpture,[111] as were in all probability also the Rhine and the Rhône. The fact that Florus writes nothing specific about their appearance probably means that they were made of less conspicuous materials.

Florus provides our only explicit evidence of the material used for the personifications. However, sources tell explicitly that personifications paraded in funeral processions could be of bronze. According to Dio Cassius, Pertinax' funeral presented all the subdued peoples represented by bronze figures arrayed according to the fashion of their countries (τὰ ἔθνη πάντα τὰ ὑπήκοα ἐν εἰκόσι χαλκαῖς, ἐπιχωρίως σφίσιν ἐσταλμένα).[112] The practice of parading the peoples subordinate to Rome in noble imperial funeral processions goes back at least to Augustus. Besides images of the emperor's ancestors, relatives, and other prominent Romans, his funeral procession displayed representations of all the peoples that he had subdued. Dio Cassius' description of Augustus' funeral is very similar to the one concerning Pertinax, except for the fact that here Dio writes nothing of the material used for the personifications: καί τις καὶ τοῦ Πομπηίου τοῦ μεγάλου εἰκὼν ὤφθη, τά τε ἔθνη πάνθ᾽ ὅσα προσεκτήσατο, ἐπιχωρίως σφίσιν ὡς ἕκαστα ἀπηκασμένα ἐπέμφθη, 'An image of Pompey the Great was also seen, and all the peoples he [i.e. Augustus] had subdued, each adorned according to the custom of its country, appeared in the procession'.[113]

[108] Zinserling (1959/60: 424–5); cf. Klementa (1993: 108).

[109] In the grand procession of Ptolemy Philadelphus, a mechanical statue representing Nysa could stand up, pour a libation, and sit down again, Ath. 5.198e–199a. Rice (1983: 62–8); Coleman (1996: 56–8). No such mechanical devices are attested for the sculptures shown in the Roman triumphal processions.

[110] Flor. *Epit.* 2.13.88.

[111] In ancient art as well as in literature, the Oceanus is depicted as a river. He is the largest of all rivers and the father of all other streams, which flow from him (Hom. *Il.* 21.195). The vast River Oceanus encircles the world, forming a world sea, an 'ocean', *Roscher* III:1 (1897–1902), s.v. 'Okeanos', 809–20 (P. Weizäcker); *RE* XVII:2 (1937), s.v. 'Okeanos', 2308–62 (H. Herter); Tandoi (1962: 137–68); Romm (1992: *passim*), For representations in Roman art, see Klementa (1993: esp. 72–102); *LIMC* viii (1997), s.v. 'Oceanus', 1:907–15 (H. A. Cahn).

[112] Dio Cass. 75.4.5 (apud Xiph.).

[113] Dio Cass. 56.34.3. Tacitus (*Ann.* 1.8.3–4) writes that the senate suggested that placards announcing the names of the peoples that Augustus had conquered should be carried ahead in the funeral procession.

In contrast to actors, sculptures could be made in supernatural dimensions for large audiences to perceive even from rather long distances. Callixenus, in his description of the grand procession held by Ptolemy Philadelphus in Alexandria, refers to statues of several metres in height.[114] In Rome, Persius' depiction of the future triumph of Caligula includes huge representations of the River Rhine, *ingentes Rheni*.[115] The problem with such gigantic statues, as stressed by Zinserling, was their weight. To overcome this difficulty, statues made for processional use were often made of lighter material. Thus, the sculptures displayed in Sulla's funeral were made of wood from the frankincense and cinnamon tree, and the famed statue of Caesar shown among the gods in a *pompa circensis* was of ivory.[116] At other times, wax, plaster, or terracotta may have been used, materials which could have been painted or covered with a surface of more precious materials.[117]

Notwithstanding, when it comes to triumphal personifications, no source says that a particularly light material was chosen. Quite the contrary, Florus maintains that the statue of the Oceanus was *ex auro*, of gold. Of course, gold stressed the importance of the conquests on display and added wealth and splendour to the processions. As for the issue of weight, triumphs included massive statues of other kinds, for among the sculptures taken and displayed as booty were those of gold and bronze and also of marble. However, sources suggest that, while the looted statues were transported predominantly on wheeled carts,[118] male bearers carried the personified representations on *fercula*. Most probably then, the personifications of peoples and rivers were made of lighter materials gilded or covered with thin layers of precious metals. In all likelihood, we should not take Florus literally when he maintains that the Oceanus displayed by Caesar was *ex auro*, but rather assume that the river was *auratus*, golden.[119]

[114] Ath. 5.198c, f, 200d. Rice (1983: 59); Köhler (1996: 84–7).

[115] Pers. 6.47.

[116] Sulla: Plut. *Sulla* 38.2; Caesar: Dio Cass. 43.45.2. Livy describes a procession to the temple of Juno at the Aventine performed in 207 BC that included two statues of the goddess made of cypress wood (Liv. 27.37.12). Suetonius (*Tit.* 2) refers to an equestrian ivory statue of Britannicus that was carried in a *pompa circensis*.

[117] Rice (1983: 59).

[118] The statues displayed by Aemilius Paullus in 167 BC filled 250 wagons according to Plutarch and 500 according to Diodorus Siculus, Plut. *Aem.* 32.4–5; Diod. Sic. 31.8.11–12 (apud Sync.).

[119] Dio Cassius (53.30.6) accounts for a golden effigy of Marcellus carried into the theatre. The *Historia Augusta* (S.H.A. *M. Ant.* 21.5) describes an *imago aurea* of Marcus Aurelius' dead son that was to be carried in the circus procession. Smith (1988a: 75) assumes that the peoples shown in Augustus' funeral were bronze statues, more specifically the very ones that adorned the *Porticus ad Nationes*. One cannot rule out the possibility that bronze and gold representations used in triumphs could at times have been statues, which were temporarily borrowed from their public settings in Rome. However, Pomponius does Porphyrio maintain that representations were produced specifically to be used in the triumphs (*ad Epist.* 2.193). Also, many personifications were shown in conquered poses and in grief, suggesting a specific triumphal function.

Gentes *and* nationes: *peoples on parade*

All in all, some eight passages in the ancient literature could be taken to refer to the triumphal display of personified peoples and their lands (*gentes*, *nationes*).[120] Besides, Dio Cassius' descriptions of the funeral processions of Augustus and Pertinax provide help in the reconstruction.[121] Our sources suggest that they were introduced in the late Republic and exploited to some extent first by Pompey the Great.

Introducing peoples into the displays: Pompey and Caesar

Somewhere by his theatre in the Campus Martius, Pompey erected an assembly of what Varro (according to Pliny) called *quattuordecim nationes* and Suetonius *simulacra gentium*, made by a certain Coponius.[122] To our knowledge, this was the first Roman major monument to display an assembly of peoples. As is often noted, the number of *nationes* (14) set up by Pompey coincides with the number of peoples over which he celebrated his great triumph in 61 BC.[123] In all probability, therefore, the monument represented the peoples subdued by Pompey and displayed in his procession.

The sculptures at the theatre prove Pompey's willingness to manifest his conquests by way of personified peoples, and one would expect some ancient testimony for such representations in his triumph. But although Pompey's celebration of 61 BC is the one most abundant in ancient evidence, no author speaks explicitly of any such display. Still, there is a passage in Appian's account which I propose to read as a description of personifications of peoples. In his report on the contents of the two-day parade, Appian tells of θεῶν τε βαρβαρικῶν εἰκόνες καὶ κόσμοι πάτριοι, 'representations of barbarian gods dressed according to the fashion of their countries'.[124] Appian's gods cannot possibly be

---

[120] Ovid. *Pont.* 2.8.39–40, *Trist.* 4.2.43–6, *Ars* 1.225; Lucan. 3.76–8; Sil. *Pun.* 17.636; Flor. *Epit.* 2.13.88–9; Plin. *Nat.* 5.5.36–7; Claud. 24.25.

[121] Dio Cass. 56.34.3, 75.4.5 (apud Xiph.).

[122] Plin. *Nat.* 36.5.41–2: *idem* [i.e. *Varro*] *et a Coponio quattuordecim nationes, quae sunt circa Pompeium, factas auctor est.* Suetonius (*Nero* 46.1) describes how the statues appeared in Nero's nightmares: . . . *modo a simulacris gentium ad Pompei theatrum dedicatarum circumiri arcerique progressu*, 'now was surrounded by the images of the peoples, which had been dedicated by Pompey's theatre and prevented him from moving forward'. Pliny's *circa Pompeium* suggests that the statues stood around the theatre, and Suetonius' *circumiri* likewise indicates a circular placing. Cf. Josephus *AJ* 15.272–3, who describes the theatre of Herod in Jerusalem as being encircled by 'trophies of the peoples, which he [Augustus] had conquered in the war, all of them made for Herod of pure gold and silver'.

[123] Nicolet (1991: 38); Kuttner (1995: 80); Ostrowski (1996: 268); Cancik (1997: 131); Parisi Presicce (1999: 87); Bellemore (2000: 122). Pliny quotes the *praefatio* of the triumph, which listed thirteen nations plus Kings Mithridates and Tigranes (*Nat.* 7.26.98). Plutarch, in his description of the triumph (*Pomp.* 45.2), tells of fourteen nations plus the pirates, all named on a placard displayed in the procession; cf. Diod. Sic. 40.4.

[124] App. *Mith.* 117, literally 'representations of barbarian gods and native ornaments'.

sculptures of deities taken as booty. This is clear from several circumstances. First, the representations are labelled εἰκόνες. This term is used also by Dio Cassius to denote the personifications shown at Pertinax' funeral,[125] but is never employed for sculptures taken and shown as booty.[126]

Second, Appian starts his processional account by describing the spoils, valuables as well as arms, and continues with the prisoners and hostages, staged war scenes, and the θεῶν τε βαρβαρικῶν εἰκόνες καὶ κόσμοι πάτριοι. Hereafter follows an inscription, the triumphator, and the soldiers. Thus, Appian basically follows the typical order of a Roman triumphal procession: spoils, prisoners, representations, triumphator, army. Now, had the barbarian gods been sculptures taken as war booty, one would have expected them to be listed among the rest of the spoils in the beginning of the description.[127] Instead, they appear just before the triumphator further back in the procession. This placement had originally been reserved for the most prominent prisoners, but was later given also personifications of important enemy peoples and rivers. The sequence suggests that the εἰκόνες should be read as plastic personifications, in all probability representing conquered peoples. Personifications of cities were rare, and personifications of rivers were displayed half-naked in the triumphal processions and not in native costume.

Finally, the interpretation of the barbarian gods as subdued peoples is strengthened by the striking resemblance between Appian's statement that the gods were dressed in κόσμοι πάτριοι, native dress, and Dio Cassius' accounts of the personifications of peoples shown in Augustus and Pertinax' funeral processions.[128] Here the subject peoples (τὰ ἔθνη) were represented by εἰκόνες, which were arrayed ἐπιχωρίως, according to the fashion of their countries.

If the proposed reading of the passage in Appian is correct, it means that personifications of peoples were viewed in a Greek source as gods. Indeed, we must remind ourselves that the distinction between abstract personifications on one hand and divinities on the other is not always a clear one. So for instance, Pax and Concordia not only constituted abstract conceptions, but were divinities with their own temples. Rivers were both personifications and gods. Nor are personifications of cities and tutelary deities of cities always separable. In a few special cases, the same goes for the personifications of peoples and their lands. Africa had temples dedicated to her and was, according to Pliny, addressed in

[125] Dio Cass. 75.4.5 (apud Xiph.). In his description of Augustus' funeral, Dio (56.34.3) accounts for an εἰκών of Pompey immediately before describing the peoples, possibly suggesting that they too were shown by way of εἰκόνες.

[126] The terms applied to statues taken as booty are instead ἀνδριάντες (statues of men), ἀγάλματα (statues of gods), and κολοσσοί (colossal status).

[127] See above on p. 84.

[128] Dio Cass. 56.34.3, 75.4.5 (apud Xiph.).

prayers.[129] However, it is most important to note that it was the people of Africa who worshipped the representation of that region. In Rome, there were at no time cults directed towards representations of foreign peoples and their lands.[130] In the triumphal accounts too, no source written in Latin describes the personifications as gods. Instead, to the writers working within the Latin tradition, the personifications symbolized and embodied the captive people of a specific ethnic group or from a certain region (*gentes, nationes*).

After Pompey, representations of peoples and their lands appear in the sources describing the triumphs held by Caesar in 46 BC. Lucan includes a Gallia as he points to the first of Caesar's celebrations: *ut vincula Rheno | Oceanoque daret, celsos ut Gallia currus | Nobilis et flavis sequeretur mixta Britannis*, 'that he might have put chains on the Rhine and the Oceanus, and had noble Gaul following lofty chariots together with fair-haired Britons' (3.76–8).[131] Florus refers to all Caesar's triumphs. In mentioning the fourth celebration, he suggests the display of Hispania and Mauretania: *Quartus Iubam et Mauretaniam et bis subactam ostendebat Hispaniam*, 'The fourth showed Juba and Mauretania and Spain, twice subjected.'[132]

The identification of Gallia, Hispania, and Mauretania as personifications is not unproblematic. Possibly, Lucan and Florus write of the general display of booty and captives from these lands rather than the specific exhibition of personified representations. Still, in the passage from Lucan, the poet mentions not only Gallia, but also the Rhine and the Oceanus, both rivers that were certainly personifications.[133] Very likely then, Gallia too was a personification. In Florus' passage, the identification of Hispania and Mauretania is less clear. It could be noted, however, that in the description of all Caesar's triumphs, Florus emphasizes the visual impact of particular prisoners and representations rather than the collective display from the conquered lands.[134] He stresses very emphatically the presence of the Rhine, the Rhône, the Oceanus, the Nile, Arsinoë, and Pharus. In

[129] Plin. *Nat.* 28.5.24. Temples: Houghtalin (1993: 37 n. 4).

[130] Cancik (1997: 141). Houghtalin (1993: 518) attests to the veneration of three 'provinces', Africa, Dacia, and Britannia. The goddess Africa was worshipped on that continent long before the Roman arrival. Evidence of the cult of Dacia and Britannia comes from the late 2nd and early 3rd cents. AD and is limited to frontier and military zones.

[131] Lucan complains that Caesar chose to celebrate triumphs not only for his victories in Gaul but over his fellow Romans as well. The passage quoted above forms part of a depiction of how his triumphal manifestation of Gallic victory would have appeared had it been the only parade performed. Without doubt, Lucan modelled his image on the Gallic triumph, as it had already been celebrated.

[132] Flor. *Epit.* 2.13.88–9. In reality, Caesar's fourth triumph in 46 BC was held over Africa and his fifth, held only in 45 BC, celebrated his victories in Spain.

[133] Flor. *Epit.* 2.13.88–9; cf. Cic. *Marc.* 9.28–9.

[134] *Caesar in patriam victor invehitur, primum de Gallia triumphum trahens; hic erat Rhenus et Rhodanus et ex auro captivus Oceanus. Altera laurus Aegyptia: tunc in ferculis Nilus, Arsinoe et ad simulacrum ignium ardens Pharos. Tertius de Pharnace currus et Ponto. Quartus Iubam et Mauretaniam et bis subactam ostendebat Hispaniam. Pharsalia et Thapsos et Munda nusquam. Et quanto maiora erant, de quibus non triumphabat!*

the relevant sentence *Quartus Iubam et Mauretaniam et bis subactam ostendebat Hispaniam*, the word *ostendebat* underlines the visual exhibition. Juba was certainly present in person, possibly suggesting that the other two, Mauretania and Hispania, were shown as individual captives as well.

In Roman official art, the majority of the preserved personifications of peoples and their lands (usually labelled 'province personifications') come from the second century AD.[135] They first appear, however, on coins in the first half of the first century BC. According to the study by Houghtalin on Roman 'province personifications', late Republican art depicted Hispania, Africa and Sicily, Macedonia, Crete and Cyrene, and Gallia,[136] hence embracing the personifications suggested in Republican triumphs: Gallia, Hispania, and Mauretania (iconographically similar to Africa).[137]

From the sources we cannot tell whether Pompey was the first to show personifications of *gentes* and *nationes* in a triumph, but, most likely he was the first to fully exploit their potential, in his processions as on coins and in sculpture. Pompey may have launched the personification of Africa in Rome at the time of his African triumph around 80 BC.[138] Among preserved coins, an aureus with a representation of Africa on the obverse and an image of Pompey riding a triumphal car on the reverse was possibly issued by Pompey at the time of one of his later triumphs, in 71 or 61 BC.[139] We have seen that Pompey erected representations of the subjugated *nationes* at his theatre complex, dedicated in 55 BC, and from the time of the civil war between Caesar and Pompey, personifications of peoples and their lands become more common.

Imperial continuations: the issue of *provinciae captae* and *piae fideles*

After Pompey and Caesar, personifications of peoples next appear in Pliny's account of Balbus' African parade in 19 BC.[140] Among the many representations

---

[135] Toynbee (1934: 22).

[136] Houghtalin (1993: 481–3, with further references).

[137] Although Mauretania did not become a Roman province until the reign of Claudius and does not appear in Roman art until the 2nd cent. AD, personifications of Africa appear on Mauretanian coins long before this date and could well have been used by Caesar to personify his victories there. The iconography of Africa, Mauretania, and Numidia are intimately connected.

[138] Houghtalin (1993: 81–2 n. 13) suggests that the Roman iconography of Africa was based on the goddess Africa as it appeared on the Numidian coins of King Iarbas, whom Pompey defeated in his African campaign. If he is correct, the creation of the Roman iconography of Africa could be linked to Pompey, who may have launched personifications of Africa already at the time of the African triumph around 80 BC, as one of the first such representations.

[139] Toynbee (1934: 35, pl. X.6); Crawford (1974: no. 402, 83, 412–13); Ostrowski (1990a: no. 1, 81); Houghtalin (1993: no. 26, 47, 61); *LIMC* i (1981), s.v. 'Africa', no. 2, 251 (M. Le Glay). Castritius (1971) prefers a date sometime after the death of Pompey, when other coin types featuring the personification of Africa appeared as a means of propaganda in the civil war between Caesar and the followers of Pompey. A gem dated to the 2nd or 1st cent. BC possibly shows a personification of Africa, *LIMC* i (1981), s.v. 'Africa', no. 13, 251 (M. Le Glay); Houghtalin (1993: no. 25, 35, 61).

[140] Plin. *Nat.* 5.5.36–7, quoted below.

of towns, peoples, rivers, and mountains, Pliny includes the following *gentes* or *nationes*: *Niteris*, *Bubeium* (*natio vel oppidum*), *Enipi*, *Viscera*, and *Tamiagi*. For Octavian's triple triumph held ten years earlier, there is explicit evidence that rivers were paraded, but most probably personifications of peoples appeared as well. Octavian in many ways sought to surpass the former glorious spectacles of Caesar and Pompey,[141] which both plausibly displayed personifications of peoples. It is also highly likely that Balbus, in his display of *gentes*, *nationes*, and other representations ten years later, was inspired by the processions performed by the governing emperor, his benefactor Augustus.

In fact, depictions in art and literary sources reveal that the age of Augustus saw a boom of larger monuments representing the peoples of the Empire. This goes for representations of single peoples and pairs of peoples, but above all for groups of peoples.[142] According to Servius, Augustus built a *Porticus ad Nationes*, where he placed *simulacra omnium gentium*.[143] Possibly, this is the monument that was later copied at the Sebasteion in Aphrodisias, where the north portico was decorated with reliefs depicting the ἔθνη from the edges of the Augustan Empire.[144] In Rome, Velleius Paterculus maintains that *tituli*, possibly accompanied by images, of Spain and all the other peoples that Augustus had conquered adorned his Forum.[145] Furthermore, fragments stemming from the altar or altar podium of the Ara Pacis depict a procession of personifications of peoples,[146] and one of the scenes represented on the Boscoreale cups, assumed to copy a larger Roman monument, shows a procession of seven female personifications proceeding towards the enthroned Augustus.[147] As stated above, personifications of the subjected peoples formed part of Augustus' funerary procession.[148] Also, Ovid twice vividly describes the appearance of Germania in

---

[141] Östenberg (1999). The *Porticus ad Nationes* was probably also intended to outdo the assembly of peoples at Pompey's theatre.

[142] Kuttner (1995: esp. 69–93). For discussions on groupings of personifications in general, Hölscher (1988: 525–31); Houghtalin (1993: 502–13); Liveriani (1995); Parisi Presicce (1999); Wiegartz (1996) on such possible personifications on the Forum Transitorium; *Provinciae fideles*, a catalogue accompanying the collective exhibition of the province reliefs from the Hadrianeum: M. Sapelli (ed.), *Provinciae fideles: Il fregio del tempio di Adriano in Campo Marzio* (Rome, 1999). See also Cancik (1997) for the cultic contexts of the personifications. Groups of peoples could at times signal defeat, at others participation.

[143] Serv. *ad Aen.* 8.721.

[144] Smith (1988*a*); Liveriani (1995: 227–9).

[145] Vell. 2.39.2, with Smith (1988*a*: 73–4); Nicolet (1991: 42–7); Cresci Marrone (1993: 181–4); Liveriani (1995: 221); Kuttner (1995: 81).

[146] Kähler (1954); De Angelis Bertolotti (1985); Smith (1988*a*: 72–3); Liveriani (1995: 220–1, with further references).

[147] Kuttner (1995: esp. 69–93).

[148] Dio Cass. 56.34.3; cf. Tac. *Ann.* 1.8.3–4, and above, p. 217.

his visions of the future triumph of Tiberius,[149] and he imagines a representation of Persia in C. Caesar's desired triumph over Parthia.[150]

After the time of Augustus, sources are fewer, but it is quite clear that the Romans continued to display personifications of peoples and their lands. Silius Italicus includes an *effigies orae Hiberae* among other representations in the poetic version of Scipio Africanus' triumph.[151] Much later, a representation of Germania appears in Claudian's depiction of Stilicho's future triumph.[152]

Thus, while personifications of peoples were probably paraded from the last century BC and throughout the Imperial age, the sources describing them are rather sparse. This is especially noteworthy for the Empire, when personifications of peoples abound in art. To a certain degree, the circumstance can be explained by the status of the sources. For the Imperial times, we simply possess less ancient written information on the triumphal processions, now much less frequently celebrated. Furthermore, the difference in frequency between the representations shown in the triumphs and those preserved in art is a result of their partly divergent functions. In Roman art, the majority of representations of *nationes* and *gentes* from the second century AD were created not to symbolize Roman conquest, but to depict the loyalty of diverse peoples towards Rome and to give form to the collective Empire. Most representations were thus of what Bienkowski in 1900 categorized as the *provincia pia fidelis*-type, personified images based on the Greek ideal form and used to represent adopted members of the Roman hegemony.[153] Representations of this type might also have been used for funeral processions, but one would not in the first place associate them with the triumphs. When, however, new territories were captured, like Judaea by

---

[149] Ov. *Pont.* 2.8.39–40, *Trist.* 4.2.43–6, both quoted and discussed below.

[150] Ov. *Ars* 1.225: *haec est Danaeia Persis*. Nicolet (1991: 45). Ovid might also be referring to personifications of peoples at *Pont.* 3.4.25: *gentes formatae mille figuris*. The *Tabula Siarensis* bears testimony to an arch erected in Rome in honour of Germanicus, decorated with golden statues of the conquered peoples, Gonzales (1984: 58, fr. II, 9–11): *Placere uti ianus marmoreus extrueretur . . . cum signis devictarum gentium ina[uratis tituloque]*.

[151] Sil. *Pun.* 17.636: *ibat et effigies orae iam lenis Hiberae*, '. . . went also an image of the Hiberian district, now pacified'. The Garamas and the Syrtis, mentioned in the same passage (17.634), might also be personifications of the peoples of these lands.

[152] Claud. 24.22–5: *hi famulos traherent reges; hi facta metallo | oppida vel montes captivaque flumina ferrent. | hinc Libyci fractis lugerent cornibus amnes; | inde catenato gemeret Germania Rheno*, 'Some would lead enslaved kings, others carry towns made of metal or mountains and captured rivers. Here would go in mourning the rivers of Libya, their horns broken, there Germania, moaning, together with the fettered Rhine.' The display of peoples, rivers, and towns was a literary topos by now, and Claudian was probably much inspired by earlier poetic descriptions.

[153] Modern scholarship on personifications of lands and peoples in Greek and Roman art started with Percy Gardner (1888). It was followed by two monographs, Bienkowski (1900) and Jatta (1908). Both of these authors aimed at identifying and categorizing the entire corpus of personifications of 'provinces' in Roman art. Bienkowski launched the two basic categories *provincia capta* and *provincia pia fidelis*, and Jatta suggested further subcategories. Jocelyn Toynbee's categorization (1934) was one of style, recognizing two basic

Vespasian and Titus or Dacia and Armenia by Trajan, personifications were created in Bienkowski's so-called *provincia capta*-style: realistic female personifications inspired by the captive inhabitants of a certain land and applied to represent newly conquered areas.[154] Although our sources are silent on the matter, Vespasian, Titus, and Trajan very probably had staged personifications of Judaea, Dacia, and Armenia, styled *provinciae captae*, led in the triumphs. Though funeral and triumphal processions merged in Imperial times, no sources suggest that triumphs ever included groups of personifications in the *pia fidelis*-style. Captives and personifications of peoples put on triumphal parade were nothing but *captae*.

Germania in chains

Most descriptions in ancient literature mention the display of personifications of peoples without providing any details on their appearance. Ovid constitutes an exception. The personified Germania appears in two passages that both describe her future presence in Tiberius' eagerly awaited triumph, which is to celebrate his victories in the North. In the *Epistulae ex Ponto*, Ovid depicts Germania in the following way (*Pont.* 2.8.39–40):

> sic fera quam primum pavido Germania vultu
> ante triumphantis serva feratur equos

So may wild Germania with trembling countenance be borne as soon as possible as a slave before steeds triumphant.[155]

In the *Tristia* 4.2.43–8, Ovid has some spectators pointing Germania out to others:

> '. . . crinibus en etiam fertur Germania passis,
>   et ducis invicti sub pede maesta sedet,
> collaque Romanae praebens animosa securi
>   vincula fert illa, qua tulit arma, manu.'
> hos super in curru, Caesar, victore veheris . . .

categories of representations: (1) the realistic, founded upon representations of individual prisoners of the particular country, and (2) the ideal, based on the Greek personifications in female form. Toynbee's classification was basically followed by Janusz Ostrowski (1990a), who opened up the category of the realistic type to include also representations of male captives. Then Liane Houghtalin published a thesis, basically following Toynbee, but preferring three categories of personifications (1993: esp. 484). Two types—one based on Greek prototypes and the other on the captive inhabitants of the country—were, according to Houghtalin, used to personify provinces of all kinds when the practice started in Roman art in the first half of the 1st cent. BC. The first type, based on Greek models, was predominantly applied to areas for which such personifications already existed, the second type for locations that lacked such prototypes. Yet another type, based on a general Hellenized or civilized look, appeared only from the 2nd cent. AD.

[154] Houghtalin (1993: 490–2).   [155] Tr. J. Dobreff.

'...See! Even Germania is borne along with her hair let down, seated in grief at the feet of the unconquered leader. Offering her proud neck to the Roman axe, she wears chains on that hand in which she carried arms.' High above them in the triumphal car, you will ride, O Caesar...

Ovid imagines the representation of Germania just in front of the triumphator in the parade. In the passage from the *Epistulae ex Ponto*, this is explicitly spelt out. Germania is carried before (*ante*) the horses driving the triumphator's car. The passage quoted from the *Tristia* forms part of a longer triumphal description, in which Ovid has some of the spectators pointing out the captive participants of the parade as they pass by. Thus, the account reflects the order in which these participants were seen. Ovid starts by describing a number of prisoners, and then he accounts for the appearance of various representations. Last in line come the Rhine and Germania, who in their turn precede only the triumphator and his army (*hos super in curru, Caesar...*). Germania's placement there emphasizes her role as a prominent and influential enemy. As such, she also appears in two other passages of Ovid. In the *Epistulae ex Ponto* 3.4, she is a treacherous opponent, who has taken active part in the war but now casts her spears aside, and in 2.8, as a fearful enemy, she is personally responsible for the death of Drusus.[156] Similarly, in the Pseudo-Ovidian *Consolatio ad Liviam*, Germania is blamed for Drusus' death, a crime for which she is to pay the capital penalty.[157]

In her appearance too, Germania is described as a living captive led in triumph. Ovid portrays her as a wild barbarian (*fera*) with undressed hair (*crinibus passis*), whose armed uprising against Rome has been suppressed. Her conquered state is emphasized. She is now a slave (*serva*) and a chained prisoner of Rome (*vincula fert*). She is subdued by the Roman conqueror, physically subordinate to him as she sits at his feet (*et ducis invicti sub pede maesta sedet*) and left at his mercy (*collaque Romanae praebens animosa securi*). The axe (*Romanae securi*) might symbolize not only Roman superiority in general, but also specifically allude to the death penalty that at times awaited the principal enemies of Rome as the triumphal procession turned to climb the Capitol. Germania bears her fate with fear (*pavido vultu*) and grief (*maesta*).[158] In all this, her captured state and the penalty that awaits her, her grief and fear, her chains and her placement,

[156] Ov. *Pont.* 3.4.97: *perfida damnatas Germania proicit hastas*; 'faithless Germania is casting away her hateful spears'; *Pont.* 2.8.47: *quem dira tibi rapuit Germania Drusum*, 'that Drusus, whom fearful Germania has torn away from you'.

[157] [Ov.] *Cons. ad Liv.* 271–2: *At tibi ius veniae superest, Germania, nullum: | postmodo tu poenas, barbara, morte dabis*, 'But for you, Germania, no right of pardon remains. You shall pay the penalty hereafter, barbarian, by your death'. I have followed Heinsius's conjecture *barbara, morte* instead of the mostly cited *barbare morte*, see *Poetae Latini Minores*, i, ed. Baehrens (Leipzig, 1879).

[158] Cf. Claud. 24.25.

Germania is depicted as a prominent prisoner led on triumphal parade. She is not an inanimate symbol of her province, but a vivid impersonation of the inhabitants of her land, a *simulacrum gentis*, embodying their sentiments and subjection.

Ovid's Germania resembles depictions of her in art, the preserved examples of which all postdate Ovid.[159] Usually represented as a *provincia capta* with barbarian looks and long loose hair, she is frequently shown seated, often as part of a trophy.[160] Germania is also recognizable from her clothing, as she almost always wears trousers. In art, dress was an important attribute, which differentiated the various peoples, especially personifications of the *capta* or realistic type. Ovid says nothing of Germania's clothes in his description, but when on parade, she was most probably dressed in her national costume. Dio Cassius' descriptions of the personifications at the funerals of Augustus and Pertinax reveal that the sculptures had been put into native dress specifically for the processional event. At Pertinax' funeral, Dio (75.4.5) writes of the bronze representations of the peoples: τὰ ἔθνη . . . ἐν εἰκόσι χαλκαῖς, ἐπιχωρίως σφίσιν ἐσταλμένα, where the passive form ἐσταλμένα (from στέλλω, 'to arrange, array, equip') unveils the fact the εἰκόνες had been dressed for the funeral. In this way too, the personifications were treated like the human captives, who were frequently dressed to emphasize their origins. For example, Appian, also using a passive form of στέλλω, writes that Pompey arrayed his prisoners according to their native customs.[161] The clothing of the personifications marked the characteristics and origins of the peoples. Colourfully attired, they would have been seen and distinguished by the remotest of onlookers. Ovid characterizes Germania as a barbarian in rather general terms, but on parade her trousers probably signified her ethnicity. In this way, she would have reminded the spectators of her *simulacra* placed in public, just as these statues in their turn would have brought her processional appearance to mind.

Simulacra gentium: terminology and identity

In most cases, Latin writers mention personifications of peoples and their lands on triumphal display by way of their particular identity only (e.g. Germania, Gallia). No specific term specifies them as works of art.[162] This is most evident when the author wishes to stress the display of one or a few

[159] Houghtalin (1993: 289–98); *LIMC* iv (1988), s.v. 'Germania', i. 182–5 (E. Künzl).

[160] Houghtalin (1993: 289–98, esp. 291).

[161] App. *Mith.* 116: καὶ πλῆθος αἰχμαλώτων τε καὶ λῃστῶν, οὐδένα δεδεμένον ἀλλ' ἐς τὰ πάτρια ἐσταλμένους, 'and a multitude of captives and pirates, none of them bound, but all arrayed in their native costumes'.

[162] The exception is Silius Italicus, who describes the representation of Spain as an *effigies orae Hiberae*, Sil. *Pun.* 17.636. The wording *orae Hiberae* is clearly poetic, as there is a close literal link between *Hiberae* in verse 636 and *Hiberus* in verse 641. The *effigies orae Hiberae* introduces a row of various representations, so possibly the term works as a general denomination of the representations on display as a group.

particular and important participants, like Ovid in his descriptions of Germania. When listing the individual representations displayed by Balbus in 19 BC, Pliny (*Nat.* 5.5.36–7) follows the same principle:

et hoc mirum, supra dicta oppida ab eo capta auctores nostros prodidisse, ipsum in triumpho praeter Cydamum et Garamam omnium aliarum gentium urbiumque nomina ac simulacra duxisse, quae iere hoc ordine: Tabudium oppidum, Niteris natio, Milgris Gemella oppidum, Bubeium natio vel oppidum, Enipi natio, Thuben oppidum, mons nomine Niger, Nitibrum, Rapsa oppida, Viscera natio, Decri oppidum, flumen Nathabur, Thapsagum oppidum, Tamiagi natio, Boin oppidum, Pege oppidum, flumen Dasibari, mox oppida continua Baracum, Buluba, Alasit, Galsa, Balla, Maxalla, Cizania, mons Gyri, in quo gemmas nasci titulus praecessit.

There is also this remarkable circumstance, that our writers have handed down the names of the towns mentioned above as having been taken by him, and have recorded that in his triumphal procession, beside Cydamus and Garama, he displayed the names and representations of all the other peoples and cities, who went in this order: the town of Tabudium, the Niteris tribe, the town of Milgris Gemella, the tribe or town of Bubeium, the tribe of the Enipi, the town of Thuben, the mountain known as mons Niger, the towns called Nitibrum and Rapsa, the Viscera tribe, the town of Decri, the river Nathabur, the town of Thapsagum, the Tamiagi tribe, the town of Boin, the town of Pege, the river Dasibari; then a series of towns, Baracum, Buluba, Alasit, Galsa, Balla, Maxalla, Cizania; mount Gyri, its representation preceded by an inscription stating that precious stones were produced in it.

Balbus' individual displays are not specified as works of art, but the peoples are, for example, a *Niteris natio* and an *Enipi natio*. They are not in the first place sculptures but the peoples of these places themselves, present as captives in person. In contrast, introducing the display, Pliny maintains that Balbus led *omnium aliarium gentium urbiumque nomina ac simulacra*, 'the names and representations of all the other peoples and cities'. Here, Pliny defines the group on display as artistic representations; they are *simulacra gentium*. The plural term *simulacra* functions as a general label, to define an assembly of personifications as works of art.

  The terms used by the ancient authors to denominate personifications shown in the triumphal processions attest to a close affinity with the art representations put up in public places. Pliny labels Balbus' peoples *simulacra gentium* and *nationes*. Both terms appear in descriptions also of the statues at Pompey's theatre. Suetonius calls them *simulacra gentium*, and in Pliny's description they are *nationes*.[163] Servius employs the same phrase—*simulacra gentium*—to describe the personified peoples that adorned Augustus' *Porticus ad Nationes*.[164] Similarly, in Greek, the peoples of the Augustan empire represented at Aphrodisias are

---

[163] Suet. *Nero* 46.1; Plin. *Nat.* 36.4.41–2.   [164] Serv. *ad Aen.* 8.721.

labelled ἔθνη on the inscribed bases,[165] the same term that Dio Cassius uses for the peoples on display in Augustus and Pertinax' funeral trains.[166]

The alternative use of *gentes* and *nationes* in Latin literature to describe peoples on triumphal display and in public settings suggests that the terms were employed without distinction to denote the same artistic and perceptive phenomenon. Both terms signified foreign less civilized peoples, races, and tribes in the first place, their lands in the second.[167] Indeed, the images were, as we have seen, animate representations embodying and personifying a group of people ethnically defined or inhabiting a particular area. The *gentes*, *nationes*, and ἔθνη were no impersonal representations of geographic areas as defined on maps. Most interestingly, the Latin writers never use the word *provincia* when referring to the personifications. Hence, even though these images are often discussed in modern literature as 'province personifications', the terminology suggests that the statues rather represented defeated peoples. In fact, several art historians claim that personifications of provinces do not exist at all, only representations of *gentes* and *nationes*.[168] Others, like Houghtalin, maintain that there were examples of province representations as well, especially from the western part of the Empire, where the Roman need to create and symbolize new territorial divisions was more pronounced.[169]

The identified personifications on triumphal parade add to the interpretation of the display as one of peoples. Of the representations specified, only Ovid's Germania could possibly represent a province, namely the *Germania Magna*, which had been lost in the Varian disaster in AD 9, but which the Romans at this time still hoped to regain. However, it might just as well be a representation of the peoples inhabiting the land of Germania. Silius Italicus' *ora Hibera*, a paraphrase for Spain, alludes rather to the area with its people than any of its provinces, and Mauretania, which Florus describes in Caesar's triumph, was not a province in the late Republic. Both Gallia and Hispania, attested by Lucan and Florus, were subdivided into further provinces at the time of the triumphs of Caesar, so his displays probably rather alluded to the people inhabiting these lands.[170] In Balbus' triumph, the obscure Niteris, Bubeium, Enipi, Viscera, and Tamiagi were all very far from being provinces. Pliny's list of small and little-known peoples, towns, rivers, and mountains is unparalleled in ancient

[165] Smith (1988*a*: esp. 53–9, pl. IX).

[166] Dio Cassius 56.34.3, 75.4.5.

[167] Saddington (1961).

[168] See Bienkowski (1900: 3–4, 11–12); Strack (1933: 139–66, esp. 139–48); Toynbee (1934: 5–6 n. 2); Smith (1988*a*: esp. 57); Ostrowski (1990*a*: 19–21); Liveriani (1995: *passim*); cf. Salcedo (1996: 17–19).

[169] Houghtalin (1993: 5–7, 499–502).

[170] While Florus (*Epit.* 2.13.88) maintains that Caesar performed his triumph *de Gallia*, the songs performed by the soldiers at the Gallic procession included verses of how he had subdued the Gauls, *Galliae*, Suet. *Iul.* 49.

prose, and, in fact, Pliny himself marvelled at the fact that the names of the places had been preserved. Nothing suggests that the display itself was unique, though. Rather, Balbus' representations very plausibly reflect a most common kind of triumphal exhibition, giving physical form to the complete conquest of a certain area by displaying even the smallest places and groups of peoples subdued. In fact, several writers attest to the general display of *simulacra* of all kinds, and beside a Germania or a Gallia, there were in all probability rows of smaller, less important peoples and localities paraded.

Although the evidence as a whole does not always allow a precise identification of the diverse personifications on parade, the Romans clearly preferred to show peoples, representing both large and small groups and areas, rather than the administrative units of provinces in the triumphal processions. This is evident from the terminology used and the specific displays known, particularly that of Balbus. Thus, again, sources suggest the display of conquest rather than the established Roman Empire.

Flumina: *staging the rivers*

Influenced by Greek art, reclining river personifications appear in Roman painting in late Republican or early Augustan times.[171] The motifs are mythological or literary, and the rivers are either domestic or of the underworld. Representations of foreign rivers emerge much later. There are no preserved Republican examples and, in contrast to the many references to representations of peoples set up under Augustus, nothing in the sources suggests the existence of monuments with reclining rivers during his age. In fact, the figure seen on the arch of Titus belongs to the earliest representations of this type, and only a handful reclining foreign river personifications can be dated before the second century AD.[172] This century witnessed a profound increase in the popularity of river personifications and produced the great majority of the examples preserved in art.[173]

[171] Klementa (1993: 65–6, 203–4); Ostrowski (1991: 35–6, 48), both with further references. According to Klementa, the reclining type employed in Roman art stems primarily from a Hellenistic personification of the Nile, created sometime during the first half of the 2nd cent. BC. Roman art also produced river images in the form of heads or masks, standing and seated figures, and figures emerging from the waves, Ostrowski (1991: 27–32). The reclining river was, however, by far the most popular type.

[172] There is also an early example of a statue of the Nile, dated to AD 63–79, from a garden in Pompeii, Klementa (1993: 13, 204). Pliny (*Nat.* 36.11.58) states that Vespasian dedicated a statue of the Nile, made of black basalt, in the Templum Pacis. In AD 85, Domitian issued a sesterce showing his subjection of the Rhine, represented by a reclining personification (Fig. 25); *RIC* ii (1926), no. 259, 187, no. 286, 190; Ostrowski (1990*b*: 313, 1991: 51); Klementa (1993: 133); *Trionfi romani*, 198, II.3.10. Statius also describes an equestrian statue of Domitian, the brazen hoof of the horse trampling on the hair of the captive Rhine, *vacuae pro caespite terrae | aerea captivi crinem terit ungula Rheni*, Stat. *Silv.* 1.1.50–1.

[173] Klementa (1993: 195); see also Ostrowski (1991: 43–59).

In contrast to the rather late appearance of foreign river personifications in art, there is explicit evidence that conquered rivers were exhibited in the triumphal parades from late Republican times. Florus and Lucan, in the passages discussed already above, both attest to the presence of rivers in the processions held by Caesar in 46 BC. Florus states that Caesar in his Gallic parade paraded the Rhine, the Rhône, and the Oceanus (*hic erat Rhenus et Rhodanus et ex auro captivus Oceanus*) and in his Egyptian the Nile (*tunc in ferculis Nilus*).[174] Two of these rivers, the Rhine and the Oceanus, also appear in Lucan's version of the Gallic parade (*ut vincula Rheno Oceanoque daret*).[175]

After Caesar, subdued rivers next appear in Octavian's triple triumph held in 29 BC. Propertius testifies to the presence of the Nile,[176] and Vergil includes the Rhine, the Euphrates, and the Araxes in his depiction of Octavian's triumph.[177] In Balbus' African parade ten years later, two rivers, the Nathabur and the Dasibari, appear among the variety of representations listed by Pliny the Elder.[178] The display of these obscure watercourses, otherwise unknown, attests to what must now have been a rather familiar sight in the processions. Several sources also show that the practice continued in the Imperial age.[179] Ovid depicts the exhibition of several rivers, such as the Rhine, the Tigris, and the Euphrates.[180] Tacitus tells of the presence of *simulacra fluminum* in Germanicus' triumph in AD 17,[181] and the river shown on the arch of Titus suggests its Flavian display. The poetic works of Persius and Silius Italicus provide further testimony. Persius writes of how *ingentes Rheni* are to be staged in Caligula's Germanic ovation, and Silius Italicus includes representations of the Ebro and the Baetis in his depiction of Scipio Africanus' procession.[182]

Thus, the abundance of river personifications preserved in art from the second century AD is not matched by a similar peak of references to their triumphal

---

[174] Flor. *Epit.* 2.13.88–9.

[175] Lucan 3.76–7.

[176] Prop. 2.1.31–2: *aut canerem Aegyptum et Nilum, cum attractus in urbem | septem captivis debilis ibat aquis*, 'Or should I sing of Egypt or of the Nile, as he, having been forced to Rome, walked weakened together with his seven captive streams'.

[177] Verg. *Aen.* 8.726–8. Östenberg (1999).

[178] Plin. *Nat.* 5.5.36–7, quoted above p. 228.

[179] Literary sources also tell of mountains displayed in triumphs, Ov. *Pont.* 2.1.39, *Trist.* 4.2.37–8, *Ars* 1.219–21; Plin. *Nat.* 5.5.36–7; Tac. *Ann.* 2.41; Sil. *Pun.* 17.637–8, 640–1; Zonar. 7.21.10; Claud. 24.22–3. However, most accounts are short and general in character, providing very little information on the appearance of these representations. In Roman art, mountains were often shown personified, in male as well as in female form, and it is likely that mountains were staged and perceived similarly to the rivers.

[180] Ov. *Trist.* 4.2.41–2, *Pont.* 3.4.107–8, *Ars* 1.223–4. Ovid also mentions the general display of *flumina*, *Pont.* 2.1.39, *Trist.* 4.2.37–8.

[181] Tac. *Ann.* 2.41.

[182] Pers. 6.47; Sil. *Pun.* 17.636–42. In the later Empire, Claudian depicts the presence of Libyan streams, *amnes Libyci*, and the Rhine in his vision of Stilicho's triumph, Claud. 24.24–5.

FIGURE 25 The Rhine
frequently appears in
descriptions of triumphs
and pictorial memorials of
successful wars. This
sesterce from AD 85 shows
Domitian in military attire
trampling on a rather small
reclining figure, which
represents the Rhine.
The coin celebrates the
emperor's victory over the
Chatti, for which he held
a triumph in AD 83.

display. The discrepancy can again be explained by the fact that fewer triumphs
were held during the Principate and that the sources to their contents are less
exhaustive. More specifically, although personifications were often employed in
Roman art to represent military subjection, this was far from their only context.
Rivers were widely employed to illustrate mythological events, and they were
used for cultic functions or for purely decorative purposes, in public as well as in
private contexts. Thus, although the personifications shown in triumphs and
those preserved in art were similar in form, their messages were not identical.
This is reflected also in the specific rivers chosen for representation. The Rhine is
the most frequently recorded of all rivers in the Roman triumphs,[183] reflecting the
continuous military campaigns in its northern lands. Yet, very few depictions of
the river have survived, the earliest being from Flavian times (Fig. 25).[184] Clearly,
the Rhine had a great symbolic value within the military and political sphere,
which was not matched by a similar significance in a mythological setting. Rivers
like the Nile, the Oceanus (and the Tiber) were more suited to this field.

The differences in frequency and contents between river personifications
attested in the triumphs and those preserved in art can thus be explained in
terms of partly diverse spheres of function. Still, it is noteworthy that, in contrast
to the personifications of peoples, the earliest references to rivers on triumphal
display are not matched by any preserved river personifications in art. As we shall
see in the following, conquered rivers played an important part in the martial and
triumphal manifestations of the Romans from the time of Caesar.

[183] The Rhine appears in seven out of the approximately twelve references to rivers on triumphal display.
[184] Klementa (1993: 132–3); *LIMC* vii (1994), s.v. 'Rhenos, Rhenus', i. 632–5 (R. Vollkommer),
Vollkommer (1994).

The great rivers of the world: Caesar and his followers

No source indicates that rivers appeared in Roman triumphal processions before Caesar. As for Pompey, there is nothing in his victory celebrations that emphasizes the conquest of rivers. Rather, both Pompey himself and his supporters, contemporary and later, suggest that he claimed the conquest of the world by stressing the subjugation of the three parts of the *oikumene* and of a multitude of diverse peoples. In contrast, Caesar's conquests of the Nile, the Rhine, and the Oceanus, all great rivers of the world, were stressed as major accomplishments in the literary accounts of his campaigns. Catullus describes the Rhine as a *monumentum Caesaris*,[185] and Ovid counts the Nile among Caesar's chief military achievements.[186] Cicero too emphasizes Caesar's subjection of rivers in a passage in *Pro Marcello* (9.28–9), which runs:

Obstupescent posteri certe imperia, provincias, Rhenum, Oceanum, Nilum, pugnas innumerabilis, incredibilis victorias, monumenta, munera, triumphos audientes et legentes tuos.

Doubtless, generations yet to come will be struck dumb when they hear and read of your commands, your provinces, the Rhine, the Oceanus, the Nile, your countless battles, your incredible victories, your monuments, your largess and your triumphs.

All three rivers mentioned by Cicero, namely the Rhine, the Oceanus, and the Nile, appear in Florus' account of Caesar's triumphs of 46 BC and two in Lucan's.[187] In Cicero's enumeration of Caesar's martial achievements and triumphs, their presence reflects the enormous importance of the subjection of these rivers and also most certainly the prominence of their visual appearance in his victory processions.

   Among the rivers put on show by Caesar, the Nile had seen battles fought on its water as part of the Alexandrian siege.[188] Captives from these naval skirmishes were led together with the river in the Egyptian parade.[189] Of the Gallic river displays, the Rhône had formed the scene of war at an early stage of the campaign. Caesar had suppressed the Helvetii, located on the northern banks of the Rhône, when they tried to cross the river into Roman territory.[190] Caesar's major achievements, however, concerned the Rhine and the Oceanus. Both

---

   [185] Catull. 11.10–12: *Caesaris visens monimenta magni, | Gallicum Rhenum, horribile aequor ulti- | mosque Britannos*, 'to visit the monuments of great Caesar, the Gallic Rhine, a terrifying water, and the Britons, remotest of men'.

   [186] Ov. *Met.* 15.752–9, esp. 753–4.

   [187] Flor. *Epit.* 2.13.88–9; Lucan 3.76–7.

   [188] Ov. *Met.* 15.753–4.

   [189] Appian (*BCiv.* 2.101) writes that Caesar introduced a kind of Egyptian triumph, in which captives taken in naval battles on the Nile were shown.

   [190] Caes. *Gall.* 1.1–12; Flor. *Epit.* 1.45.2–4.

watercourses were subdued in 55 BC, when Caesar became the first Roman to cross the Rhine and soon thereafter the Channel in his invasion of Britain. The subjection of the Rhine was clearly demonstrated by the bridges which Caesar threw across the river in 55 and 53 BC respectively.[191] Scholars also assume that knowledge itself of the Rhine in Rome originated in Caesar's description of the river in the first book of *De Bello Gallico*.[192]

Rivers on triumphal display symbolized the defeat of their lands and peoples. The Rhine, the Rhône, and the Oceanus transmitted messages of subjection of the peoples of Germany, Gaul, and Britain, and the Nile represented the conquest of Egypt. But rivers were much more than territorial emblems. In particular, they were perceived as barriers and boundaries.[193] The Nile, the Rhine, and the Oceanus were, together with the Euphrates and the Tigris, the great rivers of the world, and as such they came to constitute frontiers between the Roman sphere and the world outside. In the *De Bello Gallico*, Caesar himself repeatedly stresses the Rhine as the border between Gallia and Germania.[194] The Oceanus marked the northern frontier facing the British Isles, and the Nile indicated the south-eastern limits of the Roman realm.[195]

Since the great rivers were situated on the edges of the Roman territorial extent, they came to represent the worldwide domination of Rome. In Latin literature, the major rivers of the world were often used as symbols of the greatness of the Roman Empire. The Rhine and the Nile, for example, are not infrequently contrasted as its north-western and southern extremities, the Rhine and the Euphrates as its north-western and eastern.[196] Caesar used the rivers to demonstrate global conquest when he in his Gallic triumph paraded the Rhine, the Rhône, and the Oceanus, and then staged the Nile in his Egyptian procession, conducted in the same month. Others followed his example. As stated above, Propertius attests to the presence of the Nile in the *triplex triumphus* held by Octavian in 29 BC,[197] and Vergil depicts the Rhine, the Euphrates, and the Araxes

[191] Caes. *Gall.* 4.17–18, 6.9; App. *Gall.* 1.5; Flor. *Epit.* 1.45.15.

[192] *EV* IV, s.v. 'Reno (*Rhenus*)', 435 (R. F. Rossi).

[193] Plin. *Pan.* 16.5; Tac. *Ann.* 1.9.5. Guillaumin (1987); Rüpke (1990: 52); Braund (1996: 43–4, 46).

[194] e.g. *B.Gall* 1.1.3, 1.31.11, 1.35.3, 1.37.3, 1.43.9, 2.4.2, 4.3, 5.41; cf. Serv. *ad Aen.* 8.727. See also *EV* iv, s.v. 'Reno (*Rhenus*)', 435 (R. F. Rossi); Sallmann (1987: 123–5); Schulz (1998).

[195] For a discussion of the Nile as it appears in Roman literature, see Postl (1970), and for its representations in art, *LIMC* vi (1992), s.v. 'Neilos', i. 720–6 (M.-O. Jentel); Klementa (1993: esp. 9–51). The Rhône had constituted the border between the Roman province and the Helvetii before Caesar's arrival.

[196] Sen. *Dial.* 10.4.5 (Rhine, Euphrates, Danube), *Herc. F.* 1323–4 (Thanais, Nile, Tigris, Rhine, Tagus); *Anth. Lat.* 421.1–2 (Rhine, Oceanus, Euphrates), *Anth. Lat.* 425 (Rhine, Euphrates); Philo, *Leg.* 10 (Rhine, Euphrates); Mart. 4.11.7–8 (Rhine, Nile). Binder (1971: 269–70). Cf. Plut. *Alex.* 36.2, where we are told that the Persian king had water from the Nile and the Danube brought to Susa and stored in its treasury as a symbol of the vastness of his empire.

[197] Prop. 2.1.31–2.

as participating in the procession represented on the shield of Aeneas.[198] I have argued elsewhere that this poetic parade well reflects the contents of Octavian's triple triumph.[199] The Rhine was most certainly exhibited, and the Euphrates and the Araxes might have been present as well. By parading the Nile, the Rhine, and very possibly other rivers too, Octavian used the display of important *flumina* to boast of his conquest of the world.

The great rivers were not only borders between Rome and unconquered lands, but between the *oikumene*, the inhabited world, and the territory on the other side too. The Oceanus, believed to encircle the world,[200] marked the border between the Roman and the non-Roman area and also between *oikumene* and the world beyond.[201] Thus, the Britons, living on the other side of the Oceanus, were, in Vergil's words, 'wholly cut out from the entire world'.[202] The Nile too, was perceived as a frontier to an unknown domain.[203] The location of its sources, supposedly placed in an antipodal continent outside the *oikumene*, was a matter of much debate and mystification. In Lucan's *Pharsalia*, Caesar, following the *exemplum* of Alexander, sets out to trace the river's spring.[204] Not dissimilarly, in Silius Italicus' description of Scipio Africanus' triumph, the poet depicts the display of the Baetis river, the city of Gades, and the Calpe mountain, all placed on the fringes of the world.[205]

By subjecting the Nile and above all by crossing the Oceanus, Caesar actually traversed the edges of the world and conquered lands on the other side.[206] In Velleius Paterculus' words, through his British campaign, he tied the other world, *alter orbis*, to the known one.[207] The display of the great rivers in his

[198] Verg. *Aen.* 8.726–8: *Euphrates ibat iam mollior undis, | extremique hominum Morini, Rhenusque bicornis, | indomitique Dahae, et pontem indignatus Araxes*, 'the Euphrates went by, with waves already tamed; the Morini, the most distant of men; the Rhine of two horns; the unconquered Dahae; and the Araxes, indignant at its bridge' (tr. R. Gurval).

[199] Östenberg (1999).

[200] e.g. *Anth. Lat.* 419.3–4; Plut. *Pomp.* 38.2–3.

[201] Flory (1988); Romm (1992: esp. 140–9).

[202] Verg. *Ecl.* 1.66: *et penitus toto divisos orbe Britannos*.

[203] Romm (1992: 149–56).

[204] See the discussion and references in Romm (1992: 152–6).

[205] Sil. *Pun.* 17.637–9: *terrarum finis Gades ac laudibus olim | terminus Herculeis Calpe Baetisque lavare | solis equos dulci consuetus fluminis unda*, 'Gades, at the world's end and Calpe, the limit of the achievements of Hercules in ancient times, and the Baetis, accustomed to bath the sun's horses in the sweet wave of its water.'

[206] Plut. *Caes.* 23.2: 'in his attempt to occupy it [i.e. Britannia] he carried the Roman supremacy beyond the confines of the inhabited world'. Schulz (2000b: esp. 290–6) maintains that while Pompey had taken the Roman realm to the edges of the world, Caesar expanded it beyond the edges. He also argues (pp. 286–96) that Caesar's idea of invading Britain was shaped already during his visits to Gades in the 60s, the motif being primarily to challenge Pompey as world conqueror *terra marique* by crossing the Oceanus.

[207] Vell. Pat. 2.46.1; cf. Flor. *Epit.* 1.45.16: *Omnibus terra marique peragratis respexit Oceanum et, quasi hic Romanis orbis non sufficeret, alterum cogitavit*, 'Having traversed all lands and seas, he turned to the Oceanus,

triumphs was therefore not only a manifestation of the subjection of frontier
countries, but of lands outside of the known world as well. In this capacity, the
Oceanus formed the most important of Caesar's river displays. Flory has shown
that the cuirass made of British pearls, which Caesar dedicated in the temple of
Venus Genetrix in Rome, should be read as spoils from the Oceanus, himself a
captive in the triumphs.[208] Caesar's example was later followed by Caligula,
whose seemingly strange conduct of collecting shells on the shores of the
English Channel and claiming that they were spoils of the Oceanus should be
read as a reference to his famous predecessor.[209] Caligula may have chosen
to follow Caesar also by displaying a sculptured personification of the Oceanus
in his subsequent victory procession, as might later emperors engaged in British
warfare. The Oceanus plays a prominent role in the *Laus Caesaris*, a laudatory
poem celebrating Claudius' British campaign, and the river was probably present
in one or both of the emperor's triumphs over Britannia too.[210] Representations
of the Oceanus on Imperial display might even have been of gold, the material
Caesar used to emphasize his extraterritorial conquest.

What did the rivers look like?

The river carried in triumph on the frieze on arch of Titus displays an iconography typical of river personifications in Roman art: a reclining old man with
long hair and a full beard, the upper part of his body naked and a cloth covering
his hips and legs (Fig. 24).[211] Rivers are at times equipped with characteristics that
specify their identities, but are more often shown with general river attributes.
The water-pouring urn on which the personification on the arch of Titus leans
and the bundle of reeds that he holds in his hand are such common river features.
From iconography only, the identity of this river cannot therefore be determined.
But since the depiction on the arch of Titus commemorates the Jewish triumph
held by Vespasian and Titus, it is commonly surmised that the personification is
meant to represent the River Jordan.[212] The assumption is plausible, but there is

and, as if this world of ours did not suffice for the Romans, set his thoughts on the other'. See also Val.
Max. 3.2.23; Lucan. 2.571; Sen. *Dial.* 6.14.3; *Anth. Lat.* 419.3–4; Suet. *Iul.* 25.2. Romm (1994: 140–9);
Schultz (2000: 294–5).

[208] Flory (1988).

[209] Suet. *Cal.* 46; Dio Cass. 59.25.1–5 (apud Joann. Antioch.). Flory (1988). The passage has been much
discussed in modern literature, see Wardle (1994: 313–14).

[210] *Anth. Lat.* 419–26, esp. 419.3–4, 421.1–2, 423.3–6, 425.3–4, 426.3–4. For the poem, see in particular
Tandoi (1962), but also Borzsák (1994). According to Suetonius, Claudius placed a naval crown on the
palace as a sign that he had crossed and thus in a way subdued the Oceanus, *traiecti et quasi domiti Oceani
insigne*, Suet. *Claud.* 17.3.

[211] Pfanner (1983: 83–4 (Figur 35), Abb. 47, Taf. 79.1–2, 80.2, 85.4, 86.4, 6–7, 87.1–2); Klementa (1993:
108–9, 194). For river representations in general, *LIMC* iv (1988), s.v. 'Fluvii', i. 139–48 (C. Weiss).

[212] Vessberg (1952: 132); Ostrowski (1990b: 311); Klementa (1993: 108).

another possibility, namely that the representation was meant not to be identified as a specific river, but rather a vanquished river in general. In fact, the very unspecific depiction both of the river and the rest of the contents in the preserved scene speaks in favour of such an interpretation.

Turning to the literary evidence, Ovid, in his numerous triumphal depictions, gives several rather detailed portraits of rivers paraded. At times, the descriptions must be taken as literary conventions, at others, they are probably reflections of how the rivers appeared in the triumphs.[213] The distinction is not always easy to make, as rivers represented in both triumphs and monuments must have constituted incitements in the creation of poetic stock epithets and conventions.[214] Poets may also have been inspired by written statements announced on the accompanying *tituli*.[215] The influence could also have worked the other way, with literary descriptions influencing the artistic creations.

In a future imaginative triumph, Ovid has one of the spectators pointing out the River Rhine in this manner: *cornibus hic fractis viridi male tectus ab ulva, | decolor ipse suo sanguine Rhenus erat*, 'this thing with broken horns and poorly covered with green sedge was the Rhine himself, discoloured with his own blood'.[216] Also, in Claudian's much later description of Stilicho's future triumph, the rivers of Libya walk in mourning with horns that had been broken: *hinc Libyci fractis lugerent cornibus amnes*.[217] Vergil includes a *Rhenus bicornis* among the peoples and rivers paraded on the shield of Aeneas,[218] and Servius (*ad Aen*. 8.727) comments:

'bicorniis' autem aut commune est omnibus fluviis, aut proprie de Rheno, quia per duos alveos fluit: per unam qua Romanum imperium est, per alterum qua interluit barbaros, ubi iam Vahal dicitur et facit insulam Batavorum.

For the epithet 'two-horned' is either common to all rivers, or characteristic of the Rhine, since the river runs in two streams; in one that moves through the Roman Empire and in another that flows between barbarians in a place which is called Vahal and makes up the island of the Batavians.

Indeed, ancient writers commonly assumed that the Rhine flowed in two streams. The idea appears to have originated in the writings of Strabo and in

---

[213] Ovid himself acknowledges the triumph as a source of inspiration, Ov. *Pont.* 3.4.25–6: *sed loca, sed gentes formatae mille figuris | nutrissent carmen proeliaque ipsa meum*, 'but the places, the peoples formed in a thousand shapes, the very battles would have fed my verse'.

[214] Tandoi (1962) stresses the triumphal procession as a major source of inspiration for depictions of foreign lands in the Latin poets.

[215] Tandoi (1962: 113–14); Östenberg (forthcoming).

[216] Ov. *Trist.* 4.2.41–2.

[217] Claud. 24.24. The verse might well have been inspired by Ovid's triumphal poetry.

[218] Verg. *Aen.* 8.727.

particular of Asinius Pollio.[219] Modern scholars at times follow Servius and
assume that *bicornis* is a literary epithet symbolizing the Rhine's double course.[220]
However, it should be noted that Servius allows for the possibility that not only
the Rhine, but all rivers were two-horned. And, in fact, in Latin literature, several
rivers are described as carrying horns. For example, Ovid calls the Granicus
bicornis, and Vergil depicts the Eridanus as carrying *gemina cornua* and describes
the Tiber as *corniger*.[221] In Claudian's description of Stilicho's triumph, the rivers
of Libya are horned too.[222] Nor is the River Rhine itself always described as
bicornis. Martial depicts him as carrying not two horns, but one.[223]

The horned rivers were not only a literary convention, but an iconographic
trait as well. In Greek and Roman art, a number of river personifications have
horns on the front of their heads, the Rhine as well as other rivers.[224] The horns
shown on anthropomorphic images of rivers were reminiscences of earlier
representations, when they appeared in the form of bulls.[225] This circumstance,
together with the fact that horns were not exclusively reserved for the Rhine,
strongly implies that the literary description of the Rhine as *bicornis* was not in
the first place dependent on the number of its streams. Rather, the attribution of
horns to the Rhine and other rivers should be seen in the context of a literary and
iconographic tradition, which depicted river personifications as horned.

In consequence, it seems likely that personifications of rivers were shown
horned also in triumphs, as described by the poets. Of particular interest, then,
is the fact that both Ovid and Claudian describe the horns as broken (*cornua
fracta*). That the horns symbolized the strength of the rivers is obvious, as is the
fact that broken horns implied the Roman subjugation of these powers. In fact,
also in non-processional contexts, Latin poets allude to the lost strength of enemy
rivers by depicting their horns as broken.[226] Does this mean that Ovid and
Claudian's descriptions of the *cornua fracta* were mere literary conventions, or

[219] *EV* iv, s.v. 'Reno (*Rhenus*)', 436 (R. F. Rossi). After Asinius Pollio, only Pliny diverges in opinion and
maintains that there were three streams.

[220] Eden (1975: 191–2); Vollkommer (1994: 4).

[221] Ov. *Met.* 11.763; Verg. *Georg.* 4.371, *Aen.* 8.77.

[222] Claud. 24.24.

[223] Mart. 7.7.3: *fractusque cornu iam ter improbo Rhenus*. Further references to horned rivers in the Latin
sources: Ov. *Fast.* 3.647, *Met.* 13.894, 14.602; Stat. *Theb.* 7.66; Val. Fl. 1.106; Claud. 26.603. *Contra*
Vollkommer (1994: 4), who claims that 'bicornis' was a characteristics of the Rhine.

[224] A number of horned personifications of the Oceanus have been preserved, Klementa (1993: 216–17).
At times, the horns are shaped as crab claws, *LIMC* viii (1997), s.v. 'Oceanus', i. 907–15 (H. A. Cahn).

[225] Fest. p. 496 L, s.v. 'taurorum': *taurorum specie simulacra fluminum, id est cum cornibus, formantur,
quod sunt atrocia ut tauri*, 'images of rivers are shaped as bulls, that is, they carry horns, since they are wild as
bulls'; Hom. *Il.* 21.237–9; Serv. *ad Aen.* 8.77. *EV* iv, s.v. 'Reno', 436 (R. F. Rossi); Klementa (1993: 216–17).

[226] Mart. 7.7.3: *fractusque cornu iam ter improbo Rhenus*, 'and the Rhine, his persistent horn now broken
thrice'; Claud. 21.220–1: *Rhenumque minacem | cornibus infractis adeo mitescere cogis*, 'and you forced the
threatening Rhine to grow mild with broken horns'.

could rivers on triumphal display actually have been represented with their horns broken? The question of the *cornua fracta* forms part of the larger problem presented above concerning the value of the triumphal descriptions as sources for the appearance of the rivers, and it must be discussed together with the other visual references.

Ovid's description in the *Tristia* of the Rhine, *cornibus hic fractis viridi male tectus ab ulva,* | *decolor ipse suo sanguine Rhenus erat,* 'this thing with broken horns and poorly covered with green sedge was the Rhine himself, discoloured with his own blood',[227] is matched by a similar depiction in the *Ex Ponto*. Here too, Ovid imagines the Rhine being led in a future triumph over Germania: *squalidus inmissos fracta sub harundine crines,* | *Rhenus et infectas sanguine ploret aquas,* 'Let squalid Rhine lament its locks hanging down long beneath broken reeds and its water dyed with blood'.[228] And again, in the *Ars Amandi*, Ovid depicts the two great rivers of Mesopotamia in a future Parthian triumph to be held by C. Caesar: *Hic est Euphrates, praecinctus harundine frontem;* | *cui coma dependet caerula, Tigris erit,* 'This is Euphrates, his forehead girdled with reeds; he with the dark-blue locks hanging down will be Tigris'.[229]

Ovid emphasizes the loosely hanging long hair of the rivers and the crown of reeds on their heads, traits which reappear in literary descriptions of rivers outside of the triumphal context as well.[230] Now, the long hair is a typical iconographic trait of personified rivers in Roman art, and they frequently also wear crowns of reeds.[231] In fact, both Pfanner and Klementa point out that the river on the arch of Titus might have a crown of reeds on his head.[232] Ovid's descriptions of the rivers thus fit well the preserved imagery not only as regards the horns, but also with respect to their hairstyle and crowns of reeds. Again, the question is whether or not the poet describes the triumphal appearance of the Rhine when he depicts its crown as broken (*sub harundine fracta*).

In discussing these issues we must keep in mind that, although Ovid writes with indisputable poetic licence, two of the three quotations above form part of passages which are formulated not as descriptions from the poet's point of view, but as utterances of some spectators explaining the contents of the procession. The description of the River Rhine in the *Tristia* is embedded in a longer commentary by some viewers in response to questions from others. In the *Ars*

---

[227] Ov. *Trist.* 4.2.41–2.

[228] Ov. *Pont.* 3.4.107–8. The reading of *ploret* is far from clear, but I have chosen to follow this R. Ehwald's conjecture in the Teubner edn (Leipzig, 1884). Based on the different manuscripts, other editions prefer *portet, portat, potat,* or *potet* instead of *ploret. Monstret* has also been proposed.

[229] Ov. *Ars* 1.223–4.

[230] See e.g. Ov. *Met.* 9.3, 13.894.

[231] *LIMC* iv (1988), s.v. 'Euphrates', i. 70–4 (J. C. Balty). Klementa (1993: 215–16), proposes that the trait originates in the lotus crown depicted on the head of the Hellenistic representations of the Nile.

[232] Pfanner (1983: 84 (Figur 35)); Klementa (1993: 108).

Amandi, the description of the Tigris and the Euphrates likewise forms part of an explication on a triumphal parade made by a young man to impress the accompanying girl. In both cases, the self-styled cicerones ask their fellow spectators to look at the appearance of each of the participants as the procession passes by and then they name them. For example, the prisoner who is seen wearing purple is pointed out as the leader in the war and the one who hides his face is explained as a traitor who led the Roman soldiers into a trap. Likewise, when the rivers pass by, their specific appearances are pointed out and identities given, in this style: 'Look at the one who is discoloured by blood, he wears broken horns and a covering of green sedge—that is the Rhine!' 'That is Euphrates—the one who wears a crown of reeds!' 'The other one, who has blue hair, that is the Tigris!' To be sure, poetic licence and literary conventions were involved, and Ovid's descriptions cannot be taken as historical accounts word for word.[233] However, the realistic settings of the passages in Ovid encourage us to interpret his depictions of the rivers as trustworthy reflections of possible triumphal appearances of these representations. His descriptions of the rivers with broken horns and crowns of reed would have made little sense to the readers in Rome, who were very familiar with the appearance of the processions, if these were but literary conventions.

In Ovid's descriptions of the rivers on parade, there is also an emphasis on colour. The hair of Tigris is *caerula*, dark blue, and the sedge that covers the Rhine is *viridis*, green. Furthermore, the Rhine himself or his waters are discoloured by blood (*decolor suo sanguine*; *aquae infectae sanguine*). Again, the expressions are conventional depictions that appear also in other poems,[234] but this circumstance does not exclude the use of colours in the triumphs. The parades were, after all, pregnant visual spectacles. We know that prisoners and personifications of peoples were dressed in colourful clothes to mark their origins. On the rivers, the dress was less pronounced, and although the mantles draped around their loins could have been made of a separate coloured cloth, other means of colouring must have been used as well.

If we take Ovid's descriptions as reasonable reflections of the processional appearance of the rivers, their hair may at times have been painted blue, the sedge that was shown on the rivers green, and the water that poured from the overthrown urn red. The river sculpture itself could also be visually marked by colour, and we have already seen that Florus writes of a golden statue of the Oceanus. In art, a few reclining river personifications executed in black stone, marble, or basalt have been preserved, most identified as the Nile.[235] In fact,

---

[233] Ovid himself contrasts his position at the Black Sea, where he can see the triumph only as mental images, to the spectators who might enjoy the real sight, *Trist.* 4.2.57–66.

[234] Hor. *Carm.* 2.1.34–6; Prop. 3.3.45; Stat. *Theb.* 12.409–10; [Ov.] *Cons. ad Liv.* 385; Sil. *Pun.* 7.149–50; Min. Fel. 7.4.

[235] Klementa (1993: 223–4). Of six preserved black examples, four represent the Nile and two are unidentified.

Pausanias states that, whereas all other statues of rivers are made of white stone, the Nile is executed in black stone, as it runs through Ethiopian lands.[236] Pliny gives a specific example; he states that Vespasian dedicated a statue of the Nile, made of black basalt, in the Templum Pacis.[237] Although there is no explicit evidence, the Nile was very likely black in triumphs too. By way of such displays, the African origin of the river would have been signalled, even more so if the statue was presented together with other rivers shown in different materials and representing other parts of the world.

Flumina captiva

Rivers led on triumphal parade were no spiritless images, no inanimate localities. Like the subjugated peoples, they were present in person. Hence, although rivers were represented by sculptures, the ancient sources never address or describe the specific streams displayed as works of art. They are plainly *Rhenus* and *Oceanus*. This is not just a poetic phenomenon. Florus too, writing of Caesar's triumphs, uses *simulacrum* only in describing the Pharus, while the Nile is just *Nilus*, appearing together with Arsinoë as the principal captives on display (*Altera laurus Aegyptia: tunc in ferculis Nilus, Arsinoe et ad simulacrum ignium ardens Pharos*).[238]

Shown in person, rivers on triumphal parade were categorized, displayed, and described as living captives, and their treatment does not differ significantly from how human prisoners were paraded. Florus' Oceanus is *captivus*, and Claudian tells of the triumphal display of *captiva flumina*.[239] As captives, the rivers may have borne chains. Depicting Caesar's Gallic triumph, Lucan imagines the Rhine and the Oceanus in chains (*ut vincula Rheno Oceanoque daret*).[240] The *vincula* here have been interpreted as symbols of the bridges that Caesar built across the Rhine.[241] True, the building of bridges is often described as taming the rivers,[242] but in the triumphal procession, it is likely that real chains gave physical form to the taming.

[236] Paus. 8.24.12.

[237] Plin. *Nat.* 36.11.58.

[238] Flor. *Epit.* 2.13.88–9.

[239] In Statius' description of Domitian's equestrian statue, the hoof of the horse tramples on the hair of the Rhine, who is *captivus*: *captivi crinem terit ungula Rheni*, Stat. *Silv.* 1.1.51.

[240] Lucan. 3.76–7.

[241] J. D. Duff in the Loeb Classical Library edn. Vergil in fact mentions a bridge in describing the River Araxes in Octavian's procession on the shield of Aeneas; Araxes is *pontem indignatus* (*Aen.* 8.728). The bridge probably works both as a learned allusion to the one built over the Araxes by Alexander the Great and as a symbol of Araxes' vanquished state as he appeared in the procession. Information such as *pontem indignatus* might have been shown on *tituli* carried before the river representation.

[242] Verg. *Aen.* 8.728; Flor. *Epit.* 1.45.15; Amm. 24.3.9. Kleiner (1991). Bridges as chains were not involved in the case of Oceanus, although symbolically Caesar broke the power and thus fettered the Oceanus by crossing the channel to Britain.

In fact, human captives, demonstrably fettered, were described as carrying *vincula*, as was the personification of Germania discussed above.[243] Also, Claudian describes the Rhine on parade as *catenatus*,[244] a term that is often applied to the human captives, when led chained in the processions.[245]

Ovid's description of the River Rhine runs: *squalidus inmissos fracta sub harundine crines…ploret*, 'Let squalid Rhine lament its locks hanging down long beneath broken reeds'. This strikingly resembles his depiction of one of the prominent prisoners on triumphal parade: *squalida promissis qui tegit ora comis*, 'the one who now conceals his squalid face with his hair, hanging down long'.[246] Ovid uses *squalidus* to describe both the prisoner and the Rhine, an adjective which has the double meaning of 'rough, unkempt' and 'in mourning'. Just like the human captives, rivers expressed subjection and grief. Ovid's Rhine is said to lament its sorry condition (*inmissos…crines, Rhenus et infectas…ploret aquas*),[247] and in Claudian's description, the rivers of Libya went in mourning (*Libyci…lugerent…amnes*).

The rivers led on parade mourn their subjugation and lost powers. After all, rivers were potent natural forces. To bridge or to cross them were considered major enterprises and surrounded by scrupulously performed ritual undertakings.[248] Their display as *captivi* transmitted a clear message that their formerly fierce and unrestrained powers had been tamed and brought under Roman control.[249] Civilization now mastered Nature.[250] Propertius describes the Nile as being *debilis*, powerless, a state envisioned also by the broken horns. Vergil stresses the tamed power of the rivers when he writes that the Euphrates walked in Octavian's triumphal procession with milder waves, *Euphrates ibat iam mollior undis*. Servius comments on the verse: *sentiens quasi se esse superatum*, 'it is almost as if he feels that he has been defeated'.[251]

---

[243] Prisoners: Ov. *Pont.* 2.1.43–4, *Am.* 1.2.30; Germania: *Trist.* 4.2.43–6.

[244] Claud. 24.25.

[245] Hor. *Epod.* 7.8; Val. Max. 6.2.3; Lact. *Inst.* 1.11.2. At other times, the chained prisoners are described as *vincti*.

[246] Ov. *Pont.* 3.4.107–8, *Trist.* 4.2.34.

[247] However, as noted above, the reading *ploret* is far from clear in this passage, see n. 228.

[248] Braund (1996) provides an excellent and concise insight into the various capacities and identities of rivers in the ancient thoughtworld. See also Holland (1961: 8–20). In Plutarch's *Crassus* 19, a number of terrifying portents break out as Crassus and his army cross the Euphrates.

[249] e.g. Sil. *Pun.* 17.641–2.

[250] Cf. Kleiner (1991).

[251] Serv. *ad Aen.* 8.726. Servius compares Vergil's description of the Euphrates to the very similar depiction of the river by Horace, *Carm.* 2.9.21–2: *Medumque flumen gentibus additum | victis minores volvere vertices*, 'the river of the Medes, added to the vanquished nations, rolls in smaller eddies', The similarity in the two poets' descriptions might be explained not only by the mutual influence of the two poets on each other's writings, but could be seen as a result of a common source of inspiration: the triumphs of 29 BC, Nisbet and Hubbard (1978: 137). Here, the information about Euphrates' milder waves might have been inscribed on a *titulus*.

As captives, rivers were carried on *fercula*, as were the most eminent prisoners from time to time.[252] They are sometimes described as walking, a term often applied to prisoners but never to the inanimate spoils.[253] Their location was also among the captives. Here, due to its realistic setting, Ovid's lengthy triumphal description from the *Tristia*, where spectators point out some of the participants as they pass by, is particularly revealing.[254] The account starts off with the prisoners, and then representations of diverse kinds appear. Last of these are the Rhine and Germania, who in their turn precede the triumphator himself and the army. Thus, the Rhine and Germania, the most distinguished captives, appear right in front of the triumphator, the spot traditionally reserved for the most eminent enemy prisoners. Silius Italicus too has the representations of rivers and peoples appear after the prisoners in his description of the triumph of Scipio Africanus.[255]

The appearance, placing, and perception of the prominent rivers in the triumphal processions reveal their status as mighty enemies of Rome. And in fact, numerous passages in Latin literature, poetry and prose, describe rivers as taking active parts in battle. They could act as instigators of wars and rebellions against Rome. In the *Georgics*, Vergil portrays the threats to Rome as coming from two opposite sides of the earth. In the West, Germania, and in the East, the River Euphrates prepares war: *hinc movet Euphrates, illinc Germania bellum*.[256] Battles were also fought against the rivers themselves. Florus justifies Caesar's attack on the Rhine, as it was not right that the river should harbour and protect Rome's enemies.[257] The same author characterizes Caesar's war with the Veneti as a combat against the Oceanus, who himself seemed to take part in the battle.[258] The rivers were forced to retreat, as when the *Laus Caesaris* describes the Oceanus as fleeing before the Emperor Claudius.[259] They were defeated, and they acknowledged their vanquishment. On Caesar's return from Britain, which is interpreted as a campaign against the Oceanus as well as the Britons, Florus states that 'Oceanus himself was calmer and more favourable, as if he admitted to being

---

[252] Prisoners: e.g. Sen. *Dial.* 7.25.4; Sil. *Pun.* 17.629.

[253] Verg. *Aen.* 7.826–8; Prop. 2.1.31–4.

[254] Ov. *Trist.* 4.2.19–56. In the *Ars Amandi* (1.219–28), Ovid describes the rivers before the leading prisoners, and in the *Ex Ponto* (3.4.99–112), he refers to the rivers after the arms, valuables, trophies, cities, but before the captive kings.

[255] Sil. *Pun.* 17.629–46. Silius also describes the personified city of Carthage and the captive mountains at this location. Only an image of Hannibal, the principal enemy, appears between the personifications and the triumphator.

[256] Verg. *Georg.* 1.509, cf. 4.560–1. Clauss (1988). See also Prop. 4.10.39, where the Rhine himself throws Viridomarus and his Gallic warriors over the river to threaten Rome.

[257] Flor. *Epit.* 1.45.9–10: *Nec Rhenus ergo immunis; nec enim fas erat ut liber esset receptator hostium atque defensor*.

[258] Flor. *Epit.* 1.45.5–6.

[259] *Anth. Lat.* 425.3: *Oceanus iam terga dedit*. For the image of the Oceanus as a fighting enemy, cf. the description of the river in Pedo, discussed by Romm (1992: 144).

his [Caesar's] inferior'.[260] And finally, triumphs were celebrated over the rivers. Thus, Ovid anticipates a future Germanic triumph as being held over the Rhine, *alter enim de te, Rhene, triumphus adest*.[261] Rivers might also join the Roman cause. On the well-known introductory scene of Trajan's column, the Danube allows the Roman army to cross its bridge, thereby opening the country of the Dacians to Roman subjection.[262]

Rivers were thus presented as living, forceful enemies in war and as defeated prominent captives in the triumphal processions. But rivers had other capacities as well. Literary texts and inscriptions often describe rivers as old men endowed with profound wisdom and prophetic gifts, distinguishing them as fathers of their countries and as gods.[263] In Roman times, the cult of rivers centred particularly on the Tiber and the Nile, but offerings and altars were erected to other rivers such as the Rhine.[264] Many sculptures of reclining rivers were placed in temples, and shines were built in their honour.[265] However, when rivers were put on triumphal display, the Roman never addressed or described them as gods. They treat them as they treat all defeated human adversaries. We have seen elsewhere in this study that the very idea of a captured god was unthinkable,[266] and one wonders to what degree the divine aspects of the rivers troubled the Romans as they led the Rhine and the Oceanus as chained prisoners in their victory parades. In his article on ancient perceptions of rivers, David Braund writes that 'River deities have multiple identities, for they flow like rivers from one form into another'.[267] When on triumphal parade, the rivers' identities were those of powerful enemies, who had participated in the war and been defeated. They represented their countries, now conquered,

---

[260] Flor. *Epit.* 1.45.18–19: *ipso quoque Oceano tranquillo magis et propitio, quasi inparem ei se fateretur.*

[261] Ov. *Pont.* 3.4.88; cf. Prop 3.4.3: *parat ultima terra triumphos | Thybris, et Euphrates sub tua iura fluet.*

[262] On Trajan's coins too, the Danube (or the Tiber, Ostrowski (1991: 52)) is represented as assisting the Roman cause, *RIC* ii (1926), 283, nos. 556–9, pl. X, 180. In Pliny the Younger's *Panegyricus*, the Rhine and the Euphrates approve of Trajan (*Pan.* 14.1), and the Rhine and the Danube delight at the failures of Domitian (*Pan.* 82.4).

[263] Braund (1996: 44–5). For rivers in Roman culture, see Jones (2005). The Homeric Oceanus is the father of all gods as well as the creator of all other rivers, seas and springs, cf. Verg. *Georg.* 4.382: *pater rerum.* The Rhine is bestowed with the epithet *pater* on an inscribed altar, found in Strasburg, *LIMC* vii (1994), s.v. 'Rhenos, Rhenus', i. 632 (R. Vollkommer), Vollkommer (1994: 2, with further references). Rhenus is *pater* in Mart. 10.7.1, and Propertius calls Viridomarus *genus Rheno* (4.10.41). *Tiberinus* is called *pater* in Liv. 2.10.11. The Nile was at times identified with Osiris, at other described as one of the sons of the Oceanus, at others again as the father of Aegyptus, *LIMC* vi (1992), s.v. 'Neilos', i. 720 (M.-O. Jentel). Divine implications: Varro *Ling.* 5.71; Cic. *Nat. Deor.* 3.52; Plin. *Epist.* 8.8; Tac. *Hist.* 5.17; Plut. *Luc.* 24; Sidon. *Carm.* 7.40–4; Nonn. *Dion.* 43.410.

[264] *CIL* iii. 3416, 5863, 10263, 10395, *CIL* xiii. 5255, 7790–1, 8810–11. Latte (1960: 131–2); Wissowa (1971: 217–19); Ostrowski (1991: 13–14, 41–7); Braund (1996: 44–5).

[265] Plin. *Epist.* 8.8. Klementa (1993: 224–5).

[266] See above, pp. 82–6, 89–90, 219–21.

[267] Braund (1996: 45).

their settings as distant borders, now controlled, and the forceful Nature itself, now mastered. Their divine expressions, on the other hand, were not susceptible to conquest. As gods, the rivers were venerated; as natural forces, they were fought, subjugated, and led in triumph.

WAR SCENES

The Roman triumphal procession exhibited episodes from the victoriously concluded war. For example, Josephus describes how Vespasian and Titus in their Jewish parade staged scenes with slaughtered enemy battalions, Jews led into captivity, cities conquered, sanctuaries set on fire, and devastated landscapes.[268] Most modern studies read the scenes as 'triumphal paintings' celebrating the military achievements of the triumphator, who after the parade placed them in a public setting or a temple. However, it was maintained above that battle paintings put up in the cityscape were not produced for processional display. Here I aim to strengthen the argument that the war scenes performed in triumphs in many aspects differed from the commemorative paintings set up afterwards. The first part of the analysis focuses on the form of the war scenes staged in the parades. How was the war presented and what did the scenes look like? The second part instead focuses on the contents. What were the subject matters and function of the war scenes on triumphal display?

How were the war scenes staged?

Latin writers comment only sparsely on the triumphal display of war scenes, and their testimonies are also very general in character. Ovid was clearly more interested in the prisoners, peoples, and rivers paraded, and he notes only briefly the battles (*proelia*) put on display.[269] Tacitus mentions that the triumph held by Germanicus in AD 17 included representations of battles (*simulacra proeliorum*).[270] Also, Silius Italicus includes a scene showing Hannibal in flight in his version of Scipio Africanus' triumph.[271]

Appian's descriptions of γραφαί
In contrast, several Greek passages give detailed accounts of war episodes staged in Roman triumphs. Most important are Josephus' description of Vespasian and

---

[268] Joseph. *BJ* 7.139–147, quoted below.
[269] Ov. *Pont.* 2.1.37–9, 3.4.25–6.
[270] Tac. *Ann.* 2.41: *Vecta spolia, captivi, simulacra montium fluminum proeliorum*, 'Spoils, prisoners, and representations of mountains, rivers, and battles were carried'.
[271] Sil. *Pun.* 17.643–4.

Titus' Jewish triumph and Appian's account of the triumphs held by Scipio Africanus, Pompey, and Caesar. Appian's use of the word γραφή in these descriptions forms our only explicit evidence that paintings formed part of the scenes:

1. Triumph of Scipio Africanus in 201 BC (App. *Pun.* 66):

πύργοι τε παραφέρονται μιμήματα τῶν εἰλημμένων πόλεων, καὶ γραφαὶ καὶ σχήματα τῶν γεγονότων

Towers were borne along as representations of the captured cities, and γραφαί and σχήματα showing the events.[272]

2. Triumph of Pompey in 61 BC (App. *Mith.*117):

τῶν δὲ οὐκ ἀφικομένων εἰκόνες παρεφέροντο, Τιγράνους καὶ Μιθριδάτου, μαχομένων τε καὶ νικωμένων καὶ φευγόντων. Μιθριδάτου δὲ καὶ ἡ πολιορκία, καὶ ἡ νὺξ ὅτε ἔφευγεν, εἴκαστο, καὶ ἡ σιωπή. ἐπὶ τέλει δὲ ἐδείχθη καὶ ὡς ἀπέθανεν αἵ τε παρθένοι αἱ συναποθανεῖν αὐτῷ ἑλόμεναι παρεζωγράφηντο, καὶ τῶν προαποθανόντων υἱέων καὶ θυγατέρων ἦσαν γραφαί, . . .

There were carried images of those who were not present, of Tigranes and of Mithridates, representing them as fighting, as vanquished, and as fleeing. Even the besieging of Mithridates and his silent flight by night were represented [literally 'the night when he fled and the silence']. Finally it was shown how he died, and the daughters who chose to perish with him were painted beside, and there were paintings of the sons and daughters who died before him, . . . [273]

3. Triumphs of Caesar in 46 BC (App. *BCiv* 2.101):

τὰ δὲ Ῥωμαίων φυλαξάμενος ἄρα, ὡς ἐμφύλια οὐκ ἐοικότα τε αὐτῷ καὶ Ῥωμαίοις αἰσχρὰ καὶ ἀπαίσια, ἐπιγράψαι θριάμβῳ, παρήνεγκεν ὅμως αὐτῶν ἐν τοῖσδε τὰ παθήματα ἅπαντα καὶ τοὺς ἄνδρας ἐν εἰκόσι καὶ ποικίλαις γραφαῖς, χωρίς γε Πομπηίου· τοῦτον γὰρ δὴ μόνον ἐφυλάξατο δεῖξαι, σφόδρα ἔτι πρὸς πάντων ἐπιποθούμενον. ὁ δὲ δῆμος ἐπὶ μὲν τοῖς οἰκείοις κακοῖς, καίπερ δεδιώς, ἔστενε, καὶ μάλιστα, ὅτε ἴδοι Λεύκιόν τε Σκιπίωνα τὸν αὐτοκράτορα πλησσόμενον ἐς τὰ στέρνα ὑφ᾽ ἑαυτοῦ καὶ μεθιέμενον ἐς τὸ πέλαγος, ἢ Πετρήιον ἐπὶ διαίτῃ διαχρώμενον ἑαυτόν, ἢ Κάτωνα ὑφ᾽ ἑαυτοῦ διασπώμενον ὡς θηρίον· Ἀχιλλᾷ δ᾽ ἐφήσθησαν καὶ Ποθεινῷ καὶ τὴν Φαρνάκους φυγὴν ἐγέλασαν.

Although he took care not to inscribe any Roman names in his triumph (as it would have been unseemly in his eyes and base and inauspicious in those of the Roman people to triumph over fellow-citizens), yet all their misfortunes were represented in these processions and the men also by various representations and pictures, all except Pompey, whom alone he did not venture to exhibit, since he was still greatly regretted by all. The people, although restrained by fear, groaned over the domestic ills, especially when they saw L. Scipio, the general-in-chief, wounded in the breast by his own hand, casting himself into the sea, and Petreius killing himself at the banquet, and Cato torn open by himself

---

[272] Zinserling (1959/60: no. 8a, 406–7, 425–8); Mansuelli (1979: 46).
[273] Zinserling (1959/60: no. 17a, 411–12); Hölscher (1980: 354); Holliday (1997: 146).

like a wild beast. They applauded the death of Achillas and Pothinus, and laughed at the flight of Pharnaces.[274]

According to Appian, Scipio Africanus paraded towers as representations of the captured cities and γραφαί and σχήματα of the events. In Pompey's triumph, Appian describes the display of γραφαί showing the sons and daughters of Mithridates, while the daughters who died with him were παρεζωγράφηντο, 'painted beside'. In his account of Caesar's triumphs, finally, Appian states that the 'misfortunes' and the men were shown by way of representations and paintings, ἐν εἰκόσι καὶ ποικίλαις γραφαῖς.

Now, the word γραφή signifies 'painting', but it might also be used of a written text. In fact, Zinserling interprets the γραφαί in Appian's triumphal descriptions as inscriptions.[275] However, a number of circumstances suggest that in the three passages quoted above, Appian uses γραφή in the meaning of 'painting'. Most revealingly, in Caesar's triumphs, Appian on one hand points out that the triumphator refrained from inscribing the names of his Roman adversaries, on the other he maintains that they were instead shown ἐν εἰκόσι καὶ ποικίλαις γραφαῖς. Texts and γραφαί are opposed also in the description of Pompey's parade, as Appian immediately after his account of the representations explicitly mentions the display of an inscription, labelled not γραφή, but πίναξ and διάγραμμα.[276] In the case of Pompey, there is also the fact that Appian uses a form of ζωγραφέω, which is applicable to painting, but not writing.[277] And finally, there is the context itself—inscriptions were used for the display of shorter texts only, not for more detailed descriptions of events.[278]

In this context, another possible interpretation of γραφαί needs to be pointed out. The word is used also for embroidered tapestries, and the adjective ποικίλος, which Appian applies to the γραφαί shown in Caesar's triumphs, is often employed to describe what is embroidered or woven in many colours.[279] In his detailed account of the Jewish triumph performed by Vespasian and Titus (quoted below), Josephus writes that the stages upon which the war scenes were shown were 'enveloped in tapestries interwoven with gold'.[280] These tapestries might have been purely decorative, but it cannot be excluded that they showed scenes from the war as well.[281]

---

[274] Zinserling (1959/60: no. 18a, 412–13); Holliday (1997: 145–6).

[275] Zinserling (1959/60: 426), who reads the καὶ γραφαὶ καὶ σχήματα τῶν γεγονότων in the account of Scipio's triumph as 'texts and paintings representing the events'.

[276] App. *Mith.* 117.

[277] LSJ, s.v. 'ζωγραφέω'.

[278] See Östenberg (forthcoming).

[279] LSJ, s.v. 'ποικίλος'.

[280] Joseph. *BJ* 7.141.

[281] Woven curtains were used on the Roman stage. The so-called *aulaeum*, a drop curtain, had interwoven figures that became fully visible when the curtain was raised after the show (Verg. *Georg.* 3.24–5).

Woven tapestries might have been used for the war scenes, and paintings were certainly employed. Besides Appian's γραφαί, a passage in Pliny the Elder reveals that in the first half of the second century BC, Greek painters were brought to Rome specifically to adorn the triumphal processions. In the thirty-fifth book of the *Naturalis Historia*, dealing with painting, Pliny writes that Aemilius Paullus, having defeated Perseus, asked the Athenians to send him their most learned philosopher to educate his children and a painter to adorn his triumph, *pictor ad triumphum excolendum*.[282] To meet these two demands, the Athenians chose one person only, Metrodorus, as he was skilled in both arts.

'Triumphal paintings' revisited

How, then, are we to envisage the appearance of these painted (and possibly woven) representations? In modern scholarship, they are often assumed to have been painted on panels, *tabulae*.[283] The idea is based on the fact that several Latin authors describe how victorious Roman generals produced painted *tabulae* representing battle scenes to commemorate their martial acts. In the triumph, it is argued, a sequence of events was shown in one and the same painting, or the diverse episodes were displayed by way of a series of paintings.[284] However, as shown above,[285] Latin writers never employ the term *tabula* to account for a representation made for triumphal display. Instead, the paintings that were (depicted on) *tabulae* were produced specifically for exhibition in a public place or a temple.

Unlike paintings fixed in one place, any processional exhibition of painted scenes would have involved major difficulties as regards visibility and practicability. While three-dimensional models and personifications could easily have been produced in lighter materials in considerable sizes and perceived by spectators from all distances and angles, the contents of two-dimensional paintings would not easily have been discernible for a crowd of thousands of spectators. In order to render the details of such paintings visible from large distances, the paintings would have had to be of huge dimensions.[286] At the same time, huge paintings

---

[282] Plin. *Nat.* 35.40.135. Pliny does not state explicitly that Metrodorus was employed to produce paintings for the triumph. Rather, he was asked to adorn it (*ad triumphum excolendum*), a task that perhaps made use of his capacities both as an artist and as a philosopher.

[283] Holliday (1980: 5; 1997: 134; 2002: 80, cf. 87).

[284] Zinserling (1959/60: 428); Vessberg (1941: 39). Holliday (1997: 145) believes that there was a development from depictions in one painting to series of paintings. Mansuelli (1979) goes deeply into the discussion of how the narratives of the paintings were depicted in one single painting and in a sequence of paintings respectively.

[285] See above, pp. 82, 194–9.

[286] Several scholars interpret the *tituli* seen for instance on one of the larger panels and on the smaller frieze of the arch of Titus as 'triumphal paintings', Vessberg (1952: 131); Ryberg (1955: 147); Mansuelli (1979: 49). In view of the small dimensions of these *tituli*, clearly intended for shorter written labels, this assumption must be dismissed.

would have offered serious problems concerning their processional transportation.[287] Also in contrast to three-dimensional models and personifications, two-dimensional paintings would only have been readable from the front, a major disadvantage when it comes to a processional display.

With these considerations in mind, it becomes even more obvious why the type of paintings commissioned by Messala, Scipio Asiaticus, Tiberius Gracchus, and Hostilius Mancinus (all discussed above) were not intended for processional display.

This is especially evident in the two latter cases, where the texts explicitly describe a multitude of events all depicted in one and the same painting. The contents and meaning of such multi-scened paintings would simply not have been comprehensible in a processional context. They demanded an audience which was able to reflect on the details of the works, not just get a quick glimpse of them passing by in a parade. In fact, the scenes of these paintings were not even always easily grasped when viewed at close range. This is clearly illustrated by the case of the painting commissioned by Hostilius Mancinus, which, exposed in the Forum, showed a plan of the city of Carthage and the battles fought there.[288] Hostilius himself, Pliny states, was present in the Forum and helped the people to understand the painting by describing the single events depicted on it one by one.[289] If these kinds of paintings needed specific explanations even when viewed under such favourable circumstances, one can easily imagine how fruitless it would have been to display them in a procession, where spectators could hardly discern their details.

Instead of representations that showed a multitude of events in one and the same painting, we must therefore imagine diverse scenes shown separately from each other. In fact, this is how the war scenes appear in Josephus' detailed description of Vespasian and Titus' Jewish triumph of AD 71 (*BJ* 7.139–47), an account that deserves to be quoted in its entirety:

θαῦμα δ' ἐν τοῖς μάλιστα παρεῖχεν ἡ τῶν φερομένων πηγμάτων κατασκευή· καὶ γὰρ διὰ μέγεθος ἦν δεῖσαι τῷ βεβαίῳ τῆς φορᾶς ἀπιστήσαντα, τριώροφα γὰρ αὐτῶν πολλὰ καὶ τετρώροφα πεποίητο, καὶ τῇ πολυτελείᾳ τῇ περὶ τὴν κατασκευὴν ἦν ἡσθῆναι μετ' ἐκπλήξεως. καὶ γὰρ ὑφάσματα πολλοῖς διάχρυσα περιβέβλητο, καὶ χρυσὸς καὶ ἐλέφας οὐκ ἀποίητος, πᾶσι περιεπεπήγει, διὰ πολλῶν δὲ μιμημάτων ὁ πόλεμος ἄλλος εἰς ἄλλα μεμερισμένος ἐναργεστάτην ὄψιν αὐτοῦ παρεῖχεν· ἦν γὰρ ὁρᾶν χώραν μὲν εὐδαίμονα δῃουμένην, ὅλας δὲ φάλαγγας κτεινομένας πολεμίων, καὶ τοὺς μὲν φεύγοντας τοὺς δ' εἰς αἰχμαλωσίαν ἀγομένους, τείχη δ' ὑπερβάλλοντα μεγέθει μηχαναῖς ἐρειπόμενα καὶ φρουρίων ἁλισκομένας ὀχυρότητας καὶ πόλεων πολυανθρώπους περιβόλους κατ' ἄκρας ἐχομένους, καὶ στρατιὰν ἔνδον τειχῶν

---

[287] Mansuelli (1979: 49) touches on the practical issues involved in displaying paintings. He is sceptical to whether all 'triumphal paintings' were carried in the parades.

[288] Plin. *Nat.* 35.7.22–3.

[289] Plin. *Nat.* 35.7.22–3: *et ipse adsistens populo spectanti singula enarrando,* ...

εἰσχεομένην, καὶ πάντα φόνου πλήθοντα τόπον, καὶ τῶν ἀδυνάτων χεῖρας ἀνταίρειν ἱκεσίας, πῦρ
τε ἐνιέμενον ἱεροῖς καὶ κατασκαφὰς οἴκων ἐπὶ τοῖς δεσπόταις, καὶ μετὰ πολλὴν ἐρημίαν καὶ
κατήφειαν ποταμοὺς ῥέοντας οὐκ ἐπὶ γῆν γεωργουμένην, οὐδὲ ποτὸν ἀνθρώποις ἢ βοσκήμασιν
ἀλλὰ διὰ τῆς ἔτι πανταχόθεν φλεγομένης· ταῦτα γὰρ Ἰουδαῖοι πεισομένους αὑτοὺς τῷ πολέμῳ
παρέδοσαν. ἡ τέχνη δὲ καὶ τῶν κατασκευασμάτων ἡ μεγαλουργία τοῖς οὐκ ἰδοῦσι γινόμενα τότ᾽
ἐδείκνυεν ὡς παροῦσι. τέτακτο δ᾽ ἐφ᾽ ἑκάστῳ τῶν πηγμάτων ὁ τῆς ἁλισκομένης πόλεως
στρατηγὸς ὃν τρόπον ἐλήφθη, ...

But nothing in the procession excited so much astonishment as the structure of stages that
was carried by; indeed their massiveness afforded ground for alarm and misgiving as to
their stability, many of them being three or four stories high, while the magnificence of
the building was a source of delight and amazement. For many of the stages were
enveloped in tapestries interwoven with gold, and all had a framework of gold and
wrought ivory. The war was shown by numerous representations, in separate sections,
affording a very clear and vivid picture of its episodes. Here was to be seen a prosperous
country devastated, there whole battalions of the enemy slaughtered; here a party in
flight, there others led into captivity; walls of surpassing compass demolished by engines,
strong fortresses overpowered, cities with well-manned defences completely mastered
and an army pouring within the ramparts, an area all deluged with blood, the hands of
those incapable of resistance raised in supplication, sanctuaries set on fire, houses pulled
down over their owners' heads, and, after general desolation and woe, rivers flowing, not
over a cultivated land, nor supplying drink to man and beast, but across a country still on
every side in flames. For to such sufferings were the Jews destined when they plunged into
war; and the art and magnificent workmanship of these structures now portrayed the
incidents to those who had not witnessed them, as though they were happening before
their eyes. On each of the stages was stationed the general of one of the captured cities in
the attitude in which he was taken.

Josephus confirms the use of multiple scenes by stating: διὰ πολλῶν δὲ
μιμημάτων ὁ πόλεμος ἄλλος εἰς ἄλλα μεμερισμένος, 'the war was shown by
numerous representations, in separate sections'. After this follow his accounts of
each of the individual events staged in the procession: 'Here was to be seen a
prosperous country devastated, there whole battalions of the enemy slaughtered;
here a party in flight, there others led into captivity...' Separate scenes, thus, each
telling of one event, that could easily be seen and comprehended by the spectators.

In his description, Josephus emphasizes the visual impact of the representations. Thus, 'the art and magnificent workmanship of these structures now
portrayed the incidents to those who had not witnessed them, as though they
were happening before their eyes'. They also afforded 'a very clear and vivid
picture (ἐναργεστάτην ὄψιν) of its [the war's] episodes'. Similarly, Appian, quoted
above, writes that the representations shown in Caesar's triumphs caused groan-
ing, applause, and laughter.[290] In exile, Ovid laments the fact that he has not been

---

[290] App. *BCiv.* 2.101.

able to view the battle scenes put on parade in Rome, which would have inspired his poetry[291] Silius Italicus also attests to the superiority of the war scene on parade in catching the sight and evoking the emotions of the spectators: *sed non ulla magis mentesque oculosque tenebat, | quam visa Hannibalis campis fugientis imago*, 'but no sight attracted the eyes and minds of the peoples more than the image of Hannibal in flight over the plains'.[292]

Polybius too stresses the vivacity of the triumphal displays. He writes that in the Roman triumph, the generals bring the spectacle of the achievements (ἡ τῶν κατειργασμένων πραγμάτων ἐνάργεια) before the eyes (ὑπὸ τὴν ὄψιν) of the citizens.[293] Here, the word ἐνάργεια is crucial, as it stresses the vivacity of a performance, emphasizing that it makes something so alive that it seems to take place clearly before your eyes.[294] Josephus uses a similar vocabulary (ἐναργεστάτην ὄψιν) when he describes the vividness of the sight offered by the war scenes.

Would paintings alone, seen from quite a distance, have been able to generate such strong emotions in a people who were constantly exposed to a rich canvas of spectacles that emphasized powerful visual effects, like bloody gladiator fights, dramatic horse races, and executions staged as mythical scenes? I believe not. This is not to say that the art of painting could not provoke strong feelings or that paintings were not used in the triumphal procession. The point is that paintings needed close readings and were therefore alone not suited to the role of transmitting strong visual effects in the specific situation of a parade.

Tableaux: multimedial stagings

To reconstruct the appearance of the war scenes, Appian's accounts of the triumphs of Scipio Africanus, Pompey, and Caesar, all quoted above, are crucial. Reading the passages closely, one notices that Appian never uses the term γραφαί on its own, but always combines it with another term that implies the involvement of a second art form. In Scipio Africanus' triumph, Appian writes that there were both γραφαί and σχήματα representing the events, καὶ γραφαὶ καὶ σχήματα τῶν γεγονότων. In Caesar's processions, he maintains that the events and the men were shown by way of representations and paintings, ἐν εἰκόσι καὶ ποικίλαις γραφαῖς. And finally, in the triumph held by Pompey, Appian mentions both εἰκόνες representing Mithridates and Tigranes and γραφαί showing the sons and daughters of Mithridates.

---

[291] Ov. *Pont.* 3.4.25–6: *nutrissent carmen proeliaque ipsa meum*.

[292] Sil. *Pun.* 17.643–4.

[293] Polyb. 6.15.8.

[294] On ἐνάργεια, see e.g. Zinserling (1959/60: 414).

If γραφαί in Appian's descriptions refer to paintings (or possibly woven tapest-ries), what are the meanings of the accompanying σχήματα and εἰκόνες? The term εἰκών could refer to any kind of artistic representation, and in the processional context, it is applied to both sculptures and models. Dio Cassius uses the term for the personified peoples in Pertinax' funeral parade.[295] In another passage, he takes εἰκόνες to be the city models that Caesar and his commanders showed in 45 BC.[296] Zonaras too uses εἰκόνες to describe the general display of cities, mountains, rivers, and lakes in Roman triumphs.[297]

Appian's εἰκόνες could be taken as a general term for a variety of artistic forms used to represent people and events. They might also be sculptures, represented in simple postures. However, the word εἰκών, like its Latin equivalents *simulac-rum* and *imago*, has further implications. The term could signify a 'semblance' in general, a 'similitude', 'phantom', or a 'living image'.[298] For example, both Polybius and Herodian use εἰκόνες to describe the images of actors wearing wax masks and representing the deceased at Roman funerals.[299] Should perhaps the εἰκόνες shown together with paintings in Appian's accounts be interpreted as human actors?

To discuss this possibility, we need to look closer at σχήματα, which is the other term used in combination with γραφαί in Appian's triumphal descriptions. According to Appian, there were in the triumph of Scipio Africanus besides towers representing captured cities 'γραφαί and σχήματα showing the events' (καὶ γραφαὶ καὶ σχήματα τῶν γεγονότων). Now, if the γραφαί were paintings, what were the σχήματα shown together with them?[300] The basic meaning of σχῆμα is 'form, shape, figure'. In the plural sense, it often, like its Latin equivalent *gestus*, denotes 'gestures' or 'postures' of athletes, orators, dancers, and actors.[301] When Appian later in his book on the Punic Wars describes the sentiments at the time of the final fall of Carthage in 146 BC, he writes that the Romans were up all night and remembered together the long wars with the Carthaginians. The people recalled events from the war by way of spoken words and also by gestures (σχήματα) performed by the body.[302] Furthermore, in the description of Scipio Africanus' triumph itself, Appian uses a form of the verb σχηματίζω to describe

---

[295] Dio Cass. 75.4.5 (apud Xiph.), cf. Dio Cass. 56.34.3.

[296] Dio Cass. 43.42.2.

[297] Zonar. 7.21.10.

[298] LSJ, s.v. 'εἰκών'.

[299] Polyb. 6.53; Hdn. 4.2.10. Both the masks themselves and the actors carrying them are εἰκόνες. For the masks used at the funeral display of ancestors, see esp. Flower (1996).

[300] In translations, commentaries, and other modern works, γραφαί and σχήματα are often read together as 'pictures (of the events)', e.g. Mansuelli (1979: 46). Others read the γραφαί as inscriptions and the σχήματα as 'triumphal paintings', Zinserling (1959/60: 412, 426), cf. Hölscher (1980a: 352–3).

[301] LSJ, s.v. 'σχῆμα'; *EAA* vii (1966), 'schemata', 96–107 (A. Giuliano). Appian not infrequently uses the term to denote a person in disguise, dressed up as someone else, *BCiv.* 4.13, 4.35, 4.45, 4.47.

[302] App. *Pun.* 134: literally, 'they matched the appearances of the words to the gesture of the body', . . . καὶ ἐς φαντασίας τῶν λεγομένων τῷ σχήματι τοῦ σώματος συνεφέροντο.

the gestures of one of the dancers in the processions, performing an act in imitation of the triumphator.[303]

Thus, the interpretation of σχήματα as 'gestures' is close at hand also in Appian's καὶ γραφαὶ καὶ σχήματα τῶν γεγονότων. The reasonable interpretation of this passage would then be to imagine painted backgrounds picturing the settings of the scenes (γραφαί) against which simple dramatic postures or movements showing the events were carried out (σχήματα). Triumphal war episodes would hence have been staged not unlike theatrical scenes with dramatic acting taking place in front of painted background settings.[304]

Appian's account of Scipio's procession is very much a general depiction of the typical Roman triumph and, if the above interpretation is correct, paintings and gestures showing episodes from the war were probably regular features of the victory pageants. Also, Appian's εἰκόνες in Pompey and Caesar's triumphs seem similar to the σχήματα in Scipio's parade. Possibly, in Caesar's triumphs, the suicides of Scipio, Petreius, and Cato, the deaths of Achillas and Pothinus, and the flight of Pharnaces were shown by way of 'gestures' and the backgrounds (such as the sea into which Scipio threw himself and the banquet where Petreius committed suicide) by way of paintings. Similarly, in the triumph of Pompey, the εἰκόνες that represented Mithridates and Tigranes as fighting, vanquished, and fleeing were probably human actors, who performed simple movements against painted settings. These included, among others, the paintings (γραφαί) of the sons and daughters who had died before Mithridates as well as the daughters who died with him and who were 'painted beside'.

In fact, Appian's 'gestures' have close parallels in Josephus' account of the Jewish triumph performed by Vespasian and Titus (quoted above). Josephus describes war scenes, which were set on high structures of πήγματα. The word πῆγμα, transliterated into Latin as *pegma*, could mean anything fastened together, but was mostly used to denote either a bookcase or a movable platform or scaffold used in the theatre.[305] Josephus' choice of the term suggests that the war scenes were shown not primarily as paintings, for which a structure with numerous platforms would have been superfluous.[306] Instead, the function of these platforms must have been to house some forms of representation that needed a floor, such as sculptures, models, or actors. And, in fact, concluding

---

[303] App. *Pun.* 66: τούτων δέ τις ἐν μέσῳ, πορφύραν ποδήρη περικείμενος καὶ ψέλια καὶ στρεπτὰ ἀπὸ χρυσοῦ, σχηματίζεται ποικίλως ἐς γέλωτα ὡς ἐπορχούμενος τοῖς πολεμίοις, 'One of these [dancers], in the middle of the procession, wearing a purple cloak reaching to his feet and golden bracelets and necklace, caused laughter by making various gesticulations, as though he was dancing in triumph over the enemy.'

[304] Valerius Maximus (2.4.6) and Pliny (*Nat.* 35.7.23) date the introduction of painted scenery on the Roman stage to 99 BC, but such sceneries might well have been in use considerably earlier, Beacham (1991: 65, 67).

[305] LSJ, s.v. 'πῆγμα'; *OLD*, s.v. 'pegma', with further references; Beacham (1991: 180–1).

[306] *Contra* Holliday (1997: 134 and n. 43), who maintains that the πήγματα showed cloth paintings.

his description (7.147), Josephus explicitly states that, on each of the πήγματα, the general of one of the captured cities was placed, in the very posture in which he had been taken. These postures (τρόποι) of the captive generals correspond to the gestures, σχήματα, described by Appian. Perhaps, there is some difference in nuances, as τρόποι are more static poses, while σχήματα imply simple movements. In oratory too, the *gestus* included both posture and gesticulation.[307] We do not know who performed Appian's gestures, but in the Jewish triumph, Josephus is explicit. The prisoners themselves were forced to perform their own roles as defeated enemies.

Josephus uses very general terms to describe the scenes staged on the πήγματα. Besides the τρόποι performed by the prisoners, he maintains that the war was shown by numerous representations, διὰ πολλῶν δὲ μιμημάτων. The word μίμημα is basically equivalent to the Latin *imitatio* and generally means 'anything imitated'.[308] The term has strong connections with the field of (mimic) drama and words like μιμητής, which could imply an actor who impersonates a character.[309] The phrase διὰ πολλῶν δὲ μιμημάτων might refer to some kind of acting,[310] but most likely Josephus intends a broader spectrum of representations as well. Later in the passage, he uses the word τέχνη to describe the marvellous art of the structure, a word, which is mostly applied to the skill in metalwork and other handicraft.[311] Other artistic forms were employed too. Draped around the structures were rich tapestries, and the background settings were also very probably shown in painting. Models of diverse types, representing cities and buildings, might have been placed on the platforms, as cities being vanquished also form a recurrent theme.[312]

Josephus' πήγματα were in all probability multimedial stagings. To get an impression of what the scenes might have looked like, we might consult a painting in the Naples Museum, which shows a large roofed *ferculum* carried in procession (Fig. 26).[313] The scene is not triumphal, but shows a procession organized by a guild of carpenters. In this context, the interesting aspect concerns

[307] Quint. *Inst.* 11.3.65–88. Graf (1991: 37–8).

[308] LSJ, s.v. 'μίμημα'.

[309] Diodorus Siculus uses the term to describe the actor who played the part of the deceased in funeral processions, by wearing his mask, 31.25.2. Similarly, Suetonius labels the actor *archimimus*, Suet. *Vesp.* 19.2. μίμημα is also related to μιμνήσκων and μιμνήσκομαι, 'to remember', 'to call to mind', which could be done through the means of historical writing, or, as here, of art and drama.

[310] No ancient account gives evidence of the employment of professional actors in the triumphal processions. However, the *Historia Augusta*, describing the procession at the *decennalia* celebration of Gallienus in AD 262/3, accounts for the presence of *carpenta cum mimis et omni genere histrionum*, 'carts with mimes and actors of all kinds', S.H.A. *Gall.* 8.3. Merten (1968: 79–84).

[311] Joseph. *BJ* 7.146. LSJ, s.v. 'τέχνη'.

[312] Perhaps, these cities were shown by way of models of the type depicted by Ovid (*Pont.* 2.1.37–9), represented with razed walls and executed in expensive materials.

[313] Abaecherli (1935/36: 2, pl. I.3).

FIGURE 26 Painting from Pompeii that shows a staged tableau carried on a bier in a procession. The scene includes people involved in forms of tree-work, and the *ferculum* has been read as the float of a guild of carpenters. We should imagine similar arrangements in the triumph, with events from the war performed by acting, sculptures, models, and paintings, all on the same scene.

the diversity of media used on a platform carried in parade, including both statues (or gestures) and some acting. Certainly, in the triumphs, there would have been enough room on *fercula* and πήγματα to allow for a multitude of artistic performances.

The triumphal war scenes were characterized by a pronounced vivacity, which showed the events of the war to the spectators as if actually taking place before their very eyes. When used in the theatres, πήγματα were movable, could open and close, raise and lower scenes and actors.[314] Perhaps, these mechanical abilities were exploited in the procession as well, turning the stages in order to face the spectators in all directions. The war scenes were probably performed all along the triumphal route. We know that the procession passed through the theatres and the circuses,[315] and the parade probably halted along the way, in order to give a more advanced performance in the places where a larger number of spectators could easily view such stagings.

[314] Sen. *Epist.* 88.22: *pegmata per se surgentia* . . . Beacham (1991: 180–1).
[315] Plut. *Aem.* 32.2; Joseph. *BJ* 7.131.

We know of other types of dramas in Rome where war scenes were staged. In Republican times, there were dramatic plays called *fabulae praetextae*.[316] Very little evidence of the genre has survived, but the titles and preserved lines reveal that they were concerned with episodes from Roman history, not least with the wartime accomplishments of influential generals. For example, we know of a play named *Clastidium*, which Naevius wrote for M. Claudius Marcellus, and an *Ambracia* created by Ennius for M. Fulvius Nobilior.[317] Plays with similar content were still shown in Julio-Claudian times. This is evident from Horace's description of a theatrical play with battle scenes followed by a triumphal procession and games,[318] and from Suetonius' account of battle scenes that the Emperor Claudius staged in the Campus Martius.[319] Here, the storming and plundering of a town as well as the surrender of the kings of Britain were staged as if the war had been real (*ad imaginem bellicam*). Clearly, the scenes staged in the triumphs formed part of an established Roman tradition of recalling the events of war by way of drama.[320]

What did the war scenes show?

In the procession organized by Antiochus IV at Daphne outside of Antioch in 166 BC,[321] Polybius (preserved in Athenaeus) accounts for the display of statues of all the gods and heroes, which were accompanied by representations of their principal myths. These were shown through stories (κατὰ ἱστορίας) told ἐν διασκευαῖς πολυτελέσι, again a wording with a multitude of possible meanings.[322] The word διασκευή appears elsewhere in Greek literature in the meaning of 'theatrical performance'.[323] The passage has a striking parallel in Ptolemy Philadelphus' Alexandrine procession, where, according to Callixenus, the gods were shown accompanied by their appropriate διασκευή, which told the story (ἱστορία) of each of them.[324]

---

[316] For modern scholarship on the *praetextae*, see Flower (1995: 170 n. 1).

[317] There has been much debate about what occasions were used for performances of the *praetextae*. The proposals include: the triumphs themselves, the games held after the triumphs, the games held when the temples vowed during the war were inaugurated, and the funeral of the general. Flower (1995) argues for the dedications of temples as the only plausible occasions. Her idea has met with some acceptance. For the setting of these performances, see also O'Neill (2004).

[318] Hor. *Epist.* 2.1.189–98.

[319] Suet. *Claud.* 21.6: *edidit et in Martio campo expugnationem direptionemque oppidi ad imaginem bellicam et deditionem Britanniae regum praeseditque paludatus.*

[320] In 1994, T. P. Wiseman proposed a vivid and influential Republican dramatic tradition (*praetextae*), which played an important role in creating and shaping the Roman concept of its own history. Wiseman later developed his ideas in *Roman Drama and Roman History* (1998).

[321] For the celebration at Daphne, see Bunge (1976); Edmondson (1999: 84–9).

[322] Polyb. 30.25.13–15 (apud Ath. 5.195a–b).

[323] Dio Chrys. (32.93–4) writes of stage plays performed ἐν ταῖς κωμῳδίαις καὶ διασκευαῖς. The term διασκευή could also mean equipment, elaboration, or construction (cf. κατασκευή in Joseph. *BJ* 7.139).

[324] Ath. 5.197d.

As in the Hellenistic East, the *pompae circenses* in Rome included a parade of the gods, who were accompanied by their attributes and 'stories'. Dionysius of Halicarnassus tells of how the images of the gods were carried together with their σκευαί and their σύμβολα.[325] The gods themselves seem mostly to have been represented by way of statues, but the use of acting—probably to represent 'stories'—is attested as well. The *Liber Prodigiorum* states that a boy fell from the processional *ferculum* as he was playing the role of Victoria.[326]

Thus, in the Hellenistic East as well as in Rome, gods on parade were accompanied by representations of their myths and stories. Turning our attention again to the triumph, a passage in Pliny the Younger reveals a very similar practice. Pliny (*Pan.* 17.1–2) imagines a future triumph of the Emperor Trajan, describing how the prisoners followed illustrations of their own exploits in the war:

videor ingentia ducum nomina nec indecora nominibus corpora noscitare; videor intueri immanibus ausis barbarorum onusta fercula et sua quemque facta vinctis manibus sequentem, ...

I seem to recognize the high-sounding names of chieftains whose persons are not unworthy of such names, to behold the biers loaded with the savage, daring attempts of the barbarians, and each prisoner, hands bound, following his own deeds, ...

The fettered prisoners are most certainly identical to the chieftains, whose names Pliny recognizes. Also, without doubt, the deeds, *facta*, preceding each prisoner correspond to the attempts, the *immanes ausi* mentioned before. This signifies that Pliny, in order, imagines the display of the names of the prisoners, the biers showing their deeds, and finally the prisoners themselves. Hence, each prominent prisoner was preceded both by a placard announcing his name and by some kind of representations of his exploits in war. As in the parades discussed above, the principal participants of the Roman triumphal procession were thus shown together with representations and explanations of their 'stories'.

The observation encourages us to consider the function of the triumphal war scenes in general. From the literary descriptions, it seems that the aim of the tableaux was not primarily to provide a complete display of every event that had taken place during the war. More surprisingly, and contrary to a common assumption,[327] the war scenes are not described as depicting the martial deeds of the triumphator, showing him in victorious engagements on the battlefield. In fact, no sources describe the scenes as performing the whereabouts and doings of

[325] Dion. Hal. 7.72.13. Other sources tell that the gods were carried on *fercula* and their attributes (*exuviae*) on *tensae*, Suet. *Iul.* 76; Fest. p. 500 L, s.v. 'tensam'. Abaecherli (1935/6).

[326] Obseq. 70 [130]: *Puer in pompa Victoriae cultu cum ferretur, ferculo decidit.* Abaecherli (1935/6), 3.

[327] See e.g. Flower (1996: 215); Holliday (1997: 134): 'The main purpose of triumphal paintings was to advance the personal prestige of the *triumphator* by documenting those achievements that had led to his triumphal celebration.'

the Roman army, whether on the march, in their camps, or even in battle. This is important, since in this respect the subject matters of the scenes shown on parade differ from the ones depicted on the column of Trajan, for which these 'triumphal paintings' are generally believed to constitute the forerunners.[328] On the column's reliefs, we find the Roman army and its leader, the emperor, engaged not only in battle—battle scenes make up only about one quarter of the space—but above all in preparing and closing battle. The Roman army and the emperor appear on the majority of the scenes. The army is shown on the march, building roads and camps, and in battle; the emperor is sacrificing to the gods, addressing the army, and supervising the battles.

In contrast, the war scenes staged in triumphs seem to have focused exclusively on the enemies of Rome, their bellicose acts, military subjection, and subsequent fates. A particular emphasis is put on the disastrous consequences of the war for the conquered. Thus, the tableaux described by Josephus focus on the devastation of the Jewish land, cities and country alike, and the general message of the scenes shown by Vespasian and Titus is clearly expressed in Josephus' concluding remark: 'For to such sufferings were the Jews destined when they plunged into war.'[329]

The sources also imply that the war scenes specifically emphasized the deeds and fates of the principal vanquished adversaries, whether shown alive or represented in their absence. Such a practice is suggested by Pliny the Younger's triumphal description, quoted above, where the leading prisoners (*duces*) followed representations of their own deeds. More important are Appian's accounts of the triumphs of Pompey and Caesar. In Caesar's triumphs, all the scenes centred on the misfortunes of the principal enemies, foreign and domestic. The representations showed Scipio, Petreius, Cato, Achillas, Pothinus, and Pharnaces as they fled, were killed, or committed suicide. According to Appian, Caesar considered it too blunt to expose the names of his fellow Romans in the procession. Still, he did not refrain from showing what obviously formed an essential part of the contents of a Roman triumph—the vanquished principal enemies and their 'stories'. Similarly, in Appian's description of Pompey's triumph, all the scenes focused on Mithridates and Tigranes. The overcoming of these two principal adversaries was staged in sequence, showing them in combat, vanquished, and fleeing. These scenes were followed by the death of Mithridates and by the fates of his relatives.

I have noted the similarity in terms used in the descriptions of the triumphal and funeral representations. Here, further affinities become clear. The mimic

---

[328] Felletti Maj (1977: 59); Settis (1988: 94–8, 232–4); Kleiner (1992: 215, cf. pp. 47–8).
[329] Joseph. *BJ* 7.145–6.

actor, who personified the deceased at the funeral, focused on one man's deeds, his acts, his speech, and his movements.[330] According to Polybius, the spectators, who watched the performance, recalled the facts of the life of the departed as they were brought before their eyes (ὑπὸ τὴν ὄψιν). The dramatic scenes elicited strong sympathies from the public. In the triumphs too, the staged scenes centred on the deeds of a few men; attitudes or movements were employed and the tableaux caused emotional reactions. There might have been further parallels too. We saw above that prisoners and dressed-up captives were asked to speak as part of the performance, and actors employed to represent captives in the tableaux might well have imitated speeches as well. In fact, gestures and voice formed the cornerstones of a Roman oratorical performance,[331] which like these scenes aimed at emotional reactions in the audience. It cannot be excluded that, similar to the practice of having mimic actors study the movements and speech of famous Romans during their lifetime, certain actors were employed to learn to imitate Rome's principal adversaries with the specific aim of performing their roles at the triumph.

The interpretation of the war scenes as 'attachments' to the principal enemies at first seems out of place in Josephus' description of the battle scenes shown on the πήγματα in the Jewish triumph (quoted above). Instead, these scenes showed a variety of events, such as soldiers led into captivity, temples on fire, houses torn down, and devastated landscapes. Except for Josephus' emphasis on the general disastrous fate of the rebellious Jews, no immediate or at least only very vague thematic and chronological threads are apparent. But then, Josephus concludes the account with a statement that, on each stage, a general from one of the conquered cities was placed in the very attitude in which he had been taken. In this, he provides us with the single common subject matter of the scenes. Clearly, these captive generals cannot have been displayed detached from the rest of the scenes, but they must have formed integral parts of the visual contents of the πήγματα. In fact, being the one recurrent element of the πήγματα, the captive generals in all probability formed the very objects of the scenes.

We saw above that the triumphal accounts of Pliny the Younger and Appian suggest that the war scenes: (*a*) focused on the principal enemies, (*b*) demonstrated their exploits in the war, and (*c*) showed their final fates. Applying the same model to Josephus' account of the Jewish triumph, the principal enemies (*a*) should be identified with the generals of the captured cities, who were placed on the πήγματα. Their fates (*c*) were made visible by their very presence and by their staged appearance in the poses in which they had been captured. Following the scheme, the scenes staged on each of the single platforms most likely focused

---

[330] Polyb. 6.53; Diod. Sic. 31.25.2; Hdn. 4.2.10; Suet. *Vesp.* 19.2. Sumi (2002).
[331] Quint. *Inst.* 11.3.65–88. Graf (1999).

on the former exploits (*b*) of the general displayed on that very πῆγμα. Thus, the captured generals were not put on the stages as ornaments to the rest of the scene, but the performance of the stages focused on the generals and was composed as to tell their 'stories'.³³²

To sum up, the aim of the staged war scenes was not to retell the detailed martial achievements of the Roman army and its triumphant general. The *res gestae* of the triumphator were instead told in many other ways, not the least in the *fabulae praetextae* and in the *tabulae*, written and painted, put up after the triumph in temples and public places. In the Republican triumphal procession, the deeds of the triumphator appeared in the dances performed by the Lydi and above all in the songs sung by the army following the triumphator in the parade.³³³ Interestingly, both these types included strong elements of apotropaic irony and laughter. It seems that the deeds of the triumphator were not to be boasted about in the ritual context of the procession.³³⁴

The dramatic tableaux were instead intimately attached above all to the principal prisoners. In function, the scenes had affinities with the written *tituli*, which accompanied prisoners, spoils, and representations, identifying them by spelling out their names and at times describing the reasons for their presence. But while the *tituli* were restricted in space and could show but shorter names and messages, the staged war scenes offered unlimited means of spectacular and detailed display. Polybius, Appian, Josephus, Ovid, and Silius Italicus all emphasize the vivacity of the scenes and the strong emotions they triggered. Through these representations, the spectators of the triumphal procession were able to experience the war as if it took place right before their very eyes. They saw, they wept, they laughed, they applauded. Very probably, the mimic acting included both body movements and speech, imitating closely the defeated enemies of Rome.

Crime and punishment were two main components in the triumphal display of captured enemies, and the war scenes attached to the prisoners also focused on these two aspects. By staging the misdeeds performed by the principal enemies in war, the scenes identified and explained their crimes against Rome that had also brought about their punishment—triumphal presence and death. If the prisoners were led alive, scenes depicting their crimes were shown close by, while their final

³³² Other war stories might have centred on the capture of specific cities. For example, when Appian writes of how, in the typical Roman triumphal procession of Scipio Africanus, 'towers were borne along as representations of the captured cities, and γραφαί and σχήματα showing the events', he may refer to a combined display of cities and scenes focusing on the events taking place at these very cities.

³³³ Lydi: App. *Pun.* 66. Songs sung by the army: Liv. 7.38.3, 10.30.9–10, 39.7.3–4; 45.43.8; Suet. *Iul.* 49, 51, 80; Vell. Pat. 2.67.4.

³³⁴ O'Neill (2004), discussing Plautus' *Amphitruo*, emphasizes that the *carmina triumphalia* exposed the triumphator to humiliation in order to reincorporate him into normative society. As captives on parade were severely humiliated too (certainly in a much more cruel way), this aspect is one that reveals the parallel of exposure between the Roman triumphator and the prime enemy, discussed also above.

destinies were emphasized by their very presence and by their captive attitudes or carrying of chains. If, on the other hand, the principal enemies had fled or died, they were instead represented above all by actors. In these cases, the war scenes not only manifested the enemies' acts in war, but were also highly concerned with their final fates, defeat, and death. Similarly, we saw that the statue of Cleopatra that Octavian exhibited in 29 BC displayed her dying. In this way, the scenes compensated for what the triumphal procession lacked due to the absence of the captives themselves: the display of their final subjection and punishment.

FIVE

Staging the World

PARADING WORLD ORDER

Romans and others

The triumphal procession staged spoils, captives, and representations in marked polarization to the celebrating Romans. By this repeated ritual performance, with vibrant emotion, Rome time and time again emphatically expressed and created views of what she was and should be. In the triumph, Rome defined herself by displaying others. Similar mechanisms are visible in many other times and places. For instance, Hölscher has exposed how the Greeks portrayed other peoples as contrasts in order to set, in negative terms, ideal concepts of and normative limits to their own society.[1] As another example, to quote Sitta von Reden on the work of Hartog:[2] 'Herodotus' narratives are not faithful renditions of the customs of foreign people; rather in reporting the different and often grotesque habits of others, the ethnographer inscribes himself and his own culture into his text, thereby acting upon his own culture in an ordering and normative way.'[3]

To clearly distinguish Romans from other participants, the triumphal performance required a fixed and easily legible role-playing. A series of visual codes were employed. First, in manifest contrast to the captives paraded, the Roman participants were wreathed. The wreath or crown was a traditional and powerful symbol of victory.[4] The triumphator carried both a laurel wreath and a golden crown, the latter symbolically held by a slave.[5] Senators, soldiers, lictors, musicians, processional officials, and sacrificial servants proceeded wearing laurel, olive, or myrtle wreaths.[6] Golden crowns were carried on biers, and there were also the *dona militaria* shaped as crowns, adorning individual soldiers and whole

---

[1] Hölscher (2004*b*); Hall (1991). Hölscher (2004*b*: 34–5) writes: 'In tali opposizioni viene formulata *in negativo* una autodefinizione della società specifica.'

[2] F. Hartog, *The Mirror of Herodotus* (1988).

[3] Reden (1997: 168).

[4] Baus (1940: 143–230).

[5] In a *triumphus*, the triumphator wore a laurel wreath, in an *ovatio* instead the myrtle wreath. For the slave and the golden crown, see Östenberg (2008).

[6] Gellius (5.6.4) and Festus (p. 211 L s.v. 'oleagineis coronis') both claim that the civil participants bore olive wreaths. However, according to Pfanner (1983: 87), the triumphal frieze on the arch of Trajan at

legions or particular divisions. Even the Roman horses were wreathed,[7] as were the liberated Romans who at times followed the triumphator.[8] All Roman participants also held a spray of laurel or olive in their hands.[9] In fact, both a terracotta plaque from the Augustan age and the frieze on the arch of Trajan at Benevento show servants who are interpreted as distributing laurel or olive sprays from a basket, probably to the spectators.[10] In this way, the onlookers would have been embraced as active participants in the victory rite. Wreaths and crowns, many in symbolic laurel, permeated the triumph, from the Roman trumpeters who opened the parade to the soldiers who closed the train.

Second, victors and subjugated were distinguished by way of written placards that identified spoils, captives, and representations.[11] These *tituli* defined and confirmed conquest by giving name to the far-flung and exotic, specifying unknown currencies, royal children, and conquered cities. They also measured conquest, by announcing the exact amount and weight of spoils, and they described the former crimes of the captives. At the same time, no source testifies to any such written placards as accompanying Roman participants, giving their names or identifying their actions.[12] We have seen that war scenes staged the defeat of captives rather than any specific Roman accomplishments. Both written and scenic explications thus worked as visual tools, signalling to the spectators that the display that followed should be read as 'others' as opposed to Romans.

Third, the triumphator constituted the fixed point of the parade, dividing the exhibits into two main groups. Spoils, captives, and representations, forming the group of 'others', were without exception paraded before him in the train.[13] Behind him came only representatives of Rome, the family of the triumphator, the army, the senators and the magistrates.[14] The triumphator also formed the visual peak of the performance. The procession intensified as it proceeded,

---

Benevento represents all Roman participants, military and civil alike, with laurel wreaths. For laurel wreaths, see e.g. Ov. *Trist.* 4.2.51–2; App. *Pun.* 66.

[7] Ov. *Trist.* 4.2.21–2.

[8] Plut. *Sulla* 34.1.

[9] e.g. Plut. *Aem.* 34.6–7; App. *Pun.* 66.

[10] Adamo Muscettola (1992: esp. 8–9, figs. 10, 11). Plaque: Museo Nazionale, Rome (inv. 72823), *Trionfi romani*, 127, I.2.8.

[11] Östenberg (forthcoming).

[12] There is one known exception, Caesar's placard announcing *Veni, vidi, vici* in his Pontic triumph, Suet. *Iul.* 37.2.

[13] Before the triumphator, there were also Roman participants, such as the sacrificial oxen and their attendants, processional officials, and soldiers carrying the spoils and leading the captives.

[14] Octavian changed the placement of the magistrates. Earlier on, the Roman magistrates had introduced the parade into the city, but in his triumphs of 29 BC, they instead walked at the back together with the senators, Dio Cass. 51.21.9.

leading the spectators' gaze from the masses of riches to the more pronounced emblematic objects last in the row of spoils and the most eminent prisoners last of the captives. The imprisoned main adversary formed a climax of relief, joy, and fascination when staged in visual submission to the triumphator, who represented victorious Rome. These two figures, the principal captive and the triumphator played the main characters on the triumphal stage, and they acted in intense interplay. The glory of the victorious general was much dependent on the former actions, reputation, and bravery of his adversary, who, much stressed by Mary Beard, even threatened to steal the show.[15] Many processions from other times and places show similar arrangements, staging the important elements in the midst. Thus, as Muir puts it, 'the core of meaning and the centre of society are at the heart of the procession'.[16]

The triumph lacked Roman traitors; captives on parade were by definition non-Romans. Caesar's actions in 46 BC form an exception, as he ventured to display representations of his Roman adversaries in flight and death. His example was not followed. A central function of the triumph was to perform and confirm Roman mastery, and the role-playing was fixed. Non-Romans played the defeated, Romans the victors.

For the same reason, only Latins and Italian *socii* seem to have been allowed to walk with the Roman soldiers behind the triumphator.[17] Even as Rome came to rely more and more on foreign mercenaries and allied troops, no source mentions any such contingents among the celebrating soldiers at the rear of the parade. For example, Masinissa and his Numidians were not shipped to Italy to be present at Scipio Africanus' triumph. When Anicius Gallus triumphed over King Gentius and the Illyrians in 167 BC, Roman and Latin soldiers followed the triumphal car.[18] Attalus, Eumenes, and Prusias, allied kings of Asia and Bithynia, were present as guests of the triumph,[19] but there is no sign of any soldiers from their troops in the parade, though they had assisted in the Roman cause. Similarly, although Lucullus had chosen to rely solely on ships and crews of the eastern allies in his campaign,[20] there are no indications that these allies participated among the victorious Romans in the parade. Lack of evidence makes it impossible to exclude non-Roman and non-Latin army divisions from all celebrations. Still, the soldiers on the triumphal march sang songs in praise and

---

[15] Beard (2007: e.g. 107–11).

[16] Muir (1981: 203).

[17] Liv. 39.5.17, 40.43.7, 41.13.7–8, 45.43.7–8. At times, the allies are described as *Latini*, at others they are plainly *socii*.

[18] Liv. 45.43.7–8.

[19] Eutrop. 4.8.

[20] Plut. *Luc.* 13.4; App. *Mith.* 77. Keaveney (1992: 84–5).

jesting of the triumphator and they sang in Latin.[21] Even if present, foreign soldiers would have played a Roman role.

The triumph was a mass spectacle that created a joint space of psychological participation. The ritual shaped a sense of oneness, and as spectators carried their laurel or olive sprig and stood packed together to watch and read the parade, they joined in the emotional sharing. As in Roman rhetoric, which also addressed large crowds, the concept of *enargeia* (in Latin *illustratio, evidentia, sub oculos subiectio*) was crucial. The basic idea of *enargeia* is to move the spectators to powerful emotions by presenting them with emphatic images of reality.[22] Thus, in Greek triumphal descriptions, the notion of *enargeia* abounds, as do phrases related to *sub oculos subiectio* and similar expressions in the Latin accounts.[23]

The triumph was an emotional event, manifesting collective joy at victory and deliverance from fears. People reacted with relief, contempt, and at times with esteem as they saw formerly awed enemies subdued. They looked with pity upon innocent children led in parade and they applauded or even laughed at the failed attempts of formerly feared adversaries. Literary accounts using *enargeia* often act on conflicting emotions,[24] and in the triumphal parade too (and in their descriptions), sentiments are contrasted: the captives cry, the crowd delights. At other times, the reactions of the vanquished were paralleled by those of the spectators, as when Perseus' children, accompanied by a crying retinue, triggered tears in the spectators. Here, both the on-lookers and those looked upon cried; but for very different reasons—the subjugated as signs of submission, the viewers out of pity, the emotional privilege of the conqueror.

Presence confirmed conquest; hence the need for images replacing absent enemies. Pompey's triumph demanded the presence of Mithridates and Tigranes; Octavian's parades the image of Cleopatra. Only by setting eyes on feared adversaries or their stand-in representations was Rome able to validate their defeat and abolish their threat. Relief from fear is in fact a recurrent theme in the manifest displays, and Polybius maintains that when Scipio in 201 BC put Punic defeat on parade, the people in Rome were reminded of their former perils and expressed intense gratitude for their deliverance.[25]

The visual rhetoric of *enargeia* played a crucial role in creating emotional reactions among the spectators, fundamental for shaping Roman oneness. Humiliation

---

[21] Suet. *Iul.* 49, 51, 80; Vell. Pat. 2.67.4.

[22] For *enargeia*, see Zanker (1981); Vasaly (1993: *passim*); Walker (1993); Manieri (1998); Scholz (1999).

[23] The concept of *enargeia* was central both in the staging of the parades and in the ancient descriptions of triumphs, actual and imaginary, Brilliant (1999: 224, 226–7); Beard (2003*b*).

[24] Thucydides (7.71.3), in a famous description of the Athenean defeat in Sicily, paints the battle scene from the perspective of the spectators on the shore, contrasting their emotions—those who rejoice in victory and those who lament defeat. Walker (1993: 355–61).

[25] Polyb. 16.23.5–6. Cf. Cic. *Verr.* II.5.26.66–7.

and mocking was another means by which the audience participated actively in celebrating its own identity as victors.[26] Scorning and laughing are potent shapers of group formations, and in the exposure of the crimes and punishment of the defeated, the spectators joined in sentiments of superiority, both militarily and morally. By reading, viewing, and even ridiculing the deeds and defeat of the vanquished, they also participated in Rome's execution of that punishment.

Parading others

Conquest, not loyalty

Several chapters in this study show that the triumphs presented all kinds of gifts together with objects taken as booty. Certainly, the meaning and function of the two phenomena, gifts and spoils, were interlaced. The defeated were frequently ordered to bestow gifts, as were allies. Others brought the gifts in gratitude, signalling submissive loyalty.[27] Still, even if gifts might be spoils in all but name, nomenclature mattered. While spoils always implied pure conquest, gifts signalled some degree of voluntary acting and loyalty, both for the donor and the recipient. Thus, the ways in which spoils and gifts were staged in the triumphal procession are bound to reveal Roman manifestations of herself and her relations to the surrounding world.

Interestingly then, the Roman general turned spoils as well as gifts over to the quaestors on the battlefield, and once back in the city, he paraded them side-by-side in the triumphal procession. Whether taken as booty or bestowed as gifts, the art and valuables were displayed as wealth, ordered in gold, silver, bronze, and ivory. Even the money presented by foreign cities as contributions to games were included in the sums paraded, and spoils and gifts were not entered as different categories in the records. Similarly, although hostages and prisoners had varied origins, differed in character, and filled divergent purposes, they too were led together, intermingled as captives. Status was the determining factor in both spoils and captives; those linked to a royal context were given particular prominence. In this respect, the triumph did not parade loyalty, only conquest; or rather, even loyalty was staged as conquest.

Among all objects displayed, the golden crowns formed an exception, being specifically defined as gifts. Crowns had in the East long been bestowed on individual martial conquerors and athletic winners, and some descriptions suggest that there were occasions at which golden crowns might have been displayed as emblems of personal honour close by the triumphator. Not least, this is how

---

[26] Cf. Coleman (1990: 47).

[27] For the variety of functions and symbols inherent in gifts, see the classic study by Mauss (1970).

they appear in Plutarch's description of Aemilius Paullus' triumph. Notwith-standing, all through the period in focus here, the crowns were recorded in the treasury as spoils taken up by the Roman state, and the clear majority of parades also counted the crowns as loot of gold and paraded them among other booty far ahead of the triumphator. Again, gifts appeared as and among other spoils, parading Rome as sole master.

That the prime message of the triumph was conquest is further seen in the type of personifications chosen for the parades. Unlike many preserved examples in art, which show *nationes* and *gentes* as loyal (the so-called *provincia pia fidelis*-type), triumphs seem to have paraded peoples only as vanquished (*provincia capta*). Triumphal displays thus differ from the funeral processions of the emperors, which included assemblies of incorporated lands and peoples, very probably represented as *piae fideles*. Augustus' funeral parade is the first known to have shown statues personifying the various peoples of the empire, but Roman funerals had long before this presented loyal peoples, formerly conquered, in prominent positions. At the funeral of Aemilius Paullus, many Iberians, Ligurians, and Macedonians, the three very peoples that Paullus had conquered, were present to pay him honour.[28] The young and strong even took turns in carrying his bier—decorated with images of the Macedonian triumph—and the elderly followed, calling upon Paullus as benefactor and preserver of their countries. Here, we are very far away from Paullus' triumphs held over these peoples, where Iberians, Ligurians, and Macedonians were led as humbled captives and their former assets carried into the Roman treasury.[29] The case of Marcellus reflects the same difference between the triumphal display of conquest and the post-triumph exhibitions of loyalty. The year after Marcellus' ovation held over Syracuse, a delegation from that city complained to the senate about the Roman looting of their temples. After some debate, the senate ratified Marcellus' actions, and immediately the delegates from Syracuse threw themselves at his knees, begged him to forgive them, and to take the city under his protection and patronage, a request that Marcellus approved.[30] These cases reflect Hellenistic ruler cult, but also Roman traditions of clientship.[31] The very conquest of a city or a land impelled the victorious general, and Rome too, to take responsibility as *patronus* over the defeated peoples. Thus, monuments and funerals celebrated patronage of the subjugated. These were post-triumphal celebrations, however. The triumph itself transmitted only messages of Roman conquest.

---

[28] Plut. *Comp. Tim. Aem.* 39.8–9; Val. Max. 11.10.3.

[29] We know that Paullus defeated the Iberians, but it is unclear whether he celebrated this victory with a triumph or not.

[30] Liv. 26.32.8.   [31] Rives (1993: with further references).

Spoils and captives

Spoils and captives formed the two basic categories in the processional staging of
non-Roman participants. In fact, a triumphal parade was supposed to include
both looted goods and vanquished captives to be complete. Thus, when Caligula
set out to celebrate an ovation after his phoney campaign at the English Channel,
he arranged for two displays in particular: shells from Oceanus, since, as Dio
maintains, he needed booty for his procession,[32] and fake prisoners, Gauls
dressed up as Germans. Similarly, Domitian purchased men to play the role of
German prisoners and brought out valuable objects from the Imperial
depository to adorn his triumph with the two basic categories of display: spoils
and captives.

In various ways, ancient triumphal accounts mark spoils and captives as the
two distinct categories of processional display. Florus, in his description of
Dentatus' parade held over Pyrrhus and the Samnites explicitly separates the
captivi, on one hand, from the *pompa* consisting of the booty of valuables, on
the other.[33] Ancient authors also use different terminology for the transport
of the two categories. Captives are mostly described as led, *ducti*, while
forms of *ducere* never appear in the descriptions of spoils. These were instead
carried or driven, *lata* or *vecta*. Thus, in describing the triumphs of P. Cornelius
Cethegus and M. Baebius Tamphilus, Livy states that the triumphators paraded
only sacrificial animals, since there was nothing captured that could be carried
(*ferretur*) or led (*duceretur*), referring to the absence of spoils and captives.[34]

Terms applied also reveal the different processional placement of spoils and
captives. The phrase *ante currum ducere*, 'to lead before the triumphal car', was
specifically applied only to captives.[35] In contrast, spoils might be carried in front,
praelata.[36] Again, the triumphator, the visual zenith, forms the point of reference.
The captives were led before his car, while the spoils were carried further ahead;
the soldiers are instead mostly described as following his chariot, *secuti*.[37] Thus,
Livy writes of the triumph of L. Furius Purpureo: *Neque captivi ulli ante currum
ducti neque spolia praelata nec milites secuti*, 'There were no captives led before his

---

[32] Dio Cass. 59.25.3.

[33] Flor. *Epit.* 1.13.27: *tum si captivos aspiceres, Molossi, Thessali, Macedones, Brittius, Apulus atque Lucanus; si
pompam, aurum, purpura, signa, tabulae Tarentinaeque deliciae.*

[34] Liv. 40.38.9.

[35] See e.g. Liv. 3.29.4–5, 4.10.7, 6.4.2, 7.27.8, 31.49.3, 33.23.5, 34.52.9–10, 37.59.5–6, 39.7.2, 40.34.8; Aug.
Anc. 4; Ov. *Ars* 1.215 (*ibunt ante duces*); Eutrop. 4.2.3, 4.8.2–3, 4.27.6; Oros. 5.15.19; Ampel. 16.4. Abaecherli
(1935/6: 8 and n. 131).

[36] Liv. 3.29.4–5: *Ducti ante currum hostium duces, militaria signa praelata, secutus exercitus praeda onustus*;
4.19.7: *Consul triumphans in urbem redit Cluilio duce Volscorum ante currum ducto praelatisque spoliis*; 31.49.3:
Neque captivi ulli ante currum ducti neque spolia praelata nec milites secuti.

[37] Liv. 3.29.4–5, 31.49.3, 41.13.8.

chariot, no spoils carried ahead, no soldiers who followed.'[38] In numerous other descriptions too, the spoils are listed first and the captives second,[39] reflecting the basic order of parade. The triumphs of Flamininus and Aemilius Paullus tell the same story. Both celebrations lasted for three days and paraded the captives in front of the triumphator's car only on day three. The first two days saw spoils of all kinds, weaponry as well as art and valuables.

The categorization of displays as spoils and captives most certainly had roots far back in time. Accounting for the triumph held by A. Postumius Albus in 496 BC, Dionysius of Halicarnassus describes the presence of captured weaponry, military stores, and prisoners.[40] Diodorus Siculus' description of T. Siccius Sabinus' parade, held in 487 BC, includes spoils (λάφυρα), prisoners (αἰχμάλωτοι), and the celebrating general and his army.[41] The following year, Sp. Cassius Vicellinus led home 'captives and spoils, the adornments of a triumph'.[42] The testimonies to these early triumphs are far from trustworthy in detail, but they nevertheless reveal that spoils and captives were considered key elements of parade, together with the triumphator and his army. Naturally so, as spoils of weapons and other valuables of the van-quished together with prisoners of war formed the two basic profits gained from victorious campaigns.[43] The division of animate beings and inanimate things also has close parallels in Roman views of private ownership. In Roman law, the household, *familia*, consisted of two clearly distinguished parts, the things, *res*, and the people, *personae*.[44] The triumphal procession manifested the property of Rome as a community, and the rooted concept of *res* and *personae* might have contributed to the fixed structure of display.

The processional arrangement of spoils loaded on carts followed by captives led on foot was probably self-evident in the early days of the triumphs. More remarkably, the triumphs kept this basic division throughout the centuries. From the third century BC, the processions eventually developed into lavish spectacles with abundant displays. The wealth paraded multiplied, and novel displays were constantly added. Yet the parade remained in its essential structure the same, and even in the days of Trajan, the spectators set eyes first on spoils of all kinds, then the captives, followed by the triumphator and his army.

[38] Liv. 31.49.3.
[39] See e.g. Liv. 26.21.6–10, 34.52, 37.46.3–6, 37.59.3–6, 39.5.13–17, 40.34.7–8, 45.43.4–8; Diod. Sic. 31.8.10–12 (apud Sync.); App. *Pun.* 66; Plut. *Aem.* 32–4; App. *Mith.* 116–17; Flor. *Epit.* 1.28.12–14; cf. Liv. 3.29.4–5, 4.10.7.
[40] Dion. Hal. 6.17.2.
[41] Diod. Sic. 8.67.9.
[42] Dion. Hal. 8.69.1.
[43] See e.g. Dion. Hal. 3.42.4, 5.47.1; Diod. Sic. 12.64.2–3; Plut. *Publ.* 23.1.
[44] *RE* VI (1909), s.v. 'familia', 1980–4 (R. Leonhard); *RE* XIX:1 (1937), s.v. 'persona', 1040–1 (R. Düll).

The masses of novelties captured in the campaigns of the third and early second centuries challenged the arrangements of the Roman triumph. Where should the statues representing gods be placed? How were the golden crowns to be displayed? The banqueting items, should they be arranged according to type, material, or contents? What were to be the processional role of the elephants, the ships, and the catapults? The issues had implications far beyond the ceremony itself. Rome's close encounter with cultures outside Italy, her continuous victories abroad, and her rapid development into a number one power forced the community to deal with questions of identity and views of the world. As loads of spoils and captives unknown to most people poured into the city, the issue of how to present conquest became crucial. Categorization was an essential tool in presenting the world to Rome.

Still, the sources reveal minimal difficulties in the presentation of novelties. Mostly, the Romans seem simply to have taken up the new encounters and transformed them into customary displays of spoils and captives. Inanimate items of worth were paraded as gold, silver, bronze, amount and weight; living creatures as traditional captives, whether hostages, animals, or trees. This basic traditional division offered apt means for Rome to embrace the new within the frames of the well-known, thus at the same time restaging the celebrations of distant ancestors and expanding her realm to the edges of the earth. Through the ancient ritual, still in its essential structure recognizable, Rome manifested her identity based on traditional values and *mos maiorum*; yet she did so while incorporating and exploring dramatic changes.[45] The strength of the triumph was its sensitivity to both flexibility and frame.

At times, the categorization of the novelties must have been quite straight forward. Rams were clearly weaponry, as were catapults. Novel valuables from the Hellenistic kingdoms were spoils placed where enemy possessions had always been presented, after the weaponry but before the captives. The basic concern with wealth resulted in the categorization according to type: gold, silver, and bronze.

At other times, the categorization was less clear. Statues were humans or gods on one hand but had a material value on the other. Trees were living items, but as logs they would have been pure booty. Most challengingly, the representations produced specifically for the parades, what was their character? Were they spoils, captives, or did they form a third category of their own? In fact, spoils, captives, and representations appear at first glance to form three distinct groups of displays, and this study started out from this tripartite classification. Through the analyses of each separate subgroup of items, people, and images, it became clear,

---

[45] Darnton (1985: 121), writes of the parade in 18th-cent. Montpellier: 'But the language of the processions was archaic.'

however, that only the first two categories, spoils and captives, correspond to the ancient Roman division. The representations were not perceived as a particular kind of display to be distinguished from spoils and captives obtained in war because they had been produced for the parade. Rather, they, as everything else, gave physical form to Roman conquest. Models of cities and towns were categorized and presented among the spoils of weapons, while personifications of peoples and rivers were led as captive enemies of Rome, placed among other prisoners and represented in submission, grief, and fear.

Cities and towns were displayed as models to give form to their conquest but also to avoid parading them as anthropomorphic beings in fetters. Similarly, looted statues were paraded among the spoils both due to their material value and in order not to present them as captive gods. The two phenomena were clearly linked. As seen, the Romans mostly did not hesitate to plunder foreign temples, nor to parade the sacred loot in their triumphs. Doubts were roused only when cities might not have been taken justly. The triumphal exposure of statues from sacred contexts touched on the Roman anxiety that, in capturing cities, you had to proceed justly or next time the city of Rome itself might be endangered.

In the Roman world, warfare had to be conducted in accordance with the rights of war, and the conquest of cities was a particularly delicate affair.[46] Cities were most pregnant symbols and kernels of civic life.[47] They were sacred elements with religious boundaries and close to divine identities. Thus, in times of crises, the cities of Carthage, Syracuse, and Rome themselves appear in ancient descriptions to speak on behalf of their population and gods.[48] The ancient conception of a city was an alliance of peoples and gods at a fixed place, and its preservation depended on the worship of and sacrifice to the gods in the temples of that place.[49] When gods were robbed from their shrines, the very existence of civic life was threatened, just as the gods were attacked when cities were taken.[50] Hence, both in violating temples and conquering cities, you risked performing an impious act, thereby angering the gods. The Greek victors at Troy were punished for having violated the temples in the destruction of the city. Rome had no second thoughts about killing and enslaving thousands of people. Through their very rebellion, these peoples had proved guilty and they were justly punished. When on triumphal parade, they were humiliated and the spectators rejoiced in their display. By contrast, the cities themselves were innocent, as were their gods.[51] Having them dragged in person would have been an act of utmost impiety and hubris.

---

[46] Laurence (1996: esp. 113).   [47] Purcell (1995: 133).

[48] Cic. *Nat. D.* 3.42; Sil. *Pun.* 4.408; cf. App. *Pun.* 81.   [49] Laurence (1996).

[50] Vasaly (1993: 135).   [51] Laurence (1996: 115).

In Rome's self-perception, the gods had ordained her world domination. In fact, in the very performance of Roman victory, the triumphs themselves staged the continued favour of the gods. But the approval of the gods depended on unbroken *pietas* and justice. If Rome failed her moral responsibilities, the gods might abandon her, affecting the city and her boundaries, people, houses, and temples. Hence, Livy's judgement on Marcellus that, by looting the sanctuaries of Syracuse, he chanced attacks on the temples in Rome too. The careful display of sacred statues and cities in the triumphs reflects the concern for pious actions and for the well-being of Rome. When the triumphs, probably from the late Republic, introduced personifications of captured cities into the displays, this was most likely a reflection of Rome's confidence in her newly established *imperium*.

MESSAGES AND MEANINGS

Embracing foreign wealth

Wealth was a central theme in the triumphal display. The procession itself was a conspicuous spectacle, staged with visual splendour. There were river personifications in gold, city models in ivory, tapestries in gold and purple, processional apparatus of citrus wood, tortoise shell, and silver. All participants wore costly dress, from the triumphator adorned in gold and purple to the mass of anonymous captives, arrayed for the parade to conceal any wounds or disfigurements.[52] The spectators too wore festal outfits to mark the occasion.[53] The staging of the parade as a spectacle of opulence contributed to a joint sense of festivity and transmitted messages of a prosperous and powerful state.

In the procession, there were also masses of looted valuables and extravaganzas. The triumph brought in novel luxuries and paraded riches in unprecedented numbers. The shields, statues, household goods, torcs, temple treasures, and golden crowns were displayed and registered as gold, silver, bronze, and ivory. Amount and weight was manifested through a spectrum of visual means: a multitude of loaded biers and carts, masses of men and mules carrying and driving the goods, bearers using cushions and support-crutches to ease the burden of *fercula*. Conquest was defined and confirmed by written placards that announced numbers and weight. Future incomes were on parade too, in the explicit advertisements of indemnities, taxes and tributes to be collected from the subjugated as well as in the manifestation of enlarged territorial control as such. On a few occasions, a whole day's parade did not suffice to bring the obtained

---

[52] Joseph. *BJ* 7.138–9.   [53] Plut. *Aem.* 32.2.

riches into the city. Only after two or three days of continuous display did Rome embrace her newly won wealth.

After the procession, Rome allotted pieces of booty to allied states, thus manifesting her role as benefactor of the loyal. The larger part of the wealth was, however, taken up by Rome herself. In one of its prime aspects, the triumph was a religious procession to the principal sanctuary of the city, and the gods received their due share of the affluent spoils, in sacrifices, games, and dedications. Hence, the triumph proclaimed civic piety, as it wound its way through city space, past temples that commemorated previous victories.

The parade headed for the temple on the Capitoline hill, but the other principal objective was the state treasury, taking up and recording the wealth in the name of the community. Thus, the assets and valuables paraded confirmed the wealth of the very Roman people who watched. In this, as in many other aspects, the spectators were no mere observers, but active partakers. At times, the wealth paraded even went straight into the pockets of the citizens, as refunds of former financial contributions and as the abolition of future taxes. At others, the spoils displayed reappeared as yet other expressions of communal wealth, for example, as buildings and other adornments of the city. Certainly, the wealth did not accrue to all spectators, and warfare frequently enriched triumphators, emperors, and generals of rank.[54] Still, private profits were kept away from this celebration of the community, and the procession staged the spoils as property of the *populus Romanus*.

Besides a religious procession and a civic rite, the triumph was a political parade. In fact, one of the characteristics of political ritual is that it defines community through an excessive display of wealth and other resources.[55] The Athenians of the fifth century BC each year paraded the tribute paid to the state treasury by subject allies through the theatre as part of the public celebration of the Great Dionysia.[56] In Hellenistic times, the royal processions advertised the great wealth of the king by parading enormous amounts of riches. The rich display of these feasts confirmed strength and supremacy both within and outside the community.[57]

In Rome too, the inexhaustible loads of spoils manifested and confirmed the strength of the community in financial, political, and military terms. The display was linked both to performed accomplishments and to future control; as conquest had realized the wealth displayed, the wealth now promised still new conquests

[54] Traditionally, spoils of war adorned the houses of the triumphant generals. Spoils thus fixed were not, however, the private possessions of the triumphator, but rather a kind of public advertisement, attached to the house itself, Plin. *Nat.* 35.2.7.

[55] Bell (1997: 129).

[56] Köhler (1996: 80).

[57] Préaux (1978: esp. 208); Austin (1986: 460); Wikander (1992: 149). For rituals aiming not only at consolidating internal values but also at making symbolic statements for outsiders, see Baumann (1992).

and yet further incomes. The state recorded the wealth brought in and specified it in detail. As the confiscated goods were led on a symbolically pregnant route from the scene of the war straight into the treasury, they stated both the strength of Rome and the disarming, financially and militarily, of the subjugated. The message was thus twofold, and furthermore it aimed both at the Roman community itself, defining its identity as financially and politically supreme, and at the world at large, stating the mastery of Rome and deterring any revolts.

The triumph of civilization

In its ritual reiteration, the triumphal procession staged world order. But the order was no static display; as procession, it was movement too. The triumph carried and led foreign objects and people from outside the city into the civic midst. At times, the act signified a true embracing, as when Rome took up the riches of the subjugated and transformed them into to Roman property. In other cases, Rome did not embrace the foreign objects and people, but staged them as 'otherness' in pronounced suppression and rejection. These two aspects, embracing and rejection, were two active forces at work in the exhibition. They contrasted and interacted, often even in the same display, and both reflected and shaped ideas about what Rome was. This is seen clearly in the wild, the outlaw, the barbarian, and other *externi*, who were staged as pronounced others in order to highlight Rome's identity as civilization. Some *externi* were displayed as a true threat to civilization. They were not taken up by Rome, but staged as suppressed and crushed. Other *externi* were embraced by civilization through their very physical leading into Rome. Here, procession was true process.

Taming Nature
The triumphal procession included several expressions of the wild Nature, staged as tamed by Rome. Among these were the foreign rivers, forceful natural powers, and mighty opponents in war, who were led as chained captives, defeated and tamed. On parade, the rivers wore their horns broken and their crowns of reed cracked. They walked in mourning 'with milder waves', deprived of their former strength, giving form to civilization's mastery over Nature. Some rivers resisted taming, though. The Rhine, potent watercourse and barbarian Germanic foe, was particularly unyielding in his resistance, which caused repeated subjugation and processional fettering. Others gave in to Roman superiority more easily and, once tamed, joined the cultured cause, by offering their life-giving qualities to civilization. They might even turn against their former countries. We saw how the Danube allows the Roman army over his streams on Trajan's column, hence opening up Dacia for Roman conquest. As a parallel, Pliny the Younger writes of

how rivers and mountains, mighty and uncontrolled enemy barriers that had formerly defended their countries, abandoned their lands and joined Trajan.[58] Like rivers, mountains had a feral character, as settings of countless undomesticated creatures and activities. They too were brought under control when led in triumph, and once tamed, they also were in league with civilization. Thus, the display of Mount Gyri, paraded by Balbus with an inscription declaring that it housed precious stones,[59] announced both the Roman control of Nature and confirmed that, once subdued, Nature was willing to cooperate with civilization and produce future riches for her master. Pearls and gems, the opulent wonders of Nature, transmitted similar messages.

The visible taming of the wild also included animals. The foreign species from far and near made a manifest contrast to the Roman animals present, all representatives of civilization: the white horses accompanying the Roman leader, horses and draught animals of diverse kinds, and in particular the hundreds of flawless white oxen, bred only to be sacrificed to Jupiter on the Capitol on the day of the celebration.

Elephants were initially displayed as ferocious opponents captured in war (*monstra, beluae, ferae*). Led into the city, however, they bowed their heads low, renounced their savage powers, and acknowledged Roman supremacy. Eventually, the elephants were even transformed into domesticated servants of Rome. Again, as wild nature had been brought under control, it offered its assistance to civilization. The change was mirrored in the transfer of the elephants from captives to escorts of the captor, accompanying the Roman victor himself into the city.

In the triumphs, exotic animals, such as tigers, lions, leopards, and hippopotami, also processed. The beasts very probably came from royal zoos, thus cultured contexts. Nevertheless, the parade presented them as Nature's wild beasts, now tamed by Rome to such an extent as to allow them into the heart of civilization. Decked out splendidly, the animals walked the very streets of the city. Just as the mass of human captives were dressed and displayed according to ethnic origin, these beasts were paraded according to species. Passing by the spectators in organized rows, their display gave form to Roman world order.

Feared barbarians

Just as natural forces and animals on triumphal display were embraced by Rome, so too were human captives. In some cases, there was not even a question of taming. Young foreign children (of status), being still innocent, might be taken up by Rome and transformed into citizens. Juba, the son of the Numidian king, was even characterized as the most fortunate captive ever. Led into civilization,

---

[58] Plin. *Pan.* 16.4–5.   [59] Plin. *Nat.* 5.5.37.

he was transformed from barbarian to learned historian.[60] Very similar is the story in Plutarch on the post-triumphal fate of one of King Perseus' young sons, who ended up a professional metalworker, adopted the Latin tongue, and was employed as a secretary to Roman magistrates.[61]

Most captives were not subject to this kind of extreme incorporation. It is commonly acknowledged that the Roman Empire developed into a well-defined formal territorial unit only in late antiquity.[62] Earlier on, citizenship certainly mattered, but the mental line in middle–late Republican and in early Imperial times was drawn between Rome and Italy on one hand and the lands beyond on the other.[63] Outside Rome and Italy, people were *externi*. They were either civilized *civitates* or they were less cultured peoples, *gentes* and *nationes*. Some of these were brutish, non-comprehensible, and morally inferior, meriting the label *barbari*. Some dwelled outside all normative society: the pirates and slaves.

During much of the Republic, the Gauls were the enemy *externi* par excellence. This was a deeply rooted tradition; ever since Allia, Gauls were seen and promoted as a threat even to the city itself.[64] In response, Roman priests were excluded from military service only as long as there was no Gallic war, and Rome had a *sanctius aerarium*, reserved for use in the event of war against the Gauls.[65] The image of the Gauls as the prime threat was fed by the Hellenistic theme of Galatian victories.[66] From the late third century, the Roman *metus Gallicus* developed almost into an obsession,[67] and the notion was both reflected in and promoted by their triumphal staging. In fact, sources suggest that the Gauls were for quite some time displayed as *the* barbarian other. In no other case does such variety of tribes appear in the lists of vanquished. The people defeated were not merely Gauls, but specified in the *Fasti triumphales* as *Galli Boii, Galli Arverni, Galli Karni, Galli Insubres, Galli Contrubrii*. The naming confirmed the defeat both of each particular tribe and of the Gauls in general. From the victories of Aemilius Papus, Flamininus, and Marcellus in the 220s BC to Marius and Catulus' celebrations in 101 BC, spoils, war chariots, standards, and vessels were all specifically defined as Gallic, and some objects, such as the *carpenta* and the torcs (and probably *carnyces*), were paraded exclusively in the Gallic processions. This emphasis on origins contrasts to the booty from most other areas, displayed with no geographic or ethnic specification. The other major exception were the

---

[60] Plut. *Caes.* 55.2; cf. App. *BCiv.* 2.101.   [61] Plut. *Aem.* 37.4.

[62] Saddington (1961: 92).

[63] The passage is based on Saddington (1961).

[64] App. *BCiv.* 2.150; Plut. *Cam.* 41.6, *Marc.* 3.2–3. Saddington (1961: 97, 100); Bellen (1985: 11).

[65] Barlow (1977).

[66] Hölscher (1990: 80–2), argues that the Roman concept of Gallic threats and Gallic victories became emphasized only at the time of Rome's encounter with the kingdoms of the East.

[67] Rawson (1985: 259); Hölscher (1990: 80–2).

temple treasures from Jerusalem, which were marked as Jewish, again to define a threatening other. Livy maintains that Marcellus in 211 BC led elephants as a symbol of Punic defeat.[68] Unfortunately, little is known of the specifics of other Carthaginian displays, but Punic triumphs most probably also emphasized the origins of spoils and captives. Together with the Gauls, the Carthaginians were the principal enemies of Republican Rome. The Punic Wars, like the Gallic encounters, lasted for a long period of time and included moments of utmost danger for Rome herself. Along with the *metus Gallicus*, there was in Rome a prevalent *metus Punicus*.[69]

During the late Republic, the Gauls lost their former role as prime *externi*. In Caesar's five triumphs in 46 and 45 BC over Gaul, Egypt, Pontus, Africa, and Spain, Gaul was not singled out as a victory over barbarians.[70] Instead, the Gallic parade was staged as the most splendid.[71] In Lucan's vision of the triumph, *Gallia* is *nobilis*,[72] and the apparatus of the Gallic procession was produced from the costly citrus wood, implying the prosperity of the area.[73]

As Gaul was embraced by civilization,[74] the role as untamed *externi* was given to barbarians further away from Rome: Germans, Britons, and Dacians. Hence, in Caesar's triumphs, while Gaul was a place of wealth, the war chariots now implied bellicose Britons. The torc, another Gallic emblem, was taken up as a military symbol in Rome. Later on, Ovid's triumphal depictions provide recurrent glimpses of German prisoners and personifications of the Rhine and the Germania, all staged as barbarians, warlike, savage, unkempt. The shift from Gauls to Germans as principal barbarian others is also reflected in Caligula's ovation, where the Gauls at his disposal had to be costumed to play the part of German prisoners. Only as tall, redheaded, long-haired, and German-speaking did they fit the role of the barbarian other.[75] Still later on, Trajan emphasized the Dacians as potent warlike enemies in his triumphs and related artworks.[76]

Unlike the Gauls (and the Carthaginians), for the period in discussion here, the Germans and Dacians did not pose any true threat to the *Urbs* itself. They had never captured the Capitol and they did not stand *ante portas*. Rome at the time of the late Republic and early Empire was confident in its world rule. Still, even in

---

[68] Liv. 26.21.9.

[69] For the concept *metus Gallicus*, see Bellen (1985), and for *metus Punicus*, Bellen (1985); Welwei (1989).

[70] Caesar himself applies *barbari* especially to the peoples living beyond the Rhine, *Gall.* 2.35.1, 4.17.10, 5.34.1, 6.10.2, 6.29.2, 6.35.6, 6.37.7–9.

[71] Suet. *Iul.* 37.1, cf. 54.2–3.

[72] Lucan 3.76–8.

[73] Vell. Pat. 2.56.2. Deutsch (1924b: esp. 258–60).

[74] Vasaly (1993: 149).

[75] Suet. *Cal.* 47; cf. Pers. 6.43–7.

[76] Seneca points out the Germans and the tribes along the Danube as peoples outside Roman civilization (*pax Romana*), Sen. *Dial.* 1.4.14.

that position, Rome needed a barbarian other to mirror its own moral and political supremacy. Germans and Dacians filled that role, in the triumphs and monuments. In contrast to the Gauls and Carthaginians, who had been equipped with defining emblems, such as *carnyces*, torcs, and elephants, Germans, Britons, and Dacians were presented as barbarians in very general terms, and they were also given symbols formerly connected to Gallic victories and triumphs. In fact, Vendries has shown that in art, the *carnyx*, from being a Gallic emblem, became a general barbarian symbol denoting victories over Germans and Dacians, although these peoples never themselves employed the trumpet.[77] Hölscher also points out that representations of defeated German barbarians in imperial art show them with Gallic attire and hairstyle.[78] The Gauls were the established adversaries, and when they were embraced by Rome, others took up their role.

Although Germans, Britons, and Dacians did not threaten Rome, they challenged Roman world order in their rebellions and they hindered complete world domination. In this capacity they smoothly filled the part as antipode of Roman community. This role was indispensable, and there was no question of embracing Germans, Britons, and Dacians in the cultured realm. Instead, in the triumphs, they were promoted as pronounced barbarians, whose uprisings had been crushed in order to preserve civilization. Their crime was twofold: they had rebelled against Rome and they had refused civilization.[79] In fact, while certain leading enemies might merit severe penalty through rebellious actions, entire barbarian peoples were by nature reserved for punishment simply through their uncultured being.[80]

Pirates and slaves also lived outside civilization. In the extraordinary performance of 61 BC, Pompey paraded all captives unbound, even the pirates. Roman imperialism included a civilizing mission,[81] and Pompey, reflecting that 'by nature man neither is nor becomes a wild or an unsocial creature',[82] had the pirates tamed by embracing them with civilization. After being led into Rome in parade and seeing their ships also displayed, the pirates were transferred to a terrestrial life; they were to inhabit cities and to work the ground. Pompey's action is exceptional, testifying to the experimental and expanding nature of the triumph at this time and the self-confidence in the newly established Roman world mastery. So great were Rome's conquests, commissioned by Pompey, that he did not even have to perform the peoples and nations crushed. Instead, they were led unbound and sent home afterwards, taken up by Roman clemency.[83]

---

[77] Vendries (1999: 388–91).   [78] Hölscher (1990: 80–2).

[79] Sallmann (1997: 120).   [80] Ibid.; cf. Veyne (1993: 355).

[81] Saddington (1961: esp. 93). See e.g. Verg. *Aen.* 6.851–3; Plin. *Nat.* 3.5.39–40.

[82] Plut. *Pomp.* 28.3.

[83] Bellen (1988: 876) argues that Pompey showed the captives unbound in reference to Alexander.

In most triumphs, however, pirates were staged as criminals, without rights and beyond salvation. Their display connoted no incorporation into Rome, but rather Rome's severe punishments of outsiders who refused and even threatened civilization. In Vergil's famous words (*Aen.* 6.852–3): Rome was 'to put culture upon peace, to spare the subjected but to crush the proud' (*pacique imponere morem | parcere subiectis et debellare superbos*). Through peace (read military subjection), Rome was to impose civilization, the *inmensa Romanae pacis maiestas*, as Pliny the Elder calls it.[84] Those who acknowledged her mastery were saved, those who opposed struck down. Pirates were by nature *superbi*, and their otherness was crushed rather than neutralized. Also *superbi*, though of a very different kind, were the Jews, who to Roman eyes persisted in spurning normative civilization as they held on to their monotheistic worship and *mores absurdi*. Not only did they reject traditional Graeco-Roman culture; in their revolt, they even challenged it. If not an impending threat to Rome, they were a threat to Roman order. Their punishment was particularly severe, and the triumph of AD 71 paraded Jewish culture not only defeated but also crushed. As a central spectacle, the sacred objects from Jerusalem both emphatically staged Jewish otherness (which was rejected), and were displayed as simple booty of gold and silver destined to enrich Rome (thus embraced).

In the Roman celebration of victory, the figure of the defeated *externus*, whether seen in the River Rhine, a Punic elephant, pirates, redheaded Germans, or the Jewish temple treasures, was crucial. Representing uncontrolled Nature, non-society, barbarity, or simply otherness, they symbolized peoples and powers that were by definition opponents of civilization and the *populus Romanus*. The Roman conception of these others was nurtured by fear of the unknown and triggered by destructive encounters such as those with the Gauls at Allia or with Pyrrhus' elephants at Heraclea and Asculum. In their challenges, pirates, Germans, and Jews confirmed their own otherness by refusing normative society. Once defeated and led in triumph, they offered Roman community a visually emphatic antipode of itself. Also, whether as real threats or being promoted as such, their display presented the spectators with a catharsis of relief as they saw and grasped the overcoming of those who, through their uprisings, indeed through their very existence, had threatened Rome.

Ambivalent kingship

Royal origins had a key position in the triumphal parade and in its recording. In contrast to other valuables, grouped as gold, silver, and bronze, ancient writers carefully describe royal emblems, such as thrones, sceptres, chariots, and dia-

[84] Plin. *Nat.* 27.1.3.

dems, item by item. These regal insignia were clearly staged as individual objects. Also, royal banqueting was promoted as one of very few themes besides the general expression of wealth. Among the prisoners and hostages too, kingly status was underlined. In the *Fasti triumphales*, victories over kings were stressed, and the king himself, as the foremost of all principal adversaries, was led in close visual interplay with the triumphator. The processional placing and importance of other captives and hostages depended principally on royal kinship.

According to Cicero, the Roman people were *dominus regum, victor atque imperator omnium gentium*,[85] 'master of kings and vanquisher and commander of all peoples'. In the triumph, spoils and prisoners with royal origins were clearly stressed to manifest Rome as *dominus regum*. Just like the *externi* discussed above, kings and royals were staged as opposites that defined and confirmed Rome herself. While, however, the barbaric, wild, and criminal was absolutely inconsistent with Rome as civilisation, Roman concepts of kings and kingship were more ambivalent, including at the same time a certain fascination and pure contempt.[86] In fact, Rome, in staging the triumphal parade, both alluded to royalty and renounced it.

Acting king: the Roman triumphator

The allusion to monarchy was explicit in the Roman leading character, the triumphator. On the day of celebration, as resplendent protagonist of the triumphal play, he appeared as king. I will not address the much-discussed issue of to what degree the triumphator embodied Jupiter and to what extent he performed the role of a king.[87] Certainly, to the spectators, the appearance of the triumphator had both royal and divine tones, as he entered the city at his most glorious moment, dressed in gold and purple, carrying a golden crown and a sceptre and towering aloft in his splendid chariot drawn by white steeds. The hint at kingship was taken further by the resemblance of the triumphs to the processions staged by the kings of the Hellenistic East. Like the royal processions of the East, the triumphal trains in Rome paraded abundant opulence, military strength, and controlled exoticism. In the Hellenistic East, military powers and great wealth were capacities closely linked to (divine) kingship, and the grand processions staged these royal abilities.[88] The triumph in Rome certainly also in its overall appearance celebrated the great martial deeds of the triumphator. But we have seen that images of the triumphant general were not on display, and that

---

[85] Cic. *Dom.* 33.90, cf. 33.89. Pompey triumphed over kings, *civitates, gentes*, and *praedones*, Val. Max. 8.15.8.

[86] Erskine (1991) argues that Roman hostility to kings developed out of the conflicts with the eastern kingdoms rather than in remembrance of its own regal period.

[87] See now Beard (2007: 219–56).

[88] Préaux (1978: 183–201, 208–12); Austin (1986: 457, 459); Wikander (1992: 148–9).

the prime glorification of his deeds came only after the parade. The wealth too was not his but Rome's.

In contrast to the Hellenistic king, who ruled also when off parade and thus staged the processions as manifestations of his own military and financial capacities, the Roman triumphator acted as king only for a day.[89] He looked like a king with divine potency, but he was only a man, a Roman magistrate. The *Fasti triumphales* uncover the *mimesis*, defining his real nature at the time of celebration; in the commemorative recording, the Republican triumphator was neither king nor god, but *consul*, *proconsul*, *praetor*, *propraetor*, or *dictator*. In effect, as the triumph staged the Roman general only in imitation of a king, the procession performed a visible renunciation of royalty.

Certainly, the political scene changed with the great generals of the late Republic, accumulating unprecedented individual wealth, powers, and triumphs. In fact, as seen, Pompey and Caesar took on some new royal and godlike attributes as they staged their great triumphal performances in unprecedented confidence.[90] Both employed elephants as kingly or semi-divine accompanists in the triumphal ritual. Caesar had white horses driving his car, another allusion to royal divinity.[91] Rome first reacted with contempt for these boastful novelties, but soon adopted them. In Imperial times, white horses became regular elements of the processions, and elephants turned into customary escorts of emperors at the circus and in triumphal art. The development of triumphal dress tells a similar story. After Pompey's third triumph, a law permitted him to wear the full dress of a triumphator and golden crown in the theatre and at the circuses, although Pompey exploited the honour only once.[92] Again, after Caesar's triumphs, the senate granted him the right to wear triumphal dress on all occasions.[93] The triumphal dress and adornments were later transformed into the official garb of the emperor.[94] In this way, gradually the late Republican general and emperor took on the image of eternal triumphator.[95]

Still, the dress and attributes of the triumphator had since time immemorial been both royal and divine. The introduction of still novel regal and divine emblems into the procession and the extended use of the triumphal dress away from the parade was in a way only an expansion of some traits within a traditional triumphal frame. By contrast, some of Pompey and Caesar's other boastful

---

[89] Cf. Beard (2003*b*).

[90] See further Hölscher (2004*a*).

[91] Dio Cass. 43.14.3. Weinstock (1971: 64–79).

[92] Vell. Pat. 2.40.4. According to the *De viris illustribus*, Aemilius Paullus already had been granted this privilege, *vir. ill.* 56.5.

[93] Dio Cass. 43.43.1. Weinstock (1971: 106–8).

[94] Alföldi (1970: 143–61).

[95] Rüpke (1990: 233–4).

announcements of omnipotent powers were in explicit conflict with the established ritual. As such, they were not only condemned at the time, but also, more
revealingly, rejected by later triumphators. Thus, when Pompey in 61 BC dared to
parade a self-portrait made in pearls, this was, from what is known, a one-off
display. Pliny reacted with contempt, and later triumphators avoided similar
announcements.[96] The boasting of the triumphator's deeds was traditionally
reserved for post-triumphal recordings; the imagery on parade was instead connected to the display of the conquered, confirming their defeat and telling their
fates for the spectators to behold. When Caesar fifteen years later, in 46 BC,
included tableaux of Roman citizens as defeated and models of allied cities as
conquered, he likewise took the triumphal celebration far beyond its traditional
framing. In staging his personal Roman enemies in the traditional roles of
defeated, Caesar in fact inverted the ritual role-playing that was the very essence
of the triumph. His displays were not well taken, and later (as previous) triumphators did everything to conceal any traces of Romans as defeated adversaries.

Caesar and Pompey took the triumphal celebration to its limits—and beyond.
Later on, Vespasian, Titus, and Trajan deliberately chose to turn to Republican
and Augustan precedence in staging triumphs of traditional valour. In Josephus'
words, the spoils paraded by Titus and Vespasian 'displayed the greatness of the
supremacy of the Romans',[97] not of the emperor. In this ritual context, traditional
values and *mos maiorum* were prime components, and even behind an emperor
riding in triumph stood a public slave as representative of the community,
requesting him to remember that he was but a man.[98]

Monarchy defeated

The procession staged the Roman triumphator, king of the day, in close visual
interplay with the defeated king, now divested of his royal powers. The vanquished king played a central role in the triumphal play, embodying nobility and
wealth. Hence, among Scipio Asiaticus' achievements, Livy gives prominence to
the fact that he had conquered the richest king in the world.[99] In another passage,
Livy expresses the very essence of the exposure of defeated royalty, 'that greatest
of shows, a captive king of highest birth and greatest riches'.[100]

---

[96] Plin. *Nat.* 37.6.14. Hubris was close at hand for both Pompey and Caesar; Beard calls Pompey's
portrait 'a nasty omen of Pompey's ultimate decapitation' (2003*b*: 31; 2007: 35–6). Throughout her book,
Beard (2007) emphasizes that there was a fine line between the momentous glory of the triumphator and
his exposure to failure and humiliation.

[97] Joseph. *BJ* 7.133–4: τῆς Ῥωμαίων ἡγεμονίας μέγεθος.

[98] Plin. *Nat.* 28.7.39. Rüpke (1990: 232–3); Köves-Zulauf (1998); Östenberg (2008).

[99] Liv. 38.60.5: *L. Scipionem, qui regem opulentissimum orbis terrarum devicerit,* ...

[100] Liv. 45.39.6.

In the display of royal defeat, the king's wealth was embraced by Rome. At the same time, monarchy itself was exposed as a vanquished and renounced antipode of Rome. Eastern kingship was led in defeat—its military potency, unlimited powers, opulent wealth, effeminate appearance, and debauched habits. Emblems of kingship, such as thrones, sceptres, chariots, and diadems, were paraded in splendid isolation to underline the failure and defeat of eastern kingship in its very essence. The vanquished king himself followed, deprived of his regalia and of his powers. The luxurious items and the objects of feasting, such as furniture, plate, and textiles, added to the message of monarchic downfall. At times, the staging of defeated kingship also included former regents. Pliny maintains that Pompey paraded a silver statue of Pharnaces I together with one of Mithridates.[101] On parade, there was also the couch of Darius and many other valuables and pieces of art coming from Darius and the former kings and queens of the Ptolemies.[102] Here, Pompey showed not only Mithridates but also his very kingdom defeated along with monarchy as a concept.

Rome's continuous victories had proved royalty worthless, and the display of vanquished kingship celebrated the supremacy of the *res publica* over monarchy. Greek and Latin writers alike paint the conflicts between Rome and the Hellenistic kingdoms as one between two confronting constitutions, the free state and monarchy.[103] By nature, these two were hostile to each other: *natura inimica inter se esse liberam civitatem et regem*.[104] The triumphal emphasis on defeated royalty thus staged the superiority of the free state, embodied by Rome. In joy and gratitude, others, now freed from despotic tyranny, joined the celebration. The cities of Asia Minor bestowed golden crowns on Manlius Vulso in gratitude for his oppression of the Galatians and also for his victory over Antiochus.[105] Through these accomplishments, Vulso had relieved the cities both of the barbarian threat, giving them peace, and of the slavery of the regent, bringing about political freedom. Hence, when displayed in the triumphs, the crowns not only announced Rome as protector of civilization, they also announced her as champion of liberty.

The world

The Roman triumphs presented spoils and captives in large numbers and of varied origins, manifesting the great extent of Roman domination. As seen, the parades also customarily proclaimed mastery over peoples and places beyond the particular area officially conquered. For example, in 275 BC, Dentatus led Molossians, Thessalians, Macedonians, Bruttii, Apuli, and Lucanians in a triumph

---

[101] Plin. *Nat.* 33.54.151–2. [102] App. *Mith.* 115–16.
[103] e.g. Polyb. 36.17.13; Liv. 45.18.1–3. Erskine (1991: 116–18).
[104] Liv. 44.24.1–2. [105] Liv. 38.37.

recorded by the *Fasti* as held over the Samnites and King Pyrrhus.[106] Moreover, many items on parade originally came from places far away. Thus Cato the Elder complains that when Syracuse was taken and their looted statues triumphantly transferred to Rome, ornaments from Athens and Corinth were introduced to the Roman people.[107]

By its very character, then, the triumphal procession was predisposed to show widespread domination. Still, for quite some time, announcements of a global hegemony seem to have been only implicitly performed. Flamininus, Scipio Asiaticus, and others certainly held glorious celebrations but, as far as we know, still staged their triumphs primarily as manifestations of royal vanquishment and confiscation of kingly wealth. Not long after Perseus' defeat in 168 BC, Polybius declared Rome as the new world power.[108] Yet the numerous accounts of the triumph held by Aemilius Paullus the following year reveal no proclamations of any Roman worldwide hegemony. Paullus displayed some naval success along with the victories on land, but there is no announcement of the triumph as a manifestation of Roman power *terra marique*. More importantly, the Macedonian triumphal celebration was in fact Paullus' second or even third. Before 167 BC, he had possibly performed a triumph for his victories in Spain and certainly one for his success in Liguria.[109] One would almost have expected the sources to announce him as *triplex* victor of the West and East alike. Still, no such claims appear.

Announcing the conquest of the world

By contrast, the triumphs held by the great generals of the late Republic explicitly boasted the conquest of the *orbis terrarum*. In particular, it was Pompey's three triumphs, culminating in the magnificent celebration of 61 BC that announced Roman mastery over the *oikumene*.

In his two-day parade in 61 BC, Pompey celebrated the vanquishment of eastern kings and pirates, thus announcing Roman domination on land and at sea. There were further ecumenical aspirations. In all probability, sculptured personifications represented the numerous peoples brought into submission. The ebony trees put on parade were advertised as coming *ex India*, outside Pompey's conquests, but alluding to Alexander's. Amazons and pirates transmitted messages of the defeat of extra-communal inhabitants. In fact, Pompey boasted his claim to world rule quite ostentatiously. He claimed that he had

---

[106] Flor. *Epit.* 1.13.27.   [107] Liv. 34.4.4.

[108] Polyb. 1.1.5, 1.3.10, 3.1.4, 6.50.6. For Greek views of Roman world rule at this date, see Vogt (1960: 154–6).

[109] The *Fasti triumphales Capitolini* and *Urbisalvienses* confirm Paullus' triumphs over the Ligurians (in 181 BC) and Macedonians (167 BC). Other sources suggest a third triumph for victories in Spain. A memorial inscription declares that he triumphed thrice (*triumphavit ter*), Degrassi, *Inscr. It.* 13:3, no. 71b, 50–1. Paullus is known to have defeated the Lusitani as praetor or propraetor in 190–189 BC, and Velleius Paterculus testifies that he held a triumph in the capacity of praetor (1.9.3).

found Asia on the edge of the Roman realm and had made it the centre.[110] In the triumph, he wore a cloak that allegedly had belonged to Alexander,[111] clearly referring to the Asian conquests and worldwide ambitions of his predecessor. Most importantly, before him in the parade, he showed off his worldwide conquest by parading a representation of *oikumene* itself. Dio Cassius (37.21.2) gives the principal evidence:

καὶ αὐτὰ μὲν ἅπαξ ἀπὸ πάντων τῶν πολέμων ἤγαγε, τρόπαια δὲ ἄλλα τε πολλὰ καὶ καλῶς κεκοσμημένα καθ᾽ ἕκαστον τῶν ἔργων καὶ τὸ βραχύτατον ἔπεμψε, καὶ ἐπὶ πᾶσιν ἓν μέγα, πολυτελῶς τε κεκοσμημένον καὶ γραφὴν ἔχον ὅτι τῆς οἰκουμένης ἐστίν.

He celebrated the triumph in honour of all his wars at once, including in it many trophies beautifully decked out to represent each of his achievements, even the smallest; and after them all came a huge one, magnificently adorned and bearing an inscription stating that it was a trophy of the inhabited world.

Dio does not describe the 'trophy' of the *oikumene*, nor is there other evidence that reveals its appearance. The *oikumene* might have been a globe or it could have been a personification.[112] What Dio does state is that the representation followed other trophies, manifesting each of the preceding achievements. In similar words, Plutarch testifies to the presence in the triumph of many trophies, representing each particular success.[113] Certainly, the recent victories over Mithridates and Tigranes formed part of the display, but in all probability, this was not all. Plutarch continues his account by stating that Pompey's greatest honour was that he held his third triumph over a third continent: 'For others before him had celebrated three triumphs; but he celebrated his first over Libya, his second over Europe, and this his last over Asia, so that he seemed in a way to have included the whole world in his three triumphs.'[114] In fact, Pompey's three triumphs (Africa around 80 BC, Spain 71 BC, eastern kingdoms in 61 BC) formed a recurrent theme in ancient literature.[115] Cicero returns as many as seven times to the fact that Pompey had triumphed thrice (*ter triumphare*), Lucan in six passages.[116] Others, such as Propertius, Velleius Paterculus, Valerius Maximus, Pliny the Elder, Petronius, Seneca, and Manilius, also testify to the *tres triumphi*.[117] As in Plutarch's praise, the point was not only that Pompey celebrated three triumphs, but even more that these parades staged victories over each of the three contin-

---

[110] Plin. *Nat.* 7.26.99.   [111] App. *Mith.* 117; cf. Plut. *Pomp.* 46.1.
[112] Weinstock (1971: 38).   [113] Plut. *Pomp.* 45.4.   [114] Ibid. 45.5.
[115] Deutsch (1924a); Weinstock (1971: 38–9).
[116] Cic. *Balb.* 4.9, 6.16, *Pis.* 24.58, 13.29, *Sest.* 60.61.129, *Div.* 2.9.22, *Off.* 1.22.78; Lucan. 6.816–17, 7.685–6, 8.553, 8.813–15, 9.177–8, 9.599–600.
[117] Prop. 3.11.35; Vell. Pat. 2.40.4, 2.53.3; Val. Max. 5.1.10; Plin. *Nat.* 37.6.13; Petron. 240; Sen. *Contr.* 10.1.8; Manil. *Astron.* 1.793, 4.52.

FIGURE 27 Reverse of denarius that celebrates Pompey's three triumphs as the conquest of the world. The three smaller wreaths surrounding the globe are probably symbols of each triumphs, the larger at the top a reference to ecumenical leadership. To the right is also an ear of corn, to the left what has been read as a stern of a ship. These symbols give form to Pompey's dominance of both lands and sea.

ents, thus embracing the entire world. Thus, for example, Velleius Paterculus (2.40.4) writes of Pompey:

Huius viri fastigium tantis auctibus fortuna extulit, ut primum ex Africa, iterum ex Europa, tertio ex Asia triumpharet, et, quot partes orbis terrarum sunt, totidem faceret monumenta victoriae suae.

This man was raised by fortune to the pinnacle of his career by great leaps, first triumphing over Africa, then over Europe, then over Asia, and the three divisions of the world thus became so many monuments of his victory.

Pompey's third and final triumph could thus claim world domination as a result of his earlier success. Very possibly then, the trophies preceding the representation of the *oikumene* in the parade of 61 BC included scenes also from earlier campaigns and triumphs, all of which contributed to absolute mastery.[118] Similarly, I would think that the three smaller wreaths depicted on a silver coin from 56 BC (Fig. 27) represent his triumphs, while the larger wreath placed at top above an image of the globe celebrates the conquest of the whole world, itself a result of the three triumphs.[119] Single representations of Africa, Europe, and Asia themselves may also have been present on parade, giving form to the Roman take-over of all three parts of the *oikumene*, the image of which followed. In fact, the idea of Europe, Asia, and Africa as the three continents of the world emerged only in the

---

[118] Ooteghem (1954: 285) and Greenhalgh (1980: 171, cf. 173) both assume that the display referred to the earlier victories. Bellen (1988) instead maintains that the third triumph should be seen as an independent spectacle with its own inherent theme, celebrating the conquest of Asia and referring to Alexander.

[119] Crawford (1974: 426, 4b).

first half of the first century BC.[120] Pompey's victories and triumphal manifestations are likely to have played a part in this development. The visual proclam-
ation of world rule in this public performance certainly made a profound
impression, as is reflected in the abundant literary commemorations.

When Caesar in 46–45 BC performed his five triumphs, he aimed at outrivalling
his former son-in-law and rival as world conqueror.[121] In fact, while it took Pompey
twenty years to parade world conquest, Caesar in 46 BC staged his victories in Gaul
(Europe), Pontus (Asia), Egypt, and Africa during a period of but one month.
Clearly, the four parades formed a unity, to which the fifth triumph of Spain was
added in the following year. The great rivers the Rhine, the Oceanus, and the Nile,
were paraded as outer markers of worldwide supremacy. The apparatus of each
parade symbolized the specific area conquered and added to the message of one
single manifestation of global conquest. Citrus wood was used throughout the
Gallic triumph, tortoise shell for the Egyptian one, acanthus wood for the Pontic
triumph, ivory for the African procession, and silver for the Spanish triumph.[122]
But there was more; for Caesar, the world was not enough. While Pompey had
taken Rome to the edges of the world, Caesar, in order to outdo him, boasted
extra-terrestrial mastery.[123] According to Cicero, Caesar defeated peoples hitherto
unknown,[124] and in the procession, the Oceanus and the Nile, and the Britons, all
novelties on parade, marked the vanquishment of the world beyond. Again, Caesar
took the very triumph beyond its traditional frames.

Octavian too boasted the conquest of the world in his three triumphs, held on
successive days in August 29 BC.[125] Ships or beaks from Actium announced victories
at sea along with those on land. Rivers from all parts of the world appeared, as did,
in all probability, representations of the subdued peoples. Like Pompey, Octavian
displayed the subjugation of the three parts of the world in three processions. They
staged the victories in Dalmatia, at Actium, and in Alexandria and displayed spoils
and captives from Europe, Asia, and Africa.[126] Octavian trumped his predecessors
Pompey and Caesar, performing universal conquest in a period of three days only.
Quite clearly, the *triplex triumphus* was staged as a single glorious manifestation of
world domination. Dio Cassius and Servius both testify that Octavian entered the
city only on the last day's parade.[127] Dio also states that the spoils from Alexandria

[120] Tandoi (1962: 143).   [121] See also Östenberg (1999).

[122] Vell. 2.56.2. Deutsch (1924*b*).   [123] Schulz (2000*b*: esp. 290–6).

[124] Cic. *Prov.* 13.33.   [125] Östenberg (1999).

[126] Verg. *Aen.* 8.714–28; Liv. *Per.* 133; Aug. *Anc.* 4; Suet. *Aug.* 17.4, 22, 41, *Tib.* 6; App. *Ill.* 28; Dio Cass.
51.21.5–9; Serv. *ad Aen.* 8.714; Oros. 6.20.1. The *Fasti triumphales Barberiniani* mention only the triumphs
over Dalmatia and Egypt, Degrassi, *Inscr. It.* 13:1, 344–5, 570. See also Prop. 2.1.31–4, 3.11.53–4, 4.6.65–7;
Hor. *Carm.* 1.37; Vell. Pat. 2.89.1–2; Macr. *Sat.* 1.12.35. Binder (1971: 258–70); Gurval (1995: 19–36);
Östenberg (1999).

[127] Serv. *ad Aen.* 8.714; Dio Cass. 51.21.9.

were so numerous that Octavian had them paraded during all three days,[128] a statement that strengthens the assumption that the processions should be viewed as a single manifestation of world rule.

The age of Pompey, Caesar, and Octavian saw changes in Rome's view of herself and the surrounding world. These conceptions formed the background of the triumphal boastings of world domination, but were certainly also given nourishment by the displays themselves. The term *orbis terrarum* appears for the first time as a political slogan defining Roman power around 90 BC, but it was only after Pompey's triumph in 61 BC that the expression became routine.[129] The phrase *imperium Romanum* too, corresponding to a defined territory, occurs first in Sallust.[130] Somewhat earlier, from around 75 BC, images of the globe appear more frequently on Roman coins,[131] and according to Cicero, the Roman *patrocinium* of the world (*patrocinium orbis terrae*) changed after Sulla into an *imperium*.[132] In 66 BC, Cicero provides literary testimony to the concept of victories and domination 'on land and at sea'.[133] Cicero refers to Pompey's command over the pirates and his statement is paralleled by Pompey's own boasting of Roman control *terra marique* in his triumphal parade of 61 BC. Somewhat later, as Nicolet has stressed, the age of Augustus was permeated by the idea of Roman world control through universal pacification, reflected in the art and literature of the time.[134] Augustus himself opens his *Res Gestae* with a declaration of the conquest of the world: *Rerum gestarum divi Augusti, quibus orbem terrarum imperio populi Romani subiecit*.[135] His triumphs performed these proclamations.

Itemizing the world: parts as expression of the whole

Pompey had his third triumph announce worldwide rule by referring to earlier celebrations. Caesar and Octavian went further and staged a row of processions celebrating victories in the three parts of the world as deliberate joint manifestations. There are no sources to give evidence that they followed Pompey's example of parading a representation of the *oikumene*.[136] Instead, their triumphs proclaimed world supremacy by the collective display of single victories. A number of great rivers and a variety of peoples were paraded, and all the single displays interacted in staging the world. For example, while the exhibition of the River Nile in itself pointed specifically to the vanquishment of Egypt, jointly

---

[128] Dio Cass. 51.21.7–8.   [129] Nicolet (1991: 31–2).   [130] Sall. *Catil.* 10.1. Richardson (1991).
[131] Nicolet (1991: 36).   [132] Cic. *Off.* 2.8.27.   [133] Cic. *Manil.* 56. Nicolet (1991: 36).
[134] Nicolet (1991). See also Cresci Marone (1993).   [135] Aug. *Anc.* 1.
[136] The senate placed a statue of Caesar riding over the *oikumene* on the Capitol, Dio Cass. 43.14.6, 43.21.2. Modern scholars have debated the appearance of this image, suggesting that the *oikumene* was represented either by a globe or by a personification, e.g. Weinstock (1971: 40–59); Picard (1973); Nicolet (1991: 39–41).

staged with the Rhine, the Oceanus, and the Euphrates, its message was greatly amplified, announcing the ecumenical conquest.

In fact, Pompey's explicit boasting of world rule by way of one single all-embracing symbol seems to have constituted an exception in Roman triumphal history. Instead, similarly to Caesar and Octavian (although on a more modest scale), processions by tradition manifested supremacy through a spectrum of single displays that only in their conjunct exhibition performed complete command. This goes for Pompey's parade as well. Along with the representation of *oikumene*, the testimony of Plutarch and Dio Cassius reveals that he paraded trophies of all Roman victories, even the smallest. The embracing symbol of the inhabited world did not suffice to confirm its conquest; each single victory required exhibition.

The triumphal procession was in its essence a manifestation of conquest by the display of its parts. Ships and terrestrial spoils together staged the *terra marique*; gold, silver, and bronze absolute wealth; tigers, lions, leopards, and hippopotami the fauna; captured soldiers and families the world of war and peace; men, women, and children the family unit. Sheer multitude counted, as did widespread origins. For example, we have seen how the Republican processions paraded coins of many diverse denominations. Written placards listed rows of names of kings, peoples, and places vanquished. Captives on parade preferably represented areas far and wide, as did images of cities, peoples, rivers, and mountains. The triumph held by Balbus over the African Garamantes in 19 BC provides a striking example. Balbus paraded representations of the cities of Garamas and Cydama along with the images and names of the Rivers Nathabur and Dasibari, the mountains Niger and Gyri, the people of Niteris, Enipi, Viscera, Tamiagi, and the towns of Tabudium, Milgris Gemella, Bubeium (town or people), Thuben, Nitibrum, Rapsa, Decri, Thapsagum, Boin, Pege, Baracum, Buluba, Alasit, Galsa, Balla, Maxalla, Cizania.[137] Pliny, our source, says nothing of any representation of Africa or even of the encompassing people of the Garamantes. Such images might have been present too, but they would not have been sufficient. Only by displaying each single unit of peoples and places to the gaze of the Roman people could Balbus confirm complete conquest of the area.

In Roman art too, although the globe was frequently used as a symbol of world conquest, personifications of the *oikumene* are rare and they are not shown in subjugated poses announcing world conquest.[138] Instead, the Romans chose to stage embodied ethnic entities in corporate assemblies.[139] The personifications formed excellent means of systemizing and bringing order to the surrounding

---

[137] Plin. *Nat.* 5.5.36–7.
[138] *LIMC* vii (1994), s.v. 'Oikoumene', 1: 16–17 (F. Canciani).
[139] Smith (1988*a*: 70–1; Kuttner (1995: 91–3).

world, and it is hardly a coincidence that the age of Augustus saw a boom in monuments of groups of personifications.

Written monuments presented parallel announcements of complete conquest by naming the single units. After his success in Spain, Pompey set up a *tropaeum* in the Pyrenees inscribed with the names of 876 *oppida* that he had defeated in *Hispania ulterior*.[140] Later, at the altar of Rome and Augustus at Lugdunum, Augustus inscribed the names of sixty Gallic tribes enrolled in his cult in 10 BC.[141] The so-called *Tropaeum Alpium* at La Turbie names forty-six Alpine *gentes devictae*, and the Augustan arch at Susa lists a group of Alpine tribes.[142]

The triumphal procession itemized Roman conquests. There was the exact number of attic tetradrachmae, the precise quantity of silver vessels, the specific figure of cities conquered, the definite number of prominent prisoners. The recording afterwards forms part of the same concept of listing and defining new conquests very precisely. '*Presence* is fully defined only by *naming*', Mary Beard writes in an article on Roman religion.[143] Similarly, we might say of the Roman triumphs that conquest was fully defined and confirmed by the visual display (and its viewing) and written nomination (and its reading) of each single part.

Parading world mastery

From the age of Augustus, Rome was established master of the world. Certainly, there were still the Parthians and the Germans fully to subdue in order to gain and regain complete control, and certainly other peoples revolted.[144] But in its overall appearance, the *orbis terrarum* was now the *orbis Romanus*. World conquest had been obtained through the victories of Pompey, Caesar, and Octavian and staged in their triumphs. By contrast, the Imperial parades neither celebrated nor performed the conquest of the world. Instead, along with the specific victories paraded, they manifested mastery of the world as already conquered. In fact, world domination seems to have been a recurrent feature of Imperial processions. Unlike Pompey, Caesar, and Octavian, the emperors did not even have to carry out victories over widespread areas nor display them in a row of parades to manifest world mastery. Instead, triumphs held also for a single

---

[140] Plin. *Nat.* 7.26.96.

[141] Strab. 4.3.2, describing written texts and εἰκόνες. Fishwick (1989); Kuttner (1995: 75). Kuttner discusses groups of peoples in written and pictorial commemorations.

[142] *Tropaeum Alpium*: Plin. *Nat.* 3.20.136–7. Sasel (1973). Susa: *CIL* v. 7231. Kuttner (1995: 75).

[143] Beard (1991: 46).

[144] For Augustus' campaigns in Germania as a way to world conquest, for his *imitatio Alexandri*, and for the Roman ideology of world rule as based on geographic misconceptions of the North, see Moynihan (1985).

success in a restricted area might be performed as a celebration of Roman universal rule.

The Jewish triumph of Vespasian and Titus reflects this process. Earlier on, Pompey had liberated all of the Mediterranean of the pirates, subdued all kings of the East, and won battles in Africa and Spain to boast the conquest of the world through a series of triumphs. Now Vespasian needed but to strike down a revolt in Judaea and capture some local ships to announce mastery of lands and seas in a single procession. Josephus testifies to the ecumenical aspirations of the Jewish triumph (*BJ* 7.132–4):

Ἀμήχανον δὲ κατὰ τὴν ἀξίαν εἰπεῖν τῶν θεαμάτων ἐκείνων τὸ πλῆθος καὶ τὴν μεγαλοπρέπειαν ἐν ἅπασιν οἷς ἄν τις ἐπινοήσειεν ἢ τεχνῶν ἔργοις ἢ πλούτου μέρεσιν ἢ φύσεως σπανιότησιν· σχεδὸν γὰρ ὅσα τοῖς πώποτ' ἀνθρώποις εὐδαιμονήσασιν ἐκτήθη κατὰ μέρος ἄλλα παρ' ἄλλοις θαυμαστὰ καὶ πολυτελῆ, ταῦτ' ἐπὶ τῆς ἡμέρας ἐκείνης ἀθρόα τῆς Ῥωμαίων ἡγεμονίας ἔδειξε τὸ μέγεθος.

It is impossible adequately to describe the multitude of those spectacles and their magnificence under every conceivable aspect, whether in works of art or diversity of riches or natural rarities; for almost all the objects which men who have ever been blessed by fortune have acquired one by one—the wonderful and precious productions of various peoples—by their collective exhibition on that day displayed the greatness of the supremacy of the Romans.

Here, we find again the recurrent theme of Roman triumphs as manifesting supremacy also outside the specific area of conquest. At this point, supremacy had come to embrace the whole world. Although the triumph officially celebrated the subjugation of a revolt in Judaea only, along with the Jewish spoils, it staged natural rarities, riches, and objects of art produced by peoples far and near and coming from all over the world. Again, the claim to ecumenical control was not made through the display of one all-embracing symbol but by the exhibition of an endless row of spoils and captives. According to Josephus, the valuables of gold and silver were so abundant that they seemed to flow in the parade like a river.[145]

In fact, to such an extent had Rome now embraced others that the whole world was transferred to the city itself. Josephus reflects this process, concluding his account by stating that after the Jewish procession Vespasian decided to build the Templum Pacis to house the spoils and other objects.[146] 'Indeed', writes Josephus, 'into that shrine were accumulated and stored all objects for the sight of which men had once wandered over the whole world, eager to see them severally while they lay in various countries'. The idea of the city of Rome as

---

[145] Joseph. *BJ* 7.134.   [146] Ibid. 7.160–1.

identical with the inhabited world appears first in Cicero, Varro, and Nepos,[147] but Ovid encapsulated the idea in its most famous form: *gentibus est aliis tellus data limite certo: Romanae spatium est Urbis et orbis idem*, 'the land of other peoples has a fixed boundary; the extent of the city of Rome is the same as that of the world'.[148] The *Urbs–orbis* theme implied Roman mastery of the world, but could also be taken to mean that the whole world might be seen in Rome. By leading the world into the city, the triumphal procession formed the supreme staging of this notion. In addition, the world was not only put on stage but also invited to watch its display as part of the performance. Ovid, painting a picture of Tiberius' triumph, reports: 'By your evidence, I learned that recently, countless races assembled to see their leader's face; and Rome, who embraces the measureless world within her vast walls, had barely room for her guests.'[149] In the triumph, Rome and the world were one.

[147] Cic. *Catil.* 1.9, *Mur.* 22, *Fam.* 4.1.2; Varro *Ling.* 5.143; Nep. *Att.* 3.3, 20.5. Vogt (1960: 156, 159–60); Bréguet (1969); Nicolet (1991: 33); Rochette (1997).

[148] Ov. *Fast.* 2.683–4.

[149] Ov. *Pont.* 2.1.21–4: *indice te didici nuper visenda coisse | innumeras gentes ad ducis ora sui; | quaeque capit vastis inmensum moenibus orbem, | hospitiis Romam vix habuisse locum.*

BIBLIOGRAPHY

The abbreviations used are those cited in the *American Journal of Archaeology* (www. ajaonline.org).

ABAECHERLI, A. L. (1935/36), 'Fercula, carpenta, and tensae in the Roman Procession', *BStM* 6, 1–20.

ADAMO MUSCETTOLA, S. (1992), 'Per una riedizione dell'arco di Traiano a Benevento: Appunti sul fregio trionfale', *Prospettiva*, 67, 2–16.

AGOSTINETTI, P. P. (1997), 'Il torques con terminazioni ad anello tra mondo italico e mondo celtico', in G. Nardi, M. Pandolfini, L. Drago, and A. Berardinetti (eds.), *Etrusca et Italica: Scritti in ricordo di Massimo Pallottino* (Rome), 497–514.

ALBRETHSEN, P. HØEG (1987), 'Carnyx: En keltisk krigstrompet som møntmotiv og romersk sejrstrofæ' (in Danish), *Nordisk numismatisk unions medlemsblad*, 5, 102–23.

ALFÖLDI, A. (1970), *Die monarchische Repräsentation in römischen Kaiserreiche* (Darm-stadt).

ALLEN, J. (2006), *Hostages and Hostage-taking in the Roman Empire* (New York).

ALPERS, M. (1995), *Das nachrepublikanische Finanzsystem: Fiscus und Fisci in der frühen Kaiserzeit* (Berlin).

AMIOTTI, G. (2001), 'Nome e origine del trionfo romano', in M. Sordi (ed.), *Il pensiero sulla guerra nel mondo antico* (Milan), 101–8.

—— (2002), 'Il trionfo come spettacolo', in M. Sordi (ed.), *Guerra e diritto nel mondo greco e romano* (Milan), 201–6.

AMY, R., DUVAL, P. M., and FORMIGÉ, J. (1962), *L'Arc d'Orange* (*Gallia*, suppl. 15; Paris).

ANDERSON, R. D., PARSONS, P. J., and NISBET, R. G. M. (1979), 'Elegiacs by Gallus from Qasr Ibrîm', *JRS* 69, 125–55.

ANDRÉ, J. (1985), *Les Noms de plantes dans la Rome antique* (Paris).

ANDREAE, B. (1974), *Römische Kunst* (Freiburg).

—— (1979), 'Zum Triumphfries des Trajansbogens von Benevent', *RM* 86, 325–9.

ARCE, J. (1980), 'La iconografia de "Hispania" in epoca romana', *Archivo español de arquelogía*, 53, 77–94.

AUBAUER, H. (1970), *Antike Stadtdarstellungen* (Vienna).

AULIARD, C. (2001), *Victoires et triomphes à Rome: Droit et réalités sous la République* (Paris).

AUSTIN, M. M. (1986), 'Hellenistic Kings, War and the Economy', *CQ* 36, 450–66.

BAATZ, D. (1994), *Bauten und Katapulte des römischen Heeres* (Stuttgart).

BACCHIELLI, L. (1988), 'Un rilievo della collezione Castelli-Baldassini con rappresenta-zione di pompa trionfale', *ScAnt* 2, 391–401.

BADIAN, E. (1955), 'The Date of Pompey's First Triumph', *Hermes*, 83, 107–18.

—— (1961), 'Servilius and Pompey's First Triumph', *Hermes*, 89, 254–5.

BALBUZA, K. (2002), 'Triumph as the Expression of Roman Ideology of Victory from Augustus to Diocletianus', *Eos*, 89, 361–6.

—— (2004), 'Triumph in the Service of Emperors' Dynastic Policy during the Principate', *Eos*, 91, 64–84.

BALDACCI, P. (1969), '*Patrimonium* e *ager publicus* al tempo dei Flavi: Ricerche sul monopolio del balsamo giudaico e sull'uso del termine *fiscus* in Seneca e Plinio il vecchio', *PP* 128, 349–67.

BALSDON, J. P. V. D. (1979), *Romans and Aliens* (London).

BARINI, C. (1952), *Triumphalia: Imprese ed onori militari durante l'impero romano* (Turin).

BARLOW, C. (1977), 'The *sanctius aerarium* and the Argento Publico Coinage', *AJP* 98, 290–302.

BARR-SHARRAR, B. (1982), 'Macedonian Metal Vases in Perspective: Some Observations on Context and Tradition', in B. Barr-Sharrar and E. N. Borza (eds.), *Macedonia and Greece in Late Classical and Early Hellenistic Times* (Washington, DC), 123–39.

BAUDOU, A. (1997), 'Note sur Papirius Maso, le triomphe, le laurier et le myrte', *EchCl* 41, 293–304.

BAUMANN, G. (1992), 'Ritual Implicates "Others": Rereading Durkheim in a Plural Society', in D. de Coppet (ed.), *Understanding Rituals* (London and New York), 97–116.

BAUS, K. (1940), *Der Kranz in Antike und Christentum: Eine religionsgeschichtliche Untersuchung mit besonderer Berücksichtigung Tertullians* (Bonn).

BEACHAM, R. C. (1991), *The Roman Theatre and its Audience* (London).

BEARD, M. (1991), 'Ancient Literacy and the Function of the Written Word in Roman Religion', in M. Beard *et al.* (eds.), *Literacy in the Roman World* (*JRA* suppl. 3; Ann Arbor), 35–58.

—— (2003a), 'The Triumph of Flavius Josephus', in A. J. Boyle and W. J. Dominik (eds.), *Flavian Rome: Culture, Image, Text* (Leiden), 543–58.

—— (2003b), 'The Triumph of the Absurd: Roman Street Theatre', in C. Edwards and G. Wolf (eds.), *Rome the Cosmopolis* (Cambridge), 21–43.

—— (2004), 'Writing Ritual: The Triumph of Ovid', in A. Barchiesi, J. Rüpke, and S. Stephens (eds.), *Rituals in Ink: A Conference on Religion and Literary Production in Ancient Rome Held at Stanford University in February 2002* (*Potsdamer Altertumswissenschaftliche Beiträge*, 10; Stuttgart), 115–26.

—— (2007), *The Roman Triumph* (Cambridge, Mass.).

—— NORTH, J., and PRICE, S. (1998a), *Religions of Rome*, i. *A History* (Cambridge).

—— —— —— (1998b), *Religions of Rome*, ii. *A Sourcebook* (Cambridge).

BECK, H. (2005), 'Züge in die Ewigkeit: Prozessionen durch das republikanische Rom', *Göttinger Forum für Altertumswissenschaft*, 8, 73–104.

BELL, C. (1997), *Ritual: Perspectives and Dimensions* (New York).

BELLEMORE, J. (2000), 'Pompey's Triumph over the Arabs', in C. Deroux (ed.), *Studies in Latin Literature and Roman History*, 10 (*CollLatomus*, 254; Brussels), 91–123.

BELLEN, H. (1985), *Metus Gallicus–metus Punicus: Zum Furchtmotiv in der römischen Republik* (Mainz).

—— (1988), 'Das Weltreich Alexanders des Großen als Tropaion im Triumphzug des Cn. Pompeius Magnus (61 v. Chr.)', in W. Will, with assistance from J. Heinrichs (eds.), *Zu Alexander d.Gr.: Festschrift G. Wirth* (Amsterdam), 865–78.

BENARIO, H. W. (2005), 'Females in Germanicus' Triumph', *Ancient History Bulletin*, 19, 176–80.

BENASSAI, R. (2001), *La pittura dei Campani e dei Sanniti* (Rome).

BERGMANN, B. (1999), 'Introduction: The Art of Ancient Spectacle', in B. Bergmann and C. Kondoleon, *The Art of Ancient Spectacle* (Studies in the History of Art, 56; Washington, DC), 9–35.

BERNSTEIN, F. (1998), *Ludi publici: Untersuchungen zur Entstehung und Entwicklung der öffentlichen Spiele im republikanischen Rom* (Stuttgart).

BESELER, G. (1909), 'Triumph und Votum', *Hermes*, 44, 352–61.

BIENKOWSKI, P. (1900), *De simulacris barbararum gentium apud Romanos*: *Corporis barbarorum prodromus* (Krakow).

BINDER, G. (1971), *Aeneas und Augustus: Interpretation zum 8. Buch der Aeneis* (Meisenheim am Glan).

BLANCKENHAGEN, P. H. VON (1962), *The Paintings from Boscotrecase* (RM–EH 6; Heidelberg).

—— and ALEXANDER, C. (1990), *The Augustan Villa at Boscotrecase* (Mainz am Rhein).

BODSON, L. (1998), 'Ancient Greek Views on the Exotic Animal', *Arctos*, 32, 61–85.

BONA, F. (1960), 'Sul concetto di "manubiae" e sulla responsabilità del magistrato in ordine alla preda', *Studia et documenta historiae et iuris*, 26, 105–75.

BONFANTE WARREN, L. (1970*a*), 'Roman Triumphs and Etruscan Kings: The Changing Face of the Triumph', *JRS* 60, 49–66.

—— (1970*b*), 'Roman Triumphs and Etruscan Kings: The Latin Word *triumphus*', in R. C. Lugton and M. G. Saltzer (eds.), *Studies in Honor of J. Alexander Kerns* (The Hague and Paris), 108–20.

—— (1974), Review of H. S. Versnel: *Triumphus: An Inquiry into the Origin, Development and Meaning of the Roman Triumph*, *Gnomon*, 46, 574–83.

—— (1978), 'Historical Art: Etruscan and Early Roman', *AJAH* 3, 136–62.

BOOS, A. (1989), ' "Oppidum" im caesarischen und im archäologischen Sprachgebrauch: Widersprüche und Probleme', *Acta praehistorica et archaeologica*, 21, 53–73.

BORBEIN, A. H. (1968), *Campanareliefs: Typologische und stilkritische Untersuchungen* (RM–EH 14; Heidelberg).

BORZSÁK, I. (1994), '*Laus Caesaris*: Ein Epigrammenzyklus auf Claudius' britannischen Triumphzug', *Acta Antiqua Academiae Scientiarum Hungaricae*, 35, 117–32.

BOURQUE, N. (2000), 'An Anthropologist's View of Ritual', in E. Bispham and C. Smith (eds.), *Religion in archaic and republican Rome and Italy: Evidence and Experience* (Edinburgh), 19–33.

BRANDS, G., and MAISCHBERGER, M. (1995), 'Der Tempel des *Hercules invectus*, die *Porta trigemina* under die *Porta triumphalis*', *RdA* 19, 102–20.

BRAUND, D. (1984), *Rome and the Friendly King: The Character of the Client Kingship* (London and New York).

BRAUND, D. (1996), 'River Frontiers in the Environmental Psychology of the Roman World', in D. L. Kennedy (ed.), *The Roman Army in the East* (*JRA* Suppl. 18; Ann Arbor), 43–7.

BRÉGUET, E. (1969), '*Urbi et orbi*: Un cliché et un thème', in J. Bibauw (ed.), *Hommages à Marcel Renard*, i (*CollLatomus*, 101; Brussels), 140–52.

BRELICH, A. (1938), 'Trionfo e morte', *Studi e materiali di storia delle religioni*, 14, 189–93.

BRENNAN, T. COREY (1994), 'M'. Curius Dentatus and the Praetor's Right to Triumph', *Historia*, 43, 423–39.

—— (1996), 'Triumphus in Monte Albano', in R. W. Wallace and E. M. Harris (eds.), *Transitions to Empire*: *Essays in Greco-Roman History, 360–146 B.C., in Honor of E. Badian* (Norman Okla.), 315–37.

BRILLIANT, R. (1984), *Visual Narratives: Storytelling in Etruscan and Roman Art* (Ithaca, NY, and London).

—— (1999), '"Let the Trumpets Roar!" The Roman Triumph', in B. Bergmann and C. Kondoleon, *The Art of Ancient Spectacle* (Studies in the History of Art, 56; Washington, DC), 221–9.

BRIQUEL, D. (1986), 'La Tradition sur l'emprunt d'armes samnites par Rome', in A.-M. Adam and A. Rouveret (eds.), *Guerre et sociétés en Italie aux V*ᵉ *et IV*ᵉ *siècles avant J.-C: Les Indices fournis par l'armement et les techniques de combat. Table ronde Paris, 5 Mai 1984* (Paris), 65–89.

BRISCOE, J. (1972), 'Flamininus and Roman Politics, 200–189 B.C.', *Latomus*, 31, 22–52.

—— (1973), *A commentary on Livy: Books XXXI–XXXIII* (Oxford).

—— (1981), *A commentary on Livy: Books XXXIV–XXXVII* (Oxford).

BROMEHEAD, C. N. (1952), 'What was Murrhine?', *Antiquity*, 26, 65–70.

BRUÈRE, R. T. (1956), 'Pliny the Elder and Virgil', *CP* 51, 228–46.

BRUHL, A. (1929), 'Les Influences hellénistiques dans le triomphe romain', *MÉFRA* 46, 77–95.

BRUNT, P. A. (1966), 'The "Fiscus" and its Development', *JRS* 56, 75–91.

BRUUN, C. (2000), '"What Every Man in the Street Used to Know": M. Furius Camillus, Italic Legends and Roman Historiography', in C. Bruun (ed.), *The Roman Middle Republic: Politics, Religion, and Historiography c. 400–133 B.C.: Papers from a Conference at the Institutum Romanum Finlandiae, September 11–12, 1998* (Rome), 41–68.

BULLE, H. (1943), 'Keltische Brautfahrt, etruskische Hadesfahrt und der genius cucullatus', *WJh* 35, 138–56.

BURASELIS, K. (1996), '*Vix aerarium sufficeret*: Roman Finances and the Outbreak of the Second Macedonian War', *GRBS* 37, 149–72.

CAGIANO DE AZEVEDO, M. (1972), 'Un trionfo e una distruzione: *M. FOLVIOS e VOLSINIUM*', *PP* 27, 239–45.

CAIROLA, A., and CARLI, E. (1963), *Il palazzo pubblico di Siena* (Rome).

CALLU, J. P. (1976), 'Eléphants et cochons: Sur une représentation monétaire d'époque républicaine', in *Mélanges offerts à Jacques Heurgon: L'Italie préromaine et la Rome républicaine* (Collection de l'École française de Rome, 27), 89–99.

CALMEYER, P. (1974), 'Zur Genese altiranischer Motive. II: Der leere Wagen', *AMIran* 7, 49–77.

CAMPS, W. A. (1966), Propertius, *Elegies Book III* (Cambridge).

CANCIK, H. (1997), 'Die "Repraesentation" von "Provinz" (*nationes, gentes*) in Rom: Ein Beitrag zur Bestimmung von "Reichsreligion" vom 1. Jahrhundert v. Chr. bis zum 2. Jahrhundert n. Chr.', in H. Cancik and J. Rüpke (eds.), *Römische Reichsreligion und Provinzialreligion* (Tübingen), 129–43.

CÀNOLA, F. (1982), 'Diodoro e la storia romana', *ANRW* II.30.1 (Berlin and New York), 724–73.

CAREY, S. (2003), *Pliny's Catalogue of Culture: Art and Empire in the Natural History* (Oxford).

CARSON, R. A. G. (1978), *Principal Coins of the Romans, i. The Republic c. 290–31 BC* (London).

—— (1980), *Principal Coins of the Romans, ii. The Principate 31 BC–AD 296* (London).

CASSON, L. (1991), *The Ancient Mariners. Seafarers and Sea Fighters of the Mediterranean in Ancient Times* (Princeton).

CASTRITIUS, H. (1971), 'Zum Aureus mit dem Triumph des Pompeius', *JNG* 21, 25–35.

CHANIOTIS, A. (1995), 'Sich selbst feiern? Städtische Feste des Hellenismus im Spannungsfeld von Religion und Politik', in M. Wörrle, and P. Zanker (eds.), *Stadtbild und Bürgerbild im Hellenismus, Kolloquium, Münich 24. bis 26. Juni 1993* (Munich), 147–63.

—— (2006), 'Rituals between Norms and Emotions: Rituals as Shared Experience and Memory', in E. Stavrianopoulou (ed.), *Ritual and Communication in the Graeco-Roman World* (*Kernos*, suppl. 16; Liège), 211–38.

CHASTAGNOL, A. (1987), 'Aspects concrets et cadre topographique des fêtes décennales des empereurs à Rome', in *L'Urbs: Espace urbain et histoire (Ier siècle av. J.-C.–IIIe siècle ap. J.-C.). Actes du colloque international organisé par le Centre national de la recherche scientifique et l'École Française de Rome (Rome, 8–12 mai 1985)* (Rome), 491–507.

CHURCHILL, J. BRADFORD (1999), '*Ex qua quod vellent facerent*: Roman Magistrates' Authority over *praeda* and *manubiae*', *TAPA* 129, 85–116.

CLAUSS, J. J. (1988), 'Vergil and the Euphrates Revisited', *AJP* 109, 309–20.

COARELLI, F. (1968), 'La porta trionfale e la via dei trionfi', *DialArch* 2, 55–103.

—— (1997*a*), *Il Campo Marzio: Dalle origini alla fine della repubblica* (Rome).

—— (1997*b*), 'Il "pecile" di Villa Adriana e la porticus triumphi', *RM* 104, 207–17.

COLEMAN, K. M. (1990), 'Fatal Charades: Roman Executions Staged as Mythological Enactments', *JRS* 80, 44–73.

—— (1996), 'Ptolemy Philadelphus and the Roman Amphitheater', in W. J. Slater (ed.), *Roman Theater and Society, E. Togo Salmon Papers I* (Ann Arbor), 49–68.

—— (1999), '"Informers" on Parade', in B. Bergmann and C. Kondoleon (eds.), *The Art of Ancient Spectacle* (Studies in the History of Art, 56; Washington, DC), 231–45.

COMBÈS, R. (1966), *Imperator: Recherches sur l'emploi et la signification du titre d'imperator dans la Rome républicaine* (Paris).

CONNOR, W. R. (1987), 'Tribes, Festivals and Processions: Civic Ceremonial and Political Manipulation in Archaic Greece', *JHS* 107, 40–50.

CORBIER, M. (1974), *L'aerarium Saturni et l'aerarium militare: Administration et prosopographie sénatoriale* (Rome).

CORNELL, T. J. (1995), *The Beginnings of Rome: Italy and Rome from the Bronze Age to the Punic Wars (c. 1000–264 BC)* (London and New York).

COTTON, H. M., and ECK, W. (1997), 'Ein Staatsmonopol und seine Folgen: Plinius, *Naturalis Historia* 12,123 und der Preis für Balsam', *RhM* 140, 153–61.

COZZA, L. (1958), 'Ricomposizione di alcune rilievi di Villa Medici', *BdA* 43, 107–11.

CRAWFORD, M. H. (1964), 'War and Finance', *JRS* 54, 29–32.

—— (1969), 'The Financial Organization of Republican Spain', *NC* 129, 79–93.

—— (1974), *Roman Republican Coinage*, i and ii (Cambridge).

—— (1977), 'Rome and the Greek World: Economic Relationships', *Economic History Review*, 30, 2nd ser. 42–52.

—— (1985), *Coinage and Money under the Roman Republic: Italy and the Mediterranean Economy* (London).

CRESCI MARRONE, G. (1993), *Ecumene augustea: Una politica per il consenso* (Rome).

CURRIE, S. (1996), 'The Empire of Adults: The Representation of Children on Trajan's Arch at Beneventum', in J. Elsner (ed.), *Art and Text in Roman Culture* (Cambridge), 153–81.

DARBY, W. J., GHALIOUNGUI, P., and GRIVETTI, L. (1977), *Food: The Gift of Osiris* (London).

D'ARMS, J. H. (1999), 'Performing Culture: Roman Spectacle and the Banquets of the Powerful', in B. Bergmann and C. Kondoleon (eds.), *The Art of Ancient Spectacle* (Studies in the History of Art, 56; Washington, DC), 301–19.

DARNTON, R. (1984), *The Great Cat Massacre and Other Episodes in French Cultural History* (London).

DAUT, R. (1975), *Imago: Untersuchungen zum Bildbegriff der Römer* (Heidelberg).

—— (1984), 'Belli facies et triumphus', *RM* 91, 115–23.

DAVIS, S. G. (1986), *Parades and Power: Street Theatre in Nineteenth-Century Philadelphia* (Philadelphia).

DAWSON, C. M. (1944), *Romano-Campanian Mythological Landscape Paintings* (Yale Classical Studies, 9; New Haven, Conn.).

DAYET, M. (1960), 'Le Denier de César au type de l'eléphant', *RÉA* 11, 42–7.

DE ANGELIS BERTOLOTTI, R. (1985), 'Materiali dell'Ara Pacis presso il Museo Nazionale Romano', *RM* 92, 221–34.

DE LIBERO, L. (1998), 'Der Raub des Staatsschatzes durch Caesar', *Klio*, 80, 111–33.

DEL MEDICO, H. E. (1964), 'La Prise de Jérusalem par Pompée d'après la légende juive de "la ville inconquise"', *BJb* 164, 53–87.

DE SANCTIS, G. (1923), *Storia dei romani*, iv 1 (Turin).

—— (1968), *Storia dei romani*, III 2, 2nd edn. (Florence).

DE SOUZA, P. (1999), *Piracy in the Graeco-Roman World* (Cambridge).

DEUTSCH, M. E. (1924a), 'Pompey's Three Triumphs', *CP* 19, 277–9.

—— (1924b), 'The *apparatus* of Caesar's Triumphs', *PQ* 3, 257–66.

DEVELIN, R. (1978), 'Tradition and the Development of Triumphal Regulations in Rome', *Klio*, 60, 429–38.

DOMASZEWSKI, A. VON (1885), *Die Fahnen im römischen Heere* (Vienna).

DOWDEN, K. (1997), 'The Amazons: Development and Functions', *RhM* 140, 97–128.

DREHER, M. (1996), 'Pompeius und die Kaukasischen Völker: Kolcher, Iberer, Albaner', *Historia*, 45, 188–207.

DREIZEHNTER, A. (1975), 'Pompeius als Städtegründer', *Chiron*, 5, 213–45.

EBERHARDT, B. (2005), 'Wer dient wem? Die Darstellung des Flavischen Triumphzuges auf dem Titusbogen und bei Josephus (*B.J.* 7.123–162)', in J. Sievers and G. Lembi (eds.), *Josephus and Jewish History in Flavian Rome and Beyond* (Supplements to the Journal for the Study of Judaism, 104; Leiden), 257–77.

ECKSTEIN, A. M. (1987), *Senate and General: Individual Decision-Making and Roman Foreign Relations, 264–194 B.C.* (Berkeley, Calif.).

EDEN, P. T. (1975), *A Commentary on Virgil: Aeneid VIII* (Leiden).

EDMONDSON, J. C. (1999), 'The Cultural Politics of Public Spectacle in Rome and the Greek East, 167–166 BCE', in B. Bergmann and C. Kondoleon (eds.), *The Art of Ancient Spectacle* (Studies in the History of Art, 56; Washington, DC), 77–95.

EHLERS, W. (1939), 'Triumphus', *RE*, 2nd edn, vii/1 (Stuttgart), 493–511.

ELBERN, S. (1990), 'Geiseln in Rom', *Athenaeum*, 78, 97–140.

ERDKAMP, P. (2006), 'Valerius Antias and Livy's Casualty Reports', in C. Deroux (ed.), *Studies in Latin Literature and Roman History*, 13 (CollLatomus, 301), 166–82.

ERRINGTON, R. M. (1993), 'Rome against Philip and Antiochus', *CAH* vii, 2nd edn (Cambridge), 244–89.

ERSKINE, A. (1991), 'Hellenistic Monarchy and Roman Political Invective', *CQ* 41, 106–20.

FALASSI, A. (1987), 'Festival: Definition and Morphology', in A. Falassi (ed.), *Time out of Time: Essays on the Festival* (Albuquerque, NM), 1–10.

FAVRO, D. (1994), 'The Street Triumphant: The Urban Impact of Roman Triumphal Parades', in Z. Çelik, D. Favro, and R. Ingersoll (eds.), *Streets: Critical Perspectives on Public Space* (Berkeley, Calif.), 151–64.

FEENEY, D. (1998), *Literature and Religion at Rome: Cultures, Contexts, and Belief* (Cambridge).

FELLETTI MAJ, B. M. (1977), *La tradizione italica nell'arte romana I* (Rome).

FERRARY, J.-L. (1988), *Philhellénisme et impérialisme: Aspects idéologiques de la conquête romaine du monde hellénistique, de la seconde guerre de Macédoine à la guerre contre Mithridate* (Rome).

—— (1997), 'The Hellenistic World and Roman Political Patronage', in P. Cartledge, P. Garnsey, and E. Gruen (eds.), *Hellenistic Constructs: Essays in Culture, History, and Historiography* (Berkeley, Calif.), 105–19.

FERRIS, I. M. (2000), *Enemies of Rome: Barbarians through Roman Eyes* (Stroud).

FISHWICK, D. (1989), 'The Sixty Gallic Tribes and the Altar of the Three Gauls', *Historia*, 38, 111–12.

FLAIG, E. (1995), 'Die *Pompa Funebris*: Adlige Konkurrenz und annalistische Erinnerung in der römischen Republik', in O. G. Oexle (ed.), *Memoria als Kultur* (Göttingen), 115–48.

—— (2003), *Ritualisierte Politik: Zeichen, Gesten und Herrschaft im alten Rom* (Göttingen).

FLORY, M. B. (1988), 'Pearls for Venus', *Historia*, 37, 498–504.

—— (1998), 'The Integration of Women into the Roman Triumph', *Historia*, 47, 489–94.

FLOWER, H. I. (1995), '*Fabulae praetextae* in Context: When were Plays on Contemporary Subjects Performed in Republican Rome?', *CQ* 45, 170–90.

—— (1996), *Ancestor Masks and Aristocratic Power in Roman Culture* (Oxford).

FLOWER, H. I. (1998), 'The Significance of an Inscribed Breastplate Captured at Falerii in 241 B.C.', *JRA* 11, 224–32.

—— (2000), 'The Tradition of the *spolia opima*: M. Claudius Marcellus and Augustus', *ClAnt* 19, 34–64.

FOERTMEYER, V. (1988), 'The Dating of the *pompe* of Ptolemy II Philadelphus', *Historia*, 37, 90–104.

FRANK, T. (1919), 'The Columna Rostrata of C. Duillius', *CP* 14, 74–82.

—— (1933), *An Economic Survey of Ancient Rome*, i. *Rome and Italy of the Republic* (Baltimore).

FREY, O.-H. (1976), 'The Chariot Tomb from Adria: Some Notes on Celtic Horsemanship and Chariotry', in J. Megaw (ed.), *To Illustrate the Monuments: Essays on Archaeology Presented to Stuart Piggott* (London), 172–9.

FUGMANN, J. (1991), '"Mare a praedonibus pacavi" (*R.G.* 25,1): Zum Gedanken der *aemulatio* in den *Res gestae* des Augustus', *Historia*, 40, 307–17.

GABELMANN, H. (1981), 'Römische ritterliche Offiziere im Triumphzug', *JdI* 96, 436–65.

GARDNER, P. (1878), *A Catalogue of the Greek Coins in the British Museum, iv. The Seleucid Kings of Syria* (London).

—— (1888), 'Countries and Cities in Ancient Art', *JHS* 9, 47–81.

GASPARRI, C. (1970), 'La donazione di Seleuco Nikator al Didymaion di Mileto', *StMisc* 15, 45–53.

GEERTZ, C. (1973), *The Interpretation of Cultures* (London).

GERDING, H. (2002), *The Tomb of Caecilia Metella: Tumulus, tropaeum and thymele* (Lund).

GIOVANNINI, A. (1996), 'Die Zerstörung Jerusalems durch Titus: Eine Strafe Gottes oder eine historische Notwendigkeit?', in P. Barceló (ed.), *Contra quis ferat arma deos? Vier Augsburger Vorträge zur Religionsgeschichte der römischen Kaiserzeit. Zum 60. Geburtstag von Gunther Gottlieb* (Munich), 11–34.

GIRARD, J.-L. (1989), 'Minerva capta: Entre Rome et Faleries', *RÉL* 67, 163–9.

GIRARDET, K. M. (1991), 'Der Triumph des Pompeius im Jahre 61 v. Chr. — *ex Asia*?', *ZPE* 89, 201–15.

GLASSBERG, D. (1990), *American Historical Pageantry: The Uses of Tradition in the Early Twentieth Century* (Chapel Hill, NC).

GOELL, H. A. (1854), *De triumphi romani origine, permissu, apparatu, via* (Schleiz).

GONZALES, J. (1984), 'Tabula siarensis, fortunales siarenses et municipia civium romanorum', *ZPE* 55, 55–100.

GOODMAN, M. (1987), *The Ruling Class of Judaea: The Origins of the Jewish Revolt against Rome A.D. 66–70* (Cambridge).

—— (1997), *The Roman World 44 BC–AD 180* (London and New York).

GÖRLER, W. (1993), 'Tiberaufwärts nach Rom: Ein Thema und seine Variationen', *Klio*, 75, 228–43.

GOWERS, E. (2005), 'Talking Trees: Philemon and Baucis Revisited', *Arethusa*, 38, 331–65.

GRAF, F. (1991), 'Gestures and Conventions: The Gestures of Roman Actors and Orators', in J. Bremmer and H. Roodenburg (eds.), *A Cultural History of Gesture: From Antiquity to the Present Day* (London), 36–58.

—— (1996), '*Pompai* in Greece: Some Considerations about Space and Ritual in the Greek *polis*', in R. Hägg (ed.), *The Role of Religion in the Early Greek Polis: Proceedings of the Third International Seminar on Ancient Greek Cult, Organized by the Swedish Institute at Athens, 16–18 October 1992* (Stockholm), 55–65.

GRAINGER, J. D. (1995), 'The Campaign of Cn. Manlius Vulso in Asia Minor', *AnatSt* 45, 23–42.

GRASSI, M. T. (1999), 'L'Africa e gli elefanti: Appunti sull' iconografia della provincia', in M. Castoldi (ed.), *Koinà: Miscellanea di studi archeologici in onore di Piero Orlandini* (Milan), 481–90.

GREENHALGH, P. (1981), *Pompey: The Roman Alexander* (Columbia).

GREGORY, A. P. (1994), 'Powerful Images: Responses to Portraits and the Political Uses of Images in Rome', *JRA* 7, 80–99.

GROAG, E. (1915), 'Beiträge zur Geschichte des zweiten Triumvirats', *Klio*, 14, 43–68.

GRUEN, E. S. (1984), *The Hellenistic World and the Coming of Rome* (Berkeley, Calif.).

—— (1990), *Studies in Greek Culture and Roman Policy* (Leiden).

—— (1992), *Culture and National Identity in Republican Rome* (New York).

—— (2006), 'Romans and Others', in N. Rosenstein and R. Morstein-Marx (eds.), *A Companion to the Roman Republic* (Oxford), 459–77.

GUILHEMBET, J.-P. (1992), 'Sur un jeu de mots de Sextus Pompée: *domus* et propagande politique lors d'un épisode des guerres civiles', *MÉFRA* 104, 787–816.

GUILLAUMIN, J.-Y. (1987), 'Les *flumina* chez César', *Latomus*, 46, 755–61.

GURVAL, R. A. (1995), *Actium and Augustus: The Politics and Emotions of Civil War* (Ann Arbor).

GUSTAFSSON, G. (2000), *Evocatio deorum: Historical and Mythical Interpretations of Ritualised Conquests in the Expansion of Ancient Rome* (Uppsala).

HALL, E. (1991), *Inventing the Barbarian: Greek Self-Definition through Tragedy* (Oxford).

HARDEN, D. B. (1954), 'Vasa Murrina Again', *JRS* 44, 53.

HARDWICK, L. (1990), 'Ancient Amazons: Heroes, Outsiders or Women?', *GaR* 37, 14–36.

HARL, K. W. (1991), 'Livy and the Date of the Introduction of the Cistophoric Tetra-drachma', *ClAnt* 10, 268–97.

HARRIS, W. V. (1979), *War and Imperialism in Republican Rome 327–70 B.C.* (Oxford).

HEFTNER, H. (1995), *Plutarch und der Aufstieg des Pompeius: Ein historischer Kommentar zu Plutarchs Pompeiusvita. Teil I: Kap. 1–45* (Frankfurt am Main).

HELLIESEN, J. M. (1986), 'Andriscus and the Revolt of the Macedonians, 149–148 B.C.', in *Ancient Macedonia IV: Papers Read at the Fourth International Symposium held in Thessaloniki, September 21–25 1983* (Thessaloniki), 308–14.

HICKSON, F. V. (1991), 'Augustus *triumphator*: Manipulation of the Triumphal Theme in the Political Program of Augustus', *Latomus*, 50, 124–38.

HIDAL, S. (2001), 'The Jews as the Roman Authors Saw them', in B. Olsson, D. Mitternach, and O. Brandt (eds.), *The Synagogue of Ancient Ostia and the Jews of Rome: Interdisciplinary Studies* (Stockholm), 141–4.

HILGERS, W. (1969), *Lateinische Gefäßnamen: Bezeichnungen, Funktion und Form römischer Gefäße nach den antiken Schriftquellen* (Düsseldorf).

HIMMELMANN, N. (1973), *Typologische Untersuchungen an römischen Sarkophagreliefs des 3. und 4. Jahrhunderts n. Chr.* (Mainz am Rhein).

HÖLKESKAMP, K.-J. (2000), '*Fides—deditio in fidem—dextra data et accepta*: Recht, Religion und Ritual in Rom', in C. Bruun (ed.), *The Roman Middle Republic: Politics, Religion, and Historiography c. 400–133 B.C. Papers from a Conference at the Institutum Romanum Finlandiae, September 11–12, 1998* (Rome), 223–50.

—— (2006), 'Der Triumph—"erinnere Dich, dass Du ein Mench bist" ', in E. Stein-Hölkeskamp and K.-J. Hölkeskamp (eds.), *Erinnerungsorte der Antike: Die römische Welt* (Munich), 258–76.

HOLLAND, L. A. (1961), *Janus and the Bridge* (Papers and Monographs of the American Academy in Rome, 21; Rome).

HOLLIDAY, P. J. (1980), '*Ad triumphum excolendum*: The Political Significance of Roman Historical Painting', *Oxford Art Journal*, 3, 3–8.

—— (1997), 'Roman Triumphal Painting: Its Function, Development, and Reception', *ArtB* 79, 130–47.

—— (2002), *The Origins of Roman Historical Commemoration in the Visual Arts* (Cambridge).

HOLLOWAY, R. R. (1987), 'Some Remarks on the Arch of Titus', *AntCl* 56, 183–91.

HÖLSCHER, T. (1978), 'Die Anfänge römischer Repräsentationskunst', *RM* 85, 315–57.

—— (1980), 'Römische Siegesdenkmäler der späten Republik', in H. A. Cahn and E. Simon (eds.), *Tainia: Roland Hampe zum 70. Geburtstag am 2. Dezember 1978 dargebracht von Mitarbeitern, Schülern und Freunden* (Mainz am Rhein), 351–71.

—— (1984), 'Actium und Salamis', *JdI* 99, 187–214.

—— (1985), 'Denkmäler der Schlacht von Actium: Propaganda und Resonanz', *Klio*, 67, 81–102.

—— (1988), 'Beobachtungen zu römischen historischen Denkmälern III', *AA* 523–41.

—— (1990), 'Römische nobiles und hellenistische Herrscher', in *Akten des XIII. Internationalen Kongresses für klassische Archäologie, Berlin 1988* (Mainz am Rhein), 73–84.

—— (2004a), 'Provokation und Transgression als politischer Habitus in der späten römischen Republik', *RM* 111, 83–104.

—— (2004b), 'Centauri e Amazzoni, Persiani e Celti come antipodi del mondo classico', in M. Capaccioli, A. Garzya, and F. Tessitore (eds.), *I mercoledì delle Accademie Napoletane nell'anno accademico 2002–2003* (Naples), 33–52.

—— (2006), 'The Transformation of Victory into Power: From Event to Structure', in S. Dillon and K. E. Welch (eds.), *Representations of War in Ancient Rome* (Cambridge), 27–48.

HOPKINS, K. (1991), 'From Violence to Blessing: Symbols and Rituals in Ancient Rome', in A. Molho, K. Raaflaub, and J. Emlen (eds.), *City States in Classical Antiquity and Medieval Italy* (Ann Arbor), 479–98.

HOUGHTALIN, L. (1993), 'The Representations of the Roman Provinces', diss. Bryn Mawr College.

HOWGEGO, C. (1990), 'Why did the Ancient States Strike Coins?', *NC* 150, 1–25.

—— (1992), 'The Supply and Use of Money in the Roman World 200 B.C. to A.D. 300', *JRS* 82, 1–31.

HUNINK, V. (1992), *M. Annaeus Lucanus Bellum Civile Book III: A Commentary* (Amsterdam).

HUNTER, F. (2001), 'The Carnyx in Iron Age Europe', *AntJ* 81, 77–108.

HYLAND, A. (1990), *Equus: The Horse in the Roman World* (New Haven, Conn., and London).

INGLEHART, J. (2007), 'Propertius 4,10 and the End of the Aeneid: Augustus, the *spolia opima* and the Right to Remain Silent', *GaR* 54, 61–81.

ISAGER, J. (1991), *Pliny on Art and Society: The Elder Pliny's Chapters on the History of Art* (Odense).

—— (1997), 'La Rue: Monument et scène. La *via triumphalis* dans la République romaine', in S. E. Larsen and A. Ballegaard Petersen (eds.), *La Rue—espace ouvert* (Odense), 107–35.

ITGENSHORST, T. (2004), 'Augustus und der republikanische Triumph: Triumphalfasten und *summi viri*-Galerie als Instrumente der imperialen Machtsicherung', *Hermes*, 132, 436–58.

—— (2005), *Tota illa pompa: Der Triumph in der römischen Republik* (*Hypomnemata*, 161; Göttingen).

—— (2006), 'Roman Commanders and Hellenistic Kings: On the "Hellenization" of the Republican Triumph', *Ancient Society*, 36, 51–68.

—— (2008), 'Der princeps triumphiert nicht: Vom Verschwinden des Siegesrituals in augusteischer Zeit', in H. Krasser, D. Pausch, and I. Petrovic (eds.), *Triplici invectus triumpho: Der römische Triumph in augusteischer Zeit* (Potsdamer Altertumswissenschaftliche Beiträge = PAWB; Stuttgart), 27–54.

JACOBSTHAL, P. (1943), 'On Livy XXXVI, 40 (Boiian silver)', *AJA* 47, 306–12.

JATTA, M. (1908), *Le rappresentanze figurate delle provincie romane* (Rome).

JENNISON, G. (1937), *Animals for Show and Pleasure in Ancient Rome* (Manchester).

JONES, B. W. (1989), 'Titus in Judaea, A.D. 67', *Latomus*, 48, 127–34.

JONES, P. J. (2005), *Reading Rivers in Roman Literature and Culture* (Lanham, Md.).

JUCKER, H. (1980), 'Zum Carpentum-Sesterz der Agrippina maior', in F. Krinzinger, B. Otto, and E. Walde-Psenner (eds.), *Forschungen und Funde: Festschrift B. Neutsch* (Innsbruck), 205–17.

KAVOULAKI, A. (1999), 'Processional Performance and the Democratic Polis', in S. Goldhill and R. Osborne (eds.), *Performance Culture and Athenian Democracy* (Cambridge), 293–320.

—— (2000), 'The Ritual Performance of a *pompê*: Aspects and Perspectives', in V. Karageorghis (ed.), Δώρημα: *A Tribute to the A. G. Leventis Foundation on the Occasion of its 20th Anniversary* (2000), 145–58.

KEARNEY, R. (2003), *Strangers, Gods and Monsters: Interpreting Otherness* (London and New York).

KEAVENEY, A. (1992), *Lucullus: A Life* (London and New York).

KLAR, L. S. (2006), 'The Origins of the Roman *scaenae frons* and the Architecture of Triumphal Games in the Second Century B.C.', in S. Dillon and K. E. Welch (eds.), *Representations of War in Ancient Rome* (Cambridge), 162–83.

KLAUSER, T. (1944), 'Aurum coronarium', *RM* 59, 129–53.

KLEINER, D. E. E. (1992), *Roman Sculpture* (New Haven, Conn., and London).

KLEINER, F. S. (1991), 'The Trophy on the Bridge and the Roman Triumph over Nature', *AntCl* 60, 182–92.

KLEMENTA, S. (1993), *Gelagerte Flussgötter des Späthellenismus und der römischen Kaiserzeit* (Cologne).

KNAPP, R. C. (1977), 'The Date and Purpose of the Iberian Denarii', *NC* 137, 1–18.

—— (1987), 'Spain', in A. M. Burnett and M. H. Crawford (eds.), *The Coinage of the Roman World in the Late Republic: Proceedings of a Colloquium Held at the British Museum in September 1985* (BAR–IS 326; Oxford), 19–37.

KOEPPEL, G. M. (1983), 'Die historischen Reliefs der römischen Kaiserzeit I: Stadtrömische Denkmäler unbekannter Bauzugehörigkeit aus augusteischer und julisch-claudischer Zeit', *BJb* 183, 61–144.

—— (1984), 'Die historischen Reliefs der römischen Kaiserzeit II: Stadtrömische Denkmäler unbekannter Bauzugehörigkeit aus flavischer Zeit', *BJb* 184, 1–65.

—— (1985), 'The Role of Pictoral Models in the Creation of the Historical Relief during the Age of Augustus', in R. Winkes (ed.), *The Age of Augustus: Interdisciplinary Conference Held at Brown University, April 30–May 2, 1982* (Louvain-la-Neuve), 89–106.

—— (1986), 'Die historischen Reliefs der römischen Kaiserzeit IV: Stadtrömische Denkmäler unbekannter Bauzugehörigkeit aus hadrianischer bis konstantinischer Zeit', *BJb* 186, 1–90.

KÖHLER, J. (1995), 'Zur Triumphalsymbolik auf dem Feldherrnsarkophag Belvedere', *RM* 102, 371–9.

—— (1996), *Pompai: Untersuchungen zur hellenistischen Festkultur* (Frankfurt am Main).

KOORTBOJIAN, M. (2002), 'A Painted *exemplum* at Rome's Temple of Liberty', *JRS* 92, 33–48.

KÖVES-ZULAUF, T. (1993), '*Minerva capta*: Eine gefangene Göttin?', in J. Dalfen, G. Petersmann, and F. F. Schwarz (eds.), *Religio Graeco-romana: Festschrift für Walter Pötscher* (Graz-Horn), 159–76.

KRAELING, C. H. (1942), 'The Episode of the Roman Standards at Jerusalem', *HTR* 35, 263–89.

KÜNZL, E. (1988), *Der römische Triumph: Siegesfeiern im antiken Rom* (Munich).

KUTTNER, A. L. (1995), *Dynasty and Empire in the Age of Augustus: The Case of the Boscoreale Cups* (Berkeley, Calif.).

—— (1999), 'Culture and History at Pompey's Museum', *TAPA* 129, 343–73.

KYLE, D. G. (1995), 'Animal Spectacles in Ancient Rome: Meat and Meaning', *Nikephoros*, 7, 181–205.

—— (1998), *Spectacles of Death in Ancient Rome* (London and New York).

LAQUEUR, R. (1909), 'Über das Wesen des römischen Triumphs', *Hermes*, 44, 215–36.

LA ROCCA, E. (1985), *Amazzonomachia: Le sculture frontonali del tempio di Apollo Sosiano* (Rome).

LATTE, K. (1960), *Römische Religionsgeschichte* (Munich).

LAURENCE, R. (1993), 'Emperors, Nature and the City: Rome's Ritual Landscape', *Accordia Research Papers*, 4, 79–87.

—— (1996), 'Ritual, Landscape, and the Destruction of Place in the Roman Imagination', in J. B. Wilkins (ed.), *Approaches to the Study of Ritual: Italy and the Ancient Mediterranean* (London), 111–21.

LAZENBY, J. F. (1996), *The First Punic War: A Military History* (London).

LEE, G. (1996), *Propertius: The Poems. A New Translation* (Oxford).

—— and BARR, W. (1987), *The Satires of Persius: The Latin Text with a Verse Translation by Guy Lee, Introduction and Commentary by William Barr* (Wolfeboro).

LEMOSSE, M. (1972), 'Les Éléments techniques de l'ancien triomphe romain et le problème de son origine', *ANRW* I.2 (Berlin and New York), 442–53.

LEVI, A. C. (1952), *Barbarians on Roman Imperial Coins and Sculpture* (New York).

LIEDMEIER, C. (1935), *Plutarchus' Biographie van Aemilius Paullus: Historische Commentaar* (Utrecht).

LINDERSKI, J. (2001), 'Silver and Gold of Valor: The Award of *armillae* and *torques*', *Latomus*, 60, 3–15.

LINTOTT, A. W. (1972), 'Imperial Expansion and Moral Decline in the Roman Republic', *Historia*, 21, 626–38.

LIOU-GILLE, B. (1992), 'Le Butin dans la Rome ancienne', in *La Rome des premiers siècles: Legende et histoire. Actes de la table ronde en l'honneur de Massimo Pallottino, Paris 3–4 Mai 1990* (Florence), 155–72.

LIVERIANI, P. (1995), '"Nationes" e "civitates" nella propaganda imperiale', *RM* 102, 219–49.

LOEWENTAL, A. J., and HARDEN, D. B. (1949), 'Vasa murrina', *JRS* 39, 31–7.

LUCCHI, G. (1968), 'Sul significato del carpentum nella monetazione romana imperiale', *RIN* 70, 131–41.

LUSNIA, S. (2006), 'Battle Imagery and Politics on the Severan Arch in the Roman Forum', in S. Dillon and K. E. Welch (eds.), *Representations of War in Ancient Rome* (Cambridge), 272–99.

MACCORMACK, S. (1972), 'Change and Continuity in Late Antiquity: The Ceremony of *adventus*', *Historia*, 21, 721–52.

MCCORMICK, M. (1986), *Eternal Victory: Triumphal Rulership in Late Antiquity, Byzantium, and the Early Medieval West* (Cambridge).

MCDONNELL, M. (2006), 'Roman Aesthetics and the Spoils of Syracuse', in S. Dillon and K. E. Welch (eds.), *Representations of War in Ancient Rome* (Cambridge), 68–90.

MADER, G. (2006), 'Triumphal Elephants and Political Circus at Plutarch, *Pomp.* 14.6', *CW* 99, 397–403.

MAKIN, E. (1921), 'The Triumphal Route, with Particular Reference to the Flavian Triumph', *JRS* 11, 25–36.

MANIERI, A. (1998), *L'immagine poetica nella teoria degli antichi: Phantasia ed enargeia* (Rome).

MANSUELLI, G. A. (1979), 'Γραφαὶ καὶ σχήματα τῶν γεγονότων (App. *Punic.* 66)', *RdA* 3, 45–58.

MARIN, L. (1987), 'Notes on a Semiotic Approach to Parade, Cortege, and Procession', in A. Falassi (ed.), *Time Out of Time: Essays on the Festival* (Albuquerque, NM), 220–8.

MARKLE, M. M., III (1977), 'The Macedonian Sarissa, Spear, and Related Armor', *AJA* 81, 323–39.

—— (1982), 'Macedonian Arms and Tactics under Alexander the Great', in B. Barr-Sharrar and E. N. Borza (eds.), *Macedonia and Greece in Late Classical and Early Hellenistic Times* (Washington, DC), 87–111.

MARÓTI, E. (1989), 'Der Feldzug des P. Servilius Vatia gegen die Seeräuber Südanatoliens', *Acta Antiqua Academiae Scientiarum Hungaricae*, 32, 309–16.

MARSDEN, E. W. (1969), *Greek and Roman Artillery: Historical Development* (Oxford).

MARSHALL, A. J. (1984), 'Symbols and Showmanship in Roman Public Life: The Fasces', *Phoenix*, 38, 120–41.

MARSHALL, B. A. (1972), 'Crassus' Ovation in 71 B.C.', *Historia*, 21, 669–73.

MARSZAL, J. R. (2000), 'Ubiquitous Barbarians: Representations of the Gauls at Pergamon and Elsewhere', in N. T. de Grummond and B. S. Ridgway (eds.), *From Pergamon to Sperlonga: Sculpture and Context* (Berkeley, Calif.), 191–234.

MARTINDALE, A. (1979), *The Triumphs of Caesar by Andrea Mantegna in the Collection of Her Majesty the Queen at Hampton Court* (London).

MATTINGLY, H., and SYDENHAM, E. A. (1926), *The Roman Imperial Coinage*, ii. *Vespasian to Hadrian* (London).

MATZ, F. (1952), *Der Gott auf dem Elefantenwagen* (Wiesbaden).

—— (1968–75), *Die Dionysischen Sarkophage* (Berlin).

MAURIZIO, L. (1998), 'The Panathenaic Procession: Athens' Participatory Democracy on Display?', in D. Boedeker and K. A. Raaflaub (eds.), *Democracy, Empire, and the Arts in Fifth-Century Athens* (Cambridge, Mass.), 297–317.

MAUSS, M. (1970), *The Gift: Forms and Functions of Exchange in Archaic Societies* (London).

MAXFIELD, V. A. (1981), *The Military Decorations of the Roman Army* (London).

MEIGGS, R. (1982), *Trees and Timber in the Ancient Mediterranean World* (Oxford).

MERTEN, E. W. (1968), *Zwei Herrscherfeste in der Historia Augusta*: *Untersuchungen zu den pompae der Kaiser Gallienus und Aurelianus* (Bonn).

MEYBOOM, P. G. P. (1995), *The Nile Mosaic of Palestrina: Early Evidence of Egyptian Religion in Italy* (Leiden).

MICHEL, O., and BAUERNFEIND, O. (1969), *Flavius Josephus, De bello judaico, ii/2. Buch VI–VII, herausgegeben und mit einer Einleitung sowie mit Anmerkungen versehen von O. Michel and O. Bauernfeind* (Munich).

MILLAR, F. (1963), 'The *fiscus* in the First Two Centuries', *JRS* 53, 29–42.

—— (1977), *The Emperor in the Roman World* (London).

MILLER, J. F. (2000), 'Triumphus in Palatio', *AJP* 121, 409–22.

MILNE, M. J. (1941), 'The Use of τορεύω and Related Words', *AJA* 45, 390–8.

MITTEIS, L., and WILCHEN, U. (1912), *Grundzüge und Chrestomathie der Papyruskunde*, i. *Historischer Teil* (Leipzig).

MOFFITT, J. F. (1997), 'The Palestrina Mosaic with a "Nile Scene": Philostratus and Ekphrasis, Ptolemy and Chorographia', *ZfK* 60, 227–47.

MOMMSEN, T. (1887), *Römisches Staatsrecht*, i (Leipzig).

MORRISON, J. S. (1996), *Greek and Roman Oared Warships* (Oxford).

MOYNIHAN, R. (1985), 'Geographical Mythology and Roman Imperial Ideology', in R. Winkes (ed.), *The Age of Augustus*: *Interdisciplinary Conference Held at Brown University, April 30–May 2, 1982* (Louvain-la-Neuve), 149–62.

MUIR, E. (1981), *Civic Ritual in Renaissance Venice* (Princeton).

MURRAY, O. (1996), 'Hellenistic Royal Symposia', in P. Bilde, T. Engberg-Pedersen, L. Hannestad, and J. Zahle (eds.), *Aspects of Hellenistic Kingship* (Aarhus), 15–27.

MURRAY, W. M. (1985), 'The Weight of Trireme Rams and the Price of Bronze in Fourth-Century Athens', *GRBS* 26, 141–50.

—— and PETSAS, P. M. (1989), *Octavian's Campsite Memorial for the Actian War* (*TAPS* 79; Philadelphia).

MUSSO, L. (1987), 'Rilievo con pompa trionfale di Traiano al museo di Palestrina', *BdA* 72, 1–46.

NEILS, J. (1992), *Goddess and Polis: The Panathenaic Festival in Ancient Athens* (Princeton).

—— (1996), 'Pride, Pomp and Circumstance: The Iconography of Procession', in J. Neils (ed.), *Worshipping Athena: Panathenaia and Parthenon* (Madison, Wis.), 177–97.

NÉMETHY, G. (1903), *A. Persii Flacci Satirae*, ed. with notes and index of words by Geyza Némethy (Budapest).

NICOLET, C. (1991), *Space, Geography and Politics in the Early Roman Empire* (Ann Arbor).

NIELSEN, I. (1994), *Hellenistic Palaces: Tradition and Renewal* (Studies in Hellenistic Civilization, 5; Aarhus).

—— (1998), 'Royal Banquets: The Development of Royal Banquets and Banqueting Halls from Alexander to the Tetrarchs', in I. Nielsen and H. S. Nielsen (eds.), *Meals in a Social Context: Aspects of the Communal Meal in the Hellenistic and Roman World* (Aarhus), 102–33.

—— (2001), 'The Gardens of the Hellenistic Palaces', in I. Nielsen (ed.), *The Royal Palace Institution in the First Millennium BC: Regional Development and Cultural Interchange between East and West* (Monographs of the Danish Institute at Athens, 4; Athens), 165–87.

NISBET, R. G. M., and HUBBARD, M. A. (1978), *A Commentary on Horace: Odes Book II* (Oxford).

NYLANDER, C. (1983), 'The Standard of the Great King: A Problem in the Alexander Mosaic', *OpRom* 14, 19–37.

OAKLEY, S. P. (1985), 'Single Combat in the Roman Republic', *CQ* 35, 392–410.

—— (1997), *A Commentary on Livy Books VI–X, i. Introduction and Book VI* (Oxford).

—— (1998), *A Commentary on Livy Books VI–X, ii. Book VII–VIII* (Oxford).

—— (2005a), *A Commentary on Livy Books VI–X, iii. Book IX* (Oxford).

—— (2005b), *A Commentary on Livy Books VI–X, iv. Book X* (Oxford).

OGILVIE, R. M. (1965), *A Commentary on Livy, Book 1–5* (Oxford).

OLIVER, A., Jr. and SHELTON, J. (1979), 'Silver on Papyrus: A Translation of a Roman Silver Tableware Inventory', *Archaeology*, 32, 21–8.

O'NEILL, P. (2004), 'Triumph Songs, Reversal and Plautus' *Amphitruo*', *Ramus*, 32, 1–38.

OOTEGHEM, J. van (1954), *Pompée le Grand*: *Bâtisseur d'empire* (Brussels).

ORLIN, E. M. (1997), *Temples, Religion and Politics in the Roman Republic* (Leiden).

ORMEROD, H. A. (1922), 'The Campaigns of Servilius Isauricus against the Pirates', *JRS* 12, 35–56.

ÖSTENBERG, I. (1999), 'Demonstrating the Conquest of the World: The Procession of Peoples and Rivers on the Shield of Aeneas and the Triple Triumph of Octavian in 29 B.C. (*Aen.* 8.722–728)', *OpRom* 24, 155–62.

—— (2003), *Staging the World: Rome and the Other in the Triumphal Procession*, diss. (Lund).

—— (2008), 'Minns att du är människa!' (Remember that you are a Man!), in P. Beskow, S. Borgehammar, and A. Jönsson (eds.), *Förbistringar och förklaringar: Kulturhistoriska essäer tillägnade Anders Piltz på hans sextiofemårsdag* (Lund; in Swedish, with English abstract), 718–25.

—— (2009), 'From Conquest to *pax romana*: The *signa recepta* and the End of the Triumphal Fasti in 19 BC', in O. Hekster, E. Stavrianopoulou, and C. Witschel (eds.), *The Impact of the Roman Empire on the Dynamics of Rituals: Proceedings of the Eighth Workshop of the International Network Impact of Empire. Heidelberg, July 5–7, 2007* (Leiden), 53–76.

—— (forthcoming), '*Et titulis oppida capta legam*: The Role of the Written Placards in the Roman Triumphal Processions', in *Les Rites de Victoire: Actes du colloque tenu à l'École française de Rome, 19–21 avril 2001* (Rome).

OSTROWSKI, J. A. (1990*a*), *Les Personnifications des provinces dans l'art romain* (Warsaw).

—— (1990*b*), 'Personifications of Rivers as an Element of Roman Political Propaganda', *ÉtTrav* 15, 310–16.

—— (1991), *Personifications of Rivers in Greek and Roman Art* (Krakow).

—— (1996), 'Personifications of Countries and Cities as a Symbol of Victory in Greek and Roman Art', in E. G. Schmidt (ed.), *Griechenland und Rom: Vergleichende Untersuchungen zu Entwicklungstendenzen und Höhepunkten der antiken Geschichte, Kunst und Literatur* (Tbilissi), 264–72.

PAGNOTTA, M. A. (1977/78), 'Carpentum: privilegio del carro e ruolo sociale della matrona romana', *AnnPerugia* 15, 159–70.

PAIS, E. (1920), *Fasti triumphales populi romani* (Rome).

PALMA, B., and LACHENAL, L. DE (1983), *Museo nazionale romano: Le sculture, I,5. I marmi Ludovisi nel Museo Nazionale Romano* (Rome).

PANCIERA, S. (1994), '*Signis legionum*: Insegne, immagini imperiali e *centuriones frumentarii a peregrinis*', in Y. Le Bohec (ed.), *L'Afrique, la Gaule, la religion à l'époque romaine: Mélanges à la mémoire de Marcel Le Glay* (CollLatomus, 226; Brussels), 610–23.

PAPE, M. (1975), *Griechische Kunstwerke aus Kriegsbeute und ihre öffentliche Aufstellung in Rom: Von der Eroberung von Syrakus bis in augusteische Zeit* (Hamburg).

PARISI PRESICCE, C. (1999), 'Le rappresentazioni allegoriche di popoli e province nell'arte romana imperiale', in M. Sapelli (ed.), *Provinciae fideles: Il fregio del tempio di Adriano in Campo Marzio* (Rome), 83–105.

PAYNE, R. (1962), *The Roman Triumph* (London).

PFANNER, M. (1980), 'Codex Coburgensis Nr. 88: Die Entdeckung der Porta triumphalis', *RM* 87, 327–34.

—— (1983), *Der Titusbogen* (Mainz am Rhein).

PHILLIPS, J. E. (1974*a*), 'Verbs Compounded with *trans–* in Livy's Triumph Reports', *CP* 69, 54–5.

—— (1974*b*),'Form and Language in Livy's Triumph Notices', *CP* 69, 265–73.

PICARD, G. CHARLES (1957), *Les Trophées romains*: *Contribution à l'histoire de la religion et de l'art triomphal de Rome* (Paris).

—— (1973), 'Le Monument de César cosmocrator au Capitole', *RA*, 261–72.

PIETILÄ-CASTRÉN, L. (1987), *Magnificentia publica: The Victory Monuments of the Roman Generals in the Era of the Punic Wars* (Helsinki).

PIGGOTT, S. (1983), *The Earliest Wheeled Transport: From the Atlantic Coast to the Caspian Sea* (London).

—— (1992), *Wagon, Chariot and Carriage: Symbol and Status in the History of Transport* (London).

PLATTUS, A. (1983), 'Passages into the City: The Interpretive Function of the Roman Triumph', *Princeton Journal*, 1, 93–115.

POLITO, E. (1998), *Fulgentibus armis: Introduzione allo studio dei fregi d'armi antichi* (*Xenia antiqua*, monographie, 4; Rome).

POLLITT, J. J. (1983), *The Art of Rome c. 753 B.C.–A.D. 337: Sources and Documents* (Cambridge).

—— (1986), *Art in the Hellenistic Age* (Cambridge).

PORTEFAIX, L. (1993), 'Ancient Ephesus: Processions as Media of Religious and Secular Propaganda', in T. Ahlbäck (ed.), *The Problem of Ritual: Based on Papers Read at the Symposium on Religious Rites held at Åbo, Finland, on the 13th–16th of August 1991* (Stockholm), 195–210.

POSTL, B. (1970), *Die Bedeutung des Nil in der römischen Literatur* (Vienna).

PRACHNER, G. (1994), 'Bemerkungen zu den erbeuteten "signa militaria" der Samniten-kriege', *Militärgeschichtliche Mitteilungen*, 53, 1–32.

PRÉAUX, C. (1978), *Le Monde hellénistique: La Grèce et l'Orient de la mort d'Alexandre à la conquête romaine de la Grèce (323–146 av. J.-C.),* i (Paris).

PRITCHETT, W. K. (1991), *The Greek State at War*, v (Berkeley, Calif.).

PURCELL, N. (1995), 'On the Sacking of Carthage and Corinth', in D. Innes, H. Hine, and C. Pelling (eds.), *Ethics and Rhetoric: Classical Essays for Donald Russell on his Seventy-Fifth Birthday*, (Oxford), 133–48.

PUTNAM, M. C. J. (1985), 'Romulus *tropaeophorus* (*Aeneid* 6.779–80)', *CQ* 35, 237–40.

RAPPAPORT, R. (1999), *Ritual and Religion in the Making of Humanity* (Cambridge).

RAWSON, E. (1990), 'The Antiquarian Tradition: Spoils and Representations of Foreign Armour', in W. Eder (ed.), *Staat und Staatlichkeit in der frühen römischen Republik: Aktes eines Symposiums 12–15 Juli 1988* (Stuttgart), 158–73.

REDEN, S. VON (1997), 'Money, Law and Exchange: Coinage in the Greek Polis', *JHS* 117, 154–76.

REINHOLD, M. (1988), *From Republic to Principate: A Historical Commentary on Cassius Dio's Roman History Book 49–52 (36–29 B.C.)* (American Philological Association Monograph Series, 34; Atlanta, Ga.).

RICE, E. E. (1983), *The Grand Procession of Ptolemy Philadelphus* (Oxford).

RICH, J. W. (1996), 'Augustus and the Spolia Opima', *Chiron*, 29, 85–127.

RICHARD, J.-C. (1966), 'Les Funérailles de Trajan et le triomphe sur les Parthes', *RÉL* 44, 351–62.

RICHARD, J.-C. (1992), 'Tribuns militaires et triomphe', in *La Rome des premiers siècles: Legende et histoire. Actes de la table ronde en l'honneur de Massimo Pallottino, Paris 3–4 Mai 1990* (Florence), 235–46.

RICHARDSON, J. S. (1975), 'The Triumph, the Praetors and the Senate in the Early Second Century B.C.', *JRS* 65, 50–63.

—— (1976), 'The Spanish Mines and the Development of Provincial Taxation in the Second Century B.C.', *JRS* 66, 139–52.

—— (1991), '*Imperium Romanum*: Empire and the Language of Power', *JRS* 81, 1–9.

—— (1996), *The Romans in Spain* (Oxford and Cambridge, Mass.).

RICHARDSON, L., Jr. (1980), 'The Approach to the Temple of Saturn in Rome', *AJA* 84, 51–62.

RIDLEY, R. (2000), 'Livy and the Hannibalic War', in C. Bruun (ed.), *The Roman Middle Republic: Politics, Religion, and Historiography c. 400–133 B.C. Papers from a Conference at the Institutum Romanum Finlandiae, September 11–12, 1998* (Rome), 13–40.

RITTER, H.-W. (1965), *Diadem und Königsherrschaft: Untersuchungen zu Zeremonien und Rechtsgrundlagen des Herrschaftsantritts bei den Persern, bei Alexander dem Großen und im Hellenismus* (Vestigia, 7; Munich).

RIVES, J. B. (1993), 'Marcellus and the Syracusans', *CP* 88, 32–5.

RIVET, A. L. F. (1979), 'A Note on Scythed Chariots', *Antiquity*, 53, 130–2.

ROCHETTE, B. (1997), 'Urbis–Orbis. Ovide, *Fastes* II, 684: *Romanae spatium est Urbis et orbis idem*', *Latomus*, 56, 551–3.

ROGER, G. M. (1991), *The Sacred Identity of Ephesos: Foundation Myths of a Roman City* (London and New York).

ROMM, J. S. (1992), *The Edges of the Earth in Ancient Thought: Geography, Exploration, and Fiction* (Princeton).

ROSEN, K. (1996), 'Der Historiker als Prophet: Tacitus und die Juden', in P. Barceló (ed.), *Contra quis ferat arma deos? Vier Augsburger Vorträge zur Religionsgeschichte der römischen Kaiserzeit. Zum 60. Geburtstag von Gunther Gottlieb* (Munich), 35–54.

ROSTOVTZEFF, M. (1942), '*Vexillum* and Victory', *JRS* 32, 92–106.

ROUVERET, A. (1986), 'Tite-Live, Histoire Romaine IX, 40: La Description des armées samnites ou les pièges de la symétrie', in A.-M. Adam and A. Rouveret (eds.), *Guerre et sociétés en Italie aux Ve et IVe siècles avant J.–C: les indices fournis par l'armement et les techniques de combat. Table ronde Paris, 5 Mai 1984* (Paris), 91–120.

—— (1987/9), 'Les Lieux de la mémoire publique: Quelques remarques sur la fonction des tableaux dans la cité', *Opus*, 6–8, 101–24.

RÜPKE, J. (1990), *Domi Militiae: Die religiöse Konstruktion des Krieges in Rom* (Stuttgart).

—— (2006), 'Triumphator and Ancestor Rituals: Between Symbolic Anthropology and Magic', *Numen*, 53, 251–89.

RYAN, M. (1989), 'The American Parade: Representations of the Nineteenth-Century Social Order', in L. Hunt (ed.), *The New Cultural History* (Berkeley, Calif.), 131–53.

RYBERG, I. SCOTT (1955), *Rites of the State Religion in Roman Art* (*MAAR* 22; Rome).

SADDINGTON, D. B. (1961), 'Roman Attitudes to the "externae gentes" of the North', *Acta Classica*, 4, 90–102.

SALCEDO GARCÉS, F. (1991), 'La iconografía de Africa en época romana: algunos aspectos', *Archivo español de arquelogía*, 64, 284–92.

—— (1996), *Africa: Iconografia de una provincia romana* (Rome and Madrid).

SALLMANN, K. (1987), 'Reserved for Eternal Punishment: The Elder Pliny's View of Free Germania (*HN* 16.1–6)', *AJP* 108, 108–28.

SASEL, J. (1973), 'Zur Erklärung der Inschrift am *Tropaeum Alpium* (Plin. *n.h.* 3, 136–137; CIL V 7817)', in *Akten des VI. Internationalen Kongresses für griechische und lateinische Epigraphik München 1972* (Munich), 476–8.

SCHILLING, R. (1977), *Pline l'Ancien, Histoire naturelle: Livre VII, texte établi, traduit et commenté par R. Schilling* (Paris).

SCHNEIDER, R. M. (1990), 'Augustus und der frühe römische Triumph', *JdI* 167–205.

SCHOLZ, B. F. (1999), '*Ekphrasis* and *enargeia* in Quintilian's *Institutionis oratoriae libri XII*', in P. L. Oesterreich and T. O. Sloane (eds.), *Rhetorica movet: Studies in Historical and Modern Rhetoric in Honour of Heinrich F. Plett* (Leiden), 3–24.

SCHULZ, A. R. (1994), *Ethnicity on Parade: Inventing the Norwegian American through Celebration* (Amherst, Mass.).

SCHULZ, M.-W. (1998), 'Die Germanen und der Rhein als biologische Grenze: Ein roter Faden durch das Gesamtwerk des B.G.', *Der altsprachliche Unterricht*, 41, 5–17.

SCHULZ, R. (2000*a*), 'Zwischen Kooperation und Konfrontation: Die römische Weltreichsbildung und die Piraterei', *Klio*, 82, 426–40.

—— (2000*b*), 'Caesar und das Meer', *HZ* 271, 281–309.

SCULLARD, H. H. (1974), *The Elephant in the Greek and Roman World* (London).

—— (1981), *Festivals and Ceremonies of the Roman Republic* (London).

SEIBERT, J. (1973), 'Der Einsatz von Kriegselephanten: Ein militärgeschichtliches Problem der antiken Welt', *Gymnasium*, 80, 348–62.

SETTIS, S. (1988), 'La colonna', in S. Settis (ed.), *La colonna traiana* (Turin), 45–255.

SHAPIRO, H. A. (1983), 'Amazons, Thracians, and Scythians', *GRBS* 24, 105–14.

SHATZMAN, I. (1972), 'The Roman General's Authority over Booty', *Historia*, 21, 177–205.

SHELTON, J.-A. (2004), 'Dancing and Dying: The Display of Elephants in Ancient Roman Arenas', in M. Joyal and R. Egan (eds.), *Daimonopylai* (Winnipeg), 363–82.

SMALLWOOD, E. M. (1981), *The Jews under Roman Rule from Pompey to Diocletian: A Study in Political Relations* (Leiden).

SMITH, R. R. R. (1988*a*), '*Simulacra gentium*: The *ethne* from the Sebasteion at Aphrodisias', *JRS* 78, 50–77.

—— (1988*b*), *Hellenistic Royal Portraits* (Oxford).

SNICKARE, M. (1999), *Enväldets riter: Kungliga fester och ceremonier i gestaltning av Nikodemus Tessin den yngre* (Stockholm).

SONNE, W. (1996), 'Hellenistische Herrschaftsgärten', in W. Hoepfner and G. Brands (eds.), *Basileia: Die Paläste der hellenistischen Könige. Internationales Symposion in Berlin vom 16.12.1992 bis 20.12.1992* (Mainz am Rhein), 136–43.

SPRINGER, L. A. (1952), 'Livy and the Year 212 B.C.', *CJ* 47, 261–4, 298–9.

STAVRIANOPOULOU, E. (2006), 'Introduction', in E. Stavrianopoulou (ed.), *Ritual and Communication in the Graeco-Roman World* (Kernos, suppl. 16; Liège), 7–22.

STOL, M. (1979), *On Trees, Mountains, and Millstones in the Ancient Near East* (Leiden).

STOLL, O. (1995a), *Excubatio ad signa: Die Wache bei den Fahnen in der römischen Armee und andere Beiträge zur kulturgeschichtlichen und historischen Bedeutung eines militärischen Symbols* (St. Katharinen).

—— (1995b), 'Die Fahnenwache in der römischen Armee', *ZPE* 108, 107–18.

STORM, C. (1992), 'Freiheit als Geschenk? Identische Mechanismen in der Darstellung des römischen Freiheitsbegriffs nach Kynoskephalai und Pydna bei Polybios, Livius, Trogus', *GrazBeitr* 18, 65–86.

STRACK, P. L. (1933), *Untersuchungen zur römischen Reichsprägung des zweiten Jahrhunderts*, ii. *Die Reichsprägung zur Zeit des Hadrian* (Stuttgart).

STRIBRNY, K. (1991), 'Zur Entstehung der Elefanten-exuvie als "Africa"-Attribut', in H.-C. Noeske and H. Schubert (eds.), *Die Münze: Bild, Botschaft, Bedeutung. Festschrift M. R. Alföldi* (Frankfurt am Main), 378–85.

STRONG, D. E. (1966), *Greek and Roman Gold and Silver Plate* (London).

SUMI, G. S. (2002), 'Impersonating the Dead: Mimes at Roman Funerals', *AJP* 123, 559–85.

—— (2005), *Ceremony and Power: Performing Politics in Rome between Republic and Empire* (Ann Arbor).

SWAIN, S. C. R. (1989), 'Plutarch's Aemilius and Timoleon', *Historia*, 38, 314–34.

TÄCKHOLM, V. (1976), *Faraos blomster* (Stockholm).

TAGLIAFICO, M. (1995), 'La deportazione degli Achei a Roma nel 167 a.C.', in M. Sordi (ed.), *Coercizione e mobilità umana nel mondo antico* (Milan), 215–23.

TANDOI, V. (1962), 'Il trionfo di Claudio sulla Britannia e il suo cantore (*Anth. Lat.* 419–426 Riese)', *StIt* 34, 83–129, 137–68.

TARN, W. W., and CHARLESWORTH, M. P. (1965), *Octavian, Antony and Cleopatra* (Cambridge).

TARPIN, M. (1999), '*Oppida vi capta, vici incensi . . .* Les Mots latins de la ville', *Latomus*, 58, 279–97.

THOMPSON, D. (2000), 'Philadelphus' Procession: Dynastic Power in a Mediterranean Context', in L. Mooren (ed.), *Politics, Administration and Society in the Hellenistic and Roman World: Proceedings of the International Colloquium, Bertinoro 19–24 July 1997* (Peeters), 365–88.

THOMSEN, R. (1961), *Early Roman Coinage*, ii (Copenhagen).

TORELLI, M. (1968), 'Il donario di M. Fulvio Flacco dell'area di S. Omobono', in *Studi di topografia romana in onore di Antonio M. Colini in occasione del suo 65° anno* (Rome), 71–6.

—— (1982), *Typology and Structure of Roman Historical Reliefs* (Ann Arbor).

TORTORELLA, S. (2008), 'Processione trionfale e circense sulle lastre Campana', in *Le perle e il filo: A Mario Torelli per i suoi settanta anni* (Venosa), 301–21.

TOYNBEE, J. M. C. (1934), *The Hadrianic School: A Chapter in the History of Greek Art* (Cambridge).

—— (1973), *Animals in Roman Life and Art*, (London).

TWYMAN, B. L. (1979), 'The Date of Pompeius Magnus' First Triumph', in C. Deroux (ed.), *Studies in Latin Literature and Roman History* (*CollLatomus*, 164; Brussels), 175–208.

ULLMAN, B. L. (1957), 'Cleopatra's Pearls', *CJ* 52, 193–201.

VALLI, B. (2007), 'I percorsi delle processioni nella Roma antica: *Ludi saeculares* e funerali imperiali', *Fragmenta*, 1, 33–59.

VASALY, A. (1993), *Representations: Images of the World in Ciceronian Oratory* (Berkeley, Calif.).

VENDRIES, C. (1999), 'La Trompe, le gaulois et le sanglier', *RÉA* 101, 367–91.

VERMEULE, C. C. (1981), 'The Basis from Puteoli: Cities of Asia Minor in Julio-Claudian Italy', in L. Casson and M. Price (eds.), *Coins, Culture, and History in the Ancient World: Numismatic and Other Studies in Honor of Bluma L. Trell* (Detroit), 85–101.

VERSNEL, H. S. (1970), *Triumphus: An Inquiry into the Origin, Development and Meaning of the Roman Triumph* (Leiden).

—— (1993), *Inconsistencies in Greek and Roman Religion*, ii. *Transition and Reversal in Myth and Ritual* (Leiden).

—— (2006), 'Red (Herring?) Comments on a New Theory Concerning the Origin of the Triumph', *Numen*, 53, 290–326.

VESSBERG, O. (1941), *Studien zur Kunstgeschichte der römischen Republik* (Lund).

—— (1952), 'Det romerska triumftåget', in M. Stenberger (ed.), *Arkeologiska forskningar och fynd: Studier utgivna med anledning av H. M. Konung Gustaf VI Adolfs sjuttioårsdag 11.11.1952* (Stockholm), 128–38.

VEYNE, P. (1983), '"Titulus praelatus": Offrande, solennisation et publicité dans les ex-voto gréco-romains', *RA* 2, 281–300.

—— (1993), '*Humanitas*: Romans and Non-Romans', in A. Giardina (ed.), *The Romans* (Chicago), 342–69.

VIANOLI, R. (1972), 'Carattere e tendenza della tradizione su L. Emilio Paolo', in M. Sordi (ed.), *Contributi dell'Istituto di stora antica*, i (Milan), 78–90.

VILLARONGA, L. (1979), *Numismatica antiqua de Hispania* (Barcelona).

VILLE, G. (1981), *La gladiature en occident des origines à la mort de Domitien* (Rome).

VISCOGLIOSI, A. (1988), 'Die Architektur-Dekoration der Cella des Apollo-Sosianus-Tempels', in *Kaiser Augustus und die verlorene Republik: Eine Ausstellung im Martin-Gropius-Bau, Berlin 7. Juni–14. August 1988* (Mainz am Rhein), 136–48.

—— (1996), *Il tempio di Apollo 'in Circo' e la formazione del linguaggio architettonico augusteo* (Rome).

VOGEL-WEIDEMAN, U. (1985), 'The Dedicatory Inscription of Pompeius Magnus in Diodorus 40.4: Some Remarks on an Unpublished Manuscript by Hans Schaefer', *Acta Classica*, 28, 57–75.

VOGT, J. (1960), 'Orbis romanus: Ein Beitrag zum Sprachgebrauch und zur Vorstellungs-welt des römischen Imperialismus', in J. Vogt, *Orbis: Ausgewählte Schriften zur Geschichte des Altertums* (Freiburg), 151–71.

VOISIN, J.-L. (1983), 'Le Triomphe africain de 46 et l'idéologie césarienne', *AntAfr* 19, 7–33.

VOLLKOMMER, R. (1994), 'Vater Rhein und seine römischen Darstellungen', *BJb* 194, 1–42.

WALBANK, F. W. (1957), *A Historical Commentary on Polybius*, i. *Commentary on Books I–VI* (Oxford).

WALBANK, F. W. (1979), *A Historical Commentary on Polybius,* iii. *Commentary on Books XIX–XL* (Oxford).

—— (1996), 'Two Hellenistic Processions: A Matter of Self–Definition', *Scripta Classica Israelica,* 15, 119–30.

WALKER, A. D. (1993), '*Enargeia* and the Spectator in Greek Historiography', *TAPA* 123, 353–77.

WALLISCH, E. (1955), 'Name und Herkunft des römischen Triumphes', *Philologus,* 99, 245–58.

WALSH, P. G. (1961), *Livy: His Historical Aims and Methods* (Cambridge).

WARDE FOWLER, W. (1916), 'Jupiter and the Triumphator', *CR* 30, 153–7.

WARDLE, D. (1994), *Suetonius' Life of Caligula: A Commentary* (*CollLatomus,* 225; Brussels).

WARMINGTON, E. H. (1940), *Remains of Old Latin,* iv. *Archaic Inscriptions* (London and Cambridge, Mass.).

WAURICK, G. (1977), 'Kunstraub der Römer: Untersuchungen zu seinen Anfängen anhand der Inschriften', in *Festschrift Hans-Jürgen Hundt zum 65. Geburtstag, dargebracht vom Kollegium des römisch-germanischen Zentralmuseums,* ii. *Römerzeit* (Mainz), 1–46.

—— (1983), 'Untersuchungen zur historisierenden Rüstung in der römischen Kunst', *JRGZM* 30, 265–301.

WEINSTOCK, S. (1971), *Divus Julius* (Oxford).

WELCH, K. E. (2006), '*Domi militiaeque*: Roman Domestic Aesthetics and War Booty in the Republic', in S. Dillon and K. E. Welch (eds.), *Representations of War in Ancient Rome* (Cambridge), 91–161.

WELWEI, K.-W. (1989), 'Zum *metus Punicus* in Rom um 150 v. Chr.', *Hermes,* 117, 314–20.

—— (2000), *Sub corona vendere: Quellenkritische Studien zu Kriegsgefangenschaft und Sklaverei in Rom bis zum Ende des Hannibalkrieges* (Stuttgart).

WESTALL, R. (1996), 'The Forum Iulium as Representation of Imperator Caesar', *RM* 103, 83–118.

WHITE, K. (1970), *Roman Farming* (London).

WHITEHORNE, J. (1994), *Cleopatras* (London and New York).

WIEGARTZ, H. (1996), 'Simulacra Gentium auf dem Forum Transitorium', *Boreas,* 19, 171–9.

WIKANDER, C. (1992), 'Pomp and Circumstance: the Procession of Ptolemaios II', *OpAth* 19, 143–150.

WISEMAN, D. J. (1984), 'Palace and Temple Gardens in the Ancient Near East', in H. I. H. Prince Takahito Mikasa (ed.), *Monarchies and Socio-Religious Traditions in the Ancient Near East: Papers Read at the 31st International Congress of Human Sciences in Asia and Northen Africa* (Wiesbaden), 37–43.

WISEMAN, T. P. (1986), 'Monuments and the Roman Annalists', in I. S. Moxon, J. D. Smart, and A. J. Woodman (eds.), *Past Perspective: Studies in Greek and Roman Historical Writing. Papers Presented at a Conference in Leeds, 6–8 April 1983* (Cambridge), 87–100.

—— (1987), '*Conspicui postes tectaque digna deo*: The Public Image of Aristocratic and Imperial Houses in the Late Republic and Early Empire', in *L'urbs: Espace urbain et histoire*

(Ier siècle av. J.-C.–IIIe siècle ap. J.-C.). Actes du colloque international organisé par le Centre national de la recherche scientifique et l'École Française de Rome (Rome, 8–12 mai 1985) (Rome), 393–413.

—— (1994), 'The Origins of Roman Historiography', in T. P. Wiseman, *Historiography and Imagination: Eight Essays on Roman Culture* (Exeter), 1–22.

—— (1998), *Roman Drama and Roman History* (Exeter).

—— (2007), 'Three Notes on the Triumphal Route', in A. Leone, D. Palombi, and S. Walker (eds.), *Res bene gestae: Ricerche di storia urbana su Roma antica in onore di Eva Margareta Steinby* (Rome), 445–9.

Wissowa, G. (1971), *Religion und Kultus der Römer* (1971).

Woelcke, K. (1911), 'Beiträge zur Geschichte des Tropaions', *BJb* 120, 127–235.

Yarden, L. (1991), *The Spoils of Jerusalem on the Arch of Titus: A Re-investigation* (Stockholm).

Zachos, K. L. (2003), 'The *tropaeum* of the Sea-Battle of Actium at Nikopolis: Interim Report', *JRA* 16, 65–92.

Zanker, P. (1990), *The Power of Images in the Age of Augustus* (Ann Arbor).

Zecchini, G. (1982), 'Cn. Manlio Vulsone e l'inizio della corruzione a Roma', in M. Sordi (ed.), *Politica e religione nel primo scontro tra Roma e l'Oriente* (Milan), 159–78.

—— (1996), 'I cervi, le amazzoni e il trionfo «gotico» di Aureliano', in G. Bonamente, F. Heim, and J.-P. Callu (eds.), *Historiae Augustae Colloquium Argentoratense* (*Historiae Augustae Colloquia*, NS 6; Bari), 349–58.

Zimmer, G. (1996), 'Prunkgeschirr hellenistischer Herrscher', in W. Hoepfner and G. Brands (eds.), *Basileia: Die Paläste der hellenistischen Könige. Internationales Symposion in Berlin vom 16.12.1992 bis 20.12.1992* (Mainz am Rhein), 130–5.

Zinserling, G. (1959/60), 'Studien zu den Historiendarstellungen der römischen Republik', *WissZJena*, 9, 403–48.

Ziolkowski, A. (1986), 'The Plundering of Epirus in 167 B.C.: Economic Considerations', *PBSR* 54, 69–80.

—— (1990), 'Credibility of Numbers of Battle Captives in Livy, Book XXI–XLV', *PP* 45, 15–36.

INDEX

Page numbers marked in italic refer to illustrations